Caspian Sea

k Sea

SINOPE

PONTUS

ANCYRA

CAPPADOCIA

PARTHIA

MEDIA

ECBATANA

LCONIUM

CILICIA

M E S O P O T A M I A

IA

TARSUS

SELEUCIA

Euphrates R.

ANTIOCH

SALAMIS

PALMYRA

Tigris R. ELAMITIS

PRUS

SUSA

SIDON

DAMASCUS

BABYLON

TYRE

PTOLEMAIS

CAESAREA

JOPPA

JERUSALEM

Persian Gulf

GAZA

RIA

A R A B I A

→ Pilgrim routes

• City with Jewish community

Nile R.

Red Sea

0   200   400

KM

UNITED SYNAGOGUE — ק״ק כנסת ישראל

Edgware Synagogue Hebrew Classes
The Shemtob Levy
P R I Z E presented
by Mr. & Mrs. Joe Wahnon
Awarded to

Raphael Zarum

For _Attendance_

Class _C.H.E_

Chairman of Education

Head Teacher

5742
1981/82

Hon. Superintendent

THE WORLD HISTORY OF THE JEWISH PEOPLE

FIRST SERIES: ANCIENT TIMES

VOLUME SEVEN: THE HERODIAN PERIOD

EDITOR

MICHAEL AVI-YONAH

ASSISTANT EDITOR

ZVI BARAS

MANAGING EDITOR

ALEXANDER PELI

JEWISH HISTORY PUBLICATIONS LTD.

THE HERODIAN PERIOD

EDITOR

MICHAEL AVI-YONAH

ASSISTANT EDITOR

ZVI BARAS

W. H. ALLEN, LONDON, 1975

CONTENTS

INTRODUCTION: THE RISE OF ROME

M. Avi-Yonah

CHAPTER I: THE FALL OF THE HASMONEAN DYNASTY AND THE ROMAN CONQUEST

A. Schalit

CONTENTS

CHAPTER II: THE END OF THE HASMONEAN DYNASTY AND THE RISE OF HEROD

A. Schalit

CHAPTER III: THE REIGN OF HEROD

M. Stern

CONTENTS

CHAPTER IV: THE HERODIAN DYNASTY AND THE PROVINCE OF
JUDEA AT THE END OF THE PERIOD OF THE SECOND TEMPLE

M. Stern

CHAPTER V: THE ECONOMY OF JUDEA IN THE PERIOD
OF THE SECOND TEMPLE

J. Klausner

CONTENTS

CHAPTER VI: JERUSALEM IN THE HELLENISTIC AND ROMAN PERIODS

M. Avi-Yonah

CHAPTER VII: JEWISH ART AND ARCHITECTURE IN THE HASMONEAN AND HERODIAN PERIODS

M. Avi-Yonah

CHAPTER VIII: THE HIGH PRIESTHOOD AND THE SANHEDRIN IN THE TIME OF THE SECOND TEMPLE

H.D. Mantel

CONTENTS

CHAPTER IX: THE TEMPLE AND THE DIVINE SERVICE

S. Safrai

AUTHORS

ILLUSTRATIONS

ILLUSTRATIONS

MAPS

PREFATORY NOTE

This volume covers a period of one hundred years of Jewish history in Palestine — from 63 B.C.E. to 66 A.D. — from the fall of the Hasmonean Dynasty to the last Procurators before the first revolt against Rome. It coincides with Rome's expansion eastward, from its earliest penetration in the eastern part of the Mediterranean basin, where Judea came within its plan of conquest. This penetration, which began with the intervention in the fratricidal war of the Hasmonean house, ended with the direct Roman domination of Judea and its complete absorption into the Roman Empire. In this historical framework and under Roman protection the Idumaean house, founded by Antipater, the father of Herod, began to emerge as an important factor. Later on the Herodian Dynasty enjoyed a unique and favorable position within the Roman Empire, whether as direct rulers of Judea, or as representatives and spokesmen of the Jewish people at the imperial court.

The impact of the Herodian Period on the Judean state and its political, domestic, economic and cultural influences, entirely justifies the title of this volume. In this context mention should also be made of the tremendous Herodian monumental construction in Jerusalem, and in all the rest of the country. The crowning achievement of this building activity was of course the Temple in Jerusalem. Remains of these buildings — seen wherever one turns, and amply illustrated in this volume — serve as fair material evidence of a prosperous, dynamic and rich cultural epoch in Judea's history. Indeed, Herod's reign and achievements were long a matter of great controversy among historians, Jewish and non-Jewish alike. Jewish historical tradition portrays Herod as a cruel tyrant and a foreign usurper who annihilated the Hasmonean Dynasty and destroyed the traditional institutions of the Jewish community. Only relatively recently has a more objective assessment of Herod's reign been suggested, one of the pioneers of this appraisal is Professor Abraham Schalit. The authors and contributors to this volume have also adopted an approach of *sine ira et studio* for the Herodian contribution to the history of the Judean state.

In a general introduction Professor Avi-Yonah describes the rise of Rome, its political and social consolidation, the different stages in its expansion and its confrontation with the Hellenistic states. Pompey's intervention in the affairs of Judea, the decline of the Hasmonean regime, the rise of the Idumaean house and the internal aristocratic opposition it aroused are described in Professor Schalit's chapters. Herod's golden age, Judea as a province, the oppressive administration of the Roman Procurators and the people's reaction are dealt with in Professor Stern's chapters. The economic and agrarian activity, social conditions, the crafts and trade of the period under consideration are discussed by the late Professor Klausner. Although written some time ago, this chapter is still a valuable contribution. Special chapters are dedicated to major Jewish institutions which always played a prominent part in the social, religious and spiritual history of Judea: The Priesthood, the Sanhedrin, the Temple and the Divine Service are discussed in chapters written by Professors Mantel and Safrai. Professor Avi-Yonah has also contributed two other chapters: one, on the Art and Architecture of this Period, and the other, on Jerusalem, its urbanic structure and its monumental edifices and their artistic aspect.

Unfortunately, Professor Avi-Yonah did not live to see the completion of this volume. He was a prolific scholar who combined original thinking with a special gift for broad synthesis. His wide knowledge of classical history and art enabled him to contribute in many fields of research, among which Palestine took the first and foremost place. His far-ranging contributions to the history of Palestine in the Hellenistic, Roman and Byzantine periods, its archaeology, geography, art and architecture, as well as to other related subjects earned him special esteem and a prominent place among the students and scholars of Ancient Palestine, its antiquities and civilization. Professor Avi-Yonah was especially devoted to the study of Jerusalem, its topography, archaeology and architecture. He published numerous works on its history and specific problems; two of his best known projects are: *The Sefer Yerushalayim*, which he edited, and the model of Herodian Jerusalem at the Holyland Hotel.

Professor Avi-Yonah's death is a great loss to the project of the WORLD HISTORY OF THE JEWISH PEOPLE, of which he was one of the most outstanding contributors, editors and promoters.

In preparing this volume his guidelines were closely followed and his conceptions adhered to faithfully, thereby assuring the maximal employment of his editorial instruction and cooperation.

Lastly we would like to thank the editorial staff of Massada Press, for their invaluable efforts in preparing this volume for publication.

ZVI BARAS
Jerusalem, November, 1974

ABBREVIATIONS FOR BIBLICAL BOOKS

Gen.	Genesis	Zech.	Zechariah
Lev.	Leviticus	Ps.	Psalms
Num.	Numbers	Cant.	Canticles
Deut.	Deuteronomy	Prov.	Proverbs
I Sam.	I Samuel	Neh.	Nehemiah
Isa.	Isaiah	II Chron.	II Chronicles
Ezek.	Ezekiel	LXX	Septuagint

ABBREVIATIONS FOR TALMUD
AND RABBINICAL LITERATURE

'Arak.	'Arakin	Meg.	Megilla
'Av. Zara	'Avoda Zara	Meg. Ta'an.	Megillat Ta'anit
B. Batra	Bava Batra	Men.	Menahot
B. Mezi'a	Bava Mezi'a	Mid.	Middot
B. Qamma	Bava Qamma	Ned.	Nedarim
Bek.	Bekorot	Neg.	Nega'im
Ber.	Berakot	Naz.	Nazir
Bik.	Bikkurim	Nid.	Niddah
Dem.	Demai	Pes.	Pesahim
'Eduy.	'Eduyyot	Qid.	Qiddushin
'Eruv.	'Eruvin	Qod.	Qoddashim
Gen. R.	Genesis Raba	R. ha-Sh.	Rosh ha-Shana
Hag.	Uagiga	Sanh.	Sanhedrin
Hor.	Horayot	Shab.	Shabbat
Hul.	Hullin	Sheq.	Sheqalim
Kel.	Kelim	Shev.	Shevu'ot
Ker.	Keritot	Suk.	Sukka
Ket.	Ketubbot	Tam.	Tamid
Kil.	Kilayim	Ter.	Teruma
Lev. R.	Leviticus Raba	Tosef.	Tosefta
Ma'as.	Ma'aser	Yer.	Yerushalmi
Ma'as. Shen.	Ma'aser Sheni	Zev.	Zevahim

ABBREVIATIONS FOR GREEK
AND LATIN SOURCES

Ant.	Josephus Flavius, Jewish Antiquities
CIL.	Corpus Inscriptionum Latinarum
Dessau, ILS.	H. Dessau. Inscriptiones Latinae Selectae
Dio Cassius	Dionis Casii Cocceiani Historia Romana
Diodorus	Diodorus Siculus, Bibliothecae historiae
Eusebius, Chron. . .	Eusebius, Chronicon
Eusebius, Hist. Eccles	Eusebius, Historica Ecclesiastica
Frey, C.I. jud.	J. B. Frey, Corpus Insipcrtionum Judaicarum, Rome, 1952
Gabba, Inscrizioni . .	E. Gabba, Inscrizioni greche e latine per lo studio della Bibbia, Turin, 1958
IG.	Inscriptiones Graecae ed. by the Prussian Academy
Jacoby, Fr. Gr. Hist	F. Jacoby, Die Fragmente der Griechischen Historiker, II, Berlin, 1929
Livy	Titi Livi, Ab Urbe condita
Macc.	Maccabees
OGIS.	Orientis graeci inscriptiones selectae
Philo, De Spec. Leg.	Philo, De Specialibus Legibus
Pliny, Nat. Hist.	Pliny, Natural History
Reinach, Textes	T. Reinach, Textes d'auteurs grecs et romains relatifs au judaisme, Paris, 1895
SEG	Supplementum Epigraphicum Graecum
SIG	W. Dittenberg, Sylloge Inscriptionum Graecarum
Strabo	Strabo, Geography
War	Josephus Flavius, The Jewish War

ABBREVIATIONS FOR JOURNALS
AND SCIENTIFIC LITERATURE

BASOR	—	Bulletin of the American Schools of Oriental Research
BIES	—	Bulletin of the Israel Exploration Society (Hebrew)
BJPES	—	Bulletin of the Jewish Palestine Exploration Society
CAH	—	Cambridge Ancient History
Graetz, Geschichte	—	Geschichte der Juden von den ältesten Zeiten bis auf die Gegenwart
HTR	—	Harvard Theological Review
HUCA	—	Hebrew Union College Annual
IEJ	—	Israel Exploration Journal
JEA	—	Journal of Egyptian Archaeology
JBL	—	Journal of Biblical Literature
JJS	—	Journal of Jewish Studies
JQR	—	Jewish Quarterly Review
JRS	—	Journal of Roman Studies
JTS	—	Journal of Theological Studies
MGWJ	—	Monatschrift für Geschichte und Wissenchaft des Judentums
PEFQS	—	Palestine Exploration Fund Quarterly Statement
PAAJR	—	Proceedings of the American Academy for Jewish Research
PEQ	—	Palestine Exploration Quarterly
QDAP	—	Quarterly of the Department of Antiquities in Palestine
RB	—	Revue Biblique
RE	—	Paulys Realencyclopädie der Classischen Altertumwissenschaft (Neue Bearbeitung begonen von Georg Wissowa, forgeführt von Wilhelm Kroll und Karl Mittelhaus)
REJ	—	Revue des Etudes Juives
Schürer, Geschichte	—	Geschichte des jüdischen Volkes im Zeitalter Jesu Christi
ZAW	—	Zeitschrift für die alttestamentliche Wissenschaft
ZDPV	—	Zeitschrift des Deutschen Palästina-Vereins
ZNTW	—	Zeitschrift für die neutestamentliche Wissenschaft

HEBREW-ENGLISH TRANSLITERATION

1. All Hebrew names found in the Bible are given as they appear in the English translation of the Holy Scriptures by the Jewish Publication Society of America, Philadelphia, 1955.

2. Those names that are familiar to the English reader are rendered in their customary, accepted spelling (e. g. Caesarea).

3. All other Hebrew names and words are transliterated as follows:

א	Not noted at beginning or end of word; otherwise by ', e. g. p^eēr or pĕ'ēr (פְּאָר), mē'īr (מָאִיר).
ב	b
ב	v
ג	g
ג	g
ד	d
ד	d
ה	h (unless consonantal, ה at the end of the word is not transliterated)
ו	w
ז	z
ח	ḥ
ט	ṭ
י	y
כ	k
כ	ḵ
ל	l
מ	m
נ	n
ס	s
ע	'
פ	p
פ	f
צ	z
ק	q
ר	r
ש	sh, š
ש	s
ת	t
ת	t (Except in the word בית – beth)

a) The *dagesh lene* is not indicated, save in the letters ב and פ. *Dagesh forte* is indicated by doubling the letter.

b) The Hebrew definite article is indicated by *ha* or *he* followed by a hyphen, but without the next letter doubled, e. g. *ha-shānā*, not *ha-shshānā*.

־	a	ֳ	e
־ֲ	ă	ֱ	ĕ
ָ	ā	וּ	ū
ָ	o	וֹ	ō
ֲָ	ŏ	ֻ	u
ֵ	ē	ִ	i
ֵ	ē, ēi	ִ	ī

Sheva mobile (נע שוא) is indicated thus: ᵉ or ĕ. Neither long vowels nor *sheva mobile* are indicated in proper names.

ARABIC-ENGLISH TRANSLITERATION

ء — ' (not indicated at the beginning of a word)		ض — ḍ	
		ط — ṭ	
ب — b		ظ — ẓ	
ت — t		ع — '	
ث — th		غ — gh	
ج — j		ف — f	
ح — ḥ		ق — q	
خ — kh		ك — k	
د — d		ل — l	
ذ — dh		م — m	
ر — r		ن — n	
ز — z		ه — h	
س — s		و — w	
ش — sh		ى — y	
ص — ṣ			

The Lām of the definite article ال is assimilated before a solar letter. Proper names familiar to the English reader are rendered in their customary spelling.

XXII

THE HERODIAN PERIOD

INTRODUCTION

THE RISE OF ROME

by M. Avi-Yonah

A. THE GROWING SHADOWS OF ROME

AT A TIME when the Hellenistic dynasties, the Ptolemies and the Seleucids, were waging the last of their many wars for the possession of Coele-Syria and Phoenicia,[1] a struggle of much greater historical importance was taking place in the western basin of the Mediterranean. Rome emerged as the victor in the second war with Carthage, a war which lasted for seventeen years and which was paradoxically illuminated on the losing side by the genius of Hannibal. Rome had thus become the strongest military power in the entire ancient world. While the Seleucid king Antiochus III was still rejoicing over his conquests, a "little cloud like a man's hand" rose out of the western sea — "and in a little while the heavens grew black with clouds and wind and there was a great rain." Five years after the defeat of Carthage Rome crushed Macedonia, and seven years later Antiochus "the Great" left the battlefield of Magnesia a vanquished man. The Maccabean revolt and the Hasmonean kingdom lived under the ever-lengthening shadow of the Roman power, which gradually drew ever nearer to Judea. In the end the Jewish people was left standing face to face with the Roman empire. The first act of this confrontation with destiny forms the contents of this and the two following volumes. Its results are felt to this day in the Exile and in the destruction of that great national symbol, the Temple; and, on the positive side, in the lonely survival of the Jews as the only people in the whole ancient world to have kept its identity. Both the end and the means — the crystallization of the Jewish nomocracy — spring from that fateful encounter of 63 B.C.E.–70 A.D. It is only meant, therefore, that we consider as a preliminary to this volume the rise of the extraordinary historical phenomenon known as the Roman empire, up to the moment when it came to dominate the history of the Jewish people.

In itself the rise of Rome has had no parallel in the story of mankind.[2] Never before or after has a single city grown into a state embracing the whole of a civilization. The seemingly irresistible growth of Roman power caused the Greek historian Polybius, who witnessed the crisis and break-through of the decisive fifty-three years from the Roman side, to enunciate the theory of the invincible Tyche or Fate, leading Rome to world domination despite all the efforts of its enemies and all its own mistakes.[3] Indeed, the empire founded at the end of the third century B.C.E. lasted six hundred years, the longest span allotted to any ecumenical state, real or professed. The causes of the rise of Rome have exercised the ingenuity of philosophers and historians down the ages; it is its ultimate decline and fall which need no explanation.

If we analyze the whole story of the Roman republic, which for all practical purposes covers our present theme, we may discern in it four distinct stages. In the first period the city of Rome obtained the hegemony of a country, Latium, a process for which many historical parallels can be found. The second stage, however, in which Rome gradually gained dominion over the whole of Italy south of the Apennines, was an extra-ordinary achievement, the solidity of which stood the test in the crucible of the Hannibalic War. The contest with Carthage — the third stage — stands out as the decisive event, in which the Roman republic, led by an iron-willed Senate, triumphed over incredible difficulties, and at the same time created the conditions for its own later ruin. Finally came the fourth period, in which Rome gained the mastery of the known civilized world. It did so by using its enormous force with a complete lack of scruple, for which it would be difficult to find a parallel in the entire political history of civilized nations, ancient or modern.

Yet even as Rome succeeded in conquering one country after another, the republic itself was undergoing a complete social and political trans-formation through a series of bloody civil wars. In the end there emerged a world power ruled by a single individual, the master of thirty legions, whose will was limited only by the need to compromise, under penalty of assassination, with a surviving aristocracy.

B. Beginnings of Rome and its Political Organization

In its obscure beginnings Rome was a small townlet, built on a convenient flat hill near the lowest bridgeable point on the Tiber, the great river of central Italy. From the beginning this bridge crossing assumed such importance in Roman history that Roman priests were ever after called *pontifices* or "bridge-makers." From its very foundation, too, the Roman community was distinguished by a quality which singled it out among the

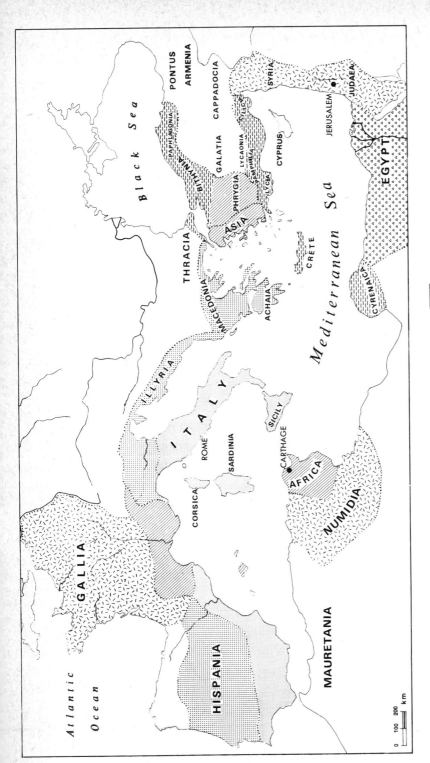

Roman conquest during Ptolemaic rule over Judaea

During Seleucid rule

In the times of Jonathan and Simeon the Hasmoneans

In the times of Jannaeus and Alexandra

In the times of Aristobulus II and Hyrcanus II

In the time of Herod

The Roman conquests in the Mediterranean Basin.

city-states of antiquity and which laid the basis for its ultimate greatness: its readiness to accept strangers and to grant them citizens' rights. While it was not unusual in antiquity to see cities rising out of a union (the so-called *synoecism* — "putting together of houses") of all the villages in a given geographical region, such a town, once constituted, normally tried by fair means or foul to keep its citizenship and the advantages connected with it as tightly closed as possible. Not so Rome; for many centuries the ranks of its citizens were allowed to grow by the incorporation of single families or of whole tribes. The division into patricians and plebeians, which troubled the early days of the republic, was a class distinction and not an ethnic one. Already in the so-called reform of Servius Tullius the old organization by families (*curiae*) was replaced by one based on propertied classes, which served also as the basis of the military establishment of the state, the centuries. By a typically Roman device, the seeming equality of the citizens was heavily weighted in favor of the rich and powerful; if they were united on any issue the 98 centuries of the propertied classes could outvote the other 95. The dominance of the landed aristocracy (for there was as yet little trade) was further strengthened by their exclusive privileges in matters of religion and by the interpretation of the as yet unwritten laws. Even during the monarchy the heads of the patrician families, assembled in a consultative assembly, the Senate, exercised considerable power. When the kings were replaced by two magistrates elected annually, first called praetors and later consuls, the power of the Senate, which now included all former high officials of the state, increased by leaps and bounds. The authority of the state, the *imperium*, was exercised by the consuls and the judges, also called praetors; it was absolute outside Rome, but within the city itself it was limited by the right of appeal to the people against a capital sentence. The original patrician stock was soon exhausted by the insistence of the nobles on marrying exclusively within their own ranks; of the patrician families known from the annals of the early republic only twenty-four are listed among the high officials in the decisive fourth, third and second centuries B.C.E. This lesson in the dangers of exclusiveness was not forgotten in the creative period of the Roman republic.

Another typically Roman quality — at least in better times — was the ability to compromise. No political or social conflict was allowed to proceed, to the extreme of bloody civil war or revolution, as happened only too often among the logical Greeks. Thus the struggles between the patricians and plebeians were at first mitigated by allowing the plebs its own magistrates (the tribunes, with a power of veto in all affairs of state and their own assemblies), while the patrician monopoly of legal knowledge was broken by the codification of the law in written form, the Twelve Tables. The social distress of the landless classes was somewhat relieved by distribution of public lands, the fruits of the first Roman conquests. Access to the magistracies was at first made possible for the plebeians by various constitutional fictions, such as the replacement of patrician consuls by "military tribunes with consular power," who could be also plebeian. New offices, such as the quaestors, were almost from the outset open to the lower class.

C. ROMAN DOMINATION OVER LATIUM AND ITALY

The same spirit of compromise and gradualness also marked Rome's foreign relations. The Cassian treaty (493 B.C.E.) between Rome and the Latin cities established perpetual peace, an alternation in military command, and a community of private rights between citizens of the contracting parties. Soon the Hernici joined on the same terms. Thus united, the Latins could face the other Italian tribes in their neighborhood, the Sabines, Aequii and Volsci. The Sabines, including the famous Claudian *gens*, were gradually absorbed into the Roman people. The other tribes were step by step pushed back by the Latin alliance. On its northern frontier the Roman republic profited from the decline of Etruscan power, The capture of Veii in 396 B.C.E. marked the turning point of the struggle, not only on account of the military success, but because the captured land could be distributed among four new Roman tribes. The Latin allies received lands of other conquered cities as their share. Because her territory was compact and her citizens were numerous and united, Rome could assume the leadership of the Latin league. For all these early years the Roman peasants, banded together in legions, waged annual campaigns during the spring, when work in the fields could be interrupted. The capture of Veii, about eight miles north of Rome, needed — according to tradition — no less than ten such spring campaigns. The Romans as yet enjoyed no overwhelming superiority in numbers, weapons or leadership; they were, however, solid, obstinate and patriotic. They were also always ready to learn from their enemies; new weapons or tactics which had been found effective against the Romans themselves were soon adopted in their own ranks.

After the disaster on the Allia (390 B.C.E.) in which the Roman army was heavily defeated by the Gauls and the city itself had to be ransomed from the barbarians, Rome was provided with its first wall. The city's territory was enlarged by the grant of citizenship to Tusculum (now

Tivoli). The Roman hold upon Latium was strengthened. By annexing Antium, Rome gained a harbor and two additional tribes.

Roman domination over Latium was put to the test in 340 B.C.E., when war broke out between the allies. The settlement of 338 marks the first definitive step of the republic towards its future hegemony in Italy. The inhabitants of the towns nearest to Rome were granted full citizenship. Another group retained its municipal status, but their citizens had the right to trade and intermarry with Romans; if they chose to settle in Rome, they could become full citizens. The rest were granted the right of trade and intermarriage with Rome only, but not among each other. All cities of the second and third class were obliged to furnish troops and to allow Rome to direct their foreign policy. The allied armies were supported at the expense of Rome — it was of course true that the campaigns were as yet of short duration and limited scope. A fourth form of submission was exacted from Antium, where a colony of Roman citizens was settled to guard the harbor.

The establishment of Roman domination over Latium was followed by a period of social and economic reforms. These consisted mainly in the admission of plebeians to all offices, including that of consul and the still more prestigious one of censor. The nobles of the two classes were blended into one aristocracy, within which the earlier distinctions became mainly formal. Meanwhile the population of Rome continued to grow apace. Many Latins took up residence in Rome and gradually became citizens; so did the sons of freed slaves, the so-called *libertini*, who were all enfranchised by a most liberal interpretation of the law. By 287 B.C.E. it was resolved that a plebeian might become dictator (a temporary magistracy with supreme powers), and that the decisions of the plebeian assemblies, the *plebiscita*, should have the force of law.

The last phases of this "Struggle of the Orders" were resolved at the most opportune moment, when Rome and its allies were about to achieve the conquest of central Italy and to face the Greek cities of the south. The decisive step taken by Rome was the granting of potential citizenship to the cities of the fertile Campania, from Fundi to Capua. A Latin colony was established at Cales in 334 B.C.E., and Neapolis (Naples) was granted protection against the Samnites further inland. The rivalry over Campania led to the great Samnite wars, which continued for two generations. The warlike mountain tribes of the Samnites, and their allies, inflicted on the Romans some of their most grievous defeats: the memory of the surrender at the Caudine Forks (321) and the lost battle of Lautulae (314) rankled for a long time. In their adversity the Roman leaders began to evolve the methods which were to lead them finally to world power. The legionary phalanx had proved too unwieldly in the hilly Samnite regions: it was broken up into smaller and more flexible units, the maniples, which were so posted as to lend mutual support without impeding each other, and which could also operate independently. The hostile area was ringed around by a circle of allies. Rome now found that behind its enemies' country there usually existed an enemy's enemy who could be enlisted as a friend. In 312 the first great Roman road, the Via Appia, was driven into enemy territory, thereby facilitating the movement of Roman troops to the attack. Colonies, mostly peopled with Latins, were settled around the hostile regions, and later on inside them. By this sophisticated measure two aims were achieved at one and the same time: the Latins, who were settled and given land, became more firmly attached to Rome, while a wedge was driven between them and the other Italian peoples. During this period of southern and eastern advance the north was not neglected. More and more of the decaying Etruscan cities were forced into alliance with Rome, and the Gauls in the Po Valley were diked in by settling colonies on the Adriatic coast.

Hardly had Rome achieved superiority over other Italian tribes, when its power was menaced from overseas by Pyrrhus, king of Epirus. This Hellenistic adventurer had come over the Adriatic Sea at the bidding of the Greek cities of southern Italy, led by Tarentum; for they now felt their freedom seriously endangered by the Roman conquests. In the first encounter with the 25,000 mercenaries of Pyrrhus, trained in the tradition of Alexander's phalanx and reinforced by twenty elephants, the Romans were at a loss how to deal with these new tactics and the unfamiliar beasts of war. They lost the two battles of Heraclea (280), and that at Ausculum a year later. However, these "Pyrrhic victories" cost the king so many irreplaceable soldiers as to become proverbial;[4] whereas his enemies could always draw upon the whole manpower of their citizens and allies. Pyrrhus decided therefore to leave for Sicily, and later moved out of Italy altogether. Bereft of their main support, the Greek cities willy-nilly joined the Roman alliance. The last to do so were Tarentum in 272 B.C.E. and Rhegium on the Strait of Messina in 270 B.C.E. The Greeks were mostly left their autonomy, but had to supply naval aid. Only Tarentum received a permanent Roman garrison. Rome was now supreme from the Appenines to the toe of Italy.

The political organization of the Roman confederacy could serve as a model for all would-be conquerors. From the outset Rome refused to follow the normal pattern of creating an impassable barrier between the dominant and the subject nations. Instead of this, a subtle gradation of rights was introduced, which was kept flexible as well. The Romans thus achieved their aim of "dividing and ruling" their subject-allies, without rendering their situation entirely hopeless. The twin method of incorporation and alliance was used throughout Italy. Some tribes (e.g. the Sabines in 268 B.C.E.) were granted full citizenship; in some vital places Roman colonies were settled, in addition to individual allotments and whole towns which were granted Roman citizenship, but kept their local magistrates. The other allies were divided into several classes, the most privileged of which enjoyed the "Latin rights" (*jus Latinum*) of trade and intermarriage with each other and with Rome, and of Roman citizenship if they settled in the capital. The Latin colonies were another privileged class. Other allies remained citizens without voting rights, having the citizen's right of appeal against death sentences (*provocatio*) and, of course, rights of trade and marriage. Still others were left to enjoy these private rights, but no civic ones. All were obliged to follow Rome in matters of foreign policy and to furnish military contingents, while those settling on public land had also to pay rent. There was no special taxation of allies. Special territorial arrangements were made in order to split up and isolate those still considered dangerous; the tribes of the Samnite League, for instance, lost half their territory to a wedge of Roman citizens in an area from Capua to Luceria; but even they retained their autonomy. Rome guaranteed peace throughout the peninsula and its defense against external foes — a welcome relief after the ceaseless warring of the previous centuries. The combined territories of the league were 52,000 square miles, of which 10,000 were Roman land proper. The confederation could muster an army of half a million men, the potentially strongest military force in the ancient world at that time.[5]

D. The Punic Wars

It was perhaps Rome's greatest fortune that she was spared the necessity of coping with several challenges at once. All her trials came one by one. The unification of Italy was hardly completed when the dynamism of her historical development brought Rome into conflict with the great maritime and commercial empire of Carthage. The series of Punic wars, and in particular the Second or Hannibalic War, put the Roman republic and its allies to their severest test ever, but at least they had no other burden to bear at the same time.

Carthage, a Phoenician colony of Tyre, had built up a naval power, which was primarily intended to protect and expand the profitable trade monopoly of the western Mediterranean. Though they themselves, like all successful merchants, were too intelligent to relish war for its own sake, or to strive after power as an aim in itself. The Carthaginians well understood that the enjoyment of their material gains necessitated a certain armed force. They had succeeded in bottling in their main competitors, the Greeks, in the Tyrrhenian Sea, and waged a long war for a foothold in Sicily. It was here that they first came into conflict with Rome, after having joined forces with her against Pyrrhus and the Greeks of Magna Graecia. Once Pyrrhus had left — remarking caustically, "What a pit we are now leaving for the Romans and Carthaginians to wrestle in"[6] — the conflict became all but inevitable. It began at the one point where the dominions of both powers actually touched — at the Strait of Messina. There a Roman garrison at Rhegium was faced by a Carthaginian one at Messana, established originally with the consent of the Mamertines, Italian mercenaries who had held the town for twenty-five years. In 264 a party of the Mamertines appealed to Rome for help against their former friends. The Senate after some hesitation decided to accede to this request, and to break a treaty of non-interference made with Carthage in 306. Thus began a series of wars with Carthage — the so-called Punic Wars — which ended one hundred and eighteen years later with the downfall and utter destruction of the greatest enemy ever encountered by Rome.[7]

The struggle was a long-drawn one, for the antagonists were evenly matched in many respects. Both were republics in which the ruling oligarchy was under little pressure from the masses. The Roman farmers and the Carthaginian merchants showed both the willpower and stubbornness of their respective professions. The fact that Carthage had to rely on mercenaries, who were both fewer in number and less resolute soldiers than the Roman legionaries, was balanced by the initial superiority of the Punic navy and cavalry, and by the appearance among the merchant princes who ruled Carthage of some leaders of genius, in particular the Barca family. On the other hand, the average Roman aristocrat was a better leader of men than his Punic opponent. As soon as some able Roman generals succeeded in overcoming the traditional distrust of outstanding personalities inherent in all aristocracies, the chances were evened out. In the last resort the decisive move was a home thrust into the enemy's country, and here the superiority of Rome was proved in the end. The Italian alliance stood incredibly firm even when Hannibal was at the gates of Rome; when the situation was reversed, Carthage collapsed.

The First Punic War was fought out mainly in Sicily, the object of the struggle, and in the seas around it. The Carthaginians did not attempt to attack Italy, and the Roman invasion of Africa, led by Regulus, ended in disaster. The fact that the war lasted twenty-three years shows how difficult it was for either side to gain the upper hand. A new factor, which proved ultimately decisive, was the unexpected and improvised creation of a large naval force by Rome, one of the outstanding examples of Roman adaptability. The sudden appearance of a Roman fleet in 261 off the Sicilian coast must have been a terrible shock to the Carthaginians, whose whole existence was bound up with their command of the sea. By using a new-fangled boarding device, the "crow" (*corvus*), the Romans could fully utilize their superiority in fighting man to man. Yet though they won a series of naval victories at (Mylae, 260, and again at Sulci, Tyndarus, the Aegates) and lost only one battle, that of Drepana in 249, even their victories were costly. In spite of their prowess in battle, the Romans were as yet quite inexperienced in the ways of the sea, and lost many more men and ships by storms than in battle. It has been estimated that the wreck of the fleet in 255 off the coast of Africa caused the loss of fifteen percent of the ablebodied men of the Italian confederation; another fleet was lost in 249 off the coast of Sicily. Although by then the Carthaginians had been pushed back in Sicily into two strongholds on the western coast, and the eastern half of the island was held by Rome's staunch ally, Hiero of Syracuse, both sides had become so exhausted that operations were almost totally suspended for six whole years (248–242). This was the moment of truth, when the more determined of the two antagonists had to show his mettle. Rome was able to make this last effort; Carthage apparently was not. A fleet of 200 warships was built in Italy, largely on the proceeds of a patriotic loan, for the Roman treasury was by now quite empty. The sea battle at the Aegates against the last Carthaginian fleet proved decisive. Sicily fell to the victor, and with it the domination of the seas around Italy.

Already during the First Punic War certain momentous developments could be observed in the Roman ways of warfare and politics. The sacking of Agrigentum and the sale of its inhabitants into slavery was only the first of the many acts of barbarity perpetrated by the Roman army during the war. The other important change in traditional policy came at the end of the war. The old way of gradually incorporating the Roman conquests within the framework of the Italian confederation and then of the Roman republic was now abandoned. Instead, Sicily became the first of the Roman provinces. It was administered by a governor of praetorial rank sent annually from Rome the capital, and its revenues were appropriated by the state treasury. In this way the republic abandoned its old policy of gradual enlargement of its human resources by the expansion of the citizen body. It now chose the old, old path of domination by the body of citizens (or their oligarchic élite) over the mass of non-citizens, vanquished peoples outside the pale.

Certain of the old rules of "divide and conquer" were, however, still observed in the new circumstances. There were subtle gradations in the degree of servitude and in the financial charges imposed on one group of provincials and another. But whereas previous conquests by Rome held out to the vanquished the hope of emancipation and an ultimate joint responsibility in the sharing of power, this road now seemed wholly closed to them. It was of no consequence at the time that several centuries later first the Sicilians, and then the other provincials, were to obtain equal status and Roman citizenship, or that these were enjoyed by privileged individuals even earlier. What is important was the prospect that Roman domination held out for its subject cities and peoples, and here the outlook appeared hopeless indeed. In addition to suffering legal discrimination, Sicily and then the other provinces were at the mercy of the provincial governor. He was changed every year, and had every reason to squeeze the last drop of revenue from the province, legally or illegally, in order to pay off personal debts and obtain the means to advance his career at Rome. As long as the reins of power in the capital were held by the old aristocrats, extortion from the provincials were kept within certain bounds. However, with the renewed outbreak of social unrest in Rome and the ensuing civil wars, there seemed no limit to the rapacity of the provincial governors. Even those who were personally honest could not remain so without committing political suicide.[8]

There is one more observation to make on the negative effects of the First Punic War. It marked the beginning of public (as distinguished from private) dishonesty and sharp dealing. Unscrupulous practices, in particular the profiting from the difficulties of others to obtain unfair advantages, became an increasingly common factor in Roman policy. The first such occurred when the Carthaginians were sorely beset by a revolt of their mercenaries. Rome profited from their predicament by extorting the cession of Sardinia and an additional payment on threat of a renewed war. When the Barca family succeeded in creating a new Carthaginian empire in Spain in the short interval between the two Punic Wars, Rome again disregarded its undertaking not to interfere south of the Ebro. By adopting the cause of Saguntum it provoked another war, and thus sowed a wind and reaped a whirlwind.

The interwar years were marked in Rome by some internal reforms, such as the creation of the last two tribes, the number being thenceforth fixed at 35; this meant there were now 350 voting centuries. Newcomers to the citizenship swelled the ranks of the four urban tribes, and thus at first remained almost powerless; only later were they distributed more evenly. The last Gallic invasion of central Italy was beaten back on the Telamon in 226 B.C.E. In a quick riposte the Po Valley from the Alps to Istria was temporarily subdued. Another event which forecast the future was the admission of Rome to the Isthmian games at Corinth (228). This was an official recognition by the Greek community of the equal standing of the Roman people with the Hellenes. It was also a sign of the beginning of the infiltration of Greek culture into Rome that such an application for admission was ever made. The rule of Rome over the Greek cities of southern Italy (Magna Graecia) now also began to affect the victors, who could not remain entirely indifferent to the siren song of Greece.

Soon afterwards, however, the republic needed all the old qualities of Roman steadfastness and resolve, rather than those of Greek sophistication and subtlety. It had to pass its most grueling test, lasting for sixteen years — half a generation — in a cruel and terrible conflict with an adversary of genius. It was the Hannibalic (or Second Punic) War which, after bringing Rome to the brink of disaster, finally assured it of dominion over the Mediterranean basin and Western Europe.

Hannibal, the Carthaginian commander in Spain, had while yet a boy sworn to his father Hamilcar the oath of eternal enmity to Rome. By a stroke of supreme audacity he decided to carry the war right into his enemies' backyard. As the seas were ruled by the Romans, and remained so till the end of the war, Hannibal marched by land across the Pyrenees and Alps, and invaded Italy in 218. Within the space of three years he had won as many great victories (on the Trebbia, on the shore of Lake Trasimene and finally at Cannae). One Roman army after another was annihilated with enormous loss of life. The tactical masterpiece of Hannibal was Cannae. Twenty-five thousand Romans were left dead on the battlefield and ten thousand taken prisoner. Yet, in spite of all disasters, the Italian confederation remained loyal to Rome. Even after Cannae only a few towns of southern Italy — Capua and Tarentum in particular — defected to the enemy. Hannibal stayed on in the Italian countryside for thirteen long years, devastating the open country. He was, however, unable to attack any important fortress, let alone Rome itself. In 206 Hannibal's brother Hasdrubal made a desperate effort to reinforce the Carthaginian army in Italy; with its failure, the fate of Hannibal was sealed.

Throughout the war the Roman Senate made a sustained effort not only to cope with the immediate danger in Italy, but to undermine the

Carthaginian bases in Sicily and Spain. The Roman war effort in the Second Punic War is almost unbelievable by modern standards. It was indeed only made possible by the primitive character of the Italian economy. For eighteen long years armies of 18–19, sometimes even 20, 23 or 25 legions were raised year after year. Although the strength of a legion was by then much depleted, this still meant mobilizing 60–70,000 soldiers annually in addition to about 50,000 sailors. This represented seven percent of all-able-bodied males in Italy. It has been calculated that a quarter of a million men were lost in the struggle, out of the million engaged. Disregarding the danger at home, the republic continued to send armies to Spain and Sicily, at first with varying success, but victorious in the end.[9]

In the Sicilian theater of war Syracuse fell in 211 B.C.E., with much destruction of life and looting of Greek art treasures. Spain was finally conquered in 206, after twelve years of fighting and the loss of three Roman armies. By 210 even the Latin allies were weary of the struggle, but Rome went on waging a relentless war. New methods were tried with great success. One of these was the investment of the young and untried Publius Cornelius Scipio with an unlimited proconsular imperium, to last till the end of the Spanish campaign. These were, however, ominous signs for the future of the republic.

The Romans continued throughout the war to develop new tactics and to adopt new weapons. They learned the use of the siege dam and battering ram from the Carthaginians, who had it from their Phoenician ancestors, who in turn had learned it from the Assyrians. Having experienced on their own bodies the advantages of the short Spanish sword, the Romans promptly adopted the short *gladius*, in addition to the throwing javelin (*pilum*). To keep his shield in position, the Roman legionary learnt to throw his javelin and then draw his sword, which, contrary to general usage, was hung on his right. Having learned the bitter lesson of the superiority of the Numidian cavalry, the Romans succeeded in drawing the Numidians over to their side. In the last and decisive battle of Zama (202), Scipio defeated Hannibal by turning the tactics of the Punic general against himself.

The moment of victory in the Second Punic War marks a watershed in Roman history. In internal politics the authority of the Senate and its leaders was supreme, for the anti-aristocratic generals elected by the opposition (Flaminius, Varro) had failed in the field. The ten to twenty families in control of the Senate closed their ranks against any newcomers. In the second century very few men were elected consuls from outside the closed circle of the great clans (*gentes*). Even a man of genius like Scipio

Africanus, although of the noble Cornelii family, was unable to make head-way against the massive phalanx of the aristocracy. Of the 206 consulates from 200–100 B.C.E. 157 were held by members of twenty-four families, and fifty of these by the four families of the Cornelii, Claudii, Aemilii and Calpurnii; the Cornelii alone held twenty-two of them.

The almost inevitable result of this oligarchic regime was a complete lack of initiative in matters of internal policy, and in economics in particular. This happened at the very moment when reforms in this field became more and more urgently needed. The Hannibalic War had eroded the peasant class, the very foundation of the Roman state. The farmers had suffered out of all proportion to the other social groups. Besides the direct destruc-tion of their farms and the damage to their plantations and crops, it was the peasant families who bore the brunt of the massive conscription during the war years.

The soldiers returned to find their holdings devastated and their agri-culture unprofitable.[10] As a result of the victories won mainly by them-selves, masses of cheap wheat — the tribute of the conquered provinces — flooded the Roman market. The generals from the noble families came back enriched by the spoils of war and of provincial administration. They looked for a safe investment for their new wealth, and found it by leasing public lands. These had greatly increased in area (especially in southern Italy) because of the massive confiscation of the holdings of rebellious cities. The nobles also purchased cheaply the farms of the impoverished peasants. Great estates (*latifundia*) were thus formed in Italy, owned by absentee landlords and worked by slave labor supervised by resident stewards. Of slaves there were plenty — another result of the long war; for the surviving losers were now sold into slavery as a matter of course. It has been estimated that half a million people lost their personal liberty as a result of the Second Punic War. The new estates specialized in pasturage, vineyards and olive groves, which were now much more profitable than the cultivation of wheat. The agricultural manuals of Cato the Elder unconsciously reveal the mass of human misery on the landed estates with their thousands of slaves. We learn from other sources about the drift of the landless peasants into the city of Rome and the creation of a hungry and desperate urban proletariat. Their only wealth were their *proles* (offspring), who for their part seemed condemned to continue their parents' weary and hopeless existence.

By a bitter irony of fate Hannibal may indeed be said to have achieved his purpose of undermining the Roman republic, even if he ruined Carthage at the same time. The masses of the Italian allies who had remained true to their oaths throughout the war, now found themselves without a vote, the pawns of an all-powerful Roman aristocracy. They were called upon to fight wars overseas which brought no visible advantage to themselves, but only enriched the Roman generals.

The deterioration of Roman society was paralleled by a decline in the political morals of the ruling aristocracy. The anxious years of the Hannibalic invasions had left their mark even upon the proud victors, and the traumatic shock they had suffered now expressed itself in a deep suspicion and hatred of all possible rivals. Never again must they face the terrible dangers of the Second Punic War, when Rome had to fear not only Hannibal, but also a Macedonian intervention. The whole world owed them compensation for the years of suffering during the war, and there was no need to keep faith with others. The "Punic perfidy" with which the Carthaginians were habitually reproached in Latin literature, now changed camps. All means were regarded by Rome's leaders as legitimate if they were designed to forestall any danger, real or imaginary.

E. Foreign Policy and Expansion

This persistent and deep-seated trauma of the Roman leadership goes far to explain the complete absence of elementary honesty or decency in their foreign policies, from the Hannibalic War onwards. Determined to crush all political enemies, they incited every small state in their orbit against their larger neighbors. Then they turned about and beat down their former friends and allies, once the latter had grown too big for Rome's safety. Wielding the most powerful military engine in existence, Rome's leaders could mercilessly crush every enemy in sight. When in difficulties in the field, as happened more than once in Spain, they made treaties and had them later repudiated at Rome. Each conquest led to new and exposed frontiers, and hence to fresh dangers and new wars. The frontiers of the Roman empire continued to expand. Former allied states became first protectorates and then provinces of Rome. War meant booty for the generals and soldiers, and tributes for the treasury. In the second century all taxes on public land in Italy could be abolished. The provinces were now required to feed the Roman populace by supplying corn for free distribution to the residents of Rome. In the vicious circle of republican politics one factor of weakness helped feed another, and was in its turn inflated by what it fed on.

The first to feel the iron fist of Rome was Philip V of Macedonia, who had indeed afforded an easy pretext for a preventive war by his half-hearted alliance with Hannibal in Italy. In their usual insidious way the Romans incited the Aetolians and Greeks against Macedonia, and then crushed the dreaded phalanx at Cynoscephalae (197 B.C.E.). Now came the turn of the second great Hellenistic kingdom, that of the Seleucids. Antiochus III thought to profit from the Macedonian defeat and advanced into Greece. He was first expelled from Europe and then defeated decisively at Magnesia (190 B.C.E.). In this war the Romans again made use of the smaller states (Eumenes II of Pergamum and the Rhodians) to bring down the bigger one. The Seleucids had to give up all Asia Minor, which was divided between Rome's allies. Antiochus IV was then prevented from annexing Egypt, and all movements of revolt in his realm (including that of the Hasmoneans) were encouraged from Rome. When Macedonia had recovered some of its strength under King Perseus, it was utterly defeated at Pydna (168 B.C.E.) and annexed as a province in 148 B.C.E. Now came the turn of Rome's former allies. The Achaean League — the confederation of Greek cities "freed" by Flamininus in 196 B.C.E. — and the Aetolians, who were severely mauled in 189 B.C.E., were goaded into conflict with the "protecting power" and finally subdued. In Epirus seventy towns were destroyed and 150,000 people sold into slavery. The capture and sack of Corinth in 146 B.C.E. with the enslavement of its people and the plunder of innumerable works of Greek art and their transfer to Rome, was a milestone in the relations of Greeks and Romans. The new province of Achaea was one of the results of this war.

In that same year Carthage was destroyed, after having been driven to despair by the ever tightening screw of Roman demands, culminating in the "request" to leave their city and settle inland. As expected, so humiliating a demand of one of the great seafaring nations of antiquity was indignantly rejected. Carthage was then besieged and destroyed, its territory becoming the province of Africa. A long war in Spain, sullied again and again by Roman treachery, brought most of this rich country under Roman rule.

In Asia, Eumenes II of Pergamum and Rhodes, two of Rome's staunchest allies, soon came to feel the perfidy of the conquerors of Antiochus III. Eumenes and his successors Attalus II and III were humiliated and harassed in every way, until the latter in despair bequeathed his kingdom to the Romans. The inheritance was accepted, and the first Roman province on the Asiatic mainland was established in 133 B.C.E.; in typically Roman fashion it was named Asia. Rhodes was ruined by the establishment of a rival free port at Delos. In one year the customs revenue of Rhodes sank from a million drachmas to a mere 150,000. Only Egypt under the later Ptolemies continued to vegetate as a Roman vassal *de facto*.

F. Social and Political Crisis in the Roman Republic

The internal situation in Rome acted both as a spur and a brake to its imperial drive. The provinces served as a source of wealth not only to the aristocratic governors, but also to swarms of Roman capitalists, the members of a "second order" of "knights" (*equites*). They formed associations of merchants, and especially of tax-farmers (*publicani*). The heavy taxation and fines inflicted on the Greek cities in Europe and Asia (Sulla, for instance, fined the Greeks of Asia five years' tribute in one year) gave rise to a class of Roman usurers, who exploited the provinces by farming taxes and then lending the cities money to pay them. The few honest governors who tried to prevent such ruinous practices were themselves accused at Rome of extortion and taking bribes.

Wherever the Roman republic established its sway, it supported the propertied classes (the *optimates* — "good men") against the rest of the population. Timocratic constitutions were set up in the cities (the "rule of the honored" — meaning that of the rich). The resulting social unrest in the Hellenistic world found expression in the revolt of Aristonicus of Pergamum (132–129 B.C.E.) and his attempt to establish a Utopian "Sun City." The social unrest was suppressed, by the use of force when necessary. No wonder, then, that the Greeks of Asia Minor and Hellas began in their despair to look for help among the barbarian enemies of Rome.

The situation in the provinces was made far more critical by the permanent crisis in Rome and Italy. The encroachments of the ruling aristocracy upon the public domain had at last roused popular opposition. The former ability of the Roman leaders to compromise seems to have been one of the casualties of the Hannibalic War. When an agrarian reform was proposed by the people's tribune, Tiberius Gracchus, who was himself of noble descent, his proposals were vetoed by one of his colleagues. Instead of patiently renewing his proposal each year, as had once been the practice, Gracchus contravened the law by having his opponent deposed by popular vote. Now the aristocratic faction felt free to act likewise, and Tiberius Gracchus was killed in a riot in 133 B.C.E. His brother Gaius took up the fight. He succeeded in driving a wedge between the senatorial aristocracy and the financial "knights" by taking away the law courts from the Senate. The taxes of Asia were now farmed out to the "knights"; and henceforward the provincial governors, who had opposed the capacity of the tax-farmers and tried to protect their subjects, were obliged to stand trial by the friends of the very extortioners — an ironical result of a reform intended to repair the injustices of the state. Gaius Gracchus was killed in his turn; and so were Saturninus and Livius Drusus, who tried to follow in the footsteps of the Gracchi. The attempts of the reformers to settle the landless Romans in colonies on the public lands in Italy, aroused the Italian allies of Rome, who began to clamor for citizenship. The cruel exploitations of the slaves on the large estates, especially in Sicily, led to a series of slave revolts, each lasting for years and suppressed with much difficulty, particularly the final one, led by Spartacus. (135–132, 104–100, 73–71 B.C.E.)

The Roman republic, which had so far been victorious in all its wars, began to rot at its very center, from which the corruption soon spread to the periphery. In the war against Jugurtha, king of Numidia (111–105 B.C.E.), the Roman armies were handicapped by the venality of their leaders. Jugurtha summed the matter up neatly when upon leaving Rome he called it "a venal city, only waiting to find a purchaser."[11] The invasion of Gaul and northern Italy by two Germanic tribes (the Cimbri and Teutones) was defeated only after a long struggle and many disasters.

G. The Ascendency of Military Commanders

The solution of the Roman crisis came from the army. Already Marius, himself one of the *novi homines* ("new men"), had reformed the legions by abolishing the former drafting of citizens by class and replacing them by volunteers drawn from the propertyless and landless masses. Only the officer corps remained largely the preserve of the aristocracy. The new army, detached from the land and from citizen politics, was entirely dependent on its generals. If victorious, they gave their soldiers booty, and provided them with land. All aspiring politicians in Rome were now forced to become military leaders. They had been taught by the bitter experience of the reformers of old that their own personal safety and advancement in the state depended on the armed forces at their disposal. They had also, of course, to have the support of a party, which could supply the necessary political and administrative cadres to carry out their policy; but the final decision rested within the camp.

The first to fully grasp the new reality was Sulla. When his adversaries in Rome voted him out of command of the troops destined for Asia, he marched his soldiers into Rome and overturned the legal government. He proved thereby that the army in its new Marian mold would serve its general even against the republican establishment. But as the raising and maintenance of large armies required some definite pretext, we note that the republic, while undergoing internal convulsion, was engaged in perpetual wars of conquest. The Roman empire grew by leaps and bounds at the very time when the Roman civil wars were at their height.

One of the longest of these armed conflicts, and the one which affected the whole of Asia Minor and Greece, were the two wars against King Mithradates VI Eupator of Pontus (northern Asia Minor), the first lasting from 88 to 86 and the second from 74 to 63 B.C.E. This energetic ruler, of Persian descent but with a smattering of Greek culture, formed the grand design of banishing the Romans from the East. Having beaten two Roman armies and occupied the whole of Asia Minor, he sent an army to Greece, which was enthusiastically received at Athens. In 88 B.C.E. Mithradates ordered the wholesale extermination of the Romans and Italians living in Asia — men, women and children. It is the best proof of the malign character of Roman rule in Asia that his order was obeyed by almost all the Greek cities — eighty thousand people were massacred in one day. The Roman effort to reconquer the lost provinces was hampered by the revolt of the Italian allies, who demanded their citizens' rights, and by political upheavals in Rome itself. Sulla, who commanded in the East, was cut off from his homeland, but still continued to fight Mithradates until the latter agreed to evacuate Asia and return to his native Pontus. In the meantime the war with the Italian allies had been concluded by a settlement enfranchising practically the whole of the peninsula.

The last opponents of Rome among the Samnites were destroyed by Sulla upon his return to Italy (83 B.C.E.). As a dictator Sulla tried to bolster up the authority of the Senate, but this could not last; the aristocracy was too weakened and too divided. Sulla's other innovation had more lasting effects. He introduced the systematic proscription and extermination of his political opponents by drawing up lists of those condemned to death and ordering the confiscation of their property; rewards were offered to the killers of the condemned. Sulla's democratic enemies had done the same thing, but less systematically. In such a way the civil wars, which lasted for over half a century, decimated the ruling Roman aristocracy. The stage was left empty and ready to be occupied by the quiet and efficient civil servants of the empire, recruited from the Italian municipalities and the provincial colonies.

The resistance against Sulla continued under Sertorius in Spain (80–72 B.C.E.), but in Rome all was quiet. The dictator abdicated in 79 B.C.E. and within a decade his reforms were annulled by two of his henchmen, Pompey and Crassus. The Mithradatic War was renewed on a smaller scale in 74 B.C.E. The king of Pontus now allied himself with Tigranes of Armenia and the Cilician pirates. The latter, who had begun to infest the

Mediterranean after the breakdown of the Rhodian sea power, had even threatened the corn supply of Rome. Lucullus, who had succeeded in expelling Mithradates from Bithynia and Paphlagonia, failed in Armenia. He was replaced by Pompey, who had cleared the seas from the pirates. From 67 to 64 B.C.E. Pompey fought in Asia, conquering the Pontic kingdom, advancing up to the Caucasus and the Caspian Sea, and marching across Asia Minor from north to south. In 64 B.C.E. he took Antioch and put an end to the last remnants of Seleucid power. In the same year he arrived at Damascus, and learned there of the situation in Judea.

Pompey's conquest of the Orient led to two decisions of lasting importance. One was the Roman resolve to make the Euphrates their frontier. The earlier experiences of Lucullus in Armenia, and the later disaster at Carrhae, where a Roman army was annihilated from a distance by the Parthians archers, showed the wisdom of this policy. Instead of wandering about in the wildernesses of Persia or the mountains of Armenia, the Romans stopped at a more or less defensible line, formed by the Euphrates in the north and the Arabian desert in the south. They abandoned the lands eastward to the Parthians, and their dependents the Palmyrenes and Armenians. Although there were to be occasional future clashes with the kings of the East, mainly over Armenia, and sporadic attempts to extend Roman rule over Mesopotamia, the eastern frontier remained stabilized for almost two centuries.

H. ROME AND THE HELLENISTIC WORLD

In the lands behind that frontier the Romans stood before a historical dilemma. During the centuries of Hellenistic rule the original impetus of Alexander and his successors had long become a spent force. Since the late third century B.C.E. Hellenism in Asia had been in full retreat. The decline of the Seleucid state and the loss of one province after another, whether by conquest or revolt, had brought some of the native rulers, such as the Itureans and the Hasmoneans, to the very shores of the Mediterranean, the inner sea of the Hellenistic world. The new conquerors could ostensibly try either to compromise with the native rulers, who certainly represented the majority of the population of the Orient, or to prop up the failing Greek or Hellenized cities and resume the work left unfinished by Alexander and his successors. This dilemma existed, of course, only on the surface. The Romans had been infected with the Greek virus centuries ago, from the moment, in fact, when they had come into contact with Greek literature, philosophy and art. Although their philhellenism might sometimes prove a useful political tool, it was nevertheless to a great extent genuine, especially in those areas of human endeavor in which the Romans were themselves uninterested. If it was not a matter of *parcere subjectis et debellare superbos*, the Roman aristocrat willingly admitted the superiority of Greek culture. In the West he could hope to Latinize the conquered provinces, and largely succeeded; but in the East he had no choice but to try and Hellenize them. For the cultures of the East, their religions and their art, he had nothing but contempt. It was only very slowly and gradually that he came to understand, in the wake of his Greek mentors, the spiritual forces behind these strange and, to his eye, uncouth phenomena.

Historians have been divided on the motivating power behind Roman imperialism. Some have considered it the result of a deep inner urge, an absolute will to power, while others have held that the Roman empire, like the British, was built "in a fit of absence of mind."[12] As we have seen, the Roman empire was certainly not the result of a deep-laid plan systematically carried out through the centuries. Its expansion was based on two factors: fear of the repetition of a Hannibalian attack on Italy, causing the Romans to look for more and more security by dominating every possible source of attack; and the material advantages to be derived from the rule over rich lands and peoples for both nobility and commoners alike. The security of Italy involved not only the physical safety of the Roman homeland from assault by foreign armies, but also the maintenance of an undisturbed supply route for the corn necessary to feed Rome's citizens — theoretically the sovereign masters of the empire — after the ruin of Italian agriculture. Thus the safety of the sea routes from piracy was a basic tenet of Roman policy; this in turn involved the domination of all the Mediterranean's coastal areas without exception — it was on this point that Roman imperial policy became incompatible with the independence of a Jewish state.

In carrying out their policy of domination first by protectorate and then by annexation, the Romans were guided by a deeply rooted belief in the inherent superiority of their people and its institutions over all others. Rome stood midway between the strong but uncouth barbarians of the North and West and the soft, civilized degenerates of Greece and the Orient. This feeling of superiority, embodied in the concept of the *maiestas populi Romani* to which all must bow, was not based — as it was with the Oriental peoples such as the Assyrians, Babylonians or Persians — on the religion of a national god more powerful than all the others. The Roman superiority complex was indeed to a certain extent camouflaged by a Stoic philosophy taken over wholesale from Hellenistic Greece: the idea that the "just man" — that is the Stoic — was alone entitled to guide the less enlightened. The Stoic creed only gave a respectable expression, in contemporary philosophical terms, to a fundamental belief of every Roman, lettered and unlettered alike. This belief gave the Roman leaders their admirable steadfastness in bad times and their detestable arrogance in good. Such gestures as that of one Roman ambassador who offered the Carthaginians the choice of peace or war in two folds of his toga, or of another who presented an ultimatum to Antiochus IV before the walls of Alexandria, drawing a circle round the king and asking him to decide before leaving it — are manifestations of the Roman sense of destiny in all its harshness and crudity.

The problem confronting those who had to encounter the Romans was therefore not whether a conflict could be avoided — it could not — but what their chances were when it occurred. Here the Romans had an enormous advantage over the Hellenistic monarchies who had so far dominated the East, over Macedonia and over the barbarians of the West. The latter were divided into many warring political entities. Macedonia had a brave and loyal populace, but was too small and had no room for maneuver, besides being handicapped by the need to keep in line with Greece with its fissiparous tendencies and its memories of "liberty" of the city states. The Hellenistic monarchies of the East had no reliable source of loyal manpower, and were rent with dynastic troubles.

In contrast with these adversaries the Romans possessed a relatively huge reservoir of manpower; they had the best and most highly trained infantry of the period, at a time when professional armies were dominant. They were impelled to use their superiority by the very instability of their home politics. The deadly struggle between the Senate aristocracy and the "popular" factions made the command of an army and a province a vital necessity for every aspiring politician. To keep the army loyal and contented its commander had to supply it with booty and hence engage in a policy of conquest. This was pursued with a doggedness that nothing could stop; typical is the example of Sulla who, though officially an outlaw, continued to fight an external foe before moving against his enemies at home. The only real limits to Roman aggressiveness were the forests of Germany or the deserts of Parthia, where the Roman legions could not operate effectively. In all other areas there was no escaping the superiority of Roman arms: sieges might last for years, but in the end the obstinacy of the besiegers carried every fortress. *Romanus sedendo vincit* — "The Roman conquers by just sitting still" — summed up the perseverance with which such sieges were conducted. The same is true of their rule — unique among armies of antiquity — of entrenching themselves in a camp after a day's march — another example of the tenacity of purpose that marked Roman warfare.

In their political behavior in the provinces the Romans were sure, by virtue of their crushing military superiority, of being able to carry out any policy that served their interests, however unpopular or unjust. They preferred to support a timocratic minority, which was dependent on them for the safety of its members and their property, than to carry out plans of reform; indeed, reformers were suspected of wishing to upset the status quo, of which Roman suzerainty was an integral part.

The strength of Roman policy, as that of the Roman army, was such that it could be carried out without much thought or intelligence; it was enough to follow the rules. Caesar, who was a master politician, subdued the Gauls with less effort than did Pompey the East; the latter was certainly no more skillful than the average politician of his time. Hence we need not wonder that Pompey soon made up his mind to lend the full weight of the Roman power to prop up the declining Hellenistic culture of the East, even if that meant supporting a rich and cultured minority against the mass of the people. The results of this fateful decision were many and varied; its disastrous effect on the history of the Jewish people (of all nations with whom the Romans came into contact the Jews were the one they least understood) both in its own country and in the Diaspora will form the principal content of this and the following volumes.

CHAPTER I

THE FALL OF THE HASMONEAN DYNASTY
AND THE ROMAN CONQUEST

by A. Schalit

A. Queen Salome Alexandra

THE REIGN OF Queen Salome Alexandra (76–67 B.C.E.) was the last peaceful moment before the outbreak of the storm which overwhelmed the Hasmonean dynasty. As has been explained in the previous volume, Salome handed over the conduct of her home policy to the Pharisees, while she herself kept control over foreign affairs, in which she seems to have shown both intelligence and some measure of military enterprise. Thus she attempted to intervene in Syrian affairs and to derive some benefit from the turmoil in that country. Her younger son, Aristobulus, was despatched with an army to Damascus, ostensibly to defend the city from the tyranny of Ptolemy Mennaeus, the ruler of Chalcis, but actually in order to conquer the city and add it to the Hasmonean state.[1] This attempt failed, however, and Damascus became temporarily a Nabataean possession.

Roman intervention in Syrian affairs was now inevitable. For more than twenty years since the death of Antiochus IX Cyzicenus,[2] the stepbrother of Antiochus VIII Grypus,[3] Syria had known no rest. Chaos ruled throughout the whole country, with no end in sight to the political turmoil. The five sons of Grypus (Seleucus VI, Antiochus XI, Philip, Demetrius III, Eucaerus or Acaerus,[4] and Antiochus XII) each in turn fought Antiochus X Pius,[5] the son of Antiochus Cyzicenus. Finally, the endurance of the Greek cities of Syria was exhausted. They summoned Tigranes of Armenia to occupy the country and so put an end to the disorder and anarchy that had paralyzed the lives of its inhabitants for decades.[6]

Tigranes did not hesitate; he occupied Syria and ruled it for fourteen years (83/82–70/69 B.C.E.).[7] The Armenian "King of Kings" was a dangerous neighbor for the Hasmoneans. Salome realized that sooner or later Tigranes would try to conquer her kingdom as well, in order to extend his control over the whole eastern shore of the Mediterranean. The queen decided to pay tribute to Tigranes and thus ensure peace and the continuance of the rule of the Hasmonean dynasty. This fact, too, testifies to her realistic and cautious political outlook. Rather than engage in knight-errantry, she weighed only the realities of military power. Tigranes accepted the submission of Salome[8] in his camp outside Accho-Ptolemais, while besieging Cleopatra Selene.[9] However, even had this act of submission not been made, the Hasmonean state would still have been saved in the long run by Lucullus' victory over Tigranes.

Lucullus could not complete his overthrow of the "King of Kings," as his men refused to continue the war into Armenia;[10] but he did take Syria away from Tigranes and handed it over to Antiochus XIII "Asiaticus," the last of the Seleucids.[11] In this way the dangerous Armenian neighbor vanished from the borders of the Hasmonean kingdom. The latter was, however, merely granted a short breathing space, for the first active interference of the Roman army in the affairs of Syria foreshadowed her coming invasion of that country. One may surmise that Lucullus refrained from a total annexation of Syria because of his preoccupation with the serious war in the East against Mithradates, and because of the intrigues against him at Rome, which finally led to his removal from the eastern command. Yet even without a formal annexation, Syria had now entered the vassalage of Rome. It must have been obvious to any clear-sighted observer that complete subjugation was merely a matter of time, and a short time at that.

After Syria came the turn of the Hasmonean state. Subjugation of the northern part of the Mediterranean's eastern littoral necessitated the subjugation of its southern part as well. This meant the conquest of the Hasmonean state, for the whole of that coastal strip was considered by all ancient conquerors, the Romans included, as a single geopolitical area. One additional political factor must be kept in mind. Rome did not customarily allow any country, great or small, to remain an independent state within her sphere of influence, without attempting to annex it or at least to turn it into a Roman protectorate. The internal logic of Roman imperialism forced that world power to extend its hand to the Hasmonean state also, perhaps initially in a clasp of friendship, but later, at the right moment, in the fist of military conquest. In 69 B.C.E., a breathing space was granted both the Hasmonean and the Syrian state alike. Rome was troubled by important matters relating to her administration of the East in general, and had no time to spend on the total subjugation of these weak countries. They would in any case fall into the hands of Rome when the time was ripe.

The expected change occurred some years later. Pompey was charged with conducting the difficult war against Mithradates VI, king of Pontus. Pursuing the defeated king he vanquished all of the neighboring countries as far as the Caucasus. The eastern littoral of the Mediterranean entered within his plan of conquest for the East.[12] This special task was entrusted to the legate, Marcus Aemilius Scaurus.[13] At Damascus, which had already been taken by Lollius and Metellus,[14] two officers in the Roman army, Scaurus learned of the struggle between Hyrcanus and Aristobulus, the sons of Jannaeus Alexander and Salome Alexandra, for the Hasmonean throne. Hyrcanus, the elder son, had been appointed to the High Priesthood on his mother's accession after Jannaeus' death (76 B.C.E.).[15] With the High Priesthood, Hyrcanus was also made heir to the secular power, a state of affairs unacceptable to his brother Aristobulus.

While Salome was yet alive but fatally ill, Aristobulus decided to act in order to win the crown and High Priesthood. He was assisted by the Sadducees and opposed by the Pharisaic counsellors of the queen. Josephus relates that Aristobulus, who was supported by the officers and the army, seized twenty-two Judean fortresses within a short space of time. He also gathered a mercenary army from Lebanon and Trachonitis, whose dynasts (μόναρχοι) trusted his ability to seize the whole kingdom and recompense them for their assistance.[16] Salome's counsellors were afraid that if Aristobulus became king he would take his revenge on the Pharisees; for during Salome's reign they had perpetrated many acts of cruelty and violence against the Saducean companions of Aristobulus and his father, Jannaeus. On the authority of the dying queen they confined Aristobulus' wife and children as hostages in the citadel overlooking the Temple.[17]

B. The Fratricidal War of Aristobulus ii and Hyrcanus ii

On Salome's death the two brothers began to wage open war. The majority of Hyrcanus' men deserted him for Aristobulus. Hyrcanus was defeated in a battle near Jericho and forced to flee to Jerusalem. There he seized the citadel where his brother's family were kept confined. Once Aristobulus had overcome Hyrcanus' men who had fled to the Temple court, the two brothers came to an agreement. Hyrcanus gave up the High Priesthood and the crown in favor of Aristobulus, and retired into private life, bereft of all power.[18] As a mark of reconciliation the two brothers exchanged dwellings. Aristobulus was installed in the royal palace and Hyrcanus took up his residence in the house Aristobulus had occupied in private life.[19]

The reconciliation did not last long, however. Hyrcanus had an old

Idumaean friend named Antipater who, according to Josephus,[20] came from a rich and noble family; according to Nicholaus of Damascus he was descended from a Jewish family which had returned from the Babylonian exile.[21] Antipater's father, whose name was also Antipater or Antipas, had in his time been appointed by Jannaeus and kept on by Salome as governor of Idumaea. He had succeeded in winning the friendship of his neighbors the Arabs (undoubtedly Nabataeans), as well as of the inhabitants of Gaza and Ascalon.[22] It is possible that the younger Antipater succeeded to this post after the death of his father. At all events, like his father he was close to the royal family and among the close friends of Hyrcanus, the heir apparent. There is no doubt that his influence on Hyrcanus was already strong in the days of the old queen; Antipater was even then preparing the ground for his own rule, as the chief counsellor of the future king.

When Hyrcanus was deposed, however, Antipater saw that his plan had been quite set at nought by Aristobulus. He therefore attempted to arouse the hostility of the deposed monarch towards Aristobulus with the assertion that the latter intended to kill him. The new king, he argued, could not regard his throne as safe while Hyrcanus lived. Antipater's plan was to smuggle Hyrcanus to the Nabataean king, and to persuade the latter to help Hyrcanus regain his kingdom in return for twelve Nabataean cities which Jannaeus had conquered long ago.[23] Antipater's insinuations finally had the desired effect, and his plan was carried out. Aretas, king of the Nabataeans, marched against Judea with a large force and defeated Aristobulus in battle. The majority of the king's men now deserted him for Hyrcanus, and Aristobulus was forced to flee to Jerusalem. Since Hyrcanus enjoyed the support of the people (viz. the Pharisaic counsellors of the late Queen Salome and the men of their faction, who hated and feared Aristobulus), Aristobulus took refuge on the Temple Mount in order to defend himself from there. The Sadducean priests faithfully fought for him.[24] It was then the time of the Passover, and many of the Jewish nobles had left the country and had taken refuge in Egypt.[25] The siege was conducted with equal stubbornness on both sides. Josephus reports that the bitterness shown by the besieging forces was so great that they did not refrain even from desecrating the sanctity of the holiday by refusing to supply the Temple with animals for the daily sacrifice, even though they had been paid one thousand drachmas a head. He also reports the story that a certain saintly man, called Onias, was killed by some extremists in Hyrcanus' camp for refusing to curse Aristobulus' men and thus hasten their overthrow. Our source continues that for this deed the punishment of heaven was brought down on the whole country, and the year's crops were lost.[26]

This was the state of affairs in Judea when Marcus Aemilius Scaurus arrived. As soon as he was informed of the fratricidal war within the Hasmonean house, the quaestor decided to extract from the enmity of the brothers and their respective partisans whatever profit he could both for Rome and himself. The arrival of the Roman legions in Syria did not escape the attention of the factions in Judea. Both brothers immediately sent delegations to Scaurus in order to plead before him each side promising a bribe of four hundred talents.[27] Scaurus decided in favor of Aristobulus, not only because the king had created the impression of being more generous and more moderate, but also because he was the effective ruler of the country.[28] Hyrcanus, on the other hand, did not seem to be capable of fulfilling his promises, which were more extravagant than those of Aristobulus, as indeed were also his demands.[29] Scaurus thus espoused the cause of Aristobulus, and after ensuring his bribe, ordered Aretas to lift the siege of the Temple Mount, threatening him with his legions if he failed to obey. After Aretas had complied and Scaurus had returned to Damascus, Aristobulus pursued Hyrcanus and his patron, the king of the Nabataeans, as far as Papyron, apparently near Jericho,[30] where he inflicted a severe defeat on their forces. In this battle (64 B.C.E.) the brother of Antipater the Idumaean was among the slain.[31]

Aristobulus thus seemed to be winning the conflict; but not in the opinion of Antipater, Hyrcanus' Idumaean counsellor. He was aware of a fact which Aristobulus and his counsellors had failed to grasp: not Scaurus, but Pompey, would be the ultimate arbiter in deciding the quarrel. Antipater, therefore, reserved his last effort for a showdown with his adversaries the moment the Roman general arrived.

C. POMPEY INTERVENES

Pompey spent the winter of the year 65/64 in Aspis (Ἀσπίς), the exact location of which is still uncertain, but is known to have been situated in Armenia Minor.[32] In the spring of 64 he left for Syria with the intention, as Plutarch relates,[33] of reaching "the Red Sea by way of Arabia in order to take into his conquest the Ocean which surrounds the inhabited world. In fact, he was the first to conquer Libya up to the Outer Sea and he again established the Roman frontier in Spain as far as the Atlantic Ocean, and thirdly in his pursuit of the Albanians, he all but touched on the Hyrcanian Sea."[34] He seems to have spent the winter of 64/63 in Antioch.[35]

The delegations of the two brothers first reached some place in Syria, most likely Antioch, well before the arrival of Pompey at Damascus.

Antipater the Idumaean represented Hyrcanus and a certain Nicodemus represented Aristobulus. Nicodemus brought Pompey a most precious gift from Aristobulus, in the shape of a vine or bower made of gold, which according to Strabo was worth five hundred talents.[36] He also complained to Pompey about the sums that Aristobulus had been obliged to pay Gabinius[37] and then Scaurus. Such a complaint was, of course, exceedingly ill-advised, especially in the case of Gabinius, who was one of the general's most important officers. The fact that Nicodemus complained to Pompey against the Roman general's confidant, no doubt on the express instruction of Aristobulus, clearly reveals the latter's complete lack of political acumen.[38] In this way Aristobulus quite gratuitously increased the number of his enemies in the general's entourage even before the start of actual negotiations. The resulting prejudice against Aristobulus among the leading members of Pompey's staff must have influenced the general himself, even before he had had the opportunity of examining the differences between the brothers on their merits.

Pompey gave no definite reply to either party, but contented himself with hearing their complaints. He ordered them to come to him in the spring, when he returned to Damascus; for he wanted more time to consider the matter.[39] The Hasmoneans duly presented themselves on the general's arriving to Damascus.[40] In addition to these two parties, however, a third delegation, composed of Pharisees, appeared on behalf of "the people." The Pharisees drew Pompey's attention to the fact that the Jewish nation had always been ruled by priests. The Hasmonean brothers, though priests themselves, stood accused of betraying their office and enslaving the nation with an alien form of government.[41] In spite of this charge of the Pharisees against the very fact of Hasmonean rule, the two brothers continued to abuse each other.

Hyrcanus complained to Pompey that though he was entitled to the crown by right of primogeniture, Aristobulus had appropriated most of the country, leaving him with but a small part of it.[42] Antipater, who undoubtedly was Hyrcanus' spokesman before Pompey, was not satisfied with this accusation alone (the general, after all, could regard it merely as a matter of Jewish internal politics). He therefore advanced an additional charge, one that would be of far greater cogency for Pompey. This referred to the hatred which the Jewish nation felt for Aristobulus, and which Aristobulus felt for the Hellenistic world. The king was described as the sworn enemy of the Greek cities bordering on Judea, which had suffered from his assaults. These were the very cities which Pompey was interested in fostering and protecting for reasons of Roman imperial policy.[43] Antipater's aim was obviously to stamp Aristobulus with the same political image as that of his father Jannaeus, who was hated by the neighboring Gentiles as their mortal enemy, and who had devoted most of his life to the destruction of the centers of Hellenic culture around Judea and the incorporation of their lands within the Jewish state.

Another crime of which Hyrcanus and Antipater accused Aristobulus was the commission of acts of piracy along the shores of Palestine.[44] Such a charge was of special significance for Pompey, as he himself had originally been given the task of crushing the plague of piracy in the eastern basin of the Mediterranean. Aristobulus was thus arraigned at the same time as the enemy of Rome herself and the one who had endangered its maritime traffic. It was surely impossible to leave such a man as Aristobulus on the Hasmonean throne — this quarrelsome rebel, hated by the Jewish nation and the enemy of the new *pax Romana*. To give substance to these charges, testimony was supplied by one thousand notables, whom Antipater had gathered especially for the purpose.[45]

Aristobulus claimed in his defense that he had had no choice but to wrest power from the incompetent grasp of Hyrcanus so as to prevent it from passing altogether from the Hasmonean dynasty into the hands of strangers. He (Aristobulus) had not assumed the title of king as a usurper, but had merely revived the usage of his father, Alexander.[46] Aristobulus also brought witnesses to support his claims. These were, however, Sadducee nobles dressed in the finery of Hellenistic courts, and their appearance made an adverse impression on Pompey and his officers.[47]

The general's initial assessement after hearing all the parties was unfavorable to Aristobulus. He seemed to Pompey to be a man of violence, who should be rendered powerless. It seems that Pompey had even then resolved not only to reduce the size of the Hasmonean state by leaving it only the purely Jewish territories, but to limit the power of the ruling house as well. Gabinius and Scaurus too, for the personal motives explained above, presumably did their best to turn Pompey against Aristobulus. However, the Roman commander-in-chief decided to postpone his decision for the moment, contenting himself with administering a summary rebuke to Aristobulus.[48] He bade all the Jewish parties await his decision until after he had managed to settle the Nabataean problem. To curb Aristobulus' rashness, Pompey ordered him to remain in the Roman camp and to accompany the army. Aristobulus seems to have guessed at the general's intentions. Possibly he was suspicious that Pompey would use him as a hostage in order to exploit the Hasmonean state for his own ends — all behind a mask of courtesy and honor.[49] In addition, Aristobulus acted from the typically "Hasmonean" motive of pride. Josephus contends that Aristobulus regarded it as a personal degradation to have to curry favor with Pompey in order to further his interests.[50] He finally left Pompey's camp near Dium without asking leave.[51]

D. POMPEY IN JUDEA
THE SIEGE OF THE TEMPLE

This impetuous action of Aristobulus aroused Pompey's wrath. He was now forced to change his plans, and decided to postpone his expedition against the Nabataeans in order to pursue Aristobulus. However, he cautiously avoided sending a military force to arrest the king in flight, but tried at first to use persuasion. When the Roman army reached Coreae on the Judean border,[52] Pompey requested Aristobulus, who had fled to the nearby fortress of Alexandrium, to come to the Roman camp. Submitting to the entreaties of his companions not to provoke the Romans, Aristobulus consented to enter Pompey's camp. There he stated his case to the general in the matter of his quarrel with Hyrcanus. Pompey acted with restraint and permitted Aristobulus to return to the fortress. The negotiations were resumed several times, once even at the instigation of Hyrcanus. Aristobulus still hoped to save his throne by flattering Pompey and pretending to obey his every command. He nevertheless always made a point of returning to the fortress in order to safeguard his position and to be prepared for future trouble, should Pompey decide to transfer power to Hyrcanus. In such a case, Aristobulus was ready to fight.[53]

Pompey finally showed his cards by requesting Aristobulus to surrender all his fortresses. Aristobulus did in fact obey, but withdrew to Jerusalem fully determined to fight for his throne. Pompey, not wishing to give his adversary time to prepare for war, went in immediate pursuit. On reaching Jericho, Aristobulus once more approached Pompey with a request for a full pardon in return for absolute submission and the payment of a large sum of money. Pompey accepted, and sent Gabinius to take Jerusalem and the money. Aristobulus' men shut the city gates in the face of Pompey's legate and refused to pay the money. When Pompey heard of this he had Aristobulus arrested, and marched on Jerusalem. The people in the city were divided. The majority, who were followers of Hyrcanus and the Pharisees, wanted peace; the partisans of Aristobulus were resolved to resist. The peace party prevailed and opened the city gates to the Romans. Aristobulus' men managed to escape to the Temple Mount and destroyed the bridge connecting the city with the Temple. Part of the Roman army under the legate Piso occupied the main section of the town, including the royal palace. Pompey himself turned his attention to the Temple Mount, the strongest part of the city. At first he tried to persuade the followers of Aristobulus to submit willingly, but without success. Pompey thereupon moved up his full force and besieged the Temple. He chose the easier northern side of the Temple Mount for his assault; but this too was well fortified with high towers and defended by a deep fosse.

The strict observance of the Sabbath was one of the causes of the defeat of the Sadducean defenders. To prepare the ground for the battering rams, which had been brought from Tyre, the Romans were forced to fill in the valleys surrounding the mount on three sides — including the western city side, where the bridge had been destroyed. The valleys were crossed by means of dams constructed of timber and earth. Noticing that the Jews fought on the Sabbath only in order to ward off assaults, the Romans stopped attacking them on that day and busied themselves merely with preparing the siege-dams.

The siege was difficult, for the Jews fought bravely; but finally, after three months of ceaseless attacks, the Romans succeeded in breaching the wall of the Temple on a fast day. They slaughtered the Jews en masse, though some were taken prisoner, including Absalom, the father-in-law of Aristobulus. Having, so to speak, defeated the God of Israel, Pompey exercised his right as conqueror and entered the Holy of Holies, thereby arousing the anger of the nation. He refrained, however, according to Josephus, from touching the Temple's treasures, and on the day after the massacre ordered the Temple to be cleared of all signs of the struggle.[54]

E. POMPEY'S SETTLEMENT

Aristobulus was dethroned and taken in chains to Rome together with his family. One son alone, Alexander, managed to escape on the journey to Rome. The Hasmonean kingdom was abolished. Most of the Sadducees, who had been the most active opponents of the Roman conquest, were executed. The walls of Jerusalem were left breached for two reasons: to prevent the city from again becoming a center of revolt, and to show the world how that rebellious city had been dragged down from its eminence as capital of a sovereign state to the status of an unwalled tributary town.

Hyrcanus received only a grudging reward from Pompey, in the form of his confirmation as High Priest and leader of the people.[55] The main blow, however, fell on the Jewish state, which had been established by the joint endeavors of the people and the Hasmonean dynasty. In accordance with

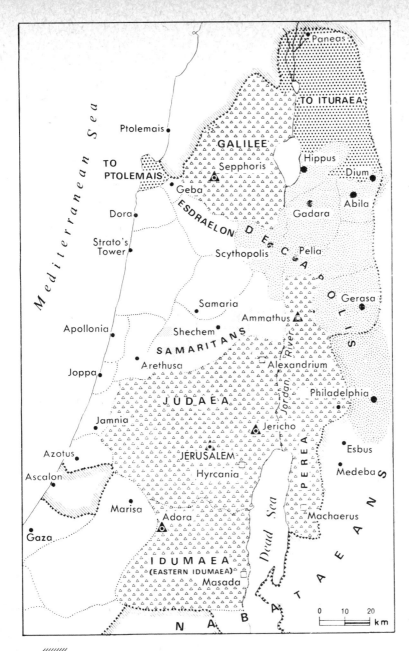

Border of Judaea before Pompey's arrangements

Judaea after Pompey's arrangements

Areas of Judaea given to Ituraea and Ptolemais

Land of Samaritans

• Independent city under proconsul of Syria

● City of the Decapolis

▲ Gabinius' Synedria

□ Jannaeus' fortresses

.... Municipal boundaries

Pompey's territorial arrangements

his pro-Hellenic policy in the East, Pompey deprived the former Hasmonean state of all its past conquests along the shore of the Mediterranean in the west, and across the Jordan in the east. Josephus lists the following towns which were now lost to Judea as a result: Gadara, Hippus, Scythopolis, Pella, Dium, Samaria, Marissa, Azotus, Jamnia, Arethusa, Gaza, Joppa, Dora, and Strato's Tower (later Caesarea).[56] All these cities were declared "free," and annexed to the new province of Syria.[57] Jerusalem was made a tributary town (*civitas stipendiaria*),[58] while Judea was divided into districts for the systematic levying of taxes — the chief function of a conbuered country in the *imperium Romanum*.[59] Responsibility for the collection of the tax was no doubt placed on the shoulders of Hyrcanus,[60] while as a High Priest he had the right to administer the nation's internal affairs according to the laws of Israel. In other words, the Jewish people received self-government in accordance with the Roman principle of *libertas*, as was customary for a city with the status of *civitas stipendiaria*.[61]

These changes clearly indicated that the former Hasmonean state was gradually being turned into a Roman province, although this was not effected in 63 B.C.E. At first Judea was not even annexed to the province of Syria, as were the Hellenistic cities which were separated from the Hasmonean state. But the existing political and legal status of the Jewish remainder of the Hasmonean state was obviously temporary. The country was under the jurisdiction of Hyrcanus, but his authority as High Priest emanated politically and legally from the juridical authority of the Roman governor in Syria. The governor could always intervene in Hyrcanus' affairs for any reason he saw fit.[62]

Pompey's motive in introducing an intermediate stage is clear enough. He understood that the small Jewish nation was different from other peoples of the East. These were easily subdued and ruled, whereas the Jews had their own highly distinctive culture and a well developed national consciousness. It would probably be impossible to place them under direct Roman rule without an intermediate stage. Judea's annexation to the province of Syria or its establishment as a seperate province would both cause endless difficulties. That Pompey realized this explains his decision to leave the Jews a shadow of their former independence in the form of the "interregnum" of Hyrcanus. It would last until the country was ready for complete Roman subjugation.

F. The Significance of Pompey's Conquest

We may now examine the full significance of Pompey's conquest in 63 B.C.E., when the Jewish people came under the mastery of Rome. We must discover how the ruling circles in Judea reacted to their imperial conquerors, for in doing so we shall be able to reveal the basis on which Judeo-Roman relations were established, and how they developed up to the destruction of the Temple.

According to Josephus, the responsibility for the fatal result of the civil war in Judea lay with the sons of Salome Alexandra. The crown of Israel passed into the hands of those who were neither priests nor of royal blood; financial ruin befell the country following the Roman conquest and the extortion of an enormous sum of money (10,000 talents) from Judea; the Hasmonean conquests which had been won at such immense sacrifice were lost, and the reduced Jewish territory placed under the yoke of Rome. In Josephus' view, Aristobulus and Hyrcanus shared responsibility for this state of affairs, since their quarrel for the crown had opened the door of the country to the Romans.[63]

There is obviously some truth in this assessment. The quarrel of the Hasmonean brothers certainly paved the way for Pompey and his legate, Scaurus, to gain control over the Hasmonean state, although this in itself did not reduce the Jewish nation to Roman rule. By examining the characters of Aristobulus and Hyrcanus we may be able to judge how far each contributed to the fateful events of 63 B.C.E. and the ruin of the Hasmonean dynasty.

Josephus describes them as two totally different characters. Hyrcanus is portrayed as a weak man whose only wish was to live in peace and quiet.[64] This is the view taken by most historians, with the exception of Laqueur in his hypercritical book *Der jüdische Historiker Flavius Josephus*.[65] According to Laqueur, Hyrcanus had a strong personality and a distinct will to rule; and indeed there are grounds here for questioning the accepted view. A study of Hyrcanus' life leaves no doubt of his craving for power, and of his reluctance to relinquish it throughout his life. Hyrcanus never gave up the struggle for power, and never despaired even in the most hopeless of circumstances.

One cannot overlook the influence of Antipater the Idumaean, who constantly guided Hyrcanus in all his actions. Yet even Antipater would hardly have been able to follow the course he did if Hyrcanus had really been the man Josephus describes. We must conclude, therefore, that Hyrcanus shared those two qualities common to most of the Hasmoneans —

an uncontrollable desire for power, and a blind obstinacy in which the possibility of failure was never considered. (His daughter, Alexandra, seems to have inherited this side of his character.) Hyrcanus however, lacked that capacity for action and that uncompromising strength of will usually found in men who yearn for the power of kingship.

With Hyrcanus, a lack of political ability thwarted a lust for power — a judgement shared by Josephus in *Antiquities*. He was thus a tool in the hands of the Idumaean, the man chiefly responsible for the destruction of the Hasmonean royalty; Hyrcanus himself clearly hoped to preserve the integrity of the Hasmonean kingdom as he had received it from his mother. But at the critical moment Hyrcanus was incapable of making a stand. He had no idea where to draw the line with Antipater, or how to restrain the Idumaean and his sons. Under these conditions the kingdom of Jannaeus and Salome Alexandra could not long survive. Power passed from the weak hands of their offspring into those of the energetic Idumaean, who was supported by two young but talented sons, Phasael and Herod. Even while Antipater was alive, Hyrcanus had become a mere figurehead. After Antipater's death, Phasael and Herod completed their father's work, slowly concentrating all power into their own hands by mutual cooperation. When Phasael died, Herod continued alone assisted, of course, by the Romans. Finally, Herod established his rule over the whole country, liquidating the last remnants of the Hasmonean dynasty, including Hyrcanus himself.

In contrast to his brother, Aristobulus is described as "an active and bold man" ($\delta\rho\alpha\sigma\tau\acute{\eta}\rho\iota\sigma\varsigma$ $\kappa\alpha\acute{\iota}$ $\delta\iota\epsilon\gamma\eta\gamma\epsilon\rho\mu\acute{\epsilon}\nu\sigma\varsigma$ $\tau\grave{o}$ $\varphi\rho\acute{o}\nu\eta\mu\alpha$).[66] He loved the life of the army, though this alone does not necessarily mean that he possessed any military talent. What we know of his way of life attests to an authoritarian spirit. He dressed in magnificent robes and insisted on being surrounded with a splendid court, including a band of nobles, who apparently formed an élite military unit.[67] According to Josephus, he resembled his father Jannaeus in every way; this was also the opinion of his contemporaries, especially the Pharisees, who feared him. However, these external features could not hide a lack of true military skill, and as a politician he was a complete failure, though of a different kind from his brother Hyrcanus. Aristobulus lacked the two main qualities needed by the expert politician; he had neither self-control, nor the capacity for cool, rational appraisal without which it is impossible to suit the action to the needs of the hour. His inherent rashness clouded his powers of judgement, and prevented his profiting by seizing the right moment.

This political deficiency became most evident when the Roman legions arrived. Unable to control his stormy temper, he made the fatal mistake of resorting to force without reflecting on the change in the balance of military power. His guiding principle should have been to safeguard the independent state he had inherited from his father.[68] That independence had been gained at the expense of the degenerate Seleucid empire and the Hellenistic cities of the coast and of Transjordan. The Hasmoneans had been able to establish their rule only because of the decline of the Seleucid kingdom which had begun in the middle of the second century B.C.E. For the Hasmonean state to survive the Seleucids had always to remain weak, but never entirely disappear and so make room for a stronger power. The moment the Romans entered Syria, they ended the existence of the Seleucid state and found themselves in direct contact with the Hasmoneans. The fate of the whole of Judea was involved, for it was considered by the Romans as part of Syria and its conquest by Pompey as merely the right military consequence from a geographical reality. Therefore Josephus is definitely wrong in stating that the quarrel between Hyrcanus and Aristobulus opened the gates of the country to Pompey's armies: Pompey's arrival was in any case inevitable.

Had Aristobulus been a true politician and able to read the signs of the times, he would have immediately drawn the correct conclusions from the presence of Roman legions in Syria. The shortsightedness of Aristobulus and his advisers made the Romans from the very beginning of their conquest regard the Jews as a discontented and rebellious people, whom it was necessary to crush. Pompey, mistrusting the insolent Aristobulus, identified him with the Hasmonean dynasty in general. Not only was it not safe to leave such a man in power: it would be expedient to abolish the rule of the whole Hasmonean dynasty. The Romans, moreover, could not allow the Jews to retain their conquests, since these made them too important a factor in Syria.[69]

The inheritance of Jannaeus Alexander thus passed away with Aristobulus. Rome felt obliged to force the rebellious Jews into her imperial framework. Toward this end, she replaced the national dynasty first by Antipater the Idumaean, and on his death by his sons, who received unlimited power. Such was the result of the events of 63 B.C.E.[70]

G. The Reforms of Gabinius

Pompey left Marcus Aemilius Scaurus as commander of the troops in Syria and of the whole area from the Euphrates to Egypt. Scaurus wanted to set out on the expedition against the Nabataeans, which Pompey had earlier planned but had been forced to postpone because of his confrontation with Aristobulus. The difficulties of such an expedition, however, were so great that the Roman commander contented himself with a bribe of 300 talents from Aretas, in return for leaving him alone. The intermediary in the deal was Antipater, who guaranteed payment of the sum — proof of the great wealth he had already amassed. Antipater also supplied the army on its way through the desert. It is not known if Scaurus made any changes in Pompey's administrative reform of Judea. It seems that he did not generally interfere in the affairs of Hyrcanus and Antipater, or in the internal frictions among the Jews.[71] The same may be said of the governors of Syria who succeeded Scaurus: Marcus Philippus, who governed in 61–60 B.C.E.[72] and Lentulus Marcellinus, who served in 59–58 B.C.E.[73] Both of these, however, continued the war against the Nabataeans.[74]

During this time Judea was not at rest, though there seem to have been no open disturbances. These began with the appointment of Aulus Gabinius as governor of Syria (57–55 B.C.E.).[75] Gabinius followed an active policy of restoring the situation as it had been prior to the Hasmonean conquests. He began to rebuild the Hellenistic cities destroyed by Jannaeus, and to resettle Gentiles there in place of those whom the Hasmoneans had either slain or driven out. The moving force behind the opposition was Alexander, the son of Aristobulus who had escaped his captors on the way to Rome. He first tried to restore the walls of Jerusalem, which had been breached by Pompey, but was prevented from doing so by a superior force of Roman colonists and their slaves.[76]

In spite of this failure, Alexander was able to amass a considerable army (10,000 foot soldiers and 1,500 horsemen) and to rebuild the fortresses of Alexandrium, Hyrcania and Machaerus.[77] Mark Antony (the future triumvir) was despatched against him with a force of Roman volunteers, undoubtedly raised from the Romans resident in Jerusalem. They were accompanied by Hyrcanus' men under the leadership of Peitholaus and Malichus. Antipater, too, was not slow to send auxiliaries. All of these formed the vanguard; the main force under the command of Gabinius himself came later. Alexander was defeated in a battle near Jerusalem, and withdrew to Alexandrium. There Gabinius besieged him, offering peace on the condition that he surrender his fortresses. Gabinius left Mark Antony to finish the siege, while he himself took part of the army to restore the Hellenistic cities. Among the cities mentioned by Josephus as having been restored by Gabinius are Samaria, Azotus, Scythopolis, Anthedon, Raphia, Dora, Marissa, Gaza, Apollonia, Jamnia and Gabala.[78]

Having finished this task, Gabinius returned to Alexandrium. The capture of this fortress he considered of major importance for the furtherance of Rome's Hellenistic policy in the East; moreover this matter had been personally entrusted to him by Pompey before the latter's departure from Syria. Alexander finally capitulated, handing over first the fortresses of Hyrcania and Machaerus, and at last Alexandrium too. His only stipulation was that he could withdraw when it suited him. Alexander's mother, who was anxious for the welfare of her husband and children then in captivity in Rome, was instrumental in arranging this treaty. Gabinius destroyed the fortresses to prevent them from serving as future strongholds of resistance.

Gabinius realized, however, that the spirit of revolt in Judea was not extinguished. The rebellion of Alexander was a sign of deep popular resentment against the new order. If the Roman authorities wished to root out the danger, they would have to deal with the people, the overwhelming majority of whom supported Aristobulus and his dynasty in their revolt against the legates of Rome. The steps which Pompey had so far taken in Judea were obviously inadequate. A different form of administration was required, one that had already been established in the other countries of the East that Pompey had conquered. Rome must strike at the national unity of the Jews in order to prevent a united stand behind their national dynasty. The plan was not new; it had repeatedly proved itself even in conquered territories inhabited by a refractory populace. It was based on the well-tried principle of *divide et impera*. Macedonia, for example, had been divided by the Roman commander-in-chief, Lucius Aemilius Paulus, into four separate provinces. The inhabitants of each province were denied the rights of marrying and owning land outside their own territory. The internal administration was conducted by elected councils (*synhedria*), one to each province. No connection was allowed between them; they formed four closed and entirely separate administrative units.[79]

These councils probably had an aristocratic, or more correctly, timocratic membership. In administering the conquered territory, the Romans usually adopted a system similar to the one used in republican Rome, in which citizens were qualified by their ownership of property. The aristocratic or wealthy elements of a conquered people were induced to support the conquerors by being granted special rights, lands or titles of honor, including sometimes Roman citizenship. Whenever the Romans wished to bring an influential tribal leader over to their side he was offered the exalted title of "ally and friend of the Roman people."[80]

The results of this policy were disastrous for the people of Macedonia. The nation's unity was destroyed and its economy ruined. Land lost its value, leaving the field wide open to Roman speculators, who provided loans to impoverished farmers at usurious rates, and then acquired their lands by default.

These "reforms" of Lucius Aemilius Paulus had served more than once as an example for later Roman conquerors in their administration of newly conquered territory. In Macedonia the Romans had discovered an effective way of crushing a proud people, who remained obdurately attached to a national and imperial tradition. Gabinius apparently now saw himself faced with a similar problem in Judea. Here, too, the conquering Romans found a stubborn people with its own peculiar culture and a strong national and political consciousness marked by a love of freedom and a hatred of slavery.

Gabinius saw no other alternative but to copy the measures of Paulus in Macedonia, if he wished to establish control over the rebellious Jews. The actions of both are indeed similar, although we have no evidence that Gabinius forbade *conubium* between the areas of his *synhedria*. He seems to have been satisfied with the sole prohibition of *commercium;* but this in itself was enough to bring economic misfortune on the country.

We have already noted that there was a large Roman colony in Jerusalem when Gabinius was proconsul — the *conventus civium Romanorum* who prevented Aristobulus' son Alexander from establishing himself in Jerusalem. They were the *cives Romani qui negotiantur; negotiatores* — the speculators who followed in the wake of the Roman army. At first, no doubt, their numbers were small, but when Gabinius' destructive reforms began to have their effect, they came in droves. The policy which had brought economic disaster to Macedonia after the battle of Pydna, produced similar results in Judea after the collapse of the Hasmonean dynasty.

The comparison between Gabinius in Judea and Lucius Aemilius Paulus in Macedonia is reinforced by the fact that Gabinius apparently placed his five *synhedria* on an aristocratic-timocratic basis, by restoring the nobles to their former power. These nobles were chiefly priests, with whom Gabinius filled the *synhedria*. They were allowed to administer the people's internal affairs according to Jewish law, though even here they were supervised by the Romans, especially in agricultural matters. Capital punishment was most probably in the hands of the Roman officials alone, since it was through this prerogative that the executive task of Roman officialdom in Judea was most clearly expressed.

We may sum up, therefore, by saying that Gabinius' reforms were completely different in character from those of Pompey. The latter chose to follow a road he thought was long but safe, by introducing Roman order into Judea slowly and without causing internal unrest. The "inter-regnum" of Hyrcanus and Antipater was a means to this end. Gabinius abandoned this method as unsuitable for the rebellious Jewish people. He attempted instead to subjugate the Jews by means of administrative decrees, which were chiefly directed against Jewish economic strength and national unity. In this way he hoped to hasten the absorption of that rebellious group into the Roman empire.

CHAPTER II

THE END OF THE HASMONEAN DYNASTY AND THE RISE OF HEROD

by A. Schalit

A. The Revolts Against Gabinius

ANTIPATER WAS the man mainly responsible for Hyrcanus' victory over his brother, Aristobulus, in the struggle for the Judean throne.[1] As we have seen in the previous chapter, he was perceptive enough to grasp what the Hasmoneans had overlooked: that the Hasmonean ideal of total independence had irrevocably passed away with the arrival of Roman imperialism in Syria and Palestine. He adroitly concluded that the Jews must affect a friendship with the Romans if they were to hang on even to the restricted internal autonomy usually granted by Rome to compliant allies. The Hasmonean dynasty was deprived of power because it and its supporters were regarded as hostile by the Romans. A man was needed who could master the unrest in the country and carry out Roman policy vigorously and faithfully. Such a one was Antipater. Hyrcanus' status was not entirely negligible, as he held the religious office of High Priest which Antipater could not fill because of his Idumaean origins. This function, however, was now entirely meaningless in a political sense, especially after the administrative reforms of Gabinius. Even the shadow of autonomy still remaining to the Jews was firmly in the grasp of Antipater, now the unflinching supporter and confidant of Rome in Palestine.

In those tempestuous times, when Gabinius was dividing up the country and eradicating the last relic of Judean independence, the Romans were in real need of a firm and unwavering grasp on their new conquest. That need was made all the greater when Aristobulus, accompanied by his younger son, Antigonus, arrived suddenly from Rome and set himself up at the head of his supporters. He at first tried to rebuild the ruined fortress of Alexandrium as a focal point and refuge for a general insurrection against Roman rule. The attempt failed; for although the people flocked to his side, he was no match for the well-trained Roman army. Defeated, he retired with the remainder of his force to the ruined fortress of Machaerus. There he put up a half-hearted resistance for a few days, but was prevailed upon to surrender and returned to Rome on the instructions of Gabinius. His other children, who had remained in Rome, were returned by the Senate to their mother, in accordance with Gabinius' promise.

Throughout these events Antipater took Gabinius' part, both for political and personal motives. He had good reason to be afraid of Aristobulus; on the latter's arrival, therefore, Antipater sent his children to his old ally, Aretas the king of the Nabataeans.[2] In pursuit of his policy, Antipater made himself highly useful to Gabinius in his expedition to Egypt to restore Ptolemy XI Auletes ("the Flute-player") to his throne. Antipater persuaded the regular Jewish forces at the border fortress of Pelusium to come over to Auletes' side and to open the gates of Egypt to the Romans.

Meanwhile, however, Judea was undergoing fresh disturbances. Aristobulus' son Alexander had raised the standard of rebellion and gathered a large army around him. He ranged the whole country, killing any Roman he found in his path. Those who managed to escape took refuge on Mt. Gerizim, where Alexander besieged them.

When Gabinius returned from Egypt he at first tried to come to terms with the rebels, with Antipater as mediator. While some rebels were persuaded into leaving the camp, it appears that the force remaining loyal to the Hasmoneans was not insignificant: according to Josephus no fewer than 10,000 men fell in the ensuing battle near Mt. Tabor. Though this figure is undoubtedly exaggerated, the Jewish losses were serious and broke the backbone of the revolt. Though Gabinius was recalled at that very point and had to give up his post as legate of Syria, he had succeeded in pacifying the country.[3]

The sources make no further mention of Aristobulus' son Alexander, except that he was later executed on the instructions of Pompey (see below). One should not assume, however, that he merely disappeared from the scene or abandoned his aspirations. It seems more likely that he was compensated in a different way by his marriage to Hyrcanus' daughter, Alexandra. This marriage had been proposed by Antipater in order to strike a compromise between the conflicting ambitions of Hyrcanus and Aristobulus, and offered Alexander good prospects of one day attaining the High Priesthood.[4]

B. Judea in the War Between Caesar and Pompey

The calm before the Judean storm did not last long. In 54 B.C.E. Marcus Licinius Crassus arrived in Syria to succeed Gabinius. His intention was to start hostilities against the Parthians, for which he needed money, and aroused fierce Jewish resentment by robbing the Temple of its treasures for this purpose.[5] However, greater trouble followed when Gaius Cassius Longinus (Crassus' quaestor) took the command in Syria into his hands in an attempt to defend the province from the Parthians after Crassus' defeat at Carrhae (53). A fresh rebellion broke out under Peitholaus, a former supporter of Hyrcanus who went over to Aristobulus when the latter escaped from Rome and renewed his attempt to gain the throne. Cassius crushed the revolt with the utmost cruelty. Josephus reports that he had 30,000 of the inhabitants of Galilean city of Tarichaeae sold into slavery. Peitholaus was put to death on the advice of Antipater, who unhesitatingly supported Cassius, in keeping with his policy never to oppose the Roman administration and the overwhelming force it represented. Moreover, he tried to convince the Jewish nation of the soundness of his policy by explaining how dangerous for the mass of the people were these ceaseless insurrections against the Romans. These attempts at pacification were probably his principal occupation from 54 to 49 B.C.E. In addition he was responsible as "Keeper of the Jews' Exchequer" for taxing the country's population.[6]

The year 49 B.C.E. was one of hope for Antipater's enemies, when civil war broke out in Rome between Pompey and Caesar. Aristobulus was prisoner in Rome and regarded himself an ally of Pompey's enemies, a view shared by Pompey's supporters in the capital. According to Josephus, Caesar intended to send Aristobulus with two legions to Syria and Judea in order to bring them over to his side. Pompey's henchmen, however, anticipated this move and had Aristobulus poisoned. At the same time Pompey gave orders for the execution of Aristobulus's son, Alexander, so as to prevent any insurrection in Judea in favor of his enemies. The king's other children were invited by Ptolemy, the son of Mennaeus, to stay in the Lebanese Chalcis, where he was king.[7]

After Pompey's defeat at Pharsalus (48 B.C.E.) and his death on the coast of Egypt, Antipater and Hyrcanus immediately passed over to Caesar's camp. Antipater showed his customary efficiency during the short campaign in Alexandria. Caesar was in great danger, when Antipater came to his aid together with Mithradates of Pergamum. By moving up the Jewish regular army to Pelusium on the border with Egypt, he opened the doors of that country to a rescue force consisting of Mithradates' soldiers and their Jewish allies. Antipater excelled himself in the Egyptian campaign, and Mithradates duly commended him in a letter to Caesar. Reward was not long in coming.

In 47 B.C.E. Caesar went to Syria to establish a new administration there. He received Hyrcanus and his adviser as faithful allies, and bestowed on them the greatest honors. Caesar refused the claims of Antigonus, the last son of Aristobulus, who asked for his father's throne on the grounds that Aristobulus had died for Caesar. Caesar instead appointed Hyrcanus Ethnarch ("ruler of the nation") and confirmed him as High Priest. Both titles were promised to his descendents on Hyrcanus' death. In addition, Caesar increased the territory of Judea, although he did not return all the regions that Pompey had detached from the Hasmonean kingdom. The most important of these territorial concessions were the port of Jaffa and the villages of the Great Plain (the Valley of Jezreel), which he and his ancestors had once owned. He also received the lands previously held in Judea by Rome's allies, the kings of Syria and Phoenicia. Caesar also recognized the special privileges of the Jews of the Diaspora in Alexandria and in Asia Minor; these mainly included the right to live according to their ancestral laws. Hyrcanus was probably also made supreme judge in the internal affairs of the Diaspora Jews. As for Antipater, his position apparently remained much the same, even though his part in the negotiations with Caesar had been important, if not decisive. He preferred to remain in the shadows, leaving to Hyrcanus the supreme rank as ruler of Judea in the matter of foreign relations. Antipater was, however, granted Roman citizenship and the office of custodian (*epitropos*) of Judea. His duties were vaguely defined, though of course his main occupation was collecting the tribute that the Romans exacted from Judea. In spite of the vagueness of his authority, or perhaps even because of it, he was able to manuever himself into a position where his was the final decision in every matter of importance.[8]

C. Antipater and His Sons as the Real Rulers of Judea

In spite of his power, Antipater took care not to exceed the bounds prescribed for a counsellor of the legal ruler. He was intelligent enough to realize what the Jewish people thought of him, and did not aspire to a position greater than that which he had already attained. Coming from a family of proselytes, he knew that the Jews would not calmly allow him to take even the first overt step to push aside the High Priest. Antipater never entertained the idea of founding a new dynasty to replace the Hasmoneans. His sole ambition was to make himself the *de facto* head of the Judean state, while leaving the *de jure* authority to Hyrcanus. This was the fundamental difference between Antipater and his son, Herod, who aimed deliberately at the throne from the very first moment he entered political life. In order to oust the Hasmoneans, Herod intended to use Roman power, even against the wishes of the Jewish people. All this was beyond Antipater, whose sole political aim was to retain the exalted position he had reached. To this end he employed the skills of his two sons, making Phasael governor of Jerusalem and Herod ruler over Galilee. He made these appointments in order to control the two key regions of the country, in case the people should try to deprive him of his status as *epitropos*.

Nor were these precautions superfluous. The high-ranking nobles of Jerusalem who formed Hyrcanus' court had grown increasingly concerned about Antipater and his sons. They rightly feared that these Idumaeans would deprive the leading families of Judea of both power and privileges. To prevent this they must take the first opportunity of ridding themselves and the country of this family of "half-Jews." Antipater was aware of the danger to his position from this group and stationed his sons at the very places where feelings were most exacerbated — in Jerusalem and Galilee.

Hostility toward strangers or half-strangers had long taken root in Jerusalem, and an Idumaean governor must certainly have been an abomination to nobles and commoners alike. As if this were not bad enough, the same Idumaean who had appointed his son over the Holy City also determined from behind the scenes who should hold the highest secular and sacred offices of the state. He also decided which members of the noble families should be allowed to serve as officials of the state. No wonder, therefore, that these groups began in their resentment to plan a *coup d'état* to put an end to the tyranny of these foreigners.

The Galileans, on the other hand, seem to have been the strongest supporters of the Hasmoneans ever since the days of John Hyrcanus, who had liberated them from Gentile rule. The country seethed with discontent under Antipater's rule; the most extreme forms of violence were used against the neighboring Syrians or those of their own people who collaborated with the Romans. In appointing Herod over this turbulent region, Antipater obviously chose the right man for his purpose.

D. HEROD IN GALILEE

In spite of his tender age, Herod showed an iron determination. He laid hold of several Galilean "brigands," viz. opponents of the Roman rule and their Idumaean henchmen, and put them to death without a trial. This bold step from such a young ruler delighted the Syrians; but it aroused strong criticism in Jerusalem and great dismay in Galilee. The nobles in Jerusalem considered Herod's act a provocation and felt that it opened the way to radical changes in the accepted administrative practice in Judea. The stronghold and focus of power for Jerusalem's nobility was the Sanhedrin. As the national council, it had the exclusive right to inflict capital punishment. Antipater had been careful not to curtail this time-honored privilege, for he was convinced that even its slightest infringement would arouse violent opposition throughout the nation. Herod, however, dared to usurp the ultimate power of the nation's highest tribunal. In doing so he undoubtedly relied upon the Roman legate of Syria, who, according to Josephus, was exceptionally friendly to him.

By this act, therefore, Herod showed that he regarded himself as the representative of the Roman administration in Galilee, and as such not answerable to the highest council of the Jewish people in Jerusalem. The nobles of Jerusalem generally, and the Sanhedrin in particular, re-cognized the magnitude of the danger presented by Herod's effrontery in revising Caesar's favorable arrangements toward the Jews. As far as we know, the juridical reforms of Gabinius in Judea tended to abolish the authority of the Jerusalem Sanhedrin, and in particular its right to judge capital cases, and may indeed have transferred this power to the Roman magistrates. This innovation was revoked by Caesar in 47 B.C.E. By renew-ing the Ethnarchy, Caesar restored the laws of Judea as to the status they had had under Simeon the Hasmonean. Part of the revived "privilege" was the right to try capital cases, a right which was therefore returned to Hyrcanus as Ethnarch and High Priest, and which remained in Jewish hands until the establishment of procuratorial governors in Judea (6 A.D.). It is clear, therefore, that when Herod executed the "brigands" of Galilee without trial or references to the Sanhedrin, he was committing an act of rebellion against the central authority of the nation. He thus made himself liable to stand trial before this authority.

The members of the Sanhedrin petitioned Hyrcanus to put the criminal on trial and to judge him according to the law. They warned him that he would be liable to lose his crown if he were to waver. Hyrcanus was aware of the close ties between Herod and the Roman governor, Sextus Caesar; the request of the Sanhedrin was therefore most inopportune, but it was one which he could not refuse. Even Antipater felt he had no option but to agree to the demand, but secretly sent a warning to his son not to come to Jerusalem without a military escort.

Herod did not delay in coming to trial, although he knew that he was liable to be condemned to death for his illegal actions. He relied probably on his Roman citizenship, and above all on his friendship with the Roman governor. He was not disappointed. Sextus Caesar sent a stern direction to Hyrcanus to ensure Herod a favorable verdict. One may presume that Herod knew of these instructions and so had nothing to fear. Herod arrived in Jerusalem, and appeared before the judges clad in royal purple, his hair trimmed and dressed, and surrounded by a band of bodyguards. The judges recognized the deliberate mockery in Herod's conduct, as it was obligatory for the accused to dress in black and present himself before the Court as a humble suppliant. Herod obviously wished to show the members of the Sanhedrin that he had nothing to fear from them; if they dared lay a hand on him, he would defend himself by force. The judges took the hint and remained silent. Josephus relates that one member alone, called Sameas, arose and arraigned his colleagues for their cowardice. He begged them to regard Herod as a criminal to be judged with the full severity of the law. If they allowed themselves to be cowed by him, they themselves would be judged accordingly when their own end came. This admonition gave new courage to the timid judges. When Hyrcanus saw that Herod's life was now really in danger, his fear of Sextus Caesar's vengeance reminded him of his instructions, and he put an end to the proceedings of the court.

Herod, on Hyrcanus' advice, fled the city. He went to Damascus, where he was appointed *strategos* of Coele Syria. It seems probable that his Roman protector gave him permission to march on Jerusalem to exact vengeance on his enemies. When he arrived with his troops, his brother and father came down from the city and beseeched him to do nothing. With great difficulty they persuaded him to be satisfied with the great alarm he had caused the Sanhedrin and the nobles.[9]

Towards the end of 47 B.C.E. Julius Caesar left for Africa on a campaign against Pompey's supporters. At first the campaign went badly, and the dictator's enemies in the East began to hope that the turning point in their fortunes had arrived. One of them, Caecilius Bassus, killed the governor of Syria, Sextus Caesar. He gained control of Apamea but was besieged there by Caesar's supporters, assisted by Antipater. The siege was unsuccessful, however, and its outcome remained undecided until the assassination of Julius Caesar himself (15th March, 44 B.C.E.).

E. The Assassination of Julius Caesar and its Influence on Judea

This portentous event entirely changed the political situation in the Roman empire in East and West alike. Both of the leaders of the conspiracy against Caesar, Marcus Brutus and Gaius Cassius Longinus, left for the East to muster as large a force as possible against Caesar's heirs, the former to Macedonia and the latter to Syria. The arrival of that die-hard republican at Apamea marked the turning point of the siege. The two opposing forces, Bassus' men and the besiegers, both went over to Cassius. At one stroke Cassius had obtained a large army; his problem was how to keep it and finance it. Cassius distributed the burden of providing the huge sums required over the whole province of Syria. Judea too was requested to give her share, to the sum of 700 talents — an enormous amount in proportion to the diminished size of the country. No wonder, therefore, that not every city managed to collect its share in time. Cassius punished any tardiness with the utmost cruelty. Josephus tells us that the inhabitants of the cities of Gophna, Emmaus, Lydda and Thamna were sold into slavery, as they were unable to satisfy Cassius entirely. The collecting of the tax was the responsibility of Antipater and his sons, who as usual did their best to please the new Roman administration. Herod excelled above all in his determination to be the first to provide his quota, in reward for which Cassius reconfirmed him as *strategos* of Coele Syria.

Hyrcanus' role in all of these events was entirely insignificant. Antipater and his sons no longer took him into account, and did exactly as they wished in Judea. The nobles at court, however, viewed the development of events in Judea with growing concern. They were unwilling to obey Cassius' every whim, reasoning perhaps that the balance of power within the Roman empire was far from settled. The policy of the Idumaeans might finally prove worthless. In particular, the nobles felt that the barbarity of Cassius towards the Jewish nation was becoming insupportable, and that the people were groaning under their heavy burden of taxes. The aristocratic party, therefore, regarded the methods of the Idumaeans as miscalculated, and only awaited the right moment to throw off their hated yoke. Presumably, they looked forward to the victory of Caesar's successors in the hope that they would follow in the footsteps of the dictator and treat Hyrcanus and the Jewish nation honorably.

As time went on, hatred for the Idumaeans grew daily. By blindly obeying the savage commands of Cassius, they themselves had become uncontrollable tyrants, who acted in the name of the Roman and ignored the High Priest who was the legal ruler of the land. The nobles greatly feared that the Idumaeans would gain Cassius' help in order to undermine the position of Hyrcanus completely, and with it their own. The Idumaeans would then establish a dynasty to replace the Hasmoneans; for even if Antipater were satisfied to remain the omnipotent minister of Hyrcanus, who could guarantee that his sons would not try for greater things? Had not Herod shown his contempt for the people and its leaders? Had he not made it plain that he obeyed only Rome, and willingly used its force to trample on the people and its laws? It was, moreover, rumored that before Cassius left for the decisive battle against Caesar's heirs, he had promised Herod to make him king after victory. Such a rumor, though probably unfounded, was enough to stir up the profoundest apprehensions among Hyrcanus' courtiers. It was necessary to remove Antipater soon, in the hope that his sons would leave the scene after their father's death.

F. RESISTANCE OF THE JERUSALEM ARISTOCRACY AGAINST THE IDUMAEANS. THE MURDER OF ANTIPATER

In this way, an active resistance gradually crystallized against the Idumaean tyranny. At the head of the movement was an officer called Malichus, apparently an old friend of Hyrcanus. According to the *Antiquities* of Josephus, Malichus aspired to Antipater's position and become second to the High Priest. As one of those responsible for levying the tax imposed by Cassius, he tried to sabotage the whole scheme, probably intending thereby to fix the blame for its failure on Antipater and so bring down Cassius' wrath on the Idumaeans. However, Cassius trusted Antipater, and Malichus' ruse failed. According to Josephus, Hyrcanus rescued Malichus by paying the Romans 100 talents by way of ransom. It seems likely that Hyrcanus approved of Malichus' actions. He too had possibly begun to have misgiving about the Idumaeans and to consider how to rid himself of them.

Malichus himself was undeterred and began to plot Antipater's assassination. The opportunity occurred when Cassius left to fight Dolabella. Antipater, however enlisted the support of the Nabataeans of Transjordan, and Malichus was forced to change his tactics. He now tried to deceive Antipater and his sons by denying all evil intentions towards them. Probably, he and Hyrcanus were afraid to oppose the Idumaeans openly, on account of Cassius and his troops. Malichus also had to reckon with Antipater's sons, who held two of the key posts in the state. Nevertheless, Malichus continued to scheme against Antipater. According to Josephus, Hyrcanus saved Antipater in one attempt on his life, but the Idumaean was doomed. Malichus and his fellow conspirators were no longer content with only speaking about Antipater's removal. They regarded the assassination of their archenemy as the only way of salvaging what remained of the Hasmonean rule and of their own influence. The moment could no longer be deferred, for Cassius had just granted Herod increased authority (though the account of Josephus is undoubtedly exaggerated). All these factors hastened the assault on Antipater's life. Malichus managed to win the confidence of the chief butler at Hyrcanus' court, and Antipater was poisoned at a banquet.[10]

Antipater's death was the signal for a life-and-death struggle between the waning Hasmonean dynasty and the rising house of Antipater. The latter seems to have been the only one in Hyrcanus' immediate circle to have realized that total submission to the superior power of Rome was the unavoidable necessity of the moment. Antipater had tried to prove to Rome that the Jewish people was not immutably hostile to Pompey's new order in Judea. His aim was to represent the Jews as Rome's friends, and to show that Caesar's policy should be continued in Judea, regardless of whether Caesar's successors were his enemies or his supporters. In other words, Antipater hoped that the status Pompey had chosen for the pagan Hellenistic element in Palestine — that of serving as a reliable support for the Roman administration — would be granted the Jews as well. Though the undisguised hatred of Aristobulus had inspired the upper classes of Rome with a lack of confidence in the Jews, this would pass away in time. Hyrcanus' other counsellors did not understand that Antipater's policy was the last chance for the Hasmonean dynasty. As long as he lived, he struggled to pursue this policy and so prevent the country from falling into anarchy. As long as Antipater held the reins of power, he remained the best surety for the continued existence of the Hasmoneans, since he also had a personal interest in safeguarding his own position as adviser. He undoubtedly desired to rule, but only as Hyrcanus' counsellor, and not in his stead.

The assassination of Antipater thus cleared the way for the ascent of Herod and the ruin of the Hasmonean dynasty. The assassin's aim was to trigger off a political revolution in Jerusalem. Malichus' friends, we are told in the *Antiquities*, were ready to support him if the Idumaeans retaliated. They were prepared not only to defend themselves, but also to attack. Malichus' failure to act expeditiously may have been due to Hyrcanus' own indecision, since he was trying to avoid bloodshed in Jerusalem. With danger threatening, Malichus fell back on his earlier strategy and vehemently denied all share in Antipater's murder. He thereby intended no doubt to deceive Antipater's sons and to strike at the first opportunity.

The brothers reacted each in a different way. Herod was ready to march on the capital, engage his enemies and defeat them in pitched battle. Phasael on the other hand, who was governor of Jerusalem and doubtless aware of the true feelings of the population, wished to avoid a civil war in the city. His apprehensions were well founded. He and his party were isolated in Jerusalem. Not only was he hated by the common people, but by the upper classes and the sages of the Sanhedrin as well. The disturbances spread even to Samaria, the domain of Herod. We are told that Herod himself was compelled to pacify the region, and won the regard of the inhabitants after his return from Jerusalem on his father's death.

Phasael believed that the mood of the country called for a different method from Herod's. He proposed therefore, that Malichus should be removed as silently as their father had been by him. Herod apparently deferred to his brother's judgement, and both pretended to accept Malichus' declarations of innocence regarding Antipater's death. Herod, however, was not content, and marched at the head of a troop of soldiers towards Jerusalem. It was apparently the time of the Feast of Tabernacles. Hyrcanus, on Malichus' advice, forbade Herod to enter the city on the grounds that soldiers were not permitted in the city while the people were bringing festival offerings. Herod ignored the orders of the High Priest and Malichus was terrified on finding Herod's troops inside the city. Fighting did not break out, however, since Phasael still felt that civil war within the city ought to be avoided. The Idumaeans and Malichus again feigned friendship, though Malichus took the precaution of surrounding himself with bodyguards. Phasael and Herod now agreed that Malichus should be killed by the Romans, for then neither Hyrcanus nor the people could blame them for his death.

As soon as Cassius returned from his campaign against Dolabella, the Idumaeans put their plan into action. Herod sent Cassius a letter, accusing Malichus of assassinating Antipater and describing him as the mortal enemy of Rome. Hyrcanus' name was probably not mentioned, although the Idumaeans well knew that the High Priest was the ally and protector of Malichus. We must assume that Herod did not yet dare lift his hand against Hyrcanus or try to remove him from his position as Ethnarch. Such a step would have exposed his future plans and would only have aroused the masses against himself and his brother. They were not yet so important that the Roman authorities would wish to set aside decrees in favor of Hyrcanus which the Senate had passed before Caesar's death and reaffirmed after it, and to replace the High Priest with one of Antipater's sons. Herod and Phasael understood this, and therefore accused Malichus alone as their father's murderer and the enemy of Rome. Cassius agreed to their plan and placed Roman assassins under the command of Herod. Malichus had by then gone to Tyre to fetch his son, who had been kept hostage there. He apparently hoped to create disturbances in Judea as soon as Cassius was occupied in the West. Herod lost no time in sending the assassins on their errand. They overtook Malichus outside the walls of Tyre and killed him. Hyrcanus collapsed on hearing the news of Malichus' death. In the end, however, he reviled his friend as "a wicked man and a traitor against his country."

Malichus' death did not put an end to the popular enmity against the Idumaeans. Malichus' brother took his place and succeeded in occupying Masada. The people rebelled in Jerusalem under the leadership of a certain Helix (or possibly Felix), but Phasael managed to put down the insurgents even before Herod could come to his aid. Phasael nonetheless felt that his position in the city was steadily deteriorating because of the general hatred against him and his brother. He showed both intelligence and clemency by releasing the leader of the revolt. We hear of no acts of vengeance even after Herod had wrested all the key points outside of Jerusalem from the hands of the insurgents. Presumably, Phasael's prudence influenced Herod to act leniently towards their enemies.

G. The First Appearance of Antigonus in Galilee

In the midst of these disturbances in Judea, Antigonus, the youngest son of King Aristobulus, entered the political scene. Ever since his father's death, he had stayed with his brother-in-law Ptolemy the son of Mennaeus, king of Chalcis. There he had awaited the right moment to seize his father's throne. The events in and around Jerusalem encouraged him to believe that the Idumaeans were about to fall, particularly as Cassius no longer stood by them, having left with his forces for the decisive battle against Caesar's heirs. At the head of a comparatively light force, Antigonus succeeded in conquering Galilee; that region was ready to serve him as a base from which he could march on Judea and the capital. Antigonus was supported by his brother-in-law, who supplied him with money, and by Marion, a dynast of Tyre appointed by Cassius. Marion captured three towns in Galilee, apparently with the agreement of Antigonus, as the price for Marion's support. Antigonus also bribed Fabius in Damascus not to interfere in the struggle between him and Herod. In the end, however, Herod was victorious and Antigonus was obliged to withdraw. Marion alone succeeded in hanging on to the places he had occupied. They were later returned to Herod under the authority of Mark Antony.[11]

The danger from Antigonus now became so great that Hyrcanus and the Idumaeans joined forces to defend themselves against their common enemy. Both parties realized that the people favored Aristobulus' son, and that there would be a general uprising as soon as Antigonus returned to

Judea. Hyrcanus had other grounds for fear: Antigonus' revenge for the death of Aristobulus. The High Priest knew that the only one who could defend him from Antigonus was Herod, because of his close relationship with the Romans and the military force at his disposal. When Herod returned to Jerusalem after expelling Antigonus from Galilee, he was received by Hyrcanus with the greatest respect and honor. In order to strengthen their friendship, Hyrcanus gave Herod Mariamne in betrothal, the daughter of Aristobulus' son Alexander by Hyrcanus' daughter Alexandra.

This betrothal was a decisive event in Herod's life, and it left its traces in later years. Most scholars believe that it took place chiefly for political reasons. It connected Herod with the ruling house, and gained him a strong position on which to base his aspirations for power. Mariamne was a descendent of the Hasmoneans; through her, Herod could share not just their glamor, but their right to rule.

This view of Herod's motives, however, seems unfounded. Firstly, when Herod became engaged to Mariamne he was still very far from the crown. He was, after all, merely an official of Cassius; the political situation in the world at that time, before the fateful hour at Philippi, hardly allowed him to dream of a throne. Moreover, his elder brother, Phasael, was by no means his inferior either in his official position or in his political standing. Even if Herod did see himself as a future king, it is highly unlikely that, with his Hellenistic upbringing he would have attached much political or legal value to the fallen greatness of the Hasmoneans. At most he would have regarded his marriage to Mariamne as politically expedient, and not as a means to gain a footing in the royal family. He was, after all, in love with Mariamne, and this appears to have been his real reason for marrying her.

On the other hand, the motives of Mariamne's grandfather, Hyrcanus, and her mother, Alexandra, do seem to have been political and military. They wanted to gain the support of the only man who they believed could defend them from the vengeance of Antigonus. They did not realize that this defender would eventually kill not only them, but also Mariamne and her children as well.[12]

H. Herod and Phasael Confirmed as Rulers of Judea after Philippi

At the time of this change in Herod's personal life, there came the news of Philippi, a battle which was to change the history of the Roman world. Judea was in tumult. The Idumaeans had been so closely linked to the republican cause that it seemed as if they would necessarily share their downfall. This was indeed the hope of all the enemies of Herod and Phasael. When Mark Antony, the victor of Philippi, arrived in Bithynia, among the many delegations which came to honor him was one from Judea. The members of this delegation complained to Antony that the Idumaeans had seized power in Judea, leaving Hyrcanus, the legal ruler of the country, as a mere figurehead. Herod, however, knew his man and acted accordingly. With Antony money was all-important, and Herod used it generously. Antony rejected the claims against the Idumaeans, and confirmed the rule of Phasael and Herod in Judea. Other factors, too, must have played a part in Antony's decision. One of these was his former friendship with their father, Antipater, when both were serving Gabinius in Judea. But Antony also preferred Herod and Phasael for political reasons. He recognized that the Idumaeans had followed their father in keeping faith with Rome under the most difficult circumstances, while their opponents were suspected of being hostile to Roman rule in Judea.

Antony's decision encouraged Hyrcanus, who sent a second delegation to the triumvir to make three requests on behalf of "the High Priest, the Ethnarch and the Jewish people." Hyrcanus asked for the release of the Jews sold into slavery by Cassius for not paying their quota of tax. He also requested that the cities of Galilee that had been taken by Marion of Tyre should be returned to Jewish rule; and that the privileges of the Jews of Asia Minor, as granted by Dolabella, be reconfirmed by the triumvir.

In the *Antiquities*, Josephus records Antony's reply to these requests. It is in the form of a letter to Hyrcanus and the Jews, in which he informs them that he has reconfirmed the privileges of the Jews by letters addressed to the various Hellenistic cities. These privileges included the release of Jews on religious grounds from the obligation to serve in the army, and the freedom of religious worship in the Diaspora. Antony also sent instructions to the cities of Tyre, Sidon, Antioch and Aradus calling for the release of the Jewish slaves held there. The Tyrians were ordered to return the cities they had occupied in Galilee.

The opponents of the Idumaeans had not resigned themselves to defeat, and sent another delegation to complain to Antony. One hundred nobles of Jerusalem met the triumvir at Daphne, near Antioch. The delegation, however, had chosen a most unsuitable time to put forward its case, for Antony had just then become involved with Cleopatra. Valerius Mesalla and even Hyrcanus spoke up in defense of the Idumaeans. In the end Antony not only confirmed Herod and Phasael in their rule but even appointed them Tetrachs — though this was perhaps an empty title. There was no change in their official posts: Phasael continued as governor of Jerusalem and Herod of Galilee. Both were undoubtedly equal in rank, though it has often been supposed that Herod rose to power as the result of being granted by Antony a greater share of authority than his brother. The fact that Antony awarded the same title to both brothers shows this impression to be mistaken. Josephus in *Antiquities* describes their role as being "to direct the affairs of the Jews." According to his *War*, they were granted authority over "the whole of Judea."

If Antipater's sons really became rulers over the whole state, was Hyrcanus deposed by Antony? This hardly seems likely, since Josephus would certainly have mentioned a fact of such importance. There is no doubt, however, that the administrative function of the High Priest continued to diminish as the Idumaeans interfered more and more in the business of government. Nonetheless, it is clear that Hyrcanus lost neither his title nor his status as Ethnarch until the year 40 B.C.E., when he was taken prisoner by the Parthians. Antony had no reason whatever to depose so weak a ruler, who gave no trouble at all to Herod and Phasael, the two puppets of Rome. When Josephus states that they were given authority over "the whole of Judea," he refers to the *de facto* state of affairs in the country, and not to the situation *de jure*. The brothers did in fact govern Judea, each in his own territory; while Hyrcanus was confirmed *de jure* as the Ethnarch over them.

Instead of gaining an advantage from their second delegation to Antony, the opponents of the Idumaeans were the worse off for it. Even though Antony had ordered the arrest of fifteen of their company, they tried their luck a third time and sent 1,000 men to Tyre to dissuade the triumvir from supporting Phasael and Herod. This time Antony's patience was at an end, and he despatched his soldiers against the mass delegation. Many were killed and the rest fled for their lives. In addition, Antony ordered the hostages from the second delegation to be executed, in an attempt to put an end to the stubbornness of the Jews and bend them to his will.[13]

While the Idumaeans remained successful in the sphere of external relations, their position within the country deteriorated owing to the steadily growing hatred among the people. Economic factors also played their part in this development. The changes of Roman administration in the East brought no change in the method of government. Brutus and Cassius had oppressed the eastern provinces in order to pay their armies; Mark Antony proved even more grasping than his predecessors, and as violent as any Hellenistic tyrant. As principal victor at Philippi over Cassius and Brutus, the lands they had subjected he treated as his personal spoils of war which must supply him with all he needed for a luxurious life.

Matters in the eastern provinces thus went from bad to worse, until their inhabitants, groaning under an intolerable yoke of extortion, yearned for the day when they would be free from the detested Roman tyranny — be their liberator who he may. Judea was a small country, but no exception to the rule. Here too the heavy hand of Antony was felt, and the people not surprisingly turned the main brunt of their wrath against Herod and Phasael. Their opportunity came with the arrival of the Parthians in Syria under the leadership of Pacorus (son of Orodes II of Parthia) in 40 B.C.E. With Pacorus came Quintus Labienus, son of the well-known legate of Julius Caesar who deserted his leader during Caesar's Gallic campaigns, and became the sworn enemy of the dictator in the civil war. His son was sent to Orodes in 43 B.C.E. by the republican leaders, Brutus and Cassius, to ask for help. After their deaths, Labienus stayed on at court and incited the king to go to war against Rome. His task was not difficult, since the Parthians had long set their hearts on gaining control over Syria. Aware of the hatred for the Romans among the peoples of the East, the Parthians hoped to be received as liberators.

I. Syria Invaded by the Parthians. Alliance between Antigonus and the Invaders and His March on Jerusalem

War broke out in 40 B.C.E. with the invasion of Syria by the Parthian forces. The legate Decidius Saxa was defeated, and his soldiers went over to Labienus. Saxa himself was slain while fleeing from the enemy. After this victory, the invading army split into two. Labienus at the head of one section turned west to conquer Asia Minor, while Pacorus and his men turned south to capture the coastlands of the eastern Mediterranean. The invaders were everywhere received with open arms. In Judea, too, the enemies of the Romans saw their chance, and decided to settle accounts with the Idumaeans. Antigonus, who thought this the long awaited opportunity to regain the throne of his fathers, was supported by Lysanias, king of Chalcis in Lebanon. Antigonus left for a meeting with the Parthian commanders-in-chief to negotiate for their assistance. This was taken as a declaration of open war against the Roman government in Judea. Antigonus had given up hope of ever reaching a settlement with the Romans, and in appealing to the Parthians he committed himself entirely to the prospect of a Parthian victory. He judged from the initial victories of the invaders that the desired end was close at hand. The negotiations with the Parthians were concluded successfully. Antigonus persuaded the leader of their southern division to send a detachment to Jerusalem, which was to become his capital under the protection of the king of Parthia. According to Josephus, Antigonus promised his allies 1,000 talents of silver and five hundred women — the wives of his political opponents. Antigonus' plan succeeded; Judea was conquered by Parthia and proved of great value against the Romans both militarily and politically.

The Parthian army moved down the coast, and were everywhere accepted as liberators; Tyre alone shut its gates to the invaders. A separate detachment under the command of one Barzapharnes advanced inland as vanguard of the main force to help Antigonus. He undertook a forced march on Jerusalem without waiting for the main army of his allies. Numerous Jews joined up with him from the woodlands of Carmel and the Drymus forest in the Sharon plain. With evergrowing forces, he drew closer and closer to Jerusalem. The whole country now rose in revolt against the Idumaeans. In Jerusalem, too, general insurrection broke out. Finding themselves surrounded on all sides by enemies, the Idumaeans and their followers fortified themselves in the Hasmonean palace, determined to fight to the death. The pressure grew with the arrival in Jerusalem of crowds of pilgrims for the Pentecost, and soon the whole of Jerusalem, including the Temple Mount, was in the hands of the people. They now tried to storm the stronghold of the besieged Idumaeans, but as the assailants were lacking in military art, Herod managed to drive them back. Herod and his supporters, however, feared that they would finally be unable to withstand the people, since they were cut off and had no hope of breaking out of the trap. Even supposing an escape were possible, where could they take refuge? The whole country had risen against the brothers, and the road southward to Idumaea was blocked.

When Antigonus saw that he would not be able to take the palace by storm, he decided to use a subterfuge. The cupbearer of the king of Parthia, also called Pacorus, was in charge of the Parthian troops in Jerusalem. At the suggestion of Antigonus, Pacorus offered the besieged free passage to the Parthian camp in Galilee, where they could negotiate a treaty with Antigonus. Phasael thought the offer reasonable; for his soldiers could not hold out indefinitely against the besiegers. He presumably intended to escape the vengeance of Antigonus by paying the Parthians a ransom for the lives of his men. He realized that the main danger to himself and his brother came not from the Parthians but from the Hasmonean, who was set on revenge against all his opponents.

Herod, however, had no trust in the mediation of the Parthian leader. It was clear to him that the Parthians were allies of Antigonus and were merely planning to trap him, his brother and the rest of the besieged (among whom was his betrothed, Mariamne). Herod was afraid that, once outside the palace, they would be seized and their lives placed in immediate danger. He therefore warned Phasael not to be deceived by the ruses of the Parthians. Hyrcanus, for his part, was probably terrified of Antigonus' vengeance, but decided nevertheless to go with Phasael — no doubt in order to lend the delegation an official form. To the outside world he was, after all, still the ruler of the Jews, the Ethnarch. He may also have believed, like Phasael, that their only chance lay in negotiating with the Parthians, rather than resisting enemies who grew daily stronger.

Herod's warnings were in vain. Phasael and Hyrcanus started on their dangerous journey to Barzapharnes in Galilee. At first the Parthians treated them honorably, so as not to arouse any suspicion before their army had seized Herod in Jerusalem. Phasael at first distrusted Barzapharnes, having been informed of the treaty between Antigonus and the Parthians. He even received a warning from a certain rich Syrian, together with the offer of a boat waiting for him by the coast. Phasael did not heed this advice, but merely asked the Parthian commander-in-chief for a declaration of his intentions. If it was money he wanted, the Idumaeans could offer him more than Antigonus. At first Barzapharnes declined to answer, but later revealed his true colors by ordering the arrest of both Phasael and Hyrcanus.

Meanwhile, the messengers sent by Phasael to warn Herod were intercepted by the Parthians. When Herod heard of the arrest of Phasael's messengers, he saw that his only chance was to escape. His attempt was successful; not only did he himself escape together with his family and soldiers — he even managed to smuggle out his treasures. As soon as Herod's flight became known to the Parthians and the Jews, they went in hot pursuit and overtook him at a place south of Jerusalem (where he was later to build Herodium). In the ensuing battle, Herod drove off his attackers and continued his journey southwards. Joining forces with his brother Joseph, they together decided to transfer the family to Masada, along with the rest of the men who accompanied them. The women, who included Mariamne (Herod's betrothed) Alexandra her mother, and Herod's mother Cypros, were installed in Masada under the protection of the guard there.

Meanwhile, important events were happening in Judea. The Parthian horsemen plundered Jerusalem and invaded Idumaea, destroying the city of Marissa. They did not touch the property of Hyrcanus, since it now belonged to Antigonus, who was ruling Judea under the protection of Parthia. The fate of Phasael and Hyrcanus is uncertain. In both *Antiquities* and *War*, we are told that they were handed over as prisoners to Antigonus. Hyrcanus was disfigured by his nephew (according to the *Antiquities*), who bit off his ears (according to *War*). Phasael committed suicide by dashing his head against a rock. According to another passage in *Antiquities*, however, Phasael and Hyrcanus were brought before the Parthians by Pacorus, and Phasael committed suicide. Another tradition says that he fell in battle. The story concerning Hyrcanus seems improbable; he was most likely mutilated in the Parthian fashion. The manner, too, of Phasael's death sounds legendary; one may presume that he was killed by his guards while attempting to escape.[14]

J. HEROD's FLIGHT TO ROME. HIS APPOINTMENT AS VASSAL KING BY THE ROMAN SENATE

Herod did not stay long in Masada, but hurried on to Malichus, king of Nabataea, in order to collect a debt still owing to his father, Antipater. Apparently Herod had not yet heard about the fate of Phasael and Hyrcanus, and wanted the money to ransom his brother from the Parthians. Malichus, however, thought it inexpedient to welcome someone who had so compromised his position, and refused to see him. Herod wasted no time and went straight on to Egypt. From there he intended to sail for Italy, where he would request help from Antony or at least hope to find refuge. On learning the news of his brother and Hyrcanus at Rhinocorura (El-'Arish), he departed so hastily that the messengers whom Malichus had sent to appease him did not find him there. He was already at Pelusium.

The death of his brother and the captivity of Hyrcanus no doubt strengthened Herod's resolution to request Roman support for his enthronement as king of the Jews. As long as Phasael lived and Hyrcanus was Ethnarch, such an idea was impractical. Phasael's position was in no way inferior to Herod's and even if Herod had ever aspired to the crown there was no reason to assume that Rome would have preferred him to his elder brother. With the death of Phasael and the captivity of Hyrcanus, the road was clear for Herod to gain the crown. His claim was well based, since Antigonus had seized the throne with Parthian support. Herod hoped to find favor with the Romans by standing as the enemy of Antigonus, who was the ally of Rome's enemy, the king of Parthia.

Cleopatra received Herod fairly, though he probably did not disclose his plans to her regarding Judea. Had he done so, she would immediately have regarded him as her enemy and had him killed, for she still pretended to the rule of Coele-Syria, the ancient Ptolemaic province, which she regarded as her ancestral inheritance. She tried to detain Herod with the offer of the leadership of her forces, but he declined, braving instead the dangers of a winter voyage. It was only with great difficulty that he managed to reach Rhodes; his ship was almost wrecked off the Pamphylian coast. Though himself in great financial straits, he donated some money to the island, which had suffered during the wars of Cassius — a gesture typical of the man.

From Brundisium he went straight on to Rome, and there met Antony. He informed the triumvir of the events in Judea and of what had befallen him personally: Phasael's death, the imprisonment of Hyrcanus, and in particular the coronation of Antigonus under the auspices of the king of Parthia. Herod of course proposed that Antony make him king over Judea as a tributary of Rome, in place of his enemy Antigonus, the vassal of Rome's adversary. The Hasmonean dynasty would have to be replaced by a king under Rome's auspices, and conforming to the accepted political and legal framework of the Roman empire. This would be a king who was the "ally and friend of the Roman people" (*rex socius et amicus populi Romani*).

According to Josephus, Herod was surprised on being appointed king. He knew that the Romans usually granted the throne only to the descendents of the ruling dynasty. Josephus claims that when he went to Rome to complain about Antigonus, Herod had not intended the kingdom for him-himself, but for Mariamne's younger brother, Aristobulus. The whole story is undoubtedly a fabrication picked up by Josephus from Herod's own memoirs, in which the king denies filching the throne from the Hasmoneans. All that we know of Herod's character proves that he was quite incapable of such altruism. The speed with which it was decided at Rome to make him king suggests that he had come with a well-prepared manifesto ready for presentation to the Roman authorities.

There were, in fact, good reasons for accepting Herod's proposal. The Romans regarded Antigonus as their declared enemy, since he had dared to join forces with the Parthians, and had accepted the kingdom from them instead of obtaining it from Rome. Rome's view of the Hasmoneans had been unfavorable ever since the days of Pompey. Moreover, even if Rome had been willing to act merciful and not to the letter of the law, it could not have continued the rule of this dynasty. The sole legal candidate for the throne was a minor (Aristobulus, Mariamne's brother). In contrast with him there was Herod, a strong ruler and one descended from a house friendly to Rome. The triumvirs realized that only such a man could serve as a reliable and steadfast supporter of Roman rule in a country as disturbed as Judea; only he could forcibly hold the reins of government of a people as difficult to rule as the Jews. Besides, as the Sages remarked, Herod was not a priest, a fact which prevented the two powers (Priesthood and Crown) from being concentrated in the hands of one man.

All these reasons explain why Antony had no difficulty in persuading Octavian of Herod's usefulness to Rome as king of Judea. A meeting of the Senate was held, in which Antigonus was presented as the enemy of Rome for having taken his authority from the Parthians, while Herod was recommended as the man who would be of greatest use as ruler of Judea. A further point in Herod's favor was his father's faithful service to Rome. Antony's motion was accepted unanimously. The Senate voted Herod the title of King of Judea. Furthermore, the kingdom itself was increased, with the incorporation of Samaria — a territory formerly under his control — for the purpose of taxation. The meeting ended with a festive ceremony on the Capitol, in which Herod walked between the two triumvirs to the temple of Jupiter Capitolinus, and took part in the rites in his honor. The event may be regarded as a symbol of Herod's reign, which stood between two unbridgeable worlds — the spiritual world of the Jews and the material world of Rome.

K. Herod's Return and His Struggle against Antigonus

All this took place within a single week. Herod, now "king, ally and friend of the Roman people," immediately left Italy in order to wrest his kingdom from Antigonus.[15] It did not prove an easy task. The Senate offered him no assistance; it had merely given him the authority to act. Herod had to collect the forces he needed by whatever means available; effective help from Rome came only during the final stage of the struggle. By the time Herod reached Accho-Ptolemais in order to hire mercenaries, Antigonus had conquered Idumaea and had put Masada under siege. Antigonus was not disturbed even when Ventidius (Antony's legate) defeated the army of Labienus in Asia Minor, and marched on Syria and Judea. Ventidius actually camped outside Jerusalem, but did nothing to carry out the Senate's decree since, according to Josephus, he had been bribed by Antigonus. He withdrew shortly afterwards to Syria to put things in order there after the Parthian invasion, leaving behind a part of the army in charge of his subordinate, Silo. Silo proved no better than his superior, at least from Herod's point of view. He too was bribed by Antigonus, who was evidently trying to gain time until the expected return of the Parthians. Antigonus hoped that he would then easily be able to nullify Herod's initial successes.

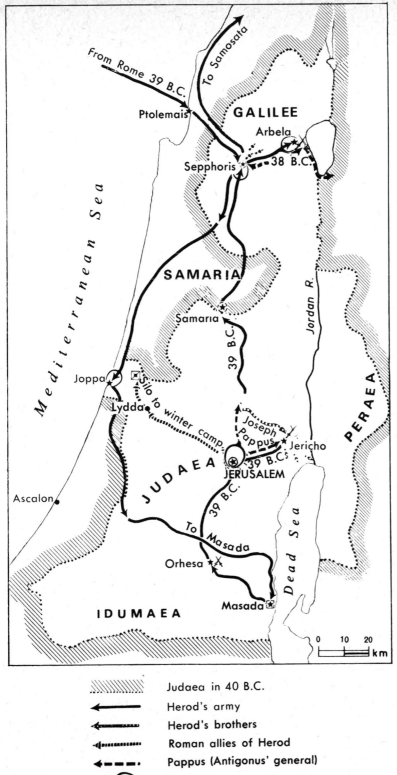

Herod's advance against Antigonus (39/8 B.C.E.)

Immediately on his arrival in Accho-Ptolemais, Herod began to act with his usual energy, mustering Gentile mercenaries as well as soldiers from his native Idumaea. According to Josephus many men from Galilee joined him, bringing him considerable victories in that region. This is doubtful, however, since Josephus does not mention the name of one single city conquered by Herod at this time. Galilee was, after all, the center of the strongest resistance against Herod during the whole of his campaign against Antigonus. It is hardly likely that the Galileans would receive him with open arms on his first incursion into their country. It was, however, logical to attempt to conquer Galilee as the first stage in the campaign, for that region had been in Herod's charge at the time of Sextus Caesar and Cassius. Furthermore, he intended turning Galilee into a base from which he could march south without fear of an attack on his rear. All the evidence shows that his efforts were in vain. He finally retreated from Galilee, and turned south through the coastal plain. Silo's forces also took part in this retreat from Galilee, which served the Roman commander as an excuse for attempting to withdraw from the whole of the combined operation with Herod. The latter now planned to gain control of the south, as a base from which he could act against Jerusalem. He took Jaffa, invaded Idumaea, and lifted the siege of Masada. This latter move was not only of strategic value, but also of personal importance for Herod himself. By freeing Masada, he could finally release his family, who had been blockaded there since his flight in 40 B.C.E. By gaining Idumaea, Herod acquired a safe base where the inhabitants were loyal to his family.

He was now so sure of victory that he dared march directly on Jerusalem in an attempt to take it by surprise attack, and thus finish the whole campaign at one stroke. It was not until Herod was already camped before the city that he realized his forces were not adequate for the purpose. Silo refused to take part in the siege because of the oncoming winter, and insisted that his forces leave for their winter quarters. This was a serious setback for Herod, for he certainly could not take Jerusalem on his own. Not only was he obliged to dispatch the Roman soldiers to their winter quarters: he also had to provide them with essentials, so that their support actually became a burden on his resources.

Antigonus was aware of these difficulties, and tried to benefit from them by appeasing the Romans, and even putting up part of the Roman forces at Lydda. He hoped thereby that Antony would soften his attitude and arrive at a compromise with him. When he discovered, however, that his hopes were vain, he cut off the supplies to Silo's troops. He also ordered the local inhabitants to leave for the mountains, and so deprive the Romans

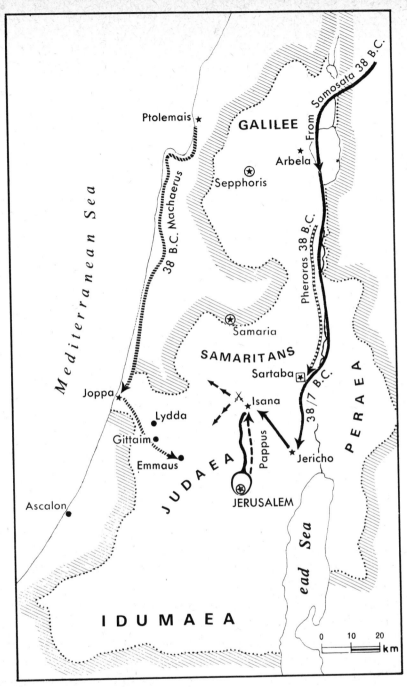

Ptolemais ★

GALILEE

From Samosata 38 B.C.

★ Arbela

Arbela

⊛ Sepphoris

Mediterranean Sea

38 B.C. Machaerus

Pheroras 38 B.C.

⊛ Samaria

Samaria

SAMARITANS

Sartaba ⊠

38/7 B.C.

X Isana

★ Isana

Joppa ★

Lydda •

Gittaim •

Emmaus •

J U D A E A

Pappus

P E R A E A

★ Jericho

Jericho

Ascalon •

⊛ **JERUSALEM**

ead Sea

I D U M A E A

| 0 | 10 | 20 |

km

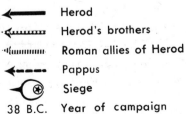

Herod

Herod's brothers

Roman allies of Herod

Pappus

Siege

38 B.C.   Year of campaign

Herod's campaign of 38/7 B.C.E.

of even daily needs. In this predicament, Silo appealed for help to Herod, who was campaigning in Galilee again, after his attempt to capture Jerusalem had failed. He hoped either to gain a foothold there or, if possible, conquer the whole of it. His family had remained behind in Samaria.

Antigonus proved himself weak and shortsighted, having neglected to fortify the territory under his control. Sepphoris was the main city of Galilee; yet it was for all practical purposes undefended, so that it fell to Herod's troops without a fight. Moreover, the Herodians found a plentiful supply of food there. The capture of Sepphoris was a great victory for Herod, since from there he could carry out incursions on every side. He overran the main part of Galilee during the winter months of the year 39/38 B.C.E. The main battle was at Arbel, where the Galileans still loyal to Antigonus were defeated. The survivors took to the caves in the vicinity, from where they continued their resistance to the Idumaean.

Herod was entitled to regard all these victories as his own achievement, since the Roman auxiliaries had taken no part in them. Herod's distrust of Silo was so great that when the latter did make an appearance, he was told that Herod could do without his help. Herod did, however, authorize his younger brother Pheroras to furnish Silo with supplies. Pheroras was also ordered to rebuild the fortress of Alexandrium.

While Herod went from strength to strength, Antigonus sat twiddling his thumbs in Jerusalem. He made no attempt to succor the Galileans, for he apparently hoped that the Parthians, who were about to renew the fight, would return to drive Herod out of the country.

In the spring of 38 B.C.E. Pacorus again invaded Syria, where Ventidius had returned as Antony's legate. Herod used the time to drive out the surviving "brigands" from the caves around Arbel. Fighting was difficult on account of the mountainous terrain, and only with much trouble and the use of special tactics did he manage to break the resistance of the ablest of the Galilean leaders.

With the clearance of the last pockets of resistance the whole of Galilee was in Herod's hands. Appointing one Ptolemy as general (*strategos*) over his newly-won territory, Herod marched to Samaria for the final battle with Antigonus. No sooner had he left, however, than the Galileans revolted and slew Ptolemy, fleeing afterwards to the mountains and marshes. This insurrection disrupted Herod's plans, and he was obliged to return and crush the revolt. He then imposed a heavy fine on the insurgent populace.

In the meantime Ventidius had defeated and killed Pacorus. After his victory, Ventidius turned against King Antiochus of Commagene, and confined him to his capital, Samosata. Once the Parthian danger had passed,

Antony instructed Ventidius to detach two legions and one thousand horsemen to help Herod. One Machaerus was put at the head of this force. Herod was again disappointed with his Roman allies. Machaerus marched on Jerusalem together with Herod, presumably in an attempt to catch Antigonus off balance. The attempt failed, and Herod accused Machaerus of incompetence. Further cooperation was impossible between the squabbling leaders. Machaerus withdrew from Jerusalem and exacted vengeance on the inhabitants of Judea. This further enraged the king, who knew that his standing with the people was weak enough without additional provocation.

After two years of fighting and failure, Herod realized that he would never accomplish his aim with the forces at his disposal. His only chance to defeat Antigonus would be to obtain aid on a much larger scale from Antony, who was already encamped before Samosata. Machaerus tried to stop Herod, but to no avail. Herod left his brother Joseph in Judea, with the specific instruction not to engage Antigonus in pitched battle during Herod's absence. The king had no intention of endangering the army that would have to fulfill such an important role in the future.

L. Herod's Decisive Victory. Conquest of Jerusalem and the End of the Hasmonean Rule in Judea

Herod reached Antony after many perils and was received with the warmest friendship. Antony agreed to put a large force at Herod's disposal to be led by Sosius, but under Herod's supreme command. Two legions would give the king preliminary aid, while the rest of the force under Sosius would come later.

Meanwhile, however, important events were taking place in Judea. Disregarding his brother's injunction, Joseph had been drawn into battle with Antigonus. His army was destroyed near Jericho, and he himself fell. Antigonus ordered his head cut off. This was the signal for the Galileans to renew their revolt and Herod's collaborators were drowned in the Sea of Galilee. A general insurrection seemed on the point of breaking out throughout the land.

As soon as Herod heard the news he rushed south with one of the legions at his disposal. The revolt in Galilee was crushed immediately, and Herod turned to Jericho, where Antigonus and his men were encamped. Herod did not dare to fight a full-scale battle, but remained satisfied with minor skirmishes until Sosius should arrive with the main force. Antigonus then committed the grave mistake of dividing his army. Keeping one part, he sent the rest to Samaria under his general Pappus, with the apparent aim of cutting his enemy's supply lines. Herod pursued Pappus and attacked him at Isana (Jeshanah, close to Beth-El), destroying the whole force. Pappus himself fell in the battle and Herod had his body decapitated in revenge for the mutilation of the corpse of his brother Joseph. Pappus' defeat swung the pendulum in Herod's favor, and only winter prevented him from marching on Jerusalem (39/38 B.C.E.).

The siege of the capital began in the spring. Herod set up his camp north of the city, as Pompey had done before him. He was now so sure of victory that he left the camp for Samaria, to celebrate his marriage with Mariamne.

After the wedding, the king returned to his camp outside Jerusalem, where in the meantime Sosius' legions had also arrived. Counting the auxiliary forces brought by Herod, Josephus put the number of besiegers at eleven regiments of foot and six thousand cavalrymen, a force undoubtedly far greater than that of Antigonus defending Jerusalem.

The defenders chose to fight to the end, for they knew they could expect no clemency from Herod or his Roman allies. Josephus relates that there was a religious revival in the city. The inhabitants put their trust in the Temple; it would defend the city and not let it fall to the enemy. Not all thought so; the most noted of the sages — an apparent reference to Hillel and Shammai — advised submission as best befitting the decree of God. After forty days, the first wall was breached; the second fell after fifteen days of incessant battering. With the Lower City and the outer part of the Temple Mount in the hands of the attackers, the defenders fled to the inner Temple and the Upper City. Hoping for their submission, Herod agreed to supply them with sacrifices for the daily ritual. When he saw, however, that they continued to defend themselves stubbornly, he pressed on and captured the rest of the city. The inhabitants were massacred by the Romans. Herod had great difficulty to get rid of his allies by giving them the treasure which he had pillaged from the nobles and the rich. Antigonus left the fortress adjoining the Temple, and prostrating himself before Sosius, begged for mercy. The Roman mocked him and put him in chains; he was brought to Antioch and executed there on the orders of Mark Antony.[16] The Hasmonean dynasty had passed away and Herod would establish his own house on its ruins. A new era had begun in the period of the Second Temple.

CHAPTER III

THE REIGN OF HEROD

by M. Stern

A. The Consolidation of Herod's Rule (37–30 B.C.E.)

THE FALL OF the Hasmonean dynasty, the conquest of Jerusalem by the Roman legions under the command of Sosius, the Roman governor of Syria, and the execution of Antigonus by Mark Antony at the instigation of Herod — all this finally made it possible to put into effect the Senate's decision to appoint Herod king of Judea. Only isolated pockets of opposition to Herod's rule remained within Judea, such as the fortress of Hyrcania.

From the outset, Herod's rule was the expression of the requirements of Roman policy in the Orient. Both the size of Herod's kingdom and its status within the empire were determined by the practical considerations of imperial policy-makers in that generation. This policy was carried out in the same way as with all allied kings during that period. Like other kingdoms of the eastern half of the Roman empire, Herod's kingdom in the first years of his rule came under the control of the triumvir Mark Antony. This state of affairs was reaffirmed by an agreement between Antony and Octavian signed at Tarentum in 37 B.C.E. Octavian's interference in the affairs of the eastern region of the empire was minimal, and his influence in that area was indirect at most.

Herod was not the only allied king in the east whose rule was maintained in those years by Antony. Among the others were Polemon, king of Pontus — whose family had proved its loyalty to Rome by taking a firm stand against the Parthians when they invaded Asia Minor — Archelaus, king of Cappadocia, and Amyntas, king of Galatia. The latter two, like Herod, owed their thrones to Antony. They were not descendants of the local dynasties, but had their crowns bestowed on them by the Romans.[1] Antony considered it prudent to support these kings. They were important to him both as loyal supporters of his policy and as rulers who knew how to maintain order in the countries placed under his jurisdiction, and whose annexation he considered unnecessary. These rulers were duty-bound to assist him both by supplying money and military aid when called upon. This necessity could well arise because of the state of tension along the Parthian frontier. Another factor was the latent antagonism between Antony and Octavian, which became more pronounced after Antony had strengthened his ties with Cleopatra.

Until after the battle of Actium (31 B.C.E.) Herod was entirely dependent upon Antony. These were years when Herod's own internal position was rather insecure. There still existed within his kingdom pockets of armed resistance among people loyal to the Hasmoneans; Herod required the presence of a Roman legion to guarantee the stability of his rule (*Ant.* XV, 72). It appears that even in Idumaea itself, the king's native province, there were some people averse to his rule. His brother-in-law, Costobar, went as far as to plan a secession of Idumaea from the kingdom of Judea with the help of elements hostile to Herod, both within the state and outside it.

In accordance with the agreements made in 40 and 39 B.C.E., the main concentrations of the Jewish population in Palestine were included within Herod's kingdom: Judea, Galilee and Peraea as well as Idumaea and Samaria. The ports of Jaffa and Gaza on the coast were also incorporated within the boundaries of his kingdom. Somewhat later the size of Herod's kingdom was reduced considerably. This was the result of Antony's gift to Cleopatra of certain of Herod's territories (specifically those bordering on Judea). Thus Cleopatra VII, queen of Egypt, became Herod's greatest enemy, till her policy threatened both his status and his personal security. It was her desire to reinstate the rule of the Ptolemaic dynasty over Judea and the neighboring lands. Antony, however, was neither willing nor able to fall in with all Cleopatra's designs on the kingdom of Judea. Not only had he to give very careful thought to the possible repercussions within Palestine itself which would follow upon dispossessing Herod of his lands, and removing the barrier between the inhabitants of Judea and a foreign ruler. He also had to consider the impact in Rome of the removal of a king whose rule had been officially sanctioned by the Senate. Nevertheless, Herod was plagued throughout this entire period by a feeling of insecurity regarding his own future, a feeling aggravated by the loss of parts of his dominions.

In pressing her case, Cleopatra made capital of the continuous internal crisis within Judea. She was thus able to join forces with elements hostile to Herod within Judea itself. These consisted of the remnants of the Hasmonean dynasty on the one hand, and advocates of the separation of Idumaea from Judea on the other. At first it seemed that Herod had made a wise

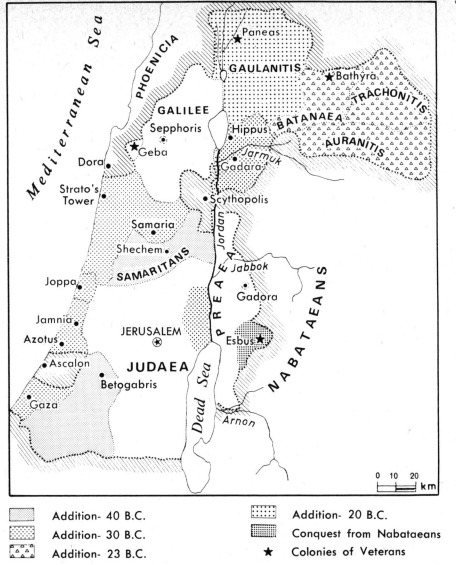

Addition- 40 B.C.

Addition- 30 B.C.

Addition- 23 B.C.

Addition- 20 B.C.

Conquest from Nabataeans

★ Colonies of Veterans

The Growth of Herod's Kingdom

move in reducing the internal tension within his kingdom by successfully negotiating with the king of the Parthians for the return of Hyrcanus II from Babylon (*Ant.* XV, 18–20). Hyrcanus had been banished during the Parthian invasion of Palestine. It is quite certain that Herod had Antony's blessing in carrying out these negotiations with Phraates, king of the Parthians. Antony realized that this was in no way contrary to his own interests, since the presence in Parthia of the former High Priest and Hasmonean ruler, highly respected by the large Babylonian Jewish community, could be a source of danger. If war should break out once more between Parthia and Rome, the Parthians could well use Hyrcanus to counterbalance Herod. However, Herod's initiative in this affair should not be considered as an expression of an independent policy, but rather as the result of coordination with the Roman rulers.[2] Herod sent as emissary to Parthia a rich Syrian, who had good connections with both the rulers of Parthia and with Herod himself; as a result of his negotiations, Hyrcanus returned to Jerusalem.

However, the return of Hyrcanus, the grandfather of Mariamne, Herod's wife, did not resolve all Herod's problems. First and foremost, the problem of the High Priesthood now became acute. Hyrcanus had been mutilated in 40 B.C.E., and could therefore not claim the title of High Priest for himself. However, the appointment as High Priest of the Babylonian Hananel, a complete stranger to the Hasmonean dynasty, raised the ire of Alexandra, the daughter of Hyrcanus and mother-in-law of Herod. She demanded reparation for the injustice done to her young son Aristobulus III, and insisted that he, as the lawful heir of the High Priests of Hasmonean descent, should be forthwith appointed. But as she was met by the refusal of her son-in-law, Herod, who feared the effect on the stability of his regime of the appointment of a Hasmonean to the High Priesthood, she decided to exploit her friendly relations with Cleopatra and to ask her to intercede with Antony. At first Antony showed little enthusiasm in the face of Cleopatra's entreaties. He soon changed his mind after receiving a report from his friend Dellius, who had visited Jerusalem and was fascinated by the beauty of Queen Mariamne and her brother Aristobulus. Antony wrote to Herod urging him to send the young man to him. But Herod decided to do all within his power to prevent Aristobulus from visiting Antony. He was afraid that this visit would endanger the future of his reign, and undermine his already unstable position among the Jews. Hope would be renewed for the complete or partial restoration of the Hasmonean dynasty. Herod therefore refused to allow Aristobulus to leave, on the pretext that he feared the outbreak of riots within the kingdom (*Ant.* XV, 23–30).

It was clear to Herod that he would be unable to withstand the heavy pressure brought to bear upon him by Antony and Cleopatra, in addition to that of his mother-in-law and wife. In his desire to prevent Aristobulus from going to Antony at all costs, he made a daring move. He dismissed Hananel and appointed the 17-year-old Aristobulus in his stead (*Ant.* XV, 31–41). Herod soon realized that his apprehensions had been fully justified and that the appointment was fraught with serious danger. Aristobulus (named Jonathan in Hebrew — *War* I, 437) had made an impressive appearance in the Temple on the Feast of Tabernacles, and the extent of the young Hasmonean's popularity with the masses was obvious to all. They were overjoyed that a descendant of the Hasmonean dynasty had been appointed to the High Priesthood. Herod decided to rid himself of Aristobulus, whatever the consequences. He now had no alternative, for otherwise the young man would sooner or later oust him completely. In such an event Roman government would accede to the demands of the Jewish masses, and prefer Aristobulus to Herod. A few days after Herod had made up his mind to take action, the king's servants drowned Aristobulus while sporting in a pool in Jericho, where Herod was staying as guest of his mother-in-law Alexandra. This was in 35 B.C.E.; Aristobulus was then 18 years old (*Ant.* XV, 50–6; *War* I, 437).[3]

The murdered youth was given a magnificent funeral, and Herod showed all the outward signs of sorrow required of him; yet he was not held to be blameless, either by Alexandra or by the people. Alexandra once again exerted her influence with Cleopatra, who induced Antony to summon Herod to explain the affair of Aristobulus. Deeply perturbed, Herod met Antony at Laodicea. A rumor spread in Judea that Herod had been tortured and summarily executed (*Ant.* XV, 71). Alexandra was filled with hope and planned to escape to the Roman legion stationed at that time in Jerusalem. But the rumor was soon dispelled; it became known that Antony had allowed Herod to remain as king of Judea and even found it necessary to stress his friendship (*Ant.* XV, 74–9). It appears that Herod succeeded in convincing Antony with weighty arguments of the virtue of his act. One has the impression that he did not attempt to deny his responsibility for his brother-in-law's murder. He did, however, justify his act with a political explanation: if he had let Aristobulus live, pro-Hasmonean riots would certainly have broken out, undermining his authority in Judea and even jeopardizing Rome's supreme power in Palestine.

At that time Antony had no one to replace Herod in Judea. Even so, the basis of Herod's rule was shaken. Antony, furthermore, took away certain territories from Herod's kingdom and presented them to Cleopatra.[4] Several towns in the coastal strip and in the Jericho Valley were no longer included within his kingdom, although the actual rule over the Jericho Valley, with its rich crop of balsam and palm trees, still remained in Herod's hands; he merely became Cleopatra's tenant and undertook to pay a rental of 200 talents annually (*War* I, 362, *Ant.* XV, 132). Herod was also required on behalf of Cleopatra to collect the annual rent due from Malichu, king of the Nabataeans, for the lands separated from *his* kingdom in the same manner. Herod's responsibility towards Cleopatra later became a source of future conflict, since it served to focus the antagonism that already existed between the kingdom of Judea and Nabataea.

The tension between Herod and the Nabataean kings continued throughout his reign. This was, in fact the situation that had existed at the height of the Hasmonean power, when the clash over territories between Jews and Nabataeans resulted in a series of wars. For some time, it is true, relations between Antipater, Herod's father, and the Nabataeans had been excellent. But Herod did not continue these relations with Malichu king of the Nabataeans, and they deteriorated when Herod fled from the Parthians. From the moment Herod was crowned king of Judea, he took up the policy of the Hasmoneans towards their Nabataean neighbors. Open warfare broke out in 31 B.C.E., because of the Nabataean king's delay in paying his debts to Cleopatra. This suited Herod's own plans, since he had decided that the time was now ripe to humiliate his enemy. The war was waged mainly in Transjordan, in the same year in which the fate of the entire Roman empire was being decided in the struggle between Antony and Octavian. It was not easy for Herod to gain the upper hand over the Nabataeans, and for quite a time neither side gained a clear advantage. The first battle, apparently fought near Dium, ended in a victory for the king of Judea. But in the second battle, near Canatha, the scales were tipped in favor of the Nabataeans, after Athenion, Cleopatra's representative in Herod's camp, betrayed the king of Judea. When Herod saw that the battle was lost, he felt his men as they retreated to their camp. The Nabataeans laid siege to the camp and succeeded in taking it, thus depriving Herod of a large part of his army. For a time he was forced to refrain from open battle with the Nabataeans, and restricted himself to forays into the areas under Nabataean rule (*Ant.* XV, 108–20; *War* I, 364–9).

Then another calamity struck Herod, in the form of an earthquake which claimed thousands of lives among the population of Judea. It was Herod's fortune, however, that the losses were mainly civilian, while his soldiers, who were camped in the open fields outside the towns, escaped unhurt. But the material losses and the effect on the morale in general were grave, and Herod seemed to have little chance of recovering his position. The nadir to which he had descended was reflected in the contempt and animosity with which the Nabataeans now treated Herod; they even murdered the emissaries he had sent to negotiate. Only by an impressive victory on the battlefield could Herod retrieve his position and lost prestige.

The decisive battle, fought not far from Philadelphia (Rabbath-Ammon), ended in a significant victory for Herod, with many enemy soldiers slain and even more taken prisoner (*Ant.* XV, 121–60; *War* I, 371–85).

The victory at Philadelphia had several important consequences. Not only did Herod overcome one of the most serious crises he had ever faced, but he had irrefutably proved his ability as a military commander. He revealed the military potential of the kingdom of Judea and established its superiority over the Nabataeans. This victory and its consequences undoubtedly impressed Octavian and, after the latter's defeat of Antony, influenced his decisions with regard to Herod. Herod's war with the Nabataeans gave him an additional advantage: since he was occupied with the Nabataeans, he could take no part in the actual fighting at Actium against Octavian and was restricted to sending provisions and money to Antony (*Ant.* XV, 189; *War* I, 388).

B. Herod's Position within the Roman Empire.
The Golden Age (30–12 B.C.E.)

Herod was faced by a new set of problems following Antony's defeat at the battle of Actium (31 B.C.E.). It was clear to him that Antony could no longer hold his ground against the victorious Octavian. On the face of it, Herod had no compelling reason to remain blindly loyal to Antony. True, it was Antony who had placed Herod on the throne of Judea, but it was also Antony who had made Herod's position insecure by allowing his policy to be influenced by Cleopatra. Herod did not hesitate for long. As a faithful son of Antipater, for whom political opportunism was a guiding principle, he abandoned the defeated Antony despite the latter's attempts to retain Herod as his ally (Plutarch, *Life of Antony*, 72). Herod's defection was especially important in that he controlled communications between Syria and Egypt, and could thus delay Octavian's advance on the Nile Valley. Herod also demonstrated how beneficial his support could be to Octavian by assisting Didius, the incumbent Roman governor in Syria, who had also joined the victor. They set out to prevent a band of gladiators, who were loyal to Antony and had been training at Cyzicus, from rushing to their master's aid in Egypt. Nevertheless, Herod could not be absolutely certain that Octavian would allow him to retain his crown, since he had after all been considered as one of Antony's supporters. It was with some apprehension, therefore, that Herod prepared to leave for Rhodes, to hear Octavian's decision. Herod left his brother Pheroras as regent over Judea; he sent his mother, sister and his children to the security of the fortress at Masada, while Mariamne and Alexandra were guarded in the fortress of Alexandrium.

Herod need not have feared. The results of his meeting with Octavian were extremely encouraging, and his enemies' hopes for his downfall completely shattered. Octavian confirmed Herod's appointment as king of Judea and showered him with honors, informing everyone that he held Herod in high esteem. Herod began to feel his position so secure that he even requested Octavian's indulgence in pardoning one of Antony's advisers by the name of Alexa, whom Octavian particularly loathed. (The request was refused — *War* I, 393; *Ant.* XV, 197.) Octavian's presence in Syria en route to Egypt afforded Herod the opportunity of giving him a royal welcome, and of supplying his army with provisions on its way from Acre to the Egyptian border. Herod presented his new master with a gift of 800 talents and also supplied Octavian's soldiers with sufficient water and wine to last them through their arduous march across the desert. On his return journey from Egypt to Syria, Octavian found Herod just as complaisant (*Ant.* XV, 7, 187–201; *War* I, 386–95), and allowed him to accompany him to Antioch (*Ant.* XV, 218).

Octavian's attitude towards Herod in leaving him as ruler of Judea was in keeping with Rome's general policy at that time. The continued existence of tributaries ruled by allied kings in the East remained one of the cornerstones of Rome's oriental policy throughout this period. The kingdoms of Galatia, Cappadocia, Paphlagonia and Bosporus still continued to exist as Roman vassals after the battle of Actium. It is important to remember that in other countries, too, Octavian often retained the same sovereigns who had ruled under Antony, though some were deposed.[5] Others, such as the king of Paphlagonia and apparently the king of Galatia, had abandoned Antony and joined up with Octavian while the battle of Actium was being waged (Dio Cassius, L, 13, 5–8). The circumstances attending the end of the reign of Malichu, king of Nabataea, are not clear. There is one theory that he was dethroned, and that his replacement by Obodas resulted from Augustus' awareness that there was no possibility of Malichu reigning side by side with Herod.[6] If this theory is correct, it would reflect Octavian's high regard for Herod; but there is no certainty regarding the fact of the dethronement itself.

Octavian was well aware that the kings of the East had supported Antony only because their lands had been under his jurisdiction; he had good grounds for believing that if he confirmed them in their rule they would be just as loyal to him. It was therefore not necessary to introduce radical changes in the countries whose kings had proved their abilities, and whose rule over their subjects seemed stable. Herod's loyalty and usefulness to Rome had been repeatedly demonstrated; he could even be said to have inherited them from his father Antipater. Herod had been one of Antony's supporters, but his relations with Cleopatra were not of the best. He did not take an active part in the battle of Actium itself and he had withdrawn his support of Antony after the defeat. He had proved himself capable and practical over the years, and again recently by the assistance he had rendered Octavian in his struggle against Egypt. His talents as a military commander had been manifested in his last battle against the Nabataeans. The Romans could certainly not have found a better candidate to rule over Judea, as long as Rome did not consider it feasible to annex Judea to Syria or to set it up as a separate province.

The stabilization of the political, military and economic situation in the Mediterranean region with the establishment of Augustus' principate, and the end of the threats that had endangered both Herod's position and the integrity of his kingdom during the time of Cleopatra, set the pattern for the golden age of Herod's reign. His rule was one of the most impressive demonstrations of the new order Augustus had introduced into the Roman empire. Octavian did not rest content with merely confirming Herod's rule within the boundaries that existed at the time of Antony's defeat, but granted him additional lands as well. Firstly, all territories were returned that Antony had severed from his kingdom at Cleopatra's behest. These comprised Gaza, Jaffa and the region of Jericho. In addition, a number of Hellenistic cities in Transjordan, such as Gadara and Hippus — cities "liberated" by the Romans from Jewish rule — were now added to Herod's kingdom. Further expansion took place in 23 B.C.E., when Trachonitis, Batanaea and Gaulanitis were added (*Ant.* XV, 343–8; *War* I, 398–9). They were annexed in order to combat the growing lawlessness in these areas whose inhabitants engaged in highway robbery and had become a menace to the neighboring populations, including the citizens of Damascus (Strabo, *Geography*, XVI, 2, 20, p. 756). The entire area had first come under the authority of Zenodorus, whose own holdings were situated northwest and west of it.[7] Zenodorus did not take sufficient action to remedy the situation. The population, suffering from the constant acts of brigandage, brought their complaints before Varro, the governor of Syria, who passed them on to Augustus. It occurred to the emperor that the best solution would be to bring these areas under Herod's jurisdiction. Herod immediately acted in the manner expected of him, and took firm steps to ensure the security of the neighboring population. In his efforts to reintroduce law and order into the area, he had to overcome numerous obstacles placed in his path as a result of Zenodorus' jealousy and the latter's relations with the Nabataeans. Zenodorus was also responsible for rousing the inhabitants of Gadara against Herod. When Zenodorus died three years later (20 B.C.E.), Augustus granted Herod his original holdings near the sources of the Jordan (*Ant.* XV, 359–60; *War* I, 400; Dio Cassius, LIV, 9, 3).[8] With the addition of these lands Herod's kingdom now included all Western Palestine with the exception of the Ascalon enclave and the coast north of the Carmel, as well as large areas east of Jordan. This virtually put an end to the division of Palestine by Pompey and Gabinius, and the Judean kingdom once again covered most of the area ruled over by the Hasmoneans in their days of glory. After 20 B.C.E. Herod's kingdom expanded no further, and if Augustus had any intention of adding to it at the expense of the Nabataean kingdom, he never carried it out.

From the beginning, Herod was granted approval by a *senatus consultum* (*Ant.* XV, 196).[9] To stress his affinity with the Roman people Herod adopted the title of "Admirer of the Romans" (($Φιλορωμαῖος$ — *OGIS*, no. 414 = *IG*, II², no. 3440). It appears that he also called himself "Admirer of Caesar" ($Φιλοκαῖσαρ$).[10] Herod was officially included among the kings who were "friends and allies of the Roman people" (*socii et amici populi Romani*). All these kings were denied any initiative in the field of foreign policy, while even in internal affairs they had to bear in mind the requirements of Rome and the policy of its princeps. Herod never attempted to hide his dependence on Augustus, nor did his subjects forget that in the final analysis the Roman emperor remained supreme ruler. The king's submission to the emperor was given expression in the oath of loyalty he was required to take (*Ant.* XVII, 42).[11]

As one of the kings in the Eastern empire, Herod's task was to maintain order within the borders of his kingdom. It was, indeed, his obvious ability to fulfill such a task that had led to his appointment in the first place. He was also required to send his forces whenever they were needed to assist Rome in its wars. During Augustus' principate there were no big wars in the Eastern empire, especially after the Euphrates border had become at least temporarily stable with an agreement between Augustus and King Phraates of Parthia in 20 B.C.E. According to this agreement the Roman prisoners and eagles taken by the Parthians were returned to Rome, thereby satisfying the honor of the Roman people.[12] Even so, Herod had a number of opportunities to offer military aid to the empire. For example, in 25–24 B.C.E. (or in 26–25 B.C.E.) when Aelius Gallus, the governor of Egypt, set out on his unsuccessful South Arabian campaign,

Herod supplied five hundred soldiers who fought in the campaign along-side the Roman legions, side by side with one thousand Nabataeans (Strabo, *Geography* XVI, 4, 23, p. 780; *Ant.* XV, 317).[13]

On another occasion, Herod himself set out from Judea at the head of a fleet to take part in an action on behalf of the empire. This was a semi-military expedition necessitated by the arrangements made in 14 B.C.E. by Marcus Vipsanius Agrippa, Augustus' right-hand man, in the Kingdom of Bosporus in the Black Sea region (Dio Cassius, LIV, 24, 4–7). Herod set sail from Judea for the western shores of Asia Minor. After a voyage around the islands (Rhodes, Cos and Lesbos) and to Byzantium, he met Agrippa at the port of Sinope on the southern shore of the Black Sea. Herod remained with Agrippa while he established Polemon king of Pontus as ruler of the Kingdom of Bosporus and ordered the affairs of other parts of Asia Minor. Agrippa was able to achieve his purpose in the Black Sea region by using only the threat of force. There was no danger attached to Herod's expedition. It did, however, provide him with an opportunity to demonstrate his loyalty to Rome, and to raise his prestige abroad. He also took advantage of the situation to assist the Jews of Asia Minor in their struggle to obtain rights within the Greek cities, and also to act as an intermediary between the Greeks and the Roman rulers.

In addition to rendering assistance to Rome in its wars, Herod was required to pay taxes in the same way, apparently, as all the kings who were allies of Rome. Antony had also imposed taxes on the kings of the East whom he had confirmed, and Augustus did not change the arrangements of his predecessor.[14] It should be pointed out that the taxes were not collected directly from the inhabitants of Judea on behalf of the Roman treasury, but were deducted by the king from his annual revenues. This prevented friction between the people and the Roman government. Payment of regular taxes to Rome did not exempt Herod from having to make contributions to the Roman emperors from his own coffers. When Antony was at the pinnacle of his power, Herod was required to buy his favor and that of his henchmen (*War* I, 358; *Ant.* XV, 5). The situation was hardly different under Octavian. When Octavian first visited Syria in 30 B.C.E., Herod presented him with a substantial gift of money. On later occasions when Augustus distributed money and gifts to the Roman people, Herod paid out large sums of money to the emperor (*Ant.* XVI, 128).

Herod's dependence upon Roman power was further demonstrated by his strong ties with the Roman governors in Syria. In all matters of major importance Herod applied for advice to the governor of Antioch. Thus for example Saturninus, governor of Syria, joined the court that sentenced Alexander and Aristobulus to death (*Ant.* XVI, 368). It was from the same Saturninus that Herod was obliged to obtain permission before taking measures against the Nabataeans (*Ant.* XVI, 277). The same governor also intervened on behalf of Herod when Nabataean agents were involved in a plot against the king of Judea — and then sent them to Rome to suffer the consequences of their actions (*Ant.* XVII, 57; *War* I, 577). Varus, Saturninus' successor as governor of Syria, took an active part in events in Judea at the time of the crisis at Herod's court when Antipater's evil schemes were uncovered (*Ant.* XVII, 89–132; *War* I, 617–40). On the other hand, at the zenith of his rule (after the year 20 B.C.E.) Herod had a certain say in the administration of Syria, since Augustus had issued instructions to the imperial procurators *in provincia* to allow Herod to take part in their decisions (*Ant.* XV, 360; *War* I, 399).

Augustus gave Herod a free hand in the internal affairs of his kingdom. Herod had sovereign rule over the lives and property of his subjects. The only restriction on his arbitary authority lay in his fear of driving his subjects into open rebellion. This would ruin Herod's image and have an adverse effect upon his relations with the Roman princeps. Augustus also agreed to allow Herod to nominate his own successor (or successors), whose appointment, however, was subject to final confirmation by the emperor. This restriction should not be interpreted as reflecting a deterioration in Herod's status during the final period of his reign. Rather it should be presumed that from the outset the freedom of appointing the king's successor was restricted by the requirement of imperial confirmation.[15] Moreover, anything connected personally with the members of the royal family, such as sentencing princes to death, could not be carried out without the emperor's consent. This requirement cannot be explained by the fact that these princes, like all members of Herod's family, were Roman citizens. It was not legal considerations that were decisive, but rather the principle that in matters which could influence the political future of Judea, no irremediable action should be taken without informing the emperor of developments and without receiving his sanction.[16] But this supervision on the part of Augustus in no way detracted from Herod's status as sovereign ruler of Judea, entitled to all the trappings of royalty and the pomp of a royal court.

In fact, Herod's position as king of Judea and his great influence within the Roman empire were determined not so much by the legal definition of his status or by virtues of resolutions taken by the Senate, but rather by his personal relationship with Augustus and the other heads of the Roman state. In this Herod successfully followed in the tradition of Antipater, who sought to forge strong ties with the heads of the Roman government, and with anyone in a position to influence the policy of state. After Actium, Octavian was the object of Herod's admiration, and to establish a close relationship with him became Herod's guiding principle. He succeeded because Augustus was well aware that Herod could cope with his task. Throughout most of his reign, Herod was a favorite of the emperor. It was only during his last years that confidence in him was shaken by the outbreak of internal strife in the Jewish court and Herod's hasty military action against the Nabataeans.

Herod's ties with the emperor were expressed in various ways. For example, he built new cities and named them after the emperor. In this, too, Herod conformed to the practice then in vogue in the Roman empire, whereby kings vied with each other in establishing cities in honor of the emperor. They even decided to complete the building of the Olympic temple to Zeus and to dedicate it to the genius of Augustus (Suetonius, *Life of Augustus*, 60). The two large cities built by Herod — Caesarea and Sebáste (Samaria) — were named after Augustus (*Sebastos* is the Greek equivalent of Augustus). In Caesarea one of the towers was named after Drusus, son of Empress Livia and the stepson of the princeps. The main demonstration of loyalty to Augustus was in the form of emperor-worship and in the erection of statues and temples in his honor. A temple of white marble was built in honor of Augustus at Panion near the source of the Jordan (*War* I, 404). At Caesarea the temple of Augustus was a prominent landmark. In this temple were statues of Rome and the emperor (*Ant.* XV, 339). At Caesarea, games were held in honor of the emperor every fourth year. The empress Livia made her own contribution to the games and the emperor supplied part of the equipment (*Ant.* XVI, 138–9). Herod's demonstration of esteem for the emperor was carried across the borders of his own kingdom of Judea and into the province of Syria, where he set up temples to Augustus in a number of cities (*War* I, 407).[17] Though he was wary of spreading the cult of the emperor and of erecting statues to him in the strictly Jewish areas of his kingdom, he managed to express his loyalty to Augustus by the enthusiasm with which he did so elsewhere.

Herod also strengthened his ties with the other leaders of the Roman state and society. First and foremost was his friendship with Marcus Vipsanius Agrippa, Augustus' son-in-law and right-hand man. Whether or not he met Herod during the latter's first visit to Rome in 40 B.C.E., they certainly became firm friends during Agrippa's prolonged sojourn in the East. In the years 23–21 B.C.E. Agrippa acted as the virtual ruler of the entire eastern portion of the empire, and Herod visited him at his residence on the island of Lesbos, apparently in the winter of 23–22 B.C.E. (*Ant.* XV, 350).[18] It was at that time Agrippa rejected the complaints of the citizens of Gadara against Herod.

The friendship between Agrippa and Herod grew during the period of Agrippa's second extended stay in the East (from 17 or 16 to 13 B.C.E.). To this period belongs Agrippa's impressive visit to Judea (15 B.C.E.) and his direct contact with the Jewish people in their land, an event without precedent in Rome's relations with the Jews. Agrippa was given a royal welcome not only by the king and his court, but also by the entire Jewish population. He stayed at Sebaste and Caesarea, was impressed by the new cities and visited three fortresses: Herodium, Hyrcania and Alexandrium. For years afterwards the citizens remembered his visit to Jerusalem and to the Temple, where he made a large number of sacrifices as a gesture of goodwill and friendship towards the Jewish people and its holy places (*Ant.* XVI, 12–15; Philo, *The Embassy to Gaius*, 294–7).[19]

In the following year (14 B.C.E.), as we have already noted, Herod visited Agrippa during his sojourn in the south of the Black Sea, and accompanied him on his journey through a number of countries in Asia Minor (Paphlagonia, Greater Phrygia and the town of Ephesus) until they reached the island of Samos. The friendship between the two was of benefit to the Jews in the towns of Asia Minor and especially in the cities of Ionia. Relations between the Greek citizens of the cities and their Jewish neighbors had deteriorated. The interests of the Jews were represented by Herod's confidant, the historian Nicolaus of Damascus. Agrippa reaffirmed the rights of the Jews. Herod's presence in the company of Agrippa enabled him to grant favors to many of the Greeks in Asia Minor and at the same time to mediate between them and his Roman friend. He made a good impression through his success in assuaging Agrippa's wrath against the citizens of Ilium, whom Agrippa had fined heavily as a punishment for failing to help his wife Julia (Augustus' daughter), who had almost drowned in the swirling waters of the Scamander River near their town. As a result of Herod's intervention, Agrippa agreed to cancel the fine. Herod also succeeded in obtaining concessions for the people of the island of Chios in the matter of payment of the amounts they owed the imperial procurators. Herod himself helped to reconstruct the magnificent city porticoes which had been badly damaged during the war with Mithradates of Pontus. (*Ant.* XVI, 22–6; Nicolaus *apud* F. Jacoby, *Die Fragmente der Griechischen Historiker*, Berlin, 1929, II, A 90 F 134).

The close friendship that existed between Herod and Agrippa was also reflected in the appearance of the name Agrippa in Herod's family. One of the sons of Aristobulus, the son of Herod and Mariamne the Hasmonean, was given this name (he was to become Agrippa I, king of Judea). In honor of Agrippa the name of the town of Anthedon[20] on the southern coast of Palestine was changed to Agrippias.

In addition to his connection with Agrippa, Herod cultivated friendly relations with many other personalities in Rome. Valerius Messalla was an old friend of Herod and his brother Phasael from the time of Antony. Another friend was Asinius Pollio, who served as a consul in 40 B.C.E., the year in which Herod was crowned in Rome as king over Judea. Pollio was a close friend of Antony at that time, and his friendship with Herod was probably derived from that. When Herod's two sons were sent to Rome to be educated in the capital of the empire, they stayed in Pollio's house (*Ant.* XV, 343).[21] Herod maintained regular contact with his friends and supporters at the emperor's court. They would inform him of the state of affairs in the capital, and especially at the court. He also heeded their advice on Judean matters, and was sensitive to their reactions to his own acts. The members of his family followed in his footsteps. The king's sister Salome was a friend of the empress Livia, and Antipater, Herod's son, made many friends in Rome. Among others he had close ties with an imperial freedwoman, a Jewess by the name of Akme, who assisted him in his schemes. The relations between Herod and the governors of the provinces of Syria and Egypt form a chapter on its own. His friendship with Titius, who served as governor of Syria during the period between Agrippa and Saturninus, is well known (*Ant.* XVI, 270).[22] A friendship also sprung up between Varus, the governor of Syria at the end of Herod's reign, and Herod's son Archelaus (*Ant.* XVII, 303). Among the governors of Egypt, Gaius Petronius (24–21 B.C.E.) was a close friend who came to Herod's aid when drought devastated Palestine (*Ant.* XV, 307).[23]

In keeping with his ardent desire to attain honor and glory in his lifetime, and the necessity of conforming to the style of other rulers in the Hellenistic-Roman eastern empire, and of the Roman élite itself in the Julio-Claudian period, Herod made gifts to various Greek cities for the construction of public buildings and for the maintenance and development of their institutions. Among the cities that profited from his generosity were those situated near the borders of his kingdom on the Palestinian coast — in Phoenicia and Syria. In the city of Ascalon — an enclave not included within the bounds of his kingdom — he maintained a palace. He also built a colonnaded street and installed fountains and public baths. In Accho-

Ptolemais he built a gymnasium; in Berytus[24] and Tyre, market places and temples. He gave Sidon a theater and in the town of Byblos he rebuilt the city walls. In the Syrian town of Laodicea, Herod constructed an aqueduct and in Antioch he paved the main street with marble along the entire length of the city and embellished it with colonnades.[25] A gymnasium and theater were his contribution to Damascus. His bounty reached the Greek mainland, the Aegean islands and Asia Minor.

Herod was honored most of all for his generous contributions to the Olympic games. He was granted the permanent title of Agonothete ("chairman of the games") after he had acted as chairman of one of the Olympiads on his way to Rome, or on his return from it.[26] Herod also gave money for the construction of public buildings in the town of Nicopolis on the western coast of Greece, built by Augustus near the site of the decisive battle of Actium. He also bestowed gifts on Pergamon, Samos and the towns of Cilicia, Pamphylia and Lycia. In Rhodes he rebuilt the temple to Apollo which had been destroyed by fire, and also gave the inhabitants of the island funds with which to build ships. At Chios he rebuilt the ruined colonnade, and on the island of Cos he established a permanent fund to pay the salary of the head of the gymnasium there. Among other cities which benefited from his generosity were Sparta and Athens (*War* I, 422–8; *Ant.* XVI, 18–19; 146–9).

As one of the kings allied with the Roman empire, Herod sought contacts with other members of the alliance. Augustus approved of such connections, and encouraged intermarriage among his vassals (Suetonius, *Life of Augustus*, 48). Following Augustus' system, Herod became friendly with Archelaus, king of Cappadocia. Herod's son Alexander later married Archelaus' daughter Glaphyra. Archelaus, like Herod, was one of Antony's former supporters, and like Herod Octavian allowed him to retain his crown. He also influenced to some extent developments in Judea. When Herod returned from Italy with his sons in 12 B.C.E. they were welcomed by the king of Cappadocia on the coast of Cilicia (*Ant.* XVI, 131). Through his friendship with Titius the governor of Syria, Herod was able to bring about a reconciliation between him and Archelaus. As father-in-law of Alexander, Archelaus kept a careful watch over developments at Herod's court in which his daughter and son-in-law were involved. For a firsthand view of the situation, he visited Judea and succeeded in reducing the tension at the court for a while. His envoy Melas also worked towards this end.

On the other hand, the Roman rulers were always suspicious of any contact between their allies in the East and the Parthians. Any suspicion by the emperor of collusion with this kingdom would be highly dangerous to Herod. Among the most serious charges brought against Herod's son Alexander was that he planned to flee to the emperor in Rome with the intention of denouncing Herod for having joined forces with the king of Parthia (*Ant.* XVI, 253).

Among the allies of Rome was Gaius Julius Eurycles, who for a time was the virtual ruler of Sparta. Apparently Herod had met Eurycles on a visit to Sparta during one of his journeys to Italy. Eurycles returned Herod's visit and while in Jerusalem played an important role in the struggle over the succession to Herod's throne.[27]

C. Relations between Herod and Augustus in the Final Period of Herod's Reign
The Nabataean Problem (12–4 B.C.E.)

In the last years of Herod's life we are aware of a certain cooling off in the relations between Herod and Augustus. This may have partly been due to Augustus' feeling that Herod was no longer successful in keeping his house in order. The internal strife surrounding the succession which beclouded all other events in Judea, in the long run reflected the king's failure and a decline in his powers of judgement. On hearing of the killings in Herod's family, Augustus is said to have remarked "I had sooner be Herod's swine (ὕς) than his son" (υἱός), and the story has an air of authenticity.[28]

However, the matter which most affected the relations between Herod and Augustus was the armed conflict which broke out between Herod and the Nabataeans. Between the years 30 and 12 we hear of no serious strain in relations nor of any armed clashes between the Nabataeans and Herod. After Malichus' reign, Herod reached a *modus vivendi* with his successor Obodas. The extension of Herodian rule to the northeast did not at first lead to any serious crisis between the two kingdoms. We hear of a change in this respect only in 12 B.C.E. The inhabitants of Trachonitis had never fully reconciled themselves to Herod's rule. He had introduced radical changes in their way of life and their economy, and they were awaiting an opportunity to throw off his yoke. While Herod was visiting Italy in 12 B.C.E., rumors spread that he had died. These rumors set off an open revolt among the inhabitants of Trachonitis, and though Herod's soldiers firmly suppressed it, this was not the end of the matter. The insurgents were aided by the Nabataeans across the border. Syllaeus, the leading figure in the Nabataean kingdom, had a personal reason for hostility towards Herod. The king of Judea had earlier prohibited Syllaeus from marrying his sister, unless he became a convert to Judaism and underwent circumcision. Syllaeus refused to fulfill this condition, as it would have jeopardized his position among the Nabataeans.

The rebels of Trachonitis were given the use of bases in Nabataean territory, from which they could make skirmishes into areas under Herod's rule, causing loss of life and great damage to property among the Jewish inhabitants of the border villages. Herod realized that these attacks would not come to an end as long as the marauders were assisted and sheltered by the Nabataeans across the border. He raised the problem with the representatives of the Roman administration in Syria, demanding that the Nabataeans hand over the rebels and repay the sum of sixty talents, which Obodas had borrowed from Herod. In the presence of the Roman officials the two parties reached an agreement to return the refugees to their respective countries. In addition, the Nabataeans undertook to repay their debt to Herod within thirty days.

When Syllaeus, however, failed to carry out the terms of the agreement according to Herod's interpretation, the king decided to put an end to his feud with the Nabataeans and their leader Syllaeus once and for all. His army crossed the Nabataean border and captured the fortress of Raepta which had served as a base for the raids against Trachonitis. In the clashes that followed the invasion many Nabataeans were killed, among them their commander Nacebos, a member of Syllaeus' family.

The impression gained from the description of events is that Herod reacted more vigorously than the Roman representatives in Syria had expected. Herod also took other steps to strengthen his hold upon Trachonitis and to establish order there. He increased the number of his supporters by introducing 3,000 Idumaean settlers into the region. Syllaeus, who was visiting Rome at the time but was kept informed of events, complained to the emperor about Herod's action. Augustus regarded Herod's action in taking the law into his own hands as an affront to the supreme authority of Rome and a violation of the principle that no king allied with Rome could make war on another without the express permission of the princeps. Augustus wrote a strongly worded letter to Herod informing him, *inter alia*, that while he had so far treated Herod as a friend, from now on he would treat him as a subject.

Syllaeus hastened to report to his countrymen on Augustus' unfavorable reaction to Herod's latest venture. Both the inhabitants of Trachonitis and Herod's Nabataean enemies across the border decided that they need no longer fear retribution on the part of Herod. The inhabitants of Trachonitis again rebelled and began to attack the new Idumaean settlers. (*Ant.* XVI, 273–92; Nicolaus *apud* F. Jacoby, *Gr. Hist.* II A 90 F 136 [1]).

In an endeavor to mollify Augustus, Herod sent Nicolaus of Damascus to Rome in order to explain the reasons for Herod's action. An opportune moment presented itself through an unexpected development within the Nabataean kingdom. Upon the death of Obodas, Aretas IV had ascended the throne. In his haste to seize the crown, Aretas had apparently neglected to obtain Augustus' prior permission, as was customary when a change was to be made among the rulers of the allied kingdoms. Syllaeus hoped to prevent Aretas from ascending the throne, and made every effort to undermine his position. On the other hand Nicolaus was helped by the emissaries of Aretas in his efforts to diminish the favor in which Syllaeus was held at the emperor's court. In this manner the way was prepared for a reconciliation between Augustus and Herod. The success of Nicolaus and his supporters was complete. Aretas was confirmed as king of the Nabataeans, Augustus was reconciled with Herod, and Syllaeus' position was shattered. A short time later, various charges were brought against Syllaeus by representatives of Aretas. To these were added other charges made by Herod's son Antipater, accusing him of plotting to murder the king. Syllaeus was found guilty and put to death shortly before Herod died (*Ant.* XVI, 293–9; 335–55; XVII, 54–7; *War* I, 574–7; Nicolaus, *op. cit.;* Strabo, *Geography*, XVI 4, 24, p. 782).[29]

The tension resulting from the invasion of Nabataea undoubtedly constituted the most unfortunate phase in the relationship between Herod and Augustus. Not only did the entire affair discredit Herod in the eyes of the emperor and his court: it also revealed how precarious was the position of an allied king within the Roman empire — even a king with relatively wide powers. The reconciliation with Augustus officially restored the relations between Herod and the emperor, and led Herod to hope that his plans for the appointment of a successor would be approved.

D. Herod's Internal Policy;
the Administration, the Royal Court, the Army, the Revenue

Within his kingdom Herod was an absolute ruler,[30] and his subjects, whether Jews or Gentiles, had no rights whatsoever. Herod's despotism was checked by only one restraint — the fear of driving his subjects to open revolt. Such an eventuality would undermine his main recommendation in the eyes of the Romans — his ability to maintain law and order within his kingdom. Herod was in fact successful in keeping Judea under control. During his entire lifetime no open revolt broke out in his kingdom, and his rule was faced with no serious threat, in spite of the numerous plots that were hatched against him. Such attempts arose out of a deep hatred for Herod, but they only affected small groups of malcontents.

The conquest of Jerusalem in 37 B.C.E. made it possible for Herod to obliterate the vestiges of the Hasmonean rule. Many of its institutions were abolished completely; others were overhauled. In certain areas Herod found it expedient to maintain the existing system, and to extend it to meet his own needs. Among the traditional Jewish institutions he inherited from the Hasmonean dynasty and considered it prudent to retain were two of the most important — the High Priesthood and the Sanhedrin. Both these were modified after Herod's accession. The High Priesthood was undoubtedly the most highly respected institution in Judea throughout the period of the Second Temple. Gentiles and Jews alike regarded the High Priest as the paramount leader of the nation in both internal and external affairs. Under Hasmonean rule the office of High Priest was combined in one person with that of king. The Jews themselves considered the office of king or Ethnarch as subordinate to that of the High Priest.

Herod was unable to combine both offices in his own person since he was not the descendant of a priestly family. Any attempt to usurp the High Priesthood would have aroused the antagonism of the whole nation. Herod was therefore faced with a serious problem, which had to be solved without delay. By appointing a High Priest from the Hasmonean family or by granting the office permanently to one of the revered priestly families, Herod would jeopardize his own position as ruler of Judea. The entire nation would have regarded the High Priest and his family as the rightful rulers of Judea. Herod's first, concern therefore, was to oust the Hasmoneans from the office of High Priest, and after the murder of Aristobulus III there were no further candidates from that dynasty. He also avoided appointing a High Priest who was in any way connected with the Hasmonean family. In addition, he abolished the custom of keeping the office of High Priest within one family, whereby a son automatically inherited it on his father's death. Thus from the time of Herod's rule onwards the exclusive right of one family to the High Priesthood was annulled, as was the custom of life tenure. It should be pointed out, however, that Herod did not actually introduce the system of regular rotation that became the practice in later generations. For many years during Herod's reign the king's father-in-law, Simeon the son of Boethus of Alexandria, served as High Priest. At all events it is certain that the relative decline of the High Priesthood began in

Herod's time; from then on it was the ruler of the land, Jew or non-Jew, who made the appointment.[31]

The Sanhedrin underwent a more serious reformation. It acted now only as the king's council on the pattern of other Hellenistic monarchies. Appointed to it were "friends of the king," his ministers and his close supporters. All important matters of state were brought before the members of the council for their opinion, and the Sanhedrin served when necessary as a court of criminal law in cases whose political implications were likely to affect the public. The king acted as chairman at meetings of the Sanhedrin, and its decisions naturally reflected his opinions.

Josephus records some of the business brought before this royal Sanhedrin. He relates, for example, how Herod informed it of his decision to appoint Aristobulus III to the office of High Priest (*Ant.* XV, 31); or how he summoned them to hear him expose the treachery of Hyrcanus II and his attempt to join forces with the king of the Nabataeans (*Ant.* XV, 173).[32] It was before this Sanhedrin that Herod announced the plans concerning the marriage of his grandsons (*War* I, 559), and laid his charge against his sister-in-law, the wife of his brother Pheroras (*Ant.* XVII, 46–8; *War* I, 571). It is not clear to what extent the composition of the royal Sanhedrin was permanent, and whether the king would co-opt additional members for specific consultations. It may be presumed that the court of 150 members appointed by Herod to judge his sons Alexander and Aristobulus at Berytus, which was attended by the governor of Syria himself, was in actual fact the royal Sanhedrin expanded for this specific purpose. Since at least some of the members of the royal Sanhedrin were not of Jewish origin, the proceedings were probably carried on in Greek, the language used by Herod in other spheres of administration and government.

Herod used public assemblies as a means of influencing the masses. Such assemblies were held from time to time in Jerusalem, and occasionally in other towns (Jericho, for example). Though mass rallies were certainly not a regular institution in Judea, they do seem to have been in use long before Herod's time for the purpose of explaining current affairs, reporting the achievements of the ruler, or obtaining the people's consent to a particular policy. In Herod's time, of course, public assemblies had no voice in matters of policy; their role was entirely passive. Herod convened a public assembly, for example, to announce his intention of rebuilding the Temple (*Ant.* XV, 381). We are also told that when Herod returned from his visit to Agrippa in Asia Minor (14 B.C.E.) he assembled the people in Jerusalem, and that persons from outside the city also participated. Herod held forth to this assembly on the successes of his journey, laying special stress on his achievement in obtaining the confirmation of Jewish privileges in the Ionian cities (*Ant.* XVI, 62–5). He also took the opportunity to announce the reduction of the tax rates by one quarter. Similarly, when in 12 B.C.E. he returned from meeting Augustus at Aquileia in Italy, he deemed it necessary to call a public assembly in the Temple court to report on the events that had befallen him. On this occasion he also presented to the people his three heirs (*Ant.* XVI, 132–5).

Another type of assembly was that called by Herod at Jericho after the attempt to remove the Roman eagle from the Temple gate (*Ant.* XVII, 161). This was not a public gathering, however, since only dignitaries and officials were invited. The manner in which the king used the public assemblies to put his adversaries to death is also of interest. A crowd murdered the military men who supported the brothers Alexander and Aristobulus (*Ant.* XVI, 393), while at Jericho others among their staunch supporters were stoned to death by the assembled mob (*Ant.* XVI, 320).

The administrative organization of Herod's kingdom largely followed the same division of the country as existed in previous generations. The kingdom was divided up into large administrative units which in general corresponded to the historic districts of Palestine: Galilee, Samaria, Judea, Idumaea and Transjordan (Peraea). To head these units Herod appointed meridarchs (*Ant.* XV, 216)[33] who were considered loyal to him and who were often his relatives by marriage. Thus his brother-in-law, Costobar, served as governor of Idumaea during the early years of his rule. The most outstanding case was that of the king's younger brother Pheroras, who while holding the position of governor of Peraea, enjoyed wide powers and held the title of Tetrarch, which Herod obtained for him from Augustus during the latter's sojourn in the East. It is interesting to note that Pheroras' son was to have inherited his father's position, though in the end he did not. It also appears that towards the end of Herod's life one of the king's cousins, Ahiab, served as governor of Judea.

The above administrative divisions covered Herod's entire kingdom. Although old-established Hellenistic cities, as well as those built by Herod, were granted a degree of autonomy and retained the trappings of government in the Hellenistic style, the king had no difficulty in supervising developments within these territories. This was done through the constitutions granted to the new cities, by stationing garrisons in them, and by appointing officials to represent the king there (*strategos* of the *polis*). The cities were generally linked to the nearest administrative division. Thus Gaza was linked to Idumaea, so that Costobar was "governor of Idumaea and Gaza" (*Ant.* XV, 254); Caesarea was likewise linked to Samaria. These divisions were subdivided into "toparchies", based on the division of the country in the Hellenistic period. The smallest administrative unit was the village.

It is quite certain that the cities were not exempted from paying taxes to the king. One of the old-established cities, Gadara in Transjordan, which served as a center of Greek culture for the area, tried to oppose Herod's despotism, but to no avail. This attempt was made during

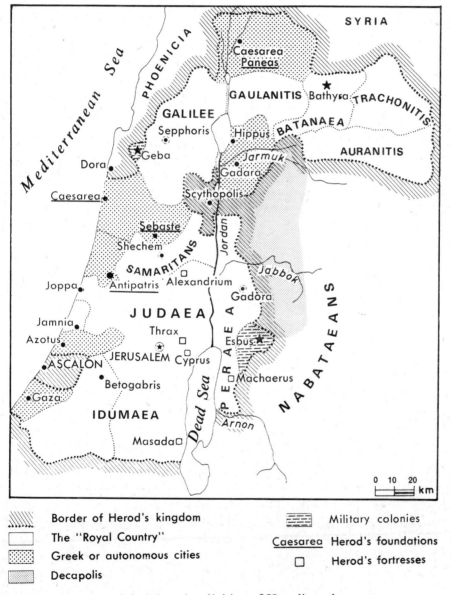

Administrative division of Herod's realm

Agrippa's first visit to the East; Agrippa arrested the city's emissaries and sent them to Herod for him to deal with. Zenodorus later urged the people of Gadara to renew their complaints during Augustus' visit to Syria in 20 B.C.E. and to demand that their city be directly affiliated to the province of Syria. But it soon became apparent that Augustus would not accede to their request; the representatives of Gadara, fearing that Augustus would hand them over to Herod for punishment, chose to commit suicide (*Ant.* XV, 351, 356–8).

The center of Herod's kingdom was the magnificent royal court, which in every respect resembled the courts of the Hellenistic kings in the East. Persons who held high positions in the government and who were permanently attached to the king, held the title of "friends" (φίλοι) and "relatives" (συγγενεῖς) of the king.

The king was the object of a personality cult. This was probably both spontaneously generated and organized from above, and embraced not only the royal court but the entire kingdom. In the non-Jewish section of the country, his subjects erected statues in his honor, as we learn from the Seeia inscription (*OGIS*, no. 415). The anniversary of Herod's accession to the throne was celebrated throughout the kingdom (*Ant.* XV, 423).

In keeping with the practice of the kings of the East, we are told of personal details connected with the king and his wives. We read of the duties of his court eunuchs, one of whom had to fill the king's goblet with wine, another to serve his meals, and a third to put him to bed (*Ant.* XVI, 230). These various eunuchs took part in the intrigues between the king and his sons.

Many of the king's assistants were Greeks. One of the most important of these was Ptolemy, who was the royal treasurer and perhaps the king's chief minister. Ptolemy was rewarded with a plot of land in Samaria (*Ant.* XVII, 289; *War* II, 69).[34] Some of the famous Greek writers of the time were to be found at Herod's court. Outstanding among them was Nicolaus of Damascus, renowned as an historian, rhetorician, dramatist, and author of works on natural science and philosophy.[35] At first Nicolaus lived under the patronage of Antony and Cleopatra. After their death he moved to Judea and became one of Herod's companions and his confidant. He was given a number of special assignments on behalf of the king. He accompanied the king on his journey to Asia Minor in 14 B.C.E., and took up the cause of the Jews of Ionia. We have evidence that Nicolaus accompanied Herod on one of his journeys to Italy and later took a leading part in appeasing Augustus following Herod's invasion of Nabataea. Nicolaus himself states that he helped to broaden Herod's education and instructed him in the art of rhetoric. When Herod's interest in rhetoric

palled they studied history together. Nicolaus also relates that it was
Herod who encouraged him to write his *Universal History*, a huge work
of 144 volumes, a good portion of it devoted to the history of Herod's
reign. Among the other writers who lived under Herod's patronage was
Philostratus, a philosopher who had also been close to Antony and Cleopatra. Philostratus' ties with Herod began in the thirties of the first century
B.C.E.[36] In addition to these there were Greek teachers in the royal household, while actors, musicians and athletes were attracted to Jerusalem by
the prizes offered by the king.

Herod's penchant for Greek civilization in its various manifestations
can be understood against the background of his ramified connections with
the Greek-speaking Mediterranean world and through the sympathetic
attitude towards Hellenism that characterized the Roman empire during
this period. It should also be noted that Augustus and his followers were
also munificent patrons of poets and writers. Some of the kings of Herod's
generation won renown as authors. Among them were Archelaus, king of
Cappadocia and father-in-law of Herod's son, and the historian Juba,
king of Mauretania. It is known that Herod himself wrote memoirs
($\dot{\nu}\pi o\mu\nu\acute{\eta}\mu\alpha\tau\alpha$) in Greek.

The Greek language served Herod not only in his contacts with the
outside world, but also as the official language of the royal court, the
administration, and the meetings of the king's council. It was also the
language most common in Herod's army. In addition to such personalities
as Ptolemy and Nicolaus, others steeped in Greek culture served in the royal
adminstration. The king's secretary Diophantus was one of these (*Ant.*
XVI, 319). Nicolaus' brother, also called Ptolemy, worked together
with him. Here and there we come across people with Roman names —
Volumnius, Iucundus, Gemellus, etc. — and there is no lack of persons of
Oriental origin, such as Corinthos the Arab, one of the king's bodyguards
who was involved in the plot against him, or Soemus the Ituraean. However,
when scrutinizing foreign names, especially Greek ones, it should be
remembered that in those times many Jews had such names too. Thus not
everyone in the service of Herod who had a Greek name was necessarily
a non-Jew. There can be no doubt, however, that the number of Greeks
in the administration, in the army and in the Herodian royal court was
quite substantial. Proof of this can be found in Nicolaus' autobiography.
Describing the turn of events after Herod's death, he states that there were
over 10,000 "Hellenes" holding positions in the administration of Herod's
kingdom, against whom the Jewish population revolted after the death of
the king (F. Jacoby, *Gr. Hist.* II A 90 F 136 [8], p. 424).

The coins minted by Herod reflect the Hellenistic character of his kingdom. Like the Hasmoneans, Herod minted no silver coins, but made do with copper. The legends on his coins are solely in Greek, and include Herod's name in both nominative and genitive form. The absence of specifically Jewish symbols is conspicuous, while pagan symbols do occur.[37]

Herod relied for his security on his own armed forces. During Augustus' principate the Roman legions were no longer based in Judea. Herod's own army was sufficiently strong to withstand an attack. Its troops were drawn from a variety of sources. Most prominent were the levies from the new cities, Caesarea and Sebaste, which supplied large numbers of soldiers first to Herod and later to the Roman army. Towards the end of Herod's reign there were 3,000 such soldiers. In addition to levying soldiers from the Hellenistic cities he had founded, Herod exploited the settlers in non-Jewish military colonies. According to the custom of the Hellenistic world these could serve as a regular force for the defense of the kingdom. Of Herod's military settlements we have records of Esbus (Ḥeshbon) in Trans-Jordan and Geba, the "city of horsemen" in the Jezreel Valley(*Ant.* XV, 294).[38] This large military representation greatly increased the relative importance of Palestine's Gentile population, and in later generations had grave repercussions on the relations between the Jews and the Roman government. Herod's forces also included mercenaries from other countries (Gauls and Thracians.)

Jews did serve in Herod's army, but as Herod regarded most of the Jewish people with suspicion, he could rely only on those elements among his Jewish subjects who were in some way different from the majority of the nation. Of these he considered the Idumaeans to be the most loyal, since he himself was of Idumaean origin. He used them as military colonists and settled 3,000 of them in Trachonitis to defend the region against robbers and marauders. Herod also placed his confidence in the Jews who had immigrated from Babylon; they too were settled in northern Trans-jordan. Only in special cases did Herod call up other Jews to his service. One of these occurred in 31 B.C.E., when he was at war with the Nabatae-ans. On this occasion he had no fear that they would desert to the enemy. In Herod's army there were officers with typically Roman names (Rufus, Gratus), who helped to raise the professional standard of his men.

As a king who did not enjoy the goodwill of the majority of his subjects, Herod was particularly sensitive to the mood of his soldiers (*Ant.* XVI, 134, 375–93; *War* I, 491). He was particularly upset, therefore, by the support within the army for his sons Alexander and Aristobulus. Antipater, another of Herod's sons, was also concerned about the coolness of the military towards him (*Ant*. XVII, 2).

The budget of Herod's kingdom was burdened with many items of heavy expenditure. One important item was the expense incurred in fostering relations with the emperor and other personages in Rome, over and above the regular payment of the annual tax to the Roman treasury. In addition, there were the considerable sums needed to maintain a magnificent court and a strong army, and the even greater ones of establishing new cities and constructing large buildings in different parts of the country. Herod's gifts to other cities outside his kingdom also added to his expenditure.

A large proportion of these expenses were covered by the income from regular taxes, the most important of which were direct taxes on agricultural produce. There were also other taxes connected with various economic functions, such as purchase and sales taxes (*Ant*. XVII, 205) and a wide variety of customs duties. Basing ourselves on contemporary sources, the income from the various parts of his kingdom reached a total of about 1,000 talents. Such unprecedented revenues stemmed partly from the development of new areas and partly from the continuous peace which permitted a revival of the country's economy. We also hear of complaints about the heavy taxes during Herod's rule and of the poverty in the country resulting from his policies (*Ant*. XVII, 308; *War* II, 85-6). It appears that these complaints were largely due to the unequal distribution of taxes, the main burden of which rested on the shoulders of the Jewish farmers and tenants of the king.

A substantial part of Herod's income came from the large royal estates. These were mainly former properties of the Hasmonean dynasty taken over by Herod. They included large stretches of fertile agricultural land in different regions of Judea, in the Jordan Valley, the Jezreel Valley and in the vicinity of Lydda.[39] Herod also probably inherited property from his father. He employed the methods used by the Roman leaders of his time (the proscriptions carried out by Antony and Octavian), confiscating the property of his many enemies who were sentenced to death or who fell in battle against him. These methods he used especially in the early years of his reign (*Ant*. XV, 5-6), but even later the continued opposition to his rule afforded him many such opportunities. In order to raise funds for his kingdom he was prepared to employ any means, and is even reputed to have tried to rob King David's tomb (*Ant*. XVI, 179-80).

The royal estates were leased to tenants who paid high rents, and served as an important source of income to Herod. On part of his private lands Herod settled soldiers who tilled the soil during times of peace and were called on to fight in times of war. The king granted plots of land as "gifts' ($\gamma\tilde{\eta}\ \dot{\varepsilon}\nu$ $\delta\omega\rho\varepsilon\tilde{\alpha}$) to his ministers and favorites, as was the custom in Hellenistic times.

The economic prosperity of Herod's kingdom was aided by the general prosperity of the region. This derived from the stable peace that began to prevail throughout the Roman empire with the beginning of Augustus' rule. The long period of civil wars in Rome, of exploitation in the provinces and of dangers threatening on land and sea now gave way to a period of security, in which international trade could develop unhindered and agriculture could flourish once more.[40] Judea also benefited from these developments. After generations of repression and revolt, of wars within and without its borders, culminating in the internecine struggles between Antigonus and Herod, Judea was at last blessed with a period of peace and security. Between 30 and 4 B.C.E., the country's peace was disturbed only by raids from across the Nabataean border. These, however, were mostly in the area of Trachonitis, and did not affect the majority of the Jewish population of Herod's domains. Herod's external relations were an important factor in the development of commerce with other countries. In this context we should mention the flow of money to Judea through the contributions to the Temple of the *half sheqel* by every male Jew, including those in other countries. Orders issued by Augustus and Agrippa explicitly permitted the Jews in the Diaspora to send such contributions to Jerusalem, in spite of the objections of the Greek cities.

Among Herod's outstanding achievements were the reclamation of soil for cultivation and the settlement of farmers in new areas. The most noteworthy example was the agricultural area in northern Transjordan which Herod turned over to agriculture and to which he brought Jews from Idumaea and Babylonia.[41] During Herod's reign these Babylonian settlers were exempted from paying taxes. They guarded the area against local bandits, and against incursions from across the border. Their presence provided the basis for the development of Gaulanitis, Batanaea and Trachonitis. The Jordan Valley was another region where important changes came about as a result of the activity of Herod and of his son Archelaus. Herod also derived income from his business undertakings abroad. One example of this was his share in the production of copper from the mines in Cyprus (*Ant.* XVI, 128).[42]

E. Herod the Builder and Founder of Cities

In one field Herod excelled all the rulers of the period of the Second Temple, including his Hasmonean predecessors — in the building of cities and the construction of impressive edifices throughout his realm. From this point of view he may be considered the equal of Solomon, the great builder king of the early period of the kingdom of Israel. Herod's sons followed in their father's footsteps. The results of their activities in town and country were apparent for many generations. Throughout the major part of his rule Herod was unable to achieve glory with impressive victories on the battlefield, owing to the severe restrictions imposed upon him by the political situation of his time. His building activities, therefore, provided an outlet for his energies, and the means for impressing observers with the splendor of his kingdom. Undoubtedly, too, some of his construction filled essential needs in the economic, military and artistic spheres.

Through Herod's initiative, Jerusalem became one of the most impressive capitals in the eastern Roman empire. His outstanding projects in Jerusalem included the magnificent royal palace and the great towers in the northwest corner of the city (Phasael, Hippicus and Mariamne); the restoration of the ancient fortress which he named Antonia in honor of his patron Mark Antony; the theater;[43] the amphitheater and hippodrome, and above all the rebuilding of the Temple — "Herod's Temple" — which replaced the old and much less impressive building erected in the days of Zerubabel. "Whoever has not seen Herod's Temple has never seen a beautiful building" (B. Batra, 4a). Herod built palaces in various places throughout the country — at Jericho, Betharamatha, Sepphoris and Ascalon. He also strengthened the ancient Hasmonean fotresses of Hyrcania and Alexandrium, and rebuilt Machaerus, east of the Dead Sea, as a stronghold against the Nabataeans. He built the fortress and palace of Herodium some 15 kilometers south of Jerusalem on the site where he drove back his enemies when fleeing from the Parthians. Herodium became an administrative center and the capital of one of the toparchies of Judea. The mighty fortresses of Herodium, Hyrcania and Alexandrium were among the places singled out for a visit by Marcus Agrippa during his stay in Palestine in 15 B.C.E.

One of Herod's outstanding achievements was the reinforcement and expansion of the Hasmonean fortress of Masada. From Josephus' detailed description and the archaeological excavations carried out on the site we are able to judge the magnitude of Herod's undertaking. The fortress of Masada was surrounded by walls which enclosed a number of palaces. One large palace to the west served as the living quarters of the royal court. Nearby were three smaller palaces, splendidly adorned and presumably the living quarters of Herod's relatives. In addition to these palaces, there was a magnificent private villa outside the walls at the northernmost extremity of Masada. Cut into the northwestern cliff were two rows of cisterns to which the waters from the river beds of two valleys were diverted, providing storage for the fortress' water supply.[44]

Herod's crowning achievement as a builder was the construction of Caesarea. The establishment of this city on the site of Strato's Tower fulfilled a vital economic need. Herod's realm did not possess a first-class harbor. The port of Jaffa and the southern ports were no longer sufficient for its needs. The new city now became the main harbor of Herod's kingdom. Caesarea was directly connected to the highly developed agricultural regions of Sharon, Samaria and the Jezreel Valley. Thanks to its unique location, it became one of the major cities of Palestine and the main rival of Jerusalem. Herod built large-scale port installations, and the port of Caesarea may possibly have outranked the harbor of Pireus. To enhance the city Herod constructed many impressive buildings. The large temple to Augustus was visible from far and wide, and contained statues of Augustus and the goddess Roma. The city was famous for its rows of towers, the most beautiful of which was named after Drusus, the emperor's stepson. At Caesarea Herod also built a palace, a theater and a hippodrome (*Ant.* XV, 331–41; *War* I, 408–15). The construction of the city took twelve years. Its completion was marked by festivities, including horse racing, gladiatorial combats, an exhibition of wild animals, and competitions in music and athletics (*Ant.* XVI, 136–8, *War* I, 415).[45]

The second largest city built, or rather rebuilt, by Herod, was Sebaste. Originally called Samaria, this town was laid waste in the time of John Hyrcanus and was restored by Gabinius, the governor of Syria. It began to thrive under Herod, who renamed it Sebaste, after the Greek version of Augustus' name. In restoring Samaria, Herod had been mindful of its strategic position. He had already had occasion to feel more secure in Samaria than in Jerusalem, and the town had served him as an important base in his war against Antigonus. He now rebuilt it as a stronghold which could be used against his dissident Jewish subjects. The town was quite large (20 stadia in circumference) and was surrounded by a strong wall. Herod also took care of its external appearance. On the western side of the hill's summit a temple to Augustus was established. Part of Sebaste's inhabitants were soldiers who had been demobilized from the king's army, while part were drawn from the surrounding villages. The number of the settlers reached a total of 6,000 and the inhabitants were granted parcels of land in the most fertile areas of Samaria (*Ant.* XV, 292–8; *War* I, 403).[46] Herod himself gave the city its constitution.

The inhabitants of this new city were grateful to their benefactor and remained extremely loyal to him. The city served as a reservoir from which soldiers were recruited for the king's army, and it continued to fulfill this function even after Herod's death, when the province was ruled directly by Rome. The unswerving loyalty shown by the citizens of Sebaste towards Herod also explains why he chose this city as the site for the execution of his sons, Alexander and Aristobulus. Sebaste differed from Caesarea and the older Hellenistic cities in that it did not have any Jewish population at all. Herod did not bring Jewish settlers to Sebaste and we may presume that later conditions prevented Jews from settling there.

Finally, the establishment of the cities of Caesarea and Sebaste tipped the numerical balance of Jews and non-Jews in the cities of Palestine in favor of the latter. In this, Herod may be regarded as continuing the policy of Pompey and Gabinius. Among the smaller towns Herod constructed were Phasaelis and Cypros[47] (in honor of his brother and mother) in the Jericho Valley, and Antipatris (in honor of his father) near Rosh ha-'Ayin.

F. The Struggle Over the Succession

From the outset Herod's rise to power was bound up with one of the most important branches of the Hasmonean family. At the height of his struggle with Antigonus Herod married Mariamne, the daughter of Alexander, who was the son of Aristobulus II, and Hyrcanus' daughter Alexandra. This marriage should have given Herod's rule a measure of legality in the eyes of the Jews. Since one of the sons from this marriage might inherit the throne of the Jewish kingdom, the marriage itself could serve as the all-important bond between the Hasmonean dynasty and Herod's reign. But events were to prove otherwise. During the war between Herod and Antigonus, Mariamnne and Alexandra identified themselves completely with Herod and his policy. The return of Mariamne's grandfather, Hyrcanus II, from imprisonment in the Parthian kingdom, reflected the understanding that existed between Herod and the branch of the Hasmonean family attached to him by marriage. However, the stumbling block for Herod was the perfectly legal claim of Aristobulus III to the position of High Priest. From the time of this episode, relations between the king and his wife Mariamne began to deteriorate rapidly, and Aristobulus' murder at Herod's instigation irredeemably contaminated the atmosphere at the royal court.

The second stage of the decline in this relationship can be dated to the execution of Hyrcanus II on the charge of having had connections with

Malichu, king of the Nabataeans. During the crisis following the defeat of Antony, when Herod was still unsure of the fate Octavian held in store for him, the fact that a former ruler of Judea was still alive seemed to Herod to be a source of supreme danger (*Ant.* XV, 161–78; *War* I, 433). The violent deaths of her brother and grandfather had their obvious effect on Mariamne's relations with Herod. Those relations became even more strained as a result of Herod's jealousy regarding his wife, a jealousy which was fanned by her enemies, especially by Salome, the king's sister. Mariamne was accused of having been unfaithful to her husband with one of his servants, Soemus the Ituraean, when Herod was overseas at his fateful meeting with Octavian. Soemus was summarily put to death. Mariamne was tried by a court composed of Herod's close supporters, and she too was sentenced to death. For some time the king postponed carrying out the death sentence and planned to hold her prisoner in one of the fortresses. However, he was persuaded by his sister Salome that this would set off riots, and he therefore decided to put the sentence into effect (*Ant.* XV, 202–36; *War* I, 438–43).

The king was overcome by profound grief at the death of Mariamne, and yearned for her so strongly that he found it difficult to go on living. He fell ill at Sebaste, and his life was in danger before he finally succeeded in overcoming the mental and physical crisis. His mother-in-law Alexandra now tried to seize the key positions in Jerusalem, but she was prevented from doing so by Herod's officers, in particular Ahiab. Ahiab informed the king, and a few days later Alexandra was sentenced to death and executed (*Ant.* XV, 247–51).

Mariamne's death left a void in the royal court. During her lifetime we find no mention of other women in connection with Herod, after the latter banished his first wife who had borne him his eldest son, Antipater. Mariamne was looked upon not as just one of Herod's wives, but as the unchallenged queen. She was a political and public figure in her own right who, in part at least, implemented the rights of the Hasmonean dynasty to the throne; her children were regarded as rightful heirs to the throne. After Mariamne's death, Herod married a number of times, and had nine wives in all. Among the most important were Mariamne II, daughter of the High Priest Simeon, son of Boethus the Alexandrian, who bore him a son named Herod; Malthace the Samaritan, mother of Archelaus and Herod Antipas, the two sons who became the main heirs to Herod's throne; and Cleopatra the Jerusalemite, the mother of Philip, another of the heirs. Other wives mentioned are Pallas, who bore Herod a son, Phasael, and Phaedra and Elpis, who bore him daughters. His brother's daughter, whom he also married, bore him no children. He also brought Doris, his first wife, back to the court.

Mariamne bore Herod five children, three of whom were boys. Only two sons were still alive — Alexander and Aristobulus. They were educated in Rome for a number of years and became closely integrated into its society and culture. In 17 B.C.E. Herod went to Rome to bring back his two sons to Judea. Their chances of inheriting the throne seemed good. Both were of striking appearance and regal bearing. Of the two, Alexander had the more impressive personality and this made him especially popular with Herod's soldiers. Herod married him to Glaphyra, daughter of the Cappadocian king Archelaus. This marriage brought Herod a special advantage in that he could always count upon help from Archelaus, who enjoyed great prestige in the East. Aristobulus married Berenice, daughter of the king's sister (*Ant.* XVI, 6–11; *War* I, 445–6).

The return of Herod's sons to Judea and their popularity among the different sections of the Jewish population brought about a renewal of the link between Herod and the branch of the Hasmonean family that had supported him. It also boded ill for those who had done their best to sever these ties and had induced Herod to carry out Mariamne's death sentence. These courtiers, headed by the king's sister, Salome, were certain that their lives were now in peril, especially as the two princes did not attempt to conceal their grief at their mother's fate. The brothers even announced their intention of taking revenge on those who had brought about her death. The king's other wives and their children they treated with utter disdain. Alexander's wife, the Cappadocian princess, insulted her sister-in-law Berenice, Aristobulus' wife. Antipater, Herod's firstborn, regarded Alexander and Aristobulus as the main obstacles to his succession to the throne. Pheroras, Herod's brother, was also in the anti-Hasmonean camp. We may presume that others, such as the Boethus family, also worked to undermine the position of the two princes.

The atmosphere at Herod's court was soon poisoned completely, and the tension between the feuding parties became the major factor in shaping events within the Judean kingdom. Herod allowed himself to be won over by the arguments of his sons' enemies, and his old antagonism towards the Hasmonean family was aroused once more. He decided to draw Antipater closer to him so as to counterbalance the two sons of Mariamne, and presented him as a potential crown prince. He also reinstated Doris, Antipater's mother, at the court. In 13 B.C.E. when Agrippa returned to Rome from the East, Herod sent Antipater with him in order to be presented before Augustus, with the aim of winning the emperor's support

(*Ant.* XVI, 66–86; *War* I, 447–51). Herod prepared the ground for his son's arrival in Rome by sending letters to his friends. Antipater, for his part, took the initiative in making further connections. During the time he was in Rome, Antipater kept a watchful eye on developments in Jerusalem and devised many schemes against his brothers, whose enemies now openly accused them of planning to depose their father. Not wishing to act on his own in the matter, Herod in 12 B.C.E. brought his two sons before Augustus, who was then staying in Aquileia in northern Italy.[48] The emperor succeeded in reconciling the two parties, and it was Alexander who made the most impressive appearance at the meeting. On this occasion, Herod presented Augustus with 300 silver talents, since money was being distributed among the Roman populace during the games then being held in the capital (*Ant.* XVI, 87–129; *War* I, 452–4). On his return journey Herod met Archelaus, king of Cappadocia, who was pleased to learn of the improved relations between Herod and his son-in-law Alexander. When he reached Jerusalem, Herod announced his intention of leaving his kingdom to Antipater in the first place and to Alexander and Aristobulus in the second (*Ant.* XVI, 130–5; *War* I, 455–66).

Herod's plan for the succession could not please Alexander and Aristobulus, since it thrust them aside in favor of Antipater, who would be given priority. Antipater was apprehensive about his future and afraid that the two brothers might succeed in outmaneuvering him, especially as they were beloved by the people.

Antipater now had Herod's trust and the support of Ptolemy, the chief minister. Salome, Herod's sister, remained hostile to Mariamne's sons, even though Aristobulus was married to her daughter Berenice. She used information she received from her daughter on Aristobulus' views and actions, in order to blacken him in Herod's eyes.

In addition to the struggle over the succession between Antipater and the sons of Mariamne, a further source of tension in Herod's court was the quarrel between the king and his brother Pheroras. It seems that Pheroras, too, was anxious about his own future. Pheroras had fallen in love with one of his maidservants (to whom he remained devoted all his life), and refused to give her up despite all his brother's attempts to persuade him to marry Cypros, Herod's daughter by Mariamne (*Ant.* XVI, 188–219).

A further deterioration in the relations between Herod and his sons followed the disclosure of intrigue between Alexander and three of the king's favorite eunuchs. Under torture the eunuchs confessed that Alexander planned to seize the throne he claimed as his by right of descent, that he was making careful preparations to put his plan into action, and that he had the support of many of the army officers. The confession caused a crisis at court. Herod completely lost his self-confidence and suspected treachery in every corner. Many persons were put to death; some of the king's closest supporters were dismissed from his service because of their contacts with his two sons. Among these were Andromachus and Gemellus; the former's son was a friend of Alexander, while the latter had been in Rome together with Alexander. One of the men tortured at Herod's command revealed that the two brothers has conspired to kill the king while he was engaged in his favorite sport of hunting. They were then to flee to Rome and request the emperor to make them rulers over Judea. This confession seemed exaggerated even to Herod. More credible was another confession exacted by torture from a young man, according to which Alexander had written to friends in Rome asking them to arrange for him to be summoned there, since he had information about contacts between Herod and the Parthians. The same young man stated that Alexander had prepared a dose of poison for himself at Ascalon. Alexander, who apparently despaired of being exonerated from the charges made against him, wrote to Herod that a plot to assassinate the king had in fact been made, but that it was Salome and Pheroras who were behind it. Friends of the king did all in their power to put an end to the animosity and mutual distrust in which the court had become engulfed. The visit of Archelaus, king of Cappadocia, came at an opportune moment, and he succeeded in bringing about a temporary reconciliation between Herod and his sons (*Ant.* XVI, 229–70; *War* I, 488–512).

But the underlying causes of the antagonism had not been removed. One event which served to make the situation worse was the visit of Eurycles the Spartan to Jerusalem. He quickly assessed the situation in Herod's court, and brought his weight to bear on the side of Antipater and against Alexander and Aristobulus. On the other hand Euaratus, an important visitor from Cos, lent his support to Alexander, but this was not sufficiently strong to counterbalance the effect of Eurycles' visit (*Ant.* XVI, 300–12; *War* I, 513–33).

The close ties formed between Alexander and Aristobulus and two retired officers (Iucundus and Tyrannus), who had lost Herod's confidence, now rekindled the king's suspicions. They were both arrested, and under torture confessed that Alexander had persuaded them to murder Herod. As a consequence of this, the commander of the fortress of Alexandrium was arrested on the charge of having promised to give the brothers refuge in the stronghold. The commander pleaded his innocence, but his own son attested to his guilt. The son also produced a letter written by Alexander, which seemed to prove his guilt. Alexander claimed that the letter was a forgery; indeed it seems that he really was innocent. The officers involved in the alleged conspiracy were stoned to death at Jericho by the mob, and we are are told that the two brothers were saved from the same fate only by the intervention of Ptolemy and Pheroras. Alexander and Aristobulus denied any attempt on their father's life, but admitted planning to escape from the atmosphere of suspicion which surrounded them. Alexander also admitted that their original goal had been to reach the court of King Archelaus in the hope that he would agree to send them on to Rome. This confession on the part of Alexander was the deciding factor for Herod. He regarded their intention of appearing before the emperor with the support of Archelaus as an open attempt to undermine his political position. Herod sent two of his men, Olympius and Volumnius, to Rome to place before Augustus all the evidence he had collected against his two sons. On their way to Rome they had orders to convey Herod's protest to Archelaus for having supported the conspiracy of Herod's sons (*Ant.* XVI, 313–34; *War* I, 535).

Augustus was impressed by the evidence, but advised Herod not to sentence his sons on his own opinion alone. The emperor suggested that a court be set up in the Roman colony of Berytus to include representatives of the Roman administration in Syria as well as Archelaus of Cappadocia. Herod chose to ignore Augustus with regard to Archelaus, but acted on the imperial advice in every other respect. A court of 150 members, including Saturninus, the governor of Syria, was convened at Berytus. The majority reached a verdict of guilty and pronounced the death sentence upon Alexander and Aristobulus, although Saturninus expressed a dissenting opinion. News of the sentence spread quickly and was received with grief and anger by both the civilian populace and the army, among whom Alexander was especially popular. One of the older soldiers, whose son was a friend of Alexander, even dared to upbraid Herod for his malevolence towards his own sons and conveyed to him the bitter resentment of the soldiers when they had learned of the verdict. However, the veteran's intervention had the opposite of the desired effect. Using the information thus gratuitously received, Herod lost no time in arresting the malcontents. Three hundred soldiers who were suspected of supporting the two brothers were put to death by the mob. Alexander and Aristobulus were brought to Sebaste and strangled there (7 B.C.E.). They were buried in the fortress of Alexandrium (*Ant.* XVI, 356–94; *War* I, 536–51, Nicolaus *apud* F. Jacoby, *Gr. Hist.* II A 90 F 136 [2], p. 423).

With the death of Alexander and Aristobulus, hopes for a descendent of

597
POMPEJUS MAGNUS
d. 48 f. Kr.

1.
Pompey the Great
Ny Carlsberg Glyptotek,
Copenhagen.

2.
Julius Caesar
National Museum, Berlin.

3.
Head of Caesar
Augustus
Vatican Museum.

4.
Bust of Agrippa Vipsanius
Uffizi, Florence.

5–10.
Coin portraits of rulers

5.
Tigranes

6.
Mithradates VI Eupator

7.
Bacchius Iudaeus

8.
Pacorus I of Parthia

9.
Marcus Antonius

10.
Cleopatra

11.
Herodian podium from Caesarea

12.
Caesarea. Roman
theater

13.
Strato's Tower at
Caesarea

14.
Aerial view of the Herodium fortress

15.
Temple of Augustus, Sebaste
Dept. of Antiq. and Museums, Jerusalem

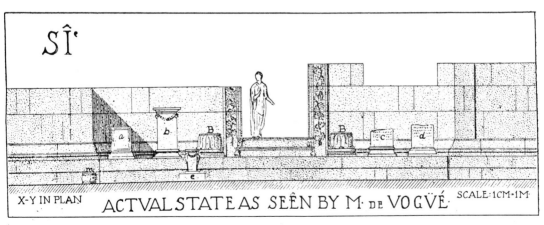

16.
Façade of the Nabataean
Temple at Seeia

. ΙCΙΛΕΙΗΡѠΔΕΙΚΥΡΙѠΟΒΑΙCΑΤΟCCΑΟΔΟΥ
ΕΘΗΚΑΤΟΝΑΝΔΡΙΑΝΤΑΤΑΙCΕΜΑΙCΔΑΠΑΝΑΙ.

17.
Dedication inscription in honor of Herod, Seeia. Dept. of Antiq. and Museums, Jerusalem
18.
Nabataean inscription in honor of Philip

19.
Graffito of *Menorah*
with seven branches,
excavated at the
Jewish Quarter of the
Old City, Jerusalem

20.
The *Menorah* symbol on coin of
Mattathias Antigonus
Dept. of Antiq. and Museums, Jerusalem

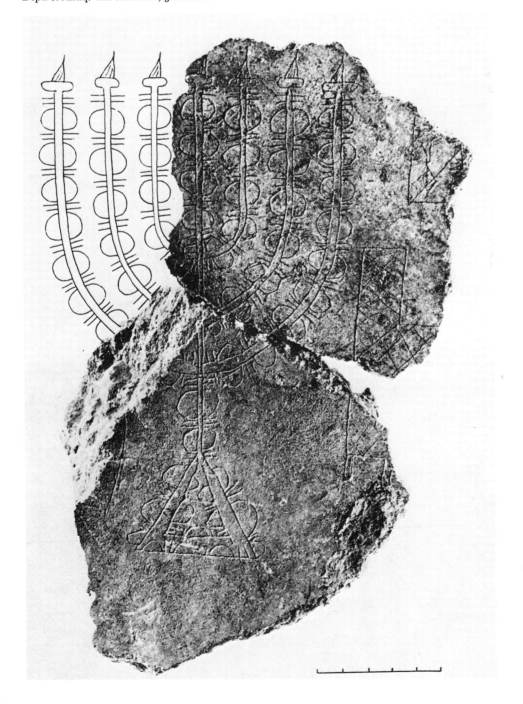

21–22.
Coins of Mattathias Antigonus, last Hasmonean King, showing Jewish symbols

21.
Coin with horn of plenty (obverse) and wreath of flowers (reverse)

22.
Coin with *Menorah* (obverse) and table (reverse)

23.
Horns of plenty motif engraved on stone piece,
Jewish Quarter, Jerusalem

24.
Herod's coins with horn of plenty (left)
and shield (right)
Archeological Inst., Hebrew Univ., Jerusalem

25.
Coins with ship and anchor
Archeological Inst., Hebrew Univ., Jerusalem

26.
City coins of Sebaste (left) and Ascalon (right)
Archeological Inst., Hebrew Univ., Jerusalem

Coins struck by Herod's sons and successors

27.

Herod Archelaus

28.

Herod Antipas

29.

Coins with portrait of
Agrippa I

30.

Coin portrait of Agrippa II

31.

Coins struck by Agrippa I

Mariamne the Hasmonean ever to gain the Judean throne were all but extinguished; Antipater now seemed clearly in line for the succession. Yet Antipater himself was to suffer a similar fate to that of his half brothers, while it was left for the son and grandson of Aristobulus to become Jewish Kings (Agrippa I and Agrippa II). Alexander's children made their success abroad and abandoned Judaism.

The Jewish people mourned the death of the brothers, who were half Hasmoneans, and their memory remained dear to many in Judea and abroad. When after Herod's death a Jew from Sidon came forward claiming to be Alexander, he was received enthusiastically by the Jews of Crete, Melos and Italy. They assisted the impostor, gave him money and treated him as though he were the real Alexander, until Augustus who had known Alexander well, himself intervened and put an end to the impersonation (*Ant.* XVII, 324–38, *War* II, 101–10).[49]

The death of the two brothers did not solve the problem of succession at Herod's court. The events of the last years of Herod's life were focused on Antipater. He was now virtually the heir to the throne, but he still felt his future to be uncertain, since it depended on his father's changing whims. Herod himself still occupied the throne, and Herod's other sons were potential rivals. Antipater endeavored to gain a firmer hold over Judea and to strengthen his position at Rome. His ally in those days was his uncle Pheroras; Pheroras' daughter even married Antipater's son (*Ant.* XVII, 18). On the other hand, his aunt Salome treated him with suspicion. Unlike Alexander, moreover, Antipater seems to have lacked any great following in Herod's army. Indeed, his part in the destruction of Mariamne's sons had earned him the hatred of many. On the other hand, a reconciliation between Antipater and pro-Hasmonean circles was made possible through Antipater's marriage to the daughter of Antigonus, the last king of the Hasmonean dynasty; the children she would bear him were no less Hasmonean than the children and grandchildren of Herod and Mariamne (*Ant.* XVII, 92).

In the meantime Herod's grandchildren — the sons of Alexander and Aristobulus — were growing up, and now they too presented Antipater with a further threat in addition to that posed by his brothers. The court was steeped in mutual hatred and suspicion, and showed all the signs of a typically Oriental court when the rule of its aging monarch was drawing to a close. Antipater pursued his course energetically. He was aided by his uncle, the brother of his mother, who married Aristobulus' widow Berenice, (*Ant.* XVII, 9; *War* I, 553) in order to gain support from both her and Salome. Antipater also devoted his attention to Saturninus, the governor of Syria, and his brother, be sending them expensive gifts (*Ant.* XVII, 6–7). He also did his utmost to enlist the support of Herod's friends in Rome.

In Judea, Antipater's friendship with his uncle Pheroras formed the cornerstone of all his actions. This was not to Herod's liking, since his own relations with Pheroras were then at their lowest ebb, owing to the activities of Pheroras' wife. Herod regarded Pheroras' house as one of the centers of resistance to his rule, after Pheroras' wife paid a fine imposed on the Pharisees for refusing to swear an oath of allegiance to Herod and the emperor. Once again it was Herod's sister Salome who urged him to take action. She kept Pheroras' house under careful surveillance, and warned Herod of the danger in the close relationship between Pheroras and Antipater. Urged on by his sister, Herod persuaded Antipater to sever all ties with Pheroras. Antipater, however, continued to maintain the relationship in secret (*Ant.* XVII, 32–51; *War* I, 566–72).

Antipater arranged things in such a manner that required his father to send him to Rome (*Ant.* XVII, 52–3; *War* I, 573). This mission had two specific purposes: to strengthen Herod's diplomatic activity against Syllaeus the Nabataean, and to obtain the emperor's agreement to Herod's latest will, according to which Antipater was to be the main successor. If Antipater were to predecease his father, the heir would then be Herod, the son of Mariamne, Boethus' daughter. Antipater's further motive for visiting Rome was to strengthen his ties with influential persons at the emperor's court. He hoped in this way to be able to manipulate the Judean court from afar. In this his hopes were not realized. The unexpected death of his ally, Pheroras, which occurred while Antipater was away in Rome, ruined Antipater's plans and undermined his position in Judea. The intensive investigations carried out among his family after Pheroras' death brought confessions, exacted under torture, confirming Salome's suspicions regarding the relations between Pheroras and Antipater. Herod became convinced that his brother and son had conspired to murder him, especially when Egyptian poison was discovered in Pheroras' house. Herod banished Doris, Antipater's mother, from the court. He also suspected Mariamne, the daughter of Boethus, of being privy to the plot. Her son's name was struck from the king's will, and her father, Simeon the son of Boethus, was dismissed from the office of High Priest (*Ant.* XVII, 58–78; *War* I, 578–600).

The first intimation of these events in Judea reached Antipater on his return journey from a successful visit to Rome. While still in Italy he learned of Pheroras' death, and on reaching the coast of Cilicia he was met by the rumor of his mother's banishment. After some hesitation in which he took counsel with his companions, Antipater decided, come what may, to continue on his way home, in the hope that his presence in Judea and his personal influence on his father would enable him to extract himself from the difficult situation in which he now found himself. The cool reception he received on disembarking clearly showed how far his position had deteriorated. When he reached Jerusalem, his father rebuffed his entreaties and summoned him before the king's council, in whose deliberations Varus, the governor of Syria, took part. The role of prosecutor was taken by Nicolaus of Damascus, whose extreme antagonism towards Antipater may be judged from the references to him in his autobiography. As Antipater was unable to prove his innocence, he was cast into chains, and Herod sent off a letter to Augustus informing him of Antipater's transgressions (*Ant.* XVII, 83–133; *War* I, 608–40).

While in Rome, Antipater had also been scheming to create a conflict between Herod and his sister Salome. He had made contact with one of Empress Livia's maidservants, a Jewish freed slave by the name of Acme, who had agreed to forge papers proving that Salome was conspiring to undermine the king's position at Rome. This plot, too, was brought to light, and Herod at first determined to send Antipater to Rome to stand trial for his crimes. He changed his mind, however, after his friends pointed out that Antipater could easily exploit his contacts in Rome in order to escape punishment. He therefore sent the emperor instead a full account of what had transpired, and in the meantime continued to hold Antipater prisoner (*Ant.* XVII, 134–45; *War* I, 641–5; Nicolaus *apud* F. Jacoby, *Gr. Hist.* II A 90 F 136 [5] p. 423 f).[50] In his reply Augustus empowered Herod to deal with his son as he saw fit, whether to put him to death or to send him into exile. (*Ant.* XVII, 182; *War* I, 661). Herod condemned his son to death; Antipater was executed, and buried in the fortress of Hyrcania (*Ant.* XVII, 187; *War* I, 664).

By this time Herod was already bedridden. As Antipater could no longer be his heir, Herod prepared a new will naming Herod Antipas as his successor; he no longer trusted his sons Archelaus and Philip, whom Antipater had discredited on account of their conduct while in Rome. Just before his death, however, Herod changed his will once more. According to this last will he appointed Archelaus as king, but left Galilee and Peraea to Herod Antipas, and Gaulanitis, Trachonitis and Batanaea to Philip. As a reward for her unswerving loyalty to her brother throughout her life, Salome received Jamnia, Azotus and Phasaelis (*Ant.* XVII, 188–9; *War* I, 664; 668).

G. Herod, the Jewish Society and Parties

Herod had received the crown of Judea by the grace of Rome and contrary to the express will of the majority of the Jewish people, who had fought devotedly for Antigonus and the Hasmonean dynasty. To the end of his days, Herod never succeeded in reaching the mass of the people, who continued to regard him as a tyrant imposed upon them by a foreign power. Yet some of his acts and achievements were received favorably by the entire nation. It was Herod who built the magnificent Temple in Jerusalem, which was universally admired; indeed, Jerusalem became in his day one of the most beautiful cities in the Orient. Herod rendered assistance to the Jewish communities in the Greek Diaspora and made use of his contacts with the heads of the Roman government to safeguard Jewish privileges in Asia Minor. He helped families and individuals from the Babylonian and Egyptian communities to attain important positions among the Jewish population of Palestine. He also strove to reach a *modus vivendi* with as wide a circle as possible. During the early days of the monarchy, the leaders of the Pharisees, Sheʿmaʿya and Avtalyon, tried to persuade the people to open the gates of Jerusalem to Herod when it became evident that there was not longer any possibility of holding out against him and the Roman army. Herod remembered this, and treated them with great esteem over the years. He was even prepared to pardon the Pharisees for having refused to swear an oath of allegiance to him (*Ant.* XV, 370). He also treated the Essenes with respect and maintained close ties with Menaḥem the Essene (*Ant.* XV 371–9).

Herod did much to develop his kingdom's economy by expanding the area under agriculture, increasing its commerce, and building a large port at Caesarea. From time to time he reduced the taxes (*Ant.* XV, 365; XVI, 64). The royal bakers baked bread for the needy, and clothes were distributed among the poor when times were hard (*Ant.* XV, 310). There was some justification in Herod's claim that none of his predecessors had done so much to improve the material standards of the Jewish people (*Ant.* XV, 383). At mass rallies he took pains to enchance his image among the people by describing his achievements and announcing his plans.

As king of Judea Herod did his utmost to defend the kingdom from attack by its neighbors; his strong stand against the Nabataeans was worthy of an heir to the Hasmonean dynasty. On occasion, he emphasized his loyalty to the Jewish religion. Augustus was well aware that Herod never ate pork (Macrobius, *Saturnalia*, II, 4, 11) and several generations later a Latin poet (Persius, *Saturae*, V, 180) referred to the Sabbath as "Herod's day" (*dies Herodis*). When his sister Salome wished to marry Syllaeus the Nabataean, Herod made his consent conditional upon his conversion to Judaism, thereby laying down a principle that was followed by his family in later generations. Even when he accused his two sons Alexander and Aristobulus of treason before a mixed court of Jews and non-Jews, he based his arguments on the laws of the Torah (*Ant.* XVI, 365).

All this did not suffice to dispel the fundamental disagreement between Herod and the Jewish people. Much of his basic conduct and policy precluded any real understanding between Herod and the majority of his subjects. The fact that Herod identified himself completely with the aims and ideology of Augustus' principate was one stumbling block in his relations with the Jews. This identification even went as far as to include emperor worship, and Herod became one of its most enthusiastic propagators outside Judea. There was also the matter of building temples and erecting statues in Herod's honor within his kingdom, although he refrained from this practice in the specifically Jewish area. It should be noted that his last serious difference with his Jewish subjects was caused by the affixing on his express orders of a golden eagle over the Temple gates. Herod did nothing to prevent his non-Jewish subjects from setting up statues dedicated to him. His total disregard for human life when pursuing his political goals, his excessive ostentation, and his lack of all moral restraint, widened the gap between Herod and the people.

Although Herod tried to avoid offending the religious feelings of the Jews, at least in the main areas of Jewish population, his conduct of affairs often brought him into conflict with Jewish tradition. His order, for example, to sell Jewish thieves into foreign bondage virtually made them certain of losing their Jewishness.[51] The holding of athletic contests, the building of a theater and a hippodrome in Jerusalem and the abhorrent practice of throwing human beings to wild animals as a form of entertainment — all these in varying degrees aroused the animosity of his Jewish subjects. Furthermore, the atmosphere at the royal court was mainly non-Jewish and reflected Herod's alienation from Jewish tradition. The presence of thousands of "Hellenes" in the administration and in Herod's army was considered by the Jews as tantamount to Gentile rule. It was against these elements that the main force of Jewish resistance was directed after Herod's death Herod's new Hellenistic cities were regarded as strongholds against the Jews, especially as he recruited his army from among their inhabitants. By setting up these cities and by drawing on them for his army, Herod in fact determined the future relationship between Jews and Gentiles in Palestine, to the detriment of the former.

There was also the belief that the king was "sucking the blood" of the people in order to find favor in non-Jewish circles both at home and abroad. (*Ant.* XVI, 154–9). Thus, while he treated the Jews with a firm hand, he acted leniently and even generously towards the Gentiles (*Ant.* XV, 356). This policy betokened the real contrast between Herod's monarchy and that of the Hasmoneans, whose memory was held dear by the majority of the nation. The destruction of the last survivors of the Hasmonean dynasty (as well as the execution of the members of the Bava family who were closely related to the Hasmoneans — *Ant.* XV, 266), and the death of Herod's two sons by Mariamne the Hasmonean — all pointed to a break between the two periods and ruined the hope of even a partial revival of the Hasmonean dynasty through intermarriage between the old and new dynasties. To this must be added Herod's basic disregard of the traditional Jewish institutions, the decline of the Jewish Sanhedrin from its primacy in Jewish public life, and the reduction in status of the High Priesthood and of entire sections of the Jewish community, who had determined its character until Herod's rise to power.

Herod was able to maintain his hold upon Judea only by virtue of a tight apparatus of control and suppression, backed by a loyal army and a chain of fortresses commanding each of the country's regions. The organization of mass assemblies was strictly banned. An efficient intelligence system was instituted (it is related that Herod would disguise himself and mix with the crowds in order to sound out the mood of the people *Ant.* XV, 367). Persons opposed to Herod or even suspected of opposition were punished with the utmost severity. Many were incarcerated in the fortress of Hyrcania and secretly put to death there (*Ant.* XV, 366). Thanks to an iron rule and brutally efficient methods, but also to a political acumen that often combined resolution and single-mindedness with indulgence and conciliation, Herod succeeded where every other ruler before or after failed. Throughout the entire period of his reign he prevented the outbreak of open revolt in his Kingdom. From time to time, however, agitation rose to the surface, and we hear of many plots to assassinate the king. Ten conspirators, one of whom was blind, planned to murder him while he was attending the theater, but failed in their bid when an informer warned Herod of the plot and all were caught. The conspirators made no attempt to deny their purpose, and were tortured to death. The informant soon met his punishment at the hands of the mob. His death brought about a chain reaction during which the repression of the people was conducted with ever-increasing harshness (*Ant.* XV, 280–91).

The last days of Herod's rule were marked by a clear deterioration in his relations with the Pharisees, three thousand of whom refused to swear an oath of allegiance and were therefore fined. It is against this background of hostility to Herod that we may understand the adherence of some of the Pharisees to Pheroras and his wife, who were opposed to the king. The influence of the Pharisees penetrated even to the royal court, where they won over one of the king's eunuchs (Bagoas) and the royal favorite, Carus, (*Ant*. XVII, 42–5). Matters came to a head at the end of Herod's reign. At the instigation of two rabbis, Judah the son of Sariphaeus and Mattathias the son of Margalius, a group of Zealots removed the eagle placed by Herod over the gate of the Temple and smashed it in the presence of a large crowd. The perpetrators were summarily executed by the authorities. No less than 40 young men were prepared to give up their lives to preserve the religious traditions of their people. On being brought before the king they proudly defended their deed in the name of their God and His laws (*Ant*. XVII, 149–67). Their open act of courage and their refusal to evade responsibility made them martyrs and heroes.

Herod's death in 4 B.C.E.[52] brought relief to the inhabitants of Judea. The people's first demand was for the execution of all those responsible for the death of the forty Zealots, whose brave act marked the renewal of active opposition to Roman authority. The king's son and heir, Archelaus, was prepared to admit that his father's rule had been harsh (*Ant*. XVII, 201), and emissaries of the Jews complained to Augustus of the great suffering inflicted upon them by Herod during his reign (*Ant*. XVII, 304–10.)

Herod's malevolent nature finds many illustrations in Jewish sources. Josephus relates that when Herod was on his deathbed, he ordered that the leaders of the Jewish community be imprisoned in the hippodrome at Jericho. He instructed his sister Salome and his brother-in-law Alexa to put all of them to death after he breathed his last, so as to stifle the people's joy at his own death. Herod's tragic fate at the end of his days was seen as an expression of God's anger at the sinful ways of the king, according to the prophecy of Menaḥem the Essene (*Ant*. XV, 376). This was also the view held by the Pharisee leaders Judah the son of Seriphaeus and Mattathias the son of Margalius (*Ant*. XVII, 150).

A harsh view of Herod, whose rule spanned times of unprecedented trouble for the Jewish people, is expressed in the pseudepigraphic work *The Assumption of Moses* written a short time after Herod's death: "And after them (the Hasmoneans) there ruled a ruthless king who was not from the priestly family, a terrible man who knew no shame and judged them as they deserved; he cut off their heads with his sword and interred their corpses in remote places so that none would know where they were buried; and he killed old people and showed no mercy on young ones; they suffered bitterly in their country because of their fear of him; and he inflicted severe punishment on them such as the Egyptians had inflicted upon them; and he punished them four and thirty years" (6, 2–7).

In the Gospel according to Matthew, Herod is portrayed as a cruel king, the murderer of the children of Bethlehem (Matthew 2:16). The Talmud also places Herod in a particularly unfavorable light. Herod was the "Edomite slave" of the Hasmonean family who "murdered the family of his masters and left no trace even of the children," and it was he who put to death all the Sages and left no one but Bava the son of Buta whose counsel he sought; he placed a wreath of leeches on his head and gouged out his eyes B. Batra 3b–4a). There is no evidence of any religious Messianic movement connected with Herod's name; the "Herodians" mentioned in the Gospels (Mark 3:6; 12:13; Matthew 22:16) were apparently a political party suporting Herod.[53]

Herod's accession to the throne marked a turning point in the history of the Jewish community during the period of the Second Temple. As had happened in the time of the religious edicts of Antiochus Epiphanes and the Hasmonean revolt, the basis of the former social structure was again shaken and its élite largely supplanted. Many of the leaders of the former period were put to death; others were deprived of their livelihood, and the majority lost their influence over the people and their standing in the administration of Judea. As could be expected, however, there was a certain continuity between the society of Herod's time and that of the Hasmoneans. But this continuity was less in evidence than the changes which took place among the élite. The first years of Herod's rule were marked by his ties with one branch of the Hasmonean dynasty, that of Hyrcanus II, whose granddaughter became Herod's wife. This fact by no means caused the supporters of the Hasmonean dynasty to shift their support automatically to Herod, but it did to some extent enable individuals to serve the new master. Later, when relations within the court deteriorated, Herod's rule had become so strong that even among the most loyal supporters of the Hasmonean dynasty there were some who were prepared to forsake their former masters in order to curry favor with the king (e.g. Dositheus' betrayal of Hyrcanus II — *Ant.* XV, 169–70, and also Sabbion's betrayal of Alexandra — *Ant.* XV, 47).

In general it may be said that those who had held leading positions in the community under the Hasmoneans no longer did so under Herod. Herod had to find leaders for the Jewish community and to base his rule on their support. The problem was solved in various ways. Under his rule there arose a new élite which was in no way dependent upon the political and social traditions of the Hasmoneans. This group continued to exist after Herod's reign, and retained its status until the outbreak of the Great Revolt against Rome.

The majority of the families which composed the new élite were un-connected with the Hasmoneans. Their advancement was due to Herod's victory, whether directly through Herod's patronage, or as the natural result of the decline of the great houses of the past. The new aristocracy was not formed from a single mold, and its origins were variegated. First and foremost was the increased importance of the Jewish communities of the Diaspora; Jewish families from Hellenistic Egypt and Babylonia formed much of the new élite during Herod's reign. At the beginning of his rule, Herod appointed Hananel, a Babylonian Jew with whom he had been friendly, to serve as High Priest. This post was later filled by Jeshua the son of Phabes, concerning whose origins scholars are divided. The name Phabes could well be of Egyptian origin, as it is similar to that we find on the Jewish inscriptions at Tell el-Yahudiye (Leontopolis; Frey: *C. I. Jud.*, II, no. 1510 = E. Gabba: *Iscrizioni greche e latine per lo studio della Bibbia* [1958], no. XIV), and it can be presumed that the house of Phabes was an Egyptian-Jewish family. Jeshua the son of Phabes was therefore the first High Priest to be descended from Hellenized Diaspora Jews in the last generations of the Second Temple.

More important than the house of Phabes for the role it was to play in the Jewish community and its institutions was the house of Boethus. The person who laid the basis for the future power of this family in Judea was Simeon the son of Boethus, an Alexandrian Jew who settled in Jerusalem. His daughter married Herod, while he himself was appointed High Priest in place of Jeshua the son of Phabes (*Ant.* XV, 320-2), and held this position for many years. In the last years of Herod's rule another High Priest, Joezer, was appointed from the same family. The houses of Phabes and Boethus were among the houses which shared the leading positions in the priesthood throughout the entire period between Herod's reign and the destruction of the Temple.

Herod's policy of assisting Jews from Diaspora communities to immigrate to Judea and of helping their advancement within the Jewish community there, encouraged the immigration from Babylonia of the house of Zamaris, which became one of the most influential families in northern Trans-jordan, an area which Herod particularly wished to develop. This Baby-lonian family undoubtedly played a vital role in that development, and the descendants of Zamaris remained loyal, to Herod and his family. Their main center was apparently at Bathyra in Batanaea, since they are known in Talmudic literature as "the Sons of Bathyra." The contacts of the sons of Bathyra reached Gaulanitis (Gamala) and spread out into Galilee. Certain rabbis in Jerusalem at the time of Hillel were members of this family, while other members were also to be found at Jamnia in the time of Johanan ben Zakkai. The rise of Hillel and the subsequent importance of his family are all part of the same process by which a new élite was established in Judea from Jewish families of the Diaspora.[54]

Some of the new houses of Herod's time, however, were from Palestine itself. Even at the time of the war with Antigonus there was a small minority within the Jewish population of Palestine which supported Herod (*Ant.* XIV, 479; *War* I, 351). At that time Herod had many supporters in Idumaea, but we also hear of certain groups among the upper classes in Galilee who were attacked by the Galileans for assisting Herod (*Ant.* XIV, 450). It is worth noting that at the end of Herod's rule High Priests were appointed from Galilee — Mattathias the son of Theophilus, and Joseph the son of Ellemus.[55]

Throughout the entire period of his rule, Herod endeavored to maintain close ties with the inhabitants of Samaria, especially the inhabitants of the city of Samaria, which later became Sebaste. Even before his final victory over Antigonus, Herod came to the city's aid by grants of money and by settling its disputes (*Ant.* XIV, 284; *War* I, 229). In Samaria Herod had loyal friends whom he could call upon for help in the hour of need, as for example when he wished to provide oil and wine to the Roman forces fighting against Antigonus. It was in the city of Samaria that Herod and Mariamne were married, and during this illness he felt more secure in Samaria than in Jerusalem. According to Josephus, Herod established Samaria — Sebaste as one of the strongholds directed against the Jewish people (*Ant.* XV, 292). One of Herod's wives, Malthace, was a Samaritan.[56]

It was in Herod's reign that the Hellenistic element in the administration and in the kingdom in general were intensified. This phenomenon could have had far-reaching repercussions on the Jewish community, but in fact there were no developments in this direction. The Jews were constantly aware of the several thousand "Hellenes" assisting the king in his rule, but these did not mix with the Jewish upper classes. In actual fact, there was no sign that the king had any intention of encouraging the mixing of Jews and Hellenes in Jerusalem, or in any of the new cities he established in his kingdom. In this connection it should be noted that in a city such as Sebaste, which among all the large cities in the kingdom had perhaps the strongest ties with Herod, there was no Jewish population whatsoever.

At the center of social life in Judea was the royal household itself. From the outset Herod appeared and acted not as an individual, but as the prominent representative of the house of Antipater, and in this he had the cooperation of his brothers and other relatives. During the difficult days of the struggle with Antigonus, Herod's brother Joseph was his confidant and right-hand man until he fell in battle. After the conquest of terusalem he promoted another brother, Pheroras, to the position of Tetrach of Peraea. Particularly prominent among Herod's other relatives was Ahiab, who was given important assignments in the administration and the army.

Those whom Herod intended for high office he attempted to bind to himself and to his family by ties of marriage. The two husbands of his sister Salome were Costobar the Idumaean and Alexa. Both were members of the new élite which had arisen within the Jewish community together with the new royal household. The descendants of Alexa were destined to fill an important role in Judea in future generations, especially his son Helcias (Hilkiah), known as "the Great" (during the time of Agrippa I), and we also hear of his grandson Julius Archelaus. It appears that one of Costobar's descendants played an important role in Jerusalem at the end of the period of the Second Temple. Helcias especially, and to a certain extent Costobar, were the founders of important families who were active not only in the time of Herod, but also in later generations. The rise and development of these two families reflects the decisive role that Herod's reign played in the history of the Jewish community in the period of the Second Temple.

Herod's reign thus marked a turning point in the social development of the Jewish community of his Kingdom. In addition to the ascendancy of new families owing their allegiance to Herod and Rome, the basis was also laid for an anti-Herodian and anti-Roman opposition with a Galilean family at its head. Both these developments were to have far-reaching consequences.

H. The "War" of Varus and the Division of the Kingdom

Herod's death was a signal for the eruption of all the resentments that had accumulated during his reign and that had reached their peak as a consequence of Herod's behavior in the last years of his life. Herod's will designated his son Archelaus as heir to the title of king and ruler of Judea, Idumaea and Samaria. To Herod Antipas he bequeathed Galilee and

Peraea together with the title of Tetrach; Trachonitis, Batanaea, Gaulanitis and the region of the Jordan sources were left to Philip, who was also to have the title of Tetrarch. Herod's sister Salome inherited Jamnia, Azotus and Phasaelis. He left silver, precious articles and expensive garments to Augustus, and a sum of money to the empress Livia. Although he had divided up the kingdom, Herod intended its various regions to maintain a degree of unity through the subordination of the two Tetrarchs to King Archelaus. For the will to take effect, however, it required the emperor's confirmation.

Upon the death of the king, Salome and Alexa assembled Herod's army in the amphitheater at Jericho and read out the message the king had prepared for them before his death.[57] In it he expressed his thanks to the soldiers for the loyalty they had shown during his life, and requested them to continue this relationship with his sons. The will itself was read by Ptolemy, Herod's chief minister, who had been entrusted with the royal seal. The soldiers spontaneously hailed Archelaus as their king, and companies of soldiers under the command of their officers marched past him and pledged their loyalty to the new ruler. Herod was given a royal funeral by Archelaus, and his body was buried in the fortress of Herodium (*Ant.* XVII, 188–99; *War* I, 666–73).

At the end of the seven days of mourning, Archelaus went up to the Temple, where he was enthusiastically received by the people. At the same time, however, demands were placed before him which he found difficult to fulfill. Some of these demands concerned tax relief and the release of prisoners. Many of the Jews gave vent to their grief over the murder of the rabbis and their disciples who had torn down the eagle from the Temple gates. They categorically demanded the punishment of Herod's closest advisers and of the High Priest Joezer the son of Boethus. Because this was the season of the Passover festival, large numbers of Jews who had made the pilgrimage to Jerusalem were gathered there, and the tension rose. Archelaus, who had already totally rejected the demands of the people, now became involved in a clash within the Temple, and his army set about and massacred the assembled crowd (*Ant.* XVII, 200–18; *War* II, 1–13; Nicolaus, *De vita sua, apud* F. Jacoby, *Gr. Hist.*, II, A, 90 F 136 [8], p. 424). Thus from the very outset Archelaus lost the goodwill of the people, who held him responsible for an act of cruelty the like of which even Herod never inflicted on them since the capture of Jerusalem from Antigonus.

Archelaus then went to Rome accompanied by his mother and Herod's veteran advisers (Ptolemy and Nicolaus). His brother Herod Antipas arrived in Rome on a mission of a different nature. He wished to persuade Augustus to recognize Herod's penultimate will, according to which he was to have been the primary heir. This demand was supported by his aunt Salome. He also placed great reliance on the powers of persuasion of the orator Ireneus. In Rome Antipas was joined by the majority of Herod's relatives who objected to Archelaus. The most outstanding of these was Salome's son Antipater (*Ant.* XVII, 219–20; 224–30; *War* II, 14–15; 20–6). In addition to Herod's sons, their relatives and companions, an independent Jewish delegation of 50 persons arrived after being granted special permission by Varus, the governor of Syria (*Ant.* XVII, 300; *War* II, 80).[58]

Augustus had in the meantime received reports from Varus and from Sabinus, procurator of finances for Syria, about the state of the property Herod had left and the annual income from the various regions of his kingdom. Augustus brought the parties before the *consilium principis*. The first to be allowed to speak was Antipater, the son of Salome, who represented the interests of Herod Antipas. His main argument was that Archelaus had assumed the powers of the monarch without waiting for Augustus to place the kingdom legally in his charge. He also castigated Archelaus for the cruelty with which he had acted towards the people, and suggested that it would be more appropriate to recognize the validity of Herod's penultimate will. Opposing him was Nicolaus of Damascus, who spoke in defense of Archelaus. Augustus decided to withhold his final decision for the time being (*Ant.* XVII, 230–49; *War* II, 26–38; Nicolaus, *loc. cit.*).

While the litigation was still in process before the emperor, news reached Rome of the outbreak of a large-scale revolt in Judea, which had gradually spread throughout all the Jewish regions of Palestine. The riots had broken out immediately after Archelaus left for Rome and were temporarily suppressed by Varus, who had left behind one legion to garrison Jerusalem. But his action was not sufficient to prevent a renewed outbreak of the revolt. A major cause of this was the untimely act of the procurator Sabinus in attempting to take over the royal fortress and to seize the treasure of the deceased king.[59]

Tension came to a head on the Feast of Tabernacles, when thousands made the pilgrimage to Jerusalem from Jericho, Idumaea, Peraea and Galilee. Many of the Jewish soldiers who had served under Herod now defected to the rebels, although three thousand of the choice soldiers from the Hellenistic cities, and first and foremost Sebaste, remained loyal to the government and fought together with the Romans. Sabinus took refuge in the tower of Phasael in Jerusalem and was besieged there (*Ant*. XVII, 254–68; *War* II, 39–54).

Meanwhile the revolt had spread throughout the entire country. In Judea a shepherd by the name of Athronges, a man of extraordinary physical prowess, was outstanding among the rebels. His four brothers, also exceedingly strong, fought together with him. Athronges fought against both the Romans and Herod's army. A company of Romans was wiped out by him near Emmaus. Many former soldiers of Herod now joined the ranks of the rebels and fought against those soldiers under the command of Ahiab who had remained loyal to the government of Judea. The inhabitants of Samaria, on the other hand, did not take part in the revolt.

In Transjordan the revolt was led by Simeon, one of Herod's slaves. At his instigation, the king's palace at Jericho was set on fire, and in other places too the royal property was damaged. Simeon fell in battle against the Romans and loyal soldiers of the Herodian army, under the command of Gratus. Other rebels in Transjordan burned down the palace at Ammathus. The revolt in Galilee was especially violent. Here the rebels were led by Judah, whose father had been put to death by Herod in the latter's youth. Judah was active at Sepphoris, the capital of Galilee (*Ant*. XVII, 269–85; *War* II, 55–65; Tacitus, *Histories*, V, 9).

It is clear that the Jewish revolts that followed Herod's death had no concerted plan or unified leadership whose guidance was accepted by all the rebels. They were in fact spontaneous uprisings of a regional nature and independent of each other. Each center of revolt had its own leader. The insurgents at Ammathus in Transjordan did not support Simeon when he burned down the royal palace at Jericho, even though he himself was from Transjordan. The rebels, including their leaders, came primarily from the lower classes. Athronges was a shepherd; Simeon was one of Herod's slaves. The various leaders adopted royal titles. This can be attributed to the tension caused by eschatological aspirations which encouraged the emergence of leaders with Messianic pretensions.

It should be noted that the strong ties between the Messianic leadership and the proletarian anti-Roman movement is one of the unmistakable signs of rebellion seventy years later. The phenomenon was personified by such men as Menaḥem the son of Judah the Galilean, who led the Sicarii, and Simeon bar Giora.[60]

Varus was forced to send large forces into the field to quell the revolt. These included two of the three legions that were then stationed in Syria, as well as large numbers of auxiliaries mainly from the army of Aretas IV, king of the Nabataeans, who was hostile to the Jews. The Roman army was concentrated at Accho-Ptolemais, and a section under the command of Varus' son was sent to fight the insurgents in Galilee. The capital of Galilee, Sepphoris, was captured and its inhabitants enslaved. Varus himself invaded Samaria at the head of the main force. From there he continued on to Judea. His Nabataean allies followed behind, plundering and pillaging the villages. Emmaus was abandoned by its inhabitants and

The Division of Herod's Kingdom between his sons

burned down at the specific order of Varus. The Romans reached Jerusalem and relieved the besieged garrison. The records tell of 2,000 crucifixions throughout the country. Ten thousand Jewish rebels surrendered to Varus through the mediation of Ahiab. The majority were freed and only the leaders were sent to Rome. Augustus punished those of Herod's relatives who had joined the revolt (*Ant.* XVII, 286–98; *War* II, 66–79). Varus returned to Antioch, leaving behind a military force in Judea to prevent a renewal of the riots.

Even before peace had returned to Judea, Augustus made his decision with regard to Herod's kingdom. He rejected the request of the Jewish delegation, which appeared before him in the temple of Apollo, to take Judea out of the hands of the Herodian family and add it to the Syrian province, even though the petition was supported by a demonstration of thousands of Rome's Jewish inhabitants. In general, Augustus approved of Herod's last will. Archelaus, who was represented by Nicholas of Damascus, was made ruler of Judea, Idumaea and Samaria, with an annual income of 600 talents. Herod Antipas was given Galilee and Peraea and an annual income of 200 talents, while Philip received the northeastern regions of Herod's kingdom and an income of 100 talents. But Augustus deviated from Herod's will on one very important point. Archelaus was for the present denied the title of king and had to make do with that of Ethnarch. In taking this step Augustus was undoubtedly influenced by Archelaus' failure to maintain quiet in Judea immediately on seizing the throne and by his lack of tact in handling the people. Augustus did, however, promise to bestow the title of king on Archelaus at some later time, once he proved himself worthy of the monarchy. In the event, Archelaus never did attain the superiority over his brothers that his father's will had prescribed.

Augustus now turned his attention to the demands of some of the older Hellenistic towns which had come within the purview of Herod's kingdom — Gadara, Hippus and Gaza. He relieved them of any dependence on rulers of the Herodian family and made them directly subject to the governor of Syria. The inhabitants of Samaria who had not participated in the revolt had their taxes reduced by one quarter (*Ant.* XVII, 299–323; *War* II, 80–100; Nicolaus, *loc. cit.*).

The period of Archelaus' rule as Ethnarch of Judea (4 B.C.E.–6 A.D.) was a disappointment from the very first. His prestige suffered when he was denied the title of king, which his father's will had led him to expect. Nor was his reputation enhanced by the events in Judea and Rome which preceded the confirmation of the will. The Jews could only be openly hostile to one who had begun his rule with a cruel massacre. After his return from Rome, Archelaus once more engaged himself in rooting out the vestiges of the revolt, and it was he who put an end to the guerilla activities of Athronges the shepherd and his brothers (*Ant.* XVII, 284; *War* II, 64).

After his appointment as Ethnarch over Judea, Archelaus added the dynastic name of Herod to his own and used it on his coins.[61] In general he attempted to emulate the manner in which his father had ruled, but he had neither his father's talent nor his ability to maintain good relations with Augustus; while he was no more acceptable to his Jewish subjects than his father had been. He also aroused their ire by divorcing his wife Mariamne and breaking Jewish law to marry Glaphyra the Cappadocian, wife of his deceased brother Alexander, who after her first husband's death had married Juba, king of Mauretania (*Ant.* XVII, 341; cf. 349–53; *War* II, 114–6).

Like his father and two brothers the Tetrarchs, Archelaus devoted his energies to development and building projects. He rebuilt the palace at Jericho which had been burned by Simeon. He also built Archelais in a flourishing date-palm region of the Jordan Valley (*Ant.* XVII, 340).[62]

As Ethnarch Archelaus aroused the anger not only of the Jews but also of the Samaritans, who seldom joined forces with their Jewish neighbors. A representative of the Samaritans accused Archelaus of cruelty towards his people against the express orders of Augustus. The emperor summoned Archelaus to Rome to face the charges against him. Unable to refute them, Archelaus was deposed and banished to Vienna in Galia Narbonensis (6 A.D.; *Ant.* XVII, 342–8; *War* II, 111–3; Strabo, *Geography*, XVI, 2, 46, p. 765; Dio Cassius, LV, 27, 6).

THE HERODIAN DYNASTY AND THE PROVINCE OF JUDEA AT THE END OF THE PERIOD OF THE SECOND TEMPLE

by M. Stern

A. PROVINCIALIZATION OF JUDEA

WHEN ARCHELAUS WAS deposed from the Ethnarchy of Judea, Augustus was presented with a choice of various forms of Roman rule which he could apply to Palestine. One of these was the incorporation of Judea into the neighboring province of Syria. (The relative insignificance of Archelaus' domain seemed to disqualify it from becoming a province in its own right, especially as the governors of Syria, after and even during the reign of Herod, held Judea under close surveillance.) Nonetheless, there were strong reasons for the Romans to refrain from taking such a step. The unique position of the Jews as regards their religion and way of life, which were totally different from those of their Syrian neighbors, necessitated exceptional care, and obliged the emperor to adopt a policy of separation between Judea and Syria. The Roman imperial government never entangled itself by treating the Jewish territory as an integral part of Syria — even though they may sometimes have changed the political organization of Judea or the extent of the territory within its rulers' control.

An alternative solution was to appoint some princeling of Herod's family as ruler of Judea. This would have been a continuation of Augustus' existing policy, by which Rome ruled indirectly through a subject-ally. It was, indeed, still customary in the empire for client princes to exist side by side with direct provincial rule, but Augustus no longer favored this policy for Judea. In this he was followed by his successors, with the notable exception of Claudius' appointment of Agrippa I as king of the Jews. Shortly after Herod's death, Augustus was petitioned by a Jewish delegation not to appoint any one of Herod's sons as ruler of Judea (*Ant.* XVII, 314; *War* II, 90–1).[1] Mindful of what the Jews had suffered during the reigns of Herod and Archelaus, the emperor judged it inexpedient to foist on them another ruler of this dynasty and thereby drive them further into opposition to Rome. The rule of Archelaus had obviously not improved relations between the Jews and the Roman authorities. Moreover, Augustus did not regard any of Herod's sons as both suitable from the point of view of imperial interests and acceptable to the Jewish people.

Augustus therefore had no other option but to create a new province, Judea, which would be governed by a man chosen from the *equites* and directly appointed by the emperor. Thus in 6 A.D. a new régime was established in Judea. It lasted until the First Jewish Revolt, with a brief interval during the reign of Agrippa I, who ruled as king over the whole country from 41 to 44 A.D. The main centers of Jewish population in Galilee and Peraea were not included in the territory administered by the early governors, but continued to be held by Herod Antipas until 39 A.D. Neither were the country's northeastern territories across the Jordan included in the new province, but were ruled by Philip until 34 A.D. Thus two of the main areas of Jewish settlement in Palestine were outside the province. This state of affairs changed only after the death of Agrippa I (44), when almost all the area of Jewish settlement was included in the province of Judea. But this situation, too, did not last long, since the Jewish cities of eastern Galilee (Tiberias and Taricheae), the whole of Gaulanitis and some parts of Peraea were added by Nero to the realm of Agrippa II. Nevertheless, the province of Judea of the later procurators comprised the vast majority of the Jews of Palestine, and certainly many more than the Judea of the earlier period.

The new province at first covered the area of Archelaus' Ethnarchy and was called officially *Judaea*. This name was retained even after additional territories were annexed to it in the course of the first century, and *de facto* until the reign of Hadrian.[2] The name "Judaea" simply reflected the fact that the Jews were the majority of the population of Palestine at that time. It was a continuation of the late Hellenistic tradition, which expressed the change affected by Hasmonean conquests whereby the whole of Palestine was regarded as Judea. The official pre-Hadrianic terminology did not include the name "Palaestina," although this term was frequently used in Greek by both Gentile and Jewish writers (such as Philo and Josephus).[3]

The foundation of the new province was connected with the appearance in Judea of Quirinius, the legate of Syria, who was entrusted with establishing the basis of the new government of Judea and with holding a census throughout the country (*Ant.* XVII, 355; XVIII 1–2; Luke 2:1–2; Acts 5:37; Dessau, *Inscriptiones Latinae selectae*, no. 2683).[4] Taking a census was quite normal on the creation of a new province. In Judea, however, the census led to disturbances, as it symbolized the country's subjection to a foreign power. It also greatly offended religious feelings in the country. In other provinces as well, the census was met with opposition and demonstrations directed against the Roman authorities. One of the rebel leaders from the time of Varus,[5] Judah of Gamala, led the revolt against the census. He and his companion, Zadok the Pharisee, roused the people to anger by representing the census as a symbol of the final and absolute subjugation of the Jews to Rome. Thanks, however, to the efforts of the High Priest, Joezer the son of Boethus, popular feeling was brought under control. Yet though Judah was killed (apparently by the Romans — Acts, *loc. cit.*), his descendants left their mark on events in Judea until the outbreak of the First Revolt.

The assistance that Joezer was able to lend the Romans in establishing their regime did not, however, strengthen his own position. On the contrary, he was dismissed from office by Quirinius himself, probably in an attempt to gain the favor of the people, who had no liking for the house of Boethus on account of its association with Herod and Archelaus. Quirinius replaced Joezer with Ananus (Ḥanan) who was head of one of the most important priestly families at the time. The influence of the house of Ananus now replaced that of the house of Boethus in the priestly hierarchy; Ananus himself retained the position of High Priest for the whole period of the first three governors, to be disposed only by the fourth.

The time of the early provincial rule was still marked by a spirit of conciliation between the Jews and the Roman authorities. The mass of the people still felt hatred for Herod and his dynasty, and thus did not regard their position as any worse under the new administration. Some of the upper class, the families of the High Priests and those related to Herod, were ready to collaborate with the Romans just as they once had supported Herod and his government. On the other hand this period saw the birth of extremist groups, who regarded any foreign rule as intolerable and who opposed Jewish submission to such a temporal power. This was the movement which led to the ferment over the census of Quirinius. Public calm was restored, however, and a head-on clash with the Romans was avoided until the procuratorship of Pilate. It was only then and thereafter that we hear of frequent disturbances, agitations, Messianic movements and a gradual disillusionment among the majority of the people with the Roman government and with their chances of cooperating with it.

The Romans for their part undoubtedly made an effort to find a *modus vivendi* with the Jews. The religious scruples of the Jews were respected and various directives were given to the administration in Judea, such as the prohibition of statues or images in Jerusalem. Things, however, did not always work out as well as could be desired. Encamped in Jerusalem was a cohort of auxiliaries enlisted from among the Gentile cities of the province. Soldiers such as these displayed a marked antipathy towards the Jews. Furthermore, the Roman governors not only preserved the right of appointing and deposing the High Priests, but also kept charge of their sacred vestments. This was felt as interference by the Romans in matters of Jewish ritual. Relations between rulers and ruled became increasingly embittered. Those who were conscious of the power of Rome tried to reconcile the two sides, since an open conflict with the superior forces of Rome could result in a disaster. Yet even the moderate element was ready at the critical moment to join the extremists, whenever Roman action endangered the existence of Judaism, as it did at the time of Gaius Caligula.

The first procurator of Judea was Coponius. He came with Quirinius, and seems to have won the respect of the Jews. There are grounds for believing that one of the gateways of the Temple was named after him (M. *Mid.* 1, 3 — the Gate of "Kiponus"). The single event of any import which occurred during his term of office, and was recorded in our sources, was the desecration of the Sanctuary by the Samaritans, when they scattered bones of the dead about the Temple area during the Passover celebrations (*Ant.* XVIII, 30).[6] Marcus Ambibulus (?) succeeded Coponius (*Ant.* XVIII, 31).[7] In his term of office, Herod's sister Salome died, bequeathing her possessions (Jamnia, Phasaelis and Archelais, the latter two near Jericho) to the empress Livia (*ibid; War* II, 167). These territories were later administered by special procurators on behalf of Livia. After her death they became imperial estates, first of Tiberius and then of his successors.

Annius Rufus was the last procurator to be appointed by Augustus (12–15 A.D.). The first nominated by Tiberius was Valerius Gratus, who served for a comparatively long term (15–26). This was in accordance with the policy of the new emperor, who preferred not to keep changing the provincial governors. Valerius Gratus dismissed Ananus, and appointed Ismael the son of Phabes as High Priest in his stead. The latter belonged to a family which had already produced a High Priest, Jeshua the son of Phabes, during the reign of Herod. Valerius, however, soon restored the house of Ananus to its former office, in the person of Ananus' son, Eleazar. He too remained in office for only a short time (not more than a year), and was replaced by Simeon the son of Camith, a *homo novus* in the priestly hierarchy. He in his turn was ousted in favor of Joseph Caiaphas. He may be compared to Ananus both as regards the length of his term and the extent of his power, in contrast to the other High Priests under the early governors. The Gospels inform us that Caiaphas was the son-in-law of Ananus and that both of them cooperated in establishing high-priestly policy (John 18:13). Caiaphas remained in office under Valerius Gratus' successor, Pontius Pilate, and was involved in the trial of Jesus. Thus Caiaphas remained High Priest throughout the terms of both Valerius Gratus and Pilate (18–36 A.D.) in spite of the fact that the former had previously made frequent changes in the office of High Priest. This durability of Caiaphas may have been due to his success in gaining the trust of the Roman authorities. It may also have depended on some sort of compromise between the high-priestly houses, a compromise that the Romans were loath to disturb.

B. The Administration of Pontius Pilate

During this period (26–36), relations between the Romans and the Jews deteriorated considerably. For the first time we hear of open friction between the two parties. The administration of Pilate is described by Philo (*Legatio ad Gaium*, 301) as a harsh and corrupt régime. We are told that Pilate was widely disliked, that he was influenced by bribery, and that he angered the Jews by his extortions and frequent executions without trial. Of all the Roman governors of Judea in the Julio-Claudian period, only Valerius Gratus served slightly longer than Pilate. This probably did not result so much from any particular efficiency or administrative ability on Pilate's part, as from Tiberius' well-known policy of not changing governors frequently. Furthermore, Pilate was supported during the first part of his administration (up to 31 A.D.) by Seianus, the commander of the Praetorian Guard and chief spokesman in Rome for an anti-Jewish policy. One should also note that there were no governors at Antioch until 32 A.D., since the legate of Syria (Aelius Lamia) had been detained at Rome by the emperor without any successor being appointed (Tacitus, *Annals*, VI, 27, 2). Lucius Pomponius Flaccus was finally chosen for this office in 32 A.D.[8] This restored Syria to its former position, in which the governor of Judea was once again overshadowed by the authority of the legate of Syria. As a result of this change and of the fall of Seianus in 31 A.D., Pilate found himself in the last five years of his rule less free to act and more sensitive to the reactions of his subjects, who could now hope to find greater sympathy at the court of Rome.

The first serious clash between Pilate and the Jews was over the introduction into Jerusalem of the ensigns of a Roman cohort bearing the image of the emperor (*Ant.* XVIII, 55–9; *War* II, 169–174). Pilate made this move under cover of darkness, as it went contrary to the customary policy of his predecessors. Although it was possibly not intended as a calculated provocation against the Jews, it nevertheless showed considerable disregard for their feelings. Pilate may well have aimed at abrogating the privileged position of the Jewish religion. Perhaps, too, the incident was connected with a change in the garrison and the encampment of a new cohort in Jerusalem.[9]

Earlier governors seem to have avoided this problem, in order not to antagonize the Jews. Pilate, however, stubbornly refused to respect previous convention, and marched his units into Jerusalem with their insignia. This action infuriated the people and they thronged to Caesarea, the capital of the province, in order to prevail upon Pontius Pilate to remove the insignia from Jerusalem. Pilate first tried to intimidate the multitude by surrounding them with his men, but the Jews stood their ground. When Pilate saw that they were strongly dedicated to their faith and were even prepared to die for their beliefs, he backed down and ordered the offending ensigns removed.

On this occasion Pilate probably yielded because he realized he had overreached himself, and was liable to find himself confronted with the revolt of a desperate people. In another case, however, he reacted quite differently, refusing to budge from what he regarded as the accepted practice of his predecessors and from what he felt did no damage to the Jewish religion. He also saw that he would be supported in his stand by the emperor. The affair concerned the aqueduct to Jerusalem, which was financed by money taken from the Temple treasury. This was met with violent reaction by the Jews who strongly resented the use of Temple funds for profane purposes. The governor was unwilling to acquiesce to the Jews' request. He disguised his soldiers in civilian dress and ordered them to attack the assembled crowd. These soldiers, who came from the Gentile cities of the province (e.g., Sebaste or Caesarea) and harbored a deep hatred for the Jews, showed more enthusiasm in executing their orders than even Pilate had expected. Many of the Jewish demonstrators were killed or wounded, and Pilate was left the cruel master of the day. (*Ant.* XVIII, 60–2; *War* II, 175–7).[10]

This same hardness may be observed in Pilate's policy regarding the coins he minted in Judea showing such pagan symbols as the *simpulum* or the *lituus*. Earlier governors had taken care when issuing their coins not to injure Jewish sensitivity in any way. They consequently avoided using any symbols on their coins that were connected with pagan worship, or could possibly suggest idolatry. With the installation of Pomponius Flaccus into office and the downfall of Seianus, the coinage of Syria was renewed and that of Pilate discontinued. Even Pilate's harsh and notorious successors (e.g., Felix) never dared to mint such coins. One cannot dismiss this matter as unimportant, for it is a clear testimony of Pilate's personality, and invalidates modern attempts to whitewash him.[11]

In the second half of Pilate's administration there occurred another incident, this time over the installation in Jerusalem of shields dedicated to Tiberius. It probably took place after the overthrow of Seianus, when Pilate wished to flatter the emperor and display his loyalty so as to cast oblivion over his former connection with Seianus. Philo claims, however, that he did this "more to vex the people than to honor Tiberius." The shields were of gold and were placed in Herod's palace. As no image was engraved on them, it could not be claimed that their display in the palace was an express transgression of Torah law. Nevertheless, the affair was without precedent and antagonized the Jews, who were now prepared to go to any extremes against anything that seemed to degrade the sanctity of Jerusalem. The inscriptions on the shields naturally contained some reference to pagan deities. All sections of the Jewish people, including four of Herod's sons, united in protesting against this act. Pilate, however, refused to withdraw the shields, maintaining that their presence neither affronted Jewish religion nor ran contrary to the declared imperial policy concerning the Jews. The Jewish representatives dared to reply that the name of Tiberius merely served Pilate as an excuse to challenge the Jews. Had not Caesar clearly shown his dislike of acts that were contrary to Jewish law? If Pilate claimed to be discharging the emperor's will, let him present them with an unambiguous document to that effect. The Jews finally sent a letter to Tiberius himself. Persuaded by their arguments, the emperor ordered the shields to be removed to Caesarea, where they were dedicated in the temple of Augustus (*Legatio ad Gaium*, 299–305).[12]

There were naturally other conflicts that find no mention in existing literary sources. The New Testament refers to the blood of the Galileans that Pilate mingled with their sacrifices (Luke 13:1)[13] There is no reason to connect this massacre with any of the episodes known to us from Josephus or Philo. One must presume that the clashes between the Romans and the Jewish populace frequently took place during the major festivals, since these provided a suitable opportunity for Messianic or social agitation. The Gospel story of the death of Jesus informs us that executions were common under Pilate. Two men were crucified along with Jesus, and they must have been condemned at about the same time. Another rebel against the Romans, one Barabas, was then also under sentence of death. Pilate's harsh policy served only to increase Jewish opposition, which in turn brought more repression and a further growth of eschatological hopes characteristic of this period. Pilate was methodical, and attempted to crush any sign of rebellion as soon as it arose. The trial of Jesus and the ruthlessness which Pilate displayed towards the Samaritans may be explained in this light. Throughout his administration Pilate found a faithful ally in Caiaphas, the High Priest. On the other hand, his relations with Herod Antipas were not always amicable (Luke 23:12). In the affair of the golden shields, for example, the Herodian dynasty made common cause with the people in defense of the sanctity of Jerusalem and the Jewish faith.

Pilate's barbarous suppression of a Samaritan disturbance proved the mistake which led directly to his dismissal. We do not know the name of the leader of this movement; it is only known that he exhorted his fellow Samaritans to follow him to Mt. Gerizim, where he promised to show them the holy vessels that Moses had hidden on the very spot. A large crowd of Samaritans gathered in Tirathana in order to make the pilgrimage to the mountain.[14] Pilate, however, put an end to their project by despatching his soldiers to Samaria with orders to set upon the demonstrators. The Samaritan council thereupon complained to Vitellius, the governor of Syria, who removed Pilate from office and ordered him to leave for Rome, to answer the charges brought against him. Pilate had to obey, leaving behind him a record of ten years of civil disturbances.

Vitellius was now made responsible for the province, and appointed one of his intimates, Marcellus, as temporary governor (*Ant.* XVIII, 85–9). Not satisfied with the mere dismissal of Pilate, Vitellius adopted various measures to ensure a lasting peace in Judea. He tried to gain Jewish goodwill by abolishing the Gentile supervision of the high-priestly vestments, and on his visit to Jerusalem (36) he removed the tax on fruit.[15] To demonstrate his departure from Pilate's policy, he also discharged Caiaphas and appointed Jonathan the son of Ananus (Joseph's brother-in-law) as High Priest (*Ant.* XVIII, 90–5). Jonathan continued to occupy an important position in Jewish society even after he too lost office.

Vitellius consistently pursued a pro-Jewish policy, and throughout his term of office was very careful not to offend the religious sensibilities of his Jewish subjects. He had at first planned to lead his legions across Judea from Ptolemais on his way to fight Aretas IV, king of the Nabataeans. Jewish officials who came to greet him, however, begged him to make a detour around Judea, as the display of Roman ensigns would offend the religious susceptibilities of the Jews. Mindful of a similar incident that had occurred under Pilate, Vitellius complied with their request and directed his forces into Transjordan by way of the Valley of Jezreel. In 37 A.D. he visited Jerusalem once more, this time in the company of Herod Antipas. He stayed there only three days, but found it necessary during this short stay to replace the High Priest Jonathan by his brother Theophilus. Though the reasons for this sudden reallocation of the High Priest's office are obscure, Vitellius may have acted in response to Jewish opposition to Jonathan. Such a motive, indeed, would have been consistent with Vitellius' indulgent policy towards the Jews.

News of Tiberius' death and of the accession of Gaius Caligula as emperor (March 16, 37 A.D.) reached Vitellius in Judea. The legate forthwith administered to the inhabitants an oath of allegiance to the new emperor (*Ant.* XVIII, 120–4).[16] Political developments at Rome were soon to produce decisive changes in Judea. For the time being, however, the only noticeable change was the appointment of a new governor of Judea, Marullus; this may even have been a confirmation of an earlier temporary appointment by Vitellius (*Ant.* XVIII, 237).[17]

C. Herod Antipas and Philip

Herod Antipas stands out as the most talented ruler and politician among all of Herod's sons. Apart from his father and his nephew, Agrippa I, he is the outstanding personality of the whole dynasty. Antipas managed to rule over his Tetrarchy for forty-three years the longest reign of any Jewish ruler of the period of the Second Temple. Although his domain included the territory of the most intractable Jews (viz., those of Galilee), he ruled in comparative peace, and had no armed rebellion to deal with either in Galilee or Peraea. His position within the empire was hardly inferior to that of his father before him. Thus there is much to support the assertion, made after Herod's death, that the latter's penultimate will was preferable to his final one. According to the former, the chief place among the king's successors was awarded to Herod Antipas and not to his brother, Archelaus, the main beneficiary under the final will, which was confirmed by Augustus.

Herod Antipas inherited his father's love for building and luxury. He is remembered, after his father, as the greatest founder of cities in his dynasty, and as the first Jewish ruler to establish a Jewish city with the constitution of a *polis*. His military abilities and success in battle did not match those of his father, but there is evidence that he kept a sizeable force and a large arsenal of weapons for an emergency. However, when the opportunity came to show his own talent in armed combat and the military strength of his Tetrarchy, he did not stand the test: he was defeated by Aretas, the

Nabataean king. It should, of course, be remembered that the military force at his disposal was much smaller than that of his father.

The troubles that beset Herod's sons in 6 A.D.[18] left Herod Antipas in a strong position which he maintained during the latter part of the principate of Augustus as well as in that of his successor. He established friendly relations with Tiberius, and was affected neither by Seianus' power nor by his fall. The reason for his cool relations with Pilate is unknown.[19]

Antipas was most active in founding cities. In all, he is said to have established three cities: Sepphoris (in its new form), Betharamatha and Tiberias. The first two had already been founded during the reign of Augustus, while the third was founded under Tiberius in the years 17–22 A.D., and was called after him.[20] Sepphoris was the capital of Galilee, but had suffered greatly in the suppression of the rebellion under Varus. It was rebuilt by Herod Antipas and renamed Autocratoris (*Ant.* XVIII, 27; αὐτοκράτωρ is equivalent to *imperator* in Latin). Betharamatha was also renamed: first Livias, in honor of Augustus' wife Livia (Tiberius' mother), and later Julias, when during the reign of Tiberius, Livia was made a member of the *gens Julia*, and became known as Julia.

Julias was naturally the center of Herod Antipas' rule in Peraea; its foundation, however, was overshadowed by that of the new city of Tiberias in Galilee. The latter assumed prime importance in the region, taking over the role of the Hellenistic city of Philoteria, south of the Sea of Galilee, after the latter had been destroyed by Jannaeus Alexander. The first inhabitants of Tiberias were a mixed lot. Some were paupers with no place in society, who sought better conditions and a higher social position by settling in the city. Antipas distributed holdings among them and built them houses. Within a few years, Tiberias became one of the great cities of Palestine. Its development was accompanied by the introduction of an administrative machinery typical of the Hellenistic *polis* in the Roman East at that time. Tiberias was exceptional in that the majority of its population was Jewish. By contrast, King Herod had never founded a *polis* in areas inhabited mainly by Jews. Tiberias was Herod Antipas' most lasting creation — as is testified by its continued existence after almost two thousand years.

As ruler of a Tetrarchy with a clear Jewish majority, Herod Antipas had to take special care not to injure Jewish religious feeling, especially since the inhabitants of Galilee and Peraea were staunch Jews. We see this careful policy in his coinage, which in contrast to that of his brother Philip bears neither the image of the emperor nor of the Tetrarch. Although his influence was felt even in Jerusalem, he held no official position in the province of

Judea; in his time the system prevailing during the period of the later procurators had not yet been established, under which appointments to the High Priesthood and the supervision of the Temple lay in the hands of Herodian dynasts ruling outside Judea.

In this period nothing is known of the activities of the sons of the Jewish extremist leader, Judah of Gamala. John the Baptist lived and worked in Herod's Tetrarchy. He raised his voice against the marriage of Herod Antipas with his niece, Herodias, for which he was arrested and executed. Jesus of Nazareth was also preaching at this time, but Antipas could not have foreseen that Jesus' disciples would lead a movement which within a few centuries was to change the aspect of the Western world.

Although Nabataea and Judea had long been enemies, a temporary basis for understanding was created between Aretas IV and Herod by their common desire to dislodge Syllaeus, the claimant to the Nabataean throne. It lasted into the times of Herod Antipas, whose marriage to Aretas' daughter assured the continuation of peaceful relations between the Tetrarchy and Aretas for a further period. Only when this marriage was annulled did matters change for the worse. Herod Antipas had fallen madly in love with Herodias, the daughter of his brother Aristobulus and the wife of another of his brothers. She favored Antipas' courtship, and agreed to divorce her husband in order to marry him. Meanwhile, these intrigues became known to Antipas' Nabataean wife, who left him at the first opportune moment for her father's kingdom. Aretas regarded the matter as a personal insult, and considered it sufficient cause for a renewal of hostilities. Border incidents soon led to a major battle, in which the Nabataeans defeated the forces of Herod Antipas. They were helped by disloyal units in Antipas' army, who hailed from Philip's Tetrarchy. Antipas now requested assistance from Tiberius in dealing with the Nabataeans, and Vitellius was ordered to lead a punitive expedition against Aretas (*Ant.* XVIII, 109–15). This expedition, however, was apparently postponed owing to the tension on the Parthian border; only after he had come to a settlement with Artabanus of Parthia and the crisis had passed did Vitellius begin his Nabataean campaign.

Herod Antipas found himself in the new and important role of mediator between Rome and the Parthians, with the aim of preventing a conflict between the two powers. The cause of the trouble, as on previous occasions was the tension over the Armenian situation. In 35 A.D. Artabanus of Parthia had tried to make his son king of Armenia after the death of Zeno-Artaxias. His plans were upset by the forceful reaction of the Romans, who assisted the brother of the king of Iberia in obtaining the crown.

However, the Parthians and the Romans decided to compromise.[21] Vitellius met Artabanus in the middle of the Euphrates on a bridge specially constructed for the purpose. Acting as host and mediator, Herod Antipas built a splendid pavilion on the bridge.[22] Even his father, Herod, does not seem to have ever attained such international prestige. Artabanus agreed to a peace and even sent his son to Rome as hostage (*Ant.* XVIII, 103).[23]

Like his father, Herod Antipas was also careful to form strong ties with the Greek world, as is attested by inscriptions from Cos and Delos, the latter referring to his connections with Athens.[24] On Tiberius' death, his position was less strong. The new emperor, Gaius Caligula, favored Agrippa, Antipas' brother-in-law and nephew. Vitellius bore Herod Antipas a grudge for having anticipated him in informing Tiberius of the treaty with the Parthians. When Vitellius learned of the death of Tiberius, he gave up his Nabataean campaign. Possibly he considered it likely that the new emperor would be grateful to Aretas for his kindness toward his father, Germanicus (Tacitus, *Annals*, II, 57, 4).

At first Herod Antipas attempted to gain the new emperor's favor, but in vain. His brother-in-law, Agrippa, had by imperial command gained the title of king in Philip's territory, while he himself still remained a Tetrarch. His wife, Herodias, persuaded him to petition the emperor for this honor, and both went to Rome for the purpose. Their mission ended in total failure, owing to Agrippa's powerful influence at the court. Herod Antipas was accused before the emperor of having amassed a store of arms for use against Rome in an alliance with Parthia.[25] He was sentenced to exile (39 A.D.), where he was accompanied by Herodias, who refused to abandon him in his misfortune. His realm was now added to the kingdom of Agrippa (*Ant.* XVIII, 240–55; *War* II, 181–3).[26]

Philip was the least colorful of Herod's successors, both from the general standpoint of political history and particularly from the point of view of the Jews. He ruled over Trachonitis, Gaulanitis and Batanaea, the development areas of Herod's kingdom in which the majority of the population were Gentiles. His coins are therefore quite different in style from those of his brother, and bear his own and the emperor's image. In contrast to most of Herod's descendants, he was known as a man of even temperament. Josephus describes his patriarchal method of judging the people while traveling throughout his territory, setting up a tribunal wherever a case was brought before him (*Ant.* XVIII, 107). Philip too, is well known as a founder of cities. He built Paneas near the source of the river Jordan, and named it Caesarea. Henceforth, it became known as Caesarea Philippi, to distinguish it from the coastal Caesarea. He also developed Beth-Saida on the sea of Galilee renaming it Julias, and it was here that he was buried (*Ant.* XVIII, 28; *War* II, 168; *Ant. ibid.*, 108). After his death (34 A.D.), his territory was taken over provisionally by the governor of Syria. At the accession of Gaius Caligula, it was bestowed upon Agrippa I, who assumed the title of king. Although we have no clear evidence of Philip's participation in the affairs of Judea, it is very probable that he was one of the four sons of Herod who protested to Pilate against the introduction of the shields into Jerusalem (*Legatio ad Gaium*, 300).

D. Caligula's Decrees

When he succeeded to the throne, Caligula was much beloved by the public. The Jews were no exception to this. Although his father, Germanicus, had spurned the Jews of Alexandria in 19 A.D.,[27] it was not certain whether his conduct on that occasion expressed his general political views, and in any case the episode would have been forgotten by most people. Thus there was no reason to assume that Germanicus' son would harbor anti-Jewish feelings, or that the Jews had cause for anxiety over the change in rule. In the past, every emperor had shown considerable sympathy for Jewish rights. Moreover, the friendly relations between the emperor and Agrippa seemed to vouchsafe the goodwill of the court.

The first two years of Caligula's rule did in fact point to a continuation of Tiberius' clemency toward the Jews. This period even brought some improvements for the Jews of Palestine, mainly through the unification of the territories of the two Tetrachs, Philip and Herod Antipas, under the kingship of Agrippa I. These dominions now formed a united kingdom (*ca.* 39 A.D.). Changes were also made in the governship of Syria. The place of the pro-Jewish Vitellius was taken by Publius Petronius, who soon showed no less a sympathy for the Jewish people. The two men were probably related.[28]

A basic change in Judeo-Roman relations followed Caligula's attempt to establish a cult of his own divinity. Previous rulers had regarded the cult of the imperial divinity merely as a political expedient, above all as an expression of loyalty on the part of the provincials towards their emperor. Caligula, however, looked on his own divinity with the fanaticism of a true believer. Emperor worship now became obligatory even in Italy and Rome. A special temple was built for the purpose in Rome, while others were set up in the provinces (e.g., in Miletus in Asia Minor). Philo caustically sums up Caligula's views on the subject (*Legatio ad Gaium*, 76)[29] and the emperor's arguments in defense of the cult.[30]

The emperor's insistence on his own divinity gave the anti-Jewish inhabitants of Egypt and Palestine a new occasion to denounce the Jews. So far a way had always been found to avoid making emperor worship a stumbling-block in Judeo-Roman relations. Matters had now radically changed, and the survival of Judaism itself was at stake. Rebellion seemed to be the only course left to the Jews.

Trouble began with the Gentile minority of Jamnia, who felt that the moment had arrived to rid themselves of the Jewish majority in the town. When reports of Caligula's dogmatic assertion of his own divinity reached the city, the Gentiles built a stone altar on which to offer sacrifices to the emperor. This action was an infringement of an ancient Jewish prerogative banning idolatry in the territory of Judea, a ban which had been respected by every Greek and Roman ruler with the exception of Antiochus IV Epiphanes. In response to the unprecedented outrage, the Jews of Jamnia smashed the altar to pieces. Their opponents complained to Herennius Capito, the imperial procurator of Jamnia, who was already on bad terms with the Jews, and who had become embroiled with Agrippa I. Capito sent a report to the emperor describing the desecration of his altar, and inciting him to vent his fury on the Jews who had dared insult his imperial godhead.

Prompted by several courtiers, including a certain Ascalonite called Apelles,[31] Caligula vowed to teach the Jews a lesson. He would forcibly install his cult in Jerusalem itself, in a manner that was both open and uncompromising.[32] His intention was to erect a colossal statue of gold in the Sanctuary proper (Philo, *Legatio ad Gaium*, 199–206; *Ant.* XVIII, 261; *War* II, 185; Tacitus, *Histories*, V, 9, 2). Presumably the statue was to have represented Zeus in the likeness of Caligula. From the very beginning this decision was expected to arouse fierce opposition among the Jews. It would be possible to implement it only by the use of the Roman army. It was also clear that the small garrison forces in Judea would not suffice to overcome the expected hostility of the Jews. The project was therefore placed in the hands of Publius Petronius, legate of Syria.

Petronius now earned a place of honor in Jewish history by risking grave personal danger in attempting to prevent a desecration of the Temple. As governor of Asia from 29 to 35,[33] he had ample opportunity to learn about the Jews in the various cities of the province. According to Philo (*Legatio ad Gaium*, 245), he seems to have had some insight into the philosophy and religion of the Jews. Josephus also depicts him as a man prepared to commit himself on behalf of the Jews and who showed respect for their God. The emperor's decree placed Petronius in a quandary. As governor of Syria and commander-in-chief on the Parthian border, he was gravely concerned over a possible Jewish revolt in Palestine, a revolt that could spread to the neighboring provinces and lead to a general insurrection against the Romans in their eastern dominions. Even the Parthians might be tempted to interfere. Artabanus of Parthia had died in 38 A.D., and though his country had been rent by civil war ever since, it was still a major power capable of causing trouble to Rome. The fact that the Romans had recently deposed Mithradates of Armenia left that country open to a Parthian invasion.

In spite of these considerations, Petronius saw no way of directly opposing the emperor's command. The most he could do was to gain time, for as yet he had no statue ready for erection in the Temple. He commissioned Sidonian sculptors to manufacture one (*Legatio ad Gaium*, 220–2), and marched some of his Syrian legions to Accho-Ptolemais. Jews everywhere trembled at the approaching disaster. Once more, as in the days of Antiochus IV Epiphanes, the basic tenets of Judaism and its continued existence was in danger. Jews of all ages thronged to Ptolemais to demonstrate their determination to suffer any sacrifice or pain for the sanctity of Jerusalem. They left Petronius with no doubt that the imperial decrees could not be implemented without a wholesale slaughter. When the governor moved on to Tiberias, he witnessed the same scene. The peasants left their fields at the height of the sowing season (autumn, 40 A.D.). For forty days Petronius was beseeched by the people to prevent the desecration of the Temple. Petronius clearly realized that this time he was not faced by an extremist or zealot movement. This was no opposition to imperial rule in principle, but a united front of the Jewish people, representing all classes and shades of ideology. Even Herod's family, headed by Aristobulus (Agrippa's brother) and Helcias, (the son of Herod's sister, Salome), presented themselves before Petronius and made it clear that if the Romans persisted in their policy, they would bring ruin to the country. Petronius was already hesitant; now he bowed to the determination of the people. He postponed carrying out the decree, thereby braving the anger of the emperor. Writing to Caligula on the difficulties he was facing, he pointed out in particular that the turbulence in Judea was liable to endanger the emperor's projected visit to the East in the coming spring (*Ant.* XVIII, 262–88; *War* II, 186–7, 192–202; Philo, *Legatio ad Gaium*, 222–53). Caligula agreed to a temporary postponement until after the end of the agricultural season. Meanwhile, Agrippa I used all his persuasion on his friend the emperor, in an attempt to change the severe decree. Agrippa was in fact risking his own position and future to avert the disaster of a Judeo-Roman clash. Agrippa's arguments, and above all his close friendship with the emperor, procured a cancellation of the worst part of the decree: the erection of an idol in the Sanctuary. Petronius was informed of this decision, but further potential dangers were contained in a qualifying clause of his instructions: if any person wished to build an altar, erect a statue or sacrifice to Caesar outside the boundaries of Jerusalem, he must be allowed to do so (Philo, *Legatio ad Gaium*, 254–334; *Ant.* XVIII, 289–301). Thus the enemies of the Jews were assured of official sanction and the stage set for further conflicts, especially in those cities where pagans lived on bad terms with their Jewish neighbors.

There is even evidence that Caligula intended to take the Jews by surprise with a plan to have a statue prepared at Rome and sent by sea to Palestine. It could then be installed in the Sanctuary in time for his planned visit. Petronius, moreover, had lost favor with the emperor, and his life was in danger (*Legatio ad Gaium*, 337; *Ant.* XVIII, 302–4; *War* II, 203). It was plain, therefore, that sooner or later the crisis in Judeo-Roman relations would recur, and that it would give rise to armed opposition, or even to general insurrection in the East. This catastrophe was averted by Caligula's assassination in Rome at the hands of a group of conspirators (Jan. 24, 41 A.D.). Tacitus records the event in his *Histories* (V, 9, 2): *dein iusssi a Caesare effigiem eius in templo locare arma potius sumpsere, quem motum mors Caesaris diremit.*

The memory of Caligula's decrees and the fear of a renewed threat of similar calamities henceforth cast a shadow on Judeo-Roman relations. It is indeed true that such decrees were almost unparalleled in ancient Jewish history; they lacked even the rational political motivation of the earlier decrees of Antiochus IV Epiphanes or the later ones of Hadrian. Thus the caprice of a pagan tyrant possessed of unlimited power exposed the threat facing Judaism even in Judea itself. Even moderate circles among the Jews were agitated. In the words of Tacitus (*Annals*, XII, 54, 1): *manebat metus, ne quis principum eadem imperitaret* — the fear remained that another emperor would issue a similar decree.

E. The Reign of Agrippa I

The short reign of Agrippa I somewhat eased the tension between Rome and Judea, thanks to the king's close ties with the imperial court. In retrospect, his reign represents the last golden age of the Jews in antiquity. It was then that the most determined effort was made to settle the differences between the Roman empire and Judaism.

Even under Caligula, Agrippa acted as the political leader of his nation and the champion of its rights. His personal history before he entered the arena of politics is known to us in more detail than that of all his Jewish contemporaries. He was the grandson of Herod. His father was Aristobulus, son of Herod and Mariamne the Hasmonean, who had been executed at Herod's command. His mother was Berenice, daughter of Herod's sister Salome. He was educated in Rome, and spent his youth among the young nobles of Roman society. Among his close friends was Drusus, the son of Tiberius, and he was on affectionate terms with Antonia, Mark Antony's daughter, who was also Tiberius' sister-in-law and a friend of Agrippa's mother, Berenice (*Ant.* XVIII, 143, 165).[34] Agrippa was also a friend of Claudius (Antonia's son), the future emperor. After Berenice's death, Agrippa fell into debt. When his friend Drusus also died Agrippa decided to leave Rome after a stay of many years and to return to Judea (*Ant.* XVIII, 143–7).

Once in Judea Agrippa did not find his prospects very promising. He was without official position and without funds. At first he went to live in the south of the country, having apparently inherited some village property there. The contrast between his former life at Rome, the hub of the world, and his present existence in the most tumbledown village of Judea (Malaatha),[35] filled him with dejection and despair. His wife, Cypros (also one of Herod's grandchildren through her mother), appealed to Herodias (Herod Antipas' wife and Agrippa's sister) to assist them in their adversity. Through this connection, Agrippa obtained the post of *agoranomos* of Tiberias from Herod Antipas.

The good relationship between the two did not last long. Agrippa could not long remain satisfied with an inferior position, and dependent on the goodwill of his brother-in-law. They soon quarreled, and Agrippa left Tiberias for Syria, where he served in the entourage of the governor, Pomponius Flaccus, one of his old friends from his Roman days. His brother, Aristobulus, was also on the governor's staff, but the two were unable to get along with each other. This mutual antagonism led to a deterioration in the relations between Agrippa and Flaccus. Aristobulus denounced Agrippa to the governor, accusing him of using his position on the legate's staff to accept bribes in return for a promise to the inhabitants of Damascus that he would help them in their quarrel with the Sidonians over some border lands.

Agrippa was obliged to leave Syria and to resume his wanderings. He was again in financial difficulties and resolved to return to Italy to try his luck a second time. After managing to raise some money in a variety of ways, he was detained in the port of Anthedon by the procurator of Jamnia for a debt to the imperial treasury.[36] Finally Agrippa succeeded in reaching

Alexandria, where once more he borrowed money from one of the Jewish leaders there, Alexander the brother of Philo. Agrippa could now embark for Italy; there he tried to reestablish his connections with Tiberius, who was then living on the island of Capri. Thanks to the help of his benefactress Antonia, he was able to repay his debts to the treasury (*Ant.* XVIII, 159–65).

Agrippa's friendship with Antonia led to one with her grandson, Gaius, the future emperor Caligula. An indiscreet remark in connection with Gaius landed Agrippa in further trouble when one of his freedmen denounced him to the emperor, claiming to have heard him express a wish for Tiberius' death so that Gaius could ascend the throne. Agrippa was put in prison (*Ant.* XVIII, 167–94) and remained there until the emperor's death (March 16, 37 A.D.).

On Caligula's accession Agrippa's fortunes were reversed. He was at once made king over the former Tetrarchy of Philip (*Ant.* XVIII, 237; *War* II, 181; Dio Cassius, LIX, 8, 2). This was the first time since the death of Herod that a Jewish ruler had been raised to the kingship. The Senate granted him the *ornamenta praetoria* (Philo, *In Flaccum*, 40), and Caligula presented him with a golden chain equal in weight to the iron chain he had borne in prison.

Agrippa's rule over Philip's territory suited Caligula's policy at that time. We know that the emperor revived the kingdom of Commagene, over which he again installed Antiochus as king. Caligula gave Antiochus additional territory in southern Asia Minor and even compensated him for the financial losses he had incurred while he was deprived of his crown (Dio Cassius, LIX, 8, 2; Suetonius, *Life of Gaius Caligula*, 16, 3). The emperor also appointed Soaemus as ruler of the Ituraeans (Dio Cassius, LIX, 12, 2). Other friends of Caligula, the Thracian princelings Cotys and Polemon, were raised to the thrones of Armenia Minor and Pontus respectively (Dio Cassius, *loc. cit.*; cf. Dittenberger, *Sylloge inscriptionum Graecarum*, No. 798). A third brother, Rhoemetalces, gained the crown of Thrace.

Agrippa was now very influential at court, certainly far more than any Jew before or after.[37] He knew every aspect of Roman society and of the imperial government, and was regarded as a member of the Roman upper classes. This intimate relationship with Rome, however, never turned into absolute identification. More than any other ruler of the Herodian dynasty, Agrippa did his best to keep the welfare of the Jews in mind.

His visit to Alexandria on his return to Judea as king of Philip's former domain (38 A.D.) produced contrasting reactions in that city. While the Jews came in their thousands to welcome him enthusiastically, the Greeks greeted him with open hostility and abuse. Such conflicting attitudes were due above all to Agrippa's new position as representative and spokesman for the Jewish people.

After Herod Antipas was deposed in 39 A.D. his former territories in Galilee and Peraea with their large Jewish populations were included in the kingdom of Agrippa (40 A.D.).[38] Nothing is known of Agrippa's policy in these regions during the reign of Caligula. Most information on this period concerns the attempts to obtain annulment of Caligula's decrees, in which Agrippa risked his position and even his life. We must remember that Caligula did not treat his allied kings with undue indulgence. He executed Ptolemy of Mauretania, while Mithradates of Armenia he deposed and imprisoned; even Caligula's old friend Antiochus of Commagene was deprived of his kingdom, despite the fact the he had once been on the same terms of friendship with the emperor as Agrippa himself (Dio Cassius, LIX, 25, 1; LX, 8, 1; Suetonius, *Life of Gaius Caligula*, 26, 1; 35, 1; Tacitus *Annals*, XI, 8, 1).

Agrippa was in Rome at the time of Caligula's assassination; the course of action he now followed was of the utmost consequence for the future of the Roman state. The candidate for the supreme position was Agrippa's friend Claudius, who was popular among the military at Rome. A proposal had been raised in the Senate to restore the republic, and the danger of open strife was imminent. Agrippa played an important part in dissuading the Senate from taking this step, and by preparing the senators for the idea of Claudius as emperor he succeeded in preventing bloodshed.

Agrippa's success was suitably recompensed by Claudius. Once more this followed the general policy of the emperor. Claudius continued to maintain the allied kings in various parts of the empire, and even went as far as to restore Mithradates and Antiochus to their respective kingdoms of Armenia and Commagene. Agrippa, who in contrast with them had managed to retain his kingdom throughout the whole of Caligula's reign, now had his territory greatly increased (41 A.D.), to include all of the province of Judea (Judea proper, Idumaea and Samaria). The ties between Claudius and Agrippa received official confirmation in the ceremonial signing of a treaty of alliance in the Forum. Agrippa's elder brother was appointed king of Chalcis. They appeared together in the Senate to thank the assembly for the kindness shown them (*Ant.* XIX, 274–5; *War* II, 215–7; Dio Cassius, LX, 8, 2–3).[39]

The province of Judea was thus abolished, and a Jewish kingdom was restored of more or less the same dimensions as the kingdom of Herod or the Hasmoneans at the height of their power. Jews in the Diaspora and Judea alike regarded Agrippa's reign with pride and confidence. Their love for the king arose not merely on account of his Jewish birth, but because he was

prepared to watch over Jewish interests everywhere and to rule in accordance with the wishes of the majority of his brethren. He also derived
much support from the fact that he was a descendant not only of the
Herodian dynasty, but also matrilineally of the Hasmoneans.[40]

It must also be realized that Jewish attitudes had changed somewhat
in the thirty-five years of direct contact with a Roman provincial administration. The majority of the people had learned to be satisfied with a
Jewish king, if only a semi-independent one, after their accumulated
experiences of provincial government, the oppression and tension under

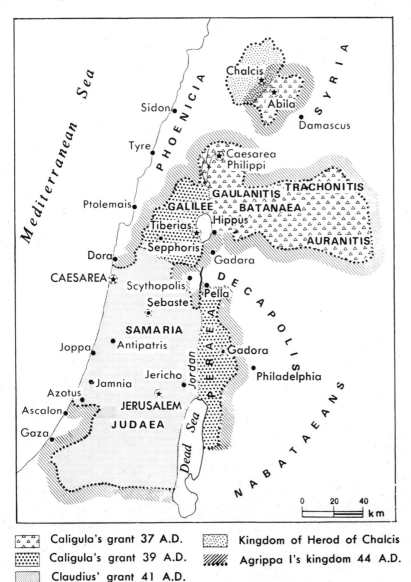

Caligula's grant 37 A.D.   Kingdom of Herod of Chalcis
Caligula's grant 39 A.D.   Agrippa I's kingdom 44 A.D.
Claudius' grant 41 A.D.

The Kingdom of Agrippa I.

the procuratorship of Pilate, and the terrible years of Caligula's reign. People were now willing to forgive certain of Agrippa's acts which would have invited severe criticism in the days of Herod. Whatever the relative merits of this or that action, the king's chief aim was always the advancement of the nation. The same could hardly be said of Herod. Josephus contrasts the two personalities, distinctly showing his preference for Agrippa the grandson, and describes the affection for the king among the majority of the people.

Agrippa for his part did his best to appear a loyal Jew in every way, at least in the Jewish regions of his kingdom. He tried by various means to win the affection of his subjects. Caligula's gift, the golden chain, he dedicated to the Temple, and he paid for the expenses of the Nazirite sacrifices from his own purse. Thus he soon acquired the image of a king who was interested in his people's affection (*Ant.* XIX, 293-4), and so he continued until the end of his reign. His popularity is also reflected in Talmudic passages, where he is represented as the ruler most acceptable to the nation. "The minister of the synagogue," the Mishnah tells us, "lifted the scroll of the Law and gave it to the head of the synagogue; the head of the synagogue gave it to the [High Priest's] deputy; the deputy gave it to the High Priest; the High Priest gave it to the king; and the king received it standing, but read it seated. King Agrippa read it standing, and the sages praised him. When he reached the verse, *Thou mayest not put a foreigner over thee*, he wept. They said to him, 'Do not fear, Agrippa, you are our brother, you are our brother'" (M. Soṭa 7, 8).[41] There were of course, some Jews who took offense at Agrippa's behavior outside Judea. Josephus records the incident of a certain extremist called Simeon, who harangued the crowds in Jerusalem on the shortcomings of the king while the latter was absent from the city. Simeon even went as far as to claim that Agrippa ought to be excluded from the Temple. The king later replied politely to Simeon's outburst, and even managed to appease him.[42] Such an occurrence would have been impossible under Herod.

Agrippa owed much of his popularity to the special consideration he showed for the views of the Pharisees. He obviously took great pains to reach an understanding with the Pharisee leaders. On the other hand, his cooperation with the Pharisees was clearly of no influence in his nominations to the High Priesthood. He could have appointed men of Pharisaic outlook or at least have sometimes chosen the candidate from elsewhere than among the traditional high-priestly families, who were almost all Sadducees. However, Agrippa remained faithful to the policy of Herod and the procurators and continued to choose High Priests from the well-defined oligarchy. One fact alone is of interest in this respect: under Agrippa, the family of Boethus returned to its former glory after it had been partially eclipsed by the family of Ananus following the deposition of Archelaus. On his accession to the throne, Agrippa dismissed Theophilus the son of Ananus, the High Priest appointed by Vitellius who had served for four years. His place was taken by Simeon Cantheras of the house of Boethus.[43]

With the return of the High Priesthood to a descendant of Boethus, the old alliance between the houses of Boethus and Herod was revived. The former had originally risen to eminence through its connections with the Herodian dynasty. However, in contrast to their protracted tenure in the days of Herod, the house of Boethus did not long retain the High Priesthood under Agrippa, and the office reverted to the house of Ananus. The king at first offered it to Jonathan the son of Ananus, one of the most influential Jews of the time. He had once before held the post for a short period, but now he refused it, and the honor went instead to his brother, Mattathias, the fourth of five sons of Ananus (*Ant.* XIX 313–6). The third High Priest appointed by Agrippa was Elioneus, of the family of Caiaphas.[44] Thus all three appointments were made from among the high-priestly aristocracy. In spite of his desire to appease the Pharisees, Agrippa was clearly unwilling to overthrow an alliance that had lasted since the days of Herod. The first to do so were the Zealots during the time of the First Revolt, when they introduced radical changes into the appointment of the High Priests.

The rule of a king of the Herodian dynasty in Jerusalem strengthened the position of the families related to it. They of course had maintained an honored status in Jewish society even under the procurators; but now they were presented with far brighter prospects. The most important of them was Helcias "the Great," who was among the representatives of the Jews at the time of Caligula's decrees. He was the son of Alexa and Herod's sister Salome. Helcias' son Archelaus was betrothed to Agrippa's daughter, Mariamne (*Ant.* XIX, 355). Helcias was Agrippa's right-hand man in administrative matters, and even succeeded to the command of the army when Silas, the former commander, fell from favor. Silas had been Agrippa's companion in his former life of poverty. A man of obscure origins, he may have been one of the Babylonian Jewish settlers of Gaulanitis. After earning the king's disfavor, he was dismissed from his post and put in prison, where he spent the remainder of his life (*Ant.* XIX, 317–25). He was executed after Agrippa's death.

Even before his rise to power, Agrippa had established connections with the Jews of the Diaspora, especially with the upper classes of Alexandrian Jewry, who regarded him as the true successor of Herod. Like his grandfather, he was on close terms with Alexander the alabarch. His eldest daughter, Berenice, even married Alexander's son, Marcus, who died shortly after the marriage (*Ant.* XIX, 276–7).

Agrippa continued to employ non-Jewish retainers and servants even after he became king. They were, however, not too conspicuous in the Jewish areas of his kingdom, and certainly did not set the tone at court. Nor did he ever disband the military units enlisted mainly from among the inhabitants of Sebaste and Caesarea. Their main camp continued to be at Caesarea, and that they never quite accepted the rule of a Jewish king was shown by later events. Agrippa was probably left no choice in the matter, since the Romans were naturally unwilling to disband troops who were both trustworthy and always at hand in Judea, or even to transfer them to another province.

Following the tradition of the Herodian dynasty, Agrippa was careful to ingratiate himself with neighboring Gentile cities. Though it is true that he quarreled towards the end of his reign with the cities of Tyre and Sidon (Acts 12:20), his relations with the Roman colony of Berytus were exceptionally friendly, and he donated a large sum of money for the construction of a theater and amphitheater there. The amphitheater was for gladiatorial displays and the theater for musical shows. For the opening of the amphitheater, a hundred pairs of gladiators were recruited from the criminals of the kingdom (*Ant.* XIX, 335–7).

As king of Judea, Agrippa had to deal with the problems arising from the spread of Christianity. He was undoubtedly severe towards the early Christians, adopting rather the Sadducean view of the problem (later expressed by such men as Ananus the son of Ananus) than that of the Pharisees, which was represented by Gamaliel the Elder. Agrippa ordered the execution of James the son of Zebedee, one of the leaders of the early Christians, and imprisoned the apostle Peter (Acts 12:1–19).[45]

The relations which Herod had fostered between Judea and Syria continued during the reign of Agrippa. The fact that Petronius was still governor when Agrippa ascended the throne made the latter's task much easier. Soon Petronius' good offices were urgently needed. In spite of the death of Caligula and the express instructions of Claudius, the Gentile inhabitants of Dora, which was officially outside Agrippa's kingdom, antagonized the city's Jewish inhabitants by setting up an image of the emperor in the local synagogue. This provocation brought back grim memories of Caligula and posed grave dangers for the future. Agrippa requested the intervention of Petronius. The latter responded promptly by despatching one of his men to arrest those responsible, and to warn the city's Gentile inhabitants that no one must suffer interference in matters of religion. Petronius also sent an official letter to Dora, in which he referred to King Agrippa's request for his personal intervention (*Ant.* XIX, 300–12). The king's connections with Vibius Marsus, the new governor in Antiocha, were less friendly.[46] A few years later, it was he who proved the main stumbling-block to some of Agrippa's more ambitious schemes.

By constantly cultivating his personal connections with the various political factors in the East, Agrippa hoped to enhance his own popularity and prestige. He was not, however, satisfied with that alone, but genuinely tried to increase the strength and security of his people. He clearly stood out from the members of his dynasty, by departing from its traditional policy of unquestioning support of the Romans in Judea. Because of his personal standing with the leaders at Rome, principally with Claudius himself, he hoped that he would not be kept under too close a scrutiny. Thanks to his ties with Claudius, he was from the very outset assured of a place of honor in the eastern empire and though his designs sometimes ended in failure, his friendship with the emperor always safeguarded his personal position.

That Agrippa's achievements did not always measure up to his political aspirations is well demonstrated by the results of his attempt to summon a general council of Rome's eastern allied kings in one of his cities. In response to his invitation, five kings came to stay with Agrippa at Tiberias. These were: Antiochus of Commagene, who had himself experienced the whims of imperial policy (he was first raised to the throne, then deposed by Caligula, and finally restored by Claudius) and to whose heir, Epiphanes, Agrippa offered the hand of one of his daughters in marriage; the two Thracian brothers, Polemon of Pontus and Cotys of Armenia Minor; Sampsiceramus of Emesa, whose daughter, Iotape, had been married to Agrippa's brother, Aristobulus; and finally, Herod of Chalcis (Agrippa's elder brother).

Besides presenting an impressive array of majesty, the congress of kings at Tiberias brought together the important links in the political and military chain that formed Rome's front against Parthia. For Agrippa, the congress may have been a manifestation of his own preeminence among the eastern kings, but for Rome it was undesirable both in the long and short term. Although they had always sanctioned such relations between the allied kings, the Romans — or at least Vibius Marsus — felt that this congress was dangerous. The legate feared that any concerted action by ihe kings might in the present critical situation jeopardize Rome's position tn the Orient. Parthia's continued conflict with Rome posed a threat to the eastern provinces, whose inhabitants could not be relied on to remain loyal to the emperor. In particular the reaction of the Jews to the decrees of Caligula had not been forgotten, while their love for their present king made him appear all the more dangerous. One should also note that the enmity between Rome and Parthia was particularly strong at the beginning of Claudius' reign, and that the problem of Armenia continued to be a bone of contention between the two powers. When Claudius restored Mithradates (previously deposed by Caligula) to the Armenian throne, Vardanes of Parthia had threatened to intervene and Marsus as commander-in-chief in the East had reacted promptly to counter the threat (Tacitus, *Annals*, XI, 9–10).[47] To complete the picture, mention must be made of the conversion to Judaism a few years earlier of the royal house of Adiabene. This petty kingdom occupied a key position in Romano-Parthian relations and was now closely allied to the Jews.

Marsus thus decided to take prompt and unequivocal action against the congress of the kings. He suddenly appeared on the scene and ordered them to leave the city without delay. They had no choice but to obey, and Agrippa, his dignity injured and his prestige weakened, henceforth regarded Marsus as his enemy (*Ant*. XIX, 338–42).[48]

Yet another of Agrippa's projects was brought to nought by the actions of Marsus. This was a scheme to strengthen the fortifications of Jerusalem and to include the "New City" within the circuit of a new strong wall. Josephus maintains that had this plan been carried out in its entirety, Jerusalem would have become wholly impregnable. To finance this project, Agrippa drew on funds belonging to the Temple. The work was stopped in its early stages by Marsus, who advised the emperor of the danger inherent in the construction of such a wall. Claudius agreed with the governor, and instructed Agrippa to abandon the project after only a small part of the wall had been built (*Ant*. XIX, 326–7; Tacitus, *Histories*, V, 12, 2).[49]

Agrippa died in Caesarea in the midst of celebrations in honor of the emperor (44).[50] He had reigned seven years and was king of the whole of Palestine for the last three of them. His Jewish subjects mourned his death deeply, but the Gentiles rejoiced, and the troops of Sebaste and Caesarea even insulted the memory of the dead king (*Ant*. XIX, 345–59; *War* II, 219; Acts 12:21–3).

Agrippa's reign was a short and transitory golden age in the Roman period of Jewish history. It is difficult to judge whether he had any far-reaching policy regarding the Jews and the empire, or what such a policy might have been. He cannot have entertained serious hopes of ever breaking away from the Roman empire by some sort of alliance with the Parthians, or by a coalition with Rome's vassals. His desire was to consolidate the position of the Jews and of the kingdom of Judea within the framework and under the protectorate of the Roman empire, with the help of friendly elements in Roman society, and particularly the imperial court.[51]

His reign had no lasting influence in the internal development of Judea, not did it leave any great mark on the structure of Jewish society of that time. It was too short to produce any effect on the relation between political and social forces in the country and abroad. Perhaps if Agrippa had reigned longer, he may have left a more lasting impression on his kingdom. The fact that the Gentiles of cities such as Caesarea hated him and rejoiced at his death shows clearly that they regarded him as a Jewish king with Jewish aspirations. As the last Jewish king to reign over Judea, however, Agrippa has been given more weight in history than the actual impact of his short reign merits.

F. The Last Procurators before the First Revolt

Agrippa's death brought about a complete change in status of Judea. At first the emperor weighed the possibility of continuing Judea as an allied kingdom, but certain reasons decided him against such a course. Most important of these was undoubtedly the feeling that a Judea under another Jewish king with Agrippa's aspirations would be disadvantageous to Rome. The minority of Agrippa's heir served as a pretext for abolishing the kingdom and for recreating the province of Judea on a border basis. It is doubtful, however, whether Claudius was really deterred from continuing the Jewish monarchy by the youth of Agrippa's heir, since he could have appointed Agrippa's brother, Herod of Chalcis, as regent. Similarly, when young Agrippa reached maturity a few years later, Claudius still remained content with appointing him ruler over areas outside Judea.

The new province was in many ways no different from the former one. The same type of equestrian governors were sent out and the garrisons were still composed of auxiliaries rather than legionaries. One major change, however, was the inclusion in the province of Galilee and Peraea, although certain parts of these areas were later detached from its territory. In contrast to conditions under the former governors, the representatives of the Herodian dynasty were now granted a privileged position in Jewish society. The authority to appoint High Priests and the supervision of the Temple and its ritual were at first granted to Herod of Chalcis, and on his death (48) to Agrippa II. In addition, both princes as well as others of the same family, continued to serve as spokesmen for the Jews and mediators between them and the emperor. Neither of them succeeded, as Agrippa I had done, in winning the love of the people of all classes, or in identifying themselves with the feelings and interests of the Jews as completely as had their predecessor in his later years.

The procuratorial government lasted twenty-two years, from the death of Agrippa I until the beginning of the First Revolt. It was marked by a growing deterioration in the relations between all classes of Jews and the Roman administration. The first Roman governors had replaced the detestable tyranny of Herod and Archelaus, while the later ones succeeded a king dear to the whole people. The Romans, moreover, were now resorting to the growing use of force and oppression. They preferred the Hellenistic elements of the mixed towns to the Jews. Extremist movements and ideologies gained increasing prevalence within Jewish society, especially among the ordinary people. Messianic hopes grew daily, undermining the order and disturbing the safety of the villages throughout Judea and of Jerusalem itself. There was constant tension between Jews and Gentiles in the Hellenistic cities of the province. Many became impoverished, and longed for social change. All these developments helped bring about the downfall of Roman administration and order in Judea.

Cuspius Fadus was the first procurator of the new province (44–46). At the very beginning of his rule the question of supervision of the High Priest's vestments once more became an issue. Fadus planned to revive the practice — abolished by Vitellius — of keeping the high-priestly robes in the fortress of Antonia under the supervision of the Roman authorities. Jewish leaders were unwilling to submit to what they considered an unjustified infringement of their recently acquired privilege. For them, this was a blow to the dignity of Jewish religion and ritual. They requested permission from Fadus himself, and from Cassius Longinus, the governor of Syria, to send a delegation to the emperor concerning the matter. They also begged that nothing should be done in the meantime to alter the *status quo*. Longinus had marched his legions to Jerusalem in anticipation of popular disturbances. The two Romans granted the Jewish request, and a delegation consisting of Cornelius the son of Ceron, Tryphon the son of Theudion, Dorotheus the son of Nathanael and John the son of John, went to Rome to present their petition to the emperor. When they arrived, they were seconded by Agrippa II, who was then staying at the court, as well as by his uncle, Herod of Chalcis, and Herod's son. The emperor accepted their plea and despatched a letter (45) to the officials of Jerusalem stating his decision to have the vestments of the Sanctuary guarded by the Jews, according to the arrangement under Vitellius (*Ant.* XX, 6–14).

Fadus also lacked another prerogative of the former governors: the appointment of the High Priests. This was granted to Herod of Chalcis (*Ant.* XX, 15), who used it to depose Elioneus, the last of the High Priests from Agrippa I's reign.

Fadus was confronted with difficulties from the first. Some of these arose from the relations between the Jews and Gentiles on the borders of the province, while others were caused by the growing Messianic movement. The focus of the trouble lay in a quarrel between Jews and Gentiles on the border of Peraea over the possession of a village adjoining Philadelphia. Some of the Jews wished to solve the problem by force without waiting for the decision of the procurator. Fadus saw this as a serious challenge to his authority and an affront to the Roman administration. Three Jewish activists were caught, one of whom was sentenced to death and the other two ('Amram [?] and Eleazar) were exiled (*Ant.* XX, 2–4). Another center of disturbance was the southern border of Idumaea, where a notorious brigand leader called Ptolemeus was caught and sentenced to death (*Ant.* XX, 5). We do not know if this man was a Jew.

During the earlier period of provincial rule the Messianic movement does not appear to have called for the active intervention of the Romans, except in the time of Pontius Pilate (e.g., the disturbances on Mt. Gerizim and the case of Jesus of Nazareth). The later procurators, however, were very much concerned with such affairs. Under Fadus, a large mob followed a certain Theudas to the Jordan, where he promised to emulate the miracle of Joshua by commanding the river to dry up and afford them passage across it. Fadus' reaction was no less harsh and peremptory than Pilate's in the Samaritan affair. He sent a squadron of cavalry against the fanatics gathered on the river bank. Most were taken prisoner, while Theudas was killed and his severed head brought back to Jerusalem (*Ant.* XX, 97–8).[52]

Tiberius Julius Alexander succeeded Fadus as procurator (46–48). He belonged to a family of Jewish notables of Alexandria, though he had abandoned Judaism for the Roman *cursus honorum*. For him the office in Judea merely served as another stepping stone in his career. Prior to this, he had held an important administrative post in Egypt, and his prospects for future promotion were bright. There is evidence that Tiberius Alexander had once been connected with the Herodian house — his father had given Agrippa I financial help in the flight to Italy, while his brother Marcus had been the first husband of Agrippa's daughter, Berenice. During his term of office, Tiberius was principally in contact with Herod of Chalcis, Berenice's second husband, who was still in charge of Temple affairs and responsible for appointing the High Priests. During the procuratorship of Tiberius Alexander, Ananias the son of Nedebeus was appointed High Priest. The latter was one of the notables of Jerusalem and a man of great wealth. (*Ant.* XX, 103).

There is no reason to believe that the Judeans received the renegade Tiberius with open arms, or that they preferred him to Gentile procurators. Under his administration, there were disturbances inspired by the two sons of Judah the Galilean, Jacob and Simeon. The procurator acted promptly and had them both crucified (*Ant.* XX, 102). Tiberius served for two years in Judea, and then was promoted elsewhere. We hear of him again fifteen years later (63), when he was one of the principal assistants to Domitius Corbulo in the war against the Parthians (Tacitus, *Annals*, XV, 28, 3).

The administration of Ventidius Cumanus (48–52)[53] was marked by continuous incidents and clashes between Jews and Romans. The first outbreak occurred during festival time, when a Roman soldier made an obscene gesture in the Temple as a deliberate insult to the Jewish religion. The congregation reacted furiously against the perpetrator of the outrage; some even included the procurator in their accusations. Cumanus sent his forces down from the Antonia to quell the riot, and many Jews were slain (*Ant.* XX, 105–12; *War* II, 224–7).

Another incident occurred a short time later. An imperial slave, Stephanus, was attacked and robbed by Jews near Beth-Horon. Cumanus responded by despatching troops against all the Jewish villages in the vicinity. During this punitive action one of the Roman soldiers desecrated a Torah scroll. The report quickly spread throughout the country and a large throng of Jews came to Cumanus at Caesarea to demand full punishment for the perpetrator. Cumanus realized the seriousness of the situation, which verged on rebellion. He took the advice of his *consilium* and commanded the offender's head to be cut off (*Ant.* XX, 113–7; *War* II, 228–31).

The situation grew worse with the outbreak of a quarrel between Jews and Samaritans, a matter which took up the remainder of Cumanus' term of office. This affair marked the nadir of the relations between these two peoples at the end of the period of the Second Temple. The tension is bitterly expressed in incidents such as had occurred under Coponius, and is well reflected in the parable of the Good Samaritan (Luke 10:25–37). Yet in certain cases, as in the opposition to the procurator Pilate and at the beginning of the First Revolt, both parties united against the common enemy. The Judeo-Samaritan confrontation reached its climax after an attack on Galilean pilgrims by villagers from Ginea (Ginae; Jenin), in northern Samaria. Crowds of angry Galileans clamored for the revenge of the martyred pilgrims. Their leaders complained to Cumanus, demanding the punishment of the guilty, but the procurator was in no hurry to carry out their wishes. Meanwhile, angry feelings raged in Jerusalem and preparations were made for a retaliatory action against the Samaritans. Prominent among the Jews was Eleazar the son of Deineus. He and another hothead named Alexander marched their men against the inhabitants of Samaria close to the toparchy of **Akrabattene**. Cumanus saw himself obliged to defend the Samaritans, and hastily brought up four cohorts of infantry and one cavalry squadron from Caesarea. In the subsequent action many of Eleazar's men were taken prisoner. The Jewish leaders in Jerusalem tried to persuade the people to remain calm and to avoid confrontation. Both sides came to Tyre to lay their claims before the governor of Syria, Ummidius Quadratus, who would make no decision until he reached the province. Once there, he suspended Cumanus from office and sent him to Rome to stand trial before the emperor. With him went Celer, a Roman tribune who had been involved in the incident, as well as Jewish and Samaritan leaders. Ananias the High Priest and Jonathan the son of Ananus, a former High Priest, were among the Jewish spokesmen. Cumanus and the Samaritans, now in the same boat, gained the support of some of Claudius' freedmen. The principal spokesman of the Jews at the court was Agrippa II, who had the backing of Empress Agrippina and one of her followers, Pallas, another of Claudius' freedmen. The latter was interested in the promotion of his brother, Felix, who had apparently already held office in Palestine (perhaps as govenor of Galilee), and was involved in a quarrel with Cumanus and the Samaritans. Claudius decided in favor of the Jews. Cumanus was sentenced to exile and the Samaritans were executed in Rome, while the tribune Celer was sent back to Jerusalem and executed there. Felix was appointed procurator of Judea (52), and his promotion was enthusiastically supported among the Jews by Jonathan the son of Ananus (*Ant.* XX, 118–37).[54]

Felix began office in an alliance with the Jews and ended it in an open quarrel with them (60). Both Josephus and Tacitus regard his procuratorship as a failure.[55] One should note, however, that for at least part of his term he worked in close agreement with influential circles in Judea. Ananias the son of Nedebeus continued as High Priest to strengthen his position in the country and advance his relations with the Roman administration. These were later maintained under the procurator Albinus. Ananias seems also to have been supported by Agrippa II, who had the power to dismiss and appoint high priests. With both of these authorities behind him, we can understand how Ananias managed to hang on to his position for a longer time than other High Priests of the same period (*circa* 47–59), though Joseph the son of Caiaphas served longer.[56] On the other hand, relations between Jonathan the son of Ananus and Felix worsened in spite of the former's connections with the procurator. Felix considered Jonathan a nuisance, as he was always giving the procurator moral counsel. Having actively supported Felix' candidature, he perhaps felt himself in some way responsible for the procurator's misdeeds. Josephus asserts that Felix decided to rid himself of him once and for all. He encouraged his assassination by the Sicarii, the extremist sect who were then beginning to take an active part in events. (*Ant.* XX, 162–5, *War* II, 256).

It is difficult to trace the progress of relations between Felix and the Herodian dynasty. They must have been very close, since Felix married Drusilla, one of Agrippa I's daughters, who abandoned her husband, Azizus of Emesa, for him. The mediator between them was a Jew from Cyprus, who is said to have been one of Felix' friends (another example of Felix' Jewish connections). Unlike other Gentile rulers of the East who married princesses of the Judean royalty, Felix could not accept, Judaism as a precondition for the marriage. As far as we know, Felix does not seem to have obtained the official blessing of the bride's brother, Agrippa II, nor of other representatives of the Herodian house. Of course, there were ways of overcoming all obstacles unofficially. Felix, at any rate, had good reason to advertise his link with the Herodian dynasty, and the child of the marriage was named Agrippa. He was killed in the eruption of Vesuvius in 79 A.D. (*Ant.* XX, 143–4).

The murder of Jonathan was by no means the only act of violence committed by the Sicarii under Felix; these soon became the scourge of Judea. At the beginning of his administration, Felix succeeded in capturing Eleazar the son of Deineus, whom he sent to Rome (*Ant.* XX, 161). His subsequent fate remains unknown. Besides the activities of the Sicarii and armed violence of various kinds, we also read of a widely supported Messianic movement founded by a Jewish prophet from Egypt. He gathered thousands of disciples, who followed him up to the Mount of Olives, where he promised to bring down the walls of Jerusalem before their eyes and deliver the Roman garrison into their hands. He himself would reign as king over the nation. Felix sent his soldiers against the assembled crowd and many were massacred. The prophet himself managed to escape to an unknown place of safety (*Ant.* XX, 169–72; *War* II, 261–3; Acts 21:38).

The suppression of this movement did not prevent the eruption of other disturbances, and certainly did not restore peace to the country. The massacre perpetrated by Felix' men merely served to increase the number of malcontents. The rebels intensified their struggle against the Roman authorities in the latter years of Felix' rule, believing any means justified in their attempt to strengthen their position. Raids were organized against villages that opposed them, their houses burnt down and their inhabitants sentenced to death. Thus towards the end of Felix' term of office his prestige in the countryside was undermined, while even in Jerusalem life was not normal (*Ant.* XX, 172; *War* II, 264–5).

One of the last changes made under Felix was the appointment by Agrippa II of a new High Priest, Ismael the son of Phabes,[57] who came from a family that had already produced several High Priests during the reign of Herod and in the time of the early Roman governors. The new appointment did not greatly change the face of things. The last years before the First Revolt were marked by an internecine struggle between rival high-priestly houses or between the High Priests themselves and the ordinary priests who had lost their rights and been deprived of their tithes. Acts of violence regularly occurred whenever the high-priestly families sent their servants to the threshing-floors to take the tithes by force (*Ant.* XX, 179–81).

Tension and clashes marked the rule of Felix in other parts of his province as well. Matters were especially critical in Caesarea, where the majority of the inhabitants were pagan and the Jews, though numerous and influential, were in the minority. In Caesarea, moreover, there was a legal aspect to the strife. This was connected with the civil rights of the Jews in that city, who based their claims on the argument that the city had been founded by a Jewish king. The Syro-Hellenic spokesmen for the pagans, while not denying this, based their case on the ancient name of the city, Strato's Tower. They also pointed out that Herod had not planned the city to be Jewish, or he would not have built temples in it or set up images of the gods. The case dragged on for years and was the cause of many a street fracas. As long as the clashes were confined to the civil population the Jews had the upper hand, but once the garrison, which was composed of soldiers from Sebaste and Caesarea, intervened on behalf of the pagans, the latter gained the advantage. Felix attempted to suppress the outbreaks, but his efforts were in vain. One case of provocation ended in a clear victory for the Jews, and the procurator ordered the soldiers to attack them. They plundered Jewish houses and killed many of their inhabitants (*Ant.* XX, 173–8; *War* II, 266–70). Felix was convinced that the final solution to the problems of civil rights in Caesarea was outside his competence, and so he sent off separate delegations of Jews and pagans to plead their respective cases before Nero in Rome.

Felix left Judea around the year 60[58] and was replaced by Festus. The Jews of Caesarea now used this opportunity to charge Felix before the emperor, but without success. No doubt the considerable influence in Rome of his brother, Pallas, stood Felix in good stead (*Ant.* XX, 182). It was about this time that the Jews of Caesarea lost their legal case, after the Syro-Hellenic delegation gained the support of Beryllus, who was very powerful at court.[59] This second defeat undermined the legal standing and prestige of the Jews of Caesarea, and tension in the city grew to a new pitch. The Jews were unwilling to reconcile themselves for long to a state of subjection, while the Greco-Syrian population regarded the emperor's decree as finally establishing the position of the Jews as citizens of the second class.

Felix' successor, Festus (60–62), found the country in a state of turmoil. All the troubles of the previous administration continued unabated. The extremist organizations were still active in the countryside; the Sicarii still terrorized Jerusalem; and hundreds of people enthusiastically followed Messianic visionaries. One self-styled prophet promised salvation to all who would follow him into the desert. Festus dealt with him just as Felix had dealt with the Egyptian prophet. His soldiers were ordered to attack and this time the "prophet" himself was among the slain (*Ant.* XX, 188).

Another incident which necessitated action by Festus, but one of a totally different sort, concerned the quarrel between Agrippa II and other Jewish leaders of Jerusalem, especially among the Priests. Agrippa had retained the right to supervise the Temple, and in order to obtain a better view of the Temple Mount, he increased the height of his palace. The priestly leaders regarded this as a desecration of the holy place, and built a wall to block out his view. The construction of this wall angered not only Agrippa, but also Festus, who thought that it hindered the Roman army in its task of keeping the peace in Jerusalem at festival time. Festus ordered the wall dismantled, but the Jews secured a deferment while they sent a delegation to the emperor, claiming that the removal of the wall was tantamount to the destruction of part of the Temple. The High Priest himself, Ismael the son of Phabes, went to Rome together with Helcias the Temple treasurer, and members of the board of the *decaprotoi*.[60] They found a supporter in the empress, Poppaea Sabina. Nero agreed to leave the wall standing, but detained the High Priest and the treasurer in Rome, possibly in order to appease Agrippa. Having lost his case, it would have been difficult for the king to face his opponents while they were still flushed with victory (*Ant.* XX, 189–195).

Agrippa II deposed Ismael, replacing him with a series of High Priests appointed in rapid succession. One of these was Ananus, the fifth of Ananus' sons, all the rest of whom had already held that office. His appointment came during a change of procurators (62), between the death of Festus and the arrival of Albinus. During his short tenure, Ananus brought a typically Sadducean outlook to his leadership of the Sanhedrin, which now decided cases in conformity with the Sadducean point of view. Among those condemned to death by the Sanhedrin was James the brother of Jesus, who was the leader of Jerusalem's Christian community. The Pharisees reacted unfavorably to Ananus, and sent a delegation to Agrippa, asking him to prevent any repetition of such deeds by the High Priest. Some even went to meet the new procurator, Albinus, on his arrival in Alexandria. They reminded him that Ananus had exceeded his powers by convening a Sanhedrin to deliver a capital sentence, without first obtaining the permission of the procurator. Albinus agreed, and sent an angry letter to Ananus, threatening punishment. Agrippa soon removed Ananus, who had served as High Priest for only a few months. Jeshua the son of Damneus was appointed in his place (*Ant.* XX, 197–203).

At first Albinus acted firmly against the Sicarii in an attempt to restore order in the country. Many of them were executed, but far from diminishing their activity, this merely served to increase it. The former High Priest, Ananias the son of Nedebeus, was Albinus' principal ally among the Jews. At this time Ananias' influence was at its peak. The Sicarii were quick to exploit the special relationship between these two powerful men. They now began to attack persons in Ananias' circle in order to put pressure on Albinus. One example was the kidnapping of the secretary of Eleazar the son of Ananias, who, they announced, would be released only if Ananias used his influence with the procurator to free ten Sicarii. Ananias accordingly persuaded Albinus to do so. Encouraged by their success, the Sicarii continued to use this method for gaining the release of large numbers of prisoners (*Ant.* XX, 210; cf. *War* II, 275–6). Albinus also saw it as a way of making money for himself. He was now willing to release those imprisoned by previous procurators or by the local Jewish authorities against a ransom to be paid by the prisoners' relatives (*War* II, 273).[61]

Under his administration, too, there were frequent changes of High Priests. Jeshua the son of Gamala, whose wife (Martha) came from the family of Boethus (Yoma 18a), was soon chosen to replace Jeshua the son of Damneus (*Ant.* XX, 213). The latter, however, would not accept his own dismissal and entered into a struggle with the new High Priest. The fight was carried into the streets of Jerusalem each of the rivals surrounding himself with a band of tough henchmen. Other leading persons of the high-priestly families, such as Ananias the son of Nedebeus, also joined in these street fights. Various other groups were drawn into these quarrels, including relatives of Agrippa II, e.g., Costobar and Saul (*Ant.* XX, 213–4).

Gessius Florus was the last procurator of Judea before the First Revolt. His administration (64–66) hastened the end which had clearly been foreshadowed in the previous procuratorships. The gulf between Jews and Romans widened, and tension among the people reached a new level. In one way Florus was even worse than Albinus, since he had no connections whatsoever with the Jewish upper classes, let alone with the ordinary people.

G.   The Status of the Province and its Governors in the Roman Empire

In accordance with the principles laid down by Augustus, the provinces of the Roman empire were divided into several classes. Some — especially those free from the threat of external danger — were left under the direct supervision of the Senate. These were termed senatorial provinces and did not have Roman legions garrisoned on their territory (there were exceptions, such as the senatorial province of Africa). In contrast to these the majority of provinces, whose security demanded constant supervision and the presence of legions, were under the direct control of the emperor. The emperor would despatch governors of senatorial rank, who bore the title *legatus Augusti pro praetore*, and had usually been consuls or praetors at Rome. Such a province was Syria, whose legates were chosen from among former consuls. The third type of province was directly under imperial control, but it was not governed, as were the first two, by senatorial governors, but by *equites* ("knights") selected by the emperor.

The richest and greatest of the provinces ruled by equestrian governors was Egypt. Its unique geographical position gave it a natural defense against external enemies; it had rich agricultural lands and a centralized organization, which for many generations had unified the country far more than other Roman provinces. The emperors were wary of sending governors of senatorial rank to Egypt. Instead, they appointed men from the equestrian order with the special title of *praefectus Aegypti* and having some legions (at first three and later two) at their disposal. The other provinces of this type could not compete with Egypt in wealth, size or status within the empire. Among these were Thrace, Mauretania, Noricum and Raetia. Judea was created a province of this type in 6 A.D. In the same year, Sardinia also changed over to the same kind of equestrian administration, and this too lasted sixty years. Cappadocia too, which up to 17 A.D. had been an allied kingdom of Rome, was reorganized into an equestrian province by Tiberius.

The common feature of all these equestrian provinces, with the exception of Egypt, was the absence of a permanent legionary garrison. When Augustus decided to make Judea a province in its own right, principally because of the special character of its inhabitants, he felt no need to station a legion on the spot; the auxiliary troops (*auxilia*) seemed sufficient to cope with all the needs of the administration. At that time Judea was surrounded by other provinces or by allied states, so that no external enemy threatened its safety. Even the internal security of the country seemed assured for the present, since Archelaus' deposition had been received quite favorably by the population. It therefore did not seem necessary to send a legionary force to the province. Moreover, such a small country seemed to require only a governor of equestrian rank.[62] It is also possible that this type of administration was less expensive to run.

There was one exception to the equestrian appointments among governors of Judea; this was Felix (52–60), who was a freedman. He rose to power under Claudius, the golden era for imperial freedom at Rome. Felix was also Pallas' brother, another freedman who had won an influential position in the imperial treasury. It is indeed possible that before his promotion to the procuratorship, Felix had been enrolled as a knight at Rome. This need not have been the case, however, since there are known instances of freedmen who received important posts in the provinces under the Julio-Claudian emperors.[63]

Whoever wished to climb the administrative ladder of the empire and attain the status of a governor of an equestrian province would have to gain experience as an officer in the legions or auxiliaries. Many had occupied posts in their native cities.[64] Moreover, a successful administration of Judea could serve as a springboard to other positions in the administrative hierarchy. Our knowledge of the previous history and subsequent fate of procurators of Judea is scant. Tiberius Julius Alexander was formerly governor (*epistrategos*) of Thebais in Upper Egypt. We find him in 66 A.D. occupying one of the highest positions in the empire, that of *praefectus Aegypti*. Some scholars are of the opinion that he even reached the supreme post of *praefectus praetorio* at Rome.[65] Albinus, too, came to Judea by way of Alexandria, though it is uncertain whether he actually held an administrative post there or merely used it as a stopping place on his way to Judea.[66] We do know that before he died he was procurator of Mauretania (Tacitus, *Histories*, II, 58–9). It has also been suggested that the first Roman governor of Judea, Coponius, had gained his experience in Syria.[67]

Felix seems to have been the administrator of Galilee or to have held some post in Judea before his appointment as governor.

A Roman knight would find the ground prepared for his promotion to the govenorship of a province, if he had already served in another post or had influential connections at court. It is certain that several of the governors of Judea received their appointment through the influence of friends at Rome. Felix was promoted thanks mainly to his brother Pallas, although he also had the support of the Jews, principally Jonathan the son of Ananus. Gessius Florus, the last procurator, owed this post to his wife Cleopatra, who was friendly with Empress Poppaea Sabina (*Ant.* XX, 252). Even Pontius Pilate may have been in some way obligated to Seianus, the commander of the Praetorian Guard, although this is a mere conjecture.

The length of the term of office was not stipulated by law. It depended on several factors: the general policy of the emperor regarding the provincial administration, the success or failure of the equestrian governor in establishing order and a working administration, his connections with influential circles in Rome, and a possible wish to promote him quickly to a higher position. It is known that Tiberius preferred to leave his men in the same office for long periods of time (*Ant.* XVIII, 172–7; Tacitus, *Annals*, I, 80).[68] Thus the two longest procuratorships in Judea were under Tiberius: those of Valerius Gratus (15–26) and Pontius Pilate (26–36). The latter would probably have continued in office until the accession of the next emperor, if his cruelty in crushing the Samaritan rebellion had not called for the intervention of Vitellius, the legate of Syria. The three governors appointed by Augustus (Coponius, Marcus Ambibulus and Annius Rufus) served for three years each.

Of the procurators following Agrippa I, Felix governed the longest (eight years). The average term of office was two years — the period served by Fadus, Tiberius Alexander, Festus and Albinus. Festus died in office. Apart from Felix, the longest tenure in the post-Agrippan period was that of Cumanus (48–52), which came to an end after the whole province had been thrown into disorder by four years of strife between Samaritans and Jews.

The salary of a procurator seems to have been 100,000 sesterces a year — a sum not overly large if compared to that of the governors of senatorial provinces (e.g. Asia, Syria etc.). We surmise, for example, that when Tiberius Alexander was promoted from his job of *epistrategos* of Thebais to procurator of Judea, his income rose from 60,000 to 100,000 sesterces.[69]

An interesting conclusion emerges from an examination of the origin of the governors in the period up to the First Revolt. The early ones (those

before the reign of Agrippa I) were all of Italian origin. The first belonged
to the family of the Coponii, who came from the ancient Latin city of
Tibur.[70] Scholars are of the opinion that Pontius Pilate traced his descent
to a Samnite family.[71] There are reasons for believing that other high posts
in the empire at this period were reserved for Italians only. We have at
least one good example in Judea from a Latin inscription first published in
1940. From this we learn that Herennius Capito, the procurator of Jamnia,
who served as representative of the empress Livia and the emperors Tiberius
and Gaius Caligula, came from the Italic city of Teate Marrucinorum.[72]
This case exemplifies the general practice in the empire as a whole. Until
the reign of Claudius the governors and their subordinates in the central
provincial administration were natives of Italy or at least the Latin West.
Later, however, the situation changed and the various branches of the
administration were filled with Greeks or Levantines. Tiberius Julius
Alexander was a Jew by birth, who had left his religion and was considered
by all as a Hellenized Oriental. Tacitus and Juvenal both regarded him as
Egyptian (*History* I, 11; *Satires*, I, 130). Felix was a Greek, he and his
brother Pallas claimed to trace their origin to the kings of Arcadia (*Annals*,
XII, 53, 2).[73] Florus came from Clazomenae in Ionia (*Ant*. XX, 252).
One may presume that men like Felix and Florus had a natural preference
for the Helleno-Syrian elements among the provincial population and would
tend to favor them in their quarrels with the Jews. Such procurators were
regarded by the Jews as their worst enemies. The origin of the procurators
and their bias in favor of the enemies of the Jews may be seen as one of
the causes of the unfortunate relations between the Roman authorities
and the Jewish people in the generation preceding the First Revolt.

The official title of the governors differed in the two periods under
consideration. We can be almost certain that the title *praefectus* was used in
the period of the first administrators of Judea, and that from the reign
of Claudius onward, it was replaced by *procurator*.[74] This is paralleled by
the evolution of the administrative terminology in the empire as a whole.
We do have evidence that the title *praefectus* was at first the most common one
for provincial governors of the equestrian class.[75] The change was made
in the days of Claudius when the term *procurator* almost completely replaced
the earlier one. Nonetheless, there is an inscription from Sardinia, which
proves that the title *praefectus* was still used in that island up to the reign
of Vespasian.[76] The decisive evidence concerning the history of these titles
in Judea comes from an inscription found in the theater of Caesarea referring to the *Tiberieum*. In it, Pontius Pilate is styled .. *praefectus Iuda(ea)e*.[77]
On the other hand, the official terminology used in the reign of Claudius

may be seen in a letter he sent to Jewish authorities in Jerusalem concerning the High Priest (*Ant.* XX, 14), in which Fadus is described as ἐπίτροπος (the usual Greek equivalent for *procurator*).

One of the important factors in the history of this period is the dependence of the administrator of Judea on the governor of Syria. This includes the general relationship between the province of Syria, which was governed by a legate of senatorial rank, an exconsul who held the title of *legatus Augusti pro praetore*, and that of Judea, which was administered by a member of the equestrian order. There is no doubt that Judea was by then regarded as a province in its own right. Her procurators depended directly on the emperor and in their territory enjoyed the extensive rights of any other provincial governor. Tacitus describes Judea at the time of the disturbances of A.D. 17 (the reign of Tiberius), and clearly states that it comprised a province on its own, side by side with Syria (*Annals*, II, 42, 5) (cf. *Histories*. V. 9, 3; Suetonius, *Life of Claudius*, 28). Likewise when Josephus describes the Ethnarchy of Archelaus and its position in the empire, he unequivocally refers to its transformation into a province (*War* II, 117). On the other hand, in the parallel passage on the creation of the Roman administration in the province, he says that Archelaus' territory was annexed to Syria (*Ant.* XVII, 355).[78] Tacitus too says that "Ituraea and Judea were incorporated into Syria after the deaths of their kings, Soaemus and Agrippa" (*Annals*, XII, 23).[79]

Likewise, there is abundant evidence of the interference by the governors of Syria in the affairs of Judea. The local inhabitants regarded them as superior to the procurators, and as an authority to which they could address their complaints against the governor of Judea. When the province was created, it was Quirinius, governor of Syria, who came to carry out the census. At the time of the massacre of the Samaritans by Pilate, the Samaritan leaders complained about him to the governor of Syria (Vitellius), who sent Pilate off to Rome for trial. Pilate had to obey since "it was impossible to oppose him" (*Ant.* XVIII, 89). Vitellius even appointed a temporary governor in place of the one he had suspended, and interfered in such purely internal matters of Judea as the changing of High Priests. The next governor of Syria, Petronius, received special instructions from the emperor Caligula to supervise the affairs of Judea, and this continued to be done in the reign of Agrippa I. When the local administration under Fadus became apprehensive of disturbances in Jerusalem over the problem of the High Priest's vestments, Cassius Longinus, the governor of Syria, thought it politic to come to Jerusalem.

The power wielded by the governor of Syria in the affairs of Judea is well illustrated by the way in which Quadratus dealt with Cumanus. Receiving a complaint from the Samaritans regarding the Jews, the governor himself went to Judea, where he ordered the execution of a number of people and then sent Cumanus to Rome, together with a delegation of Jewish and Samaritan leaders. On the very eve of the First Revolt, we hear of Jews demonstrating to the governor of Syria, Cestius Gallus, over the acts of Florus in Judea.

It is clear, then, that the Syrian governors' supervision of and interference in the affairs of Judea was habitual. In this respect there is no difference between the early and later administrators of Judea. Part of this concern may have emanated from a special authority vested in certain of the governors by the emperor. It is reasonable to assume that Quirinius had been specially instructed to carry out a census in the province and to lay the foundations for an administration. Similarly, Vitellius had more authority than the usual governor of Syria, since he was a kind of governor-general appointed over all the provinces of the eastern empire (Tacitus, *Annals*, VI, 32, 3). Quadratus, too, had the right to decide matters concerning the procurators. Nevertheless, there still remain instances that can only be explained by assuming that the governor of Syria had special rights to act in Judea.[80]

The dependence of Judea on Syria was in the main a result of the difference in the importance and prestige of their respective governors. The fact that the force of the disposal of the governor of Judea comprised only auxiliaries and was not sufficient to suppress a serious riot, let alone a full-scale rebellion, meant that in every crisis he was dependent on the legate of Syria. Only the latter could send the legions necessary to restore order. Since the procurator's decisions and actions affected a wide range of affairs, including matters of cult and religion, to which the Jews were particularly sensitive, it followed that there would be frequent need for the use of external forces. The procurator of Judea, therefore, had always to take the possible reaction of the legate at Antioch into consideration.

It should also be remembered that the governor of Syria was not an ordinary legate; his status was higher than others in the empire. From the reign of Tiberius onward, he had the powerful force of four legions at his command. He it was who held the post of commander-in-chief of the imperial forces in the East, and who was responsible for the defense of the Parthian frontier. Not only was he an ex-consul, but in some cases among the most prominent men in the Roman society of his day. He would naturally overshadow the equestrian prefects and procurators who administered Judea. For the most part, then, the description of Judea as an appendage of Syria is justified from a comparison of their respective governors. It was the governor of Syria who had greater importance and rank, who was often invested with special authority by the emperor, and who always had to come to the aid of his relatively powerless neighbor to the south.

On the other hand, we should not forget that the procurators of Judea did have much freedom of action in purely internal affairs (the judicial system, finance, the command of the local garrisons, etc.) and they were appointed directly by the emperor. Only legates with special authority, such as Vitellius, could dismiss and appoint procurators of Judea according to their idea of the needs of the empire. One should also consider that the relative power of the two governors was influenced in no small degree by their connections in Rome. Pilate was dismissed by Vitellius five years after the death of his supposed patron, Seianus.

For the native Judeans, as for other provincials, it was possible to oppose the tyrannical or oppressive measures of a governor or even to indict the governor himself if his actions had made him particularly hated. When Augustus created the principate, he undoubtedly meant to bring relief to the provinces after their suffering under the republic. It was certainly no mean achievement to put an end to the civil wars and the extortions accompanying them, which had brought economic ruin to the provinces. But even under the principate things did not always go as they should. It was still possible for governors to exploit the natives for their own benefit or to have people arbitrarily executed. Documents from Egypt and information from ancient literature on the rebellions in the west of the empire (Gaul and Britain) testify to the harsh treatment of the provincials. The history of Judea abounds in cruel and corrupt governors, such as Pilate, Felix, Albinus or Florus.

It was difficult to keep close check on the activities of the provincial administrator from distant Rome. Josephus writes that Agrippa II, when trying to pacify the crowds in Jerusalem, assured them by way of comfort that the emperor was unaware of the misdeeds of Florus (*War* II, 352). Legally the provincials could indict the governors for extortion. However, it was impossible to bring anyone to court who was still occupying a public post. They had to wait until he finished his term, or else try to influence the emperor to have him dismissed.[81] In Agrippa's speech, the people were reminded of the fact that Florus would not stay for ever, and that they could hope for fairer treatment from his successors. Nor was it an easy matter to send a delegation to Rome. Permission first had to be sought from the governor, and this was not always granted. When, for example, the governor himself was implicated in an illegality, he would hardly wish to have the matter looked into by Rome. The normal method of charging a governor was to wait until after he had left his post in the province. Cumanus, for instance, was sentenced to exile after he had been dismissed (52). In the case of Cumanus' successor, Felix, the Jews were not so successful. On handing over the reins of office, Felix was accused before Nero by the Jewish leaders of Caesarea. He would possibly have lost his case were it not for the influence of his brother Pallas, who intervened for him.

It may be assumed that the provincials often refrained from taking legal action against their governor because of the uncertain chances of success, or the governor's connections at Rome, or the enormous expense involved in the proceedings. At the same time the relatively long list of governors indicted for extortion is noteworthy. It is not divided equally among the various provinces. Delegates from a province with no special influence obviously had considerably less chance of success than those from a province which made up an important part of the Greco-Roman world.

Nonetheless, the governor always had to consider the threat of a court case, and could not entirely overlook the possibility of being indicted for his policy in the province. He usually attempted, therefore, to win the favor of influential people in the provinces in the hope that they would speak up for him in time of need.[82] The Jewish circles considered worth cultivating by the Roman adminstration were Herod's family and the upper ranks of the high-priestly houses. It was principally the Herodian princes who made most powerful impression at Rome. A good example is Agrippa II, who influenced the emperor in the legal decision against Cumanus. A procurator like Albinus even tried to appease the populace before his retirement by releasing all prisoners (*Ant.* XX, 215).[83]

Josephus asserts that as Florus' misdeeds were notorious, he planned to drive the Jews to rebellion and so prevent them from instigating any judicial examination of his office (*War* II, 282–3). Philo makes a similar statement regarding the procurator of Jamnia (Capito), who feared the results of an enquiry into his ill-gotten gains and thus wished to blacken the Jews in the emperor's eyes (*Legatio ad Gaium,* 199). There is no evidence to suggest that the procurators were inhibited in any way by the presence in Judea of other high-ranking Roman officials or by the visit of distinguished members of Roman government or society. It is true that in other provinces there were sometimes clashes within the administration itself, such as occurred in Britain during the reign of Nero. In that province there was open hostility between the governor, Suetonius Paulinus, and the financial procurator, who brought about Paulinus' dismissal (Tacitus, *Annals,* XIV,

38–9). The procurator of the imperial estate at Jamnia was in direct contact with the court (*Ant.* XVIII, 163). This of course also served the emperor as an independent source of information regarding events in Judea. It seems probable however, that important officials usually collaborated with one another against the Jews, and covered up for each other's misdemeanors.

The origin and cultural background of the post-Agrippan procurators, and the location of their headquarters in the anti-Jewish center of Caesarea, inclined them more towards the Graeco-Syrian city-dwellers than to the Jews. Nevertheless, there were strong ties between some procurators and certain Jewish circles. Most noteworthy were the relations between the Herodian dynasty and some of the administrators. Though Pilate was for a considerable time on unfriendly terms with Herod Antipas, even this was put right in the end (Luke 23:12). Festus had connections with Agrippa II and his sister, Berenice (Acts 25:13–27; 26:1–32). Felix demonstrated his affinity to the Herodian house by marrying Drusilla. At first, too, he had a strong attachment to Jonathan the son of Ananus (the former High Priest). Albinus is known to have cooperated with the ex-High Priest Ananias the son of Nedebeus. Thus in spite of the natural affinity of the procurators for the Hellenized cities, they did find some points of contact with the Jews, and both sides were able to put on the appearance of friendship. In this Florus differed from previous procurators. He played the part of the tyrant of Judea in every respect, and it is doubtful whether he had any contact at all with the Jews. Even his relations with the Herodian dynasty seem to have been quite uncordial, and neither Agrippa nor Berenice appear to have had any influence with him.

H. TAXES, JUSTICE AND THE ARMY

Under Herod and Archelaus there was no direct contact between the Roman administration and the Jewish taxpayer. The latter usually vented his anger on officials or tax-farmers acting on behalf of the Jewish ruler. The situation changed after 6 A.D., when the Roman administration itself took over the responsibility for collecting the revenue. The Romans seem to have largely adopted the methods of tax collection used in Judea under the previous régime. They were assisted by the local administrative institutions, and only necessary changes were made. There is no reason for believing that the taxes were raised above their previous level.

The taxation system in Judea was based on the census. In Egypt, for instance, a census was held every fourteen years.[84] Little is known of the situation in other provinces, and it is difficult to decide which method was prevalent in them. The creation of a new province or the basic reorganization of an existing one necessitated the holding of a census. Thus in 12 B.C.E. a census was held in Gaul by Augustus' stepson, Drusus, for the purpose of reorganizing the province (Livy, *Periochae*, 138). There was another census there in 16 A.D. (Tacitus, *Annals*, II, 6).[85] The census associated with Quirinius was carried out when Judea was created a province, and a census for the whole of Syria was held about the same time.

We do not know for certain whether any further general censuses were made in Judea other than the first one. There are stories of a population census held on the eve of the First Revolt, under Cestius Gallus in Syria and Agrippa II in Judea. These connect the assessment with the number of Passover sacrifices (*War VI*, 422–4; Pes. 64b), but it is difficult to discern what lies beneath these stories. It is possible that the violent Jewish reaction to the census of Quirinius made the Romans wary of attempting any new census, and forced them to rely on other methods of ascertaining changes in population and property. Egypt, in fact, seems to be the only clearly documented case of a province where censuses were regularly held during the Julio-Claudian period.

The land tax furnished the main part of the revenues collected by the Romans in Judea, though there are no recorded data which would allow us to estimate the amount of taxes at this period. Furthermore, the Judeans were also liable to the poll tax — well known from Egypt under the name of *laographia* (census). According to Ulpian, the jurist who lived in the Severan period, the more all-embracing *tributum capitis* in Syria was levied on every male between the ages of fourteen and sixty-five and on every female between twelve and sixty-five (*Digest*, L, 15, 3). Probably certain privileged classes in Judea, as in Egypt, were either completely exempt from the poll tax or paid according to a reduced rate. These included the inhabitants of the Greek cities, and special classes of Jewish society. The New Testament indicates that the usual poll tax in Judea at the end of the period of the Second Temple was set at a *denarius* per head Mark 12:13–17; Matthew 22:15–22; Luke 20:20–6).

There were, of course, other sources of revenue in Judea apart from the land tax and poll tax. We may complete the picture from fragmentary references in our sources or by comparison with the situation in other provinces. Josephus mentions a tax on the houses in Jerusalem, which Agrippa I cancelled for the benefit of the inhabitants (*Ant.* XIX, 299). There is no indication of the size of the total levy in Judea, or of how the administration's income and expenditure were balanced. In the speech attributed to Agrippa II at the beginning of the First Revolt it is stated that the imperial income from Egypt in a month exceeded that from Judea in a whole year (*War* II, 386). A remark of this sort, however, is not of much value. Moreover, the picture is incomplete unless we take into consideration the revenues which found their way to Rome from the vast imperial estates in the country. At any rate, there is no doubt that the taxes in Judea were felt as a heavy burden, as they were in other provinces.

In Tacitus' discussion of the events in 17 A.D., during the reign of Tiberius — an emperor who did not particularly increase taxation — he notes that Syria and Judea were exhausted by the burden of tribute and requested relief (*Annals*, II, 42, 5). The situation appears to have deteriorated under Nero.[86] Documents from Egypt and literary sources on taxation clearly show that the tribute was exacted with great severity, causing extreme hardship in the country and the flight from the town to escape the tax-collectors (Philo, *De legibus specialibus*, III, 159–62).[87]

The custom tolls were an addition to the already heavy burden of the country. It appears that an octroi was exacted at the gates of the city on fruit sold in the markets of Jerusalem. The administration obtained considerable revenue from levies on imports such as spices from Arabia. The duty on these was levied at excise offices, and was very high (Pliny, *Natural History*, XII, 63–5). Unlike the taxes, however, these duties affected only a minority of the Jewish population. We do have some information regarding the customs houses at the major ports of Judea (Caesarea and Jaffa). One of the edicts of Julius Caesar from the time of Hyrcanus II testifies to the considerable revenue from the customs at Jaffa, but we do not know anything about subsequent development at that port. We may presume that the growth of Caesarea somewhat diminished the importance of Jaffa. We know more about the customs houses inland. Zacchaeus (Zakkai), the chief tax-collector of Jericho, was in charge of the tollhouse between Judea and Peraea during the time of Herod Antipas (Luke 19:1–2). The Gospels tell us of tax-collectors in the Galilee (Matthew 9:10; Luke 5:29).

The private estates of the emperor also provided him with a considerable income. These were the result of bequests to the emperor by rulers of the Herodian dynasty. The most outstanding examples are those of Jamnia and the lands around Jericho, which Salome (Herod's sister) had left to the empress Livia. After the latter's death (29 A.D.), the estates passed to her son Tiberius, and thereafter to his successors. The world-famous balsam groves of En-gedi and the vicinity of Jericho were of great economic importance to the state treasury.

In addition to the taxes and dues exacted from the inhabitants of Judea, there was also a corvée. This was an ancient institution in the East, which the Hellenistic and Roman authorities continued to maintain. It was widely abused in the Roman provinces, as is testified by documents, especially those from Egypt. During his stay in Egypt in 19 A.D., Germanicus tried to curb this practice, and the same practice was criticized in the edict of Capito, prefect of Egypt.[88] The New Testament, too, cites examples of corvée in Judea, showing how widespread it was. In accordance with this custom, the soldiers pressed Simon of Cyrene into carrying Jesus' cross (Matthew 5:41, 27:32; Mark 15:21; Luke 23:26). It was regarded in the Mishnah as a fact of life (B.Meẓ. 6, 3; Yer. Sheq. 8, 51a).

The governors of Judea had the right to mint their own coins.[89] Examples of these have been found even in such far-off provinces of the empire as Epirus and Gallia Narbonensis.[90] The coins are usually dated by the current official era. Under Augustus the date was reckoned from the battle of Actium, and under Tiberius, Claudius and Nero by the year of their own accession. Not all governors appear to have minted coins, and only those of five have been found. These include the first two governors of the reign of Augustus, two under Tiberius (Valerius Gratus, Pontius Pilate), and on one (Felix) from the time of Claudius and Nero. The last three procurators apparently did not issue coins. Like the Jewish rulers before them, the Romans did not mint silver coins in the province, but only bronze. All of them, with the exception of Pilate, paid due regard to Jewish religious scruples. The coins show sheaves of barely, palm trees, palm leaves, bunches of fruit, cornucopiae, vine branches, leaves and figs. On the coins of Felix there are also anchors and crossed spears. Pilate's coins are exceptional in depicting pagan symbols, such as the *lituus* or the *simpulum* used in Roman sacrifices.

The governor was supreme judge in his province. In practice, civil law was still in the hands of the various autonomous Jewish institutions, following the custom in other parts of the empire, though in principle the procurator could also decide civil cases. This was sometimes a matter of course in Judea, if one of the parties was pagan. We do not know, however, what was the practice during the period preceding the First Revolt.

The exercise of criminal justice was the exclusive prerogative of the procurator. This is reflected in the Gospel of John (18:31), where the Jewish authorities admit that they have no power to execute anyone

We may compare this with the Jerusalem Talmud (Sanh. 1, 18a: "For forty years, until the destruction of the Temple, they did not judge in capital cases"; cf. Shab. 15a). As we have mentioned, Judea was not exceptional in this — the same state of affairs existed in all the other provinces. This we know from an inscription found at Cyrene, recording the fourth edict of Augustus (7–6 B.C.E.), according to which the governor himself was bound to judge capital cases or to appoint a tribunal in his place and invested with his authority.[91]

The governors were entitled to judge provincials and to carry out death sentences without the need for additonal confirmation from Rome. Josephus refers to this (*War* II, 117) when he discusses the authority of the first procurator, Coponius, to execute people.

Clearly, the procurators of Judea did not use capital punishment sparingly; indeed, we may assume that executions were a common occurrence under their rule. Judea, however, was no different even in this respect from the other provinces. Lucius Valerius Messalla Volesus, governor of Asia during the reign of Augustus, is reported to have three hundred people executed in one day (Tacitus, *Annals*, III, 68, 1; Seneca *De ira* II 5, 5).[92] In certain circumstances however, the procurators of Judea did indeed refrain from taking the decision themselves, and sent the accused to be tried at Rome. Wherever the case itself or the sentence arising from it was of political importance, it was obviously safer to pass the matter on to Rome for the emperor to decide.

In Judea, as in other provinces, an accused person who had Roman citizenship was a special case. Some were soldiers of the garrison, mainly officers of the auxiliaries such as Claudius Lysias, who is remembered for his part in the arrest of the apostle Paul (Acts 22:28). Many, however, were Jews, of whom some were freedmen (a synagogue of freedmen in Jerusalem is mentioned in Acts 6:9). Moreover, some Jews were even enrolled in the equestrian order (*War* II, 308). The rights of a Roman citizen in a province are well illustrated in the case of Paul (Acts, Chapters 21–26). Claudius Lysias wished to have him beaten, but gave up the idea when he learned that Paul was a citizen of Rome, since law forbade the flogging of Roman citizens. When Paul was brought before Festus, he demanded that his case be heard by the emperor (Acts 25:11); Festus asked the advice of his *consilium* on the matter. Application for trial before the emperor did not constitute an appeal from a lower court to a higher one, nor did the imperial justice fill the role of a court of appeal but rather that of a court of first instance.

Not every procurator, however, was as conscientious as Festus regarding the rights of Jews with Roman citizenship. Florus, at least, had some of them flogged or even crucified, even though they were of the equestrain order. Florus apparently justified his act by claiming that these were rebels against the emperor, and therefore enemies of Rome who automatically forfeited their privileges.[93]

In spite of considerable research on the subject, we still do not know the exact limits of the procurator's authority in judging such cases. Recent enquiry suggests that at this period the procurator did in fact have the right to judge Roman citizens in the province.[94] Yet if the accused could reasonably claim that he could be denied justice if his trial were held in the province itself, he could request to stand trial in Rome. When Paul demanded this right, Festus consulted his council and granted his request. Another scholar has advanced the theory that the procurators of the Julio-Claudian period were entitled to judge capital cases of Roman citizens, but only if they were clearly defined by statute laws in contrast to those which fell extra ordinem. Any other capital charge necessitated a trial at Rome.[95] Such a hypothesis, however, seems too artificial.

Many scholars hold the view that Roman law did in fact allow a Roman citizen to claim the right to be judged by the emperor, but since certain procurators were expressly granted the "right of capital punishment" (*jus gladii*), they were also authorized to judge Roman citizens. The granting of this power to them in the period under discussion is not sufficiently attested, however. In the opinion of these scholars, the authority granted to Coponius (according to Josephus) refers to this governor and does not imply that similar authority was granted to his successors. Yet it is doubtful whether Josephus was indeed referring to a power granted concerning Roman citizens to Coponius. It seems more likely that he was writing about the general authority of a governor to judge provincials in capital cases.[96] It is also highly unlikely that he intended a distinction between Coponius and his successors.

Another hypothesis currently in vogue claims that the scope of the *jus gladii* in the Julio-Claudian period was limited to cases of Roman citizens who served in the army.[97] In this way, Festus lacked the right to try Paul, who was a civilian, against his will. As pointed out above, it is difficult to arrive at a definite conclusion on this matter. We only know with certainty that Roman citizens did enjoy legal rights which were denied to provincials. These undoubtedly included, in some cases at least, the privilege of being tried before the emperor. It seems that in this, as in other matters, there was some measure of flexibility: much depended on the position of the procurator himself.

The governor was the commander-in-chief of the provincial army. Since Judea was an equestrian and not a senatorial province, there were no legions stationed there. There were only the troops of the *auxilia*, usually composed of men (with the exception of the officers) to whom Roman citizenship was granted after military service. Only at times of crisis were some of the Syrian-based legions transferred to Judea. Syria was the headquarters of the imperial forces for the eastern provinces. Its legions formed the "army of the Euphrates," (*Legatio ad Gaium*, 207); it was they who were mainly responsible for the defense of the empire against the Parthian enemy. During the Julio-Claudian period the relations between these two powers hovered between peace and war. One of the main bones of contention was the kingdom of Armenia. The might of the Roman empire was generally superior to that of the Parthian kingdom. The latter, however, had managed to gain a foothold on the Euphrates frontier and the regions bordering on it, thus threatening Roman rule in Syria and Asia Minor. Conditions in the West did not always make it possible to transfer legions from Europe in order to build up military superiority in the East. It was therefore usual for the main defense of the eastern provinces to fall on the shoulders of the garrison of Syria. We may thus understand the attitude of the Romans towards events in countries neighboring on Syria. Of these Judea was then the only province with an active anti-Roman movement, which led in time to the First Revolt. It was only gradually that the dangers and implications of the Judean situation became apparent to the emperors. These involved so many military and political problems regarding the East as a whole that the Romans, after the crushing of the Great Revolt, finally concluded that auxiliary troops were not enough for Judea and would have to be replaced by a permanent legionary force.

From the reign of Tiberius onward, four of the empire's twenty-five legions were based in Syria (double the force in Egypt; Tacitus, *Annals*, IV, 5).[98] At that time the Asian provinces had no legions at all. Of the four Syrian legions, only one was stationed at Antioch. Southwest of Antioch, at Laodicea ad Mare, was the camp of the Sixth Legion (Ferrata; Tacitus, *Annals* II, 79, 2). It is conjectured that the legion closest to Judea was the one camped northwest of Emesa, at Raphaneae. The Tenth Legion (Fretensis) was posted near the Euphrates at Cyrrhus (northeast of Antioch) adjoining the allied kingdom of Commagene (Tacitus, *Annals* II, 57, 2).

There are many recorded instances when it was necessary for the Syrian legions to intervene in the affairs of Judea. Varus marched a legionary lorce to Jerusalem (*Ant.* XVII, 286; *War* II, 67); Petronius took two fegions — half of the Syrian Army — to help him enforce Gaius' decrees (*Ant.* XVIII, 262);[99] while Cestius Gallus had an equally large number of men at his disposal for the purpose of crushing the First Revolt in Jerusalem

(*War* II, 500). The latter force was made up of the Twelfth Legion and two thousand men from the remaining legions in Syria.

In peaceful years, when there was no rebellion or threat of strife in Judea, the garrison force was enough to keep order. It was composed of some five infantry cohorts, each of which numbered 500 men,[100] and one squadron of cavalry — a total of 3000 men. The main force was enlisted from the cities of Sebaste and Caesarea and was created by Herod. These two cities continued to furnish the Romans with the recruits for the local garrison.[101] Josephus tells us that the soldiers from Sebaste and Caesarea used the occasion of the death of Agrippa I to insult his memory (*Ant.* XIX, 356). Referring to the enmity between the Jews and the pagans of Caesarea during the reign of Nero, he says that the pagans relied on the garrison of the city as it was mostly made up of soldiers from Caesarea and Sebaste (*Ant.* XX, 176). In other places, he mentions only those of Sebaste (*Ant.* XX, 122; *War* II, 236). These cohorts are also mentioned in Latin inscriptions dating after the year 70 A.D., when these units were seconded to places outside Judea (a cavalry squadron: *C.I.L.*, III, no. 2916; VIII, no. 9359). It seems likely that the official Roman abbreviation for these troops was "the Sebastenes," perhaps because Sebaste, rather than Caesarea, was the first place in which this militia was enlisted. Possibly, too, the Sebastenes supplied a larger number of soldiers to the force (*Ant.* XIX, 365; cf. *War* III, 66).

Sometimes other auxiliary forces were active in Judea. We read of an Italian cohort (Acts 10:1), one of whose centurions was called Cornelius. There is indeed epigraphic evidence for the existence of an Italian cohort in Syria, and this cohort might very well have served for some time in Judea too.[102]

The headquarters of the garrison forces was in Caesarea (*War* III, *loc. cit.*, *Ant.* XVIII, 55). In Jerusalem, too, there was usually a garrison whose main task was to ensure public order on the feast days (*War* II, 224; V, 244). Roman garrisons were also scattered throughout the various fortresses of the country, e.g., at Cypros and Machaerus (*War* II, 484–5). On the other hand, we have no real evidence for the existence of a Roman fleet at this time. It was evidently the events of the First Revolt which led to the formation of a naval force for the province of Syria (*classis Syriaca*).[103]

I. Cities: Gentile and Jewish

The Hellenistic cities of Palestine gained a new lease of life with the collapse of the Hasmonean kingdom. The advent of Pompey and Gabinius marks the beginning of a new era in their history. The reign of Herod and those of his sons in their respective territories increased the number of Hellenistic cities. These, and principally Sebaste and Caesarea, became strongholds of resistance against the Jewish majority. They came to resemble completely such older cities as Accho-Ptolemais and Ascalon, which had been outside the boundaries of Herod's kingdom and the province of Judea. Sebaste and Caesarea, as we have seen, were the main recruiting centers for the auxiliaries of the provincial forces. Ascalon, too, had its role in the imperial military scheme. At Ptolemais discharged veterans were settled, and under Claudius the city gained the status of a Roman colony. The fact that the garrison troops in Judea were based on the Hellenistic cities tightened the bonds between the Roman authorities and the local inhabitants, especially as it was the Jews who necessitated the use of the army.

In fact, with the exception of Sebaste, there was a large Jewish population in all the Hellenistic cities. Their relations with the Syro-Hellenistic majority were usually tense. The cities in Palestine and across the Jordan flourished during the first century. They continued to produce men of culture and even some who had influence at the imperial court (e.g. Apelles of Ascalon).

Ptolemais and Ascalon were not included in the province. Nevertheless, they did influence events in Judea, and their affairs were bound up with those of the province. This is also true to some extent for Tyre, whose territory bordered on the northern Jewish settlements in Upper Galilee. That of Ptolemais reached Chabulon in Galilee (Josephus, *Life*, 213) and Beth-She'arim in the Valley of Yezreel (*op. cit.*, 118). The relations of Ptolemais with the Jews of neighboring Galilee were traditionally bad. Ptolemais was one of the first cities to be attacked by the Jews at the beginning of the First Revolt (*War* II, 459). On the other hand, Josephus reports that the inhabitants of the city massacred some two thousand Jews there (*War* II, 477). The first Hellenized city south of the Carmel was Dora, which was not part of Judea. It too served as one of the centers of the Roman administration's anti-Jewish activities.

Caesarea was the capital of the province, the seat of the procurator and the headquarters of the garrison. Thanks to its function as capital and its port installations, which were the most developed on the whole of the Palestinian coast, it flourished and soon grew into a large town (*War* III, 409). The internal peace of the city was frequently disturbed by the struggles between the Syro-Hellenistic majority and the Jewish minority, which was rich and strong and claimed the rights of citizenship.

Ascalon, too, held a special position in this period. Pliny describes it as a free city (*oppidum Ascalo liberum*; *Natural History*, V, 68). Relations between its Jewish and non-Jewish inhabitants were generally hostile at the end of the period of the Second Temple. The Ascalonite, Apelles, had great influence with Gaius Caligula and was regarded as one of those mainly responsible for provoking the emperor against the Jews. At the beginning of the first Revolt the Jews also attacked Ascalon, and here too it is reported that the city's 2,500 Jews were massacred by the non-Jewish inhabitants (*War* II, 477). The Jews failed in their attempt to conquer the city. Both Philo and Josephus stress the enmity of the Ascalonites towards the Jews. Less important at this period from the standpoint of Judeo-Gentile relations was the role of Gaza, although clashes also occurred here at the beginning of the First Revolt (*War* II, 460).

Of major importance was Beth-Shean (Scythopolis), which had strong ties with the Hellenistic cities in Transjordan and was a member of the Decapolis, the league of the Ten Cities (Pliny, *Natural History*, V, 74). By the end of this period it had attained considerable size (*War* III, 446). Part of Vespasian's forces camped there in his Galilean campaign. It seems that relations between the Gentile majority and the Jewish minority were friendlier here than in other cities. The Jews even cooperated with their pagan neighbors against the Jewish rebels. This, however, did not save them from being treacherously killed by their fellow citizens during the course of the fighting (*War* II, 466–76).

Gerasa, east of the Jordan, is well known to us on account of its wonderful ruins and the exceptionally large number of its inscriptions.[104] The archaeological and epigraphical evidence shows that the city, which was liberated under the settlement of Pompey, flourished from the first half of the first century A.D. This resulted from the *pax Romana* of the Julio-Claudian period and from the fact that the city was situated near the main road from Petra, the Nabataean capital, to Damascus and the other cities of Syria to the north. The transit trade served as the basis of its economy, and the relations with the Nabataeans left their mark on the development of the city.[105] Gerasa, as other cities of the Transjordan, was administered as part of the province of Syria. Its proximity to the great center of Jewish population in Peraea resulted in close connections with the Jews of the vicinity.

Much can be learned of the history of Gerasa from its inscriptions.[106] The city was organized in the usual way of Hellenistic cities in the Orient; it had a *boule* and *demos*. Executive power was in the hands of a body of archons, at the head of which was a chairman (*proedros*). There was also the *decaprotoi* (the "first ten"), known to us from Jerusalem, Tiberias and other places of the Roman East. Like other Greek cities, Gerasa had its own gymnasium, under the supervision of a gymnasiarch elected every six months. The inscriptions mention other city officials, such as the *agoranomos* who was in charge of the city market, and officials who supervised public building.

An important Jewish settlement existed at Gerasa. Relations between the Jews and the pagan majority were friendlier than in most other cities of Palestine. With the outbreak of the First Revolt, Gerasa was exceptional in that its pagan inhabitants not only refrained from massacring the Jews, but left them with the option of staying or of leaving the city under the charge of the Gerasenes (*War* II, 480).

J. The Reign of Agrippa II

One of the peculiar facts of Jewish history in the last years before the destruction of the Temple is the unique position granted to the Herodian dynasty within the framework of the Roman empire. At the time of the early governors of Judea, Herod Antipas and Philip still ruled over large areas of Palestine, and at the beginning of Claudius' reign Agrippa I was made king over the whole country and ruled it for three years. The Romans began to regard the Herodian dynasty as a friendly house, which could be conveniently used for their political ends even outside Palestine, mainly in Syria and Asia Minor. In 41 A.D. Agrippa I's brother, Herod, was made king over Chalcis by the Romans, where he reigned until 48 A.D. Herod the Great's grandson, Tigranes, the son of Alexander and Glaphyra (daughter of King Archelaus of Cappadocia), was appointed king of Armenia by the Romans (*Ant.* XVIII, 139). Tigranes' nephew was also made king over that country (*Ant.* XVIII, 140). This branch of the family, however, became totally alienated from Judaism; we do not hear of a single instance of their intervention on behalf of the Jews. The Romans also made Aristobulus, the son of Herod of Chalcis, king of Armenia Minor (*Ant.* XX, 158; Tacitus, *Annals*, XIII, 7, 1).

Herod's sons were generally on excellent terms with the Roman officials, and some even managed to make their way into the upper class of Roman society. Salome, Herod's sister, had established friendly relations with the empress Livia. Her daughter Berenice (the mother of Agrippa I) was a good friend of Antonia, the sister-in-law of Tiberius. One of Antonia's sons (Claudius) and one of her grandsons (Gaius Caligula) ascended the throne, and Agrippa's connections with them were decisive for his career. The sons of this dynasty even gained entrance into the Roman adminstration of Syria. Agrippa I before his accession, and his brother Aristobulus, both served on the staff of Flaccus, the legate of Syria (*Ant.* XVIII, 151).

The Herodians were also considered the unofficial spokesmen of the Jews vis-à-vis the principate, even when they were not rulers in Judea itself and merely served as representatives at the court whenever they could influence the emperor in their favor. These strong ties were regarded by the Greeks, especially of Alexandria, as a nuisance. In one of the fragments of the *Acts of the Alexandrine Martyrs* the Alexandrian gymnasiarch vilifies Claudius by claiming that he was the son of the Jewess Salome (H.A. Musurillo, *Acts of the Pagan Martyrs*, Oxford, 1954, no. IV, Rec. A, col. III, 1. 11). The reference is to Herod's sister Salome, who had close ties with Livia.

After the death of Herod of Chalcis, Agrippa II remained as the central figure of the Herodian dynasty and the one closest to the Jewish people. He was the only son among the four remaining children of Agrippa I — his brother Drusus had died while still very young. Although Claudius did not allow Agrippa to succeed to his father's throne, the young prince had at least acquired a certain degree of influence. He was thus able to fulfill the traditional role of a prince of the Herodian house in the Julio-Claudian period, that of representing the Jews at the imperial court. The Jews first needed his help shortly after the renewal of the provincial administration in Judea. The intervention of Agrippa, his uncle Herod of Chalcis and his cousin Aristobulus, ensured the Jews success in their struggle over the supervision of the high-priestly vestments.

Agrippa was requested to intervene once more after the disturbances between the Jews and the Samaritans during the procuratorship of Cumanus. It was largely due to his attempts that the emperor decided in favor of the Jews. At that time, Agrippa was the ruler of Chalcis in place of his uncle Herod.[107] On his succession to that throne he began his career as an allied monarch of Rome, a career that lasted more than forty years. The territorial aggrandizement of his kingdom began some years afterwards, when he was granted the former domains of Philip; these had also formed the core of his father's kingdom. At the same time, Chalcis was taken from Agrippa's realm (*Ant.* XX, 138; 53–54 A.D.). His domain was next increased at the beginning of Nero's reign by the addition to his kingdom (54–55 A.D.) of the Galilean cities of Tiberias and Taricheae, as well as part of the territory of Peraea (*Ant.* XVIII, 159; *War* II, 252).[108] Consequently, Agrippa was now the ruler over a mostly Jewish population.

Agrippa certainly never attained the same influence or standing as his father, or even Herod Antipas. Nonetheless, he did reach a position of importance among the other kings allied with Rome. At the beginning of

Nero's reign, when the Romans were about to march against the Parthians, Agrippa too was asked to supply military assistance (Tacitus, *Annals*, XIII, 7, 1).

Faithful to the tradition of his forebears, Agrippa II showed some interest in the Greek cities outside his kingdom especially Berytus. He changed the name of his capital, Caesarea Philippi, to Neronias in honor of the emperor (*Ant.* XX, 211). The First Revolt put him in an extremely difficult position. He and his sister Berenice tried their best to calm the people of Jerusalem, but all his efforts, including the despatch of troops to the city, were in vain. He then sent forces to help Cestius Gallus recapture Jerusalem from the rebels. The rebel's victory over Gallus hastened the revolt of Agrippa's Jewish subjects. Not only Galilee (Tiberias and Taricheae) was in a state of insurrection but also Gaulanitis, led by the fortress of Gamala.

Agrippa never managed to crush the revolt in his kingdom with his own forces. He was defeated at the siege of Gamala, and did not regain his control of Tiberias. The picture changed with the arrival of Vespasian. Agrippa again actively assisted the Romans; he helped them to subdue Tiberias and took part in the siege of Gamala, in which he was wounded (Josephus, *Life*, 352; *War* IV, 14). Both he and Berenice later enthusiastically supported the Flavians in their bid to gain control of the empire (Tacitus, *Histories*, II, 81).

After the conquest of Jerusalem and the final victory of the Romans, the boundaries of Agrippa's kingdom were extended northward to include Arca (northeast of Tripoli; *War* VII, 97). It is difficult to determine in what way the romance between Titus and Berenice assisted Agrippa's advancement. Berenice took up permanent residence in Rome from 75 to 79 A.D. Towards the end of Vespasian's reign, Titus gave in to the pressure of public opinion and Berenice left the city. It is true that she returned to Rome in 79 A.D. after Titus' accession, but he was again forced to send her away.[109] Agrippa still reigned for most of Domitian's rule, but he seems to have been no longer king when Domitian was assassinated in 96 A.D.[110] Thus ended the role of the Herodian dynasty in Jewish history; Agrippa II was the last Jewish king of that house, and his territories were absorbed into the Roman empire.

CHAPTER V

THE ECONOMY OF JUDEA
IN THE PERIOD OF THE SECOND TEMPLE

by J. Klausner

IT WAS NOT until the conquests of Jannaeus Alexander that the Jews of Palestine took up trade in any great numbers. This may be explained by the fact that the country's entire coastal strip, including its harbors, was under the control of foreigners. The northern ports, from Jaffa to Accho-Ptolemais, were inhabited by Hellenized Phoenicians. The southern ports, from Jaffa to Raphia and beyond, were occupied by Hellenized Philistines; it was they who gave Herodotus the impression that the country of the Jews was called *Palaestina* (Παλαιστίνη), for he himself had never journeyed inland.

Thus the Jews were confined to the hinterland, and depended on foreigners for their exports and imports. As late as the Persian period, Jewish housewives were still weaving linen garments and girdles for sale to the Phoenicians.[1] This state of affairs served Josephus with an explanation of why the Greeks had never heard of the Jews, in spite of their being such an ancient people: "Ours is not a maritime country; neither commerce nor the intercourse which it promotes with the outside world has any attraction for us. Our cities are built inland, remote from the sea; and we devote ourselves to the cultivation of the productive country with which we are blessed."[2]

Though Josephus is obviously exaggerating for rhetoric effect, there is a great deal of truth in his statement. In the period between the Babylonian exile and the reign of Jannaeus Alexander, the vast majority of Jews were engaged solely in agriculture. Under the Hasmoneans the Jewish population began to include traders and seafarers, but was still primarily based on agriculture. Galilee, for example, was renowned for its abundant crops and flourishing plantations (vineyards and olive groves).[3] It does not, however, seem to have been a busy center of trade, despite its proximity to Phoenicia, where commerce was so prevalent an activity that the term "Canaanite" "Phoenician" (as we know from various passages in the Bible and in Greek literature) came to be used as a synonym for trader. Let us begin, therefore, with an outline of the country's agriculture during the period under discussion.

A. AGRICULTURE

Grain

In earlier times the biblical description of the Land of Israel as "a land flowing with milk and honey" was meant merely as a contrast to the wilderness from which the Children of Israel had just emerged. Much of the country was mountainous and rocky, or covered with natural forest or scrub which had to be cleared before the land could be used for planting. Moreover, the Jewish farmer of antiquity faced the problem of producing grain in a climate marked by an uneven distribution of annual rainfall. Destructive torrents descended during the short rainy season, while for almost nine long summer months the soil lay parched and vegetation withered.

Over the generations the Jewish farmer learned how to cut down the scrub, clear away stones and boulders, hoe out weeds, enrich the soil with manure, and fence in his fields with thorny hedges. With the stones he had cleared he built terrace walls to prevent further erosion by winter rains of the thin layer of fertile topsoil. Gradually he succeeded in exploiting every available square inch of rugged land or wilderness.

Thus by the time of the Second Temple Jewish agriculture had already reached a high level of development.[4] It was not confined solely to dry farming, for which the ancient Hebrew idiom בית הבעל ("House of Ba'al")[5] still preserved the idea of the dependence on the Lord (Ba'al) of heaven for a propitious fall of rain. Irrigation was also practiced; — the water of wells and springs was conveyed to the field by means of pipes, aqueducts and man-made channels. Rabbinic and Greek literature alike praise the excellence of the irrigated fields around Jericho, "city of palm trees."[6] Michmas and Zanoah (Zanuḥa) in Judea were both commended in the Mishnah for the quality of their grain.[7] Hapharaim was renowned for its abundant crops, and "to carry straw to Hapharaim" was the equivalent of carrying coals to Newcastle.[8] Excellent wheat was also grown in the valley 'Ein Soḵer in Samaria, as well as in several places in Galilee, particularly the valley of Arbel, Capernaum and Chorazin.[9] The barley crop was sufficient to provide the staple diet of the poor and to leave a remainder for export. Spelt, oats, rye and millet were also plentiful. Rice, on the other hand, had to be brought from abroad, and was only later acclimatized.

On the whole, however, the country was not overly fertile. In an average year the peasant's holding produced a fivefold crop of wheat. An exceptional harvest or a particularly rich soil would produce much more, although the biblical reference to a hundredfold yield is evidently a figure of speech.[10] In actual fact the Judean peasant could produce only ten or fifteen times the quantity he put into the soil, even in good years and on his choicest land. The harvest was stored in barns and granaries, on which the farmer would draw for his own use and for sale in the market. There were also government storehouses ("the store-house of the kings") to supply the towns with bread in case of famine, or for provisioning the army.[11] Judea generally had more than enough grain for its own needs, and sometimes exported the surplus. In the New Testament we are told that the people of Tyre and Sidon depended for their nourishment on the "king's country" (the king being Agrippa I).[12] In times of scarcity grain was imported from Egypt, as happened once or twice during Herod's reign.[13]

Vegetables

Many species of vegetables had long been grown in Palestine and could thus be considered as native plants. These included cabbages, beetroots, radishes, turnips, lettuces, horseradishes, lentils, beans and pulses. All these vegetables were sold in the market-places of Judea and formed a large part of the popular diet. Other species were introduced from abroad, as their foreign names in Hebrew testify — cucumbers (מלפפון), artichokes (קינרס), asparagus (אספרגוס), Egyptian beans, Egyptian pumpkins, Greek pumpkins, etc. Some of these were more expensive than the native types of vegetable, and were bought mainly by the rich.

Fruit

Fruit was plentiful and of excellent quality. Orchards plantations and vineyards, were planted in abundance throughout Judea. Two of the most common fruits were pomegranates[14] and figs.[15] Other native Palestinian fruits were: grapes, olives, carobs, citrons, plums, cherries, almonds, walnuts, dates, mulberries, apples, pears and quinces. Some had foreign names and were introduced from abroad, e.g. the "crustumenian" (a type of pear or quince) the peach, the medlar, etc.

Dates

Dates were grown both for home consumption and for export. Though date palms grew quite as tall and strong in the hills as in the plain, the colder mountain climate prevented the growth of a rich crop of dates. Rabbi Eliezer b. Hyrcanus once said to R. Ishmael in the course of a heated argument, "Ishmael, you are a palm of the mountains!"[16] —

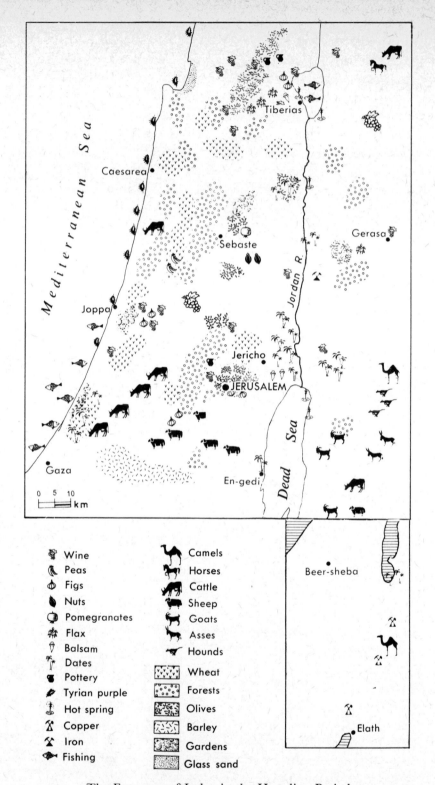

Legend:

- Wine
- Peas
- Figs
- Nuts
- Pomegranates
- Flax
- Balsam
- Dates
- Pottery
- Tyrian purple
- Hot spring
- Copper
- Iron
- Fishing

- Camels
- Horses
- Cattle
- Sheep
- Goats
- Asses
- Hounds
- Wheat
- Forests
- Olives
- Barley
- Gardens
- Glass sand

The Economy of Judea in the Herodian Period

implying that Ishmael's knowledge of the Torah was deep but that its fruits were scant. The products of this fruit were date wine and date honey,[17] which like the fruit itself were both for local consumption and for export. Pliny reports that Judea was as famous for its dates as Egypt for its perfumes, and mentions five different kinds of Judean dates outstanding for their taste and fragrance.[18] Tacitus also praises the Judean dates.[19]

Figs

Figs grew plentifully and large quantities were sold abroad, usually in the form of strings of dried figs. These were even sent to Rome: Augustus favored the type called "Nicolaite," of which the Roman Jews were also fond.[20] The most famous of this sort was the string of figs called $q^{e'}ilit$, the juice of which was slightly intoxicating.[21] The Talmud graphically illustrates the potency of fig honey: "R. Jacob b. Dostai said: 'From Lydda to Ono it is three miles; once I was too eager at a banquet and walked back on my knees because of the fig honey.' "[22]

Wine

Wine was another major item of agricultural produce. The wine of Sharon[23] was universally praised and good enough to export; it was contrasted with the wine of Carmel.[24] The wines of Ascalon, Gaza and Lydda were also well known and sold abroad. The Mishnah lists a number of other places noted for their wines,[25] though not all of them may be identified. Kᵉfar Signa supplied the wine for the offerings on the Temple altar.[26] There was a white wine (חמר חיוורין), a dark wine, and even a "black," i.e. a dark red wine. Since wine was regarded as salubrious a "spiced wine" was also produced, and is first mentioned in the Bible.[27] The Talmud called this "condiment wine,"[28] while in the Gospels[29] and Pliny[30] it is referred to as "myrrh wine."

Besides grapes and wine, the vineyard also produced raisins from dried grapes,[31] and vinegar.[32] The vineyards of Judea were the most famous of the land. The Mishnah, Barayta and Tosefta all abound in Hebrew names for every detail of the vine and its growth, as well as of the process of wine-making — proof of the importance of viticulture in Judea, where Hebrew survived as a spoken language longer than in Galilee.[33]

Oil

The number of Hebrew words connected with olive growing and the extraction and manufacture of the oil shows this to have been one of the main occupations of the Jews of Galilee and Judea during the period of the

Second Temple. Apart from being used by the local population both as a food and a medicine, oil also served as an important source of income through its extensive sale in Tyre, Sidon, Egypt and Syria. While, however, the choice wines came from Judea, the finest oils were produced in Galilee. According to the Talmud the purest oil came from Tekoa in Galilee[34] and was called "Alfa." Other outstanding oils from Galilee were produced in Meron and Netofah.[35] Those of Samaria were from Shifkon and Beth-Shean,[36] while the best oil from east of the Jordan came from Ragaba.[37] The most noted producer of oil, however, was Gischala (modern el-Jish), and its Hebrew name, Gush Ḥalav, indicates the quantity of its oil production.[38] It is most interesting to note that shortly before the destruction of the Temple, John of Gischala was granted a monopoly on the sale of oil from Galilee to Caesarea Philippi.[39] Judea, too, had its olive groves, as is demonstrated by such local names as Mount of Olives, Mount of Anointment, Gethsemane (meaning "oil press") etc.

Balsam

Balsam groves flourished particularly in Gilead and Jericho, though at a later period the trees were also cultivated along the western and northern shores of the Dead Sea between En-gedi and Betharamatha. The extract was used both as a spice and a medicine, and according to Pliny fetched twice its weight in gold.[40] Strabo relates that the Jews grew balsam trees only over a limited area so as to maintain the scarcity of the product and hence its high price.[41] The balsam of En-gedi was thus one of the most important exports of Judea.[42] We learn from Pliny that after the destruction of the Temple the Jews tried to destroy the balsam plantations in order to prevent the Romans from exploiting them.[43] The Romans saved the groves, however, and even extended their area until the price of balsam fell.

Other plants

Ḥenna blossom was used in the production of a bluish dye with which women painted their faces. Cypros, the name both of Herod's mother and Agrippa's wife, may well be derived from the Hebrew כופר[44] (ḥenna), and not, as has been assumed, from the Greek κυπρισσός. Roses were also cultivated in special flower gardens for the sake of their costly "rose oil."[45]

Livestock and animal products

One of the main occupations of the Jews in the period of the Second Temple was the raising of cattle, sheep and goats, which were all needed for the Temple sacrifices.[46] Large numbers of sheep were also imported from Moab and Nabataea, or bought from Arab herdsmen; these were the "flocks of Kedar" and the "rams of Nebaioth" of our sources. Jewish farmers who raised sheep and cattle either sold them on the open market or to a cattle trader. There was a special market in Jerusalem for fattened cattle.[47] Jewish sheep-farmers from Peraea were able to sell their wool in Judea, their major outlet being the wool market in Jerusalem.[48] The women of Judea normally used the wool for weaving, while those of Galilee used flax.[49]

Poultry

Species of domestic poultry were introduced into Palestine at a comparatively late date, though still during the existence of the Second Temple. This is indicated by the fact that all the Hebrew names for domestic fowl are derived from Sumerian via Akkadian. The word for rooster ("tarn^egol") replaced the original Hebrew word *gever*, which survives in the Mishnah. The former is a derivation of the Sumerian phrase *TARU-GALU*, meaning "large fowl," and the word for hen — "tarn^egolet" — was formed by analogy (the original Hebrew word for hen is unknown). The Hebrew *awwaz* (gander) is derived from the Sumerian *UZU*, as is the Aramaic *bar-awwaza* (duck). All these foreign derivatives indicate that domestic fowls were introduced into Judea from other countries.[50] Turtledoves and pigeons, on the other hand, were raised by the Jews for sacrificial use, and their nomenclature is basically Hebrew. The Bible, Mishnah and Talmud employ Hebrew terms for pigeon (יונה), turtledove (תור), fledgeling (גוזל), dovelet (פרידה), domestic pigeon (יונת שובך), wild pigeon (יונת בר), and Herodian pigeon (יוני הרדסאות).[51]

Hunting

Hunting was still widely practiced in Palestine during the period of the Second Temple, though it was then already in decline. It was discontinued entirely after the destruction of the Temple, mainly on account of the biblical restrictions regarding unclean animals and the rabbinical laws of ritual slaughter.

Fishing

During the time of Neḥemiah the Jews had no access to the sea, and Jerusalem had a "Fish Gate" to which the Tyrians brought their fish for sale.[52] From the time of the Hasmoneans the Jewish population of the coastal towns of Judea and Samaria probably engaged in a certain amount of fishing, but the catch can only have been sufficient for local needs.

In Galilee, however, fishing was the main livelihood for the inhabitants of the numerous villages along the shores of the Sea of Galilee (called the "Sea of Tiberias" in the Talmud and the "Lake of Gennesareth" by Josephus). Although the lake was not large it abounded in all kinds of freshwater fish, including some of the choicest species.[53] The lake was always crowded with fishing boats from the towns and villages along its shores, all of which prospered greatly by fishing. The catch was large enough to provide not only fresh fish for local consumption but salted fish for sale abroad. Hence the principal city on the lakeshore was called Taricheae ($\tau\acute{\alpha}\rho\iota\chi\circ\varsigma$ = salted),[54] a fact confirmed by Strabo.[55] Strabo also praises the local speciality, a pickle or conserve of salted fish called *muries*. The center of fishing and fish trade in Galilee later moved to Tiberias.

B. NATURAL RESOURCES

Salt, pitch, asphalt and bitumen were extracted from the Dead Sea and were sold for export. According to Josephus large lumps of pitch, like headless bulls, were often found floating on the surface of the lake. They were used for tarring ships and in medicinal preparations.[56] Judean bitumen, according to Pliny, was the best in the world.[57] "Nitrate of Antipatris" was another Judean mineral that was extracted and processed on the spot.[58]

Iron deposits were found in northern Lebanon. Josephus also mentions an "Iron mountain" on the border of Moab.[59] The name has been preserved in the Mishnah in the phrase "the thorn-palms of the Iron Mount,"[60] as well as in the Targum Jonathan[61] and the Jerusalem Targum.[62]

C. CRAFTSMEN AND ARTISANS

The works of Josephus contain few references to crafts and craftsmen, and it is to the Mishnah and Barayta that we turn for most of our information regarding the state of the crafts in Palestine during the period of the Second Temple. Too much reliance, however, should not be placed on the many Talmudic passages relating to the arts and crafts. Our idea of the day-to-day life of the Jews of Palestine at that time should be based only on factual report or straightforward, undidactic narrative.

An *uman* was an artisan skilled in a specific profession, and these were to be found in the cities, towns and larger villages of Palestine. The term "required crafts" (אומניות שוקדות) was applied to the handicrafts necessary to every region at all times.[63] It was regarded as honorable for a young man to enter a skilled trade, while certain "base crafts" were considered not suitable. The idle and unemployed were despised in Judea.⁶⁴ Most of the Tannaim had secondary occupations: the greatest of them, Hillel the Elder, was a manual worker, Joshua b. Ḥananiah, his disciple, was a charcoal burner, and Nehunyah used to dig ditches. The tradition was maintained after the destruction of the Temple. R. Johanan was a sandal maker, R. Isaac a smith, R. Judah a baker, another R. Judah a perfumer, R. Joshua a maker of grits, etc.⁶⁵ In the same tradition, Jesus of Nazareth was a carpenter and also made pack saddles,⁶⁶ while the apostle Paul wove curtains or made tents.⁶⁷

The sages enjoined every father to teach his son a craft.⁶⁸ The early sources supply us with a long list of crafts practiced in Palestine during the period of the Second Temple. There were tailors, cobblers (סנדלר; רצען is a foreign term used a little later), masons, stonecutters, woodworkers (נגר — "carpenter" — is the post-biblical term although it is an ancient Semitic word), millers, bakers (נחתום; אופים is the later term, undoubtedly of Akkado-Babylonian origin, as are all other nouns with the prosthetic *nun*), tanners (later called בורסיים from the Greek βυρσεύς), perfumers, cattle fatteners,⁶⁹ butchers, cooks and pastrycooks of both sexes, milkmen, cheesemakers, surgeons and bloodletters (אומנים), barbers, laundrymen and washer-women, smiths (goldsmiths, silversmiths, blacksmiths), dyers, weavers, embroiderers, workers in gold thread (טרסיים), carpet weavers (טפיטנים), mat-makers (חולצים), diggers of cisterns and ditches, fishermen, hunters, beekeepers, ceramic workers, potters and jug makers, coopers (who made and repaired barrels), asphalt workers and glass smelters. During the early Hasmonean period glass was still regarded as a luxury that only the rich could afford.

Sculptors are not mentioned among the artisans either by the Bible or the Talmud. Presumably there were none in Judea owing to the strict interpretation of the Second Commandment forbidding the fashioning of graven images. The Talmudic word for statue (אנדרטא) and bust (פרוטומי) are of Greek origin and are always used in connection with pagan ritual and idolworship. On the other hand the commonly used word for painter (צייר) is pure Hebrew. The painter worked in colors and dyes, but was also prohibited from painting "likenesses" (i.e. portraits) by the same biblical injunction. On the feast of Sukkot the tabernacles were often decorated with "painted sheets,"⁷⁰ presumably by Jewish artists. The reliefs depicting grapes, roses etc., found in the Tombs of the Kings and other monuments in Jerusalem were presumably executed by Jewish sculptors.⁷¹ Mention should also be made of the "engravers of inscriptions" referred to in Ben Sira,⁷² and of artistic engravers in the Bible.⁷³

We know, of course, that there were professional scribes who were employed in writing documents or copying books. They also produced their own writing material, using papyrus reeds (גומא; also פפיר in the Talmud) for the preparation of paper (נייר). The latter is an ancient word derived either from the root ניר ("fallow land" — an image for the paper waiting to be "sown" with words), or from an Egyptian root akin to יאור (river). Another synonym for paper was כרטיס — a late term derived from the Greek χάρτης. Allied professions later included scroll and parchment making and the preparation of account books (פנקס, from πίναξ). Ink was made from gallnut resin and from a cupreous form of vitriol (קנקנתום of the Talmud — from the Greek χάλκαντον).

Skills were generally passed from father to son, as demonstrated by the Talmudic expression "a carpenter and the son of a carpenter."[74] Among the builders of the wall mentioned by Neḥemiah are "Ḥananiah, one [lit. son] of the perfumers" and "Malchijah, one of the goldsmiths."[75] There were apparently families in which a profession was handed down from one generation to the next.[76] According to Christian tradition Jesus of Nazareth and his father Joseph were both carpenters. The midwife and the physician also passed on their professions to their children. Some families kept the secrets of their professions jealously to themselves, e.g. the House of Garmu and the House of Abtinas mentioned in the Mishnah.[77]

Other crafts were organized in the form of home industries in which entire families were employed. The families of the linen weavers of Beth Ashbe'a are mentioned in the Book of Chronicles (ca. 400 B.C.E.).[78] Crafts houses like *Beth Zaggag, Beth Kaddar* and *Beth Zabb'a* — all mentioned in the Talmud[79] — are none other than places where craftsmen worked together with their apprentice sons. A Hebrew inscription found in the burial cave near Bethphage in the vicinity of Jerusalem and dating from the period of the Second Temple includes a list of names of men employed in a local manufactory.[80]

Whole towns or settlements were often connected with a certain trade or industry. Migdal Ẓebo'aiya ("Magdala of the Dyers," east of Jordan), obviously included a large number of dyers among its inhabitants;[81] Beth-saida derived its name from its fishing industry; Kᵉfar Hanania and Kᵉfar Shiḥin were well-known centers of pottery production ("carrying pots to Kᵉfar Hanania" was like "carrying straw to Hapharaim").[82] Nazareth was apparently a town of carpenters. Joseph ha-Levi thought that the name Nazareth was akin to the Hebrew *nᵉsoret* (sawdust), and that Gennesaret literally meant the "Valley of Sawyers."[83]

D. Peasants and Landowners; Hired Laborers; Leasing the Land

Although craftsmen occupied an important place in the economic life of Judea during the period of the Second Temple, the majority of the population belonged in fact to the peasantry. In the Mishnah and Barayta references to farming greatly outnumber those relating to the crafts. The Gospels tell us that the disciples of Jesus almost all came from peasant stock, and most of the parables are drawn from peasant life. It was in the field of agriculture, moreover, that the Jews could compete with other countries, whereas even ordinary articles of clothing or common household objects were often cheaper to import from abroad.

Peasants

The majority of the population were smallholders ("householder" is the term used in the Mishnah, equivalent to the οἰκοδεσπότης of the Gospels). They lived in "villages" — often small or even medium-sized towns surrounded by fields, vegetable gardens, orchards and vineyards. The farmer was helped by his children as soon as they were old enough to work. In spite of his industry, however, the smallholder never became rich. Most of his produce went to feed himself and his family, and only a little remained for bartering or selling in the nearest market town, in exchange for the necessities of his household. He had no savings, so that after one or two years of drought, or a prolonged war, he often lost his land and became a hired laborer or journeyman. To avoid this the smallholder would sometimes borrow from a richer landowner, but if he failed to repay his debt he finally forfeited his land. If even this was not sufficient to cover his debt, he could be taken in service as a "Hebrew slave"; sometimes, too, his wife and children went into bondage with him.

Even if the farmer succeeded in holding on to his small plot of land until he died, only his eldest son, who according to the Torah prescription inherited double his brother's share — could hope to support himself and his family from the land. His brothers would often sell him their portion and join the ranks of the laborers. If they could not find regular work they had to make do with casual employment. Sometimes they became unemployable and ended up either as beggars or brigands.

Landowners

Some estates, of course, were large enough to produce more than the farmer needed for his own family. Such well-to-do landowners were able to supply the impoverished smallholder with a loan of money, or perhaps

with seed or food, against a mortgage on his land. Often enough the rich
would often increase their own estates in this way. These medium-sized
landowners were the mainstay of commerce, for they were able to sell
most of their harvest for cash, with which they bought goods and services
in return. There seem to have been many of this class in Palestine during
the period of the Second Temple.

Relatively few, on the other hand, were the great landowners — the
"estate owners" (בעלי נכסים) of the Talmud (עתירי נכסין in Aramaic) and "men
of valor" (גיבורי חיל) of the Bible. (In comparison, however, with the owners
of the great *latifundia* of Italy, they were relatively poor.) This class was
usually friendly towards the Persian or Hellenistic administrators, and
included the "noblemen and governors," the king, the royal family and
the high officials (in Hasmonean times and during the reign of Herod), the
high-priestly houses and some of the wealthier merchants. Some of the
great landowners are mentioned in the Talmud: Rabban Gamaliel II of
Jamnia employed workers to till his fields,[84] and also leased his fields for
a share of the produce.[85] Such was in fact the method by which great
estates were made to yield profits to their absentee landlords. Rabban
Gamaliel's position obliged him to remain in the city and to appoint a
steward (*oikonomos* or *epitropos*)[86] to manage his estate. These stewards are
also mentioned in the Gospels;[87] their duties included the general management of the estate, the supervision of the workers in the field, the collection
of their master's debts etc. The landowner could thus reside permanently
in the city and was left free to attend to his business transactions.

Hired laborers

Owners of large farms and estates could not, of course, work the land
themselves. They therefore employed laborers either on a time or a work
basis. The former were hired at a fixed rate,[88] whether for a year, a month,
one or several days, or even by the hour. No single contract could be
entered into for a period of more than six years (in contrast to the Hebrew
slave, who went free after six years). The daily laborer was usually a small
farmer from a neighboring village, or even from further afield, who had
been forced to relinquish his land. Or again, he may have been a younger
son whose impoverished father had been unable to leave him enough land
to live on. His only way of earning a living and improving his position
would be to hire himself out to a prosperous farmer for a fixed time.[89] In
Judea and Galilee such landless peasants who remained all their lives as
hired laborers on the large estates of the wealthy were referred to as לקוטות
("gleaners") by the Talmud.

The working day lasted from sunrise to sunset, with an hour's rest during the heat of the day. There was little change in wage rates from the time of the Persians to the reign of Nero.[90] The daily wage ranged from an *issar* (roman *as*) to a *sel'a* and probably averaged a *drachma* (אדרכמון)[91] or a *denarius* (דינר)[92] The *sel'a* was equal to four *denars* or a *tetradrachm*.[93]

Where professional knowledge or skill were required, the laborer might be hired out for a specific task for which he would be paid a fixed sum on its completion. Farmers and landowners were not the only ones to hire out such laborers. Artisans, too, had their employees as well as their apprentices.[94] Yet even the skilled worker could not always find employment. The repeated mention in the Talmud of the פועל בטל ("idle worker") is evidence of a significant amount of unemployment in Judea during that period. According to Josephus, over 18,000 men were left without work when the rebuilding of the Second Temple was finally completed in 64 A.D. Those in charge of the reconstruction were obliged to find additional work for them so that they and their families should not starve.[95] The Gospels mention an estate owner who recompensed laborers who had sat idle for the first hour of work and to those who had been idle all day long since no one had hired them.[96]

The Mishnah regards all employers as having entered into a contract with their workers, if not in writing then at least by word of mouth. A fine was imposed on whichever party revoked the agreement or broke any part of it, after both sides had been allowed to present their case. Numerous cases in point are cited in the Mishnah.[97] That most are decided in favor of the worker is indicative of the humanitarian attitude of the Tannaim and their solicitude for the poor.

Though the living standards and conditions of the Jewish worker were hard enough, they were never as bad as those of his Roman counterpart. Society in Palestine was less polarized and the difference between rich and poor not as marked. There was also much less opportunity for the ruthless exploitation of the laborer. The humanitarian treatment of the poor and needy enjoined by the Torah, and the democratic spirit of the Pharisees in general and of the Tannaim in particular, also did much to smooth the differences between the classes.

Leasing the land

If a landowner did not wish to work his fields himself he could lease out his land in a number of ways. Firstly, he could place it in the hands of a contractor (קבלן or קבל), who undertook to tend his fields, pay all expenses, including taxes, and comply with the legitimate requirements of the owner

— all in exchange for half (sometimes a third or a quarter) of the harvest.

Another way of farming out land was to a lessee (אריס) — the equivalent of the Roman *colonus*, a poor farmer whose holding was insufficient to supply his needs. The lessee received a deed of lease (שטר אריסות) from the well-to-do owner of an estate for part of the property.[98] Unlike the contractor, who had to supply all the means of production himself, the lessee also received seeds, implements and farm animals in exchange for his labor (called פעולה in the Talmud) and an agreed portion of the produce. Whereas the contractor hired his own laborers, the lessee tilled the land himself.

Since the lessee did not own the land himself, he exploited it without regard for its proper maintenance and improvement. In Rome this form of tenancy ruined the great *latifundia*, though in Judea its practice was not as widespread and its effects therefore not as marked. In Judea's case it was the state of protracted war and not any agricultural mismanagement that led to the country's economic ruin. Nevertheless, the existence of what amounted to a class of serfs was a divisive factor in the life of the nation, as the parable in the Gospels indicates.[99]

Thirdly, there was the leaseholder (חוכר), who differed from the contractor and lessee in that he bore the loss if the land produced less than the fee agreed on. On the other hand the surplus, too, accrued to the leaseholder, whereas the contractor or lessee merely received the share of the harvest agreed on with the landlord. In one respect the leaseholder did resemble the lessee — he paid the rent (חכירה) from the produce of the field, and not in cash.

A fourth method of hiring out the land was by means of a tenancy. The tenant (שוכר), like the leaseholder, made the profit or loss his own responsibility. Unlike the leaseholder, however, he paid his rent in cash.

Thus at the end of the period of the Second Temple the population of Judea included a minority of rich landowners, a majority of poor smallholders, and a large class of landless peasants, most of whom lived off the land either as sharecroppers, tenants or laborers. A smaller section of the working population consisted of artisans, their apprentices and hired workers.

Two other classes of workers have still to be mentioned — servants and slaves. The former were employed by wealthy families on a permanent basis, though they were free to change masters if they wished. Scholars, too, often kept personal attendants to clean their rooms, cook their meals, and look after their clothes.[100] Such tasks, however, were usually performed by male and female slaves, and it is this third class which may be treated here in a little more detail.

The "Hebrew slave"

A laborer, an artisan or even a servant was considered a free man by the law. If his work could be sold to others, his body remained his own. Not so the slave, whose only advantage was that he could never become un-employed or die of hunger. Not even the Hebrew slave could choose his own work or exchange one master for another. He was not, however, a slave in perpetuity, but rather a bondman, who in Mosaic law had to be released after a maximum of six years of service unless he himself expressly declared: "I love my master . . . I will not go out free."

The Sages devoted much discussion to the case of the Hebrew bondman.[101] We must, however, treat all references in the Talmud to slaves and bond-women with a degree of circumspection. Most of the rules of the Mishnah, Barayta and Tosefta are based on the assumption that only the work and not the body of the Hebrew slave belonged to his master.[102] Such an approach is epitomized in the dictum "Whoever buys a Hebrew slave buys himself a master."[103]

Most of these rules were undoubtedly enacted at a late period, when the Tannaim were the spiritual leaders of the Jews. Daily life during the earlier period of the Second Temple was hardly governed by such moral sensi-bilities. For the period of his service the Hebrew bondman was truly a slave in body and soul, obeying his master without hesitation, expecting to be beaten for laziness or insubordination,[104] and living off the leavings of his master's table. Unlike the hired laborer he worked without benefit of fixed hours or labor regulations, and was expected to be at his master's beck and call at all hours of the day and night. He was not, however, subject to severe cruelty, since he enjoyed a close relationship with his master and lived in a country where the democratic spirit of Pharisaism was prevalent. With the exception of Herod, only the alien rulers of Judea sold Jews as slaves after a war or rebellion. A Jew could be sold in bondage only to a fellow Jew and only to his own creditor in payment for a debt. The debt was deducted from his sale price on completion of his service.

Unlike the relatively large slave classes of Greece and particularly of Rome,[105] Hebrew slaves were never very numerous. Nevertheless they did constitute an important sociological factor in the political and spiritual upheavals during the time of the Second Temple. At the end of the period they formed part and parcel of the wider proletariat, a fact which helps explain the frequent rebellions and the various political, social and religious movements of that time. When Simeon bar Giora left Masada, his first important step towards gaining entry into Jerusalem was to declare freedom for all slaves.[106]

The "Canaanite slave"

Quite different from the status of the Hebrew bondman was that of the "Canaanite slave." The name was probably derived from the markets of Tyre and Sidon, and was used for all non-Jewish slaves. It may also have been a reference to the biblical verse: "Cursed be Canaan, a slave of slaves shall he be to his brothers . . . Blessed by the Lord my God be Shem; and let Canaan be his slave."[107] We read in the Second Book of Maccabees that the Syrian general, Nicanor, offered the slave dealers of Tyre and Sidon ninety Jewish slaves for one Syrian *talent*.[108] This may be taken as evidence that the Canaanites (Phoenicians) were the chief slave dealers in the East at that time, but not as a guide to the accepted market price for the individual slave. The author's purpose here was merely to show how cheap Jewish slaves were expected to be after Nicanor's anticipated victory. The Mishnah inform us that a slave could fetch as much as one hundred *minas* or as little as a *denarius* ("gold denar").[109] The average price lay somewhere between the two extremes, possibly in the region of one hundred *denars*; that of a female slave was somewhat lower. Physical appearance, fitness, education and race were the basis for judging the value of a slave. Syrians, for example, were often preferred, Negro slaves, too, were common, and Negro girls were highly regarded as serving maids.

No work in the house or field was beyond the capacity of an able-bodied Canaanite slave. But not all were required to perform menial tasks, and any special skill or aptitude was put to good use. Slaves worked as tailors, bakers, cooks, barbers, tutors — even pearl fishers. Some female slaves served as coiffeuses or nursemaids, while others were kept as singers and dancers.

Canaanite slaves, like cattle, were traded by bill of sale. The slave was marked in case he should escape, and sometimes he was even branded.[110] More usually, however, the mark would consist of a seal on the forehead, a bell around the neck or either of these attached to the slave's cloak. In addition he might be required to wear a special kind of cap (כבול). Even according to Jewish law Canaanite slaves were regarded as chattels of their master. They enjoyed no rights of ownership, for anything they acquired belonged to their master, including the produce of their work and the compensation received for personal injury or damaged honor. According to law, too, they had no status of marriage, divorce or widowhood, and neither their lineage nor their familial ties were recognized.

Slaves had a reputation for laziness, licentiousness and shamelessness. Their masters disregarded slaves to such an extent that they had sexual intercourse in their presence.[111] Some masters and their sons "took liberties with the serving-maids."[112] Others tyrannized their slaves and beat them mercilessly with rods, leather whips, scourges (פרגול — from *flagellum*) and metal-tipped lashes. Thirty-nine or even sixty strokes could be meted out at a time. If the slave was permanently disfigured by such cruel punishment he became free; if he died under the lash or from his wounds, his master had to answer with his life. By this law alone were slaves distinguished from animals.

Such treatment, however, cannot have been prevalent, particularly during later times. The Talmud tells us that "the hand of the slave was as the hand of his master,"[113] and "a man's slave is like his own self."[114] Indeed his actual position must have been very different from his legal one. Rabban Gamaliel "the Patriarch" mourned for his slave Tabi and received condolences.[115] In the patriarch's house old retainers were addressed as "father" and old maidservants as "mother."[116] During the period of the Second Temple, too, it is quite probable that the life of the Canaanite slaves in Judea was easier than their legal status would indicate. If not treated by their masters as members of the family they were at least regarded as part of the household. In spite of their deprivation of the rights of ownership, some slaves were allowed to save "redemption money" (*peculium*) in order to regain their liberty. It was common even in Rome for slaves to be freed simply as a token of their master's affection, and the practice must also have occurred in Judea.

Though more numerous than the Hebrew bondmen, the Canaanite slaves were never an important factor in the social or economic life of Judea. Since only the rich could afford to buy and support them in any large number, their influence among the people was morally less corrupting and politically less disruptive than their Hebrew counterparts.

E. Trade and Commerce

The reader will have noted than in the foregoing sections we have freely used Talmudic sources to shed light on the state of agriculture and other economic aspects of the life in Judea during the period of the Second Temple. This we have regarded as entirely legitimate, since neither agricultural nor other forms of production could have greatly altered in the intervening generations up to the beginning of the Tannaitic era. In the field of trade and commerce, too, we believe that many of the references in the Mishnah, Barayta and Tosefta are of relevance, at least in regard to the latter part of our period.

Centers of trade

From the reign of Alexander Jannaeus onward there were enough people in Palestine to populate several large cities and fortified towns, apart from the country's hundreds of villages and hamlets.[117] Jerusalem was the capital and largest city, whose population reached over 100,000 during the reign of Herod and his sons (the higher figures sometimes suggested seem exaggerated). In addition to the ten Hellenistic cities of the Decapolis, other towns with large populations included Caesarea, Sebaste, Hebron, Bethlehem, Lydda, Jamnia, Beth-guvrin, Tiberias, Sepphoris and Taricheae. In typically hyperbolic fashion, the Talmud tells us that there were "600,000 fortresses" from Geba to Antipatris.[118] Josephus claims that there were as many as 204 villages towns and fortresses in Galilee alone,[119] though he is surely exaggerating when he asserts that even the smallest village contained more than fifteen thousand inhabitants.[120] Dio Cassius reports that little more than fifty years after the First Revolt Hadrian conquered 50 Judean forts and 985 villages in the course of the Second Revolt.[121] This figure, too, is greatly inflated though, as in the case of Josephus, his exaggeration must have been based on a numerous population.

Phoenicans and Greeks

The first outside commercial contacts of the Jews — during the period of the First Temple and the beginning of the Second — were with the "Canaanites" (Phoenicians); indeed the name "Canaanite" was used in Hebrew as a synonym for trader. The Phoenician influence infiltrated south into Judea by way of Galilee, where the northern Hebrew tribes were intermixed with Tyrians and Sidonians. During this period the Hebrew terms used in connection with trade and commerce were confined to such basic roles as that of pedlar (רוכל — literally, one who goes on foot; רגל = רכל), merchant (סוחר — one who "travels around"), shopkeeper (חנוני;[122] חנות = stall), dealer (תגר[123] — akin to סחר), and money-changer (שולחני; שולחן = table or counter).[124] Hebrew also possessed terms for the primary concepts of commerce — trade (מסחר), gain (סחר),[125] merchandise (סחורה),[126] bargaining (מקח ומכר — literally, "buying and selling"),[127] and dealing (משא ומתן — "give and take").

From the middle of the period of the Second Temple the Phoenician influence on Jewish trade was replaced by that of the Greeks, who inherited most of the Palestinian coastal cities in both north and south, including all the ports, from the former Persian empire. It was this Greek influence which became especially marked after the conquests of Alexander the Great. A large part of the foreign trade of the Jews — all of Judea's imports in fact, as well as most of her exports — now passed through Greek hands. By the time these coastal cities were conquered by Jannaeus they had become completely Hellenized. In the period between the reigns of Jannaeus and Herod hundreds of thousands of Jews settled there and lived in close proximity with the existing non-Jewish population. From them they learned the art of trading, and many became importers in competition with their gentile neighbors — a fact which no doubt contributed to the hostility between them.

In consequence the Hebrew language adopted a whole new vocabulary of trading terms from the Greek. The word for corn factor (סיטון) is derived from σιτώνης; a retailer, especially of bread, was called פלטר, either from πρατήρ (according to Schürer and Krauss), or from πωλητήριον (according to Herzfeld); מנפול, a dealer in a single commodity, is taken from μονοπῶλης; the merchant's account book, in which he made entries of the goods he sold "on credit" (בהקפה — a Hebrew word) was called פינקס (πίναξ).

The names of cloth, and indeed of most articles of clothing, were Greek in origin: פילוסין (cloth from Pelusium), הנדוין or הנדיקי (cloth from India), קילקי (Cilician felt), דלמטיקון (Dalmatian garment), סגום[128] (Latin sagum, a coarse woolen cloak), פרגוד (a curtain or tunic — παραγαύδιον), אצטלא (robe, stola — στολή), סודר (handkerchief — σουδάριον) פיליון (felt cap — πίλιον), אנפלאות (felt socks — ἐμπίλια), and סנדל (sandal — σάνδαλον, σανδάλιον), etc.

Other words from Greek and Latin also found their way into the Mishnah and Barayta and thence into modern Hebrew. These include ספסל — subsellium (bench), קתדרה — καθέδρα (chair), וילון — velum, (veil), טבלא — tabula (table), אסקוטלא — scutella (plate), תיק — θήκη (bag), קופסא, — κάψα capsa (box, case), etc. Even the ancient Hebrew word for mirror (מראה) was replaced by the Latin-derived אספקלריה, from speculum; by way of specularia, ("window-panes"). The word for hemp — קנבוס — was imported from the Greek together with the product (κάνναβος).

Whether the use of all such foreign words necessarily implies that the articles were imported along with their names, it does indicate the extent of the Greek influence on the country's trade. It is also a measure of the Greek influence on Jewish commercial life that though Hillel the Elder used Aramaic for most of his decrees, he applied a Greek term (פרוסבול — προσβολή) to his reform of commercial practices in Judea.

Still other words with little or no direct bearing on commerce were loaned from the Greeks. The Greek word λιμήν, harbor, entered Hebrew as לימין; the letters were subsequently inverted to give the form נמל — harbor. The word טופס (official document) was adopted from τῦπος, דוגמא (example) from δεῖγμα, הדיוט (private person) from ἰδιώτης, נס (dwarf) from νавνος, ליסטיס[129] (brigand) from λῃστής, אסתניס (sensitive) from ἀσθενής, etc. The free use of such loan words by the Mishnah, Talmud and Midrash, often in place of words of Semitic origin, shows that they had already long become part and parcel of the Hebrew language.

Before the arrival of the Greeks the coins of Palestine were known by Hebrew names: *Sheqel*, called after the early Hebrew — Canaanite measure of weight; *me'a*, equivalent to the Greek μνᾶ, and the plural of which (*me'ot*) signified money in general; *peruta*, the smallest token and equal to the Greek ὀβολός. From the reign of Herod onwards all denominations were given Greek or Latin names. דינר The *denarius* or *denar* of silver or gold replaced the *sheqel*, while other coins included the פונדיון (*dupondius*), אסר (also איסר), called the "Italian asar" (from *as*, old Latin *assarius*; Gr. ἀσσάριον), טרפעיק (τροπᾱικόν), and קונטרונק (a corruption of καδράντης = *quadrans*.[130]

F. Domestic Trade and the Diaspora

Market day was a long-established institution among the Jews of Palestine. Every Friday, the day before the Sabbath, the villagers would come to the towns and cities to sell their produce. The market day was called the "Day of Assembly" (יום הכניסה); other market days were on Mondays and Thursdays.[131] At first the day of assembly, was used specifically for trading, but later for other purposes as well — weddings, court sessions, public instruction and the reading of the Torah. Every city, town and large village in Judea had its market where food, clothing and other village produce could be purchased. The small-town market seems to have been a purely Jewish institution; its Gentile counterpart was the fair (יריד).[132] Fairs were held only in the large towns possessing a non-Jewish majority (Ascalon, Gaza, Acco-Ptolemais, Antipatris, Tyre, Scythopolis and Caesarea), and were connected with the pagan religious festivals (the איד of the Mishnah; Syr. 'Ida; Arabic 'id = festival).[133] At these fairs it was possible to buy all kinds of foreign goods from itinerant salesmen, including costly perfumes and other luxury items. Slaves were also sold there.

The country's domestic trade was boosted considerably by the thrice-yearly pilgrimage to Jerusalem.[134] Every pilgrimage brought thousands of the Diaspora's Jews to the Holy Land, where they not only spent large sums of money but also engaged in trade with the country's inhabitants. They were joined in Jerusalem by the very many more thousands of pilgrims from all over the country itself. The total influx into the capital on each of the festivals cannot be accurately gauged, but it probably could not have exceeded 300,000. Various estimates cited in ancient sources are of course greatly exaggerated. The Talmud, for example, asserts that the number of Passover sacrifices was double the number of people who came out of Egypt at the Exodus.[135] Since each Passover offering served up to ten men, the pilgrims would therefore have numbered 12,000,000! Josephus' estimates also appear grossly inflated — on one occasion he mentions 2,700,000,[136] on another 3,000,000.[137] Chwolson has pointed out that Jerusalem (with a circumference, according to Josephus, of thirty three stadia, or approximately six km) could not possibly have held such a large number of people, even standing shoulder to shoulder.[138] Nevertheless even one tenth of Josephus' number of pilgrims would have generated a large amount of additional trade in the city to meet all the pilgrims' requirements during their stay, including the thousands of animals needed for their sacrifices.

It may be assumed that the influence of the Diaspora on the economy of Palestine was not confined to the pilgrimage season. Herzfeld has shown that as early as Second Temple times commerce flourished between the Jews of Babylon, Egypt, Phoenicia, Syria, Cyprus, Cyrene, Ethiopia, Arabia, the whole of Asia Minor, Greece and Italy, especially Rome.[139] The Jews of the Diaspora engaged little in the crafts, more in agriculture and most of all in trade. There must have been regular trade relations, too, between the Jews of Palestine (the metropolis) and the Diaspora (the "daughters" or "settlements" of Judea and Jerusalem, as Philo calls them). The communities of the Diaspora grew rich from trade and were thus able to send large sums of money to Jerusalem to support the Temple, the center of Judaism. We are told, for example that around the year 70 B.C.E. Mithradates of Pontus confiscated eight hundred talents of gold left on the island of Cos by the Jews of Caria and Ionia for forwarding to the Temple.[140] On a later occasion Lucius Valerius Flaccus seized one hundred pounds of gold saved by the Jews of Apamea and Laodicea for the same purpose.[141] As the Jews of the Diaspora always remained closely linked to the metropolis, their religious and national center, it is also safe to assume that their trade connections with Palestine expanded as their own prosperity grew.

G. Foreign Trade

With the development of Jewish agriculture in Palestine, the country's various districts produced commodities in excess of their own local needs. The Sharon, for example, had a surplus of wine and cattle; Jericho and the Valley of Gennesareth a surplus of fruit. The lowlands of Judea (the Shefela) produced large quantities of wine and oil. This naturally led in the first place to the expansion of domestic trade. We find that Galilee produced not only a surplus of oil and vegetables, but also supplied other parts of the country with grain. When all domestic needs had been filled, however, there still remained a not inconsiderable surplus for export in a number of commodities. Judean wine was sold to Egypt, Syria and other neighboring countries, as well as to some distant ones. Galilean oil and grain were well known and readily bought in the world market. Various kinds of fruits and fruit products were also exported, some of them to Rome.

To offset this many kinds of goods were imported. Herzfeld has enumerated as many as 240 different imported articles commonly found in Palestine, of which over half were known by their foreign names.[142] Even some items of food and drink were imported from abroad. These included Babylonian beer, Median beer and Egyptian *zythum* (barley beer).[143] Smoked fish and lentils were also brought into the country from Egypt. Other imported foodstuffs included grits from Cilicia,[144] cheese from Bythinia[145] and mackerel from Spain.[146] Although local wines were of excellent quality and sold abroad, Palestine also imported foreign wines. Greek wines were particularly popular, while the Mishnah mentions several other foreign wines — Italian, Cilician and Cypriot (though the latter's Hebrew name may refer not to Cyprus but to the caper wine mentioned in the Talmud). "Ethiopian wine" probably received its name from its dark color rather than from its country of origin. At a later period the Talmud also mentions wine of Ammon.[147]

Camels, asses and all kinds of animal hides came from Arabia. Lybian asses were much used in Palestine. Purple dye was brought from Tyre and jewelry from Alexandria. Egypt also exported parchment and papyrus to Judea. The former was used for scrolls, documents and books, and the latter in the manufacture of plaited "Egyptian baskets."[148] Woolen cloth as fine as silk was imported from Miletus in Asia Minor.[149]

H. TRANSPORTATION

Caravans and roads

Goods were carried to the inland cities by caravans of donkeys (חמרת) and camels (גמלת) — both words of Hebrew coinage. The caravans were assembled by a number of traders as a means of protecting themselves from the ambushes of highwaymen.[150]

Caravans were also used for bringing goods overland from neighboring countries (שיירת; Syr. *šayyarta*; Arab. *sayara*). The various ancient trade routes by which they came to Palestine were of great economic importance.

One led from southwest Arabia and ran parallel to the Red Sea coast and the Gulf of Elath. Along this route the treasures of Arabia Felix, Ethiopia and Africa were brought to Petra (seventy km. south of the Dead Sea). Petra was also the road junction for caravans crossing the Arabian desert from the Persian Gulf, laden with goods from Babylon and India. Both of these routes barely touched on Palestine. From Petra the road branched to Egypt, Gaza and Damascus, the latter route following the eastern shore of the Dead Sea and the east bank of the Jordan. The road to Gaza passed northwestwards along the Judean lowlands and thence led to Jerusalem, Lydda and Samaria.[151] In the Jezreel Valley it joined up with the road to Acco-Ptolemais and from there continued to Antioch, the Syrian capital.

The road from Babylon crossed the central Euphrates and the Syro-Arabian desert to Palmyra; thence it continued to the east bank of the Upper Jordan, crossed the river north of the Sea of Galilee (Gennesaret) at what was later on called the "Bridge of Jacob's Daughters" (built in Roman times), descended into the Jordan Valley down to Beth-Shean (Scythopolis), and from where it turned into the Jezreel Valley, finally joining the coastal road at the foot of Mt. Carmel.[152]

Jerusalem, too, was a road junction, with routes leading north to Damascus via Neapolis and Sebaste, west to Jaffa and south to Hebron.[153] The Romans built a road to Egypt along the entire length of the coast as far as Pelusium via Gaza, Raphia and Rhinocorura (el-Arish). The same road continued northward from Gaza to Ascalon, Jamnia, Jaffa, Caesarea and Tyre.[154] Palestine thus served as a crossroads between Africa, Asia Minor and the Orient, to which its towns and cities were directly linked by well-traveled roads.

Ships and sailors

In addition to Palestine's overland trade routes, the country was also linked by sea to the lands of the Mediterranean. Many references are found in Hebrew literature to the "countries of the sea." The "sailor from the sea" is as frequently mentioned in the Talmud as the "merchant from the caravan."

There were many Hebrew names of ships and boats. Apart from the larger type of vessel (ספינה; אניה in the Bible), there was the generally smaller אליפה (also in Syr.; Ass. *êlippu*). A large cargo boat for carrying produce was called an ארבא.[155] The small דוגית was orginally used exclusively for fishing (דייג), and was identical with the ביצית of Babylon. The Bible refers to the fishing boat as a סירת דוגה.[156] Finally the canoe — like ערִיבה was used on the Jordan for transporting produce.[157]

Jewish sailors (ספנים ;מלחים in the Bible) were not uncommon in the period of the Second Temple. They were considered "righteous" and "pious," in contrast to the "wicked" ass-drivers and camel-drivers,[158] probably since their calling placed them continually in the hands of Providence. The numerous Hebrew terms for nautical implements (apart from the Aramaic or Greek) indicate that many Jews had taken up seafaring as a vocation.[159] According to the Talmud, Midrash and classical sources, Jews frequently sailed the Mediterranean as well as the Dead Sea and the Sea of Galilee. They also knew how to navigate the Jordan river, a not insignificant feat in view of its continuous meanders and treacherous currents. Josephus tells us that the fishing town of Taricheae, on the Sea of Gennesaret, had 230 boats of four oars.[160] Many of them probably served as cargo boats as well as for fishing. The *arabarches* (this is the correct reading of *alabarches*), whom many scholars mistakenly believe to have been the head of the Alexandrian Jewish community, was in fact the official in charge of the river on the "Arab" (east) bank of the Nile.[161]

The exit ports for the Judean sea trade were Jaffa, Caesarea, Ascalon, Acco-Ptolemais and Anthedon. From there boats left for Rome, calling at Brundisium and Puteoli (Dicaearchia); Cilicia (especially Tarsus, birthplace of the apostle Paul); Gaul; and Aspamea (Spain). By the end of the period of the Second Temple the economy of Palestine was so dependent on commerce that the High Priest used to offer a prayer on the Day of Atonement: "May it be Thy will, O Lord our God and God of our fathers, that this year be one of cheapness and abundance, a year of flourishing trade."[162]

I. Markets and Merchants

The common Talmudic expression "adorning the markets with fruits"[163] referred to the ornamental display of fruit on the market stalls and counters. Goods and produce were sold wholesale at the fairs and bought retail at the shops and stalls of the market. The Bible and Talmud mention the stalls of bakers, dyers, linen merchants (חנותא דכיתנא) and perfumers, as well as markets of bakers (חוץ האופים) clothiers, wool merchants, smiths, glaziers, carpenters etc.[164] At Emmaus there was a cattle market, referred to in the Mishnah and Talmud.[165] Pedlars bought their wares in the large cities and hawked them around the smaller towns and villages. Frequent reference is made in Talmudic literature to the "pedlars that go around from town to town."[166] The term מוכרי כסות (clothes dealers) is used in the Mishnah for pedlars of clothes who carried their wares rolled on a staff which they slung over their backs.[167]

Meat was sold in the מקולי (*macellum*); the עטליז (also קטליז, אטליז; κατάλυσις) was a temporary bazaar for the caravan merchants, where cattle, meat and wine were sold. Baked bread (פת) was obtainable at the baker's (נחתום, also נחתומר) and the פלטר, where vegetables were also sold. In the market itself there were permanent shops with shutters (תריסים) which when opened served as temporary display shelves.

Sometimes the shops would be situated inside a stoa (סטיו — στόα), a covered colonnade with perhaps a domed roof at one end where the commercial exchange and eating places were to be found.[168] Antipatris had such a stoa,[169] while according to a late source Jerusalem had a "Dome of Accounting" (כיפת חשבונות) where merchants made up their accounts for the day and fixed their prices.[170] The basilica (בסיליקי) was also used for commercial purposes. "There were three kinds of basilica buildings: those attached to royal palaces, baths or store-houses."[171] There is clear evidence that the basilica at Ascalon was used for selling grain.[172]

The official in charge of the market was called the "master of the market" in Hebrew (בעל השוק; in a Phoenician inscription — רב השוק). This title was equivalent to the Greek ἀγορανόμος, which also occurs in the Talmud in the form אגורא נימוס.[173] The post is already referred to in pre-Hasmonean contexts.[174] Shortly after Herod's death we find his grandson, the future Agrippa I, appointed by Herod Antipas to the post of *agoranomos* at Tiberias.[175] The *agoronomis* was responsible for supervising the levy of taxes on all goods and produce traded in the market. He was also in charge of the market police and traffic, so that his office had an administrative and political aspect in addition to its financial duties.[176] There were also appraisers (שמאים) who assessed the value of the goods for taxation, and market commissioners (משערים בשוק) who would check the price of goods from time to time.[177]

J. Duties and Taxes

As early as Persian times the country's population already suffered high taxation. In addition to a land tax (מנדה; Akk. *mandatu*; מידת המלך in Ezra and Nehemiah), there was also a food tax (בלו; Akk. *biltu*) and a toll (הלך; Akk. *alakku*) on goods transported by road.[178] During the reign of the Seleucids the Jews paid a poll tax, land tax, cattle tax, fruit tax, and even a "crown tax" for the presentation of gold wreaths and crowns to the king.[179] The exact nature and extent of the taxes levied by the Hasmoneans is not known. It seems probable, however, that they adopted all the taxes levied in Judea by the Seleucids, though they did reduce the purchase tax on goods sold in the market.

Under the Romans the taxes were called *vectigalia* and *tributum*. The former was an import and export duty. The latter a poll and land tax based on the population census. The levying of the tax was entrusted to tax collectors (גבאים) assisted by investigators (בלשים) who checked on the payment of the tax and caught evaders. It was usual for the govenment to farm out its taxes to large contractors, who would often sub-let their right to a number of small publicans.

During Herod's reign the level of taxes in Judea was particularly high. After his death the people requested the abolition of the annual poll tax and the excessive purchase tax levied on all goods sold in the market.[180] Taxes were also severe during the time of the procurators, and included a city tax, a water tax, a food tax (on meat, salt etc.) and road tolls. Border tolls were particularly burdensome. Pliny reports that tax inspectors waited at almost every inland and coastal station for the collection of some sort of tax.[181]

Though the official levy on goods was only 2.5% of their value, the operations of the tax farmers and publicans multiplied that figure many times over. The publicans and their assistants checked the goods as they passed through the customs houses. To prevent customs evasion they used an "exciseman's staff,"[182] for scattering the merchandise and for poking into baskets and bundles. After the goods had been thoroughly examined and the tax paid into the publica's box,[183] the exciseman tied them with an "exciseman's label."[184] Sometimes investigators and spies would be sent to ascertain whether the tax was being collected in full.[185]

It is therefore not surprising that all those connected with the levying and collecting of taxes were the object of bitter hatred on the part of the people and their leaders, who regarded them as the personification of imperial rule. The tax farmer was considered by the Talmud and Midrash as on a par with the brigand,[186] and his title was synonymous with robber and oppressor.[187] Even the tax collectors were placed in the same category as thieves.[188] Publicans were excluded from giving evidence in court.[189] It was likewise forbidden to accept money from their box even for charity, since it was regarded as stolen.[190] In the Gospels, too, "publicans and sinners" are classed together in one phrase.[191] Indeed, the universal opprobrium with which the publicans and their assistants were regarded seems fully justified; for though the Roman system of tax management undoubtedly lay at the root of the evil, the immediate oppressors were the collaborators who enforced the system — the tax gatherers themselves.

K. Economic Classes — A Summary

In the foregoing pages we have seen how the country's economic development during the period of the Second Temple led to the creation of a multi-level society. At one end of the scale we find the nobility and the rich of Jerusalem;[192] at the other, the Hebrew bondman and the Canaanite slave. Most owners of land were smallholders who worked the land themselves. There was also a smaller class of more prosperous farmers who could afford to employ hired labor. Still more wealthy were the owners of large estates who increased their lands by taking over the holdings of smaller farmers unable to pay their debts. Such landowners did not need to work themselves but employed laborers and kept servants and slaves.

The other classes of the population owned no land, though some earned their livelihood through some form of tenancy or sharecropping, while others belonged to a class of landless farm workers and laborers. Craftsmen and artisans formed a small but important class, most of whom worked on their own, though some employed workers and apprentices. The last section of the earning population comprised the traders — pedlars, shop-keepers, dealers and merchants, as well as rich money changers and money-lenders who grew rich on the interest from loans to farmers and shopkeepers, or from the profits gained in changing the large sums of foreign currency brought into the country by pilgrims.[193]

Finally there were those who possessed neither land nor property. These included on the one hand, the Hebrew and Canaanite slaves; on the other the unemployed, who either begged for a living or swelled the ranks of brigands and Sicarii.[194] Still others retreated from the world by joining one of the Messianic or ascetic sects.

Yet the poor and downtrodden were after all a small minority. Since the time of the Hasmoneans the country had clearly made enormous progress both in agriculture and in commerce. Indeed, had that momentum been maintained Palestine would no doubt have become one of the most prosperous countries within the Roman empire. But history decreed otherwise. The country was placed under the strain of an ever-increasing burden of taxes made heavier by the rapacity of the publicans. Herod for his part aggravated the situation by attempting to force the economy in every direction at once. After Agrippa's death the hand of Government grew ever more oppressive as one unsympathetic procurator followed another. A Jewish confrontation with Rome now became inevitable, leading finally to the destruction of the Temple and the end of a period in Jewish history.

EDITOR'S NOTE: The above chapter has been adapted from a hitherto unpublished article written several years ago by the well-known Jewish historian of the last generation, the late Professor Joseph Klausner. While the editor is well aware that the subject now requires a thorough reconsideration, he is convinced that the author's interesting contribution affords a valuable insight into the economic and social conditions of the Jews in their homeland during the period covered by the present volume.

CHAPTER VI

JERUSALEM IN THE HELLENISTIC AND ROMAN PERIODS

by M. Avi-Yonah

IN MARKED CONTRAST with the paucity of archaeological and literary information on the Jerusalem of the First Temple, we have a relatively large number of sources on the city from the Hellenistic and Roman periods. Excavations have been going on in Jerusalem for the last 110 years. We also have at least one more or less complete description of the city on the eve of its destruction. This is the famous account of Josephus in the fifth book of his *Jewish War*, beginning in the fourth chapter and carrying on into the fifth. This description is especially valuable, written as it was for a public of Gentiles who did not know Jerusalem. One of the great difficulties in interpreting the many passages in the Bible dealing with Jerusalem is the fact that these texts were written by contemporaries who assumed in their readers a familiarity with the city as it stood. They thus felt no need to indicate the exact position of every wall or building mentioned. We, however, who lack such familiarity with ancient Jerusalem, are left groping in the dark. On the other hand, the systematic description of Josephus, although not lacking in obscure passages, does nonetheless give us a general idea of the extent of the city and its external aspect. In addition, there are dispersed throughout both the *Jewish War* and the *Antiquities* the names of many public buildings then in existence[1], while the description of the siege wall which Titus built around Jerusalem furnishes us with a considerable number of names of geographical features or structures in its vicinity. The fact that this description is a systematic one — the wall is described from the northwest in a clockwise direction and back to the starting point — adds to its value as a topographical source. On the other hand, the authors of the Books of Maccabees followed the Biblical pattern by neglecting to describe the various features of Jerusalem mentioned in their work, and thus we sometimes find it difficult to identify these structures.

A short but exact description, based apparently on the reports submitted by Titus to his father the emperor during the siege (as was the custom with all Roman generals) may be found in the fifth book of the *Histories* of Tacitus (II, 3.). In addition we have many isolated facts in Greek geographical literature[2] from the Hellenistic to the Roman period. There is also the so-called *Letter of Aristeas*, a source that purports to have been composed in the time of Ptolemy Philadelphus, but which apparently belongs to the Hasmonean period. Pesudo-Aristeas gives a somewhat fanciful description of Jerusalem in those days. The New Testament also mentions a number of place names in Jerusalem that were connected with the last days of Jesus and the activities of the apostles. We also find a number of facts about the city and a description of its ruins in various sources written after the destruction. Most important in this respect are the two tractates of the Mishnah, Middot and Tamid, which describe the Temple and the Temple services. Facts about Jerusalem before 70 A.D. are dispersed throughout the Talmud and Midrash. The halakic decisions concerning Jerusalem are especially valuable, since their authors were trying to be as factual as possible; whereas in the Aggada we often find fanciful stories that cannot be reconciled with reality. Similarly the itineraries of the first Christian pilgrims, and indeed patristic literature in general, must be used with caution on account of their numerous fanciful stories and imaginary identifications, the accumulated efforts of many generations of guides who led the pilgrims through the Holy City.

A. History of Excavations

Archaeological activity in Palestine has from the very beginning been concentrated in Jerusalem.[3] Excavations generally began later in Palestine than in other countries of the ancient East such as Egypt or Babylonia, though Jerusalem was something of an exception. This comparatively slow start, however, cannot be said to have retarded our knowledge of the Holy City. On the contrary, early excavation techniques were so primitive that we can only be thankful that work did not start seriously in Palestine until the end of the 19th century. Moreover, excavations in Jerusalem were from the very first carried out with special care. In those days it was usual to disregard all small finds, particularly potsherds, which we now know have a decisive archaeological importance in determining the period, the ethnic composition of the population and its economic life. Because of Jerusalem's

sacred character, however, early archaeologists kept every object or fragment and included them in their reports. It is of no importance, therefore,
that their datings were usually wrong: their descriptions are so precise that
we are able to determine the correct period of these finds. Moreover, from
the sixties of the last century Jerusalem's population included skilled observers interested in the antiquities of their city, who followed up every
chance discovery made in the course of new construction in the area. They
reported each such discovery to one or other of the scientific publications
dealing with the Holy Land. Thus in addition to the main excavation
reports, a considerable quantity of information has been accumulated
through such small discoveries, information which completes our knowledge
of the remains from the various periods in the life of the city.[4]

Excavations in Jerusalem started in 1864 with the clearing of the Tombs
of the Kings north of the city by the Frenchman, De Saulcy. He still believed
that he had found the tombs of the royal house of Judah, as did most of his
contemporaries who were influenced by popular legends; actually these are
the tombs of the royal family of Adiabene (see below, page 243). In marked
contrast with the hurried and unsystematic work of De Saulcy, the excavations of Charles Warren around the walls of the Temple Mount were carried
out with extraordinary exactitude and devotion. Although he was working
under the most difficult conditions, having to excavate around the walls in
tunnels so as to avoid offending Moslem susceptibilities, Warren's plans and
measurements have been confirmed by recent excavations almost down to
the last centimeter. Only where he engaged in speculation did he occasionally go wrong. Until 1968, in fact, Warren's work of a century ago comprised
the sum total of our knowledge regarding the Temple enclosure.

At the end of the 19th century, Frederick J. Bliss excavated around the
western hill (now called Mt. Zion). Continuing the earlier work of Sir Henry
Maudslay, Bliss followed the line of the wall which encircled that hill in the
time of the Second Temple. (On this wall and its archaeological importance
see below, page 226). Bliss also excavated in the valley between the two hills
and found a broad wall damming up the Pool of Siloam. He was followed by
R.A.S. Macalister, who studied many of the tombs around Jerusalem and
drew their plans; much later, in 1923 to 1925, Macalister and J.G. Duncan
excavated on the eastern hill. In 1909 to 1911, Parker organized an expedition ostensibly to study the source of the Gihon, but in fact to find the
treasures of the Temple, whose location was supposed to have been recorded
in a coded passage of the Bible. Thanks to the interest of the Dominican
Father, L.H. Vincent, the scientific results of this expedition have been
preserved for posterity. In the last years before and the first years after World

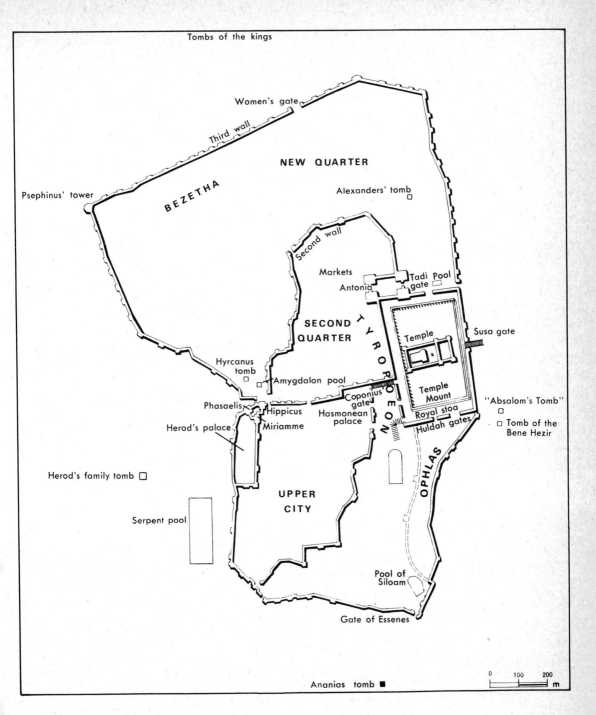

Jerusalem at the End of the Second Temple Period

War I, the southern end of the eastern hill (the so-called Ophel) was excavated by an expedition directed by R. Weill on behalf of Baron Edmond de Rothschild. The painstaking work of this, the first Jewish expedition in Jerusalem, led to the discovery of the walls of the Iron Age city and possibly also to that of the tombs of the Davidic dynasty.

After World War I, excavations in Jerusalem continued under the British Mandate. In the main, activities concentrated on the "Ophel," where J.W. Crowfoot continued Macalister's work in the years 1927 to 1929. At the same time, local Jewish bodies, the Hebrew University and the Jewish Palestine Exploration Society (now the Israel Exploration Society), began work in Jerusalem. In 1924 N. Slouchz excavated near the so-called Tomb of Absalom, and in 1925–6 L.A. Mayer and E.L. Sukenik excavated large portions of the Third Wall (see below, page 226). Sukenik and N. Avigad continued with the clearance of Jewish tombs around the city for several decades. Two important excavations were undertaken by the Mandatory Department of Antiquities. In 1937 R.W. Hamilton excavated near the Damascus Gate and along the northern line of the present wall of the Old City. From 1940 to 1946, C.N. Johns cleared the court of the Citadel around the Tower of David. During the Jordanian occupation of East Jerusalem from 1948 to 1967, Kathleen Kenyon excavated on the Ophel Hill and established the true line of the Jebusite wall. She also carried out various trial digs in other parts of the city. At Bethany the Franciscan Fathers cleared a Jewish cemetery from the time of the Second Temple, and another at "Dominus Flevit" on the Mount of Olives. In the Israeli part of the city, various tombs in the Sanhedria quarter and the Tomb of Jason in Rehavia were cleared. Since 1967, excavations have been carried on by B. Mazar along the western and southern walls of the Temple enclosure, and by N. Avigad in the Jewish Quarter of the Old City. A number of important tombs have also been cleared, including the Tomb of the Nazirite on Mt. Scopus and a tomb in Givʻat Mivtar.[5]

As a result of these archaeological activities extending over a century, very many of the important topographical problems of Jerusalem from the period of the Second Temple have been solved. Of course many problems still remain, such as the exact delineation of the Second and Third Walls, or the precise location of the *Akra*, but even on these points it is now possible, in the opinion of the majority of scholars, to arrive at a more or less correct identification.

B. Orography of Jerusalem

According to Josephus, Jerusalem was built on two hills separated by a central valley (*War* IV, 137). A glance at a topographical map will show two hilly ridges crossing the Old City from north to south. The western ridge begins at a height of 805 m., descends to 774 m. near the Jaffa Gate, rises to 777 m. in the Jewish quarter, and ends at 619 m. at the bottom of the Valley of Hinnom (Gehenna). The second, eastern, ridge is somewhat lower. It begins at 770 m., descends to 743 m. in the Temple area, and ends at 627 m. Between these two ridges lies a valley which begins at 754 m. near the Damascus Gate and ends at 617 m. in the Kidron Valley. There can be no doubt that these two ridges are the east and west hills which, according to Josephus, together comprised the area of ancient Jerusalem. Josephus continues by saying that the Upper City was built on the higher and more level of the two; the other hill on which the Lower City stood was hog-backed. The identification of these two hills, with the Upper City on the western hill and the Temple Mount and Lower City on the eastern, is generally accepted. Josephus adds: "On the exterior the two hills on which the city stood were encompassed by deep ravines, and the precipitous cliffs on either side of it rendered the town nowhere accessible" (*War* IV, 541). He also explains at the beginning of his description (*War* IV, 136) that one single wall was enough to defend the city on those sides which were surrounded by steep-sided valleys.

Thus in the time of the Second Temple, Jerusalem was divided into two parts, each of which formed a separate fortress. This was also the opinion of Tacitus, who based himself on Roman military reports. Josephus does indeed complicate his description by the mention of a third hill, which according to him existed opposite the Lower City and was separated from it by a wide secondary valley, later filled up by the Hasmoneans in order to join the Temple to the City. The topographical situation however, does not seem to confirm this. It is indeed true that a ridge 759 m. high issues from the Upper City in the direction of the Temple, but this can hardly have ever been joined to the Temple Mount. This ridge formed the site of the *Akra* (see below, page 231).

In a later chapter in which the Third Wall is discussed (*War* IV, 148), Josephus tells us how the inhabitants of Jerusalem left the "Hill" (the Upper City, apparently) and built their houses around a fourth hill north of the Temple Mount. This fourth hill is called the "Bezetha,"[6] a name of doubtful interpretation. It was included by King Agrippa I within the Third Wall. It is possible that what is meant here is the ridge north of the Old City from which the western and eastern hills both project. This ridge was included within the line of the third wall; it begins at 805 m. and descends eastward to 724 m. near the Kidron Valley.

It is easier to identify the deep valleys which surrounded the city. The one on the west and the south is the Valley of Hinnom; the second, which enclosed part of the northern and the whole eastern side, is the Kidron Valley. Both together formed a most effective defense for about three-quarters of the whole circumference of ancient Jerusalem.

C. The Temple Mount

As we have already noted, the central valley divided Jerusalem in the time of the Second Temple into two separate and independent strongholds. The taking of one did not give the enemy possession of the whole town. In 63 B.C.E., for example, Pompey occupied "the City" (meaning the Upper City), but he had to besiege the Temple Mount separately. Similarly, the fall of the Temple Mount in the month of Av, 70 A.D., did not mean the surrender of the whole town; the Romans had to mount a second attack on the Upper City, which did not fall until a month later, on the 8th of Elul. The reason for the existence of two fortified areas within the same city lies not only in its topography, but also in its history. In the time of the monarchy, from David to Hezekiah, the Temple Mount formed part of the city while the western hill was partly inhabited as an open suburb. After a short period in which the eastern half of the western hill was enclosed by a wall, this area was again abandoned under Nehemiah. It was resettled as "Antioch — at — Jerusalem" in the Hellenistic period. For the next twenty years the Temple Mount, or "Mount Zion" as it was then called, was in Jewish hands while the fortress of the Upper City, the *Akra* was held by Syrian troops and Hellenized Jews. The two fortified areas in this city were at that time hostile to each other. After a period of unity under the Hasmoneans, the separation was resumed. Herod, who together with his grandson Agrippa I determined the external aspect of Jerusalem until the destruction in 70 A.D., further strengthened the two parts of the city in order to dominate both. The fortress of Antonia (formerly called the "Baris") dominated the Temple, and Herod's palace, with its three huge towers, the Upper City.

Herod's activities radically altered the shape of the Temple Mount. In pre-Herodian times the area of the Sanctuary extended around the top of the rock that now lies inside the Dome of the Rock. At that time the Tempel area apparently did not have a definite geometrical shape: its outer walls followed the natural outline of the ground. These walls must have already existed in the time of King Solomon, since he would hardly have left his Temple unprotected. It is possible that one part of Solomon's wall, or of the later wall on the same line, was found in 1967 by Kenyon, south of the Temple Mount.

The weak spot in the defenses of the Temple Mount was the saddle which joined it to the hill on the north side. It was here, therefore, that the kings of Judah built two towers called the towers of Hananel and Meah. From these two towers ran a wall to the south following the line of the central valley. The northern wall of the Temple area made use of a small diagonal valley which descended to the Kidron from 742 m. to 680 m.; this valley is now called the Bezetha Valley. On the eastern side the Kidron served to defend the Temple Mount; on the south it was defended by the palace of the kings of Judah. During the period of the Second Temple the situation changed. The royal palace was no longer in existence, thus making it necessary to reinforce the defenses of the Temple area on the dangerous north side. Nehemiah therefore combined the two towers into a single fortress called the "Baris" (*ha-Bira* in Hebrew) and appointed a special commander for it (Neh. 7:2).

The Jews returning from the Babylonian exile undoubtedly did their best to build the Second Temple as far as possible on the foundations of the First. These were probably still visible, since only fifty years had elapsed since the destruction and the area had not been used for any other purpose, as it was after the second destruction.[7] Moreover, there were eyewitnesses still living who remembered the First Temple from their youth and could point out its exact location.[8] Around the new Sanctuary various chambers were erected and an outer court added.[9] The Babylonian exiles were apparently influenced by the prophet Ezekiel (chapter 40 *et seq.*), who drew up a plan for a new Temple somewhat different from the First. Both Nehemiah and Zechariah mention the courts of the House of the Lord (in the plural) and thereby indicate the date of this change.[10] We may assume that the various "private" chambers mentioned by Nehemiah formed part of the outer court, whereas the "chambers of the House of Our Lord"[11] and the "treasuries"[12] were inside the inner court. At that time the Temple was connected with the area outside by means of ramps. Before the inclusion of the western hill within the city there was no need for a bridge between it and the Temple.

In the time of the High Priest Simeon the Just the walls of the Temple were heightened and strengthened.[13] The inner wall was breached in the time of Antiochus IV.[14] The breaches were closed by Judah the Maccabee who with his brothers fortified "Mount Zion" against the *Akra*. The attempt by the High Priest Alcimus (Eliakim) to open the walls of the inner court ended after his sudden death.[15] The (whole or partial) razing of the *Akra* by Simeon the Hasmonean made the Temple fortress the highest part of the city.[16]   In the time of the Hasmoneans a bridge was built between the Temple Mount and the Upper City; "Wilson's Arch" now stands on its remains (see below, page 237).[17] During that same period, possibly in the days of John Hyrcanus, an underground passage was cut between the "Baris" and the Temple, making it possible for the High Priest and the King to enter the inner court from the palace without passing through the crowds.[18]

During Herod's reign the Temple underwent the greatest change in its history since the days of Solomon. The king decided to use part of the revenue he had obtained from taxation and commercial ventures to carry out a complete reconstruction of the Sanctuary and its surroundings. Undoubtedly he hoped thereby to gain the favor of his people, who hated the "Edomite slave", the slayer of the Hasmonean dynasty. With his usual energy and vision Herod extended the area of the Temple Mount to double its former size. He entirely closed the Bezetha Valley and changed the course of the central valley westwards. Thus a quadrangular esplanade was created at a uniform level. Rock which projected above the desired level in the northwestern part of the esplanade was cut away. On the other hand, the sloping ground to the southeast was raised by buttress walls and vaults, some of which were provided with a filling of earth and rubble. The shape of the Temple area as we know it today, including the Western or "Wailing" Wall, is the result of Herod's activity. He also greatly strengthened the fortification of the Temple. Even in the time of Pompey a siege of several months had been necessary to overcome the walls of the Temple, and now these were rendered still stronger. The Temple walls rose to 32 m. above the central valley, 38 m. in their northeastern corner and 47 m. in their southeastern corner.[19] These walls would have presented a threat to the rule of Herod and the Roman procurators in Jerusalem were it not for the Antonia fortress, which was built in the northwest corner of the Temple Mount. According to Josephus, "as the Temple lay opposite the town like a fortress, so did the Antonia dominate the Temple, and he who held it kept all of them."[20]

The identification of the Temple Mount has never been in doudt. Unbroken tradition which has consecrated the area now called in Arabic *Haram esh-Sherif* (the "Noble Sanctuary"), and the archaeological remains which are still visible around this area, have made the identification a certainty. According to Josephus, "the surface of the hill was widened by cutting away through many generations; also they [the people] made a breach in the northern wall and included an area as big as the whole circumference of the holy court."[21] In fact, however, the great extension of the Temple area was effected by Herod rather than by the "many generations" of Josephus, and not in the north but in the south. There the area of the Temple was almost doubled by the huge substructures erected by the king. The height of the wall, according to Josephus, was 300 cubits (150 m.) or more;[22] the blocks used in the building reached a length of 40 cubits (20 m.; this too is an exaggeration — the largest block known to us and visible today does not exceed 12 m. in length).

The Temple walls, as built by Herod, have the following dimensions: south 280 m., east 470 m., west 485 m., and north 315 m. — a total perimeter of 1,550 meters. For once Josephus gives a lower figure — 6 stadia, i.e., 1,110 meters. The area of the Temple Mount is 144,000 sq. meters, or over twice the area of the halakic Temple Mount, as given by the Mishnah (Mid. 2, 1). According to this source the Temple Mount measured 500 by 500 cubits, i.e., 62,500 sq. meters. It is clear, however, that the Rabbis did not regard the additions on the north and south as integral parts of the sacred area.[23]

The Herodian wall has been studied in its northern part from the Birket Isra'in to the northeast corner, and along the full length of the east wall. The south wall and the southern half of the west wall have been recently cleared down to the Herodian level; the line of the west wall in its northern section has been followed underground for about a quarter of its total length.[24]

The masonry of all these parts is uniformly Herodian. The stones are dressed in the typical Herodian manner: a low boss enclosed within a narrow margin surrounded by a second, wider margin.[25] The only difference in dressing has been observed in the east wall about 30 m. northward from its southern end; there the high boss on the north changes in one course to the flat dressing of the rest. This change can be explained by the addition of another section to the south for housing the royal basilica (see below, page 216f.). However, no corresponding change in the character of the masonry has been observed at this same point on the west wall. The stones which were below the level of the Herodian street encircling the wall, and which were therefore invisible (about 5 courses), have much rougher bossing and wider margins. The lowest course was placed upon the rock within a rock-cut trench. The average height of a course is 1–1.20 meters. This height is observed throughout, with the exception of the "master course" which passed below the door sills of the southern gates; the height of this course is

1.85 meters — almost twice the normal one. The cornerstone of this course measures 7 × 1.85 meters; it is surpassed in length only by some of the blocks in the southwest corner, but not in height. This cornerstone weighs more than 100 tons. In the southwest corner there are some stones with a length of 12 meters.[26]

There were two gates in the southern wall of the Temple which were called the Huldah Gates; these are now known as the Double Gate and Triple Gate. Originally both of them were double; the third opening in the Triple Gate seems a later addition. Of the Triple Gate only the western jamb is still the original one. Ramps ascended from these two gates at a slight incline to the interior of the Temple Court. According to the Mishnah[27] the public entered the Temple from the south. The Mishnah also states that there was only one gate in the west, called the "Kiponus" (Coponius) Gate.[28] In fact, there were at least three and possibly four gates in this wall. From south to north these are: (a) the gate leading to Robinson's Arch and by stairway into the Tyropoeon Valley; (b) the gate today known as Barclay's Gate south of the women's praying area at the Western Wall; it seems that stairs also led from this gate down to the Street of the Valley; (c) the third gate issuing onto Wilson's Arch which gave access to the Upper City. As this gate and the bridge led to the Xystus and the Hasmonean palace, we may assume that it was the main gate in the west wall and therefore identical with the Coponius Gate mentioned above. A fourth gate, today, called "Warren's Gate," has been presumed at the end of a long underground passage north of Wilson's Arch, but its existence has still to be verified.

On the north side there existed an underground passage between the Antonia and the Temple; no traces of it have yet been found. The Mishnah mentions only one gate on the northern side, the so-called Tadi Gate; it corresponded to the present "Gate of the Tribes." In the east there was also only one gate, called the Shushan Gate; its name was derived from a picture representing the Persian capital Susa on its portal. A second gate in the east wall may have existed near its southern end; the sill of such a gate with the beginning of an arch below it has been observed in this place. The Mishnah mentions two ramps — the "Ramp of the Heifer" and the "Ramp of the Goat" — and these may have led to the two eastern gates referred to.[29]

Porticoes extended along the walls of the outer court of the Temple. They were 15 meters in height, and had a double row of columns each 12.5 meters high.[30] The roofs of the porticoes were made of cedar wood. The width of the porticoes corresponded to their height, except for the "royal portico" or "royal basilica," which was one stadium (185 meters) long and ran almost the full length of the south wall. The basilica consisted of three halls separated by two rows of columns. The central hall or nave was 15 meters wide and 30 meters high; the two aisles were each 10 meters wide and 15 meters high, and were probably surmounted by galleries.[31] At least two columns corresponding in size to those of the outer porticoes have been found during quarrying work in Jerusalem; one of them is still visible in the Russian Compound. They were left *in situ* due to the appearance of flaws in the stone. No other traces of the porticoes of the Temple have been discovered.

Nothing remains visible of the other structures inside the court. There are records however, of underground passages and cisterns in this area. Before the construction of the aqueduct leading from the vicinity of Hebron (see below, page 247f.),[32] a great number of cisterns were cut out of the rock in the Temple area.[33] Two of these on the northern side of the sacred Rock in the center of the Temple area perhaps formed part of the *m*e*sibba* or winding underground passage connecting the "Chamber of the Hearth," one of the chambers of the inner court, with the northern gate. Another rock-hewn cistern nearby may have belonged to the "House of Ablutions" which was connected with the *m*e*sibba*. These two cisterns, together with a long passage possibly leading to the "Water Gate" of the inner court,[34] are the only fixed points, other than the Rock itself, which help us to locate the position of the Sanctuary within the outer court. If we assume, as many scholars now do, that the Rock corresponded to the site of the altar for burnt offerings outside the Sanctuary,[35] we obtain a fairly convincing picture of the shape of the Temple Mount at the end of the period of the Second Temple.

The pilgrim who entered the Temple court from the Tyropoeon or one of the Huldah gates, or who passed over the viaduct leading from the Upper City, saw a vast court paved with many-colored stones[36] and surrounded by porticoes with columns of white stone. On the south rose the higher roof of the nave of the royal basilica. On the north, the tall towers of the Antonia fortress dominated the corner of the northern and western porticoes. In the middle of the court was the *soreg*, a balustrade formed by low pillars connected by stone slabs. The pillars were apparently 1.5 meters high and there were 13 openings in the balustrade.[37] By each opening there was an inscription in Latin and Greek warning all Gentiles not to enter the balustrade, or else be responsible for their own ensuing death.[38] Beyond the balustrade was a stairway of fourteen steps leading to a platform 10 cubits (5 meters) wide. This was the *ḥel* which surrounded the Inner Temple wall with its towers. Leading from the *ḥel* and on the same level with it one entered the Court of Women, the eastern of the two courts of the inner Temple. The western court was on a higher level, about 7.5 meters above the *ḥel*; the gates of this court were approached by twelve steps. Most of the gates of the Inner Court were reserved for the priests, and hence the mass of pilgrims entered by way of the Court of Women.[39] This court was square in shape (67.5 meters on all sides) with four chambers in its corners, each of which consisted of a portico surrounding a small open court. These were: in the northwest, the "Chamber of the Lepers," with a ritual bath at its center; in the southwest, the "House of Oils" used for storing the Temple oil; in the southeast, the "Chamber of the Nazirites," where the Nazirites waited during the last hours before the termination of their vows; in the northeast, a storeroom housing wood for the altar fire. The whole of the Court of Women was surrounded by a balcony on which the women assembled on feast days. The east and main entrance of the Court of Women was a gate 25 meters high whose portals were covered with gold and silver plates. This was apparently the "Beautiful Gate" referred to in the Acts of the Apostles (3:2). The western gate of the Court of Women was the famous Gate of Nicanor, which was reached by fifteen steps "rounded like the half of a round threshing-floor."[40] The gate itself was a triple one, and above its central entrance was surmounted by a conch. The portals were made of bronze and so beautifully ornamented that this gate alone was not gilded over. According to legend, miracles occurred during the transportation of these portals from Alexandria to Jaffa.[41]

Court of Women and the Inner Court were surrounded by a wall which formed part of the defenses of the Sanctuary itself. There were six other gates in the Inner Court,[42] three on the north and three on the south. Above two of these gates there were balconies; these were the gate of the Chamber of the Hearth on the north and the House of Abtinas on the south. There were no gates in the western side of the Inner Court, since this was the nearest side to the Holy of Holies. The wall of the Inner Temple was surmounted by towers at its corners.

Porticoes surrounded the inner courts. There were also chambers along the walls of the Court of Priests, some of which served as storerooms and others for the various functions connected with the Temple ritual. One of them situated apparently in the southeastern corner, was the Chamber of Hewn Stone (*Lishkat ha-Gazit*), the seat of the Sanhedrin. The measurements of the whole Inner Court were 187 × 135 cubits (93.5 × 67.5 meters). Apart from a strip 11 cubits wide at its eastern end, the whole of this area could normally be entered by the priests alone, and was hence called the Court of Priests. Ordinary Israelites could only go into the narrow "Court of Israelites" but could approach the altar during the sacrifices in connection with various ritual practices. Opposite their court stood the high Altar of

Burnt Offerings, with horns in its four corners. The altar was approached by a ramp from the south. The slaughterhouse was opposite the altar on the north.[43] Between the altar and the slaughterhouse rose the high façade of the Sanctuary, which formed a square of 100 cubits (50 meters wide and 50 meters high).

The Sanctuary itself had the shape of a lion — "narrow from behind and wide in front,"[44] since the Holy of Holies and the hall were only 70 cubits (35 meters wide), whereas the porch in front of the hall had the full width of 100 cubits. The façade of the Sanctuary was decorated by four half-columns or half-pillars.[45] Between the two central columns the opening of the porch was 20 meters high; it was approached by twelve steps. The gate was wider at the top than at the bottom, and its lintel was built with alternate layers of stone and wood to commemorate the method used in constructing the First Temple.[46] Above the cornice of the Temple façade was a row of dentated battlements and spikes. The latter were gilded, and served to prevent birds from perching on the Temple parapet.[47] The walls of the Sanctuary were built, according to the Talmud, of white, reddish and blue marble, veined "like the waves of the sea."[48]

The entrance to the porch had no doors, but was covered with a blue, purple and red veil decorated with the signs of the zodiac.[49] Beyond the veil one could see the doors of the hall, which were covered with gold and surmounted by conches. Above the central door hung the golden vine which was built up over the years from the donations of the people.[50]

The central door of the hall was open by day. Inside, the walls were covered with gold plates decorated with palm designs. Within stood the golden candelabrum (*Menorah*), the table of the shewbread and the golden altar of incense. The candelabrum and the table are shown on the reliefs of the Arch of Titus in Rome, which depict the triumphal procession after the destruction of the Temple. At the inner end of the hall was a double veil closing off the Holy of Holies; no man entered it except the High Priest on the Day of Atonement. The Holy of Holies itself had the traditional dimensions of a cube of 20 cubits, and thus was half the height of the hall. Along the walls of the Sanctuary were three tiers of cells, around which a ramp ascended from the floor to the upper story. The latter was an empty space, the only purpose of which was to raise the height of the Sanctuary to 100 cubits.

The Second Temple in its final shape made a deep impression on all who saw it. The Rabbis said: "Whoever has not seen the building of Herod, has never seen a beautiful building in his life."[51] With its white walls and gold ornaments reflecting the light of the sun, it resembled a snowy mountain on a sunny day.

D. The Walls of the City

We have begun the description of Jerusalem with that of the Temple, which in those and subsequent generations undoubtedly was regarded as the heart of the city. We must now survey the outer limits of the town itself, beginning with the lines of the walls which defined its shape and separated it from the country round about. These walls were also an important factor in the general history of the city, but particularly, of course, in its military history before and during the revolt against Rome.

Research on the walls of Jerusalem began with a general topological study of the city.[52] At first the discussion was theoretical and was based on the passages in Josephus' *Jewish War* (Book IV, 136–76), as well as other passages dispersed throughout his writings. From the time of E. Robinson onward (i.e., from the middle of the 19th century), there has been an intensive study of the topography and its archaeological remains. More and more information has been collected on these matters, although complete agreement has not been reached on all points. The line of the First Wall is more or less agreed upon, although there are still differences of opinion about the date of its construction. The problem of the Second Wall depends on a solution to the problem of its date and to the general question of the extent of Jerusalem in the time of the Second Temple.[53] As regards the Third Wall, scholars are divided into two camps. One opinion is that this wall was identical with the line of the present north wall of the Old City. The second group believes that the remains excavated by E. L. Sukenik and L. A. Mayer in 1925/6, on a line already discovered by Robinson represent the true remains of the Third Wall.[54]

Josephus lists three walls of ancient Jerusalem. In most cases he numbers them from the point of view of the inhabitants, calling the innermost wall the first and the outermost the third. Occasionally, however, he counts them in the opposite way, as the Romans would when assaulting the city.

Although Josephus stated expressly that "the town was fortified with three walls," he adds at once, "except where it was surrounded by impassable ravines."[55] We should not, of course, take this sentence too literally; for there is no part of the Kidron Valley or the Hinnom Valley which is really impassable. What Josephus meant was that in the conditions of ancient warfare, a serious difference in height between the assailants and the defenders would make the walls of the city practically impregnable. We therefore find that Jerusalem was almost always attacked from the north side, where there were no great differences in level between the ground outside and inside the city. On the contrary, the high ground here slopes down from north to south, giving the besiegers somewhat of an advantage over the defenders. It is clear, therefore, that the three walls of Jerusalem in the time of the Second Temple were built on its north, northwest and northeast side, while the southern sections of the west and east walls and the whole of the south wall, where the defenses rested on the slopes of valleys, consisted of a single line only. Nevertheless, this southern line proved highly effective, for the city was not once attacked from that direction in the thirty sieges it had to endure.

I. THE FIRST WALL

According to Josephus,[56] the First Wall was the most ancient of the three, as well as the strongest, not only in construction, but also because of the valley in front of it and the elevation on which it was built. There is some justification in this statement. While the Third and Second Walls were breached by the Romans with relative ease, the First Wall proved the main line of defense during the siege of Titus. The line of the Third Wall, of course was a very long one, and difficult for the outnumbered defenders (25,000 against 70,000 attackers) to man effectively. The Second Wall, as we see, was constructed along a strategically weak line. On the other hand, the attacks on the First Wall were repulsed several times during the siege. Although we may attribute this in part to the desperate valor of the defenders — this was, after all, the last wall defending the Holy City — Josephus was nevertheless right in praising its strength. It is to be regretted that those parts of the wall which have so far been discovered belong to a section which was well protected by nature and therefore never seriously attacked; hence we are unable to judge its real strength.

The date of this wall is disputed as regards its northern and western sections; the solution of the problem depends on our view of the extent of the city during the time of the Israelite monarchy. It seems now that the line of this wall did not predate the Maccabean period, even though Josephus claims that it was built by David, Solomon and their successors. The archaeological finds made in the court of the Citadel, and those found earlier by Bliss, show that this section of the wall is of Hellenistic, probably Hasmonean date. Its eastern section was built at the same time, as has been established by the excavations of Dr. Kenyon.

According to Josephus, this wall began on its northern side at the tower called Hippicus (see page 234, below) and continued to the Xystus. It adjoined the Council Chamber and ended at the western portico of the Temple Mount. The Hippicus Tower is one of the three towers built by

Herod north of his palace; the Phasael Tower (the "Tower of David") was another of these. Clearly, therefore, we must look for this tower near the Citadel and the Jaffa Gate. From the Hippicus Tower, then, the First Wall ran eastwards in the direction of the Temple, taking advantage of the narrow transverse valley running west to east from the Jaffa Gate to the central valley, which thus served the wall as a fosse. The wall crossed the central valley on the line of Wilson's Arch. It is possible that this viaduct was a kind of dam, retaining the waters of the biblical "Upper Pool." In time of siege the openings in this viaduct were probably closed, and it could serve as part of the wall. In this section of the wall east of the Jaffa Gate two fragments have been found, one consisting of the remains of two towers with 18 meters of curtain between them, and the other a fragment of wall 6.5 meters long.[57]

Josephus continues his description of the wall as follows: "Starting from the same point [that is, from the Hippicus Tower] in another direction, westward, the wall continued in the direction of a place called Bethso to the Gate of the Essenes, and then continued southward above the Siloam Spring and again eastward toward the Pool of Solomon, and then past a place called Ophlas, and joined finally the eastern portico of the Temple Mount." From this description we note firstly that the wall also ran westward from the Hippicus Tower. Josephus makes no mention here of the Phasael Tower, but as we know from excavations that this tower was included in the line of the wall, it follows that the Hippicus stood to the east of it. The southward bend of the wall was found in the course of excavations inside the court of the Citadel. In all, 78 meters of the wall, including two towers, were uncovered, all belonging to the time before Herod. Herod's splendid tower was inserted into the line of this wall only at a later stage. The continuation of the First Wall southward has been cleared for almost its full length. Parts of it were found in the Armenian garden south of the Citadel. The continuation round Mt. Zion was excavated by Maudslay and Bliss in the second half of the 19th century. They reached a gate in the central valley which is most probably the one known as the Gate of the Essenes, since it led to the Judean Desert where the Essene communities lived.

As regards the mysterious "Bethso," the recent discovery of the copper scrolls in one of the Qumran caves might be of some help.[58] There, in paragraph 38, mention is made of a "cistern of Sh^{e}wa." This has been related to the biblical vale of Shaveh, also called "the King's Vale" in Genesis 14:17. Nehemiah 3:15 mentions the Pool of Siloam in the "King's Garden." By taking all these three sources together we may identify the Bethso with the Shaveh Valley or the King's Vale and place it at the junction of the Hinnom and Kidron valleys. This indicates a general south-western direction of the wall.

The other elements mentioned in this description are the Spring of Siloam, that is to say, the issue of the Siloam tunnel (the original Gihon Spring having been entirely forgotten by the time of Josephus), and the Pool of Siloam (for "Solomon"). All belong to the same vicinity, although it is difficult to understand why Josephus should mention the spring before the pool if his description goes from west to east. The position of the "Ophlas" (Ophel) south of the Temple Mount is quite clear, and so is the connection of the line of the wall with the southwest corner of the Temple area. Of this line Bliss discovered a length of 160 meters with five towers spaced at an average distance of 36 to 37 meters.[59]

The excavations have shown that the remains of the uncovered wall belong to two different periods. The upper wall was apparently built in the Byzantine period. Opinions differ with regard to the lower wall, however. Bliss himself, and those scholars who have assumed that the western hill was included in Jerusalem in the time of the monarchy, have assigned the wall to that period or at latest to the time of Nehemiah. Recent excavations have shown that this wall cannot possibly have been as early as that. In the court of the Citadel C. N. Johns has cleared a very similar wall which has been assigned to the Hellenistic period.[60] Dr. Kenyon, on the other hand, has concluded from her work at the "Gate of the Essenes" that at least the southern part of the Bliss wall is from the time of Agrippa I.[61] This would, however, imply for the Herodian period a line close to the present southern wall of the Old City, an unacceptable conclusion leaving the southern tip of the western hill outside the city walls. It seems, therefore, that the whole of the wall discovered by Bliss belongs to the Hasmonean period, when the Hellenistic "Antioch-at-Jerusalem" was united with the rest of the city. On the other hand, the "Ophel wall" discovered by Warren, which runs directly towards the southeast corner of the Herodian Temple enclosure, must be either later than the time of Herod, or at the least, contemporary. Its upper part is certainly Byzantine.[62]

Historical and topographical logic requires the existence of an inner wall protecting the Upper City on the east, since this quarter would otherwise have been at the mercy of an enemy reaching the Tyropoeon Valley from the east or south. If the Upper City was to be a defensible fortress equal to the Temple Mount, it had to be surrounded by walls on all sides, including the east. Moreover, we know from accounts of Titus' siege that after the capture of the Temple and the Lower City, the Upper City resisted alone for a whole month. The Romans were forced to construct new siege dams and attack this quarter from both east and west. If the Upper City had remained unprotected on the east, the attackers could easily have reached it by way of the central valley. No remains however, have been found on this line, apart from the deep rock cutting opposite the Western Wall area, which was probably made during the destruction of the *Akra* by Simeon the Hasmonean in 141 B.C.E.

II. THE SECOND WALL

In contrast with the more or less detailed description of the line of the first wall, Josephus mentions the Second Wall only in one short sentence: "The second wall started from the gate in the first wall, which they called Gennath and, encircling only the slope towards the north, went up as far as the Antonia."[63] The relative shortness of this line may be deduced from another passage,[64] which assigns to this wall only fourteen towers, as compared to sixty in the First and ninety in the Third Wall. The starting point of this wall, the "Gennath" gate, is unknown. There are two possible lines of this wall. If we assume that the Gennath gate is identical with the Water Gate of the Hippicus Tower, leading to the Amygdalon Pool (now called the "Pool of Hezekiah"), the wall may have followed the eastern edge of the pool, which could have served it as a fosse. On the other hand, if the gate were the one further to the east, the wall would have run along the edge of the valley from south to north. The other end of the line, the Antonia fortress, is a fixed point in the northwest corner of the Temple Mount. No remains of the Second Wall have been found so far. Present evidence, however, favors the second hypothesis, since both in Area C of Dr. Kenyon's soundings and in the excavations below the German church north of it, only a deep fill of probably Roman origin has been found. In any case the Second Wall must have reached the present Damascus Gate, since here in 1937 Hamilton found the remains of a Herodian gateway. As we shall see below, this cannot be part of the Third Wall, and hence must have belonged to the Second. If the Second Wall reached the Damascus Gate, it must have included the hill east of it and descended from that high area towards the Antonia, "encircling the slope towards the north," as Josephus has it.[65]

This line is not very sound strategically, but is the only probable one if we remember that the purpose of the Second Wall, built in the time of Herod, was to protect the market quarter in the upper Tyropoeon Valley. Under conditions of ancient warfare a flat area of about 200 meters was enough to afford the defenders reasonable protection; the effective range of ancient siege engines did not exceed that distance.[66] In fact the Second Wall did not hold out for long in the siege of Titus; the Romans breached it in five days, and their only difficulty was in afterwards taking the warren of streets and markets behind it.[67] From the descriptions of Josephus we may assume that this wall passed near the "Pool of Hezekiah"[68] and the monument of the High Priest, John (Hyrcanus).[69] A significant remnant possibly associated with this wall is a long rock cutting, resembling a rock scar with a projecting tower, which was found south of the Damascus Gate. The deep rock cutting east of the Damascus Gate might have belonged to the line of this wall.[70] A deep fosse also passed in front of the Antonia.[71] In the time of Josephus, the Second Wall actually marked the general line of the built-up area of Jerusalem, for, as he notes,[72] the Third Wall was built to include a large open area, on the assumption that the town would continue to grow northwards.

III. The Third Wall

The beginnings of this line date to the time of King Agrippa I, who set out to strengthen Jerusalem's northern defenses. According to Josephus the town would have been impregnable had the wall been completed as planned.[73] The Roman authorities ordered construction to cease, and the wall was completed only after the outbreak of the First Revolt in 66 A.D., using any material that came to hand. Josephus describes this Wall at more length than the Second but less briefly than the First.[74] "The third wall began at the tower Hippicus, whence it stretched northwards to the tower Psephinus, and then descended opposite the monuments of Helena... and proceeding through the Royal Caverns, it bent round a corner tower over against the so-called Fuller's Tomb, and joining the ancient rampart terminated at the valley of Kidron." Josephus states that the wall was completed only to a height of 25 cubits (12.5 meters) and in one place not completed at all.[75] Our source also mentions that this wall had ninety towers each 20 cubits (10 meters) wide and 45 cubits (22.5 meters) high, and spaced at 100 meter intervals.

The line of this wall has been in dispute ever since 1838, when Robinson proposed to assign to it the remains of walling visible about 500 meters north of the Damascus Gate. Most scholars of the late 19th and early 20th century have rejected that view, and have assumed that the Third Wall followed the present northern wall of the Old City. According to this theory, the tower of Psephinus which stood at the northwest corner of this wall was identical with the Herodian remains in the northwest corner of the Old City, known in Arabic as Qal'at Jalud (Goliath's Castle). This view has been recently maintained by Drs. Kenyon and Hennessy as the result of their excavations in 1964 near the Damascus Gate. Recent work outside the northwest corner of the city wall has shown that the allegedly Herodian remains at that corner of the Old City wall were of Crusader work reusing Herodian masonry. The towers discovered flanking the Damascus Gate belong to the Roman period, as has been convincingly proved by Hamilton in 1937. On the other hand, the line found by Robinson was excavated in 1925–6 by L.A. Mayer and E.L. Sukenik, who found a length of wall of about 500 meters. In 1940 a further 265 meters of wall were discovered.[76] The full stretch of wall on this line now extends for over one kilometer. In 1946 a quarry was found near the Street of the Prophets, from which stones similar in size to those used in the Mayer-Sukenik line had been removed. Since, according to the Mayer-Sukenik theory of the Third Wall, this was the area of the corner tower of Psephinus, the discovery lent further support to their identification. Moreover, the distances between the towers as indicated by Josephus (200 cubits or 100 meters) are confirmed by these discoveries. Thus, for example, 200 meters separated a tower found near the former Swedish school near the Nablus road from another tower which stood on the line of this road itself. The distance between the tower opposite the Albright Institute and the one east of it found in 1940 was 150 meters; but between that tower and the corner tower, nearer the Kidron, it was again 100 meters.

We may thus maintain, against the views of Simons[77] and Vincent,[78] that the Mayer-Sukenik wall is actually the wall as planned by Agrippa. The argument that the wall was built in a hurry and with any material that came to hand may be explained by the fact that the part excavated in this line was the hastily erected wall of the rebels. Recent excavations (1972) by S. Ben-Arieh and E. Nezer have shown its excellent planning. Vincent was unable to deny that this "rampart fantôme"[79] was a wall, and attributed it to the time of Bar-Kokhba.[80] It is impossible, however, to explain why Bar-Kokhba should have chosen to build a line of wall outside the existing wall of Agrippa and thus enlarge the line of defenses far to the north, at a time when Jerusalem was in ruins and its inhabitants few. Nor may the line of that wall be regarded as part of the Roman circumvallation, since according to Josephus this siege wall was built in three days.

We are therefore justified in attempting to fit the descriptions of Josephus to the proposed line of the Third Wall. Like the First Wall, it began at the Hippicus Tower near Herod's palace. The wall continued in a northwesterly direction along the slope of the upper Hinnom Valley, which changes direction near the Jaffa Gate. Some pieces of walling were observed along this line by Robinson. The Psephinus Tower has to be assumed at the highest point of the ridge near the present Abyssinian church (805 meters). The wall then turned and descended towards the Kidron Valley "opposite the tomb of Helena," the monument known today as the Tombs of the Kings (see below, page 243). The excavated remains were found between this slope and the Kidron itself.[81] The tower found in 1925 near the Albright Institute would then correspond to one of the "Women's Towers" flanking a gate.

The next passage in Josephus' description has caused commentators a great deal of difficulty. If we translate διά to mean "through" and assume the "Royal Caverns" to be the Cave of Zedekiah, we gain support for the theory that the Third Wall followed the line of the present wall of the Old City. If, however, we accept the meaning "besides" or "along," which is supported by Herodotus (IV, 39) — Thackeray has translated the crucial passage as "past the Royal Caverns"—then the outer line of the Third Wall, as proposed, is quite plausible. The site of the monument of the Fuller's Tomb is unknown. The last section of the wall followed the Kidron Valley till it joined the northwest corner of the Temple enclosure. One of its towers has been identified in the foundations of the Old wall south of the Stork's Tower.

The line of the Third Wall as proposed here represents a successful adaptation to the difficult terrain north of the city, which has always been the weak spot in Jerusalem's defenses. It makes use of the slope in the upper Hinnom Valley, which would thus provide part of the defense for the wall. At this point it had to cross the ridge going up from the town in a northwesterly direction. Here the corner tower of Psephinus was built, which was the strongest and largest of the towers of Jerusalem except for those protecting Herod's palace. After crossing this dangerous point they were again able to use the westward turn of the Kidron Valley, and then its continuation to the south.

The story of the siege of Titus shows how efficient was Agrippa's work. The Roman general was the only one to attack the city not from the convenient north side, but from the west near the Jaffa Gate of today.[82] This change in the line of attack was undoubtedly due to the existence of the Third Wall. It is, possible, however, that the choice was based also on another consideration. In Titus' camp there were at least two persons who were thoroughly acquainted with Jerusalem and its defenses. One of them was Tiberius Alexander, the nephew of Philo, who had been a governor of Judea and who served under Titus as chief-of-staff. The other was Josephus himself. The plan chosen by Titus upon their advice included a breach of the Third Wall near the Jaffa Gate, followed by an immediate attack on the First Wall, which was not protected by the Second in the spot. By taking the Upper City the Romans could have hoped to end the siege at one stroke. However, this plan failed; the First Wall proved too strong and the defenders too energetic. Titus was thus obliged to occupy the new town after breaching the Third Wall, and then to attack the Second Wall. The final assault came by way of the Antonia and Herod's towers north of the palace. The First Wall was finally breached through the Antonia, and this led to the fall of the Temple and the Lower City within ten days. The inner wall mentioned above (see page 223) now proved its value; it took another month for the Romans to capture the Upper City.

E. The Fortresses

The citadels built within the city were no less important for its defense than the walls themselves. These strongpoints served a double purpose: on the one hand they strengthened the line of the wall against the foe without; and on the other, they protected the rulers against their discontented subjects within. The Hellenizers in Hasmonean times, Herod and his descendants (with the exception of Agrippa I), the Roman procurators — all needed these fortresses to keep the people in submission and to protect themselves, their supporters and their soldiers in time of danger.

I. The Baris-Antonia

The oldest of these citadels was the Baris (*ha-Bira*). As we have noted (page 213), this fortress was built in the time of the monarchy or after the return from the Babylonian exile: it incorporated the towers of Hananel and Meah, which are already mentioned by Jeremiah. It stood on the saddle joining the Temple Mount to the ridge north of it. The disappearance of the royal palace which protected the Temple also made it especially necessary to strengthen the defenses on the north. Nehemiah already mentions a governor of the Bira.[83] We may assume that this fortress was included in the defenses of "Mount Zion," as the Temple Mount was called in Hasmonean times. The wall of the Temple had been already reinforced by the High Priest Simeon the Just (see above, page 213), and again by Judah the Maccabee after the liberation of the Temple area and the dedication of the Temple.[84] These fortifications were breached by order of King Antiochus V after his victory at Beth-zacharia and the reoccupation of the Temple Mount which followed it.[85] Josephus mentions on several occasions that this fortress, which he calls Baris (the Anatolian form of the Persian name for fortress), was strengthened by John Hyrcanus, and that his son Judah Aristobulus ruled from there.[86] In the Second Book of Maccabees mention is already made of the strengthening of the Temple Mount near the *Akra*[87] and of the fact that Simeon dwelt there with his family. The *Letter of Aristeas*, which was written in the Hasmonean period (although the author pretended that it was composed in the time of Ptolemy II Philadelphus, and added various imaginary and fictitious details), contains a description of the fortress near the Temple with a tower garrisoned by 500 men who changed guard from time to time.[88] The fortress of Baris was connected with the Temple by an underground passage through one of its towers called Strato's Tower (the name is identical with that of the city which later became Caesarea). We do not know which Strato this name refers to; perhaps he was the architect who built it or some governor of the fortress in the time of the Hasmoneans or earlier.

During the civil war that followed the death of Queen Alexandra, the Baris was a stronghold of the faction of Aristobulus. During Pompey's siege the Romans attacked the Temple Mount from the north, since it was too well protected on its other three sides by deep valleys — the central valley, the valley of Hinnom and the Kidron Valley. By then, however, the strong fortifications of the Temple on that side made the attack very difficult. Josephus states that it was protected by a deep fosse and high towers.[89] In the parallel account in the *Jewish War*, the "strong and beautiful" towers on that side are again referred to.[90] Pompey was forced to attack the Temple on its strong northern side just as Titus had to do later on. In Herod's siege of Jerusalem, the city was again attacked from the north. Herod first occupied the outlying areas of the Temple[91] and the Lower City.[92] Antigonus defended himself from the Baris, and at the end of the siege left the fortress to surrender.

When Herod ruled in Jerusalem, he seems to have remembered the difficulties of the long siege, and decided to strengthen the northern defenses of Jerusalem in general and of the Temple in particular. He therefore rebuilt the old Baris and called it the Antonia in honor of the Roman triumvir, Mark Antony, who was then the ruler of the eastern half of the empire, including Judea.[93] From that time onwards this fortress was the focal point of the Temple's defenses. From there the king's soldiers, and later on the Roman garrison, could control the rebellious masses which assembled especially on the occasion of the three annual pilgrimages to Jerusalem. The courts of the Temple were then full of people and the slightest spark could cause a revolt. The Antonia also served as a safe place of keeping for the sacred vestments of the High Priest, which were handed over to those in charge of the Temple only on the eve of the festivals. This was also one of the means used by Herod and the procurators to keep the Jews obedient. If necessary, the soldiers could descend from the fortress into the northern and western porticoes of the Temple which met near the Antonia.[94] At the outbreak of the First Revolt the Antonia fell into the hands of the rebels after a fight lasting two days.[95] From then on the fortress served as a strongpoint in the defenses of Jerusalem, until the Romans broke through it between the 5th and 26th of Tammuz and razed it to its foundations.

According to Josephus[96] the Antonia was built on a steep rock 50 cubits (25 meters) high. This rock was surfaced from its base upwards with flat paving stones which not only served as ornament but also made the work of the attackers more difficult. A battlement 3 cubits (1.5 meters) high surrounded the building; behind it the tower rose to a height of 40 cubits (20 meters). The full height of the tower was therefore 45 meters. The inside of the fortress served at one and the same time as a palace and a barracks. It included halls, porches, baths and courts, and could house a large garrison. At the corners of the fortress rose four towers. Three of these were 25 meters high, while the fourth one in the south-eastern corner, which dominated the whole Temple court, was 35 meters high. Including the wall below it rose to a total height of 55 meters, and was the tallest structure in the whole town.

The archaeological remains found in the area of the fortress suggested to L. H. Vincent a reconstruction of its plan.[97] According to this reconstruction, the fortress extended on both sides of the Via Dolorosa, including the convent of Notre Dame de Sion and part of the Monastery of the Flagellation. The pavement under the convent was identified with the *lithostrotos* of John 19 : 13 and the place where Jesus was judged by Pilate. The double pool extending below the convent has been identified with the Pool of Struthion mentioned in connection with the Roman assault on the Antonia in 70 A.D.[98] Recently P. Benoit has suggested a much smaller fortress, not passing north of the Via Dolorosa.

Remains of the foundations of the Antonia have been identified by Vincent on the rock surface of the Temple Mount near its northwestern corner; it seems that the present area of the esplanade included part of the fortress. Two rock cuttings are especially important in this connection: one is 107 meters in length and runs parallel to the north border of the Temple esplanade; the other one is 36 meters long and is parallel to the west border. The former is 3 to 10 meters high, rising as the rock descends eastwards in the direction of the Kidron Valley. The second rock cutting is 4.8 meters high. Here and there stones dressed in the typically Herodian style are still visible. The Antonia was rectangular in shape, with two of the four towers mentioned by Josephus in the east and two in the west. The rock-cut platform (60 × 35 meters) probably formed the base of the principal buildings. The main entrance was on the west; it was connected with the central valley and the city's main commercial thoroughfare, as well as with the road leading north, whence came the Roman governors and soldiers. There seems to have been no northern gate to the Antonia, since on that side the fortress was protected by a deep fosse. On the east a small postern has been assumed, to ensure access to the Sheep market and control over the northern gate of the Temple Mount. On the south the Antonia was connected by steps with the northern end of the west porches.

II. *The Akra*

Before the Antonia, Jerusalem's foreign garrison was stationed in another fortress, called the *Akra* in the Books of Maccabees and by Flavius Josephus. Let us examine the literary and topographical sources for the identification and location of this fortress. Whereas all are agreed on the position of the Antonia (if not on its size or plan) the site of the *Akra* is one of the main bones of contention in the topography of Jerusalem. According to I Maccabees 1:33, Apollonius, the Seleucid commander left in Jerusalem in 167 B.C.E., erected a strong wall in the "City of David" and "it became for them (the Hellenizers) an *Akra*." The *Akra*, which stood out against the Temple and had to be blockaded several times in the early years of the Hasmonean revolt, finally surrendered in 141 B.C.E. to Simeon the Hasmonean;[99] according to Josephus, he seized the fortress by main force. Simeon entered the *Akra* "with praise and palm branches and with harps, cymbals, and viols, and with hymns and songs; because a great enemy was destroyed out of Israel." (I Macc. 13:51).

According to Josephus,[100] Simeon thereupon persuaded the people to level the mound on which the *Akra* stood, so that the Temple might be the higher of the two. After three years of work, night and day, it was broken down to its base and the ground made quite flat.[101] In another place[102] Josephus mentions a hill shaped like a hog's back which supported the Lower City, and which bore the name of *Akra*. In several other places[103] Josephus equates the *Akra* with Lower City; but he contrasts the Lower City and "the Citadel" (*Akra*) as the two parts of Jerusalem captured separately by David.[104] According to I Maccabees 13:52, Simeon "fortified the Temple Mount by the *Akra* and dwelt there, he and those with him." If the Baris, the forerunner of the Antonia, was "by the *Akra*," one must have been situated fairly near the other. Obviously, then, Josephus cannot have been correct in locating the *Akra* in the Lower City; he was apparently trying as best he could to reconstruct the city mentally, as it existed before Herod.

Let us sum up the evidence on the *Akra* from the primary source, the Books of Maccabees:

(1) it was situated in the "City of David";
(2) it was outside "the City" as it existed in Hasmonean times;
(3) it was on a level with or even higher than the Temple Mount;
(4) it adjoined the Tyropoeon market;
(5) it was razed by Simeon;
(6) it was not far from Baris or Antonia.

The assumption that the *Akra* was situated in the Lower City south of the Temple conflicts with every one of these statements. In its southern position the *Akra* would indeed be in the City of David as we understand it now, but certainly not in what was believed to be the City of David in the time of Jason of Cyrene or Josephus.[105]   It would be inside the Hasmonean city and not separate from it. It could hardly be higher than the Temple Mount, for neither the existing rock surface nor the geological stratification suggest that there could have been a second mountaintop south of the Rock in the Dome of the Rock. Such an *Akra* would be quite distant from both the Tyropoeon and the Baris.[106]

We can only conclude that the *Akra* was situated across the central valley opposite the Temple. In the northeast corner of the Upper City there is a hill which is separated from the rest of the western hill by a fairly narrow neck. This hill is 726 m. in elevation and would thus have been 20 meters higher than the Temple area.[107] Remains found by Avigad in the Jewish Quarter include those of a massive wall of a fortification dating to the Hellenistic period, that was in all likelihood once part of the *Akra*.[108] The rock cuttings opposite the Western Wall which delimit this area on the east could be evidence of Simeon's activity described above.

III. The herodian Palace

Parallel to the construction of the Antonia with its towers and buildings forming a stronghold on the eastern side, Herod decided to protect the Upper City by building another fortified palace in the northwest corner of the Upper City. He probably refused to live in the old, unfortified Hasmonean palace inside the town, since he would have been unable to leave it suddenly and seek a safer refuge in time of revolt. The new site was so well chosen that it has remained the focus of civil and military power in Jerusalem from Herod's time to the present.

The Herodian palace occupied a considerable area of the Upper City. According to Josephus, its whole area was surrounded by a wall 30 cubits (15 meters) high with towers at set intervals. Inside the wall, the palace was arranged in the Persian-Hellenistic manner in a series of pavilions set in an elaborate garden. The pavilions were connected by semi-circular porches or exedrae. The palace included two large banqueting halls, living rooms and accommodation for a hundred guests. The rooms were decorated with colored marble. The halls were roofed over with very long beams, making it possible to dispense with interior columns. The description of the pools and flowing fountains inside the palace gardens shows that the aqueduct of Jerusalem must already have been operating in the time of Herod.

The two main buildings were named after the emperor Augustus (Caesaraeum) and the emperor's vice-regent, Marcus Vipsanius Agrippa (Agrippaeum).[109] The use of these two names proves that the palace was built after the battle of Actium, whereas the Antonia was constructed before that battle. Such a chronology certainly corresponds to what we generally know of Herod's mode of action. His first interest was in security; only after this was taken care of by the construction of his three towers and the fortress of Antonia could he think of embellishing either his own palace or the Temple. The foundations of Herod's palace have been found in excavations in at least four places: the court of the Citadel, the Armenian garden opposite St. James' Cathedral, near the southwest corner of the Old City wall and on "Mount Zion" outside the present city wall. They consist of a network of intersecting walls one meter thick, which were filled up with earth and rubble and supported the platform on which the palace was built.[110]

IV. The Towers

Herod reinforced the weak north side of his palace by the construction of three strong towers. One of the three towers was named after Herod's brother Phasael, who committed suicide in Parthian captivity in 40 B.C.E. The two brothers had worked closely together during their father's lifetime, and the death of Phasael opened the way to the throne for Herod himself. He also honored the memory of his brother by the foundation of a village called Phasaelis in the Jordan Valley. The second tower was called Hippicus after an otherwise unknown friend of King Herod. The third tower he named for his beloved Hasmonean wife, Mariamne, whom he had had executed in a fit of jealousy. In Josephus' *Jewish War*[111] we find a detailed description of the three towers, from which we are able to determine that the tower popularly known as "David's Tower" is built on the stump of the Phasael, a 20 meter cube. This base was surmounted by a porch 5 meters in height. At its center a second high tower rose up another 20 meters, containing living quarters and a bath. The top of the tower was ornamented by battlements, and the whole recalled the famous Pharos lighthouse of Alexandria. The total height of the Phasael was 45 meters. Its foundations descend to the rock and slope away at their lower extremity. The stones of the Phasael are typically Herodian, with a double margin and a flat boss. Excavations in the court of the Citadel have shown that this tower was inserted into the earlier wall dating from the Hasmonean period. The base of the tower is almost solid ashlar.

The sites of the other two towers are at present unknown. They were, however, close to the Phasael. The Hippicus was somewhat smaller than the Phasael (it was only 40 meters high). Its base was 15 meters in height and 12.5 meters square. On top of this was a 10 meter high reservoir, which was fed by rainwater from the roof and protected by its own double-sloped roof. The 12.5 meter space between the reservoir and the battlements was left open. The base of the Mariamne Tower was smaller still (10 meters) and the total height of the tower no more than 27.5 meters. It was the most ornate of the three towers.

The identification of the Phasael is certain, but the exact position of the other two towers is still unknown. Some believe that the Hippicus should be identified with the northwest corner of the Citadel. Excavations in the Citadel court have shown that all the existing towers except the base of the Phasael were built in the 13th and 14th centuries A.D. The two tower bases found inside the Citadel court belong to an earlier wall and are not built in the same manner as the Phasael. We must therefore look for these two towers east and southwest of the latter. It is possible that Hippicus — the stronger tower — was placed on a rocky bulge (elev. 768.4 m.) between David Street and Christ Church in the Old City. The Mariamne Tower, which being the weaker was probably not included in the lines of the walls, stood on a similar elevation (768 m.) slightly more to the south. According to this theory, the three towers formed a triangle, which was a fortress in itself.[112]

This hypothesis is supported by the account of the siege of the towers at the beginning of the First Revolt (July/August 66 A.D.). After the forces of Agrippa II abandoned the Herodian palace, the remaining Roman troops took up positions in the three towers and continued to defend themselves.[113] This proves that the three towers were not built in one line, for in that case

32.
Mt. Carmel hoard of Tyrian tetradrachms
Dept. of Antiq. and Museums, Jerusalem

33.
Air view of Ledga landscape with Roman road
(Poidebard)

34·
Site of the Antonia fortress built by Herod I

35·
Strution pool or the "twin pool" originally located under
the Antonia fortress

36.
Herod's aqueduct at Caesarea — a fair example of his
elaborate water supply system

37.
Phasael Tower, popularly called "David's Tower," one
of the three towers built by Herod to protect his royal palace

Dept. of Antiq. and Museums, Jerusalem

38.
Herodian masonry near Damascus Gate
Dept. of Antiq. and Museums, Jerusalem

39.
Herodian wall at the Cave of Machpelah, Hebron
Dept. of Antiq. and Museums, Jerusalem

40.

Plan of a Roman villa from
Tell el-Judeideh

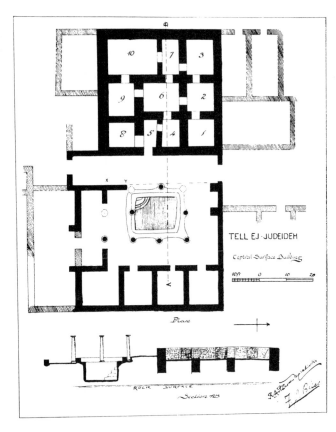

41.

Bird fresco in a private house,
excavated at Mt. Sion, Jerusalem

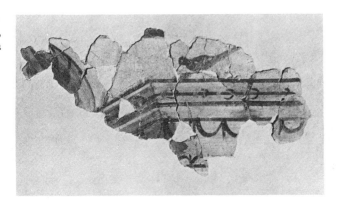

42.

Mosaic floor of the Herodian
Period, uncovered at the Jewish
Quarter of the Old City, Jerusalem

43.
Corinthian capital dating from the
Herodian Period. Found in the Old
Jewish Quarter, Jerusalem

44.
Herodian pottery. Jars and a typical lamp

45.
Fractions of stone
reliefs, probably part
of the wall and gates
from the royal
callonade built by
Herod. Excavated at
the Southern Wall,
Jerusalem

46.
Plan of burial cave
with vaults of the
Herodian Period

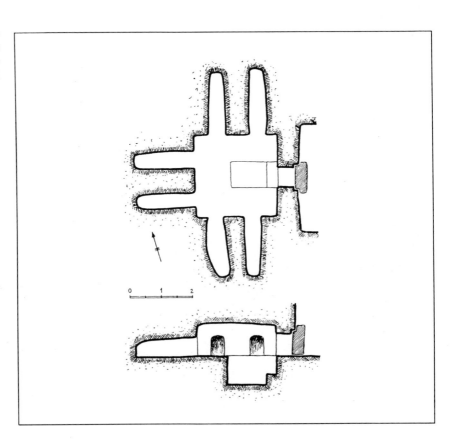

47.
Staircase leading to
Queen Helene's tomb,
known as the "Tomb
of the Kings,"
Jerusalem

48.
Burial vaults seen
inside the "Sanhedrin
Tombs," Jerusalem

49

Gable doorway of the "Sanhedrin Tombs"

50.

Ornamentation detail on burial coffin

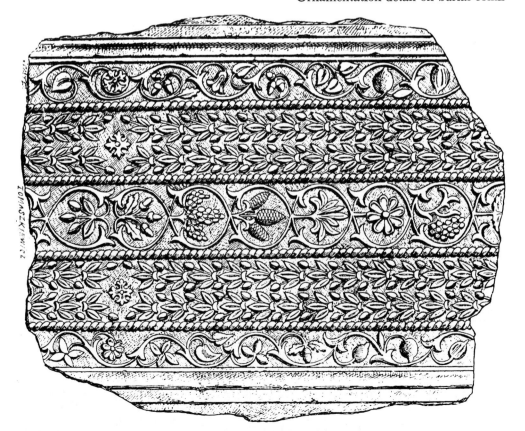

51.
Sarcophagus with stylized ornamentation from the
burial vault of a Nazirite family (Second Temple Period),
uncovered at Mt. Scopus, Jerusalem

52.
Stone ossuary with typical ornamentation from Herod's
family tomb, Jerusalem

53.
Western Wall built by Herod around the Temple Mount,
with Robinson's arch

54.
Inscription on wall synagogue built by Theodotos, dating
from Herod's time
Dept. of Antiq. and Museums, Jerusalem

55.
Greek inscription forbidding the entrance of foreigners
into the inner Temple area
Dept. of Antiq. and Museums, Jerusalem

56.
Façade of the Second Temple erected by Herod I.
Model based on Prof. M. Avi-Yonah's reconstruction
Holyland Hotel, Jerusalem

they could have been attacked separately through the curtain wall and each one isolated and destroyed. As a fortified triangle, the towers were far easier to defend.

Agrippa I competed with his grandfather in the construction of towers in Jerusalem. He built ninety towers in the Third Wall, the most important of which was the corner tower called Psephinus. This tower was 35 meters high and was octagonal in shape.[114] As it stood on the highest spot in the city (805 meters), it was possible from its roof to see the sun rising over Arabia in the east, and the whole area of Judea down to the sea in the west. "Arabia" (i.e., the mountains of Moab) can of course be seen from every high spot in Jerusalem. With regard to the Mediterranean, the height of the tower (35 meters) added the elevation of its site (805 meters) would be quite enough to command a view over Romema, the highest hill west of Jerusalem (829 meters). This tower must have been built in the days of King Agrippa, for when the Third Wall was hastily finished in 66 A.D. there was no time to build such high and massive structures. The remains at Qal'at Jalud once claimed to have been the Psephinus, hardly reach 785 meters, and are now not regarded as Herodian in date.[115]

In concluding our discussion of the walls of Jerusalem, it is worth mentioning that Josephus estimates the length of the whole wall as thirty stadia.[116] This includes the entire Third Wall and the western, southern, and eastern parts of the First Wall (the Second Wall and the northern part of the First Wall were all within the city). Taking a stadium as 185 meters, the full length of the wall would be 5,550 meters. In contrast with this figure, other estimates of the city's perimeter seem greatly exaggerated, especially by those authors who wrote before Agrippa I had almost doubled the size of the city by building the Third Wall. A Syrian topographer quoted by Eusebius[117] gives the circumference of the city as 27 stadia (5,195 meters); Pseudo-Aristeas and Timochares (also quoted by Eusebius)[118] give 40 stadia (7,400 meters); Hecataeus, who is quoted by Josephus in his book *Against Apion*,[119] estimates it at 50 stadia (9,250 meters); finally Strabo gives 60 stadia (11,100 meters) — more than double the true estimate.[120] The correct measurements are 4,200 meters for the First Wall, 4,600 meters together with the assumed line of the Second Wall, and 5,500 meters together with the Third Wall.[121]

F. THE CITY QUARTERS AND THEIR BUILDINGS

The historical circumstances of the development of Jerusalem, and in particular the various changes in the line of its walls, resulted in the separation of the city's populated areas (i.e., those parts which were outside the Temple Mount, the royal palace and the fortresses) into four quarters, each of which had its own function and character. These were the Upper City, the Lower City, the markets and the New City.

I. THE UPPER CITY

This quarter extended from the First Wall in the north to the Valley of Hinnom in the south; from east to west, it stretched from the central valley to Herod's palace. It occupied the whole area of the western hill from the saddle on which stood the three towers, as well as the transverse valley along which the First Wall ran down to the Tyropoeon. The surface of this hill was fairly flat and could be conveniently used for building. In its northwest corner there was an outlying ridge on which first the *Akra* and later the royal palace of the Hasmoneans were built. Although originally settled by Israelites during the period of the monarchy, its planning most probably only took place in the Hellenistic period as part of the "Antioch-at-Jerusalem" demanded by the Hellenizers.[122] It was therefore planned from the beginning with streets intersecting at right angles according to the so-called Hippodamian plan.

Several times Josephus calls the Upper City the "upper market."[123] This name may be derived from the "upper agora," the center of the Hellenistic city. If we are to judge from the examples of other Hellenistic cities (such as Miletus, Priene, etc.), this market-place was surrounded by colonnades. Its most likely location was the center of the Hellenistic city at the highest point of the western hill. The fact that the Hasmoneans could plan to cut the *Akra* off from the marketplace by a wall shows that they were near each other. When Herod built his palace on the western edge of the Upper City, he probably appropriated the western half of the agora, which thenceforth adjoined the east wall of the palace.[124] In a normal Greek town the temples of the gods and the gymnasium would be built near the agora.[125] Such buildings may have been planned for Antioch-at-Jerusalem as well. Some remains, including a huge column base and a matching capital, have indeed been found in the Old City, and these may have been intended for such a temple.[126] When the Hasmoneans took over the city, however, such plans were of course abandoned. Instead of a gymnasium, Jewish Jerusalem had a place called the Xystus, a square which ordinarily formed part of the group of buildings used for athletics, but which in this case served only for the gathering of large popular assemblies.

The Upper City probably had two gates on the north, one the Water

Gate of the towers[127] and the other apparently leading to the markets (either of these might be the Gennath Gate mentioned by Josephus as the beginning of the Second Wall). There must have been one gate near the towers leading westward and southward, the precursors of the Bethlehem Gate of the Byzantine period and the Jaffa Gate of our time. In the west, Herod's palace blocked the Upper City for its full length. In the south, we know of no gate apart from the Gate of the Essenes, near the Pool of Siloam,[128] but an unnamed gate has been found by Maudslay near Bishop Gobat's school. In the east there must have been one gate leading to Wilson's Arch and over the viaduct to the Temple Mount; the remains of a road from the Herodian period pointing straight towards Robinson's Arch suggest that there was another gate in the eastern wall. This latter gate was probably connected with the stairways discovered in the eastern slope of "Mt. Zion."[129]

Higher than other parts of Jerusalem, and situated on the west side of the city where it enjoyed the cool sea breeze, the Upper City was always the preferred residential quarter for the important and the rich. From the history of the first days of the revolt against Rome, we know for certain that here stood the palaces of Agrippa II and Berenice (as we have already seen on page 214, it is possible that they resided in the old Hasmonean palace built on the ruins of the *Akra*, which had passed from the Hasmoneans to the Herodians). We also know that near this palace stood the palace of the High Priest, Ananias, since both buildings were burnt in the same conflagration.[130] Elsewhere we read that the masses of the people erupted into the "upper market" and confronted "the heads of the people and the High Priests," who apparently lived there. If the "upper market" (the agora) did not actually serve for commercial purposes (the real, markets, as we shall see, were in another part of the town), at least it was situated near the storehouses and residences of the great merchants of Jerusalem.

We know about the design of the houses in this quarter through the recent excavations in the Jewish Quarter of the Old City, especially of the house belonging to the Bar Kathros family (the so-called "burnt house") and the houses near it. These houses, as well as those excavated on "Mt. Zion," were basically of the Hellenistic Mediterranean type, with a central court, rooms grouped around it, and underground kitchens, cellars, cisterns and bathing pools.[131] We know from various references to Agrippa's palace that its flat roof commanded a view of the whole city. According to Josephus,[132] the king added a vast banqueting hall from which he could look into the Inner Temple. A comparison, however, of the heights of the two buildings disproves this story. We are told that the people assembled in the Xystus below the palace could see Berenice, the king's sister, standing in the "presentation window" of the palace.[133] This feature of the Hasmonean palace had probably been copied from the Ptolemaic palaces, which in their turn had adopted it from their Pharaonic predecessors; it was possibly a kind of *liwan* or loggia open to the street. The one house which has been excavated in the grounds of the Gallicantu monastery and which has been represented as a Hellenistic house from the time of the Second Temple, is in fact a later Roman structure.[134]

II. THE LOWER CITY

According to Josephus, the Lower City extended over the eastern hill[135] which he calls the *Akra*; but in another passage[136] at *Akra* comprises only part of the Lower City, which also included an area known as Ophlas (biblical Ophel). The topographical layout of Jerusalem shows that the Lower City must have included the southern end of the eastern hill, south of the Temple Mount, i.e., the real Ophel and the City of David. This we should of course distinguish from the "City of David" or "Zion" situated on the western hill, according to Josephus and later topographers. The Lower City also included the southern part of the central valley and probably even the lower slopes of the western hill on the east, since these were outside the wall encircling the Upper City. The Lower City therefore included the oldest parts of the built-up area of ancient Jerusalem. It included the "Jewish city" from the time of the Hasmoneans, as opposed to the "Hellenistic city of Antioch" which was built in the northern part of the Upper City. Naturally, therefore, the Lower City was densely populated, the houses crowding the slopes of the hills and spilling into the valley. This part of the city had a distinctly popular character, and its inhabitants were mostly poor. Thus, for instance, when the nobles pursued the Zealot leader Menahem, who had instigated the revolt against Rome, he was able to flee to the Ophel and find refuge there among his partisans from the lower classes.[137] For the same reason, those of the rich who felt themselves nearer to the people and were opposed to the official line of compromise with the government and the Greek or Roman culture, preferred to settle in the Lower City. Here were the palaces of the royal house of Adiabene, whose members had adopted Judaism. These included the palace of Queen Helena, which according to Josephus stood in the center of the *Akra*, i.e., in the heart of the Lower City.[138] Not far from this stood the palace of a relative, the princess Grapte,[139] which was used during the siege of Jerusalem as the headquarters of John of Gischala. Helena's son Monobazos, whom the Mishnah calls "King Monobaz," had a palace (*aulê*) on the slopes of the central valley.[140] If we remember that the sons of this family fought with great distinction against the Romans during the siege to Titus, we can understand why they decided to build their palaces in a popular quarter and not among the aristocracy of the Hellenized Upper City. The corner of a large house found in 1940 during excavations in the central valley[141] may be a remnant of one of these palaces.

In addition to these palaces, the Lower City contained the archive and the municipality building (*bouleuterion*), both of which are mentioned together in the list of buildings burnt down after the capture of the Temple Mount and the whole Lower City by Titus.[142] The *bouleuterion* mentioned here is distinct from the council house (*boulê*), which was connected with the First Wall between the Xystus and the Temple Mount.[143] The archives were burnt early in the revolt, when the rebels seized and destroyed the bills of debt stored there.[144] We may assume, therefore, that the two buildings were close together and that the archives also served the needs of the municipal administration. It is possible that part of these buildings were found in the recent excavations near Robinson's Arch. Although it is not certain whether Jerusalem had a city council (*boulê*)[145] in the Greek sense or whether the Sanhedrin filled that function, we may assume that the practical needs of the local adminstration were best served by locating the offices of the municipality near a popular thoroughfare where they were easily accessible.

The Lower City was divided into two by the Tyropoeon. This name, which is mentioned only once in Josephus' *Jewish War*,[146] literally means "Valley of the Cheesemakers"; according to that source it separated the Upper from the Lower City and continued to the Siloam, an abundant spring of sweet water. In another passage[147] this valley is simply called the "central valley." It is undoubtedly the valley now called el-Wad which bisects the Old City from the Damascus Gate in the north to the Dung Gate in the south. The name "Valley of the Cheesemakers" has not yet been satisfactorily explained. Jerusalem was never a large center for dairy produce and cattle raising, and it is hardly likely that those engaged in cheesemaking should have the main valley of the town named after them, especially as this activity was not a separate craft but a part of dairy production. It has been suggested that there is a biblical reference to a "Cheese Gate" in Nehemiah 3:13, where *safot*, meaning "cream" or "cheese,"[148] is given in place of *ashpot* ("dung"), but this variant is undoubtedly a simple mistake of the copyist. Other proposals have regarded the Tyropoeon as a corruption of some Hebrew or Aramaic name with a similar sound,[149] but none of these are really convincing. The source of the Siloam's water is of course the Gihon Spring, which is connected to it by Hezekiah's tunnel.

III. THE MARKETS

The Upper part of the central valley lay between the First and Second Walls. This valley, which is joined by a transverse valley leading up to the royal towers, ended near what is now known as the Damascus Gate, and it has always been the commercial center of Jerusalem. During the monarchy, the shops of the perfume makers and the goldsmiths were located there. In the time of the Second Temple it was the site of the wool market, the clothing market and the shops of the coppersmiths.[150] The narrow streets in the market quarter were cut obliquely by the Second Wall; the fact that the Jewish defenders knew this quarter well helped them for a time to repulse the Romans who had made a narrow breach in the Second Wall and had begun to wander aimlessly in the market streets. A flanking attack from the "upper gates" in the Second Wall (perhaps the gate in the hill east of the Damascus Gate) forced the Romans to retire. Indeed, the Romans would have suffered a major defeat had their archers not been able to shoot from the part of the wall they already occupied. We should note that in this passage Josephus lists the markets as belonging to the "New City." The latter usually refers to the Bezetha quarter outside the Second Wall; since, however, he is speaking here of an area occupied after the breaching of the Second Wall, the "New City" must be that enclosed by Herod within the Second Wall. This same area, which was filled with markets in the time of the Second Temple, remained a commercial center of Jerusalem in later times as well. Here were the forum of the Roman colony and the bazaars of the Crusaders, and to this day it is the market quarter of the Old City.

Apart from the central market, there were three other places in which trade was conducted in ancient Jerusalem. One of these was the "upper market" which we have already mentioned — the *agora* of the Hellenistic city. The second was the wood market, which was placed outside the Second Wall in the Bezetha quarter because of the danger of conflagration. This we learn from the description of the attack by the governor of Syria, Cestius Gallus, at the beginning of the First Revolt in 66 A.D. When Gallus and his army reached the gates of Jerusalem he burnt down Bezetha or the "New City" and the area known as the wood market; only then did he advance into the Upper City.[151] The third market was for the sale of sheep, and was centered round the Sheep's Pool (Προβατική) mentioned in the New

Testament.[152] The Hebrew name Beth Ḥasda (Bethesda, Bezetha?) is also mentioned in this connection. The proximity of this pool to the Sheep Gate of the time of the monarchy (situated north of the Temple) is explained by the necessity of having a convenient place near the Sanctuary and yet outside the city where sacrificial animals could be brought.[153] The purchasers could take the animal through the Tadi Gate into the Temple court where they could be kept in special tents provided in the Chamber of the Hearth of the Inner Temple.[154] Here, too, we note the persistence of traditions in Jerusalem. Until quite recently the weekly sheep market was held outside Herod's Gate near the ancient Sheep's Pool; only now have the sheep been chased away by the taxis and the market moved around the corner of the wall near the Stork's Tower in the same vicinity.[155]

IV. BEZETHA OR THE "NEW CITY"

In his account of the topography of Jerusalem, Josephus adds a fourth hill to the other three hills upon which Jerusalem was built. According to him, Jerusalem's increasing population could no longer be contained within the city walls, and spread out into an area north of the Temple. This area included a fourth hill called the Bezetha, "which can be translated into Greek as the New City"; it was situated opposite the Antonia but was separated from it by a deep ditch.[156] Agrippa I enclosed this quarter with the Third Wall which, as we have seen (page 225), was completed at the beginnings of the revolt against Rome.[157] In another passage we read that the Bezetha hill was the highest of all the hills in the town, that part of the New City spread over it, and that it was the only obstacle hiding the Temple from the north.[158] We also read of the encounter between the Jewish populace and the two cohorts brought from Caesarea by the procurator Florus; these pursued the Jews through Bezetha in the direction of the Temple and the Antonia. It seems, therefore, that this quarter was situated between the road entering the city from the north and the Temple Mount.[159] Bezetha is mentioned twice more in one passage.[160] The "First Wall" (meaning the Third Wall — see above, page 225 f.) was somewhat lower in the section opposite the monument of John the High Priest (see below, page 243); the builders had neglected to fortify the less populated quarters of the New City. According to another passage,[161] the Roman siege wall continued from the Assyrian camp to the Kidron Valley through the lower parts of the New City. From these topographical data and from the excavations along the line of the Third Wall we may conclude that by the hill of Bezetha Josephus meant the hill northeast of the Damascus Gate; this is in fact 778 meters in elevation and thus higher than both the Temple Mount (743 meters) and the Upper City (777 meters). It was only after Agrippa I carried his wall over to the Psephinus Tower 805 meters above sea level that the city reached a still higher elevation. The nucleus of the "New City" was therefore the hill which on the east reached as far as the Sheep's Pool and on the west the gate in the line of the Second Wall which stood below what is now the Damascus Gate and the wood market opposite. Between this quarter and the Second Wall there was a deep cutting crossed today by the Jericho road. It is obvious that the builders of the Third Wall believed that the town would grow much larger and therefore included a large open area within their wall, mainly on the western side in continuation of the Upper City ridge as far as the "Assyrian camp" from where Titus conducted his siege.[162] This is apparently the area now known as the Russian compound.

G. The Buildings and Monuments Outside the City Wall

I. The Villages around the City

A large city such as Jerusalem was at the end of the period of the Second Temple did not necessarily stop at its walls even after these had been extended. The city, of course, had its necropolis, as well as a number of open villages and other monuments around it. Among the villages we may mention four built on the Mount of Olives and its slopes. These were Bethany,[163] Bethphage,[164] Bahurim and the so-called "Village of Agrippa."[165] On the south of the city was a village known as the "House of Pulse" ('Ερεβίνθων οἶκος)',[166] the exact location of which is not known. It is mentioned, however, as being in the line of the siege wall between Pompey's camp and the Herodian monument, and as at least the latter is known with certainty we may assume that this village was situated in what is now known as the Valley of Rephaim. We are also told, in the same passage describing the Roman circumvallation, of a rock called "the Dovecote" (Περιστερών) situated in the Kidron Valley above the Siloam ravine. It is possible that this was the place where doves were brought up for the Temple sacrifices. As is usual in the suburbs of large cities, there were many fruit and vegetable gardens around Jerusalem, especially in the area north of the city down to the Kidron Valley. There were many small patches fenced off with stone walls and crisscrossed by irrigation channels.[167] All these walls, gardens and trees were destroyed when the Romans leveled the area outside Jerusalem in preparation for their assault.[168]

II. The Necropolis

Our information about the cemeteries around Jerusalem comes from two sources, literary and archaeological. The literary sources deal only with the most important and prominent monuments which served as fixed points in the topography of Jerusalem and its surroundings. Only in two cases (the "Tombs of the Kings" of Adiabene and the "Herodian Tomb") can we identify these monuments from literary sources; in five other cases (the Tomb of the House of Nicànor, the Tomb of the Family of Calon, Jason's Tomb, the Tomb of the Bene Hezir, and the Tomb of the Nazirite) we know their names from inscriptions written on ossuaries or on the lintel of the tomb itself. Of all other important monuments mentioned in our sources nothing is left but the name. In a few cases we can at least determine their approximate location from our topographical knowledge. Thus, for instance, the Fuller's Tomb (τοῦ Γναφέως μνῆμα) [169] which is mentioned in the description of the Third Wall between the corner tower and the Kidron Valley, must have stood where the line of that wall approaches the valley. The tomb of the High Priest Ananias,[170] which was situated between the Valley of the Fountain (Job's Well in the Kidron Valley) and Pompey's camp, must have stood on the hill now known as Deir Abu Tor. Two other monuments served Josephus as important topographical landmarks in his description of the Roman attack on Herod's towers and the Antonia fortress. One of them was the tomb of King Alexander[171] (no doubt Alexander Jannaeus), which was in front of the line held by John of Gischala opposite the Antonia. It must, therefore, have stood somewhere in the Moslem Quarter of the Old City of today. The tomb of John the High Priest (undoubtedly John Hyrcanus I) was opposite the line of Simeon bar Giora near the Water Gate of the Hippicus Tower and the Amygdalon Pool (or Pool of the Towers, now called the Pool of Hezekiah). Here the Romans repeatedly attacked the First Wall, but were repulsed by the defenders.[172]

The "Tomb of Herod's Family" (τῶν Ἡρώδου μνημεῖον),[173] which according to Josephus was near the Serpents' Pool and between the "House of Pulse" and Titus' camp opposite the Hippicus Tower, can be identified with the burial cave excavated in 1894 in the area then known as Nicoforia, between the King David Hotel and the Yemin Moshe quarter.[174]

The other tomb which is mentioned in our sources and can be identified with certainty is the burial cave known as the "Tombs of the Kings." This name was given them by their discoverer, De Saulcy, on the basis of a popular legend that these were the tombs of the kings of Judah. These were indeed royal tombs, but the kings buried there were of the house of Adiabene. According to Josephus they were situated near the Women's Towers in the Third Wall north of the city, and were surmounted by three pyramids.[175] Josephus calls it the Tomb of Queen Helena,[176] and it is mentioned by later sources including Pausanias.[177] Its pyramids were still standing in the fifth century.[178]

Most of the other monuments around Jerusalem have remained anonymous. The names given to them traditionally, such as the "Tombs of the Judges" (in Hebrew, the "Tombs of the Sanhedrin"), the "Tomb of Absalom" or the "Tomb of Zechariah" etc., have no basis in fact. These tombs form part of a vast necropolis encircling ancient Jerusalem on the north, east and south. Most belonged to rich families which could afford to have a monumental tomb cut into the rock. The tombs of the poor of Jerusalem have not been preserved. Most of these monuments were discovered long ago and emptied of their contents, but even in the case of the few found intact (such as the tomb recently unearthed at Giv'at Mivtar), not much has been discovered apart from the ossuaries and some pottery and glass. The above-mentioned tomb is noteworthy in that it contains the remains of a man described as "a builder of the temple" and of another who had been crucified. A monumental tomb found in the Rehavia quarter and identified as that of a man named Jason illustrates the transition from the burial habits of the Sadducees and to those of the Pharisees. In earlier practice the dead were piled in common graves, since according to the biblical tradition it was enough for a man to be buried with his ancestors without any need for a separate interment of his bones. Later on when the belief spread in the individual resurrection of the dead, the bones were collected after a year (the flesh being regarded as sinful but the skeleton part of the essential personality) and placed in receptacles known as ossuaries.

As the monumental tombs needed a smooth vertical surface for their façade, they usually cut into the slopes of the mountains or of the valleys encircling Jerusalem (in particular the valleys of Kidron and Hinnom), or in the walls left by quarrying. No one was allowed to be buried inside the city except the kings of the House of David and the prophetess Hulda. Because of the prevailing western winds, burial sites were usually on the east or south of the city. The necropolis of Jerusalem is therefore concentrated on the northern, eastern and southern sides of the city, although occasional graves have also been found on the west.

Many of the tombs contain rich epigraphical material which helps us to classify the population of Jerusalem by the derivation of their proper names. It has been suggested that at least two groups of tombs — one found on the Mount of Olives near the "Dominus Flevit" monastery and the other near Talpiot — belong to early Judeo-Christians, because of the type of name, the signs of crosses marked on the ossuaries and various additions to the names themselves. However, the great majority of scholars are convinced that such an assumption has no basis, and that the alleged inscriptions "Jesus Woe!" etc. should be otherwise interpreted. Similarly the inscribed crosses may merely mark the position of the ossuary lid, or indicate that the ossuary was full.[179]

The monumental tombs around Jerusalem are among the most important remains of Jewish art from the time of the Second Temple, and as such their ornaments, plans and architectural details have been dealt with in the next chapter (see page 258 f.).

III. The Water Supply[180]

The problem of supplying Jerusalem with water has always exercised the city's administrators. In the period of the Second Temple, when the population reached a number only surpassed in modern times, this problem became ever more acute. The small and insignificant source of the Gihon, which since the days of Hezekiah has been flowing through a tunnel into a pool in the central valley, could not of course supply the needs of a great city. Its origin had been quite forgotten by the time of Josephus, who referred to the mouth of the tunnels as the "source of Siloam." Neither could the second source in the Jerusalem area, the one called 'Ein Rogel in the Kidron Valley, furnish much water. The only other source in the Jerusalem area was the spring of Lifta (the "Waters of Nephtoah" of Josh. 15:9), but this was far away to the west by the standards of the time. During the course of the Hellenistic period, it became necessary to store rainwater in cisterns and pools. Cisterns cut into the rock were more costly but also more efficient, because the water in them did not evaporate during the summer months. Water collected in pools dried up in the course of the summer; but such reservoirs were much easier to prepare. Thus we find both methods in simultaneous use during the period of the Second Temple. A third method — that of bringing water from a distance by means of aqueducts — was also employed in the latter half of that period.

The excavation of cisterns in Jerusalem is facilitated by the geological structure of the rock on which the city stands. The soft *mizzi hilu* rock is covered by the harder *meleki*. It was enough to cut a narrow mouth in the harder stone and widen it out when the softer layers were reached.

Such cisterns were accordingly bell-shaped. In other cases natural caverns were used; their mouths were stopped up and a narrow opening cut in the roof of the cavern. The number of cisterns in ancient Jerusalem equaled or even surpassed the number of its houses. In the latest excavations no house has been found without one or several cisterns, some of which also served as bathing pools with steps cut into their walls. The abundance of cisterns is illustrated by the Temple Mount, where 34 cisterns of various sizes have been found, with a combined capacity estimated at 40,000 cubic meters. The biggest of these, called by the Arabs "the small sea," holds 12,000 cubic meters; a second one farther to the east contains 8,000.[181] The importance of the cisterns is demonstrated by an inscription from a synagogue built by a certain Theodotos son of Vettenius. There mention is made of "house, hospice, rooms and *water installations*" which were provided for the use of poor pilgrims.[182] The remains of these cisterns have been found in the foundations of the building.

While pools were of course far fewer than cisterns, they could store much more water. As the pools were mainly in open spaces accessible to the public, we have much more information about them.

To the period of the Second Temple we must ascribe the "Pool of the Towers" (Amygdalon)[183] — now called the Pool of Hezekiah. In Arabic it is known as the "Pool of the Patriarch's Bath." Its original length was 95 meters, but at present it measures 77 × 44 m.; its depth varies from 6 to 7.5 meters. Its water came from the Pool of Mamilla, which possibly belongs to the same period, although it is not mentioned in the sources before 614 A.D. Another pool, which is mentioned in the account of the siege of Titus and was therefore already in existence in the time of the Second Temple, was the pool called Struthion[184] (Στρουθίον). It was by means of a siege dam across this pool that the Fifth Legion attacked the Antonia. Clermont-Ganneau has suggested that this pool is identical with the twin pools now below the Convent of Notre Dame de Sion. These pools are partly rock-cut and partly vaulted over. Its western part measures 49.3 × 6 meters, its eastern part 38.7 × 6 meters. The pools are 12 meters deep at their northern end and 17 meters at their southern end. Today both pools are vaulted over, but as the Struthion was apparently an open pool in the time of the Second Temple, the vaulting must be of later date if we are to accept the identification. As this pool has no natural source of water, it was connected with an aqueduct descending from the Damascus Gate, where there may have been a reservoir collecting the waters of the upper central valley.

Northeast of this was the Sheep's Pool, which is mentioned in the New

Testament.[185] In some manuscripts of the same source its Hebrew name is Beth Hasda, in others Beth Zetha. The latter form seems preferable. The present shape of this twin pool is of two reservoirs measuring 45 × 6 meters. Its depth is 11 meters. There is some doubt, however, whether the present twin pool belong to the period of the Second Temple or whether the original pool was a shallow one slightly to the east.[186]

Josephus mentions one more pool, called the Serpents' Pool (ὄφεων κολυμβήθρα).[187] This pool was situated near the Herodian monument (see above, page 243). It is therefore identified with the reservoir known today as the Birket es-Sultan, which is situated in the central part of the Hinnom Valley west of the upper city. This reservoir was made by building a dam across the valley. It has undergone many changes in the course of time, but in its original form was 40 meters long, 20 wide and 4 deep.[188]

Apart from these pools it is probable that those which already existed in the time of the monarchy were still in use. We certainly know, for instance, of a "Pool of Solomon" (Σολομῶνος κολυμβήθρα), which is mentioned in the description of the First Wall as being situated between the source of the Siloam and the Ophel.[189] This apparently refers to the pool now known as the Pool of Siloam. The wall running along the side of that pool is certainly an integral part of the First Wall, and we may therefore assume that the pool itself already existed in the time of the Second Temple. Possibly this was the "lower pool," corresponding to the central valley which was created by the First Wall in its northern crossing of the valley, the one referred to in the Bible as the "upper pool."[190]

Finally, we may mention the reservoir called the "Pool of Israel" (Birket Isra'in). This reservoir is not mentioned in any literary source, but the fact that it follows the line of the northern wall of the Temple Mount and served it as a fosse proves that it did already exist at that time. It must indeed have been a most effective obstacle, since the Roman legions preferred to attack the strong fortress of Antonia instead of crossing the pool. The reservoir itself is partly rock-cut and partly built, the wall reaching a width of 4 meters. It measured 110 × 38 meters and was over 26 meters deep. Its eastern wall had two openings (at depths of 6 and 12 meters) to, carry away the surplus of water into the Kidron Valley.[191]

Jerusalem's aqueduct, which according to Josephus[192] was 400 stadia (74 km.) long, reached the south of the city from the springs in Wadi 'Arrub near Hebron. The length of the aqueduct is due to its many windings, as its builders did not wish to use arched bridges or siphons. They preferred to follow the natural gradient, cutting tunnels through the mountain where necessary, near Bethlehem and near the city. The aqueduct crossed the

Hinnom Valley near the Serpents' Pool, and circling the Upper City, entered the Temple Mount near Wilson's Arch. On its way its waters were collected in what are popularly known as "Solomon's Pools" near the village of Urtas. This aqueduct has been attributed to Pontius Pilate on the basis of a statement by Josephus[193] that the procurator used money from the Temple treasury to carry out the work, thereby provoking a riot. According to the Mishnah[194], however, the surplus of the *sheqel* tribute could legitimately be used to repair an aqueduct. From the fact that this aqueduct did not use the usual Roman type of arch, and from the similarity of its construction and planning with the aqueducts at Hyrcania and Alexandrium, it has recently been suggested[195] that the Jerusalem aqueduct was originally built in Hasmonean times, possibly by Alexander Jannaeus.

H. The Architectural Aspect of Jerusalem in the Time of the Second Temple

Like all cities founded in remote antiquity and which continued to develop in different cultural eras, the external aspects of Jerusalem at the time of the Second Temple was extremely heterogeneous. Approaching the town, one would first notice the many walls with their high towers encircling the city. Apart from several particularly tall buildings such as the Temple and the towers of Herod, most of the houses would probably be hidden by the walls. The walls were undoubtedly built in accordance with the rulers of Hellenistic fortification, with a wide base, passages and steps within the wall, high battlements to protect its defenders, and arrow slits for the bowmen. On the roof of the towers were flat surfaces on which engines (*ballistae*) could be mounted for shooting arrows and stones. Outside the walls there was a belt of gardens, groves and vegetable fields dotted with monumental tombs. A fosse was cut in the rock between the garden area and at least part of the circuit of the wall.

The city itself was divided into old and the new sections, rich and poor quarters, public buildings, streets and markets. We may assume that the houses of the well-to-do were generally built in the Hellenistic style of the period, with a sometimes colonnaded central court surrounded by many rooms. The richest houses had also had an upper story commanding a wide view of the town and its environs (see page 237 above). The palaces, and particularly Herod's palace, were surrounded by gardens and protected from the street by a special wall. This Hellenistic style was also apparent on the Temple Mount, from the porches in the outer court to certain features (such as the Nicanor Gate and the Temple façade) of the Inner

Temple. In the ritual buildings, however, the Hellenistic style had to yield to the traditional forms of the Orient. Nor were all the palaces built on the Greek model. It seems likely, for instance, that the dwellings of the family of Adiabene which stood in the Lower City (see above, page 238) were built in their native style with an open court and a niche, the interior of the house being carefully protected from the outside, as was usual in the Orient. On the other hand the public buildings erected by Herod, such as the *boulé*, the Xystus, the agora, the theater and the hippodrome were all certainly in the current Hellenistic style, with Ionic or Corinthian capitals. The architectural details undoubtedly followed the style found in tomb façades or in the recently excavated architectural remnants of the Temple Mount, though here the masons obviously refrained from using the images of living beings in their ornament.

In contrast to these monumental buildings surrounded by their open spaces, the markets and the Lower City had the aspect of a typical oriental town. Here the houses were built of small stones; they were crowded together and had hardly any garden space, but they too had an interior court protected by a wall. The markets were possibly built in the form of a colonnaded street, and were certainly as noisy and dirty as a modern bazaar. The bridge between the Upper City and the Temple Mount was no doubt constructed mainly to enable the High Priests and other persons of rank to reach the Temple without having to cross the lower marketplace. Whereas the poorer quarters were crowded and unplanned, the Upper City was laid out in orderly fashion round its agora, the upper market. As far as we know there were no public gardens in the city, though rose gardens were cultivated for commercial purposes.[196]

In the last decades of the Second Temple Jerusalem was the focus of many opposing tendencies and styles, all expressing the Jewish way of life of that period. It was a royal capital and religious center, the focus of a wide Diaspora and the seal of illustrious rabbinical schools. But its glory was doomed. In its last terrible struggle much of its past was obliterated, and its surviving roots transplanted to a distant soil.

CHAPTER VII

JEWISH ART AND ARCHITECTURE IN THE HASMONEAN AND HERODIAN PERIODS

by M. Avi-Yonah

A. THE HELLENIZATION PROCESS AND ITS INFLUENCE ON JEWISH ART

THE GREAT ENCOUNTER between the Greco-Roman culture and Judaism, which is the theme of several volumes of this *History*, also showed its effects in the visual arts. In fact Greek art, in the perfection of its classical shaping of the human image, was possibly of even greater danger to the traditional Jewish way of life than was Greek literature. Its appeal was more universal and its message more readily comprehensible to broad sections of society. To understand Homer, Sophocles or Aristophanes required a familiarity with the arcana of the Greek language; a beautiful image of Aphrodite needed no verbal intermediary to kindle a response in the beholder. Nevertheless the imitation of Greek styles, whether in a pure form or mixed with oriental elements, began — like the whole process of Hellenization at the top of the social pyramid, if only for the simple reason that works of art cost money. Of the two great families which dominated Jewish society in the Hellenistic period, the high-priestly Oniads were on the whole more obliged to respect tradition than were their rivals, the Tobiads. We need not wonder, therefore, that the earliest extant monuments of Greco-Jewish art were discovered in the Tobiad domain, east of the Jordan, in the lands later known as the Peraea.

The difference between a traditional versus a reforming approach to Jewish art, at least in the times of the Second Temple, lies in the interpretation of the Second Commandment. The Tobiads and other Hellenizers were content to adopt the old biblical attitude as revealed in the plethora of figurative images of man and beast to be found in Israelite strata from the time of the monarchy: the cherubim in Solomon's Temple, the oxen which supported the "sea" there, the lions standing guard on the steps of Solomon's throne, the golden "calves" (bulls in actual fact) set up by Jeroboam at Dan and Beth-El, the Samaria ivories etc. It was their "traditionalist" opponents who, influenced by the austere teaching of the later prophets, expounded the Second Commandment as wholly proscribing all images of living beings, man and beast alike.

The unfinished building now known as Qasr el 'Abd at 'Iraq el Emir (Tyrus or the Birtha of the Ammonites in ancient times)[1] was probably planned as a rival temple to the one in Jerusalem. It was set up by the dissenting Tobiad, Hyrcanus the son of Joseph (who died *ca.* 175 B.C.E.).[2] This idea of a rival temple was then not as outrageous as it may have seemed in later days. Not long afterwards the exiled Oniads set up another such sanctuary at Leontopolis in Egypt, and this was accepted by the Talmudic sages as a legitimate place of worship, even if of lower rank than the Temple of Jerusalem.[3]

The Tyrus temple employs both Greek and Oriental features. The façade, with two pillars set between *antae*, recalls the rock-cut tomb façades of Jerusalem from the Hasmonean and Herodian periods. The main hall is divided into a nave and two aisles by two rows of seven columns. The capitals, with their paired horse's heads and busts are reminiscent of Persian capitals of the Achaemenid period. The frieze of marching lions around the outer wall of the building, and the fountain outside it bearing the relief of a feline, both show strong traces of Hellenistic naturalism mixed with Assyrian traditions. The plan of the temple, with its opisthodomus behind the sanctuary is basically Greek.[4]

B. HASMONEAN ART AND ARCHITECTURE

The Hasmonean dynasty, which superseded both the Oniads and the Tobiads, began its career as extreme opponents of all that the "sons of Belial" stood for, figurative art no doubt included. Gradually, however, the new rulers were forced to abandon their radical posture when they found the practice of the visual arts necessary out of purely utilitarian considerations. The mere refurbishing of the Temple with a new candelabrum (*menorah*), table of shewbreads, incense altar etc. to replace those taken away by the henchmen of Antiochus IV, required skilled craftsmanship of no mean order, the more so when the materials initially used had to be of the cheapest (Cf. Menahot 28b). No glitter of massive gold plating could cover up shoddy work in such a case.

When Simeon, the last surviving son of Mattathias the Hasmonean, proceeded to erect the family's monumental tomb at Modiin, the shaping of the base, of the pyramids and of the images of ships surmounting it obviously required both architectural and sculptural skills.[5] Similar glyptic abilities applied in miniature were required from the engravers of the dies used for the Maccabean coinage.⁶ While the prototypes of the emblems (cornucopiae, wreaths, anchors and stars) were taken from Seleucid coins, the delicate work of cutting the dies with their minuscule emblems and letters, and in particular the replacement of the pagan caduceus with the identifiable image of a pomegranate, presupposed a high standard of craftsmanship.⁷ The relief found at Jerusalem in which the pomegranate and cornucopiae are reproduced on a larger scale⁸ is convincing proof of the existence of Jewish relief sculptors in the capital during the time of the later Hasmoneans.

There are very few examples of domestic architecture of that period. In most cases only the foundations of the houses have survived, as at Gezer. The one exception, and an interesting one, is the house at Tell el-Judeideh near Beth-guvrin, which the excavators assumed to have been the residence of a commander of the late Hasmonean period. It is a large house divided into two sections. One is a typical Hellenistic *andron*, centered on a peristyle with columns of the Doric order. Attached to it is a structure with a narrow entrance and a congeries of small rooms round another courtyard — a typically Oriental women's house. This plan, then, also reflects the characteristic ambivalence of Hasmonean architecture.⁹

Two of the monumental tombs in the vicinity of Jerusalem have been assigned to this period. One of them is the tomb of a man named Jason and his family found in Alfasi Road in the Rehavia quarter.¹⁰ The tomb is approached by a forecourt. An arched opening led to an outer court, which was connected by a door in a wall to the inner court. The façade of the tomb itself was formed by a single column *in antis*, incorporating a Doric capital but a nonclassical base. This "monostyle" type of entrance is very rare; it occurs once before in the tomb of Thrasyllas in Athens (320 B.C.E.).¹¹ In Jason's Tomb the façade was surmounted by a pyramid. The rather rough drawings on the porch walls seem to represent a sea battle — probably one in which Jason took part in the time of Jannaeus Alexander (103–76 B.C.E.).¹² They also show that the king's Sadducean friends had no aversion to depicting human beings. The drawing of a crouching stag (perhaps the family crest or an allusion to a family name) is further evidence of the acceptability of figurative art among the Hasmoneans.

The other Hasmonean monument in the Jerusalem necropolis stands at the opposite side of the city, in the Kidron Valley to the east.¹³ It is the tomb of the priestly family of Bene Hezir, mentioned in I Chronicles 24:15. The identification is by inscription and is quite definite. More familiar to European travelers as the "Tomb of St. James," the monument features a plain Doric colonnade of two columns flanked by two Doric *antae* pillars.

The style is classically correct (e.g., the columns and pillars have no bases), but there are two triglyphs in the entablature between the columns instead of the usual one. The triglyphs are cut according to Greek stylistic rules, with a row of three *guttae* below each but without the *regulae*. The latter appear *above* the triglyphs, but not, as they should, in the horizontal part of the cornice. Above the cornice is a concave *corona*. The "Tomb of Zechariah,"[14] a solid rock-cut monolith (as far as we know at present) stands south of the Bene Hezir tomb, in a rock-cut space. This was in all probability the monolith (*nefesh*) of the Bene Hezir monument (compare the relation between the "Tomb of Absalom" and the "Tomb of Jehoshaphat" — see below, p. 260). The monolith has four identical façades, each composed of pillars in the corner, with a Doric capital and four disks below it. Two Ionic half columns divide the wall on each side, and two quarter columns, also Ionic, are cut in the corners adjoining the pillars. All have the correct Attic bases. The fluting of the columns is only indicated below the capitals, a not unusual Hellenistic practice.[15] Above the entablature is a convex *cyma*, surmounted by a pyramid. The Ionic capitals are quite classic in their design, with an "egg-and-dart" pattern between the volutes, and a *pulvinus* ("cushion") on the sides. The tomb of the Bene Hezir combines the orthodox use of Greek architectural forms with that of Orientalizing and Egyptianizing elements: a *cavetto* (hollow groove) instead of a frieze and a plain entablature. The interior plan of the tomb and its *koḵim* (*loculi*) is based on Egyptian-Hellenistic prototypes.

The Herodian period, following that of the Hasmoneans, is comparatively well represented in both public and domestic architecture. This is especially true of the former on account of its monumental character. In their constructions in the Jewish part of the kingdom, Herod and his dynasty seem to have adhered strictly to the most rigid interpretation of the Second Commandment. Apart from a few figures of birds in fresco on the wall of a house in the Upper City, no image of a living being has been found in any Herodian structure either in Jerusalem or even at Masada or Herodium. These were royal fortresses where no rabbi probably ever set foot; yet all the finds are aniconic. However, neither Herod nor his grandson Agrippa I disdained the art of the Hellenic sculptor outside the Land of Israel. In the Nabataean temple at Seeia in the Hauran[16] there once stood a statue of King Herod himself. The coins which Agrippa I struck at Caesarea carry likenesses of both the king and his son;[17] whereas those from his Jerusalem mint were entirely devoid of images.

C. Herodian Architecture in Jerusalem

The Herodian architecture in Jerusalem (and to a lesser extent in Hebron, too) is monumental both as regards the dimensions of the whole complex as well as those of its parts. This breadth of conception reflects the sudden enlargement of the Hellenistic world horizon following Alexander's conquests. Like the Seleucids and the Ptolemies, Herod felt he had room to spare; it was no longer necessary to observe the restrictions imposed by the cramped area of a typical Greek *polis*. Moreover, being an autocrat both by circumstance and conviction, Herod needed to consult no one; nor did he normally feel obliged to apply to any public body for permission to carry out a project, or to seek approval from his subjects once it had been completed. He could build to the limit of his power and his purse. The tower of Phasael (popularly called the "Tower of David") rising from its solid square base (twenty meters by twenty) is but one example of the strength and magnificence of Herodian architecture.[18] Its huge stones have the typical double draft of the period: a broad outer margin and a narrow inner one around a flat boss. Another and even more impressive example is the outer supporting wall of the Temple esplanade. The giant blocks (ten to twelve meters long and one meter high) form large solid masses of masonry, subdivided by their drafted edges. The effect is one of invincible strength and austere beauty.[19] In the upper part of these walls (as in the Herodian walls still standing at Hebron around the Cave of Machpelah) the surface was divided up by a series of flat pilasters.[20] This architectural feature recalls the enclosure walls of the earlier Babylonian brick temples and of the Parthian palaces contemporary with Herod.[21] The architectural fragments found in the excavations outside the west and south walls of the Temple enclosure[22] belong most probably to Herod's "Royal Stoa" which extended along the south wall of the esplanade. Their basic "grammar of ornament" is classical Greek. The execution, however, in which each pattern is broken up into sharply defined areas of light and shade, is essentially Oriental. So too is the preference for the "allover" type of ornament and for stylized or geometrical forms.

Another fine example of Herodian architecture is a Corinthian capital found in the Upper City.[23] It strongly resembles in simplified form the Augustan variants of this order; very similar capitals have been found in the "Tombs of the Kings" (see below, p. 259).

The one building project for which Herod needed the consent of his subjects was the complete reconstruction of the Second Temple.[24] Were it not for the fact that the divine service continued uninterruptedly, we should properly call it the Third Temple. In rebuilding the Sanctuary Herod was bound to preserve the dimensions and general layout as set forth in the Scriptures. All he could do to bring his Temple closer to the grandiose ideal of the great Hellenistic-Oriental sanctuaries (then being built at Palmyra and Heliopolis), or to the past glories of Didymae or Ephesus, was to profit from a variant reading in II Chronicles 3:4 and to double the height of the façade. It was now constructed as a square of one hundred cubits (approx. 50m.) in height and width. He also had to retain the traditional overhanging lintel over the huge gate of the Porch. However, as far as one can judge from the representations of the Temple façade on the Bar-Kokhba tetradrachms and in a fresco of the synagogue at Dura-Europus, Herod's architects managed to follow the Oriental tradition while making use of Hellenistic architectural details, in about the same proportion we find at contemporary Palmyra. The façade was divided by four monumental half columns or pillars, with capitals of the Corinthian order, and crowned with a crow-stepped balustrade. Herod lavishly furbished his Temple with the most costly building materials, including marbles of different hues, some veined like waves of the sea (the Talmud mentions[25] three kinds; *shaysha'*, *koḥala'* and *marmara'*, possibly referring to white, blue and pink stone). Gilt was applied unstintingly, so that Josephus could compare Herod's Temple to a "snowy mountain glistening in the sun."[26] Even the Sages, who had no great affection for Herod, were forced to admit that "he who has never seen [Herod's Temple] has never seen a beautiful building in his life."[27] The diminishing holiness of the Inner Court, the Court of Women and the Outer Court, all with their porticoes and gates, afforded the architects and artisans a freer hand in catering to the taste of the period, always, of course, in conformance with the strict interpretation of the Second Commandment. In these outer courts the wishes of the many donors from the Diaspora had doubtless to be taken into account. The cast and chased bronze ornaments of the Nicanor Gate[28] must certainly have reflected the trends of contemporary Alexandrian art. The same must have been true of the "Beautiful Gate" leading to the Court of Women, and of all the other gates except the Shushan Gate. The latter, with its portrayal of the palace of Shushan, was probably decorated in the Parthian style.

In striking contrast to Herod's avoidance of the use of human and animal forms throughout the Temple area was his insistence on affixing the image of an eagle to the Temple gate — an act which provoked a riot.[29] The mere suspicion that the trophies over Herod's theater represented men stirred the people's anger.[30] Even later on, the fact that Herod Antipas had furniture adorned with figures of animals was enough to rouse popular fury.[31]

D. Herod's Palaces at Herodium and Masada

Herod's other major works, his palaces at Masada and Herodium, differ greatly from the monumental splendor of his buildings in Jerusalem or even Hebron. At Herodium[32] the structure was designed to serve a triple purpose, that of palace, fortress and tomb. The site itself was an artificial truncated cone, crowned by a round curtain wall with one round tower in the east and three semicircular towers at the other three points of the compass. The plan seems to have been inspired by the circular mausoleum which the emperor Augustus, Herod's patron and "friend," had just built at Rome.[33] The tomb itself (which has not yet been discovered) may presumably have been included in the solid round tower, facing eastwards the sun rising over the mountains of Moab. The confined area within the round curtain wall necessitated a most careful and well-balanced use of the space available. The eastern half of the circle adjoining the round tower was used for the construction of a rectangular court with two exedras, surrounded by colonnaded porticoes. The western half was bisected by a large hall with two square niches. It was flanked on the north by a hypocaust bath and on the south by another hall, possibly used then or at a later date as a synagogue. The palace rooms may have been set in an upper story, now destroyed, or even have been outside the fortress in the as yet only partly explored structures north of it. These include long corridors, a pool with a circular pavilion in its center, storehouses, possibly a stadium etc. The style of the architecture at Herodium was almost purely Hellenistic.

At Masada[34] there was no problem of space. In fact the buildings were thinly scattered on the surface of the fortress plateau. Planned as a last refuge and possibly also as a hunting lodge in the Judean desert, Masada was not built in the solid fashion of the other Herodian monuments. Its situation on a table mountain, isolated on all sides, made a strong fortification wall seem unnecessary. The main palace, the baths, barracks and storehouse for the fortress garrison were mostly low structures, with only a few second stories. However, Herod's penchant for daring feats of engineering found full expression in the building of his private three-level palace at the north end of the fortress. Here a modest villa stood on the upper terrace, with a wide semicircular platform in front of it. From it the paranoic tyrant could gaze with contempt at the human ants crawling in the wide expanse of the plain one thousand feet below. The second terrace of this palace had a circular colonnaded building (a *tholos*); its function is not clear. The lowest terrace, erected in part on huge supporting walls overhanging the void, included what was probably an open court surrounded by columns that may have served as a banqueting hall. It was protected against the outside by a window-pierced wall with a corridor running around it. Below this hall were more rooms and private baths, literally hanging over the abyss.

The other palace at Masada seems to have been used for ceremonial purposes. It comprised several blocks of rooms, each functional in character. Besides the special palace storerooms and the artisans' quarters attached to it, there was another bath, paved with mosaics. The main architectural attractions of this palace were the monumental entrance, whose stucco walls were made to simulate ashlar masonry, and the throne hall, preceded by a separate court. The entrance to the hall was monumental in character, featuring two columns flanked by *antae*. Although the palace itself was based on the standard plan of a rich Hellenistic mansion, the replacement of the usual porch by an Oriental type of portal drew attention to the hierarchical importance of the hall behind it.

As at Herodium, the plans of the buildings at Masada show an intelligent, functional and original solution of the architectural problems. This good planning — entirely typical of Herod's projects — is in stark contrast to the shoddy execution of the buildings. Most of the walls are of local sandstone, plastered over. The Corinthian capitals are of purely Vitruvian design and conform to the severe Augustan style; they are cut in stone, in two blocks set one upon the other. The columns, however, consist of sandstone drums stuccoed over and provided with the classical flutings. The few Ionic capitals are probably from the upper stories. The roofs seem to have been of light reed construction and plastered over. Some of the molded stucco is quite good. Most of the walls, however, are painted with a dreadful imitation of veined marble, worthy of a small bourgeois at Pompeii — and this in the abode of a rich and powerful monarch! The mosaics at Masada are of two kinds: some, in black and white geometric patterns, closely imitate contemporary Augustan work in Italy.[35] More interesting are the colored mosaics, which show a meaningful translation of common Greek patterns, especially of the floral type, into something orientally rich and strange. The dominant symbols are those representing the Seven Kinds of produce — grapes, figs, pomegranates, dates, etc. — with which the Holy Land is blessed (Deut. 8:8).

One remarkable point about the planning of Masada is the considerable influence of Nabataean art in its overall design. This is also evident in such details as the columns or pillars attached to the walls. The Nabataean kingdom was just across the Dead Sea opposite Masada, and (as we know from the Judean Desert documents) there was much intercommunication between Jews and Nabataeans. The rock-cut façades at Petra did not, of course, present the same static difficulties as the mainly freestanding structures at Masada; yet they have much in common with the *tholos* on the middle north terrace or the rear wall of the banqueting hall below.

E. Domestic Architecture in Jerusalem

A number of private dwellings of Herodian date have recently been excavated in the Jewish Quarter of the Old City of Jerusalem and on "Mount Zion" both formerly part of the aristocratic Upper City.[36] One of these, apparently belonging to the Bar-Kathros family, was left untouched after the conflagration of 70 A.D. This and the other houses found nearby employ the common Hellenistic plan, in which the rooms are arranged around a courtyard reached from outside by means of a narrow entrance. The number of stepped baths and cisterns is remarkable. In one house a mosaic pavement was found composed of purely geometric ornaments rather in the style of the Masada mosaics. Among the findings were a marble table whose edge was decorated with an "egg-and-lotus-flower" design and rosettes.[37] In one of the houses on "Mount Zion" frescoes recalling Pompeian wall decorations were found, even including pictures of birds, a sign of a private liberalization of the kind that only became general a couple of centuries later. Another house was covered by a Herodian road leading straight towards "Robinson's Arch" in the west wall of the Temple — remarkable evidence of Herod's careful town planning.

Herod's palace itself has been totally destroyed, but recent finds have at least given us an idea of its size. The platform on which it was built was no less than 350 meters long, extending from the Citadel to the southwest corner of the Old City.[38]

F. Herodian Monumental Tombs

As in the case of Hasmonean art and architecture, so too with regard to the Herodian period (up to the destruction of Jerusalem in 70 A.D.) we must turn to the ornaments and contents of the tombs to obtain a clearer idea of the prevailing trends in art. In the Jerusalem necropolis several outstanding monuments have been assigned to the time of Herod. Most of these tombs are rock-cut (some are partly rock-cut and partly built). For their ornamental façades a vertical rock face was chosen, most often to be found in disused quarries (as in the Sanhedriya tombs). Frequently, however — particularly with the funerary monuments of the very rich or very influential — it was specially cut for this purpose (e.g. the Tombs of the Kings, the "Tomb of Absalom"). The internal plan of these tombs is fairly simple — a central hall, with *kokim* or side rooms driven from it into the rock. Owing to the prevailing custom of burial in two stages, a pit was usually provided for in the hall. There the bodies were deposed provisionally until the bones could be transferred to ossuaries. The entrance to the tombs was sometimes protected by a *golel* (rolling stone); in the more sumptuous there was often a court in front of the façade with benches around its walls. The inner walls of the tombs were lined with slabs cut to resemble ashlar masonry whenever this seemed desirable or necessary. The main interest of these monuments from the point of view of art history lies in their ornamented façades and in the decorated sarcophagi and ossuaries in which the dead (or their bones) were laid to rest.

Among the monumental Herodian tombs in the Jerusalem necropolis the largest are the Tombs of the Kings, once believed to be the burial place of the kings of Judah, but now generally identified with the "Monument of Helena"[39] erected by the widowed queen of Adiabene. The monument consists of an impressive staircase 30 meters long, followed by a large rock-cut court (25.8 × 27.4 m and 8.5 m deep). The entrance to the porch of the tomb was once divided by two columns with Ionic capitals, which stood between two ("semidetached pillars") with Doric capitals. Above the façade there were originally three tall conical pyramids, by which the monument was still known as late as the fifth century A.D. What has remained is a rock-cut cornice with triglyphs and metopes, the latter filled with round shields. We again notice (as in the Tomb of the Bene Hezir) that the number of triglyphs between the columns is twice the correct classical number. This cornice is a piece of architectural pretense; it is not even placed on top of the epistylion, as in the earlier tomb, but "floats" freely above it, while its alternation of metopes and triglyphs is interrupted in the center by two "acanthus cups" with two wreaths and a triple bunch of grapes in between. The latter is an ancient Jewish symbol, recalling the golden vine of the Temple and repeated on coins of Bar-Kokhba. It is indeed significant that this symbolic arrangement weighed more with the architect or his patrons than the classical correctness of the frieze. In addition there is a ribbon of acanthus leaves (with various fruits worked into it) extending either side of a central rosette between the cornice and the top of the columns, and descending at right angles down the corner pillars.

The leaves of this garland are cut very flat, with strong contrasts of light and shade in each leaflet.

Similar pseudoclassical arrangements may be observed in various other tombs.[40] In the "Tomb of the Frieze" in Samuel Road, the frieze is above the two pillars in the corners of the entrance; it has rosettes in all the metopes, except for a wreath in the central one, and is surmounted by a concave cornice ornamented in the classical style. Another tomb in the vicinity, the "Two-Story Tomb," has a correct Doric frieze over Egyptian column-capitals, but is surmounted by a dwarfed second story. In a third monumental tomb, called Umm el-'Amed, the walls of the court and porch are dressed to resemble a wall of ashlar masonry blocks, complete with margins. Here too there are two Ionic columns between two *antae*, surmounted by a Doric frieze with rosettes in the metopes. This frieze extends along the whole length of the façade as far as the two pillars in the corner of the court, the whole in imitation of a built wall with a monumental entrance at its center. In the so-called "Tombs of the Sanhedrin" (also known as the "Tombs of the Judges" — both appellations are popular inventions),[41] as well as in both "Tomb of Jehoshaphat" and the "Grape Tomb," the entrance is surmounted by a triangular gable, sometimes complete with rock-cut *acroteria*. The gable is filled with floral ornament, a vine trellis or a tracery of acanthus leaves issuing from a central design and spread flatly over the surface. Botanical niceties are usually disregarded — grapes, pine cones, pomegranates and citrons all spring from the acanthus stem. The main point to note is the decorative effect of the flatly spread and highly stylized ornament, which is laid out in a lace-like design over the whole surface, thus illustrating the *horror vacui* typical of Orientalizing art.

Perhaps the most strikingly elaborate of these Herodian tombs is that known as the "Tomb of Absalom".[42] Actually it is but the "pillar" (*nefesh*) of the adjoining burial cave known as the "Tomb of Jehoshaphat" — both names are quite unhistorical. The "Tomb of Absalom" is a freestanding structure with an inner chamber once used for burials. The square base (7 × 6.8 m.) is rock-cut to a height of 8 m. It has Doric corner pilasters and Ionic half columns in between, both surmounted by a Doric frieze (with two triglyphs between each column). The metopes are filled with round shields. Above the frieze is an Egyptian *cavetto* cornice. The rest of the 20 m. high structure is built. A square base is followed by a round drum with a molded base and cornice; the whole resembles a *tholos* without the columns and the interposed statues commonly found in Greco-Roman monuments. The drum ends in a rope ornament. Above it rises a conical concave pyramid, ending in a lotus-flower ornament. The whole mixture of style bears a striking resemblance to some of the Nabataean monuments at Petra. However, as the "Tomb of Absalom" was partly built and not all hewn out of the rock, the architect could not allow his fancy equally free rein.

Apart from the tomb façades, we may learn much about the dominant trends of Herodian art from the burial containers found inside the tombs themselves. These are of two kinds: full-length sarcophagi with floral ornament in relief; and ossuaries, of which about a thousand have so far been found. These are limestone boxes 50–80 cm. long, 20–30 cm. wide and 30–40 cm. high, with a flat, curved or gabled lid; they were used for collecting the bones of the dead in a second burial.

G. Sarcophagi and Ossuary Ornamentation

In general the sarcophagi are ornamented in relief with garlands and rosettes, most of the ossuaries, on the other hand, are decorated by means of a technique known as notch carving ("Kerbschnitt") borrowed from woodwork. Rulers and compasses were used to set out the most common type of ossuary ornament. This consisted of two metopes framed in straight or wavy borders, with a six-petaled compass-drawn rosette inside each metope. The whole design is sharply gouged out, creating contrasting surfaces of light and shadow. This basic design is varied by a multitude of additions, flowers and trees, often strongly stylized, as well as by representations of buildings and architectural details (columns, doors etc.), or various objects such as cups and other vessels.[43]

The sarcophagi, which were obviously more costly than the ossuaries and hence used mainly in the burials of the rich, more closely resemble the tomb façades in their ornament.[44] Thus, for example, a sarcophagus found in the Tomb of Herod's Family in Jerusalem is decorated on its long side with a winding plant issuing from a central acanthus cup; rosettes are used to fill the spaces between the convolutions. Two ornamented sarcophagi have been found in the Tombs of the Kings. One shows a row of rosettes with circular fillers in between. The other has a lid with a most interesting design: two long strips, each containing two stylized olive branches within a rope design, run the length of the lid. Around them is a winding vine sprouting not only bunches of grapes, but also all kinds of other fruits or leaves such as pomegranates, acorns, lotus flowers, ivy leaves, pine cones etc. The whole decoration strongly recalls Palmyrene ornament of the same period, in which naturalism is combined with stylization. Several more sarcophagi have recently been added to those already known. In a tomb at "Dominus Flevit" at Bethany a number of sarcophagi were found[45] adorned with various kinds of molded ornaments. Most of the elements already mentioned are reproduced here: a winding plant ornament bearing various kinds of fruit with a rope design in the center; molded rosettes; and an acanthus cup issuing forth rows of myrtle leaves entwined with ribbons etc. A similar find was made in 1967 on Mount Scopus, in the tomb of a Nazirite family.[46] The cover, decorated with myrtle leaves and ribbons, recalls one of the "Dominus Flevit" coffins. In the center of one of the long sides we see a stylized lily (?) with vine tendrils stemming symmetrically from it; these bear triple bunches of grapes and leaves of various designs. The whole is executed in a flat stylized manner.

There also exists at least one wooden coffin, found in the "Cave of the Pool" in Naḥal David near En-gedi.[47] It is remarkable for its unusual material, and for its decoration of bone inlay, reproducing the rosette ornament common on ossuaries.

The sarcophagi and ossuaries so far discussed represent two different artistic traditions. The sarcophagi follow the trend of Hellenistic-Oriental art prevailing in the other countries of the Roman East, especially at Palmyra and the Nabatene.[48] In all these countries the aristocracy aimed at adapting the artistic elements of the dominant Greco-Roman tradition to their own ancestral culture. The Jewish upper classes, of course, could assimilate only part of classical and Oriental tradition, in particular the geometric and floral ornament, but not the figurative art. The treatment of the plant motifs on the sarcophagi combines Greek naturalism with such Oriental features as the stylized arrangement of the winding branches (following a strict geometrical line), the transformation of the organic plants into a pattern, incorporation of many botanical species into one plant, and the spreading of the detail over a flat surface with no consideration either for the natural appearance of the fruits and leaves or for the laws of gravity. In some cases, as in wreath ornamentation, the single flowers are represented by circular blobs, each pierced in its center.

There is no parallel in the classical world for the ossuary ornament. These geometric rosettes and "endless" patterns, the "conceptual" representations of objects, the *horror vacui* with its compulsive filling of the whole surface, the sharply cut design based on an optic contrast of light and shadow in a lace-like pattern, entirely different from the soft glyptic transitions of Greco-Roman reliefs — all this can, however, be paralleled in ancient Oriental art, as well as in nearly contemporary Parthian art at Assur, Babylon and Hatra. It has been suggested that the ossuary design was brought over by Jews returning from the Babylonian exile and that it became "consecrated" in the course of time; they had learned it from the same Mesopotamian prototypes that had also served the Parthians.[49]

It should be noted, however, that although the sarcophagi and ossuaries represent different artistic traditions, the two have many elements in common. This is true both with regard to the basic ornamental conceptions, such as symmetry and patterning, as well as to many details of execution. Some sarcophagi are ornamented in the flat design of the ossuaries, while some ossuaries are decorated with the raised (glyptic) rosettes, wreaths and "handles" more typical of the sarcophagi. Both may therefore be regarded as different expressions of the same artistic conception. Although most of the elements of this art are derived either from eastern or from western prototypes, the particular selection and transformation they have undergone justifies us in reading the art of the Hasmonean and Herodian periods in Judea as a specifically Jewish creation.

CHAPTER VIII

THE HIGH PRIESTHOOD AND THE SANHEDRIN IN THE TIME OF THE SECOND TEMPLE

by H. D. Mantel

A. Judea as Temple-State

DURING MOST OF the period of the Second Temple, the High Priest was not merely a religious officer as he was in the First Temple,[1] but also a political figure and even a political leader. Under the Roman domination, his political status went through several changes, to understand which we must first make a brief study of the office from the beginning of the Persian period.

Most historians and biblical commentators assign an important political role to the High Priests,[2] beginning with Joshua the son of Jozadak, who, it is argued, replaced Zerubbabel as governor of Judea.[3] This is to overlook, however, that Zerubbabel's place was taken by other governors, as Nehemiah testifies,[4] and as is evidenced by the coins found at Beth-Zur and Tell Gamma with the legend, "Hezekiah Peḥa,"[5] bearing out Porten's original hypothesis.[6] The names Urio, Hananah, Jehoazar, Ahzai and Jehezekio, stamped on the "Yehud" jars which were also found in Beth-Zur, are thought by Avigad to have belonged to Temple treasurers,[7] though some doubt the "Yehud" reading.[8] The inscription *pḥw'* (governor) found on other jars Cross reads as *pḥr* (potter).

In view of these differences we may seek a clue to the political status of the High Priest by examining the nature of the Jewish state in the Persian, Ptolemaic and Seleucid empires. The terms of Cyrus' edict ordering the reconstitution of the Jewish state specify that the purpose was לבנות לו בית בירושלם אשר ביהודה — "to build Him a house in Jerusalem, which is in Judah."[9] This is tantamount to saying that Judea was to be a Temple-State, examples of which abounded in the Persian and Hellenistic empire. While their constitutions were not identical, a general outline may be obtained from their description in Strabo's *Geography*.

Of the Temple-State of Comana in Cappadocia he writes:[10] "It is a considerable city; its inhabitants, however, consist mostly of the divinely inspired people (θεοφορήτων) and the temple servants who live in it. Its inhabitants are Cataonians, who, though in a general way (ἄλλως = other-wise) classed as subject to the king, are in most respects (τὸ πλέον = mostly) subject to the priest." The Temple-State was composed of three classes of people: common people, who were the minority; religious devotees, and temple priests and servants, who together constituted the majority. While the king imposed taxes and decided on matters of state such as war and peace,[11] the High Priest was in charge of routine, day-to-day affairs.[12]

Strabo continues: "The priest is master (κὐριός) of the temple, and also of the temple-servants, who on my sojourn there were more than six thousand in number, men and women together."[13] Elsewhere, Strabo gives different figures for the temple servants. In Morimene, at Venasa, there were three thousand.[14] He also explains that the High Priest was not empowered to sell them (πλῆν τοῦ πιπράσκειν).[15] In other words, their labor was at his dis-posal, but not their bodies. Thus, he could probably not force mates upon them in order to produce slaves for him. Furthermore, "considerable territory belongs to the temple, and the revenue is enjoyed by the priest."[16] Elsewhere Strabo states that it was the work of the temple servants on the sacred lands that yielded the priests their yearly revenue.[17]

On the status of the High Priest, Strabo writes: "He is second in rank in Cappadocia after the king (δεύτερος κατα τιμήν μὲτα τοι βασιλεά).[18] Later he adds that the priest holds his position "for life" (δια βιόν)[19] and that his son "succeeded" him (ἢν ἱερωσύνην παρέλαβεν).[20] The Temple-States were thus feudal states, managed by hereditary High Priests, and under the sovereign-ty of the king. Though they had no political power, they probably enjoyed, as Rostovtzeff infers, considerable political influence.[21]

The image of Judea, as it emerges from the books of Ezra, Nehemiah, Haggai, Zechariah and Malachi, conforms on the whole to Strabo's de-finition of the Temple-State. The narratives, visions, oracles and addresses in these books center around the temple cult, the High Priest and the priests. Even Zerubbabel, the Davidic heir, is a religious figure. All this, and the Torah, are inseparably interwoven with Judah (Judea) and Jerusalem.[22] The temporal sovereign is the Persian king, the "peḥa" is his deputy and "we are bondmen,"[23] to whom the kings of Persia permitted "to set up the house of our God, and to repair the ruins thereof, and to give us a fence in Judah and in Jerusalem".[24] The political significance of the High Priesthood is indicated by the fact that the Persian satrap, Bagoas, actively supported Jeshua in his bid to replace his brother Johanan as High Priest.[25] In the Book of Judith,[26] set in the Assyrian period,[27] and in the legends on Simeon the Just,[28] the High Priest appears as the political head of the state. Indeed, the cooperation of all classes in Judah in building the walls of Jerusalem[29] was in harmony with the strongly democratic character of the Temple-State, where resources and labor were pooled in behalf of the community.[30]

With regard to the Hellenistic period, no one questions the political supremacy of the High Priest in the absence of a royal governor. Hecataeus of Abdera[31], the *Letter of Aristeas*,[32] the Tobiad story[33] and Ben Sira[34] are unanimous in their testimony on this point. There are, indeed, very few references in our sources that are inconsistent with the political role assigned to the High Priest in the Temple-State.

That Judea was a Temple-State is confirmed by other considerations, too. The "divinely inspired" free people who, we are told, comprised the majority of the population in a Temple-State, accord with the manifestly religious character of the Sons of the Golah (Captivity). They had left the pleasant and prosperous cities and villages of Babylonia[35] for insecure and poverty-stricken Judea[36] because of their desire to live in the proximity of the Temple in Jerusalem.

The role of temple servants (ἱερόδουλοι) in the Temple-States seems to have been filled by the Nethinim.[37] No satisfactory theory has yet been proposed regarding their task in the Temple.[38] They consisted of 33 or 35[39] families, and in the fifth century numbered 392 persons, together with "Solomon's servants" (עבדי שלמה). It is hard to fathom what there was for them to do in the pitifully small Temple,[40] which reportedly had 4089 priests[41] 47 Levites, 128 singers, and 139 porters,[42] in addition to the "ministers of this house of God"[43] included in the edict of Artaxerxes. The Nethinim were not even needed as חוטבי עצים — "hewers of wood" for the altar, since the various clans took it upon themselves "to bring it [wood] into the house of our God, according to our father's houses, at times appointed year by year."[44]

We may solve this problem if we assume that the Nethinim worked the Temple lands for the benefit of the High Priest, just as the ἱερόδουλοι did in all Temple-States. Indeed, Josephus translates Nethinim (Ezra 7:24) as ἱερόδουλοι, "temple servants"; and similarly I Esdras.[45] It would expain, incidentally, why the Nethinim are classified in the Ezra list with "Solomon's servants."[46] The latter were in some way in the service of the Davidic house, while the Nethinim performed functions in behalf of the Temple. This explains, too, why Solomon's servants are here mentioned for the last time.[47] They relinquished their status when Zerubbabel was removed from office. If, as is probable, the Davidic estates were amalgamated with the temple lands, Solomon's servants would then become temple servants.

It is generally recognized that the Nethinim were not slaves during the period of the Second Temple.[48] In a sense they belonged to the priestly élite, as they are listed with "the priests, Levites, singers, porters,"[49] and elsewhere even with the priests and Levites alone,[50] though of course at the end of the list.[51] It is worth noting that the Babylonian temple servants, the *širkutu*, were financially independent, could own slaves, marry as they pleased, and even belong to the nobility.[52] We must bear in mind, however, that the books of Ezra-Nehemiah and Chronicles may each present a one-sided viewpoint, that of the Sons of the Golah and the Levites respectively. The priests, who tried to deprive the Levites of the tithes,[53] may have shown a less favorable attitude toward the Nethinim.

Our theory would also explain the source of the High Priest's wealth. Throughout the period of the Second Temple the High Priests constituted the highest aristocracy of the land, both politically and socially.[54] It is inconceivable that their economic status depended on the shaky foundations of voluntary contributions shared with the ordinary priests.[55] Writing in the early Hellenistic period, Hecataeus of Abdera, who seems to have gathered his information on the Jews from priests, reports that the (High) Priests had larger estates than the rest of the people.[56] This, however, raises a twofold question. How did they acquire these lands, and was not this acquisition a clear violation of the Torah that "The priests the Levites, even all the tribe of Levi, shall have no portion nor inheritance with Israel?"[57] Finkelstein suggests that they accumulated their wealth by demanding high dowries.[58] Yet the ordinary priests and Levites remained poor, despite their superior lineage.[59] Nor was it characteristic of the Sadducean High Priests[60] to evade the plain words of Scripture by means of ingenious interpretations.[61]

It seems farfetched to suggest that the High Priests got their wealth from the fields dedicated for sacred use as *ḥerem*.[62] Such dedications are conceivable in a prosperous country, where large tracts of land lie fallow, but not in small and indigent Judea.[63] The injunction "Everything devoted in Israel shall be thine"[64] (that is, Aaron's) and, "every devoted thing in Israel shall be theirs"[65] may refer to relatively small dedications, not necessarily to large fields. Josephus, at any rate, does not mention the *ḥerem* among the priestly sources of income.[66]

Finkelstein suggests that "the priests seized the land and themselves became the wealthiest people in the country."[67] If this theory must assume complete anarchy and confusion in the early days of the Second Temple, the evidence does not support it.[68] If, however, it merely means that the Persian authorities empowered the High Priest to appropriate lands for the Temple, this would correspond to the situation in all Temple-States, where the High Priest "supervised in person the fixing of the boundaries of lands and fields" as well as "the allotment of land."[69] Since temple land was not theoretically the property of the High Priest, the scriptural prohibition against the priests owning land[70] was not infringed.

The temple lands of the Zadokite High Priests were subsequently appropriated by the Hasmoneans.[71] After the deposition of the Hasmoneans their land may have been put at the disposal of the high priestly families.[72]

The sacred character of Jerusalem is also confirmed in the edict of Antiochus III, where on account of the piety ($\delta\iota\grave{\alpha}$ $\tau\grave{\eta}\nu$ $\epsilon\grave{\upsilon}\sigma\acute{\epsilon}\beta\epsilon\iota\alpha\nu$) of the people and the sanctity of the Temple, he prohibits the introduction of impure things into the city.[73] Similarly, Demetrius II declared, "Let Jerusalem be holy" ($\kappa\alpha\iota$ $\iota\epsilon\rho o\upsilon\sigma\alpha\lambda\eta\mu$ $\check{\epsilon}\sigma\tau\omega\tilde{\alpha}\gamma\acute{\iota}\alpha$),[74] under the authority of the High Priest.[75]

Some scholars question whether the High Priesthood in the Ptolemaic period was inseparable from political authority,[76] and refer to the case of Joseph the Tobiad. This of course is a purely theoretical question, for there is no evidence that Joseph the Tobiad was anything but a tax-collector outside Judean territory.[77]   Actually, Josephus' use of the term $\pi\rho\acute{o}\sigma\tau\alpha\sigma\iota\alpha\nu$ ("chief magistracy")[78] may simply be as a synonym for the "high priestly office" ($\grave{\alpha}\rho\chi\iota\epsilon\rho\alpha\tau\iota\kappa\tilde{\eta}\varsigma$ $\tau\iota\mu\grave{\eta}\varsigma$.[79] In any case, the Tobiad story is suspect,[80] and even if we assume it to be reliable in a general way,[81] we certainly cannot depend on its details.[82]

B. The Temple-State under the Hasmoneans

The Temple-State came to an end with the rise of the Hasmonean dynasty. Judea ceased to be confined to Jerusalem and the villages around it. The Jewish state now included extensive territories and almost thirty Hellenized cities on all sides of the compass — the coast, Galilee, Transjordan and Idumaea.[83] For the head of a sovereign state to retain the title of High Priest was not only incongruous, but also politically dangerous. The inhabitants of the Hellenized cities in particular could thus be led to believe that their subjugation to the Jews was only temporary, since the High-Priestly authority was by definition confined to the Temple-State, or at most to fellow religionists. Moreover, High Priests of Temple-States were never sovereign, but always subordinate to a king. John Hyrcanus may have been partly motivated by such considerations in forcing Judaism on the Idumaeans,[84] and Aristobulus in converting part of the Ituraeans in Galilee.[85] Yet in Samaria John Hyrcanus was content with destroying the temple on Mount Gerizim,[86] expecting perhaps that the Samaritans would now recognize the Jerusalem Temple and its High Priest.

At this point we must explain why the Pharisees' objected to the Hasmoneans' assuming the functions of both king (or prince) and High Priest. According to Josephus they resented the assumption by Jannaeus of the title of king,[87] and called upon John Hyrcanus to give up the High Priesthood.[88] The Talmudic tradition, indifferent to historical detail, assigns both stories to "King Jannaeus."[89]

The two cases are in fact different. Of John Hyrcanus they demanded: רב לך כתר מלוכה, הנח כתר כהונה לזרעו של אהרן "Let the royal crown suffice thee, and leave the priestly crown to the seed of Aaron."[90] As it stands, the statement contains two factual errors: John Hyrcanus did not assume the royal title,[91] and was himself of the seed of Aaron.[92] The distortion no doubt arose from the need of using picturesque language as a means of preserving an oral tradition. The prosaic rendition of Josephus is more reliable: "Give up the High Priesthood and be content with governing the people" (το ἀρχειν τοῦ λαοῦ).[93]

What the Pharisees wanted of John Hyrcanus was that he give up the High Priesthood. The reason is not far to seek. We may assume that it was not this single incident alone that caused Hyrcanus to become a Sadducee. The Pharisees, having noticed his tendencies toward Sadduceeism,[94] now insisted on his relinquishing the High Priesthood. This incident was merely the final straw that led him to break with the Pharisees.[95]

The situation changed when Jannaeus, already a Sadducee,[96] illegally and arbitrarily assumed the title of king.[97] The people demanded that he give up both the kingship and the High Priesthood;[98] since he would do neither, only his death would satisfy them.[99] In the case of his children, Hyrcanus and Aristobulus, Josephus reports that "the nation was against both and asked not to be ruled by a king."[100] The reason was clear: "It was the custom of the country to obey the priests," whereas "these two were seeking to change their form of government in order that they might become a nation of slaves." In other words, while Judea was a Temple-State, the High Priests made no exorbitant demands on the people, and they lived simply and peacefully. But the two brothers, wishing to play the part of Hellenistic princes,[101] imposed heavy taxes and military levies on the people, thus turning them into "a nation of slaves."

C. The High Priesthood in the Roman Period

Under Roman domination, both the Jewish state and the High Priesthood underwent several political transformations. Pompey reduced the Jewish state to the area inhabited by Jews,[102] thus excluding the Hellenistic cities but leaving the villages of eastern Idumaea, Jewish Peraea east of the

Jordan, and Galilee. The Jewish state could no longer be classified as a Temple-State, i.e. a temple city with its surrounding villages. Because of its homogeneous population, however, the state still revolved around the Temple in Jerusalem. The religious devotion of the population[103] still qualified it as *θεοφορητοι* — a "divinely inspired people." The slaves of the High Priests[104] may have been considered as temple slaves, *ἱεροδουλοι*. The fact that Antiochus III's edict does not include them among the Temple officials[105] does not rule out this possibility, since they worked for the High Priests and not for the Temple directly. The Jewish state now began to approximate a "theocracy,"[106] a term which Josephus invented for it. Hyrcanus was now deprived of his title of king,[107] but Pompey restored him to the High Priesthood (*ἀρχιερωσύνην*) and permitted him the "leadership of the nation" (*τοῦ ἐθνους προστασίαν*).[108] In the light of the above discussion, we can understand the need for both titles. As High Priest (*ἀρχιερευς*), only his religious authority extended to all Jews everywhere,[109] while his political rule was limited to the Temple-State of Judea. But as "leader of the nation" (*ἔθνος*), his political authority also came to include all other territories occupied by Jews.[110]

Josephus remarks that six years later, when Gabinius divided the country into five synods,[111] or *synhedria*,[112] "the people were removed from monarchic rule and lived under an aristocracy."[113] Presumably, Jerusalem and its vicinity remained a Temple-State under the High Priest, while other districts were governed by collaborating Jews, not necessarily priests. This arrangement followed the general Roman policy of weakening or even abolishing Temple-States and replacing them with secular entities.[114]

There is no real foundation for the accepted view that the "aristocrats" in the various districts were simply priests.[115] Ordinary priests were not independent: they were accustomed to take orders from the High Priest, or as Josephus puts it, under his "direction" (*ἡγεμονίαν*).[116] Moreover, an exclusively priestly rule was never a Jewish form of government. In the days of Nehemiah the people were governed by חורים וסגנים — "nobles and rulers."[117] In the Book of Judith, the "elders" are mentioned as the High Priest's council,[118] had they been priests, they would not have been called elders. In the Tobias story, again, the highest council is not composed of priests, but referred to as *πλῆθος* ("the people").[119] The First Book of Maccabees distinguishes between the various leaders: "priests and people and leaders of the nation and elders of the country."[120]

Finally, the Romans in the provinces preferred to hand over the rule to the well-to-do, whom they regarded as the aristocracy (timocracy).[121] Subsequently, when Julius Caesar wished to reward Hyrcanus II for his loyalty to Rome, and enlarged the Jewish state by granting it the city of Joppa and the Valley of Yezreel,[122] he again conferred two titles on Hyrcanus, those of High Priest and Ethnarch ("ruler of the nation").[123] Caesar himself explained that Hyrcanus and his sons "shall be High Priests and priests of Jerusalem and of their nation" with the same authority as their forefathers.[124] And, "being also Ethnarchs, [they] shall be the protectors of those Jews who are unjustly treated" (i.e. anywhere in the Roman empire). This meaning of the title Ethnarch is confirmed by the fact that the title was held by the Patriarch (*Nasi*) in the post-destruction era, when the only justification for its use was that he had authority over the Jewish communities throughout the Roman empire.[125]

Under the Herodians, Palestine was a Roman province ruled by the Roman Senate. The High Priest was purely a figurehead with no political power, arbitrarily appointed and removed by the kings.[126]

Under the procurators, the Jewish government became, according to Jeremias, "a pure theocracy,"[127] where the priesthood was the primary representative of the nobility. The High Priest was now the head of the Sanhedrin. All the sources are in general agreement as to the form of government in this period. According to Josephus the Jewish state was now ruled by the "aristocracy."[128] "Aristocracy" meant in the first place the council of the High Priests. Various High Priests are mentioned as performing important political tasks. In 52 A.D. a former High Priest, Jonathan the son of Ananus, led a delegation to Umnidius Quadratus, the governor of Syria.[129] He and the High Priest Ananias were then sent as ambassadors to Caesar.[130] This Jonathan was also responsible for persuading Caesar to appoint Felix as procurator of Judea.[131] Two High Priests, Ananus the son of Ananus[132] and Jeshua the son of Gamala,[133] played an important role in the revolt against Rome.

It is generally believed, however, that the aristocracy included others besides the High Priests, since Josephus refers also to "the first of the city," "leaders of the people," "the notables," "the leading men," "the nobles and the most eminent citizens."[134] In one passage he enumerates all the groups represented in the "aristocracy" — the "principal citizens" (δύνατοι), the "chief priests" (ἀρχιερεῦσιν) and the "most notable Pharisees" (Φαρισαίων γνωρίμοις).[135] This agrees with the reference of the Gospels to "the chief priests [ἀρχιερεῖς] and the scribes [γραμματεῖς] and the principal men of the people [πρῶτοι τοῦ λαοῦ]".[136]

Curiously, the Talmudic Aggada has occasion to refer only to the "great men of Jerusalem,"[137] that is, the wealthy and influential. On the other hand, Jeremias' description of this government as a "pure theocracy" is an exaggeration. The group of High Priests, consisting of the incumbent and former High Priests ἀρχιερεῖς were not the only members of the "aristocracy" or *synedrion*, though in the trial of Jesus the opinion of the High Priest Caiaphas carried the day.[138] Thus in the trial of Peter and the apostles, it was R. Gamaliel whose voice was decisive in acquitting them.[139]

Moreover, in the spiritual and religious realm, the Sanhedrin of the High Priests and notables were not the sovereigns of the people. Most of the people followed the Pharisaic leadership,[140] whether that leadership controlled the Sanhedrin in the *Lishkat ha-Gazit* ("Chamber of Hewn Stone") of the Temple or whether it merely consisted of a council of scholars.[141] The Essenes or the Qumran sect certainly did not look to this Sanhedrin for religious guidance.[142]

The last stage in history of the High Priesthood comprised the four years of the First Revolt, between 66 and 70 A.D. The High Priest had now no political responsibilities.[143] This division of authority between the political and religious may have been in accordance with Pharisaic doctrine, as implied in the Pharisees' demand of John Hyrcanus: רב לך כתר מלכות, הנח כתר כהונה לזרעו של אהרן — "Give up the High Priesthood and be content with governing the people."[144] Priestly government was not a Pharisaic principle, the popular demand not withstanding.[145] The ultimate ruler of the Jews should be a Davidic king.[146] Until the redemption, the Pharisees taught כל ישראל ראויים למלכות — "Every Israelite is eligible to the kingship."[147] When Simeon the Hasmonean was appointed "leader ἡγούμενον and High Priest" over the nation, it was only "until a true prophet should arise," that is, until the Redemption.[148]

"Theocracy" in the sense of priestly rule, as Josephus describes it,[149] was never in force in Israel. During the period of the First Temple the (High) Priests were officers of the Davidic kings,[150] and in religious influence the prophets rivaled the priests.[151] The rivals of the priests during the period of the Second Temple were at first the "Sons of the Golah," with leaders like Ezra the Scribe;[152] in the second half of the Persian period, they were the Elders and the disciples of the prophets.[153] At the beginning of the Hellenistic period came the men of the Great Synagogue, followed by their successors, the Pharisees.[154] Other rivals in religious influence were the authors of the apocryphal literature, including the Dead Sea sect.

The difference among the sects involved not only the question of the Oral Law, but also the identity of the ultimate Redeemer. While the Pharisees looked toward a descendant of the House of David, the priestly circles believed in a Zadokite;[155] some priests apparently believed — at least for a while — that the Redeemer would come from the Hasmonean dynasty.[156]

Among the ordinary people, however, theocracy was always the ideal constitution, in the sense of an obligation on the part of every Jew to abide by the Covenant with God and to obey His commandments as interpreted by the prophets and the Sages.

D. The Officials of the Temple

Next in rank to the High Priest was his deputy or captain, s^{e}gan ha-kohanim,[157] who succeeded him if he became disqualified.[158] He stood at the right of the High Priest while the latter performed his functions.[159] He was in charge of the priests,[160] and of supervising the ritual and the High Priest's vestments;[161] he also had the power to make arrests in the Temple area.[162] It was the captain of the Temple, Eleazar b. Ḥanina, who ordered the discontinuation of sacrifices for Rome and the emperor, and thus initiated the Great Revolt.[163]

Büchler has shown that the s^{e}gan was a Pharisaic priest, installed under the pressure of the Pharisees in the last decade of the Temple, to ensure the practice of their doctrine in the performance of the ritual. Previously, a brother or close relative of the High Priest had acted as his deputy.[164]

Two other groups of powerful officials in charge of the Temple treasury were members of the leading priestly families,[165] the amarkalim, (at least seven) and the gizbarim (at least three).[166] Jeremias suggests that the amarkal was an overseer of Temple property while the gizbar was a financial officer. Those of the officers on the lists of the Tosefta[167] and the Mishnah[168] who were in charge of the shewbread, salt, wood, seals (or tokens), drink offerings, bird offerings, incense, curtains and vestments, were called gizbarim, while the trenchdigger, gatekeeper, jailer, herald, the director of music, etc. were amarkalim.[169] In fact, however, the Tosefta clearly distinguishes between these officers, who are called m^{e}munim, and the two other classes of officials, whose work is also clearly defined. "The three gizbarim, what did they do? Through them were redeemed objects vowed to the Temple, devoted property, votive offerings, second tithes, and all sacred work [involving financial transactions] was done by them."[170] The amarkalim, in turn, held the keys to the ʿazara (inner court), meaning the store-rooms of the ʿazara, and kept them open only while the gizbarim were inside.[171]

Büchler, on the basis of the Targum, applies the title amarkalim to the elders of the families, who slept with the keys of the ʿazara on the eve of their turn of Temple service.[172] These keys, however, were evidently for the ʿazara proper, which was opened at dawn to allow the priests to enter, and remained open all day.[173] The Targum[174] is probably of post-destruction origin, when the Persian term *amarkal* assumed the general meaning of "respected official,"[175] based on R. Judah's interpretation *mar-al-kol*, i.e., "ruler over all."[176] Still, the identification may be right.

Other Temple officers included the heads of the *ma'amad*[177] (of laymen) and of the *mishmar*[178] (of priests), two groups who served in a regular order in the Temple, as well as two permanent *katholikoi*,[179] but no clear records exist of the functions of the latter three.[180]

E. The Relationship between the High Priest and the Sanhedrin

In his capacity as head of state during most of the period of the Second Temple, the High Priest presided over the supreme political and judicial body, which in the Roman period was known as the Sanhedrin.[181] The question dividing historians is whether the Sanhedrin was also invested with religious authority, or whether there was a separate religious Sanhedrin under the dominance of the Pharisaic scholars.[182] To clarify the issue, let us briefly examine the sources dealing with the relationship between the High Priest and the Sanhedrin.

Josephus relates that in pursuing the Roman policy of *divide et impera*,[183] Gabinius divided the country into five συνέδρια[184] or σύνοδοι.[185] This is the first mention of the Sanhedrin in Jewish history. Gabinius' object was of course to diminish the political power of the Sanhedrin in Jerusalem. There is little reason to believe that the division also affected the religious supremacy of the Jerusalem Sanhedrin.[186] This would point to the existence of a separate religious Sanhedrin at that time (57 B.C.E.). A few years later Julius Caesar re-unified the country, not only confirming Hyrcanus as High Priest (ἀρχιερεύς), but also bestowing on him the title of Ethnarch (ἐθνάρχης).[187] This latter title apparently meant that Hyrcanus, and his descendants after him, were to protect[188] and exercise supreme religious authority over[189] all the Jews in the Roman empire.[190] This, "if . . . any question shall arise concerning the Jews' manner of life . . . the decision shall be with them."[191] It was apparently on this authority that the High Priest sent Paul to arrest the followers of Jesus in the Damascus Jewish community.[192] After the destruction of the Temple, the Patriarchs (another form of Ethnarchs[193]—that is, the *Nesi'im*), inherited the same authority.[194] Being the protector of Jewish rights was not equivalent to being the arbiter on questions of religious law. Nor did Roman recognition mean that the Jews regarded the High Priest as the leading expert in Jewish law. The Jews of Egypt presented their religious problems to the "Sages," that is, the Sanhedrin in Jerusalem;[195] and it was Hillel, their head, who handed down their solution.[196] Apparently, then, the Sanhedrin in Jerusalem which decided on religious matters[197] was a Pharisaic one. Opponents of this conclusion would argue that "Sages" here refers to the scholars at the head of the Pharisaic sect,[198] or that the formulation of the story is late. This story would merely mean, then, that the Pharisees also had followers in Alexandria.

Josephus relates that when Herod was *strategos* in Galilee he was brought to trial before the Sanhedrin in Jerusalem for the murder of a number of patriots. The presiding officer of the Sanhedrin was Hyrcanus.[199] In another version of the story, there was no trial; Hyrcanus simply freed Herod.[200] The Talmud, apparently referring to the same event, presents the case as if Hyrcanus himself had to stand trial before the Sanhedrin as the one responsible for Herod.[201] At all events, this story is irrelevant to the issue of whether the High Priest presided over the religious Sanhedrin, since Herod was tried for a political murder. The question before the Sanhedrin may have been whether the murders were justified in order to prevent massacres by the Romans.[202] The political nature of the trial is attested by the fact that the governor of Syria, Sextus Caesar, "sent express orders to Hyrcanus to clear Herod of the charge of manslaughter."[203]

Another political trial took place before the Sanhedrin when, the tables turned, Herod the king charged Hyrcanus with treachery.[204] In another version, Herod put Hyrcanus to death without benefit of trial, since it was the prerogative of the king to execute rebels.[205] Nor does Josephus state if there was a trial, or whether the president of this Sanhedrin was Herod himself, the High Priest or someone else. In condemning his wife Mariamne, he set up a special court of those "who were closest to him" and read the charge before them.[206] In this trial, apparently, he was not a judge.

The court that tried his two sons for treachery was a *synedrion* set up in Berytus, consisting of the Syrian governor, the king of Cappadocia, and other Roman officials;[207] according to another version, it also included some of his own relatives.[208] Nothing may be learned from these cases about the permanent Sanhedrin in Jerusalem. Nor are we any wiser from the incident in which Herod "summoned the Jewish officials" (τέλει)[209] to Jericho to lay charges against the pious Jews who had removed the eagles from the gates of the Temple. His pretext was that the latter had committed "sacrilege" (ἱεροσυλοῦντας)[210] — מעילה in Talmudic terminology — the unlawful use of sacred property.[211] But in reality he regarded their action as a personal insult.[212] Nor does this court seem to have been the regular Sanhedrin, but one specially composed of his trusted officials. In Jewish law, neither sacrilege of Temple property (m^e'ila)[213] nor insult to the king is subject to capital punishment by the Sanhedrin.[214] These trials mentioned by Josephus seem, therefore, to have been all *ad hoc* courts, most of them for political offenses, one for murder, one for adultery and one for sacrilege. None of them needed the Great Sanhedrin of the *Lishkat ha-Gazit*, as described in Tannaitic literature: all of them could be judged by any court of twenty-three. There is nothing in Josephus, then, that refutes the view first presented by Büchler that Herod left religious matters to the Sanhedrin holding its regular sessions in the *Lishkat ha-Gazit* of the Temple, as maintained by Tannaitic literature.

Referring to the time when the procurators ruled the land and internal affairs were in the hands of the priests, Josephus relates two contradictory stories about the Sanhedrin. The Sadducean High Priest Ananus "convened the judges of the Sanhedrin" in order to condemn James, the brother of Jesus, for transgressing the Law.[215] This Sanhedrin was no doubt a Sadducean one, presided over by the High Priest. Moreover, its members were either ignorant of the law[216] or simply disregarded it, for the people in Jerusalem who adhered to the Law objected to the verdict.[217] On the other hand, the Sanhedrin which Agrippa II convened to permit the Levitic singers to wear a priestly uniform, and this over the violent objection of the priests,[218] was obviously a Pharisaic one. It is evident, too, that it was not the High Priest who presided over this Sanhedrin.

It is not necessary to assume that these two Sanhedrins were convened during two different stages of the struggle between the sects. They could simply have been two kinds of courts, one of priestly and the other of non-priestly and Pharisaic composition. The Pharisees regarded singing in the Temple as an integral part of the ritual,[219] and so they had no objection to the Levitic singers wearing the priestly uniform. It may seem strange that this Pharisaic Sanhedrin was convened to deliberate on a halakic question, not by its Pharisaic head, but by the king. The explanation is provided by Josephus. The Levitic singers, he writes, "urged the king," in his royal capacity and as "curator of the temple" (ἐπιμέλειαν τοῦ ἱεροῦ), to convene the Sanhedrin for this purpose, in order to "mark his reign" through this innovation.[220] Having convened the Sanhedrin, Agrippa himself took no part in its deliberations.

During the four years of the First Revolt (66–70), when the membership of the Jerusalem Sanhedrin was determined by the Jews themselves,[221] it did not coincide with the "aristocracy"[222] of which it was composed during the Roman domination, as Kuenen,[223] Schürer[224] and Jeremias[225] think. The high officials were now appointed by a popular assembly. Those elected to the supreme control of affairs did not include High Priests in office. In describing them Josephus first mentions a layman, Joseph the son of Gorion, and only next a former High Priest, Ananus.[226] Formerly, the High Priest would have occupied the leading position over all other members.[227] Two functions are attributed to this Sanhedrin: it conducted the affairs of the state, and appointed generals (στρατηγοι) for the various parts of the country.[228]

The moderate rebels were later replaced by extremist Zealots who, Josephus says, instituted mock trials and courts of justice. They summoned seventy of the leading citizens to the Temple to act as judges in the trial of Zacharias the son of Baris, whom they accused of treason.[229] No indication is given as to the identity of the presiding officer. Here, too, the role of the Sanhedrin was political, not halaḵic.

In summing up Josephus' references to the Sanhedrin during the Roman period we note that, except when the Herodians were kings, the state was headed by High Priests who also presided over the Sanhedrin in political trials. Herod appointed Sanhedrins *ad hoc* to try cases in which he had a personal interest. During the First Revolt, the High Priest was not the head of the state, nor did he preside over trials. Josephus does not describe how halaḵic decisions were made. In the case of the Sanhedrin on the Levitical singers, Agrippa II's role was limited to convening it. We are virtually certain that it was composed of Pharisees and not presided over by the High Priest. It was distinct from, though contemporaneous with, the political Sanhedrin under the direction of the High Priests.

A similar picture emerges from the Gospel narratives. Except under the Herodians, the High Priests were responsible to the Romans for the peaceful administration of the country; they presided over cases which had political implications, such as those connected with the rebellion against the Romans.[230] The Sanhedrin was composed of "all the chief priests and the elders and the scribes,"[231] and was apparently equally divided between Pharisees and Sadducees.[232] They did not meet in the Temple,[233] and had no compunction about meeting at night[234] or even on festivals.[235] No halaḵic decisions are recorded. When there arose the issue of the belief in the resurrection, the Sanhedrin was simply paralyzed, since this dogma was the subject of controversy between the Pharisees and Sadducees.[236]

As distinguished from the Hellenistic sources, the Talmudic passages deal chiefly with the halaḵic aspects of the Sanhedrin's function. The Sanhedrin met in the *Lishkat ha-Gazit* in the Temple and was the final authority on *Halaḵa*.[237] Doubtful cases were sent to "the Sages in the *Lishkat ha-Gazit*."[238] Questions of priestly genealogy were also within its province.[239] It held regular daily sessions between the morning and the evening *tamid* (public sacrifice), i.e. between 7.30 a.m. and 3.30 p.m., but there were no sessions on Sabbaths and festivals.[240]

The juridical competence of the Great Sanhedrin was limited to the judging of "a tribe, a false prophet, or the High Priest." It also decided on "voluntary wars," (*milḥemet reshut*), on additions to Jerusalem's and the Temple's territory, on the appointment of Small Sanhedrins for the various tribes, on the proclamation of an Apostate City,[241] and in cases of a Rebellious Elder.[242] It also dealt with questions concerning the sacrificial red heifer, and with the appointment of a king or a High Priest.[234] Finally, it supervised the administration of the "water of bitterness,"[244] and the ceremony of breaking the heifer's neck to atone for an anonymous murder.[245] With the exception of the decision on voluntary wars and the appointment of the king and High Priest (as in the case of Simeon the Hasmonean in 142 B.C.E.[246]), all its actions involved the definition and administration of *halaḳot*.

Clearly not all of the seventy-one members were present all the time. As long as twenty-three were in attendance, however, all the juridical functions of a Small Sanhedrin, including capital punishment, could be lawfully discharged.[247] Nothing is said of the High Priest's role in the Great Sanhedrin, except that "he can judge and be judged."[248] On the other hand a non-Davidic, Herodian king "can neither judge nor be judged."[249] Both rules are in agreement with the Hellenistic sources which report of trials under the presidency of the High Priest, but do not refer to the king as presiding over trials. Incidentally, the Mishnah's ruling on Herodian kings, rather than on Davidic, refutes the contention that the Talmudic rules are irrelevant to the current situation and reflect only what the Tannaim considered ideal.[250]

In Rabbinic literature, the president of the Great Sanhedrin in the *Lishkat ha-Gazit* is the *Nasi*, the leading Pharisaic scholar. Of the *zugot* ("pairs") the Mishnah says: "The former [of each pair] were *Nesi'im*, and the others were *Avot beth-din*."[251] Of their successors the Barayta states: "Hillel, Simeon, Gamaliel and Simeon held the office of *Nasi* during the last hundred years of the Temple."[252] R. Judah, a second century Tanna, says: "The people of Galilee need not assign their share [in the public property of the *Nasi*], since their fathers [of the Temple days] have done so for them already."[253]

However, it has been argued that the *Nesi'im* were presidents of Pharisees, not of the Sanhedrin.[254] This meaning of the term has no support from the text, but is necessary if we assume that there could be only one Sanhedrin at a time and that according to the Hellenistic sources its presiding officer was the High Priest. We have seen, however, that neither assumption is correct. In the time of Agrippa II there was, in addition to the political Sanhedrin dominated by the High Priests, also a Pharisaic Sanhedrin which often issued decisions contrary to the priestly views.[255] Moreover, in none of the Hellenistic sources does the High Priest have any connection with a *Halaka*-making body.

In their performance of the Temple cult the High Priests were bound to the Pharisaic *Halaka* by means of an oath.[256] When the Boethusian High Priests wished to have the date of the New Moon determined according to their reckoning rather than that of the Pharisees, they even resorted to the hiring of false witnesses.[257] It is hardly conceivable, therefore, that this *Halaka* was formulated by a body headed by Sadducees and Boethusians, as many of the High Priests were.

Thus, in one case the *halaka* was decided in the *Lishkat ha-Gazit* on the basis of a testimony that it was "a tradition from R. Me'asha, who received it from his father [*Abba*], who received it from the *zugot*, who received it from the Prophets as a *halaka* given to Moses from Sinai."[258] Yet none of the later authorities mentioned were recognized by the Sadducees; nor did they recognize the validity of any *Halaka*, or of the Midrash, which was another source of halakic decision.[259] Some High Priests were known not to have been scholars,[260] even if they were not Sadducees. They would have been extremely uncomfortable presiding over a scholarly disputation. The logical assumption, therefore, is that the halakic Sanhedrin in the *Lishkat ha-Gazit* was composed and headed by Pharisaic scholars.

The sources, being of diverse nature, have given rise to a variety of views and interpretations.[261] Scholars who see a contradiction between the Hellenistic and Rabbinic sources, regard one or the other as unreliable. To Wellhausen[262] and Schürer,[263] the Talmudic sources are late, anachronistic and Utopian, while Jost[264] thinks that the Hellenistic sources are inaccurate. Hoffmann[265] maintains the accommodating theory that the Sadducean High Priests seized the presidency from the legitimate *Nesi'im* on those occasions when they happen to be mentioned in the Greek sources.

Other scholars deny that any contradiction exists, since there were two or three Sanhedrins functioning side by side. Geiger,[266] Derenbourg[267] and Schreier[268] cite various *baraytot* which report that there were three Small Sanhedrins of twenty-three members each, one consisting of priests, one of Levites and one of Israelites. When the three courts united to discuss special problems, they constituted, together with the presiding officer (the High Priest) or officers (*Nasi* and *Av beth-din*) a Great Sanhedrin of seventy or seventy-one. Unfortunately, there is no evidence that the three courts held common meetings. Nor are we certain as to the number of its members, as the more reliable texts[269] have only three members for each court, rather than twenty-three.[270]

Büchler was the first to suggest that there were two leading Sanhedrins in Jerusalem, a Pharisaic one in the *Lishkat ha-Gazit*, and the other a criminal court with a political character.[271] All the reconstructions along this line,[272] though differing on the precise nature of the political Sanhedrin, are based on two premises. First, the term "Sanhedrin" is applicable to various types of council-courts, political, military, administrative,[273] and even social.[274] Secondly, the Hellenistic and Talmudic sources deal with a different aspect of Jewish history.

We may thus sum up the two sides of the debate. One side argues as follows:

1. In antiquity the political ruler was generally the religious head of the state.[275]

2. The title *Nasi* as applied to the leading Pharisaic scholars need not refer to the presidency of the Sanhedrin, but only of the sect.[276]

The conclusion here is that there was only one Great Sanhedrin in Jerusalem, presided over by the head of the state. According to some scholars (Schürer, etc.), it was this Sanhedrin, composed of Sadducees and Pharisees, that enacted the *halakot*; others believe that this was done by a committee of Pharisee scholars, headed by a *Nasi* of their own, and appointed by the Sanhedrin (Chwolson, Dubnow, Klausner). Safrai's suggestion (above, n. 254) implies that the Pharisaic *Halaka*, like the Qumran rules (*Serek*), was a sectarian affair and independent of the Sanhedrin.

The opposing argument may be presented thus:

1. As neither Queen Salome Alexandra[277] nor Herod[278] could or would preside over the halakic sessions of the Sanhedrin, we need not assume this presidency for the High Priests. Indeed, the elders of the Court reminded the High Priest that he was "our delegate and the delegate of the Court,"[279] not its head.

2. There could be no mixed halakic Sanhedrin of Pharisees and Sadducees, since the Sadducees denied the validity of *Halaka* altogether.[280]

3. The Pharisaic *Halaka* seems to have been the official law of the land, as is shown by its abolition and restoration by John Hyrcanus I[281] and Salome Alexandra[282] respectively. With only one exception the victories of the Pharisees over the Sadducees which are celebrated in the *Megillat Ta'anit*, all concern rules of the Temple cult; while the

abolition of the *Sefer Gᵉzerta* ("Book of Decrees") affected judicial rules of punishment. These represented the last stage in the gradual identification of Judaism with Pharisaism.[283]

All this supports the Talmudic tradition that there was a separate halakic Sanhedrin in the *Lishkat ha-Gazit* in the Temple, composed of Pharisaic scholars and headed by their leader, the *Nasi*. During the rule of the procurators, a council consisting of the acting and former High Priests — all of them owing their appointments to the procurator — headed the political Sanhedrin of the country.

While the Great Sanhedrin was a national institution, there were Small Sanhedrins of twenty-three members[284] in the capital cities of each region.[285] At least one member of each of the latter was a full-fledged scholar, called a *mufla* or *muflag*, but the title of the others, *yoʿeẓ*[286] (βουλευτής), reveals that these Small Sanhedrins constituted the city council[287] (βουλή), with the authority to impose capital punishment.[288] The villages came under the jurisdiction of the cities,[289] and according to Josephus[290] were governed by seven appointed leaders.

CHAPTER IX

THE TEMPLE AND THE DIVINE SERVICE

by S. Safrai

THE MAIN SOURCE of knowledge concerning the Temple service and an understanding of the status and role of the Temple in the life of the community during the final generations of its existence is the Tannaitic literature, especially the Mishnah. The information is scattered throughout various tractates, particularly those of the orders of Qodashim and Mo'ed. Most of the order of Qodashim deals with laws connected with the Temple, and two of its tractates, Tamid and Middot, are devoted to recording the order of daily service and the dimensions of the Temple and its courts. Tamid belongs to the early strata of the Mishnah. The tractate does not mention the name of a single Tanna, either as supporting or dissenting.[1] Its language is archaic, and includes expressions which are rarely used in the Mishnah and are closer to the later books of the Bible. The tractate ends on a poetic note: "This was the order of the regular daily service of the house of our God. May it be His will that it shall be built up again speedily in our days. Amen."[2] According to a Tannaitic tradition, and indeed to both Talmuds, R. Simeon of Mizpeh was the Tanna responsible for Tamid.[3] R. Simeon lived during the time of the Temple,[4] and remained alive for a long time after its destruction, for he is always referred to as "Rabbi," a designation found only in connection with Tannaim who lived after the destruction.[5] According to the testimony of both Talmuds, the Mishnah of Middot derives from R. Eliezer b. Jacob. He, too, was contemporaneous with the destruction, and he describes the dimensions of the Temple and many of its arrangements as an eyewitness. He belonged to a priestly or a Levitical family, and recalls what happened to his mother's brother while the latter was on guard in the Temple (1, 2). He sometimes mentions that he has already forgotten a certain detail: "The wood chamber — R. Eliezer b. Jacob said: I forget what it was used for" (5, 4). These two tractates, as can be inferred, were not included in the Mishnah of R. Akiba, the source of R. Judah ha-Nasi's Mishnah, and for that reason have no parallel *barayta* collections in the Tosefta in our possession.

In the order Mo'ed, most of tractate Yoma is devoted to a description of the service of the High Priest on the Day of Atonement, and many chapters of tractates Pesaḥim, Sukka, Rosh ha-Shana, Ta'anit and Ḥagiga discuss *halakot* connected with the Temple and the pilgrimage thereto. Much information about the Temple arrangements and its officers may be gleaned from tractate Sheqalim. In the other orders of the Mishnah, too, there are isolated *mishnayot* and even whole chapters that record *halakot* and various facets of Temple life. The third chapter of Bikkurim records the order of the first fruit offerings, and the seventh chapters of Soṭa the order of the Torah reading by the High Priest on the Day of Atonement, and by the king at the *haqhel* (assembly) ceremony on Sukkot. Both these chapters mention the conduct of King Agrippa in connection with those practices.[6] It is probable that both belong to the same period, namely, to the first years after the destruction, and that both are from the same source that aimed at recording and preserving the character of Temple life for the future. The first chapter of Kelim details ten degrees of holiness connected with the Temple. Similar matters are found in many chapters of the Mishnah.

Apart from the two Tannaim already mentioned, others who testified or transmitted evidence concerning the Temple and its service included R. Ẓadok and his son R. Eleazar, R. Zechariah b. Kabutal, R. Hananiah the prefect of the priests, R. Ṭarfon, R. Johanan b. Gudgada, R. Joshua b. Hananiah, Abba Shaul b. Boṭnit and Rabban Johanan b. Zakkai. All were of the generation of the destruction and most had ministered in the Temple either as ordinary priests and Levites or in the highest offices save that of High Priest. Conspicuous among those of following generations who passed on their knowledge about Temple life are R. Judah b. Ilai, the disciple of R. Ṭarfon, and Jose b. Ḥalafta of Sepphoris, who also transmitted many traditions concerning the attachment of his native town to the Temple.

Next to the Mishnah, the most important source are the works of Josephus — the *Jewish War*, the *Antiquities of the Jews*, particularly Books III, V and XX, and *Against Apion*. For many incidents the Tannaitic literature and Josephus supplement one another, but they differ in many details and we cannot be certain in advance which of the sources is to be preferred. Both the Tannaim and Josephus wrote as eyewitnesses, and both strove to be accurate, the former so as to establish the *Halaka* for the Temple to be built in the future, the latter to preserve an account for history. Both also utilized literary sources, and some of these most certainly derived from different eras. It will never be possible to know which *halaka* and which factual account was contained in these sources. Hence each case must be investigated, as far as possible, on its own merits.

Much information is contained in the books of the New Testament and in Christian apocryphal traditions, including the papyrus fragments.[7] Of writers in the era before the destruction of the Temple, mention must be made of Philo of Alexandria who also visited the Temple at least once and almost certainly wrote as an eyewitness. Many details are contained in his works, especially in the books dealing with the laws. Of the noncanonical writings, particular attention should be given to Ben Sira, the last chapter of which describes the High Priest Simeon the son of Onias ministering at the Altar. This is not a description of the service of the Day of Atonement, for it contains nothing to connect it with that day. It is simply the order of service of the regular daily sacrifice. Ben Sira's description of the service bears no resemblance to any presumed description of the service in the time of the First Temple. Yet it also differs in many respects from the description in the Mishnah, representing a halfway stage between the biblical era and the era of the Pharisee Sages and the Mishnah. Some information is contained in the Books of Maccabees and in the Testaments of the Twelve Patriarchs, particularly in the Testament of Levi, and in the description in the *Letter of Aristeas*. Other meager details may be garnered from Greek writers, particularly Hecataeus of Abdera and Plutarch.

A. The Temple

1. THE TEMPLE AND ITS COURTS.

THE SECOND TEMPLE differed from the First in its arrangements and manner of functioning. The service was performed by twenty-four priestly courses, in conjunction with twenty-four divisions, consisting of priests, Levites and Israelites jointly. The attachment of the people for the Temple was expressed in many ways, including participation in the divine service. The various courts of the Sanhedrin held their sessions in the Temple buildings. Within the confines of the Temple was a synagogue where the public was taught the Torah. All these developments necessitated changes in the construction of the Temple, particularly in the manner in which its courts and chambers were used.

The outermost boundary of the Temple was the Temple Mount. Its dimensions according to the Mishnah were "... five hundred by five hundred cubits. Its largest open space was to the south, the next largest to

Plan of the Second Temple and the Temple Mount

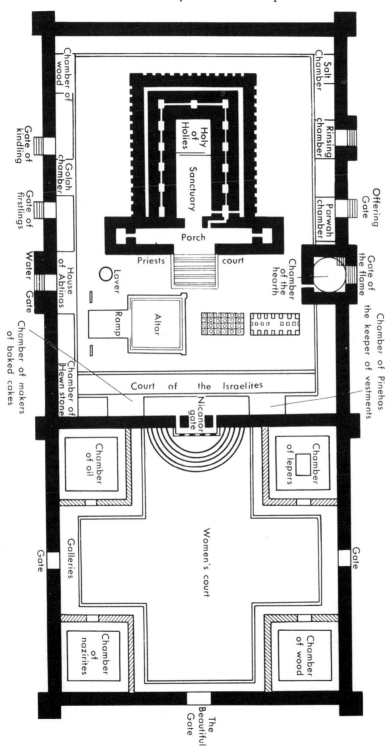

the east, the third largest to the north and its smallest to the west; the place where its measure was greatest was where its use was greatest" (M. Mid. 2, 1). Two gates on the south side provided the main entry into the Temple. From the archaeological research now in progress at the southern and western walls of the Temple Mount it has become clear that there was a large open space on the south side from which people ascended to the Temple Mount. Israelites who journeyed to Jerusalem but had not yet purified themselves, as well as respectful Gentiles visiting the Temple, were permitted to enter the outer Temple court. No part of the Temple service took place there, but it served as a meeting place of the crowds who took part in the service. When the eve of Passover occurred on the Sabbath, thus preventing those sacrificing their paschal lambs from carrying them to their houses in the town, the Mishnah tells us that ". . . the first group left [the Temple] and remained within the Temple Mount" (Pes. 5, 10). Crowds of pilgrims from the Land of Israel and the Diaspora congregated within the magnificent colonnades that surrounded the Temple Mount,[8] and listened to the Torah discourses and reflective sermons of scholars and preachers. In the area of the Temple Mount sat a court of twenty-three — one of the three courts of which the great Sanhedrin was composed.[9] In this area there was also a house of study used by the Sanhedrin on Sabbaths and festivals, when it did not sit as a court, as the Tosefta testifies: "On Sabbaths and festivals they would enter only into the place of study on the Temple Mount."[10]

The Temple Mount was apparently also the venue for all business dealings connected with the Temple, such as the purchase of doves, oil and wine required for the sacrifices.[11] Here, too, were located the money changers who "sat in the Temple" to change the different currencies into the "money of the Sanctuary." This busy commercial activity often sorely offended the pilgrim who went up to the Temple, particularly as members of the High Priesthood exploited it to augment their own incomes.[12]

Most of those entering the Temple came from the south,[13] and pilgrims were also wont to circle right round the rampart and the balustrade (soreg) which surrounded the inner wall and prostrate themselves thirteen times, as stated in the Mishnah: "Inside the Temple Mount was a balustrade [soreg] ten handbreadths high. It had 13 breaches which the Grecian kings had made; these were fenced up again, and over against them 13 prostrations were decreed" (M. Mid. 2, 3). The Mishnah appears to be referring to the breach made by Alcimus in the Temple walls in order to destroy the boundary limiting the entry of Gentiles to that locality alone (I Macc. 9:54), though the Mishnah attributes the action of the Jewish High Priest to his Gentile masters. The second area of sanctity was the rampart (*hel*), which was merely a terrace ten cubits wide surrounding the court. The rampart, too, played no direct part in the Temple service, but a court of twenty-three was located there.[14]

From the rampart they ascended through a number of gates into the Court of Women, the third area of sanctity where those who had bathed that day for uncleanness were forbidden to enter until sunset (M. Kelim 1, 8). In contrast to the Temple Mount and the rampart which surrounded the Temple on all four sides, the Court of Women only extended on the east side and served as a kind of secondary court to the Temple. In its four corners were four chambers whose function was directly connected with the service and the ministration of those coming to complete their sacrifice. One of these, the Chamber of the Nazirites (where Nazirites prepared their sacrifices on completing the period of their vow) was in the south-eastern corner (M. Mid. 2, 5). Another of the chambers in the west, near the steps, leading to the Inner Court, housed the musical instruments of the Levites (M. Mid. 2, 6). In the Court of Women there took place all those congregational ceremonies connected with the divine service as it developed during the time of the Second Temple. Here the High Priest read the Torah on the Day of Atonement after completing the sacrificial rite and the burning of the incense (Yoma 69b); here the king or the High Priest read the Torah during the *haqhel* assembly ceremony of the Feast of Tabernacles (Soṭa 41b); and here, too, the rejoicing took place at the *Beth ha-Sho'eva* water-drawing festival, while on the fifteen steps in the west stood the Levites playing their instruments throughout (Suk. 5, 1).

Such an outer court of the inner enclosure is alluded to at the beginning of the period of the Second Temple,[15] but it is not referred to as the Court of Women except in the Talmudic literature and by Josephus when writing of Herod's building.[16] The court was so called not because no men were to be found there — its chambers served both priests and Israelites, and the usual way into the inner enclosure was through the court itself[17] — but because women generally did not go further than the end of the area of the court, though they were not forbidden to enter the inner enclosure.[18] It is also possible that it was first designated the Court of Women after balconies were built there for the women taking part in the festivities of the *Beth ha-Sho'eva* water-drawing: "When the court saw that they behaved frivolously they made three balconies surrounding the three sides where the women saw the rejoicing of the water-drawing, so that when they saw it they were not wont to mingle."[19]

The inner enclosure was elevated above the Court of Women and was

usually simply called "the Court" (*'azara*). This court was divided into
the Court of Israelites and the Court of Priests, the former extending only
over a narrow area along the eastern wall of the court. The whole court
was 185 cubits by 135 cubits, and the Court of Israelites 11 cubits by
136 cubits (M. Mid. 2, 6). Ends of flagstones separated the Court of Israelites from the Court of Priests.[20] In one section of this partition stood the
platform on which the Levites sang (*ibid.*). The Israelites went beyond the
partition only to approach the altar on offering a sacrifice, or during the
Feast of Tabernacles when they circled the altar with their palm branches.[21]
It was in the inner court where the main service and ritual of the Temple
took place. One of the chambers at the side of the wall of the court was the
Chamber of Hewn Stone (*Lishkat ha-Gazit*) in the form of a "large basilica"
(Yoma 25a). This served as the seat of the Sanhedrin, but it was also
much used for the daily service. The other chambers connected with the
sacrificial rites of the priests were also built in the wall of the court on
both sides of its gates; one of these, for example, was the Chamber of the
Hearth.[22] At the center of the Court of Priests stood the altar of the whole-
offering, to its north the slaughterhouse and to its south the laver.[23] Most
of the daily services were performed in the open court, both congregational
and individual sacrifices being offered upon the altar in the court. The
Levites stood upon the platform, and when blessing the people the priests
stood on the steps leading up to the porch (M. Tamid 7, 2). Other ritual
observances for which the community depended upon the Temple and its
priests were performed within the area of the court at the Gate of Nicanor.[24]
The people gathered in the court for prayer at the time of offering incense
(Luke 1:10). In the Sanctuary itself only the burning of incense was performed, morning and evening, and the lamps kindled. The only exception
was on the Day of Atonement, when several of the services were held in the
Sanctuary, and incense burned in the Holy of Holies.

2.   THE TEMPLE AND THE CITY OF JERUSALEM.

The life of Jerusalem was bound up with the Temple and influenced by
it in many ways. Many Jews from other cities in Palestine and the Diaspora
visited Jerusalem for shorter or longer periods, as we know from literary
references[25] and from the many tombstone inscriptions that have been
discovered around the city.[26] References to synagogues catering to pilgrims
from different parts of the Diaspora occur in the literary sources. The
inscription of Theodotus testifies to the building of a synagogue with an
attached hospice for the purpose of "giving hospitality to the needy from

foreign parts."[27] According to the *Halaka*, Jerusalem was considered an expanded precinct of the Temple, as indeed it was in actual fact. The Book of Deuteronomy imposes the duty of carrying tithes to the place of God's choice: "... and thou shalt eat there before the Lord thy God" (14:26). A similar injunction existed with regard to sacrifices which were partly eaten by their owners, and which the Talmud refers to as of lesser sanctity (Deut. 12:7). The early *Halaka* required tithes, peace offerings, and paschal offerings to be eaten in the Temple court, in that section later called the Court of Women. It is already stated in Ezekiel that the place for cooking holy meats to be eaten by the priests was in the "inner court": "that they bring them not forth into the outer court" (46:20), and that the outer court was for "boiling places where the ministers of the house shall boil the sacrifice of the people" (46:24). The boiling of lesser sacred meat in the court almost certainly carried with it the duty of eating it there, just as the cooking of the priest's sacred meats in the inner court implied a prohibition against removing them from that court. Describing the Passover sacrifices in the reign of Josiah, the Second Book of Chronicles (35:13) states "they [the Levites] roasted the passover with fire according to the ordinance; and the holy offerings cooked they in pots, and in cauldrons, and in pans, and carried them quickly to all the children of the people." Obviously, the Levites did not carry the Passover sacrifices to the people's dwellings, but into the Temple court. The later *Halaka* reads: "The firstling of beasts, the tithe, and the Passover lamb were of the lesser holy things; they were slaughtered anywhere in the court and could be eaten throughout the city by anyone."[28] That this actually occurred is attested to by Josephus and by the fact that Jesus ordered his disciples to prepare the Passover in the house of one of the inhabitants of the city.[29] Similarly, Onias the Circle-maker turned to those who begged him to pray for rain and said: "Go out and bring in the Passover ovens that they be not softened" (M. Ta'an. 3, 8). Thus the ovens were in the private possession of the Jews and not of the Temple, as stated in the books of Ezekiel and Chronicles. This *Halaka* is taken from the teaching of the Pharisees. The author of the Book of Jubilees protests against it and requires that the eating of the passover and of the second tithe should take place only within the Temple area.[30] It is probable that with the growth of the population and the increase in the number of pilgrims, the *Halaka* was changed and the boundaries of the Temple court were extended to include the whole of Jerusalem. Most people accepted this *Halaka*, though certain circles opposed it. However, the sanctity of Jerusalem did not apply to the whole of the city but only to its older sections. A Tannaitic tradition transmitted by Abba Shaul[31] states: "There were two reservoirs [clefts in the hills] in Jerusalem, a lower and an upper one; the lower one was sanctified by all these[32] but not the upper one. When the exiles went up, however, they sanctified it, without a king, and without the Urim and Tummim. At the lower one whose sanctity was complete the ignorant ate lesser sacred meats and "Associates" [i.e., those versed in the Torah] ate sacred things but not second tithe. At the upper one whose sanctity was incomplete the ignorant ate lesser sacred meats but not second tithe, while Associates ate neither lesser sacred meats nor second tithe. Why then was it included in Jerusalem?[33] Because it was the weak point of Jerusalem from where it could easily be captured." From the *barayta*'s references to the "weak point of Jerusalem," the place was apparently in the north of the city. This tradition may therefore be speaking of Bezetha, the new city that Josephus mentions in his *Jewish War V*, (151) and that was finally added to the city with the building of the Third Wall by Agrippa I. Yet this is so, the *barayta* attributes events belonging to the time of Agrippa I to a much earlier period. Since it is difficult to ignore the Tannaitic tradition, it would be better to connect this tradition with older sections of the city which were already added in Hellenistic times but not regarded as part of the city. In that case the new town, Bezetha, would not be regarded at all as part of the city in which it was permitted to eat sacred meats.

The city's attachment to the Temple also found expression in the rules of purity whose purpose was not only to ensure the sanctity of the city itself, but also to make it easier for pilgrims to purify themselves before entering the Temple. The author of the *Letter of Aristeas* already states: "There are steps too which lead up to the crossroads and some people go up and others down and they keep as far apart as possible from each other on the road because of those who are bound by the laws of purity, lest they touch anything which is unlawful."[34] Talmudic tradition enumerates a series of *Halakot* applicable only to Jerusalem: ". . . the dead are not lodged overnight in it, nor may human bones be kept there . . . nor may tombs be maintained there except for those of the dynasty of David, and the tomb of the prophetess Huldah which were there from the time of the early prophets . . . nor may refuse be heaped up there because of uncleanness, nor may ledges of balconies be protruded into the public thoroughfare because of overshadowing uncleanness."[35] Even some of the Gentile rulers and armies took account of this fact, and Antiochus III forbade the bringing of unclean dead animals into the city (*Ant.* XII, 145–146). In a later time Hyrcanus II enjoined Herod not to bring alien soldiers into Jerusalem because the people were purifying themselves for the festival.[36]

B. Those Performing the Sacred Service and those Participating in it

1. THE PRIESTS.

The daily service of the Temple was performed chiefly by the priests, who alone were permitted to approach the altar and to enter the Sanctuary. They offered the congregational and the private offerings, burnt the incense, lit the candelabrum in the Sanctuary, and blessed the people. Even in the services pertaining to the Levites, such as the singing and guarding, the priests took part in a manner emphasizing their superior status. They blew trumpets at the beginning of the singing and during intervals (M. Mid.), and where priests and Levites guarded together, "the priests keep watch above the Levites below" (1, 5). Even in those services permitted by *Halaka* to non-priests (Levites and Israelites), the priests were mindful of their dignity and did not permit non-priests to approach. The *Halaka* permitted slaughter by a non-priest, but we find in practice that only priests did the slaughtering.[37] Mishna Yoma states (6, 3): "All were eligible to lead away [the scapegoat], but the High Priests had established the custom not to permit an Israelite to take it away."

The priests were divided into twenty-four courses, each of which served one week. This number is already established in I Chronicles 24:7–18, and these courses, including their names, remained until the end of the Temple's existence.[38] The courses were subdivided into families, each of which served one day in the week of the course. The number of families in each course was not the same. According to the *barayta* it varied between four and nine,[39] and the division of the families to the seven days of the week was adapted accordingly. In charge of the course was "the head of the course," and his second-in-command was "the head of the father's house," assisted by "the elders of the father's house," in whose possession were the Temple keys that were to be delivered to the elders of the course coming on duty.[40]

Most of the priests, particularly the ordinary priests, did not live in Jerusalem, and indeed priests are found living together as a number of families or in larger communities throughout the length and breadth of the land. The Hasmonean priestly family lived in Modiin, and priestly families were to be found in Sepphoris, Gophna, Zeredah, Jericho and elsewhere.[41] They would travel to Jerusalem when their period of service was due and return to their towns when it was finished. During their stay in Jerusalem they slept in the Temple: "The Chamber of the Hearth was vaulted; it was a large chamber and around it ran a raised stone pavement; and there the eldest of the father's house used to sleep on the ground."[42] Different sources from the beginning of the Hellenistic era onward give different numbers for the total complement of priests, but an estimated total cannot be established from them. Either the number is much exaggerated, as in the *Letter of Aristeas* (95) — which speaks of 700 priests taking part in the service at the same time who were relieved by others when they tired — or it cannot be understood which priests are to be included in the given number, as in the testimony of Hecataeus of Abdera (*Against Apion* I, 22), who refers indefinitely to 1500 priests.

For the sacrifice of the daily offering, about 20 priests were drawn by lot. In addition many priests ministered to the offerings of individuals.[43] It is not possible to determine the extent of participation in the Temple services by priests who came from the Diaspora. From a *Halaka* in the Mishnah it may be inferred that these priests could minister, for it states: "Priests that have ministered in the house of Onias may not minister in the Temple of Jerusalem" (M. M^en. 13, 10). Thus an ordinary priest who came from outside the Land of Israel could minister, but there is no evidence from the sources to what extent these went up and ministered with the course to which they belonged. From one *mishna* it is known that priests from Babylon or Alexandria were present in the Temple on the Day of Atonement, and took a share when the sacrificial meat was apportioned. Mishnah M^enaḥot states: "If [the Day of Atonement] occurred on the eve of the Sabbath, the he-goat of the Day of Atonement was eaten in the evening. The Babylonians ate it raw since they were not squeamish." The *barayta* says that they were Alexandrians, not Babylonians.[44] According to the Book of Leviticus (21: 17), only priests without a blemish were fit to minister, but even blemished priests were not excluded from the Temple. They went up to Jerusalem with their courses and were entitled to eat of the congregational and individual sacred offerings, receiving their share when the holy things were apportioned.[45] One *barayta* (Tosefta, Sukka 4, 3) teaches in the name of R. Judah: "The one distributing the shewbread stood on the pavement in the porch, breaking off pieces and putting them down. Each one came and took his portion. The portions of the blemished priests were carried out to them, since they could not enter between the porch and the altar." Nor were they completely excluded from ministering, for they too participated in many ministrations not connected with the offering of sacrifices,[46] such as placing the willow branch around the altar, and in the priestly blessing.

There are many references in the sources to the loyalty of the priesthood to the Temple and to the service. They were diligent in their ministration in normal times and devoted to it in adversity. The Temple was a fortified area within the city of Jerusalem and was more than once besieged by enemies. Even during those dangerous days the priests continued at their posts. The Temple's requirements were many, and though the altar was not idle even during periods of famine, the priests did not touch the food stores in the Temple.[47] "Priests are diligent" is a common expression in the *Halaka*, and while Talmudic literature often complains of the denigration of the Temple and its service by priests, all such references are to the High Priesthood alone.

2. THE LEVITES.

The status of the Levites in the Temple is one of the obscure topics of Israel's history, arising from differences in the various traditions that have come down to us. Indeed, many of the problems have always been disputed. Moreover, the very fact that the term "Levite" sometimes includes the priests — for they too were descendants of Levi — makes it impossible for these problems ever to be solved.

From the sources it can be concluded with certainty that from the Hellenistic era onwards the Levites lost much of their status in the Temple. Whereas the Levites are continually mentioned in descriptions of the dedication of the altar in Ezra and Nehemiah,[48] and still more frequently in the Books of Chronicles, they are ignored completely in the Books of Maccabees,[49] when the dedication of the altar by Judah the Maccabee is described, as well as in Ben Sira's account of the service performed by Simeon the son of Onias.[50] In the period with which we are dealing, the Levites were denied all connection with the altar and its sacrifices: they are mentioned in the sources merely as singers and gate-keepers. In these two activities the priests also took part, though their superior status was stressed. Criticism of the night watch was directed only against the Levites who stood guard outside, and not against the priests who guarded within.[51]

However, the distinction between them is most conspicuous in connection with the singing. For while the Levites took part with lyres, harps and cymbals — instruments that do not appear until the late books of the Bible — the priests had possession of the trumpets which are already mentioned in Numbers (10:10). These were not only blown on all of the festive occasions, such as the water libation and the Passover offering. Even at the daily offering the priests blew before the wine libation, before the Levites began singing and between each of the parts of the song, and only when the priests blew did the people prostrate themselves.[52] The priests were also in possession of the horn (*shofar*)[53] which in the time of the Temple was connected mainly with the Temple and the New Year offering (see below). Whereas the priests with their trumpets stood close by the Altar, the Levites remained at the boundary between the Court of Priests and the Court of Israelites.[54] In addition to harps, lyres and cymbals, the Levites also played flutes during the festivals. According to Tannaitic tradition, Israelite families also took part in this activity, while minors from among well-born Jerusalem families took part in the singing.[55]

In the First Book of Chronicles (ch. 9) the Levites are divided by families into singers and gate-keepers, and these divisions were carefully preserved during the entire existence of the Temple.[56] The gate-keepers had to close the gates, guard the Temple area at night, and supervise the daytime visitors to the Temple to ensure that none entered in impurity. They were also responsible for the cleanliness of the Temple.[57] It is probable that the *hazzanim* (superintendents) — the public servants mentioned in the literature in connection with the Temple — were Levites, since in Talmudic literature the terms Levites and *hazzanim* are sometimes interchangeable.[58]

In many *Halakot* connected with the service the Levites were assigned an inferior position to the priests. Until the final years of the Temple the Levites fought for the right to wear special garments during their ministration. The dispute arose out of contradictory traditions, and it was only during the last years of the Temple that a decision was arrived at in their favor by a Sanhedrin convened at the command of Agrippa II.[59] Though a priest with a physical blemish was unfit to minister, the *Halaka* was widely held that Levites were not thus disqualified.[60] The decline in their status was also expressed by the fact that, in the Second Temple, the tithe which according to the Torah belonged to the Levites (Numbers ch. 18) was also, or even exclusively, distributed among the priests.[61]

Like the priests, the Levites were divided into twenty-four courses, each ministering one week, but there is no reference in the sources to an explicit division into families after the manner of the priests.[62]

3. ISRAELITES.

Israelites entered the Temple for three main purposes:

1) in order to perform a religious duty, such as coming as pilgrims, bringing first fruits, tithes and gifts, offering vow and freewill offerings, or such obligatory offerings as those of the Nazirites on completing their vows or of lepers on becoming clean, etc.;

2)   to act as spectators of the service, and as worshipers either during the service or at some other time;

3)   to participate in the service together with the priests in some special function as in the divisions (ma'amadot).

Besides the pilgrimages, which will be dealt with later, there were thus many occasions which brought Israelites to the Temple. An Israelite would almost certainly combine many things on one visit to the Temple. Many visited the Temple to cleanse themselves from severe impurity by means of the ashes of the red heifer. Though the ashes were available in the twenty-four regions — since they were divided among the twenty-four courses[63] and the sources refer on many occasions to the presence of the ashes of the red heifer in Judea, Galilee, Trans-Jordan, and even as far south as in 'Ezion Gever (Asia),[64] they were apparently not available in every locality. Thus many went to the Temple to be cleansed, particularly before the festivals,[65] and there was even a fixed time in the Temple for the purification of the unclean.[66] Many Israelites came daily to the Temple to observe the service, to receive the priestly blessing, to pray when the incense was being offered, and to prostrate themselves before the Lord on hearing the daily psalm sung by the Levites.[67]

The participation of Israelites in the service took the form of divisions (ma'amadot) and of this the Mishnah (Ta'anit 4, 2) teaches: "What are the ma'amadot? In that it is written: 'Command the children of Israel and say unto them, My oblation, My food for My offerings made by fire, of a sweet savour unto Me, shall ye| observe to offer unto Me in their due season' [Num. 28:2] — how can a man's offering be offered while he does not stand by it? Therefore the early prophets ordained twenty-four courses, and for every course there was a ma'amad in Jerusalem, made up of priests, Levites, and Israelites." The founding of the ma'amadot gave expression to the idea that the divine service of the Temple was not the exclusive affair of the priests performing it, but an obligation imposed upon the whole people, for whom the priests were agents.[68] The ma'amadot were founded when congregational offerings were already being made from communal funds, and not when an individual could donate a congregational offering, which was the view of the Sadducees and apparently the custom in early years.[69] The division into ma'amadot was based upon a geographical division into twenty-four regions, for the terms ma'amadot and pelakim (regions) are identical and interchangeable in Talmudic literature.[70] The sources do not indicate who went up with the ma'amad from the region, how many there were or how they were appointed. It was the duty of the members of the ma'amad to stand next to the priests during their ministration. After the sacrifice had been offered they gathered to pray for the welfare of the community, for the children, for pregnant women and nursing mothers, and for those crossing the seas and deserts. On most weekdays they fasted.[71] There is no mention of the *ma'amadot* outside the Talmudic literature, and it seems very likely that this institution belongs wholly to the final stages of the Temple's existence.

Before an Israelite entered the Temple court he bathed in water; this was required even if he was clean, and he could do so in one of the many ritual baths to be found in the Temple courts or in front of the gates.[72] It appears to have been the custom to enter the Temple only in white garments, for this was regarded as indicating modesty and piety.[73]

In halakic sources there is no explicit mention of an Israelite being forbidden entry into the Temple court, but it can be inferred from those sources, as well as from incidents related by Josephus, that the gates of the Temple court were closed to transgressors who disregarded or rejected the ways of the community. Thus the Mishnah (*'Eduyyot* 5, 6) states: "R. Judah said: God forbid that it should be Akabya that was put under the ban! — for the Temple court was never shut against any man in Israel so wise and sin-fearing as Akabya b. Mahalaleel." The purpose of this *mishna* was to reject a tradition that Akabya b. Mahalaleel had been excommunicated. In such a case, it argued, the Temple court would have been shut against him, and the Temple court was not readily shut against anyone as sin-fearing as he.[74] In his account of Agrippa I, Josephus (*Ant.* XIX, 332–334) relates: "There was a certain man of Jerusalem whose name was Simeon and who was held to be erudite in the law. He got together a great multitude when the king was in Caesarea and had the impudence to accuse him of being wicked, and said that he could justly be excluded from entering the Temple, as only those behaving well had the right." From the continuation of this account it appears that the cause of Simeon's anger was the king's visit to the theater in Caesarea. This transgression, Simeon held, merited the king's exclusion from the Temple for having rejected the ways of the community. Sacrifices, too, were not accepted from every Israelite, even though they were received from Gentiles. The *barayta* in Ḥullin (5, 1) teaches that "sacrifices are accepted from Israelite transgressors so that they should repent, but not from apostates, those who make libations of wine [to idols], and those who publicly desecrate the Sabbath."

4.   THE TEMPLE OFFICERS.

The priests, who were replaced each week, were supervised by a fixed staff of officers who inspected and trained the priests in their services, superintended the guarding of the Temple, announced the closing and opening of the gates, supervised the sale of libations and birds to those bringing offerings, and administered all that was done in the daily service of the Temple. The Mishnah (Sheqalim 5, 1) has preserved a list of some of the officers of the Temple: "These are the officers who served in the Temple. Johanan b. Phineas was over the seals, Ahijah was over the drink offerings, Mattithiah b. Samuel was over the lots, Petahiah was over the bird-offerings . . . Ben Ahijah was over bowel sickness, Nehunyah was the trench digger, Gabini was the herald, Ben Geber was over the shutting of the gates, Ben Bebai was over the knout, Ben Arza was over the cymbal, Hygros b. Levi was over the singing, the House of Garmu was over the preparation of the Shewbread, the House of Abtinas was over the preparation of the incense, Eleazar was over the hangings, and Phineas was over the vestments." The names mentioned in this *mishna* appear to belong to the last generation before the destruction of the Temple.

It is not to be assumed that the functions mentioned in this *mishna* were the only ones supervised by officers, or that these were the most important officers. This list, like those in many other cases, is not a systematic one, but was compiled in circumstances of which nothing is known and must be regarded as not comprehensive. Tractate Tamid (5, 2) mentions several officers not included in this *mishna*, such as the officer who attended the High Priest when he was offering incense. More than one person served in the offices enumerated, for the *mishna* continues: "nor were less than two persons suffered to hold office over the public in aught concerning money, save only Ben Ahijah who was over bowel sickness and Eleazar who was over the hangings, whom most of the congregation agreed to accept." The offices passed down from father to son, and in several cases (e.g. the House of Garmu who were in charge of the shewbread, and the House of Abtinas of the incense), *baraytot* state that they refused to disclose the nature of their work to anyone outside their own families.[75] The Tosefta of Sheqalim (2, 14) has a parallel list supplementing that of the Mishnah: "These are the officers who were in the temple: Johanan b. Gudgada was over the shutting of the gates, Ben Tutafas was over the keys, Ben Rifai was over the palmbranch, Arza was over the platform, Samuel was over the ovens, Benjamin was over the baked cakes, Ben Maklit was over the salt, Ben Pelek was over the wood." This list enumerates offices mainly of a lower status than those of the Mishnah and contains chiefly Levites. Johanan b. Gudgada was a Levite ('Arakin 10a). Arza was almost certainly a Levite, and several of the other functions enumerated in the *barayta* are ascribed by the Book of Chronicles to Levites.[76]

5. THE HIGH PRIESTHOOD.

During the period of the Second Temple the service was divided among twenty-four priestly courses, and all those tracing their descent from the tribe of Levi participated in the divine service. This division prevented the Temple service from becoming the private concern of the High Priest and his family, but on the other hand it enhanced his status *vis-à-vis* the other priests. The people were greatly attached to the Temple throughout its entire existence, a fact which added to the High Priest's importance. His exalted social and political status during this period derived, at least in principle, from his office. It was the High Priest who became leader of the people and head of the Sanhedrin — not the other way around. During this era the main institutions of the community were centered round the Temple, and all were subject, in greater or lesser degree, to the authority of the High Priest.

The unique status of the High Priest was not only expressed by his position at the very top of the grades of those who performed the divine service, but also in many laws and customs which singled out his status. Thus the daily offering was supplemented by a baked meal offering in the name of the High Priest; the service of the Day of Atonement could be performed only by a High Priest; in addition to the white garments of his fellow priests, he also wore lordly golden raiment of eight garments as described in the Book of Exodus (ch. 28). The baked meal offering was part of the daily offering and was included with the other services connected with the daily offering for apportioning by lot.[77] It was a "private offering," an officer was in charge of it, and a special chamber was assigned to it.

The High Priest was not subject to the distribution of services in accordance with the weekly courses, but could offer the daily sacrifice or the incense whenever he so desired, and could take any part of a sacrifice he preferred.[78] Either to avoid harming the rights of those priests who were officiating according to their courses, or because he was busy with communal and political affairs, the High Priest did not minister every day. However, both the Talmud and Josephus relate that he often participated in the service on Sabbaths and festivals.[79] The sources particularly mention the ministration of the High Priests during the Feast of Tabernacles, when crowds of people were assembled in the Temple court and the service was conducted with festivity and great magnificence. Thus we read that John Hyrcanus wore the golden raiment ministering in the Temple during the Feast of Tabernacles, while Alexander Jannaeus, whose appearances in the Temple were certainly infrequent, approached the altar on the Feast of Tabernacles. The young Aristobulus, brother of Mariamne, also ministered at the altar on the Feast of Tabernacles.[80]

On other special occasions, too, the High Priest took part in the service. The burning of the red heifer was valid if performed by any priest,[81] yet we always find that the High Priest attended to it. The Tosefta (Para 3, 8) relates that R. Johanan b. Zakkai had difficulties with a Sadducean High Priest who refused to follow the teaching of the sages in burning the red heifer, and in its account of the sacrifice of the red heifer the Mishnah itself records: "And they said to him, My Lord the High Priest, immerse thyself this once" (Para 3:8). According to the Mishnah (Soṭa 7, 8), the king used to read the Torah before the people at the *haqhel* ceremony during the Feast of Tabernacles to mark the termination of the Sabbatical year, and also records the case of King Agrippa reading the Torah. However, throughout most of the period there was no king of Israel, nor was the king always able to read the Torah. Josephus, for his part, states that it was the High Priest who read it (*Ant.* IV, 209), and does not mention the king. This may either be because he was referring to the situation in his own time, or because he inclined to glorify the priestly status.

6. THE CAPTAIN

Second in rank to the High Priest was the captain, or to give him his full title, "the Captain (*segan*) of the Priests." The captain took the place of the High Priest if the latter became disqualified, accompanied him when he officiated, and supervised the daily offering. It was he who gave the sign for beginning the song when the service ended.[82] It is almost certain that the *segan* of the Hebrew sources is identical with the στρατηγός of Josephus and the Christian Gospels, not only because the Septuagint translates the word *segan* in the Bible by στρατηγός, but mainly because of the similarity between the functions of the two. During the final years of the Temple the captain appears to have belonged to the Pharisee party, and when he accompanied the High Priest at the service he also made sure that the latter did not follow the Sadducean custom. The Mishnah (Yoma 4, 1) relates: "He shook the casket and took up two lots... The captain was on his right and the chief of the father's house on his left.

If the lot bearing the Name came up in his right hand the captain would say to him, 'My lord high priest, raise thy right hand.'" According to R. Akiba the purpose of raising the hand was "to prevent the Sadducees getting the upper hand over us" (Tosef. Yoma 3, 12). The office of High Priest remained with the Sadducees throughout, but during the final years of the Temple the captains apparently came from among the Pharisees. Two of the captains known to us by name were Pharisee scholars, the one being the Tanna R. Hanina, called "captain of the priests," and the other the commander, Eleazar b. Hananiah, who was one of the political opponents of the Sadducee High Priesthood and presumably their religious antagonist too. He is probably the Eleazar b. Hananiah, one of the disciples of the School of Shammai, who is also mentioned in Talmudic literature in connection with the Temple.[83]

These, then, were the ones who took an active part in the Temple service. Let us now deal briefly with those who only visited the Temple, or took no more than a small share in its service.

7. THE WOMEN

Both tradition and *Halaka* attest to the great attachment of the women to the Temple. During the Feast of Tabernacles three balconies were prepared in the Court of Women to enable them to watch the festivities of the *Beth ha-Sho'eva* water-drawing ceremony (see above). Women and girls also took part in the pilgrimage during Passover. The *Halaka* exempted women from the commandment of appearing before the Lord. They were, however, obliged to take part in the festival rejoicing, chiefly expressed in the peace-offering sacrifices.[84] It may be inferred from a halakic teaching in the Mishnah of Keritot (1, 7) that many women brought sacrifices to the Temple: "If a woman suffered five issues that were in doubt or five miscarriages that were in doubt, she may bring but one offering . . . Once in Jerusalem a pair of doves (the required sacrifice) cost a golden denar. Rabban Simeon b. Gamaliel said: By this Temple: I will not suffer the night to pass before they cost but a silver denar. He went into the court and taught: If a woman give birth five times she need bring but one offering and may then eat the sacrifices, and she is not bound to offer the others. And the same day the price of a pair of doves stood at a quarter denar each."

Of the five or six Nazirites whose names are recorded, three were women: Queen Helene, Berenice the sister of King Agrippa, and an unknown woman named Miriam of Tadmor (Palmyra).[85] There are numerous tombstone inscriptions in Jerusalem bearing names of women from other cities and from the Diaspora.[86] However, the contribution of the women to the Temple service was small. The Mishnah testifies only that they wove the veils, two of which were prepared annually by eighty-two maidens.[87]

8. GENTILES

Josephus does not exaggerate when he writes in *War* IV, 262 that the Temple in Jerusalem was held in honor by Hellenists and barbarians alike. Gentiles made the pilgrimage to Jerusalem and brought their sacrifices from distant lands. The Talmud tells of a Gentile who went up several times from Nisibis for the Passover festival, and similar cases are brought by the Gospels and by Josephus.[88] The *Halaka* permits vows and free-will offerings to be accepted from Gentiles, and R. Simeon even taught: "The court ordained seven things and this was one of them: If a Gentile sent his burnt-offering from beyond the sea and sent the drink-offering also, these are offered; but if not, they are to be offered at the cost of the congregation."[89]

C. The Daily Service

The main Temple service of the day was the sacrifice of the daily offering of two lambs, one in the morning and the other in the afternoon. The service commenced with the morning daily sacrifice and closed with the afternoon daily sacrifice. Other offerings due that day were brought in between, including voluntary offerings such as whole-offerings, peace offerings, thanksgiving offerings and various types of meal offerings, and obligatory offerings such as sin offerings, guilt offerings and the purification offerings of men and women.

The Torah makes no mention of the prayers accompanying the sacrifices. It does not say that the priestly blessing was to be pronounced daily or on any specific days of the year, nor is any explanation given of the connection between the priestly blessing and the Temple and its altar. By the time of Ben Sira it was already the practice for the High Priest to bless the people at the conclusion of the daily sacrifice. In a variety of ways, prayers and Torah readings were gradually added to the Temple service. At the most exalted moment of the Temple service, when the High Priest entered the Holy of Holies to offer incense on the Day of Atonement, he added a short prayer, and when he had completed the service of that day he read to the people from the Torah. The poetry of the psalms was cultivated by the Levites, and some were sung daily during the wine libation and at each festive ceremony. The main occupations of the *ma'amad* of priests, Levites and Israelites were prayer and reading the Torah. On Sabbaths, New Moons and festivals, additional offerings were brought after the morning daily offering. Their number and nature varied for each festival. These additional offerings were attended by special ceremonies, such as the offering of the *'omer* on the second day of Passover, the two loaves on the Feast of Weeks, and the water libation during Tabernacles. Some of these, such as the water libation, were connected with altar, while others had very little or no direct connection, such as the blowing of the horn (*shofar*) and the taking of the palm branch.

The special precepts for the festivals, whether laid down in the Torah or introduced during the period of the Second Temple, are mostly connected with nature and its changes: "said R. Akiba: the Torah said, Bring barley on Passover which is the barley season that thereby cereals may be blessed, bring first fruits of wheat on the Feast of Weeks, which is the wheat season, that thereby the fruits of the trees may be blessed, pour water during Tabernacles for this is the rain season."[90] Most of these observances were carried out with the participation of those celebrating the pilgrimage.

1. THE WATCH

The night watch was regarded as part of the daily service. The Mishnah of Tamid, which deals with the daily offering, commences with a description of the guard posts. These were ceremonial rather than for protection against unauthorized entry. The guards stood at twenty-four posts: five by the five gates of the Temple, four at the four corners within, five at the five gates of the Temple court, four at its four corners without, one at the Chamber of Sacrifice, one at the Chamber of the Veil, and one behind the place of the ark cover. The remaining three places were guarded by priests: the Chamber of Abtinas, the Chamber of the Flame, and the Chamber of the Hearth. The latter was guarded by priests alone, while in the Chamber of the Flame the priests stood guard in the upper chamber above the portico while the Levites were below. The function of the Chamber of Abtinas is not clear from the Mishnah.[91] Each guard post comprised about ten men; for when Josephus states that the gatekeepers who closed the gates numbered about 200, he seems to be referring to those who both closed the gates and remained on guard.[92] The posts were inspected by the officer of the Temple Mount who "used to go round to each post with lighted torches before him." Philo, too, speaks of guards who went the rounds of the Temple by day and by night in order to safeguard its ritual cleanliness. Josephus relates that the Temple watch was increased after the incident in which the Samaritans introduced impurity into the Temple at night during the procuratorship of Coponius (6–9 A. D.).[93]

2. THE DAILY OFFERING OF THE MORNING AND AFTERNOON

The daily service commenced shortly after dawn with the stentorian cry of the herald: "Priests to the service and Levites to the platform and Israelites to the division."[94] The herald's cry aroused the sleepers, and got them on their feet, but the gates of the Temple court were not opened until the arrival of the officer in charge of the lots, who first cast lots for removing the ashes from the altar. Those wishing to participate in this ballot bathed early before the arrival of the officer, since it was forbidden to enter the Temple court without bathing.[95] This was the only balloting that took place in the Chamber of the Hearth outside the boundary of the Temple court.

After the ballot the officer opened the wicket leading from the Chamber of the Hearth of the Temple court, and entered followed by the priests "carrying two lighted torches, [who] separated into two parties, the one going along the colonnade eastwards and the other going along the colonnade westwards. They kept diligent watch as they went until they came to the place where the baked cakes were made" (which was on the east side by the Gate of Nicanor). "When both came thither they called 'Is all well?' 'All is well!'" (M. Tamid 1, 3). They then removed the ashes and arranged the wood piles on the altar, after which they assembled in the Chamber of Hewn Stone for the main balloting for the daily sacrifice.

Thirteen priests were chosen for the daily sacrifice, nine for the actual sacrifice, and four for services connected with it, viz., removing the ashes from the inner altar, removing the ashes from the candelabrum and preparing it again, offering up the meal offerings, and pouring the wine libation (M. Yoma 2, 3). Those who had been chosen in the ballot for the daily offering washed their hands and feet, and then waited "until the east was alight" before commencing the day's service. When the watchmen informed them that the whole east was alight, the officer ordered the lamb brought from the Chamber of Lambs, while at the same time those who had the right to the services in the Sanctuary, namely, to remove the ashes from the candelabrum and from the inner altar, went to open its gates.

They carried four utensils in their hands — the ash bin for removing ashes from the altar, the oil jug for the candelabrum and two keys.

The gates of the Sanctuary were not opened from the outside, but first they opened the wicket on the north of the Sanctuary, entering the Sanctuary thereby, and only when the trumpets sounded were the gates opened.[96] "The slaughterer never slaughtered until he heard the noise of the opening of the great gate." (M. Tamid 3, 7). The opening of the Sanctuary gates signaled the commencement of the day's service and the closing of its gates terminated it. Any sacrifice slaughtered while the gates were not open was invalid. The gates remained open the whole day but the veil was not drawn back. Only on festivals and special occasions was the veil drawn back so that those entering the Temple could see into the Sanctuary.[97]

After the slaughtering, when the limbs of the daily sacrifice were ready to be carried up to the altar, the priests assembled in the Chamber of Hewn Stone and together with the populace read the Ten Commandments (according to the ancient formula, before the Ten Commandments were omitted as a result of heretical claims), the *Sh^ema'* ("Hear, O Israel"), and the three blessings. It is not known when the people first entered the Temple, but it may be assumed that when the trumpets were blown for the opening of the gates of the Sanctuary, the gates of the Temple were also opened for the populace. At all events, the people were already present in the Chamber of Hewn Stone before sunrise, and read the *Sh^ema'* with the priests.[98]

When this was over and prayers had been recited, the priests cast lots for the incense. In this ballot only those priests participated who had never offered incense. "He said to them, Ye that are new to the incense come and cast lots" (M. Tamid 5, 2). This was regarded as one of the most important of the day's services because it was performed inside the Sanctuary, and it was cast for on its own. They then cast lots for the last time to carry the sacrificial limbs on to the altar (M. Yoma 2, 3). He who had obtained the right to offer incense favored one next to him with the coal pan to collect coals from the altar for burning the incense. When the two priests came between the altar and the porch, the officer took the shovel and threw it down — its mighty noise is the subject of many legends — as a signal for the division and all the people in the Temple to prepare for what was to follow. The priests now drew near to enter the Sanctuary, the Levites prepared to begin their song, and the chief of the *ma'amad* made the unclean stand at the eastern gate, apparently for the purpose of purification.[99] The two priests who were to burn the incense and collect the coals from the altar reached the steps of the porch, preceded by the two who were to remove the ashes from the altar and the candelabrum. The first of these entered, took the ash bin with the ashes of the altar, prostrated, and withdrew backwards. The second kindled the western lamp in the event that he found it extinguished. He then took the oil jug, prostrated, and withdrew. (On their previous entry they had removed the ashes, but not their vessels.) The priest who had the right to collect the coals from the outer altar entered the Sanctuary first, heaped the coals upon the altar of incense, prostrated himself, and withdrew. Now the priest who was to burn the incense entered with the incense dish in his hand. He was allowed to hand the ladle with incense "to his friend or kinsman" so that he should help him to fill his hands with the incense. The officer accompanied him and instructed him how to burn it. Before the incense was burned all the people departed from between the porch and the altar, "and the officiant did not offer the incense until the officer said to him: 'Offer the incense!' ... if he was the High Priest, the officer said to him: 'My lord High Priest, offer the incense!' When all were gone away he offered the incense, prostrated himself and came away."[100] While the incense was being offered the people assembled in the Temple court for prayer. Outside the Temple, too, the people set aside this time for prayer, particularly at the time of the afternoon incense.[101]

After the incense had been offered all the priests entered the Sanctuary, prostrated themselves, and withdrew. They then stood upon the steps of the porch to pronounce the priestly blessing over the people, together with those who had participated in offering the incense. Even priests with physical blemishes who were forbidden to approach the altar, now ascended and joined in the blessing.[102] The Bible states that Aaron alone blessed the people (Lev. 9:22), a practice that was still continued in the days of Ben Sira, when only the High Priest Simeon blessed the people. In the latter days of the Second Temple however, the priestly blessing was pronounced by all the priests even if the High Priest participated. When the ineffable name was uttered during the blessing, all the people fell upon their faces and prostrated themselves.[103] Now came the last part of the service — the carrying up of the limbs, the meal offering of flour, the baked meal, and the libation of wine upon the altar. Before the libation two priests blew a straight blast, a wavering blast and a straight blast on their trumpets. The trumpet blowing took place before every important ceremony performed publicly. When the officiant stood ready to pour the wine the captain waved a cloth as a signal, whereupon Ben Arza clashed the cymbal and the Levites broke forth into singing,[104] accompanied by musical instruments. One of the psalms was designated for each day. The daily psalm was divided into two or three stanzas. After each stanza the priests blew, and at each blowing there was a prostration. The end of the singing terminated the service of the morning daily offering.[105] The members of the course now applied themselves to the morning prayers and to the reading of the Torah, while the priests offered the many and varied offerings, voluntary and obligatory, brought by the people.

At a half after the eighth seasonal hour, the offering of private sacrifices ceased and the offering of the afternoon daily sacrifice commenced. For the most part the afternoon daily offering resembled that of the morning, but with a few changes. The removal of the ashes, the recital of the priestly blessing, and the arranging of the wood piles on the altar took place in the morning only. In the afternoon, on the other hand, two logs of wood were carried up to the altar to preserve the perpetual fire and all seven lamps of the candelabrum were lit, for in the morning they merely trimmed the lamps and left one lamp burning.[106] All who were chosen in the morning ballot also ministered in the afternoon, except for the incense, for which lots were cast anew.[107]

When the afternoon daily sacrifice was ended the Sanctuary gates were closed; it is almost certain that the other gates were closed with them, and that no further sacrifices were offered. Several halakot relating to prayer have reference to the closing time of the Sanctuary gates, but the sources do not indicate at what hour this took place. From Talmudic discussions it would appear to have been close to sunset.[108] After the gates of the Temple court were shut, the priests remained within to offer the limbs and bespoken parts that they had not managed to offer during the course of the day. The limbs and bespoken parts remained upon the altar the whole night and were consumed by the altar fire. Only at the beginning of the following day were the ashes removed.[109] Care had also to be taken to supply wood for the altar fire so that it did not die out. The sources do not state through which wicket the priests went in and out, though presumably they did so through one of the wickets leading from the Chamber of the Hearth where the priests stayed the whole night. In the evening the priests assembled for their meal of the sacred meats. Though this is not explicitly stated in the sources, it seems reasonable to assume that the priests did not sit down to a meal while the sacrifices were being offered, since even the ordinary people had their meal only in the evening or shortly before it.

The regular sacrifice of the morning and afternoon constituted the main divine service and the main assignment of the altar. Overwhelming importance was attached to the offering of the daily sacrifices, and its threatened cessation was regarded with the greatest apprehension. Even when stress and siege overtook the city and the Temple, all sections of the people acted with great devotion to ensure the continuation of the daily sacrifice.[110]

3. THE SABBATH

All the work connected with the altar was permitted even on the Sabbath. The fire was kept burning upon the altar, the daily sacrifice slaughtered, the incense offered, and the lamps kindled. It was not permitted, however, to defer any work which could be performed before the Sabbath. Thus, for example, the twelve loaves of shewbread were arranged upon the golden table in the Sanctuary on the Sabbath, but all the work connected with their preparation was performed on the eve of the Sabbath.[111] No private offerings were offered on the Sabbath, only the congregational, daily and additional offerings. The priestly courses changed on the Sabbath, and included in the morning prayer of the priests and people after the slaughter of the daily sacrifice was a blessing for the departing course (according to the Babylonian Talmud, the outgoing course blessed the incoming one): "He who has caused His name to dwell in this house, may He cause love, brotherhood, peace and fellowship to dwell among you."[112] After the morning daily offering the additional offering of two lambs was brought. According to the Talmud (Rosh ha-Shana 32a), this service had its own hymn, "Give ear, ye heavens" (Deut. 32).

The arrangement of the shewbread followed the additional offerings. The outgoing course had already brought the shewbread and placed it before the Lord, and had burned the two ladles of frankincense that accompanied it. The following was the order of its service on the Sabbath when the fresh bread was brought in and that of the previous week removed and shared among the priests.[113] The Mishnah states: "Four priests entered, two having in their hands the two rows [each of six loaves], and two the two dishes [with frankincense]; and four went before them, two to take away the two rows [of the old bread] and two to take away the two dishes. Those bringing in stood on the north side facing south, and those carrying out stood on the south side facing north. As the latter were removing [the old loaves], the others would be arranging [the fresh loaves], so that the handbreadth of the one extended into the handbreadth of this other." The removed bread was placed upon a golden table in the porch. They burned the removed frankincense upon the altar, and its burning made the removal loaves permissible to the priests. The twelve loaves were shared equally between the two courses, and, according to R. Judah, in the following manner: "The one distributing the shewbread stood on the pavement in the porch, breaking off pieces and putting them down, and each one came and took his share. The portions of those with blemishes was carried outside, since they could not enter between the porch and the altar."[114] The Aggada relates that in the days of Simeon the Just, "a blessing was sent upon the '*Omer*, upon the two loaves, and upon the shewbread, so that every priest who obtained an olive's bulk, ate it and became satisfied, while some ate and left over. Thenceforth a curse was sent upon the '*Omer*, two loaves and shewbread, so that a priest received a piece as small as a bean: the modest priests refrained from taking it and the voracious ones took and devoured it. It once happened that one of them grabbed his own portion and that of his fellow, and until his dying day he was called 'the grasping one!' "[115]

Most of the sacred food of the altar to which the priest was entitled during his days of service could be eaten only in the Temple court and only by males. Little of it could be eaten in Jerusalem, and even this could not be carried away to his home. From his service he could take away only the skins of the sacrifices, and the sages frequently contended with the powerful priests to prevent them exploiting the ordinary priests in the division of the skins.[116]

4.   THE THREE PILGRIMAGE FESTIVALS

During the three pilgrimage festivals the arrangements of the Temple were changed. For besides the additional offerings and the special precepts of the day, the priests had to manage the many private sacrifices of the pilgrims, which, in contrast to the Sabbath, were allowed on the festival.[117] To cope with these numerous sacrifices they commenced the daily service earlier. As the Mishnah relates: "Every day they removed the ashes from the altar at cockcrow, or near to it, either before it or after it; but on the Day of Atonement they did so at midnight, and on the pilgrimage feasts at the first watch. And before cockcrow the Temple court was filled with Israelites." On the pilgrimage festivals the gates of the Temple were opened to the people at midnight.[118] During festival time it seems almost as if the Temple was removed from the authority of the priests and the Sadducee High Priests and handed over to the ordinary people, who conducted the worship in accordance with the teachings of the Sages and their Pharisee customs. In order to facilitate movement between the city and the Temple, and to allow as many into the Temple as possible, the laws of uncleanness were made easier not only outside the Temple and within the Temple itself.[119] During the festival the veil that hung before the entry into the Sanctuary was drawn back so that people could see into the Sanctuary, while the Temple vessels were brought out into the court so that the people could go near and inspect them.[120] Priests from all the courses, both those living in the Land of Israel and those from the Diaspora, went up to the Temple during the festival, and the *Halaka* asserts that all of them had a right to those sacrifices brought on account of the festival. The Mishnah even records the customs of the Alexandrian, or Babylonian, priests.[121]

a) PASSOVER

The special character of this festival with regard to the Temple lay in the sacrifice of the paschal lamb on behalf of all the celebrants who had made the pilgrimage to Jerusalem. The celebrants combined into groups, since there were those who held that the paschal lamb could not be slaughtered on behalf of an individual and that a quorum of ten was required for each paschal offering. The Mishnah refers to groups of women, to groups of slaves, and also to groups of priests,[122] for they too offered their paschal lambs together with the rest of the people. The paschal lamb was eaten, at least during the period of the Second Temple, in the houses and in the courts, but it was slaughtered in the Temple court and its blood sprinkled upon the altar. In contrast to the sacrifices offered at other times, however, the Passover sacrifice was slaughtered by the Israelites themselves, as is testified both by Talmudic sources and by Philo.[123] It was slaughtered during the afternoon of the 14th of Nisan, Passover eve, and the Mishnah (Pᵉsaḥim 5, 5f.) has preserved a description: "The Passover offering was slaughtered in three groups . . . When the first group entered and the Temple court was filled, its gates were closed. A straight note, a quavering note and a straight note were blown. The priests stood in rows and in their hands were basins of silver and basins of gold. In one row the basins were all silver and in another all gold . . . An Israelite slaughtered and the priest caught [the blood for sprinkling], passing it to his fellow, and his fellow to his fellow, each receiving a full basin and passing back an empty one. The priest nearest the altar tossed the blood in one action against the base [of the altar]. When the first group went out the second group came in, when the second went out the third came in . . . [Meanwhile the Levites] sang the *Hallel* (Pss. 113–8). If they finished it they sang it anew, and if they finished it a second time they sang it a third time, although it never happened that they thrice completed it. R. Judah says: Never did it happen during the third group that they reached "I love" (Ps. 116) since its people were few." When the slaughtering was completed the priests swilled the court (*ibid.*, 5, 8). The Passover offering was brought on the eve of Passover even if this fell on the Sabbath. From the *barayta* we may infer that this ruling goes as far back as the time of Hillel, and tradition connects Hillel's promotion to the presidency of the Sanhedrin with his decision regarding this matter.[124]

At the termination of the first day of the festival the people took part in the reaping of the '*Omer* of barley which was usually brought from Beth Miklah in the Brook of Kidron. If, however, the nearby grain had not ripened, they brought it from a distance — the Mishnah states that it was once brought from the valley of 'Ein Soker in Samaria.[125] As is well known, the Sadducees and Pharisees differed as regards the day for bringing the '*Omer*. According to the Sadducees this was the morrow of the Sabbath after the festival, while the Pharisees brought it on the morrow of the first day of Passover. In order to discredit the view of the Sadducees the '*Omer* was reaped with great publicity, and even on the Sabbath. In this case, too, the Mishnah records the order of reaping: "And the town nearby all assembled there together that it might be reaped with much pomp. When it grew dark he called out to them, 'Is the sun set?' and they answered, 'Yea!' . . . He used to call out three times for every matter, and they answered, 'Yea!' 'Yea!' 'Yea!' Wherefore was all this? Because of the Boethusians who used to say that the reaping of the '*Omer* does not take place at the close of the festive day" (M. M^en. 10, 3). After it had been prepared in the Temple court it was waved before the Lord, its handfull was offered and the remainder shared among the priests. The offering of the '*Omer* permitted the eating of the new harvest: "After the '*Omer* had been offered they used to go out and find the market of Jerusalem full of meal and parched corn" (*ibid.* 5).

b) FEAST OF WEEKS

In the sources and in the early authorities there is no explicit connection between this festival and the giving of the Torah. Its character is chiefly that of a harvest festival and its specific ritual in the Temple — the offering of the two loaves — is connected with the wheat harvest. After the frankincense had been burned, the two loaves were shared among all the priests whether on duty or not, as was the rule for all offerings brought in consequence of the festival. The offering of the two loaves permitted the new harvest to be brought upon the altar, for until then no meal offerings were allowed from the new harvest. Commencing with the Feast of Weeks and until Tabernacles, the firstfruits of the Seven Species were brought to the Temple. Some no doubt combined the bringing of their firstfruits with their pilgrimage for the festival.

c) TABERNACLES

In Tannaitic literature the Feast of Tabernacles is called simply "the Festival." This itself indicates the unique place allotted to it, and indeed the literature of our period relates that it was celebrated with great show and splendor and with large assemblies.[126] The number of additional sacrifices was far greater than for other festivals; on the first day thirteen bullocks, two rams, fourteen sheep and one he-goat were offered. The offering of the sacrifices was accompanied by the singing of *Hallel* and the playing of the flute, an instrument used only on the most festive occasions. Of the twelve days in the calendar on which *Hallel* was sung and the flute played, eight belonged to Tabernacles.[127]

The special Temple rites for the day were many. The Bible mentions only the taking of the palm branch, but the Tannaim discuss a number of other customs practiced in the Temple. In addition to the willow sprigs taken together with the palm branch, willow branches were placed upright around the altar, and willow branches were also beaten on the ground on the last day of the festival. A libation of water was added to the libation of wine, and during the nights of the festival they celebrated the rejoicing of *Beth ha-Sho'eva* all night long in the Temple court. The whole atmosphere of the festival was one of joyful celebration; the custom of taking palm branches in procession was a popular expression of rejoicing, and is recorded in other connections.[128] During Tabernacles the people participated equally with the priests in all the religious duties of the festival except in the water libation, which was poured by the priests alone. They encircled the altar with their palm branches and willow sprigs, and the whole populace took part in the rejoicing of *Beth ha-Sho'eva*. During Tabernacles the people virtually took possession of the Temple. When a Boethusian High Priest appeared to be evading or ridiculing the water libation by pouring it at his feet, the whole populace pelted him with their *etrogim*; when the Boethusians attempted to prevent the erecting of the willow bough on the Sabbath by placing large stones upon them on the eve of the Sabbath, the people found out and rolled off the stones.[129]

During the early years the ritual of the palm branch was basically performed in the Temple. This seems to be the plain meaning of the Mishnah, which in presenting the precept describes only how it was performed in the

Temple. Philo, too, in the section he devotes to Tabernacles, makes no mention of the practice at all, so that he apparently regarded it as connected with the altar alone. The same is implied by Josephus, and also by Plutarch, who speaks of taking the palm branch in connection with entering the Temple.[130]

The whole populace took part in the circuits around the altar, even though during the rest of the year ordinary Israelites were not allowed to approach it: "What was the arrangement for the circuit? All Israel, great and small, take their palm branches in their hands and their *etrogim* in their left hands and encircle it once, but on that day [of *Hoshana Rabba*] they encircle it seven times."[131] Besides its inclusion in the "Four Species," the willow, as we have seen, was also utilized on its own as a decoration around the altar. The Mishnah states: "There was a place below Jerusalem called Motza. Thither they went and cut themselves young willow branches. They came and set these up at the sides of the altar so that their tops were bent over the altar. They then blew a straight, a quavering, and a straight blast" (Sukka 4, 5).

At the end of the first day of Tabernacles the *Beth ha-Sho'eva* rejoicing began. The people danced in the Temple court to the light of bonfires: "Men of piety and good deeds before them with burning torches in their hands . . . And Levites [played on] harps, lyres, cymbals and trumpets and countless musical instruments, on the fifteen steps leading down from the Court of the Israelites to the Court of the Women." Some of the greatest scholars, such as Hillel the Elder and Rabban Simeon b. Gamaliel, took an active part in the festivities, dancing for the crowd, regaling them with words of wisdom, or juggling with eight lighted torches. Among the dancers were "men of good deeds" who had never fallen into sin and repentant sinners who regretted their youthful transgressions.[132] It is usual to connect the name *Beth ha-Sho'eva* ("Place of Drawing") with the water drawing but in the whole of the description of the rejoicing no reference can be found to the drawing of water. The only certain things about the narrative are the bonfires and lighted torches. It would seem, therefore to be connected with the Aramaic-Syriac *Shuvta* — i.e., the rejoicing of the bonfire.[133]

The rejoicing of the water drawing continued throughout the night, and at cockcrow a large concourse accompanied by trumpets went to draw water from the Pool of Siloam to pour upon the Altar during the morning daily sacrifice. In the Mishnah and the Tosefta there are remnants of farewell salutations uttered when people took their leave of the Temple and of one another: "When they departed what did they say? Beauty to thee, O Altar!" "And when they took leave of one another, one said to the other, The Lord bless thee from Zion, And see the good of Jerusalem all the days of thy life, And see thy children's children. Peace be upon Israel.''

d. THE DAY OF ATONEMENT

The distinctive feature of this day in the Temple was the service of the High Priest that once a year atoned for the iniquities of the people. The whole of the service — the daily offering, the additional offerings, and that specific to the day — was performed by the High Priest alone. Only ancillary service and ritual performed outside the Temple, such as the burning of the High Priest's bullock and the sending away of the scapegoat, were performed by other priests or even by Israelites.

On this day the people assembled in the Temple to witness the service. In particular they watched the High Priest ministering in the Sanctuary, and anxiously followed his entry into the Holy of Holies and his exit therefrom. The inhabitants of Jerusalem and pilgrims from all over the country and the Diaspora — nobles, priests, ordinary Jews — all thronged to the Temple to behold the sacred ritual. When the bullock was being burned it was necessary to post guards ". . . because of the pressure of people to prevent them jumping or falling into the fire.''[134] The people did not take part in the service itself but followed it in silence. Only when they heard the ineffable name pronounced by the High Priest, "those near fell upon their faces and those at a distance would say, 'Blessed be the name of His glorious kingdom for ever and ever. Neither of them moved from there until it [the ineffable name] escaped their memory.''[135]

Seven days before the Day of Atonement the High Priest was set apart in a special chamber in order to avoid ritual uncleanness and to prepare himself for the service. On the night of the Day of Atonement he remained awake all night for fear of an unclean issue, and men of Jerusalem used to keep him occupied so that he did not doze. They read to him, or he himself read, from the Scriptures. It also became the general custom to remain awake all night, and as a memorial to the Temple even after its destruction.[136]

The priest commenced the service at midnight in order to have enough time to complete all the services of the day. The services of the daily and the additional offerings were performed by the High Priest in his raiment of gold, but those specific to the Day of Atonement, such as the offering of the two goats and the burning of incense in the Holy of Holies, were performed in white garments. Whenever he changed from one set of garments to the other he bathed, and at the conclusion of each part of the service he washed his hands and feet, bathing five times and washing ten times during that day. After all the service of the daily and additional offerings, he confessed his sins and cast lots for the two goats, to determine which was to be sent to Azazel and which offered to the Lord. He then made confession again upon his bullock, but on this occasion included his fellow priests in the confession. After slaughtering the bullock he went to offer the incense in the Holy of Holies, a ceremony for which much preparation was required. He burned the incense upon the sh*tiyya* (foundation) stone and withdrew, saying only a short prayer in the Sanctuary so as not to alarm the people. The two Talmuds preserve various and alternative prayers recited by the High Priest. The text of the Babylonian Talmud reads: "May it be Thy will, O Lord our God, that this year be both warm and rainy; let there not depart a ruler from the house of Judah; let not Thy people Israel require to sustain one another; and let not the prayers of travellers come before Thee." The Jerusalem Talmud adds the following: ". . . and for the people of the Sharon he prayed, May it be Thy will, O Lord our God and God of our fathers, that their houses become not their graves."[137]

After offering the incense, sprinkling the blood towards the veil, and slaughtering the goat for the Lord, he made confession over the second goat in the name of the whole people, and the goat was sent to the wilderness of Judea. The priest who was entrusted with despatching the scapegoat passed ten stations before reaching the ravine down which he cast the animal. Those in Jerusalem were informed by the waving of cloths that the goat had reached its destination. When this was known the High Priest began the last stage of his service. This took place in the Court of Women, the most spacious part of the Temple area, and consisted of a reading from Leviticus (chapter 16, etc.), followed by the recital of eight blessings — for the Law, for the Temple service, for the thanksgiving, for the forgiveness of sin, for the Temple, for the Israelites, for Jerusalem, and for the priests — and concluding with a prayer. When the High Priest had finished his prayer, all the people took their books and read from them.[138]

The solemn ceremony of the High Priest's service on the holiest day of the year, climaxed by his entry into the Holy of Holies — all made a deep and lasting impression upon the people. After the destruction, the memory of the lost splendor was kept alive in a number of literary forms. One version of the Temple service is incorporated in Mishnah Yoma. By the amoraic period there already existed different versions of the order of service to be read during the prayers of the Day of Atonement. These orders of the service were not always written in conformity with the Mishnah or the *Halaka* of Mishnah Yoma. Even the orders of service from a later date compiled by Eleazar ha-Qalir and other *paytanim* are based on sources earlier than the Mishnah. The Egyptian papyri contain fragments written in Hebrew from the end of the second or the beginning of the third centuries, which testify to the custom of writing down the High Priest's order of service in order to read it in the synagogue on the Day of Atonement.[139]

e) THE TEMPLE SINGING

The term "singing" in the Mishnah includes vocal music and the instrumental music accompanying it. Singing was an accompaniment of the daily offering on weekdays and Sabbaths, of the additional offerings, of the people's sacrifices, and of its assemblies during special seasons and festivals. The vocal music consisted chiefly of excerpts from the Book of Psalms and poetic sections from the Torah such as the poem "Give ear, ye heavens" (Deut. 32) and the like. The music came from harps, lyres and cymbals, in addition to two trumpets which announced and concluded the singing. The late scriptural sources already mention all the instruments used in the service, though not in connection with the daily offering and not as if regularly used. Ben Sira mentions singing but not musical instruments in connection with the daily offering. A *barayta* appended to Mishnah Tamid enumerates the psalms that were sung each day of the week: "These were the psalms which the Levites used to recite in the Temple: On the first day of the week they would recite, 'The earth is the Lord's and the fulness thereof; the world and they that dwell therein' etc." (Ps. 24). The massoretic text of the Psalms testifies to the specific use of Psalm 92 which begins: "A Psalm, a song for the Sabbath day." The Septuagint translation contains evidence for most of the daily psalms. For the first day, Psalm 24 (23 in the Septuagint) has the heading τῆς μιᾶς σαββάτον, and so too for the other daily psalms. The *baraytot* contain evidence that certain psalms were introduced for the days of the week and others sung on special occasions and festivals, and some of them have been confirmed by the headings in the Septuagint translation. Every festive occasion in the Temple had its own specific psalms. When the first-fruits were brought Psalm 30 was sung, at the rejoicing of the *Beth ha-Shoe'va* the fifteen psalms (120–134) commencing with "A song of degrees," and so on. Besides the weekday and festival psalms, the *Hallel*, consisting of Psalms 113–118, was sung on festivals during the sacrifices of the people. It was accompanied by the flute which also accompanied the singing when the first fruits were brought. Isaiah (30:29) already mentions the playing of the flute while the pilgrim came to the house of God "on the night when a feast is hallowed."

When singing the Levites used to stand on the platform between the Court of Israelites and the Court of Priests, and during the rejoicing of *Beth ha-Sho'eva* they stood upon the fifteen steps descending from the Court of Israelites to the Court of Women. The Mishnah ruled that there were to be not fewer than twelve Levites on the platform, and these were joined by minors from the children of "the Jerusalem nobility" in order to lend flavor to the music. Of the instruments the Mishnah asserts: "They never played on less than two harps or on more than six . . . They never played on less than nine lyres and their number could be increased without end; but of cymbals there was only one."[140]

The psalms sung by the Levites in the Temple comprised not only religious hymns but also ethnical and social teaching: "Who shall sojourn in Thy tabernacle? Who shall dwell upon Thy holy mountain? He that walketh uprightly and worketh righteously, And speaketh truth in his heart . . . He that putteth not out his money on interest, nor taketh a bribe against the innocent. He that doeth these things shall never be moved" (Psalm 15).

D. The Temple Administration and Treasury

1. THE TEMPLE TREASURY AND ITS OFFICERS

The Temple treasury consisted of numerous chambers. In the Sheqel Chamber were stored the half sheqels which were sent as an obligatory contribution by all Jews in the Land of Israel and the Diaspora, and which constituted the chief source of the treasury's income. In addition, Mishnah Sheqalim mentions the Chamber of Utensils, to which people brought offerings of utensils for the sacred service, the Chamber of Secrets, for "the poor of good family [to receive] support therefrom in secret," and the Chamber for Temple Repairs. The Mishnah enumerates thirteen "*shofar* chests," i.e., boxes shaped like *shofars*, being wide below and narrowing upwards, which were for receiving money for designated sacrifices, whether obligatory or voluntary. If a person needed to offer a pair of birds he put the money into the designated chest and birds were purchased with the money. Money that did not suffice for a complete sacrifice was put into the chest and went towards the cost of a sacrifice.[141]

The Temple's income was undoubtedly very great. The half-sheqel dues alone amounted to vast sums, and the Talmudic sources refer to the surplus from the Sheqel Chamber.[142] Other offerings and gifts also brought much money to the Temple. Mishnah Middot relates: "A golden vine stood over the entrance to the Sanctuary, trained over posts; and whoever gave a leaf, or a berry, or a cluster [of gold] as a freewill offering brought it and hung it thereon. R. Eliezer b. Zadok said: It once happened that 300 priests were appointed to it" (to remove it from its place).[143] It was customary for people to dedicate a field or a house for sacred purposes, or the valuation of a person: "Once the mother of Yirmatia said, "I vow my daughter's weight [if she recovers from her illness]. [When she recovered] she went up to Jerusalem and weighed her against gold." (M. Araḳ. 5, 1). The halaḳic sources speak not only of the redemption of persons but also of fields and houses, and make no provision for these consecrated properties to remain under Temple ownership. Nowhere do we find, in fact, that the Temple owned land or immovable property after the manner of other temples in the ancient world.[144] Despite this, many services and functions were financed out of the Temple treasury. From the contributions deposited in the chambers all the daily sacrifices were paid for and all expenses connected therewith, such as the wages of the women who wove the veil, the purchase of the red heifer designated for the purification of all Israelites, and the like. Other institutions connected with the Temple were also maintained from these contributions. Those appointed to judge cases of robbery received their salary from it, as did the scribes who corrected the Temple scrolls. All the communal needs of the city of Jerusalem were also met from the Temple funds: "The aqueduct, the city wall and its towers, and all the city's needs, were provided from the residue of the chamber."[145] When Pontius Pilate took the "money of the sacrifice" to spend on the aqueduct for Jerusalem, the revolt which this caused among the populace may have arisen from the governor's interference with consecrated monies rather than from the use to which those monies were put.[146] It appears, too, that all the Temple's expenses connected with the Sanhedrin and with those public requirements enumerated in Mishnah Sheqalim — such as repairing the roads leading to Jerusalem, the ritual baths, and the like — were provided for from the offering of the chambers.[147]

At the head of the administration of the Temple treasury were a group of men designated treasurers and supervisors. In practice the treasurers dealt with all the Temple's financial business and managed all the functions of the Temple that were not directly related to the service: "What was the work of the three treasurers? They redeemed vows of valuation and of worth, sanctified objects and the second tithe, and all the work of the holy place was performed through them." They also supervised the offering of the chamber, and supplied all the requirements of the altar. The Mishnah also enumerates seven supervisors who were over the treasurers, the latter acting only under their control and with their permission.[148] These two categories of office are frequently mentioned together; they are not mentioned as having authority over the daily service, but only as administering the affairs of the Temple, particularly the various Temple stores. They also appear as representatives of the High Priesthood. From the poetical complaint of Abba Shaul b. Boṭnit and Abba Jose b. Johanan of Jerusalem against the priesthood, they also appear to have kinsmen of the family of the High Priesthood: "Woe is me because of the House of Boethus, woe is me because of their curse. Woe is me because of the House of Kathros, woe is me because of their pens. Woe is me because of the House of Elhanan, woe is me because of their whispering. Woe is me because of the House of Elisha, woe is me because of their fists. Woe is me because of the House of Ishmael b. Piabi who are themselves high priests, their sons treasurers, their sons-in-law supervisors, and their slaves come and beat us with sticks."[149]

In addition to these, the *barayta* in Sheqalim of the Jerusalem Talmud (5, 49a) mentions another category of officer over the treasurers and the supervisors: two *katholikoi* (financial officers). According to the *barayta* the order of the hierarchy was: High Priest, *katholikos*, supervisor, treasurer. From the *barayta* it would appear that the chief business of the *katholikos* was to supervise financial matters on the highest level, and this too seems to be the use of the word in aggadic *midrashim* even when unconnected with the Temple. Save in the aforementioned *barayta*, the *katholikos* is not listed among the officers of the Temple. He may, in fact, be identical with one of the officers already mentioned, such as the captain (*segan*) or the head of the priestly division.

2.   THE HALF SHEQEL

The half sheqel is first mentioned in the Book of Exodus (30:11), and later in the Book of Kings in connection with Jehoash and Josiah. It does not, however, appear as an annual fixed due or in connection with sacrifices. The monies were collected only for the repair of the House of the Lord.[150] In the Book of Nehemiah it was stressed for the first time that the offering of the half sheqel (there it specifies a "third of a sheqel") was for the purpose of offering sacrifices: "Also we made ordinance for us, to charge ourselves yearly with the third part of a sheqel for the service of the house of our God; for the shewbread, and for the continual meal-offering and for the continual burnt-offering . . . and for all the work of the house of our God" (10:33–34). During the period of the Second Temple the

Pharisees came to adopt the view that the offering of an individual could be accepted for the daily service. Pharisees and Sadducees argued fiercely over this *halaka* until it was finally decided that all the services in the House of God were to be maintained from the equal offering of the whole populace.[151] According to the *halaka* every male Israelite with the exception of minors was obliged to give the half sheqel. However, if a father had begun to pay on behalf of a son who was a minor, the payments could not be discontinued, though his property was not taken in pledge for it. The half sheqel was not accepted from Gentiles at all. The Sages held that priests, too, had to pay the half sheqel, but the latter considered themselves exempt. We find Rabban Johanan b. Zakkai arguing against this attitude of the priests, just as he argued against them in other matters both during the Temple's existence and after.[152]

The half sheqel was the equivalent of two Roman denars or two Greek drachmas. Its collection was proclaimed on the first of Adar so that the new sheqalim could be used for the first of Nisan, the beginning of the Temple year. The collection took place not only in Jerusalem but in all parts of the country. Thus the Mishnah teaches: "On the fifteenth thereof [of Adar] the tables [of the money changers] were set up in the provinces."[153] When Jesus came to Capernaum, the collectors of the half sheqel approached Peter (δίδραχμα λαμβάνοντες) and demanded the half sheqel from them (Matthew 17:24). The money changers remained in the provinces until the 25th of Adar. After that date they sat in the Temple only, and began to impound pledges from those who had not brought their offering. The collectors compared lists in their possession with the lists of the offerings, which were compiled in several cities and sent to Jerusalem.[154] Even those who dissociated themselves from the Temple sacrifices, or even refrained from entering its courts, nevertheless used to send the half sheqel. Thus the Essenes sent their sheqels though they offered no sacrifices in the Temple, while Jesus and his associates, though not recorded as having brought an offering with them when they came to the Temple, paid their sheqels in Capernaum.[155]

The obligation of paying the half sheqel also applied to the Diaspora, and was customarily collected there. Josephus relates that Nehardea and Nisibis served as collecting centers, and a large escort accompanied the money to Jerusalem. Philo reports a similar practice among the Jews of Rome.[156] Tannaitic sources state that they took up an offering three times a year — half a month before Passover "on behalf of the Land of Israel," half a month before the Feast of Weeks "on behalf of the cities surrounding it," and half a month before Tabernacles "on behalf of Babylon, and on behalf of Media, and on behalf of distant lands." Concerning this last collection the *barayta* states: "This was the richest of all, for it contained gold coins [staters] and gold darics." The gold coins were used in exchange for many of the half sheqel "on account of the burden of the journey."[157] The money was sent half a month before the festivals, since this was the time when pilgrims both from the Land of Israel and from the Diaspora made their journey to Jerusalem.

The money collected in half sheqels and other donations by the Jews of the Diaspora amounted to large sums. It was not surprising, therefore that the non-Jewish inhabitants of those cities attempted to lay hands on the money either for local needs or at least to prevent the Jews from using it. Both Josephus and Philo make it clear that this was already an officially recognized privilege of the Jews in the time of the emperors. Such contributions were considered as "monies of the Sanctuary," and anyone touching them could be punished for sacrilege.[158]

3.   THE NEEDS OF THE TEMPLE AND THEIR PROVISION

The Temple treasurers were obliged to supply the Temple not only with the congregational offerings, daily and additional, but also with those offerings which individuals either could not bring or found it difficult to bring themselves. The treasurers bought animals for the congregational offerings alone, since each individual brought his own with him, or bought it from the cattle merchants in Jerusalem (M. Sheqalim 7, 10). Wine, flour and oil, however, were mostly purchased from the treasurers, for not all who brought sacrifices could bring with them oil, as this needed to be prepared and guarded according to the Sanctuary's strict requirements of purity. This was especially difficult for those coming from abroad, and quite impossible for a Gentile bringing his offering to the Temple. A pair of doves was the obligatory sacrifice in a number of instances. They had to be offered, for example, by a woman after childbirth, by a person who had suffered a discharge, or had recovered from leprosy. Doves were also brought as freewill offerings. The private person, of course, could not always bring the doves himself. It is in this connection, therefore, that the Mishnah refers to the special *shofar* chests. Anyone liable to the sacrifice placed the appropriate sum of money in the chest, and every day a number of sacrifices were offered corresponding to the amount of money deposited (M. Sheqalim 6, 5).

Of the libations (wine, oil, flour) the Mishnah states: "If anyone wished for drink offerings he would go to Johanan who was over the seals, give him money, and receive from him a seal; he would then go to Ahijah who was over the drink-offerings, give him the seal, and from him receive drink-offerings" (*ibid.*, 5:4). There were four or five seals, depending on the type of sacrifice (*ibid.*, 5:3). The individual could also bring his own drink offerings, and detailed *halakot* explain when and in what circumstances people are believed with regard to purity for the Sanctuary, as well as where it was possible to purchase these commodities in a condition of purity fit for the altar.[159]

The Mishnah and *barayta* of Menahot record detailed traditions concerning the localities from which the congregational offerings were brought. These were chosen either because they were known for the good quality of their products or because of the season of the year when the fruits of that locality ripened. Flour and wine were brought mainly from the Judean region (Michmas, Beth Rimah, etc.), and oil from Galilee (Tekoa, Gischala), rams from Moab, calves from Sharon and sheep from Hebron.[160] The doves were reared in cedars on the Mount of Olives.[161] Much salt was needed for the sacrificial service, since the Torah commanded, "with all thine offerings thou shalt offer salt" (Lev. 2:13). The Tosefta states that they chiefly used Sodom salt.[162]

Together with the daily offering every morning and afternoon, an offering of incense was burned in the Sanctuary, incense being the only offering that could not be brought by the individual either in an obligatory or voluntary capacity. The Torah mentions four only of its ingredients: stacte, onycha, galbanum and frankincense (Ex. 30:34), but the Tannaitic tradition, presented as a *halaka* handed down to Moses on Mt. Sinai, enumerates eleven spices, to which were added *ma'ale 'ashan* — ("smoke-raiser") and Jordan-resin.[163] According to various traditions there were several gardens in the vicinity of Jerusalem where these spices were grown, and indeed most of them do appear to have grown around Jerusalem.[164]

4. HEAVE OFFERINGS, TITHES AND TEMPLE

A frequently quoted *halaka* throughout Talmudical literature is that heave offerings, tithes and other priestly dues connected with plants or living creatures, such as the dough offering, the first shearing of the wool, the redemption of the firstborn, etc., were given directly to the priests in his village or town, there being no necessity or religious duty to take them up to the Temple in Jerusalem.[165] Indeed Josephus confirms that the tithes and heave offerings were taken directly by the priests from the fields and granaries.[166] In early times, however, priestly dues were brought to Jerusalem and handed to the Temple treasury. The books of the Bible written at the beginning of the period of the Second Temple state this repeatedly both in rebuking the people and in reasserting the covenant of faith to fulfill the precepts.[167] According to the plain meaning of the verses the priestly dues were brought to the Temple for distribution among the priests engaged in the divine service. For some time during the existence of the Second Temple this custom continued to be observed. We read in I Maccabees (3:49–50) with regard to the gathering of the people in Mizpeh: "And they brought near the priestly garments and the firstfruits and the tithes and they confirmed the Nazirites who had completed their days and called aloud to heaven saying, what shall we do with these and whither shall we carry them." In a later chapter (10:31), the letter of Demetrius to the Jewish people promises that "Jerusalem will be sacred and it and its environs shall be freed from tithes and taxes." These words can only mean that the tithes brought to Jerusalem were to be exempted from payment to the government.[168] Something of the same nature is implied in the Book of Judith (11:13), which tells us how the people of Bethulia guarded the heave offering and the tithes in their city, in order to send them later (apparently when they made the pilgrimage at the festival) to Jerusalem for the priests. The Book of Tobit, too, relates that Tobit used to carry up his tithes to Jerusalem (1:6). The Gospel of St. Luke writes: "And when the time came for their purification, in accordance with the law of Moses, they brought him up to Jerusalem to present him before the Lord" (2:22), i.e., to redeem him in Jerusalem and to give the redemption money to the Temple. The facts are clear and emphatic in Philo, who details the priestly dues and then adds: "And in order that none of the givers should insult [the priests], [the Torah] commands that they first bring the gifts to the Temple from where the priests receive it later" (De Spec. Legibus, I, 152). This custom was especially prevalent among the Jews of the Diaspora. Although the Halaka affirms that heave offerings and tithes do not apply outside the Land of Israel, many were nevertheless accustomed to set them aside, in greater or smaller degree, and the practice was usually bound up with a pilgrimage to Jerusalem. We already find that the pro-consul of Asia Minor ordered the inhabitants of Miletus to allow the Jews to donate the monies to the Sanctuary and to deal with the fruits in accordance with their laws,[169] i.e., to send the half sheqel, the heave offerings and the tithes to Jerusalem.

It is impossible to determine when the previous fixed custom was discontinued and the halaka introduced whereby heave offerings and tithes were given to the priests in the towns and villages. In Antiquities (XIV, 203)

Josephus states that Julius Caesar decreed that the Jews "should pay the tithes to Hyrcanus and his sons just as they also paid them to their ancestors." Thus the authority of the early custom had already been undermined in the time of Hyrcanus, and there were even some who did not bring their tithes to Jerusalem. Hyrcanus seems to have attempted to revive the bringing of the heave offerings and tithes. Apparently he did not succeed even though he appointed a double set of inspectors to collect the tithes. The Mishnah records that he did away with the "avowal of the tithes,"[170] the declaration made by an Israelite when he set aside all his tithes and delivered them for their proper purpose. Thus when Philo refers to the bringing of priestly dues to the Temple he is mainly describing the usage of the Diaspora, where those who did set aside heave offerings and tithes carried them or their value to Jerusalem. Even after the destruction they continued the custom of sending their tithes to the Land of Israel to maintain the central institutions which they regarded as substitutes for the Temple.[171]

E. The language of the Temple

The language used at the service and in other activities of the Temple was Hebrew. Throughout Talmudic literature there are scattered sayings, readings, benedictions and fragments of prayer taken from the life of the Temple. There are several score of these dicta, the greater number being in Hebrew. It is impossible to accept the view of several scholars,[172] that all these expressions are translations from the Aramaic vernacular of the people in the later period of the Temple. Tannaim and Amoraim were particular to transmit things in their original form and language, and even if they had translated all the traditions from Aramaic to Hebrew, this could hardly have been done in such a smooth and consistent form, since the Talmudic literature was edited neither at one time nor by one school. We possess but few traditions from the life of the Temple concerning the use of Aramaic. In Mishnah Sheqalim (5, 3) Ben Azzai states that the seals handed to those paying for drink offerings were "inscribed in Aramaic." Describing the making of the girdle, Josephus notes that the girdle "is called by us himyana" (Ant. III, 156). He almost certainly means that in the priestly circle they called the girdle by its Aramaic name of himyana, and he also usually speaks of kahanaya (priests) and kahana rabba (high priest). It is not surprising that the Aramaic used by the people of Jerusalem, in the provincial towns, and in the Diaspora, also penetrated into the Temple, but these few traditions do not suffice to set aside the many traditions testifying to the predominant use of Hebrew in the Temple. The fragmentary inscriptions found in the recent excavation outside the Temple court, near the southern wall, are quite convincing proof that Hebrew was used in the Temple, at least in written form.

F. The Pilgrimage

The pilgrimage was one of the most conspicuous expressions of the people's attachment for the Temple and Jerusalem, and the occasion which provided most opportunity for each to influence the other. On the three festivals, tens of thousands from the Land of Israel and the Diaspora went up to the Temple at the coming of each appointed season. The pilgrimage was a factor of great importance in the life of the Jewish individual, who prepared himself for the time when he would appear in the courts of the House of the Lord. He had to collect the not inconsiderable sum of money for the expenses of the journey and for the many sacrifices bound up with the pilgrimage. On returning to his home and village, the influence of his visit was conveyed through his account of the majesty of the Temple, the splendor of the city, and the elevation of spirit he had experienced while staying in the courts of the House of the Lord and in the city's places of learning.[173] He may, indeed, even have been stimulated and strengthened for his own study of the Torah.[174]

Economically, too, the pilgrimage was of great importance for Jerusalem. Three times a year thousands of pilgrims spent large amounts of money during their stay in the city, both for their own maintenance and in the distribution of charity. Perhaps more important, however, was its national and political consequence. The pilgrim came to Jerusalem with the experience of his town or village; he returned home bearing the feelings and aspirations of a whole nation. On several occasions Josephus stresses that the revolts against the government broke out chiefly during festivals.[175] The mere fact that tens of thousands of people were concentrated in Jerusalem made such disturbances possible. It was natural, therefore, that those preaching revolt used the time of the pilgrimage for rousing the people against foreign rule.

1.   THE PRECEPT OF PILGRIMAGE

In three places in the Torah it is written: "Three times in the year all thy males shall appear before the presence of the Lord."[176] In the time of the Second Temple these verses were explained not as a duty upon every male to make a pilgrimage three times a year, but merely to "appear before the presence of the Lord." Anyone entering the Temple at these seasons, however, was obliged to offer sacrifices: "and they shall not appear before the Lord empty" (Deut. 16:16). In the whole of Tannaitic literature there is no discussion of the precept of making a pilgrimage, but only of which duties the person is obliged to perform when he did make the pilgrimage. Mishnah Ḥagiga, which is mainly devoted to the matter of the pilgrimage, commences: "All are subject to the command to appear [before the Lord] excepting a deaf-mute, an imbecile, a minor . . ." but the *mishna* actually refers to the pilgrimage offerings. For the following *mishna* continues: "The School of Shammai say: The pilgrimage offering [must have the value of at least] two pieces of silver." The Jerusalem Talmud explains the first *mishna* similarly, but in the Babylonian Talmud there is a discussion on whether the pilgrimage is a permanent duty that must be fulfilled three times a year.[177] Typical of the development of the *Halaka*, in its explanation of this precept, is the *barayta* of R. Jose the Galilean which states: "Israel were commanded three precepts when they make the pilgrimage, the appearance [i.e. the pilgrimage offering], the festal [offering] and the rejoicing [offering] . . . the appearance differs from the other two in that it is wholly consumed before the Most High" etc.[178] The *barayta* speaks only of the precepts that were to be observed when they made the pilgrimage, and "appearance" simply means the appearance or pilgrim's offering. Maimonides, however, construes this *barayta* in conformity with the conclusion of the Babylonian Talmud: "Israel was commanded three precepts on each of the three pilgrimage festivals these being: the appearance, as it says, 'all thy males shall appear,' and the festal, as it says... and the rejoicing, as it says... the appearance mentioned in the Torah means that we appear before His presence in the Temple court on the first day of the festival and bring a burnt offering" (beginning of *Hilkot Ḥagiga*). It would seem that in practice, too, the pilgrimage was not regarded as a fixed duty. One *barayta* in Tractate Peṣaḥim relates that in consequence of a dispute whether the festal offering that accompanied the paschal offering could be brought on the Sabbath or not, a certain Sage, who differed from his colleagues in holding that the festal offering overrode the Sabbath but was not permitted to act accordingly, solved his conflict of conscience by moving away from Jerusalem. "Judah b. Durtai," says the *barayta*, "dissociated himself, he and his son Durtai, and they went to dwell in the south."[179] Had that Sage regarded the pilgrimage as a fixed duty, he would have effected nothing by his move, since in any case he would have needed to make the pilgrimage, and so have become liable for the sacrifice. Many accounts in the Talmudic literature and elsewhere of God-fearing men who observed the precepts strictly, mention the pilgrimage as being made once a year or even only occasionally, and not as a regular practice three times a year.[180] When Josephus speaks of the people of Israel assembling three times a year, he apparently is not referring to all Israel. Philo, too, treats the pilgrimage as a matter of exceptional piety, and thus could not have regarded it as imperative for all Israel on each of the three festivals.[181]

2. THE PILGRIMAGE FROM THE LAND OF ISRAEL AND FROM THE DIASPORA

On each of the three festivals many tens of thousands went up both from the Land of Israel and the Diaspora. Most, of course, came from the Land of Israel, on whose inhabitants the precept was regarded as chiefly binding.[182] Of these, moreover, the majority came from nearby Judea and Idumaea. Josephus states this explicitly in reference to the pilgrims who came during the Feast of Weeks following the death of Herod: "And the pilgrims from near, from Judea, were still greater in number." Of the years just before the destruction Josephus relates that when Cestius Gallus came to Lydda he found it deserted, for all the people had gone up to Jerusalem to celebrate the Feast of Tabernacles.[183] The Mishnah itself gives us an idea of the principal region from which the pilgrimage was made: "What counts as *a journey afar off* [for bringing the Passover offering]? Beyond Modiin, or a like distance in any direction" (Pᵉsaḥim 9, 2). When the ascent to Jerusalem was made for other purposes, too, such as for the *ma'amadot* (divisions) and the wood offering, the participation of the inhabitants of Judea was greater than those dwelling in other districts. Most of the families enumerated in Mishnah Ta'anit (4, 5) who used to bring the wood offering at fixed times were descended from Judea, while the *barayta* (Ta'anit 27a) stresses the great part played by Jericho in sending the *ma'amadot* to Jerusalem.

Nevertheless many made the pilgrimage from other parts of the country too. Of the pilgrimage from the Peraea there is little information just as indeed there is of Jewish Transjordan in general.[184] Such is not the case with regard to Galilee, however. Traditions in the Talmudic *Halaḵa* and Aggada record the widespread practice of caravans and individuals making the pilgrimage on each festival. The Jerusalem Talmud and Midrashim recount legends and miracles that happened to scholars and ordinary people when they went up to Jerusalem. The subject of the legend may be the synagogue beadle, or the women of Sepphoris, or R. Hanina b. Dosa.[185]

Tradition may connect the institution of one *halaka* or another with something that befell a certain man from Meron on his visit to Jerusalem, or someone named Arsela of Sepphoris who was staying in the Temple on the Day of Atonement.[186] The Christian Gospels, particularly those of Luke and John, frequently speak of the ascent to Jerusalem of Jesus in the company of his family and friends.[187] The writings of Josephus also contain many references to pilgrims from Galilee, and even mention the paths they customarily used. From his account we may gather that they went mostly by way of Samaria, 'Ein-Gannim, and Shechem, which was a three-day journey from Galilee to Jerusalem.[188] This route was preferred for a number of reasons. There was no need to descend into valleys and then climb hills, there were settlements along the whole route, and water was always available to the pilgrim. Two other routes, however, were also frequently traveled — the one through the valley of the Jordan and Jericho and thence to Jerusalem, or down Mt. Ephraim, and then to K^{e}far Othnai, Antipatris and Jerusalem.[189]

It is almost certain that there were fewer pilgrims from the Diaspora than from the Land of Israel itself, though even those were many. Philo testifies to "many tens of thousands from innumerable localities travelling on each festival to the Temple, some going overland, some by sea, from east and west, from north and south."[190] From Josephus and the New Testament, particularly Acts, it is possible to compile a long list of towns from which pilgrimages were made at the three festivals. Philo and Josephus report[191] that the half sheqels were carried in caravans by the townspeople, and from the Mishnah we know that these reached Jerusalem for the special seasons. We may well conclude, therefore, that the sheqels were sent with the pilgrims, and that the pilgrimage, like the contribution of the half sheqel, embraced a large section of the Diaspora. Throughout the literature there are references to the presence in Jerusalem during the festivals of Jews from Babylon, Persia, Media, pilgrims from Egypt, Alexandria, Cyrene, Ethiopia, Syria, Pontus, Asia, Cilicia, Tarsus, Phrygia and Pamphylia.[192] Many places, either collectively or through local benefactors, erected synagogues and hospices in Jerusalem for their own pilgrims. Talmudic literature mentions a synagogue of Alexandrians (or possibly of Tarsiots) existing in Jerusalem. The Acts mention a synagogue of Freedmen, frequented by Jews from Cyrene, Alexandria, Cilicia and Asia. In the excavations on the Ophel the remains of a group of buildings have been discovered, which according to an inscription were built by Theodotus the son of Vettenius, as a synagogue with water installations "in order to accommodate the needy from foreign parts."[193]

How many pilgrims were there on any particular festival? The sources speak of the numerous pilgrims who filled the city and its environs, but it is doubtful whether even a rough estimate can be made. Several scholars[194] have attempted to do so from the description in Mishnah Pesaḥim (5, 5), which relates that the Temple court was filled three times with the slaughter-ers of the Passover offering, and that when Passover eve fell on the Sabbath all three groups remained within the Temple Mount, as they were not permitted to carry the sacrifice outside its boundaries (*ibid.*, 5, 10). These scholars calculated the area of the Temple court or of the rampart, estimated the density of the crowd, and so arrived at the number of slaughterers. This they multiplied by ten, since both Josephus and the Talmud[195] state that at least ten persons were counted for each Passover offering. Based on these calculations, one scholar reached a figure of 100,000 pilgrims, while another put the figure at 125,000. Despite the ingenuity of these calcula-tions, however, there is no real basis for such estimates. First of all, it is impossible to ascertain the area into which the celebrants were crowded, since we do not know where outside the Court of Israelites (which was a small area of 135 × 11 cubits) the celebrants were allowed to remain. They were certainly not allowed between the altar and the porch, and we have no way of telling whether there were not other buildings in those areas that are unknown to us. Most important of all, there is nothing on which to base an estimate of the degree of crowding, and it is certain that the round number of ten per sacrifice given by the Talmud and by Josephus is not sufficiently accurate to be used as a multiplier. It is quite possible, for instance, that the average number for each sacrifice was not more than seven or eight, while on the other hand it may even have reached fifteen. The only inference to be drawn from the Mishnah is that those Talmudic traditions that speak of 12,000,000 people in Jerusalem, or even the more modest figure of 3,000,000,[196] are very far from the reality as portrayed in the Mishnah's factual narrative of the order of offering the Passover sacrifice.

3.   THE PILGRIMAGE AND THE STAY IN JERUSALEM

Chapter 3 of Mishnah Bikkurim records the arrangements for carrying up the firstfruits: "All the smaller towns of the *ma'amad* [the Tosefta has "the region"] gathered together in the town of the *ma'amad* and spent the night in the open place of the town and did not go into the houses; and in the early morning the officer [of the *ma'amad*] said, *Arise ye and let us go up to Zion unto the house of the Lord our God* . . . The ox went before them, having its horns overlaid with gold and a wreath of olive leaves on its head. The flute was played before them until they drew near to Jerusalem." This description of the caravan gathering together in the town of the *ma'amad*, or of the region, was also formerly applicable to the pilgrimage, as may be inferred from sources both prior to and later than the Mishnah. Isaiah 30:29 says: "Ye shall have a song as in the night when a feast is hallowed; and gladness of heart, as when one goeth with the pipe to come into the mountain of the Lord." The flute accompanied those going up to the mountain of the Lord on the festival. In a late midrash of Lamentations Rabba (1, 52) contrasting the sorrow of the pilgrimage after the destruction with the splendor and rejoicing during the time of the Temple, the homilist draws on the descriptions in this chapter of the Mishnah: "In the past I used to go up with singing and psalms . . . in the past I used to go up with multitudes upon multitudes of celebrants." Another expression of rejoicing on the festival was the wearing of wreaths. The author of the Book of Jubilees (16:30) connects this custom with the Feast of Tabernacles, when not only the ox but the celebrants themselves wore olive wreaths on their heads.[197] Many of the psalms that express yearning for the House of God and His holy habitation are almost certainly connected with the pilgrimage in caravans and reflect the rejoicing of the pilgrim.[198]

The communal pilgrimage bore not only a festive character but was associated with some of the religious ethical thought of those generations. This connection is well illustrated in the Psalms: "Who shall ascend into the mountain of the Lord? And who shall stand in His holy place? He that hath clean hands and a pure heart" (24:3–4), or "Who shall sojourn in Thy tabernacle? Who shall dwell upon Thy holy mountain? He that walketh uprightly, and worketh righteousness" (15:1–2), etc. On a practical level, the beginning of Mishnah Bikkurim rules that those whose produce is tainted with stealing may not bring firstfruits.

Pilgrimage in organized caravans did not prevent individuals and families from making the journey to Jerusalem on their own initiative, and they did so both for the firstfruits and for the festival. Jews living outside the Land of Israel, however, frequently went up in caravans either in imitation of the custom in Israel or for their own safety and that of the money and offerings they carried with them.[199] The women in the family also participated in the pilgrimage. The Talmudic *Halaka* asserts: "Israel was commanded three precepts when making the pilgrimage, the appearance-offering, the festal-offering, and the rejoicing-offering . . . the rejoicing-offering differs from the other two since it applies to both men and women."[200] Josephus, the Talmud and the Christian Gospels all record the custom of pilgrimage together with wives and daughters.[201] R. Eliezer, of the generation of the destruction, held, as did other Sages, that "it is not commendable for a man to leave his household on the festival."[202] The verse "All thy males shall appear" was explained as referring merely to the appearance offering, which was incumbent upon males alone.

The pilgrims used to arrive well before the festival. This was particularly so in the case of the pilgrims from abroad, who needed seven days to purify themselves from the uncleanness of Gentile lands. Josephus relates that on the 8th of Nisan pilgrims were already present in Jerusalem for the celebration of the Passover. It was in this connection that Hyrcanus requested Herod not to bring an army of Gentiles into Jerusalem, since the people were purifying themselves for the festival. When Paul, too, arrived in the city from abroad he purified himself before entering the Temple.[203]

As we have already mentioned, the appearance before the Lord in the Temple was bound up with the offering of several sacrifices. First was the appearance offering itself, brought in the form of a burnt offering, to which were added peace offerings essential for the rejoicing. The sacrifices were offered on the first day of the festival, or on the remaining days which were regarded as complementary to the first day; also on the six days following the Feast of Weeks, since this festival lasted only one day.[204] The pilgrims stayed in the city itself, in the surrounding villages, and in tents pitched in the fields on the city's outskirts.[205] We may judge from the literature of that period that one of the effects of the pilgrimage was to create a spirit of brotherliness among its participants. Indeed, custom and *Halaka* fostered this idea. The *Halaka* eased the laws of uncleanness during the festival both within the Temple and outside it, so that the normally stringent purity practices should not prevent a person from having contact with his fellow. Householders in Jerusalem were forbidden to take rent from the pilgrims, and received only the animal hides from them as gifts.[206] The pleasant atmosphere that prevailed in the city among the pilgrims themselves and between them and the local inhabitants is also implied in the Tannaitic tradition: "Ten miracles were wrought for our ancestors in Jerusalem . . . no man said to his fellow, 'I have not found an oven in Jerusalem to roast the paschal sacrifices'; no man ever said to his fellow, 'I have not found a bed to sleep in Jerusalem'; no man ever [said] to his fellow, 'The place is too strait for me that I should lodge in Jerusalem'" (*Avot de-R. Nathan*, Version I, ch. 35).

Although the pilgrims were allowed to lodge outside the city, they were required to remain within its walls on the day they offered their sacrifices and to eat the paschal lambs there. On the days preceding Passover, Jesus stayed outside the city, but before Passover eve he ordered his disciples to go to one of its inhabitants and set aside a place for their meal.[207] Though the man was not necessarily one of the followers of Jesus, it was taken for granted that he would invite the members of the group into his house.

4. THE WOOD OFFERING

The book of Nehemiah (10:35) states: "And we cast lots, the priests, the Levites, and the people, for the wood-offering, to bring it into the house of our God, according to our fathers' houses, at times appointed, year by year, to burn upon the altar of the Lord our God, as it is written in the Law." The duty of bringing wood to the Temple was thus divided among "fathers' houses" (this appears to be the correct reading and is adopted in several versions of the Septuagint: εἰς οἴκους, and in the Vulgate: per domis); and this custom continued throughout the whole period of the Second Temple. There was a tradition among the older families of bringing wood at fixed seasons for the continual fire on the altar. Josephus mentions this custom with reference to the last years of the Temple, and R. Eliezer b. Zadok, a contemporary of the destruction, also testifies to it.[208] It was not their exclusive privilege, however, for they were joined on several occasions by the ordinary people. Thus Josephus says: "And the eighth day was the festival of the wood-offering, when all the people were accustomed to bring wood for the altar." Mishnah Ta'anit (4, 5) specifies the seasons for bringing the wood offering: "The wood-offering of the priests and people was brought [on the 9th of Ab][208a]. On the 1st of Nisan [it was brought] by the family of Arah of the tribe of Judah; on the 20th of Tammuz by the family of David of the tribe of Judah; on the 5th of Ab by the family of Parosh of the tribe of Judah; on the 7th of the same month by the family of Jonadab the son of Rechab; on the 10th by the family of Senaah of the tribe of Benjamin; on the 15th by the family of Zattu of the tribe of Judah together with the priests and Levites and all whose tribal descent was doubtful, and the family of the Pestle-smugglers and the family of the Fig-pressers. On the 20th of the same month [it was brought] by the family of Paḥath Moab of the tribe of Judah; on the 20th of Elul by the family of Adin of the tribe of Judah; on the 1st of Tebet there was no ma'amad since on that day there was the *Hallel*, an additional offering, and a wood-offering." Thus there were two wood offerings in the month of Ab, on the 9th and on the 15th (the one referred to by Josephus) when the people could bring wood offerings to the Temple. The wood-offering seasons were a kind of minor pilgrimage for these families and for those who joined them, and Josephus even refers to it as the festival of the wood offering. The *Halaka* required those participating in the wood offering to stay overnight in Jerusalem in the same manner as all celebrants who brought their offerings to the Temple.[209]

G. THE PLACE OF THE TEMPLE IN THE LIFE OF THE PEOPLE

The period of the First Temple saw the establishment of several mutually independent authorities in the life and thought of the nation — the monarchy, the prophets, the Temple and the priesthood. Their independence of each other was not merely in the history of their development, but also in theory and in practice. Neither the kings nor the prophets received their power from the Temple and its priests. Though the king was sometimes anointed in the Temple by the High Priest, or achieved his rank through the power and influence of the priesthood, there was in fact no necessity for the king to be anointed in the Temple itself, nor did the custom become permanent. The prophets made their demands upon the people through the power of the word of God as revealed to His messengers, and they received neither inscription nor authority from the Temple. Nor was the Temple the only place for the service of God. Its uniqueness as *the* place of worship emerged only at the end of a long process of consolidation lasting for generations.

The First Temple, then, occupied an important place in the life of the nation but did not encompass every spiritual and practical sphere of activity in Israel. This was not so in the case of the Second Temple. The beginning of the settlement during the return to Zion centered around the altar and the Temple. It is true that in the course of the Temple's existence the sacrificial service of God no longer came to comprise the sole form of the nation's religious and social life. To a great extent the stress moved to the study of the Torah. The synagogue, the place of learning, and eventually even the functions of administration and justice, were not entrusted to the care of the priesthood. Nevertheless, every one of these institutions and fundamental aspects of religious, social and national life was bound up with the affairs of the Temple. The city of Jerusalem, with the Temple at its center, served not only as the generator of all these ideas and social currents, but also as their mold and principal vehicle, even if, paradoxically, the very power of the Temple and its priests was inevitably eroded in the process.

In the course of the Temple's existence we witness the development of the synagogue, which was at first intended primarily for reading the Torah, and to which prayer was added later. This institution represented a twofold innovation. From the religious aspect it meant that man's connection with his Creator was no longer expressed by the offering of a sacrifice to the Lord, but by reflection, prayer, and the study of the Torah. Its communal and social significance lay in the fact that the service of the Lord was not implemented through the medium of a priest, but directly by the congregation, all of whose members were of equal standing. What determined the sacred status of the synagogue meeting was nothing more than the assembly of ten Israelites. Not only was this institution common in Jerusalem: it was even combined with the service in the Temple.[210] During the service of the daily offering the priests assembled for prayer in the Chamber of Hewn Stone; the men of the *ma'amodot* gathered in the synagogue; on the Day of Atonement and at the *haqhel* (assembly) celebration the High Priest read from the Torah scroll. Moreover it even appears that the origin of the synagogue was connected with some of the activities in the Temple. Our first sources for the existence of a synagogue of this nature are the Books of Ezra and Nehemiah, which record the reading of the Torah in the presence of the congregation.[211]

Thus there is no justification for regarding the foundation of the synagogue as an attempt to fill the vacuum created by the destruction of the First Temple, since the basic elements of the synagogue — the public reading of the Law and congregational prayer — were first instituted by Ezra and Nehemiah. Even during the hundreds of years of the Second Temple's existence the synagogue and its activities did not take the place of the sacrificial service, but existed side by side with it, adding breadth and depth to the religious-spiritual experience, to social thought, and to the significance of congregation and assembly.

Tradition generally regards the institution of prayers as corresponding to the various sacrifices. Thus the morning prayer corresponds to the morning daily offering, the afternoon prayer to the afternoon daily offering and so on. In consequence the evening prayer, which had no corresponding offering, occupies a somewhat uncertain place in the *Halaka*.

While at prayer, the individual or the congregation would face towards Jerusalem and the Temple.[212] Several other liturgical principles of the synagogue are based on Temple practices, and only spread to the synagogue in the course of the years. Most of them, however, were not adopted by the synagogue on the destruction of the Temple, but were already current during its existence. The priestly blessing, for example, was recited in the Temple, though after the destruction R. Johanan b. Zakkai decreed that the priests should not ascend the platform of the synagogue wearing shoes, as a sign of mourning for the Temple. The actual practice of reciting the priestly blessing outside the Temple had already spread before his time, during the Temple's existence.[213] The same applied to the carrying of the palm branch and the blowing of the *shofar*. These two practices were at first only connected with the altar and the sacrifices, but they had already spread into the synagogues while the Temple was still standing.[214]

In the course of time the reading of the Torah was supplemented by its interpretation and study. This activity, too, was connected with the Temple. Tannaitic tradition speaks of a place of learning in the Temple Mount or the rampart, where the Sanhedrin assembled on Sabbaths and festivals not as a court — since cases were not tried on the Sabbath — but as a place of learning (see above). Josephus relates that in the time of Herod, Judah the son of Sariphaeus and Mattathias the son of Margalius, the two Sages who stirred their disciples to pull down the golden eagle that Herod had erected above the Temple gate, ". . . were wont to instruct daily in the Temple in the presence of many youths who drank in their words thirstily." The Gospels speak of Jesus teaching daily in the Temple, and after his death the Judeo-Christian apostles gathered daily in the Temple and some of them preached before the people. Of R. Johanan b. Zakkai it is written that he used "to sit and expound in the shade of the Temple."[215]

We know very little of the personalities of many of the Tannaim from the time of the Temple. Most of them were connected with Jerusalem, and their attachment to the Temple was great even if their meeting and activity in the Temple were not always to the liking of the High Priesthood. One tradition recorded in Tractate Yoma clearly illustrates the conflict between the High Priesthood and the Sages: "It once happened that a High Priest left the Temple [on the Day of Atonement] and everyone was following him. When they saw Shemaiah and Abtalyon they left him and followed after Shemaiah and Abtalyon. Eventually Shemaiah and Abtalyon came to take leave of the High Priest. He said to them, 'May the descendants come in peace.' They replied, "May the descendants of Gentiles who do the deeds of Aaron come in peace, but the descendant of Aaron who does not do the deeds of Aaron, he shall not come in peace.'"[216]

The Temple was also used as a repository for the care, preservation and dissemination of sacred writings, historical notes and genealogical records. The scroll of the Law that served as the master from which copyists corrected the scrolls was deposited in the Temple.[217] This copy seems to have been already in existence in the very first years of Hellenistic rule in the land, for we are told that Eleazar the High Priest sent Ptolemy the book of the Law and requested him to return it to him. He cannot have been referring to any ordinary copy written in Hebrew, for such must certainly have been available in Alexandria, but to the accurate copy from which they were corrected, and it was this that was sent to Alexandria for the translation of the Torah into Greek.[218] It was apparently this copy, too, that was used for reading out on festive occasions in the Temple, as when the High Priest read the Torah on the Day of Atonement or at the *haqhel* ceremony. It is also highly probable that this was the scroll referred to by Josephus as the one Titus took back to Rome with the booty (*War* VII, 150).

Several sources in the Talmud mention 120 scriveners who received their salaries from the offering of the Chamber.[219] They not only copied the scrolls and scrutinized them for errors, but also took care of the transmission of the text. In one place we read that the text was determined according to the version of the majority of several scrolls that were in the Temple court "There were three scrolls that were in the Temple court; the scroll of Ma'on, the scroll of Hi', and the scroll of Za'atutim. One had written [for Deut. 33:27] *ma'on qedem* [eternal dwelling place] and the two *me'ona elohei qedem* [the eternal God is a dwelling place]; the sages abrogated the one and confirmed the two."[220] Besides the scrolls of the Torah and the prophets, other books were also preserved and cared for in the Temple. The Second Book of Maccabees contains a letter to the Jews of Egypt informing them that Judah the Maccabee had gathered all the books that had been scattered and was willing to send them to Egypt should they so desire (II Macc. 2:16). It seems to have been merely one of the functions of the Temple to supply books to Jews in the country and the Diaspora. On several occasions Josephus mentions the existence of non-sacred writings stored in the Temple, such as accounts of the wars of the Jewish nation, and genealogical records of priestly families in Israel and in the Exile.[221] In a *barayta* incorporated in the gaonic literature we read: "The elders of the School of Shammai and the elders of the School of Hillel wrote the Scroll of the Hasmonean House, and they wrote the *Megillat Ta'anit* in the upper chamber of Hananiah b. Hezekiah b. Garon."[222] In this upper chamber of Hananiah b. Hezekiah (a probably more correct version reads Eleazar b. Hananiah, who is identical with Eleazar the captain of the priests),[223] the Book of Ezekiel was saved from obscurity: "Howbeit, may that man be remembered for good, and his name is Hananiah b. Hezekiah: but for him the Book of Ezekiel would have been hidden since it contains words contradicting the words of the Torah. What did he do? 300 measures of oil were carried up to him and he stayed in an upper chamber, and reconciled them." This upper chamber was almost certainly in the Temple area, since "the 18 decrees" within the boundaries of the Temple.[224]

In addition to the Temple scroll, other books from the Temple were plundered by Titus, some of which Josephus later succeeded in obtaining from him (*Life*, 75). And so the Talmudic tradition testifies: "When the enemies entered the Temple the Ammonites and Moabites entered with them. Everyone ran to plunder silver and gold but the Ammonites and Moabites ran to plunder the Torah (Lamentations Rabba 1, 38).

The courts of twenty-three, from which the Sanhedrin in the Chamber of Hewn Stone was constituted, also sat within the Temple boundaries. According to both halakic and aggadic tradition, the seating of the Sanhedrin in the Temple was not a matter of chance. The priests and Levites formed a substantial, and at times a decisive, element in its composition, and the Sanhedrin's decision was not binding unless taken in the Chamber of Hewn Stone and only when the Temple service was maintained. The verse in Deuteronomy (17:9) — "And thou shalt come unto the priests, the Levites, and unto the judge that shall be in those days" — is taken to mean that when there is a priest (performing the service), there may be judgment (of capital cases), and when there is no priest, the judge may not function.[225] The subsequent verses (17:10–13) impose the death penalty on the one who rebels against the decision of the court in "the place which the Lord shall choose." Thus the *Halaka* construes that "if he encounters them at Bethphage [near Jerusalem] and rebels against them ... one might think this is regarded as rebellion [to impose the penalty], but the Scripture says: *and thou shalt arise and get thee up to the place*, teaching that the place conditions the act" (Sanhedrin 14b).

The Temple was a place of many and diverse activities, but to the people it represented above all the dwelling place of the Lord God who had singled them out from the nations of the world. All those social and religious values with which it became associated did nothing to diminish its image for the Jews as the unrivaled center for the service of God through the offering of sacrifices in the name of all the people. But even for the individual and his personal religious experience, the Temple service was of paramount importance. The offering of sacrifices purified him and atoned for his sins, and served as a medium for his spiritual elevation and refinement. The Temple and its sacred utensils brought the earthly world in contact with the whole of the heavenly system, and were regarded as a source of blessing for all the nations of the world.[226] There was a fervent belief that the Temple would stand as long as heaven and earth existed. That the Temple had in fact existed for so long, and had been rebuilt in even greater splendor than before, merely served to strengthen the belief in its eternality. Hence the people's great devotion to the Temple in time of peace, the strength of its resistance when the enemy breached its walls, and the utter despair and desolation of soul as the Temple was reduced to rubble and ashes.

By its destruction the image of the world was harmed, the orderly framework of the nation was demolished, and — in the words of the Talmud (Berakot 33b) — "an iron wall intervened between Israel and its Father in Heaven."

NOTES

INTRODUCTION
THE RISE OF ROME

1   See *The Hellenistic Age*, Jerusalem, 1972, pp. 79 ff., the 6th Volume of THE WORLD HISTORY OF THE JEWISH PEOPLE

2   The Histories of Rome are innumerable: we shall list here only the classical history of Th. Mommsen, *Römische Geschichte*, Breslau, 1854–5, and the main studies that have appeared in this century. See Bibliography to Introduction.

3   Polybius I, 1, 5; 3, 6.

4   Plutrach, *Pyrrhus*, 21.!

5   T. Frank, *An Economic Survey of Ancient Rome*, I, Baltimore, 1933, pp. 13–19.

6   Plutarch, *op. cit.*, 23.

7   The principal sources for the Second Punic War are Livy, Books XXI-XXX, Polybius and Appian.

8   The most famous case of such corruption, that of Verres in Sicily, as exposed by Cicero, occurred somewhat later than the events in the end of this chapter.

9   T. Frank, *op. cit.*, I, p. 56; J. Kromayer, *Roms Kampf um die Weltherschaft*, Leipzig, 1912, pp. 37–40.

10   T. Frank, *op. cit.*, I, pp. 76 ff.

11   Sallust, 35, 10.

12   Bengtson, *Grundriss der römischen Geschichte und Quellenkunde*, München, 1967, pp. 465–6.

CHAPTER I

THE FALL OF THE HASMONEAN DYNASTY
AND THE ROMAN CONQUEST

1 *Ant.* XIII, 418; *War* I, 115.

2 Porphyrius *apud* Eusebius, *Chronicon*, ed. Schöne, I, Berlin, 1866, pp. 260; he was given this cognomen as he was educated in Cyzicus (*Ant.* XIII, 271); Appian, *Syriaca*, 68–9.

3 Cf. Appian, *loc. cit.*; he was called "Aquiline" (ὁ Γρυπός) as opposed to σιμός (snub) on account of his aquiline nose (cf. Justin, XXXIX, 1, 9).

4 Εὔκαιρος — Ἄκαιρος "Propitious" or "Unpropitious"; the cognomens testify to the praise of his supporters or the mockery of his opponents According to A. R. Bellinger, "The End of the Seleucids," *Transactions of the Connecticut Academy of Arts and Sciences*, 38 (1949), p. 76, the cognomen Ἄκαιρος was given him by his Jewish supporters when he intervened in the war between the Pharisees and Jannaeus.

5 Appian, *Syriaca*, 69; Porphyrius *apud* Eusebius, *Chron.* I, 259–62.

6 On the endless wars and internal turmoil in Syria during this period, see Bellinger, *op. cit.*, and also E. Schürer, *Geschichte des jüdischen Volkes im Zeitalter Jesu Christi*, I, Leipzig, 1901, p. 175 f.

7 Cf. Appian, *Syriaca*, 48; 69; Justin, XL, 1, 1–4; Bellinger *op. cit.*, p. 80 ff. and Schürer, *op. cit.*, I, p. 175 f.

8 The genuineness of this submission is attested by Josephus in *Ant.* XIII, 420: ... καὶ ἐδέοντο χρηστὰ περὶ τῆς βασιλίσσης καὶ τοῦ ἔθνους συγγινώσκειν and also in *War* I, 116: Τιγράνην ... συνθήκαις καὶ δώροις ὑπηγάγετο. The Hasmonean kingdom had even then become a dependent state.

9 *Ant.* XIII, 419–20; *War* I, 116.

10 Concerning Lucullus' war against Tigrances, see Rice Holmes, *The Roman Republic*, I, Oxford, 1923, p. 191 ff.

11 Cf. Justin, XI, 2, 2; Appian, *Syriaca*, 49; also M. Gelzer, *Pompeius*, München, 1949, p. 83, 101; B. Niese, *Geschichte der griechischen und makedonischen Staaten seit der Schlacht bei Chaeronea*, III, Gotha, 1903, p. 310; and Schürer, *Geschichte*, I, p. 178.

12 Pompey's aim was to conquer as much territory as possible in remote lands of the East where the Roman army had never before set foot. He hoped by this to gain the admiration of his contemporaries, who would regard him as a second Alexander the Great; cf. Diodorus XL, 4.

13 *Ant.* XIV, 29; *War* I, 127

14 *Ant.*, *ibid.*; *War*, *ibid.* (Μέτελλος, Λόλλιος).

15 *Ant.* XIII, 408; *War* I, 109.

16 *Ant.* XIII, 422–7; *War* I, 117.

17 *Ant.* XIII, 426, 428–9; *War* I, 118; concerning the violence of the Pharisee advisers of Salome Alexandra, see *Ant.* XIII, 408–17; *War*, I, 113–4.

18 One must draw this conclusion from *Ant.* XIV, 6 in conjunction with XIV, 42, 97; cf. XIV, 43–4. We read in *War* (I, 121) of the two brothers' agreement that Aristobulus should rule and Hyrcanus be stripped of all power and live as "the king's brother" (Ὑρκανὸν δὲ ἐκστάντα τῆς ἄλλης ἀπολαύειν τιμῆς ὥσπερ ἀδελφὸν βασιλέως). Aristobulus undoubtedly took both titles, the High Priesthood — regarded by the people as the greater of the two offices — and the crown — since in the opinion of Aristobulus Hyrcanus lacked all ability to rule (cf. *Ant.* XIII, 423). On the question of whether or not Hyrcanus received the title of "the king's brother," see Schalit, *BJPES*, 6 (1936/7), pp. 145–8.

19 *Ant.* XIV, 4–7; *War* I, 120–2.

20 *Ant.* XIV, 8; cf. also XIV, 403; *War* I, 123.

21 *Ant.* XIV, 9, where Josephus remarks that these are merely Herod's praises. I have discussed this question in my book: A. Schalit, *König Herodes*, Berlin, 1969, 474; 677 f.

22 The appointment and friendship probably began well before the conquest of Gaza by Jannaeus. The Hasmoneans' aggressive policy towards Gaza — as well as towards the Hellenistic cities — was not to the liking of Antipas, who passed these views on to his son, Antipater. I discuss all these points in my book (*op. cit.*, p. 4 f.; 677 f.).

23 Cf. A. Schalit, "Alexander Jannai's Conquests in Moab (Hebrew), *Eretz-Israel*, I (1951), p. 104 ff.; *Theokratia*, I (1967–69), p. 3 ff.; The return of the cities was also the idea of Antipater, as, indeed, was the whole plan.

24 *Ant.* XIV, 8–20; *War* I, 123–6. The Sadducee priests who fought on Aristobulus' side were undoubtedly the same group who occupied the highest positions of state during the reign of Jannaeus, who were then deposed in the reign of Salome Alexandra, and later returned to power during the short term of Aristobulus. They unanimously championed Aristobulus and his cause (*Ant.*, *loc. cit.*).

25 *Ant.* XIV, 21. A similar flight of nobles from Jerusalem occurred after the victory of Cestius Gallus in 66 A.D. (*War* II, 556).

26 *Ant.* XIV, 21–8. The Onias of Josephus is undoubtedly Ḥoni ha-Mᵉ'agel ("the Circle-maker") of the Mishnah and Talmud (cf. *Ant.* XIV, 22); M. Ta'an. 3, 8; Ta'an. 23a; Yer. Ta'an. 3, 9–10; commentary to *Mᵉg. Ta'an.* 2, 34 (cf. ed. Z. Lichtenstein, *HUCA*, VIII–IX [1931–2], p. 348 f.). Traces of the events in Josephus are found in Talmudic sources (cf. *Ant.* XIV 26–7): Soṭa 49b; Mᵉn. 64b; B. Qamma 82b; *Ant.* XIV, 28, where a mighty storm is mentioned as having befallen the country as a punishment from heaven for the murder of Onias. The Talmud states that the country was disturbed in an area of 400 parasangs after Hyrcanus' soldiers hoisted up a pig on to the wall instead of a ritually clean animal; cf. Dio Cassius, XXXVIII, 11, on the earthquake that shook many cities in Asia in 64 B.C.E. All the sources quoted here were gathered by J. Derenbourg, *Essai sur l'histoire et la géographie de la Palestine*, I, Paris, 1867, p. 112; see also J. Klausner, *History of the Second Temple* (Hebrew), (2nd ed.), III, Jerusalem, 1951, p. 217 ff. The droughts mentioned by Josephus (*Ant.* XIV, 28) are apparently hinted at in M. Mᵉn. 10, 2, where it is mentioned that the 'omer was brought from Gannot Ẓerifin and the two loaves from the valley of 'Ein Soḵer, i.e. from places distant from Jerusalem. These normally came from the immediate vicinity of Jeru-salem, but it seems that owing to a local drought the 'omer and loaves had to be brought from a distance; cf. Derenbourg, *op. cit.*, p. 114, no. 4.

27 Thus in *Ant.* XIV, 29–30; in *War* I, 128 we are told that Aristobulus paid 300 talents; on bribes paid by Hyrcanus, Josephus offers no information.

28 Josephus does not explain what type of "long thought out" requests these were, though Aristobulus probably claimed, as he later did before Pompey, that he and not his brother was fit to rule. Aristobulus' bribe to Scaurus had no political effect; Scaurus, who was a soldier and unconcerned with Roman policy in the East, remained satisfied with accepting it. Pompey, on the other hand, was primarily a politician with an interest in Rome as a world empire. The claim of Aristobulus, that he and not Hyrcanus was fit to carry on the Hasmonean dynasty, was of no real concern to Pompey. The one question was whether Rome could profit from Aristobulus' rule. Thus while Scaurus preferred Aristobulus, Pompey acted in his brother's favor.

29 Josephus makes no mention of Hyrcanus' exaggerated claims. Hyrcanus' representatives probably stressed his right of primogeniture and the fact that Aristobulus had deposed him by force. Antipater was apparently not among the delegation, or Josephus would have mentioned it. Scaurus the soldier would naturally have had more affinity towards a man who had proved his ability to act in the struggle for power. Hyrcanus had shown weakness, and had lost his right to rule the moment he proved incapable of defending himself. Such a man had no right to request others to repair the damage his personal failure had produced. What was more, he promised less money than his brother, and he could not even back that promise fully. He thus seemed "poor and miserly" (*Ant.* XIV, 31: πένης ἦν καὶ γλίσχρος).

30 Cf. A. Schlatter, *Gesch. Israels v. Alexander d. Grossen bis Hadrian*, Stuttgart, 1925, p. 393 n. 31; M. Avi-Yonah, *The Holy Land, from the Persian to the Arab Conquests* (536 B.C. to A.D. 640) (transl. from the Hebrew), Michigan, 1966, p. 133.

31 The majority of the manuscripts of *Antiquities* endorse the reading Φαλλίων (others suggest Κεφαλλίων; cf. Schalit, *König Herodes*, p. 6, n. 24). In this way they resemble the MSS of *War*. The Latinus has "Cephalon." The Idumaean equivalent is unknown. The whole passage on Scaurus appears both in *Ant.* XIV, 29–33 and *War* I, 128–30. Indeed, a sarcophagus inscribed "Antiochus son of Phallion" has been found at Scythopolis; see A. Rowe, *Topography and History of Beth-Shan*, Philadelphia, 1930. On Papyron see Schalit, *König Herodes*, p. 741 f.

32 According to Dio Cassius, XXXVII, 7, 5, Pompey spent the winter of 65/64 at his camp at Aspis (Πομπήιος δὲ ἔν τε τῇ Ἀσπίδι καὶ τότε ἐχείμασε). Rice Holmes discusses the point in his work *The Roman Republic* (I, p. 433 f.): "... and Niese remarks that the words καὶ τότε prove that he wintered in the same country as in the preceding year, when he had a camp in Armenia on the upper Kur. Mommsen concludes that his quarters were near the Caspian Sea. Plutarch, however, relates that after he had subdued the Albanians he returned to the Lesser Armenia; and since Dio says that in the winter of 66–65 he encamped in Anaitis, Théodore Reinach infers that the camp was in Acilisene, another name of Anaitis. Reinach also remarks that Aspis is otherwise unknown, but, as Dio's subsequent narrative shows, must have been in the Lesser Armenia. ... we may accept Reinach's view and conclude that Pompey spent the winter of 65–64 in that part of Acilisene which was on the right bank of the Euphrates." Gelzer (*Pompeius*, p. 103 and n. 104, *ibid.*) agrees with this; W. Fabricius (Theophanes v. Mitylene, 1888, p. 196) accordingly corrects Theophanes *apud* Dio Cassius, XXXVII, 7, 5. In spite of this, R. Dussaud *Topographie historique de la Syrie antique et médiévale*, Paris, 1927, p. 237, maintains that Aspis was in Syria, identifying it as '...à Afis, localité entre Sermin et Qinnesrin ... Cette ville, qualifiée de 'place admirablement défendue par l'art et par la nature,' semble avoir été choisie par Pompée pour y passer

l'hiver de 64–63." Marcus is also convinced that the place was in Syria.

33 Plutarch, *Pompey*, 38 2–3.

34 Cf. the description of Pompey's triumph: Plutarch, *Pompey*, 45; also Cicero, *Pro Sestio*, 67; *Pro Balbo*, 16. The passages are partly in Gelzer, *Pompeius*, p. 107, n. 137.

35 Cf. *ibid.*, p. 108, and the passages in n. 146.

36 *Ant.* XIV, 35–6. The name τερπωλή given to the work of art, as Marcus explains in his note on p. 466, is really parallel to the Hebrew expression עדן ('Eden). One should therefore not suppose it represented the Garden of Eden as described in the Bible, but that it was probably a work in the Alexandrian-Hellenistic style; cf. *König Herodes*, p. 8, n. 28. The quotation of Strabo *apud Antiquities* must, I think, continue up to the words τὸν Ἰουδαίων δυνάστην, as Reinach suggests. It is uncertain whether Schürer (*Geschichte*, I, p. 295, n. 12) agreed with him. If the words Ἀριστόβουλον μὲν οὖν τοῦτο λέγεται πέμψαι τὸν Ἰουδαίων δυνάστην were written by Josephus, then it would be impossible to understand λέγεται. Josephus had no doubt that Aristobulus gave the present, and quotes Strabo as proof. If we regard the words as Strabo's, the text becomes quite clear.

37 Nothing is mentioned before about gifts of money to Gabinius.

38 Cf. also Gelzer, *op. cit.*, p. 112.

39 *Ant.* XIV, 37–8.

40 On his way to Damascus, Pompey instituted reforms in several places; in Apamea he destroyed the fortress built by Antiochus Cyzicenus (*Ant.* XIV, 38); he destroyed the fortress Lysias (on the location of which cf. Strabo, XVI, 2, 10, p. 753), of Silas the Jew (*Ant.* XIV, 40); cf. Gelzer, *op. cit.*, p. 111; another Jewish ruler, Bacchius Judaeus, was also defeated; his name appears on a coin issued by the aedile, Aulus Plautius, in 54 B.C.E., depicting his surrender (cf. Schürer, *Geschichte*, I, p. 295, n. 14). Josephus mentions another ruler, Dionysius of Tripolis, who was executed (*Ant.* XIV, 39). S. Reinach (*Actes et conférences de la société des études juives*, 1887, p. CXCVI ff.: addendum to *REJ*, [1887]) believes Dionysius was none other

than Bacchius Judaeus, (q.v. Klebs, *RE*, vol. 2, pp. 2789). In contrast, Ptolemy the son of Mennaeus, who was the ruler of Heliopolis and the Lebanese Chalcis, had to appease Pompey with 1,000 talents (*Ant.* XIV, 39; cf. Strabo, XVI, 2, 10, p. 753). It will be noted that the sequence of events in *Antiquities* is confused: the delegation sent to Damascus in the spring of 63 B.C.E. (XIV, 34) is mentioned before the first delegation to Pompey in the winter of 64/63 at Antioch (or perhaps another place; cf. *supra*). It was this last-mentioned delegation which presented the golden bower to Pompey. Schürer, *Geschichte*, I, p. 296, n. 15, follows Niese (in *Hermes*, 11 (1876), p. 471) in maintaining that it was given to him at Damascus, i.e. in the spring of 63 B.C.E.; cf. Marcus' note to *Ant.* XIV, 34.

41   *Ant.* XIV, 41. Concerning the meaning of the alternative form of government, see A. Schalit, *Hellenistic Age*, Jerusalem, 1972, pp. 288 ff.

42   *Ant.* XIV, 42. Marcus is convinced that Idumaea remained under the control of Antipater and Hyrcanus. If this is true then one must conclude either that Scaurus' lieutenants did not carry out their task completely, or that Antipater managed to wrest Idumaea from Aristobulus after Scaurus' return to Syria.

43   On Pompey's Hellenizing policy in the East, cf. Gelzer, *op. cit.*, p. 84.

44   According to Diodorus, XL, 2, Pompey rebuked Hyrcanus for all his misdemeanors against the Romans. R. Laqueur *Der jüdische Historiker Fl. Josephus*, Giessen, 1920, p. 149 suggests that the source used by Josephus in the piracy charge against Aristobulus actually referred to Hyrcanus; this is attested too by Diodorus; *Ant.* XIV, 43.

45   *Ant.* XIV, 43; *War* I, 131.

46   *Ant.* XIV, 44. From here one may conclude that Jannaeus Alexander and not Judah Aristobulus was the first Hasmonean king; for a discussion of the whole question see *Hellenistic Age*, pp. 223 f., 226. See *König Herodes*, p. 743 f., Appendix II.

47   *Ant.* XIV, 45.

48   *Ant.* XIV, 46. Josephus' words: Πομπήιος

δὲ τούτων ἀκούσας καὶ καταγνοὺς ᾽Αριστοβούλου βίαν...

49   *Ibid.*, ... θεραπεύων ἅμα τὸν ᾽Αριστόβουλου According to Josephus (*ibid.*), Pompey intended by this action to prevent Aristobulus from blocking the roads to Palestine against the Romans.

50   *War* I, 132: ἀδοξήσας δὲ πρὸς τὰς θεραπείας καὶ μὴ φέρων δουλεύειν ταῖς χρείαις ταπεινότερον τοῦ σχήματος...

51   *Ant.* XIV, 47; *War* I, 132. The latter version has Διοσπόλεως and also Δίον ἡλίου πόλεως. Most scholars identify the place with Tell el-Ash'ari, east of the Sea of Galilee; cf. *ZDPV*, 20 (1897), p. 167; Schürer, *Geschichte*, p. 177 VII, n. 345; F. M. Abel, *Géographie de la Palestine*, II, Paris, 1938, p. 306 f.

52   *Ant.* XIV, 48-9; *War* I, 133-4. Pompey marched by way of Pella-Scythopolis-Coreae (Κορέαι). The latter was a border settlement of Judea. On its location, see Gildemeister, *ZDPV*, 4 (1881), p. 245 f.; it is in the vicinity of the Arab village of Qarawa near Wadi Fari'a in the Jordan Valley, two hours' walk north from Mt. Sartaba. Scholars identify Coreae with Tell Mazar, three miles northwest of where the Jabbok flows into the Jordan and the same distance northeast of Alexandrium (cf. Abel, *op. cit.*, II, p. 301); Moulton, *BASOR*, 62 (April 1936), p. 14; Avi-Yonah, *The Holy Land*, p. 15).

53   *Ant.* XIV, 49-51; *War* I, 134-36.

54   *Ant.* XIV, 152-73; *War* I, 137-153. According to Dio Cassius XXXVII, 16 the Temple's treasures were plundered, cf. *König Herodes*, p. 678 f. Regarding the exact dating of the conquest, see Schürer, *Geschichte*, I, p. 288, n. 23; Herzfeld (*MGWJ*, 4 [1855], p. 109 ff.) has pointed out that Josephus was deceived by non-Jewish sources, who always referred to the Sabbath as a "fast day," leading him to conclude that the city was taken on the Day of Atonement. This is confirmed by Strabo, XVI, p. 763, who was aware that the conquest took place on a Saturday (Chronos' day); it was the end of the summer. But see now Schalit, *König Herodes*, p. 764 ff.; appendix IX.

55   *Ant.* XIV, 73; *War* I, 153.

56 *Ant.* XIV, 74–6; *War* I, 155–6. The list, as Schürer shows (*op. cit.*, I, p. 299, n. 25; II, p. 102), is not complete; cf. also Schalit, *Roman Administration in Palestine* (Hebrew), Jerusalem, 1937, p. 4 and notes 3–11. His criterion for determining whether a particular city in the Hasmonean state had won freedom under Pompey was if its chronology was reckoned from the year of Pompey or Gabinius (63 or 57 B.C.E.). In fact, we do find this chronological system in use among various cities previously held by the Hasmoneans but not mentioned by Josephus as having been taken from them: e.g., Raphia, Gerasa (cf. Schürer, *Geschichte*, II, pp. 109, 179 f.). Abila should also be mentioned, as it too was liberated from the Hasmoneans (*ibid.*, p. 163). Josephus mentions that Gadara was rebuilt by Pompey to please his *libertus*, Demetrius, and also that the latter furnished the general with loans for his eastern war and hoarded up a huge fortune (cf. the charming story in Plutarch, *Cato Minor*, 13; *Pompey*, 40, 1–3). Demetrius was widely thought to be richer than his master, Pompey (Seneca, *De tranquillitate animi*, 8, 6; Plutarch, *Pompey*, 40, 5; cf. also the story in Dio Cassius, XXXIX, 38, 6 of the rumors that Demetrius provided the money for Pompey to build his theater in the Campus Martius in Rome, near the Circus Flaminius). With regard to the location of Arethusa, the order of Josephus' list would place it near Jamnia and Azotus (as Marcus claims); Avi-Yonah, *The Holy Land*, pp. 80, 87, 145 locates it at Aphek-Pegae; Klein (*BJPES*, 3 [1935–6], 109 ff.) near the modern village of 'Artas, in the vicinity of Solomon's Pools between Jerusalem and Hebron. On the changes made by Pompey in the southern part of Syria, cf. T. Marquardt, *Römische Staatsverwaltung* (3rd ed.) I, Darmstadt, 1957, pp. 405 ff.; E. Kuhn, *Die städtische und bürgerliche Verfassung des römischen Reichs*, II, Leipzig, 1864, p. 178.

57 *Ant.* XIV, 76; *War* I, 157.

58 *Ant.* XIV, 74: καὶ τὰ μὲν Ἱεροσόλυμα ὑποτελῆ φορου Ῥωμαίοις ἐποίησεν; *War* I, 154: τῇ τε χώρᾳ καὶ τοῖς Ἱροσολύμοις ἐπιτάσσει φόρον. On the details of the legal status of this, see: Schalit, *op. cit.*, (n. 56), p. 59 ff.; Marquardt, *op. cit.*, I³, 405 ff.

59 Cf. Pompey's division of the country for the purposes of tax-gathering and the former Jewish administrative division dating from Hasmonean times (see Schalit, *op. cit.* (n. 56), p. 19 ff.; *König Herodes*, p. 14 f.; 196 ff.).

60 Cf. *Ant.* XX, 244: Πομπήιος ... τῷ δ' Ὑρκανῷ πάλιν τὴν ἀρχιερωσύνην ἀποδοὺς τὴν μὲν τοῦ ἔθνους προστασίαν ἐπέτρεψεν, διάδημα δὲ φορεῖν ἐκώλυσεν. Antipater supervised the tax-gathering for Hyrcanus, though the special title for this (ἐπίτροπος) was only later given him by Gabinius (cf. *infra*).

61 Such cases were called αὐτονομία in the Hellenistic East. Cicero used both expressions to describe his work in Cilicia. Cf. *Ad Atticum*, VI, 2, 4: *Laetari te nostra moderatione et continentia video. Tum id magis faceres si adesses. Atque hoc foro quod egi ex Idibus Februariis Laodiceae ad Kalendas Maias ommnium dioecesium praeter Ciliciae mirabilia quaedam effecimus. Ita multae civitates omni aere alieno liberatae, multae valde levatae sunt, omnes suis legibus et iudiciis usae* αὐτονομίαν *adeptae revixerunt.*

62 Sextus Caesar, for example, intervened in the case against Herod for the murder in his youth of Hezekiah the Galilean and his followers. Hyrcanus neatly twisted the law at the Syrian legate's request (*Ant.* XIV, 170; *War* I, 211).

63 *Ant.* XIV, 77–8.

64 *Ibid.*, XIII, 407; XIV, 13. Hyrcanus did not believe Antipater's provocative words: Φύσει χρηστὸς ὢν καὶ διαβολὴν δι᾽ ἐπιείκειαν οὐ προσιέμενος ῥαδίως. Josephus adds: ἐποίει δ᾽αὐτὸν τὸ ἄπραγμον καὶ τὸ παρειμένον τῆς διανοίας τοῖς ὁρῶσιν ἀγεννῆ καὶ ἄνανδρον δοκεῖν; compare XIV, 44, where Aristobulus explains to Pompey how Hyrcanus lost his power: ὁ δὲ τοῦ μὲν ἐκπεσεῖν αὐτὸν τῆς ἀρχῆς τὴν ἐκείνου φύσιν ᾐτιᾶτο ἄπρακτον οὖσαν καὶ διὰ τοῦτ᾽ εὐκαταφρόνητον. In *War* (I, 109), Josephus states that Hyrcanus was appointed High Priest because he was the first-born: καὶ ἄλλως ὄντα νωθέστερον ἢ ὥστε ἐνοχλεῖν περὶ τῶν ὅλων cf. *War* I, 120.

65 p. 134 ff.

66 *Ant.* XIV, 13; cf. *ibid.*, XIII, 407; XIV, 43, 46.

67 Cf. especially *Ant.* XIII, 411–8, where we learn of the connection between

Aristobulus and his band of Sadducee nobles.

68 Aristobulus forgot how in Queen Salome Alexandra's days Hasmonean independence was preserved probably because Tigranes had been driven out of Syria and the danger to the Hasmonean dynasty thereby removed.

69 That the relations between the Jews in Palestine and the Roman conquerors could have been more friendly from the beginning is proved by the friendly attitude of Julius Caesar to Aristobulus. Josephus relates that Caesar gave orders in 49 B.C.E. for two legions to be handed over to Aristobulus to enable him to conquer Judea and Syria for him; he himself was then busy preparing an army against Pompey. Nothing came of this, however, as Aristobulus was poisoned by supporters of Pompey who had remained in Rome even after Caesar took the city: *Ant.* XIV, 123–4; *War* I, 183–4.

70 I refer to this in my book *König Herodes*, p. 16ff.

71 On Scaurus' position under Pompey, see: *Ant.* XIV, 79–81; *War* I, 157–9. Of interest in connection with Scaurus' campaign against Aretas the Nabataean is a coin bearing the inscription: *Aretas, M. Scaur. Aed. cur., ex S. C.* (Eckhel, *Doctrina Num.* V, 131). Cf. the general article in *RE*, vol. 1, 588 f.; Schürer, *Geschichte*, I, p. 304.

72 Cf. Appian, *Syriaca*, 51; see Schürer, *Geschichte*, p. 304.

73 *RE*, vol. 4, p. 1389 f.; Schürer, *Geschichte*, I, p. 305.

74 Appian, *loc. cit.* (n. 72).

75 Cf. Schürer, *Geschichte*, I, p. 305 f. It seems that Gabinius' actions in Syria

were not too oppressive, since Cicero criticizes him for not permitting the Roman publicans to exploit the inhabitants of the province as they wished.

76 *Ant.* XIV, 82; *War*, I, 160. I have shown in *Roman Administration in Palestine*, p. 35 ff. that those Romans who lived in Jerusalem during the time of Gabinius were none other than the *conventus civium Romanorum*, i.e. Roman citizens, most of whom were *equites* engaged in trade and usury, or in freehold and tenant farming. These men were particularly numerous throughout the eastern provinces and became a plague in the country where they practiced usury and extortion on the inhabitants; it is sufficient to mention the role of the *negotiatores* of Asia Minor, who were massacred at the command of Mithradates Eupator. The presence of such men in Jerusalem clearly indicates the economic plight of Judea in the years immediately following the conquest (on the legal meaning of the *conventus* and its various types, see Kornemann *RE*, vol. 4, p. 1173 ff.; Schulten, "De conventibus civium Romanorum").

77 *Ant.* XIV, 83; *War* I, 161.

78 *Ant.* XIV, 84–8; *War* I, 162–6. The name Gabala (Γάβαλα) is uncertain. The variants Γάμαλα, Gadara (Lat.) also occur.

79 Cf. Livy, XLV, 29, 10: *Pronuntiavit deinde (sc. Paulus) neque conubium neque commercium agrorum aedificiorumque inter se placere cuiquam extra fines regionis suae esse . . .*; 32, 2: *pronuntiatum, quod ad statum Macedoniae pertinebat, senatores, quos synhedros vocant, legendos esse, quorum consilio res publica adminstraretur.*

80 *Ant.* XIV, 91.

CHAPTER II

TH END OF THE HASMONEAN DYNASTY
AND THE RISE OF HEROD

[1] A Christian tradition (cf. Justin Martyr, *Dialogus cum Tryphone Judaeo*, 52; Eusebius, *Historia eccles.* I, 7, 11; cf. I, 6, 2–3; Syncellus, ed. Dindorf, I, p. 561), connects Antipater's family with Ascalon. According to Africanus, his father was a slave in the temple of Apollo at Ascalon. While still a child, he was taken prisoner in an assault on the temple by the Idumaeans, and grew up among them. This tradition is recorded by other Christian writers as well. However, it seems likely that Josephus is correct in stating that Antipater was born into a rich and noble Idumaean family (*Ant.* XIV, 8; 10; *War* I, 123). He also states that even in the days of Jannaeus Alexander and Salome Alexandra, this family was extremely powerful among the Idumaeans, since Antipater had been a friend of Hyrcanus and had been appointed governor of Idumaea (*Ant., ibid.*, 10). Cf. also: Schürer, *Geschichte*, I, p. 292, n. 3; W. Otto, *Herodes, Beiträge zur Gesch. des letzten jüdischen Königshauses*, Stuttgart, 1913, p. 1.

[2] *Ant.* XIV. 92, 96–7, 122; *War* I, 171–4.

[3] On Gabinius' march to Egypt, cf. Dio Cassius, XXXIX, 56–8; Cicero, *In Pisonem* 49; Plutarch, *Antony*, 3; Appian *Syriaca*, 51; *Ant.* XIV, 98; *War* I, 175. On Antipater's assistance to Gabinius' army, see: *Ant.* XIV, 99; *War* I, 175; On Alexander's rebellion, see: *Ant.* XIV 100–2; *War* I, 176–7. On Gabinius' recall from Syria, see E. Meyer, *Cäsars Monarchie und das Prinzipat der Pompeius*, Gotha, 1920, pp. 165 ff., 202 ff.

[4] Cf. H. Willrich, *Das Haus des Herodes zwischen Jerusalem und Rom*, Heidelberg, 1929, p. 21.

[5] On Crassus' election as proconsul of Syria see Dio Cassius, XXXIX, 33–6; Livy, *Epit.*, 105; Plutarch, *Pompey*, 52; *Crassus*, 15; Appian, *Bellum civile*, II, 18. On the pillaging of the Temple, see: *Ant.* XIV, 105–9; *War* I, 179.

[6] On Cassius' defense policy, cf.: Dio Cassius, XL, 28–9; Livy, *Epit.*, 108; Justin, XLII, 4, 5. Cicero, *Epist. ad Atticum*, V, 20, 3; *Epist. ad familiares*, II, 10, 2; *Philippics*, XI, 14; *Ant.* XIV, 119. The reference to Antipater's advice on removing Peitholaus is plausible, since the latter was undoubtedly one of those who disturbed Antipater's plan for pacifying Judea and bringing a lasting peace. The title "Keeper of the Jews' Exchequer" (ὁ τῶν Ἰουδαίων ἐπιμελητής) is mentioned in Strabo (the fragment is preserved in *Ant.* XIV, 139; here: ὁ τῆς Ἰουδαίας ἐπιμελητής), as well as by Josephus (*Ant.* XIV, 127). Presumably, it was Gabinius who granted the title to Antipater (on the relationship between the two men, see: *Ant.* XIV, 103; *War* I, 178). Ἐπιμελητής is but an equivalent of ἐπίτροπος, i.e. the Latin *procurator*, an official who dealt mainly with financial matters. No doubt the Roman administration made him responsible for levying the taxes imposed on the Jews. However, Antipater was also greatly concerned with the preservation of peace in the country (cf. *Ant.* XIV, 156–7).

[7] *Ant.* XIV, 123–5; *War* I, 183–5. See also Dio Cassius, XLI, 18. The murderer of Alexander was under the instructions of Pompey; he was the father-in-law of the general, Quintus Metellus Scipio, proconsul of Syria at the time (49–48). On the invitation to the surviving children of Aristobulus, see *Ant.* XIV, 126 and *War* I, 185–6. The same passage mentions the marriage of one of Aristobulus' daughters to the son of Ptolemy Mennaeus; however, the old king killed his son, and himself married the beautiful Hasmonean.

[8] The death of Pompey is hinted at in the Psalms of Solomon, 2:30–36. The Pharisee author of the work sees in the violent death of Pompey the hand of the Lord, since the general had dared to desecrate the Holy of Holies. For him it is an overwhelming proof that God is "a great and righteous king, who judges (all) that is under heaven" and casts down the proud who do not

recognize him. On the war in Alexandria and Antipater's part in it, see: *De bello Alexandrino*, 26 ff.; *Ant.* XIV, 128–36; *War* I, 187–93. On the rejection of Antigonus' claim to his father's throne and Hyrcanus' appointment as High Priest and Ethnarch, see: *Ant.* XIV, 140–143; cf. 194, 199; *War* I, 195–199. On the return of Jaffa, the Jezreel Valley towns and the lands of the kings of Phoenicia, see *Ant.* XIV, 202–7, 209 (cf. Schalit, *König Herodes*, p. 753 ff.). Josephus does not specify the extent of these transferred lands, but probably refers to the private property of the Seleucid kings in Palestine which the Hasmoneans had formerly made their own. With the disintegration of their state, these lands were confiscated by Pompey as Roman property (*ager publicus populi Romani*). When Caesar now presumably awarded them to Hyrcanus, he was giving him back his ancestral inheritance. On the civil rights of the Jews of Alexandria, Josephus mentions them as being conferred by Julius Caesar: *Ant.* XIV, 188; *Against Apion*, II, 37. In the first source, Caesar is said to have expressly set forth on bronze tablets that the Jews were Alexandrians. Cf. *ibid*; 188: ... οὐ μὴν ἀλλὰ καὶ Καῖσαρ Ἰούλιος τοῖς ἐν Ἀλεξανδρείᾳ Ἰουδαίοις ποιήσας χαλκῆν στήλην ἐδήλωσεν, ὅτι Ἀλεξανδρέων πολῖταί εἰσιν...; in c. Ap. II, § 37 we read: ... καὶ τὴν στήλην τὴν εστῶσαν ἐν Ἀλεξανδρείᾳ καὶ τὰ δικαιώματα περιέχουσαν, ὁ Καῖσαρ ὁ μέγας τοῖς Ἰουδαίοις ἔδωκεν ... Doubt is cast on the truth of Josephus' claims by the famous letter of Claudius Caesar (on this subject, see H. I. Bell, *Jews and Christians in Egypt*, Oxford, 1924, p. 14 ff.). On the rights of the Jews of the Diaspora, cf.: Schürer, *Geschichte*, III, p. 97 ff.; J. Juster, *Les Juifs dans l'empire romain*, I–II, Paris, 1914. This is the source of the suggestion that Caesar made the High Priest supreme arbiter in the internal affairs of the Diaspora Jews, since it had been the tradition in the Diaspora that important cases were decided by the High Priest. On the relationship between the Diaspora communities and the High Priest, we learn from the Elephantine papyri (fifth century B.C.E. *et seq.*). I Macc. 15, 22 f. sheds light on this relationship in the second century B.C.E. It is quite probable that Hyrcanus brought this tradition to Caesar's notice and had it ratified by law. On the personal rights of Antipater and his appointment as *epitropos* of Judea, see: *Ant.* XIV, 137; *War* I, 199.

9 With regard to the position of the Hasmoneans in Galilee, one should remember that Jannaeus Alexander was educated there, according to a reliable historical source (*Ant.* XIII, 322), although Schürer doubts it (*Geschichte*, I, p. 276 n. 10). The Galileans apparently felt a warm affection for their hero king. We hear of no resistance on their part to Jannaeus' home or foreign policy. Antigonus seems also to have derived a large part of his forces from the Galilee. His father Aristobulus apparently enjoyed good relations with the Galileans, although we have no explicit evidence of this. One should note that the decisive battle which broke the backbone of the rebellion of Alexander, the son of Aristobulus, took place near Mt. Tabor (*Ant.* XIV, 102; *War* I, 177). Hence one may conclude that some of his forces came from the Jezreel Valley and Galilee. Josephus mentions the appointment of Phasael and Herod in *Ant.* XIV, 158 (cf. *War* I, 203). On the execution of the "brigands" at Herod's command, see: *Ant.* XIV, 159–67; *War* I, 204–9. The term "brigands" in Josephus refers to those who resisted Roman rule in Judea. He uses the terminology of his non-Jewish sources, who regarded the rebels as robbers of the peaceful inhabitants; thus *Ant.* XVII, 271 (= *War*, II, 56); XX, 5; *Life*, 105; *War* II, 253, 275, *et passim*. On the Sanhedrin's right to try cases of capital punishment, cf.: Juster, *op. cit.*, II, p. 127 ff.; Schürer, *Geschichte*, II, p. 260 ff. On the legislation of Gabinius, see A. Schalit, *Roman Administration in Palestine* (Hebrew), Jerusalem, 1937, pp. 36, 60–1; cf. *supra* on the reforms of Julius Caesar in Judea. See *Ant.* XIV, 165 on the attitude of Hyrcanus' courtiers to Herod's actions, where the courtiers say to Hyrcanus: ἢ οὐχ ὁρᾷς Ἀντίπατρον μὲν καὶ τοὺς παῖδας αὐτοῦ τὴν ἀρχὴν διεζωσμένους, σαυτὸν μέντοι τῆς βασιλείας ὄνομα μόνον ἀκούοντα; On Antipater's caution and Hyrcanus' behavior (as well as

Sextus Caesar's warning), cf.: *Ant.* XIV,
168–9; *War* I, 210; *Ant.* XIV, 170; *War* I,
211. On how the trial was conducted, see
Ant. XIV, 171–9. There is no doubt that
Sameas was none other than Shammai the
Elder. For more details of whose activities
see the following chapter. A parallel
account of this story is found in the Baby-
lonian Talmud, Sanhedrin, 19 ab. According to this source the event concerned
Jannaeus and Simeon ben Sheṭaḥ. There
are no grounds for concurring with the
opinion already expressed by J. Derenbourg
*Essai sur l'histoire et la géographie de la
Palestine*, I, Paris, 1867, p. 146 ff., that the
Talmudic account actually did refer to
Herod and Shammai, but that their names
were disguised in the usual manner of the
Aggada; cf. Klausner, *History of the Second
Temple* (Hebrew), (2nd ed.) III, Jerusalem,
1951, p. 174 *et seq*. On the appointment of
Herod as *strategos* in Coele Syria in return
for a bribe, cf. *Ant.* XIV, 180; but also cf.
War I, 213.

10 We learn of Julius Caesar's war in
Africa principally from the *Bellum Africanum*
(anon.); cf. Rice Holmes, *The Roman Republic*,
III, Oxford, 1923, p. 236, ff. Veith-
Kromayer, *Antike Schlachtfelder* III/2, Berlin,
1912, p. 761 ff.; Dio Cassius, XLVII,
26–7; Appian, *Bellum civile*, III, 77; IV, 58.
On the fighting at Apamea and Antipater's
part in it, see: *Ant.* XIV, 268–9; *War*
I, 216–7; Appian, *loc. cit.;* Dio Cassius,
XLVII, 27; Strabo, XVI, p. 752. On the
turn of events at Apamea, when Cassius
arrived following the dictator's assassination, see: *Ant.* XIV 272; *War* I, 218–9; Dio
Cassius, XLVII, 28; Appian, *Bellum civile*,
III, 78; IV, 59; Cicero, *Philippics*, XI, 4,
30; *Ad Brutum*, III, 3; *Ad familiares*, XII, 11;
12. For a description of the harsh rule of
Cassius in Judea, see: *Ant.* XIV, 272, 275;
War I, 219–20; 222. On the part played
by the Idumaeans in increasing the hardship
of the people, see: *Ant.* XIV, 273–4; *War*
I, 220–1. On the appointment of Herod
as *strategos* of the Syrian army, cf.: *Ant.*
XIV, 280; *War* I, 225 (ἐπιμελητής). In these
passages, Josephus mentions the rumor of
Cassius' promise to Herod. On Malichus,
cf.: *Ant.* XIV, 84; *War* I, 162; on his

relations with Antipater: *Ant.* XIV, 273.
The subversion of Malichus in the matter
of the taxes may be deduced from the fact
that Cassius was angry with him and
wished to kill him, and that Hyrcanus paid
a ransom for his life, viz. the quota imposed
on him by Cassius. Josephus does not
explicitly state that Malichus had disobeyed
orders. Antipater's appeal to his Arab
friends for help against Malichus is mentioned in *Ant.* XIV, 277, and the circumstances
of Antipater's death in *Ant.* XIV, 281 and
War I, 226.

11 *Ant.* XIV, 281 tells us of the state of
readiness of Malichus and his men following Antipater's death. In a later passage
(282) we read that Malichus denied his
guilt (cf. *War* I, 227, where Josephus
states that the people were angry and
Malichus appeased it by his denial). The
story, however, does not seem reliable;
Josephus may have obtained his sources
from Antipater's family. It is also possible
that "the people" who were angry were
Antipater's followers. On the retaliation of
the Idumaean brothers for the murder of
their father, see: *Ant.* XIV, 283–4; *War* I,
227. On the disturbances in Samaria, cf.
Ant., XIV, 284; *War*, I, 229. On Herod's
march on Jerusalem, see: *Ant.* XIV, 285–6;
War, I, 229. Concerning Malichus' death,
cf.: *Ant.* XIV, 288–93; *War* I, 230–5. On
the insurrection in Jerusalem: *Ant.* XIV,
294–6; *War* I, 236–7. On Antigonus' attempted conquest on Galilee and his
retreat, cf.: *Ant.* XIV, 297–9; *War* I,
239–40.

12 On the betrothal of Mariamne and
Herod, cf. *Ant.* XIV, 300; *War* I, 240–1.
Among those who have interpreted the
betrothal as a political arrangement, we
may mention: W. Otto, *Herodes, Beiträge
zur Geschichte des letzten jüdischen Königshauses*, Stuttgart, 1913, pp. 23.

13 On the battle of Philippi, cf.: Dio
Cassius, XLVII, 42–9; Appian, *Bellum
civile*, IV, 105–31; *Ant.* XIV, 301; *War* I,
242. See also the discussion in Veith-
Kromayer, *op. cit.* (n. 10 above) IV, p.
654 ff. On the delegation to Antony and
the latter's decision in favor of the Idumaeans, cf.: *Ant.* XIV, 301–3; *War* I, 242.

On Hyrcanus' request to Antony, see *Ant.*
XIV, 304; Antony's reply is found in
ibid., 306–13. Antony's letter to the inhabitants of Tyre regarding the return of
the Galilean territories: *ibid.*, 314–8; on
the return of the captives: *ibid.*, 319–22;
his letters to the Sidonians, Antiochians
and Aradians: *ibid.*, 323. On the privileges
of the Jews granted by Dolabella: *ibid.*,
225–7. On the second delegation and the
negotiations at Daphne: *ibid.*, 324–6; *War*
I, 243–4. On the appointment of the
brothers as Tetrarchs: *Ant.* XIV, 326; *War*
I, 244. On the third delegation and the fate
of its members, and the prisoners from the
second one: *Ant.* XIV, 327–9; *War* I,
245–7.

14   On Antony's extortions in Asia Minor,
we are principally informed by Appian,
Bellum civile, V, 4–6; 75; see also Dio
Cassius, XLVIII, 24; cf. also the discussion
by Broughton in T. Frank, *An Economic
Survey of Ancient Rome* IV, Baltimore,
1933, p. 585 ff.; D. Magie, *Roman Rule in
Asia Minor*, I, Princeton, 1950, p. 427 ff.
and II 1278, n. 1. Antony's extravagant
living consumed vast sums of money which
the provinces were expected to supply (for
a fuller description see Plutarch's *Antony*,
56 f.). Typical too, is the story of the orator
Cestius Pius (Seneca, *Suasor*, I, 6) concerning Antony's stay in Athens (winter of
39/38 B.C.E.). The Athenians had been
very obsequious to Antony, suggesting
that "the new Dionysus" (Νέος Διόνυσος), as
he had been called, should marry Athene.
Antony thereupon demanded a dowry of
1,000 talents. Their claims that even Semele
(Σεμέλη), the mother of Dionysus, had
married Zeus without money, were to no
avail, and they were forced to pay the full
sum; cf. Schalit, *König Herodes*, p. 73, n. 66.
On the legation of Quintus Labienus to the
Parthians, cf.: Dio Cassius, XLVIII, 24, 5;
Justin XLII, 4, 7; Plutarch, *Antony*, 28, 1.
Labienus called himself "Labienus Parthi-
cus imperator" on the obverse of a coin he
struck (Grueber, *Coins of the Roman Republic
in the British Museum* II, London, 1910,
p. 500; cf. Dio Cassius, XLVIII, 26, 5;
Strabo, XIV, p. 660). An expression of
Eastern hatred for the Occident is found in

the "prophecies" of the eastern Sibylline
Oracles. On this see: A. Peretti, *La
Sibilla babilonesse nella propaganda ellenistica*,
Firenze, 1943; H. Fuchs, *Der geistige
Widerstand gegen Rom*, Berlin, 1964. On the
downfall and death of Lucius Decidius
Saxa, see Dio Cassius, XLVIII, 25, 3–4
On the war of Labienus in Asia Minor and
the suffering and destruction it caused, see:
Dio Cassius, XLVIII, 26, 3–4; Appian,
Bellum civile, V. 65. Epigraphic evidence is
of supplementary importance, cf.: Magie,
op. cit., II, p. 1280 f. n. 10. M. Rostovtzeff,
*The Social and Economic History of the Hel-
lenistic World*, Oxford, 1941, p. 1012, n.
125. On the agreement between Antigonus
and the Parthians, the march on Jerusalem,
and the initial battles with the Idumaeans,
cf.: *Ant.* XIV, 330–9; *War* I, 248–53.
On Phasael's decision to negotiate with the
Parthian commander: *Ant.* XIV, 340–1;
War I, 254–5. On the journey of Phasael and
Hyrcanus and their fate: *Ant.* XIV, 342–
8, 365–9; *ibid.*, XV, 12–13; *War* I, 256–60;
269–72. On Herod's flight: *Ant.* XIV,
352–8; *War* I, 263–7.

15   On Herod and Malichus the Nabataean,
see: *Ant.* XIV 370–5; *War* I, 274–8. Herod
in Egypt and his relationship with Cleopatra: *Ant.* XIV, 375–6; *War*, I, 278–9.
His journey to Italy and the negotiations
with Antony: *Ant.* XIV, 386–7. The
ceremony on the Capitol and Herod's
departure for Judea: *ibid.*, 388–9; *War* I,
285. For the debate in the Senate, and its
decision to grant Herod the kingdom, see:
Ant. XIV, 384–5; *War* I, 284.

16   On the siege of Masada by Antigonus:
Ant. XIV, 390–1; *War* I, 286–7. On the
defeat of Labienus: Dio Cassius, XLVIII,
39–40; Plutarch, *Antony*, 33, see also the
discussions on the subject in: Rice Holmes,
The Architect of the Roman Empire, Oxford,
1928, p. 121; Magie, *op, cit.*, I, p. 431 f.
Ventidius in Syria and Judea: *Ant.* XIV,
392–3; *War* I, 288–9; Silo in place of
Ventidius in Judea; *Ant.* XIV, 393; *War* I,
289; Dio Cassius, XLVIII, 41. Herod
reached Ptolemais about two weeks before
the end of the winter of 39/38 B.C.E. He
thus left for Rome at a time when the winds
were fiercest; his stay at Rome was very

short (*Ant.* XIV, 376, 387). On Herod's unsuccessful march against Galilee, his retreat and invasion of Idumaea by way of the coastal plain: *ibid.*, 394–8; *War* I, 290–4. The attempt to seize Jerusalem: *Ant.* XIV, 400–5; *War* I, 294–6. Antigonus' attempt to appease the Romans: *Ant.* XIV, 409–12; *War* I, 300–2 — Josephus describes only Antigonus' efforts to harass Herod's men and to supply food for the Romans. The battles with the Galileans and the conquest of Sepphoris: *Ant.* XIV, 413–9; *War* I, 303–8. Clearing out the "brigands" of Galilee: *Ant.* XIV, 421–33; *War* I, 309–16. On Ventidius' victory over the Parthians: Dio Cassius, XLVIII, 39–41; Plutarch, *Antony*, 34; Justin, XLII, 4, 8–10 (see Rice Holmes, *op. cit.*, p. 121). Herod's journey to Samosata: *Ant.* XIV, 438–47; *War* I, 321–7. The defeat and death of Herod's brother, Joseph: *Ant.* XIV, 448–50; *War* I, 323–5. The events outside Jericho and the defeat of Pappus at Isana (Jeshanah): *Ant.* XIV, 451–64; *War* I, 331–41. The conquest of Jerusalem by Herod: *Ant.* XIV, 465–91; *War* I, 343–57.

CHAPTER III

THE REIGN OF HEROD

1 On Antony's policy in the East in those years, see: J. Raillard, *Die Anordnungen des M. Antonius im Orient* (Diss.), Zürich, 1894; L. Craven, *Antony's Oriental Policy until the Defeat of the Parthian Expedition*, Univ. of Missouri Studies, 3 (1920), no. 2; R. Syme, *The Roman Revolution*, Oxford, 1939, pp. 259–75; H. Buchheim, *Die Orientpolitik des Triumvirn M. Antonius*, Heidelberg, 1960.

2 Antony himself negotiated with them prior to his expedition aganist the Parthians in 36 B.C.E. (Plutarch, *Life of Antony*, 37; Dio Cassius, XLIX, 24, 5).

3 The doubts expressed by H. Willrich, *Das Haus des Herodes zwischen Jerusalem und Rom*, Heidelberg, 1929, p. 52, concerning the reliability of the charge of Herod's responsibility for the murder, derive from his desire to exonerate Herod.

4 The question of the chronology of Antony's gifts to Cleopatra is a point of controversy among the scholars, arising from the apparent discrepancy between Plutarch, *Life of Antony*, 36, 3, and Dio Cassius, XLIX, 32, 5 (36 B.C.E.) and what transpires from Josephus (34 B.C.E.). It seems to me that Antony's territorial gifts with regard to Palestine were presented to Cleopatra in two stages. In the first stage (36 B.C.E.) Jericho was taken from Herod, while the coastal towns (Joppa and Gaza) were cut off from his kingdom only in 34 B.C.E. Of the numerous discussions on the subject cf. J. Kromayer, *Hermes*, 29 (1894), pp. 571–85; J. Dobiáš, *Annuaire de l'institut de philologie et d'histoire orientales et slaves*, 2 (1934), pp. 287–314; Buchheim, *op. cit.*, pp. 68–74.

5 On Octavian's relations with the kings of the Roman eastern empire, cf. D. Magie, *Roman Rule in Asia Minor*, I, Princeton, 1950, pp. 440–5; G. W. Bowersock, *Augustus and the Greek World*, Oxford, 1965, pp. 42–61.

6 This, for example, is the opinion of Bowersock, *op. cit.*, p. 57, but there is no solid evidence to support it.

7 On Zenodorus' lands see: Schürer, *Geschichte*, I, pp. 714–6; A. H. M. Jones, *The Cities of the Eastern Roman Provinces* 1971, Oxford, pp. 269–270.

8 For Augustus' other arrangements during his sojourn in the East, cf. Dio Cassius, LIV, 9, 2.

9 Dio Cassius LIII, 25, 1 regarding Polemon, who belonged to Herod's generation and class. On Herod's legal and political status, cf. A. Schalit, *King Herod* Hebrew, Jerusalem, 1960, pp. 85–94; Schürer, *Geschichte*, I, pp. 401–4; P. C. Sands, *The Client Princes of the Roman Empire under the Republic*, Cambridge, 1908, pp. 226–8; W. Otto, *Herodes*, Stuttgart, 1913, pp. 57–9; E. Bammel, *ZDPV*, 84 (1968), pp. 73–9.

10 Cf. *IG*, II² no. 3441. See also B. D. Meritt, *Hesperia*, 21 (1952), p. 370. In this connection also *SEG*, XII, no. 150. See also *IEJ*, 20 (1970), pp. 97–8, a stone weight discovered a short time ago.

11 Cf. P. Herrmann, *Der römische Kaisereid*, Göttingen, 1968, pp. 90–9, and especially pp. 98–9.

12 Cf. Dio Cassius, LIV, 8, 1–3, Monumentum Ancyranum, 29. See also J. G. C. Anderson, *CAH*, X, 1934, pp. 254–65; N. C. Debevoise, *A Political History of Parthia*, Chicago, 1938, pp. 136–42; K. H. Ziegler, *Die Beziehungen zwischen Rom und dem Partherreich*, Wiesbaden, 1964, pp. 45–57.

13 Cf. also Pliny, *Natural Histori*, VI, 160–1; Dio Cassius, LIII, 29, 3–7; A. Kammerer, *Pétra et la Nabatène*, Paris, 1929, pp. 196–206; Anderson, *op. cit.*, pp. 247–54. Shelagh Jameson, *JRS*, 58 (1968), pp. 76–8, gives the earlier date.

14 Cf. A. Momigliano, "Ricerche sull' organizzazione della Giudea sotto il dominio romano," *Annali della R. Scuola Normale Superiore di Pisa*, (Ser. II) 3 (1934), p. 43 (350). F. M. Abel, *Histoire de la Palestine*, I, Paris, 1952, p. 362, is still of the opinion that Herod was not required to pay taxes to Rome.

15 In a number of places in Josephus

reference is made to Herod's having been granted unlimited powers to leave his kingdom to his heirs in whatever way he saw fit. Cf. *Ant.* XV, 343; XVI, 92; 129; *War* I, 454; 458. On the other hand, it transpires that his decisions on this matter required Augustus' approval — cf. *Ant.* XVII, 53; *War* I, 573. We also note that after Herod's death Augustus did not fulfill the terms of Herod's will in their entirety, but introduced an important change in the status of his son Archelaus. One cannot accept the view of Otto, *op. cit.*, p. 66, that after a time Herod's power was curtailed, since this was a restriction affecting all the allied kings.

16   Herod executed his brother-in-law Aristobulus, Hyrcanus II and Mariamne without requesting permission from the Roman authorities. In the case of Aristobulus III, Herod was indeed summoned by Antony to explain his action, while Hyrcanus II was killed during the war between Antony and Octavian. Neither were strictly members of the ruling royal house. In Herod's approach to Augustus in connection with the misdeeds of his three sons, the latter's Roman citizenship should not be regarded as of significance, as is the claim of E. Täubler, *Klio*, 17 (1921), pp. 98–101. In this connection see also H. Volkmann, *Zur Rechtsprechung im Principat des Augustus*, Munich, 1935, pp. 159–61. Rome was approached not out of any legal obligation connected with Roman citizenship, but from purely political considerations relating to Herod, in that he was required to take into consideration matters which in Augustus' view would have their effect on the future of his kingdom.

17   On the Augustus cult cf. L. Cerfaux et J. Tondriau, *Le culte des souverains*, Tournai, 1957, pp. 313–39; K. Latte, *Römische Religionsgeschichte*, Munich, 1960, pp. 306–9.

18   On the date cf. M. Reinhold, *Marcus Agrippa*, Geneva, New York, 1933, p. 84, n. 47.

19   See also V. Gardthausen, *Augustus und seine Zeit*, I, 2, Leipzig, 1896, pp. 841–2; R. Daniel, *M. Vipsanius Agrippa* (Diss.), Breslau, 1933, pp. 31–3; R. Hanslik, *RE*, pp. 1262–3, *s.v.* Vipsanius.

20   On Anthedon cf. M. Avi-Yonah, *The Holy Land from the Persian to the Arab conquests* (536 B.C. to A.D. 640) (transl. from the Hebrew), Michigan, 1966, p. 100; Abel, *Géographie*, II, pp. 244–5.

21   The majority of scholars tend to identify this Pollio with Asinius Pollio; cf. recently A. Momigliano, *CAH*, X, 1934, p. 327; L. H. Feldman, *Transactions of the American Philological Association*, 84 (1953), p. 79. On the other hand R. Syme, *JRS*, 51 (1961), p. 30, suggests that he be identified with Vedius Pollio, see also M. Grant, *Herod the Great*, London 1971, p. 145. Willrich, *op. cit.*, pp. 184–5, considers that the Pollio with whom Herod's sons stayed in Rome was a Jew. But it appears that the majority opinion is correct.

22   On governor Titius cf. R. Hanslik, *RE*, (2e Reihe), vol. 6, pp. 1559–62.

23   On Petronius cf. A. Stein, *Die Präfekten von Ägypten in der römischen Kaiserzeit*, Bern, 1950, pp. 17–18.

24   On Herod and Berytus see also *Académie des Inscriptions et Belles-Lettres, Comptes rendus*, 1927, pp. 243–4.

25   On Herod and Antioch cf. W. Weber in *Festgabe für* Adolf Deissmann, 1927, pp. 26–8; G. Downey, *A History of Antioch in Syria*, 1961, pp. 173–4.

26   On the connection between the emperor's family (Tiberius and after him Germanicus) and the Olympic games, cf. for example *SIG³*, nos. 782, 792.

27   On Eurycles' visit to Judea see also E. Kjellberg, *Klio*, 17 pp. 53–7. On his personality and family cf. K.M.T. Chrimes, *Ancient Sparta*, Manchester, 1949, pp. 169–204; G. W. Bowersock, *JRS*, 51 (1961), pp. 112–8.

28   Cf. Macrobius, *Saturnalia*, II, 4, 11. It may be presumed that Marcobius' remarks are based on a source dating to Augustus' times. Cf. G. Wissowa, *Hermes*, 16 (1881), p. 499.

29   On the two phases in the removal of Syllaeus, the last of which ended in his death, cf. Otto, *op. cit.*, p. 129, note; Volkmann, *op. cit.*, pp. 167–9.

30   On Herod's rule within his kingdom, cf. Schalit, *op. cit.*, pp. 85–239; M. Avi-Yonah, *The Holy Land*, 1966, pp. 94 ff.;

Otto, *op. cit.*, pp. 59–64; H. Bengtson, *Die Strategie in der hellenistischen Zeit*, II, Munich, 1944, pp. 265–70.

31 On the development of relations between the High Priesthood and the authorities at the end of the period of the Second Temple, cf. E. Bammel, *ZDPV*, 70 (1954), pp. 147–53; E. M. Smallwood, *JTS*, (n.s.) 13 (1962), pp. 14–34.

32 Cf. Momigliano, *op. cit.* (n. 14 above), p. 65 (372).

33 Cf. M. Stern, *The Documents on the History of the Hasmonean Revolt* (Hebrew), Tel Aviv, 1972, pp. 63–4; Bengtson, *op. cit.*, p. 267.

34 Cf. Avi-Yonah, *The Holy Land*, p. 153; Abel, *Géographie*, II, p. 251.

35 On Nicolaus cf. P. Jakob, *De Nicolai Damasceni sermone et arte historica quaestiones selectae* (Diss.), Göttingen, 1911; R. Laqueur, *RE*, vol. 17, pp. 362–424; B. Wacholder, *Nicolaus o Damascus*, Berkeley–Los Angeles, 1962; G. W. Bowersock, *Augustus and the Greek World*, Oxford, 1965, pp. 134–8. The remaining fragments of Nicolaus' historical writings (the *Universal History* and the *Autobiography*) are collected in F. Jacoby, *Die Fragmente der Griechischen Historiker*, Berlin, 1929, II A 90.).

36 The ties between Philostratus and the Judean monarchy in the time of Herod are reflected in a poem of the Crinagoras of Mitylene in *Anthologia Graeca*, VII, no. 645 — A.S.F. Gow and D. L. Page, *The Greek Anthology*, *The Garland of Philip*, I, Cambridge, 1968, no. XX, p. 210. See also C. Cichorius, *Römische Studien*, Leipzig-Berlin, 1922, pp. 314–8. The author of this work considers this Philostratus as also being the author of a special work on the Jews, an opinion worth consideration.

37 Cf. Y. Meshorer, *Jewish Coins of the Second Temple Period*, Tel Aviv, 1967, pp. 64–8.

38 On the site of Geba (el-Harithiya?), see B. Maisler, *HUCA*, 24 (1952/3), pp. 75–84.

39 On the royal estates and their development, see A. Alt, *Kleine Schriften*, II, Munich, 1953, pp. 389–91.

40 Cf. F. Oertel, *CAH*, X 1934, pp. 382–424.

41 Cf. S. Appelbaum, *Studies in the History of the Jewish People and the Land of Israel*, in Memory of Zwi Avineri (Hebrew), Haifa, 1970, pp. 79–88.

42 On the mines in Cyprus in the period of the Roman Empire, see Galen *Opera* (ed. by C. G. Kühn) vol. XII, pp. 226; 234; XIV, p. 7.

43 On Herod as a builder of theaters, cf. E. Frézouls, *Syria*, 36 (1959), pp. 210–2.

44 On excavations at Masada, cf. Y. Yadin, *IEJ*, 15 (1965), pp. 1–120; *id. Masada*, London, 1968.

45 On the excavations at Caesarea, cf. A. Frova *et alii*, *Scavi di Caesarea Maritima*. Milan, 1965.

46 On the excavations at Samaria, cf. G. A. Reisner, C. S. Fisher, D. G. Lyon, *Harvard Excavations at Samaria*, 1908–1910, I, 1924, pp. 170–80; J. W. Crowfoot, K. M. Kenyon, E. L. Sukenik, *Samaria-Sebaste I: The Buildings at Samaria*, London, 1942, pp. 31–5, 39–41, 123–9.

47 On Cypros see G. Harder, *ZDPV*, 78 (1962), pp. 49–54; on Phasaelis see *ibid.*, pp. 54–60.

48 It seems that this was Herod's last journey to Rome. Cf. L. Korach, *MGWJ*, 38 (1894), pp. 533–5; E. Schwartz, "Die Aeren von Gerasa und Eleutheropolis," *Nachrichten von der königlichen Gesellschaft der Wissenschaften zu Göttingen, Philologisch-historische Klasse*, 1906, p. 356, n. 2; Otto, *op. cit.*, p. 125, note; T. Corbishley, *JRS*, 24 (1934), p. 43. Josephus in *Antiquities* XVI, 271, 273, 276 refers to this journey and not any later one.

49 On similar cases in the history of the Roman empire, cf. F. Millar, *A Study of Cassius Dio*, Oxford, 1964, pp. 214–8.

50 See also E. Täubler, *Byzantinische Zeitschrift*, 25 (1925), pp. 33–6.

51 This was in keeping with the practice of the Greeks to ensure that a citizen should not serve as a slave in the town of his birth. Cf. *Dikaiomata*, herausgegeben von der Graeca Halensis, Berlin (1913), pp. 122–4. See also; A. Schalit, *King Herod* (Hebrew), 1960, pp. 125–30.

52 The arguments for setting the date of Herod's death in the spring of 4 B.C.E. are clearly set forth in Schürer, *Geschichte*, I,

p. 415, n. 167. W. E. Filmer, in JTS, 17 (1966), pp. 283–98, objects to the accepted method and proposes 1 B.C.E. as the year of Herod's death, but his arguments are unconvincing. Cf. now T.D. Barnes, *JTS*, (n.s.). 19 (1968), pp. 204–9. Another alternative date proposed by Barnes, i.e. December of 5 B.C.E., has a very slight basis, and relies on the late Hebrew gloss of the M*g. Ta‘anit*.

[53] Cf. the various opinions on the Herodians in H.H. Rowley, *JTS*, 41 (1940), pp. 14–27; H. W. Hoehner, *Herod Antipas*, Cambridge, 1972, pp. 331–342.

[54] On Herod's policy and the country's social development, see M. Stern, *Tarbiz* (Hebrew), 35 (1966), pp. 235–53.

[55] In *Antiquities* XVII, 78, Mattathias the son of Theophilus is referred to as being of Jerusalem, but this only proves that he lived in Jerusalem at that time. From the Talmudic sources it appears that Joseph the son of Ellemus, who according to *Ant.* XVII, 166 was a relative of Mattathias, came from Sepphoris in Galilee. Cf. Tosef. Yoma 1, 4; Yer. Yoma, 1, 38d; Yer. Hor. 111, 47d, Yer. M*g. 1, 72a, Yoma 12b; M*g 9b; Hor. 12b.

[56] Cf. also G. Alon, *Studies in Jewish History* (Hebrew), I, Tel Aviv, 1957, pp. 73–4.

[57] The tradition that Herod ordered his sister Salome and her husband to imprison all the Jewish leaders at Jericho and execute them upon his death is certainly a legend arising out of hostility to Herod. In Otto's opinion (*op. cit.*, p. 148), the intention was to use the leaders as hostages as a guarantee that there would be no riots after Herod's death.

[58] On these events, cf. Täubler, *op. cit.*, pp. 36–40; Hoehner, *op. cit.*, pp. 19–39.

[59] Our sources, which rely mainly on Nicolaus, who sympathized with Varus, put the blame mainly on Sabinus. However, Varus' character as described in other sources and in other circumstances is far from sympathetic; cf. Velleius Paterculus, II. 117; Florus, *Epitoma*, II, 30, 31. Velleius Paterculus stresses the fact that Varus came as a poor man to a rich province (Syria) and left it a poor province as a rich man (*Pecuniae vero quam non contemptor Syria, cui praefuerat, declaravit, quam pauper divitem ingressus dives pauperem reliquit*).

[60] See M. Stern, *Encyclopaedia Judaica*, Year Book, 1973, p. 147.

[61] See Meshorer, *op. cit.*, p. 69; also Dio Cassius, LV, 27, 6. According to Dio Cassius, Herod (Archelaus) was found guilty by his brothers, and because of this was exiled.

[62] On Archelais see M. Avi-Yonah, *The Holy Land*, pp. 104, 164; Abel, *Géographie*, II, p. 249.

CHAPTER IV

THE HERODIAN DYNASTY AND THE PROVINCE OF JUDEA AT THE END OF THE PERIOD OF THE SECOND TEMPLE

1 A similar petition from the inhabitants of Cilicia and Commagene was made after the death of their kings (Tacitus, *Annals*, II, 42, 5).

2 Cf. M. Noth, *ZDPV*, 62 (1939), pp. 127–9; R. Syme, *JRS*, 52 (1962), p. 90.

3 Cf. Philo, *De Abrahamo*, 133; *Vita Mosis*, I, 163; *De virtutibus*, 221; *Quod omnis probus liber sit*, 75; *Ant.* XX, 259.

4 The problem of the census of Quirinius has given rise to a lengthy controversy among scholars. This results from the discrepancy between Luke, who places the census in the reign of Herod, and the remarks of Josephus, who relates it to the creation of the province in 6 A.D. It is hardly possible that Josephus was mistaken, expecially as the creation of the province would have been the natural occasion for a census. Most scholars therefore conclude that Luke was mistaken. There are no real grounds for assuming that there were two censuses, and that Quirinius twice served as legate of Syria. The extensive literature on Quirinius includes: Schürer, *Geschichte*, I, pp. 508–43; E. Groag, *Jahreshefte des österreichischen archäologischen Institutes*, 21–22 (1922–4), Beiblatt, pp. 445–78; R. Syme, *Klio*, 27 (1934), pp. 131–8; F. M. Heichelheim, *Roman Syria*, apud T. Frank, *An Economic Survey of Ancient Rome*, IV, Baltimore, 1938, pp. 160–2; A. G. Roos, *Mnemosyne*, 3rd Series, 9 (1941), pp. 306–18; S. Accame, *Rivista di Filologia*, 72–3 (1944–5), pp. 138–70; D. Magie, *Roman Rule in Asia Minor*, II, Princeton, 1950 pp. 1322–3; R. K. Sherk, *The Legates of Galatia from Augustus to Diocletian*, Baltimore, 1951, pp. 21–4; H. Braunert, *Historia*, 6 (1957), pp. 192–214; B. Levick, *Roman Colonies in Southern Asia Minor*, Oxford, 1967, pp. 203–14.

5 On the identification of Judas, who stirred up trouble at the time of Quirinius' census, with Judas the son of Hezekiah, who was active in the "war" of Varus, see: J. S. Kennard, *JQR*, 36 (1945–6), pp. 281–6;

M. Hengel, *Die Zeloten*, Leiden-Cologne, 1961, p. 337. For a different view, see H. Kreissig, *Die sozialen Zusammenhänge des judäischen Krieges*, Berlin, 1970, pp. 114–6.

6 Some scholars connect this event with the famous edict of Nazareth, which forbade the removal of bodies from their graves: see J. Carcopino, *Revue historique*, 166 (1931), pp. 88–91. Others followed him, e.g. J. Irmscher, *ZNTW*, 42 (1949), pp. 181–2. On the inscription itself, see E. Gabba, *Iscrizioni greche e latine per lo studio della Bibbia*, Turin, 1958, no. XXVIII. See also: J. H. Oliver *Classical Philology*, 49 (1954), pp. 180–2; F. de Visscher, *Le droit des tombeaux romains*, Milan, 1963, pp. 161–95.

7 The name Ambibulus is an emendation of the editors. The MSS have Ἀμβιβοῦχος.

8 The procuratorship of Pomponius Flaccus lasted only a short time. See Tacitus, *Annals*, VI, 27.

9 On the episode of the standards, see C. H. Kraeling, *HTR*, 35 (1942), pp. 263–89.

10 S. Zeitlin, in *The Rise and the Fall of the Judaean State*, Philadelphia, 1967, p. 143, has conjectured that the money used by Pilate for the aqueduct had been specially set aside for the sacrifices of Nazirites. Josephus contains not any hint of this.

11 On the coins of Pilate and their special characteristics, see E. Stauffer, *La nouvelle Clio*, 1–2 (1949–50), pp. 495–514. The numismatic material strengthens our impression of the uncompromising character of Pilate and disproves modern attempts to whitewash him. Among those who defend him are: H. Peter, *Neue Jahrbücher für das klassische Altertum*, 19 (1907), 1–40; E. Fascher, *RE*, vol. 20, 1950, pp. 1322–3; J. Blinzler, *Der Prozess Jesu*, Regensburg, 1960, pp. 187–93; P. L. Maier, *HTR*, 62 (1969), pp. 120–1.

12 On the episode of the shields see Maier, *op. cit.*, 109–21. The affair must not be

confused with the episode of the standards.
Cf. also E. M. Smallwood, *Philonis Alexan-drini Legatio ad Gaium*, Leiden, 1961, p.
302. It seems reasonable to ascribe the
incident of the shields to the period after
the downfall of Seianus in 31 A.D. It is
doubtful, however, whether it occurred
during the Passover of 32 A.D., as has been
claimed by A.D. Doyle, *JTS*, 42 (1941),
p. 193.

13 See also J. Blinzler, *Novum Testamentum*,
2 (1958), pp. 24–49.

14 Cf. L. Haefeli, *Geschichte der Landschaft
Samaria*, Münster, 1922, pp. 108–10.

15 The exact date of Pilate's downfall is
uncertain, owing to contradictions implied
in *Antiquities*. It is certain that on being
deposed by Vitellius, Pilate reached Rome
after the death of Tiberius (*Ant.* XVIII,
89). Hence it seems that he was deposed
some time before 16 March, 37 A.D., the
date of the emperor's death. See U.
Holzmeister, *Biblica*, 13 (1932), pp. 228–
32; E. M. Smallwood, *JJS*, 5 (1954), pp.
12–21; Blinzler, *Der Prozess Jesu*, pp. 194–
196; J. Jeremias, *Jerusalem zur Zeit Jesu*,
Göttingen, 1962, p. 219, n. 8.

16 See P. Herrmann, *Der römische Kaisereid*,
Göttingen, 1968, pp. 105–107.

17 The previous governor had been
Marcellus, whow as appointed by Vitellius.
Because the names are similar, we may
presume that they actually hint at the
same man, and that the emperor ratified
the appointment made by Vitellius; see F.
Westberg, *Die biblische Chronologie nach
Flavius Josephus und das Todesjahr Jesu*,
Leipzig, 1910, p. 64.

18 See Strabo, *Geography*, XVI, 2, 46, p.
765 (according to the comments of W.
Otto, *Herodes*, Stuttgart, 1913, pp. 178–80).

19 On the relations between Herod Anti-pas and Pilate, see Blinzler, *op. cit.*, p. 211.

20 On the date of the foundation of
Tiberias, see M. Avi-Yonah, *IEJ*, I (1950–
51), pp. 160–9. He prefers the date 18 A.D.
Y. Meshorer, *Jewish Coins of the Second
Temple Period*, Tel Aviv, 1967 p. 74, dates
it at 19–20 A.D. See also T. Rajak, *Classical
Quarterly* (n.s.), 23 (1973), p. 349, n. 7.

21 On these events see J. G. C. Anderson,
CAH, X, 1934, pp. 748–50.

22 *Ant.* XVIII, 96–105, describes these
events as belonging to the end of Tiberius'
reign in contrast to Suetonius, (*Life of Gaius
Caligula*, 14, 3), and Dio Cassius (LIX,
27, 3), who both place them in the reign of
Gaius Tacitus, too, in one of the lost books
of the *Annals*, seems to ascribe them to the
reign of Gaius. For arguments in favor of
Josephus' version, see E. Täubler, *Die
Parthernachrichten bei Josephus*,(Diss.), Berlin,
1904, pp. 39–62. For arguments on the
other side, see A. Gartzetti, *Studi in onore di
Aristide Calderini e Roberto Paribeni*, I, 1956,
pp. 211–29.

23 *Ant.* XVIII, 103, reports that at this
time a Jew of gigantic stature arrived in
Rome, who was called "Giant" (γίγας). C.
Cichorius *Römische Studien*, Leipzig-Berlin,
1922, p. 421, links this with the words of
Columella (*De re rustica, III*, 8, 2), who
seems to have been in Rome when the Jew
was there, and describes him as taller than
even the tallest of the Germans.

24 Cf. Dittenberger, *OGIS*, nos. 416–7.

25 J. P. V. D. Balsdon, *The Emperor Gaius*,
Oxford, 1934, p. 197, has suggested that
Herod Antipas was at one time a secret
ally of Artabanus of Parthia.

26 *War* II, 183, reports that Herod Antipas
was exiled to Spain; according to *Ant.*
XVIII, 252, it was to Lugdunum in Gaul.
O. Hirschfeld, *Kleine Schriften*, Berlin, 1913,
p. 173, n. 2, tries to reconcile the two
passages by conjecturing that the place
referred to was Lugdunum Convenarum
in the Pyrenees.

27 *Against Apion*, II, 63; see U. Wilcken,
Hermes, 63 (1928), pp. 51 f.; D. G. Wein-gärtner *Die Ägyptenreise des Germanicus*,
Bonn, 1969, pp. 91–5.

28 Cf. Tacitus, *Annals*, III, 49; Suetonius,
Life of Vitellius, 6; see M. Stern, *Zion*, 29
(1964), p. 163, n. 58.

29 See Suetonius, *Life of Gaius Caligula*,
22; Dio Cassius, LIX, 26, 5; *Ant.* XVIII,
256; cf. also Seneca, *De ira*, I, 20, 8–9.

30 On the divinity of Gaius and his cult,
see H. Wilrich, *Klio*, 3 (1903), pp. 439–48;
G. Herzog-Hauser, *RE, Supplementband* vol.
4, 1924, pp. 833–4; L. Cerfa x et J.
Tondriau, *Le culte des souverains*, Paris-Tournai 1957, pp. 342–7.

31 See Suetonius, *Life of Gaius Caligula*, 33; Dio Cassius, LIX 5, 2.

32 These developments may have taken place at the beginning of summer, 40 A.D. Differences between Philo and Josephus, however, make it impossible to determine the chronology of the events under Caligula with any certainty. For discussions on the subject, see J. P. V. D. Balsdon, *JRS*, 24 (1934), pp. 19–24; E. M. Smallwood, *Latomus*, 16 (1957), pp. 3–17; P. J. Sijpesteijn, *JJS*, 15, (1964), pp. 87–96.

33 See R. Hanslik, *RE*, vol. 19, p 1199.

34 On the role of Antonia in promoting Agrippa, see E. Ciaceri, *Processi politici e relazioni internazionali*, Rome, 1918, pp. 322–31.

35 Cf. A. Alt, *Kleine Schriften*, III, Munich, 1959, pp. 395–6.

36 A. H. M. Jones, *The Herods of Judaea*, Oxford, 1938, p. 187. Jones conjectures that Agrippa was in debt to the treasury since he had borrowed money from people whose property was confiscated by the emperor. Cf. Ciaceri, *op. cit.*, p. 328, n. 2.

37 Dio Cassius (LIX, 24, 1) emphasizes the negative influence of Agrippa and Antiochus of Commagene on the emperor.

38 One may perhaps associate these events with an epigram of Philippus of Thessalonica, in which he describes the gift of a wonderful carpet sent by Cypros (Agrippa's wife) to the emperor — see *Anthologia Graeca*, IX, no. 778; A. S. F. Gow and D. L. Page, *The Greek Anthology*, *The Garland of Philip*, Cambridge, I, 1968, no. VI, p. 300.

39 It is possible that an inscription mentioning the return of King Agrippa refers to this period and not to the reign of Agrippa II. This is also the opinion of Dittenberger in his commentary to *OGIS*, no. 418.

40 The fact that Agrippa I was descended from kings who were mainly High Priests, viz. Hasmoneans, is stressed in Philo, *Legatio ad Gaium*, 278 (πάππων δὲ καὶ προγόνων βασιλέων ἔλαχον, ὧν οἱ πλείους ἐλέγοντο ἀρχιερεῖς).

41 A number of scholars, however, are convinced that there are strong arguments for associating this Jewish tradition with Agrippa II; cf. A. Büchler, *Die Priester und der Cultus*, Vienna, 1895, pp. 12–16; I. N. Epstein, *Prolegomena ad litteras tannaiticas* (Hebrew), Jerusalem-Tel Aviv, 1957, p. 40–1.

42 Cf. G. Alon, *Studies in Jewish History* (Hebrew), Tel Aviv, 1957, I, p. 116–7.

43 Attempts to identify Simeon Cantheras with Simeon the Just of the Talmud, (Soṭa, 31a) have been made by P. Winter, *Zeitschrift für Religions-und Geistesgeschichte*, 6 (1954), pp. 72–4.

44 See also Jeremias, *op. cit.*, p. 108, n. 7.

45 On the persecution of the Christians by Agrippa, see E. Meyer, *Ursprung und Anfänge des Christentums*, III, Stuttgart-Berlin, 1923, pp. 174–7; M. Goguel, *La naissance du Christianisme*, Paris, 1946, pp. 503–4.

46 R. Hanslik, *RE*, 2e Reihe, vol. 8, pp. 1973–5.

47 Tacitus in fact dates these events to 47 A.D. They must, however, have taken place earlier, since Vibius Marsus was dismissed shortly after Agrippas' death. See J. Dobiáš, *Dějiny rimské provincie syrské*, Prague, 1924, p. 422, n. 49.

48 See also V. M. Scramuzza, *The Emperor Claudius*, Cambridge, Mass., 1940, p. 195. Actually, Agrippa managed to build only a little of the third wall. It was finished in haste during the First Revolt; see M. Avi-Yonah, *IEJ*, 18 (1968), pp. 98–122.

50 This refers to the festivities celebrating the triumph of Claudius after his first conquest of Britain. See Kirsopp Lake, *The Beginnings of Christianity*, 1, 5, London, 1933, pp. 446–52. There is no evidence that Agrippa was poisoned by his enemies, as others have suggested; cf. Zeitlin, *op. cit.*, II, p. 202.

51 A very disparaging view of Agrippa's character is expressed by H. Dessau, *Geschichte der römischen Kaiserzeit*, II, 2, Berlin, 1930, p. 793. A fair appraisal of Agrippa's aims and aspirations during his reign is given by Ciaceri, *op. cit.*, pp. 319–62.

52 Acts 5:36, where the execution of Theudas is mentioned as taking place before the disturbance associated with Judah the Galilean. This is a mistake of the

author of Acts; cf. E. Haenchen, *Die Apostelgeschichte*, Göttingen, 1961, p. 211.

[53] From Josephus we learn only his cognomen, Cumanus; the nomen, Ventidius, is found in Tacitus, *Annals*, XII, 54, 2.

[54] There seems to be disagreement between Josephus and Tacitus on the subject of the quarrel between the Jews and the Samaritans under Cumanus. In the same passage Tacitus states that Felix' administration was in Samaria while Cumanus ruled over Galilee. It is possible that Felix held some post in the country during the procuratorship of Cumanus and perhaps was governor of Galilee — but not of Samaria, as Tacitus infers, while Cumanus was procurator of both Samaria and Judea proper. Of the many discussions of the problem, see: H. Graetz, *Geschichte*, Leipzig, III, 2, 1906, pp. 728–30; Dobiáš, *op. cit.*, pp. 430–2; A. Momigliano, "Ricerche sull'organizzazione della Giudea sotto il dominio romano", *Annali della R. Scuola Normale Superiore di Pisa*, 3 (n. s.) (1934), pp. 388–91; M. Aberbach, *JQR*, 40 (1949–50), pp. 1–14; E. M. Smallwood, *Latomus*, 18 (1959), pp. 56–7; E. Schwartz, *Gesammelte Schriften*, V, Berlin, 1963, pp. 152–4.

[55] B. W. Henderson, *The Life of the Emperor Nero*, Philadelphia — London, 1903, pp. 364–6; the author, who is not particularly noted for his love of the Jews, paints far too fair a picture of Felix.

[56] Graetz (*op. cit.*, III, 2, pp. 724–7) reduces the term of office of Ananias, though his arguments are not sufficiently convincing.

[57] It is impossible to identify Ismael the son of Phabes with the High Priest of the same name, who served at the time of Valerius Gratus, though he could well be a descendant. The error appears in S. Munk, *Palestine, description géographique, historique et archéologique*, Paris, 1845, p. 575.

[58] The length of Felix' term of office is also a matter of controversy; some wish to date his last year earlier, though *circa* 60 A.D. seems preferable. See: Schürer, *Geschichte*, I, p. 577, n. 38; E. Meyer, *op. cit.*, (n. 45), III 53–4; J. Felten, *Neutestamentliche Zeitgeschichte*, I, Regensburg, 1925, p. 224, n. 4. Those who prefer an earlier date

include: Lambertz, *RE*, vol. 22, pp. 220–7; C. Saumagne, *Mélanges Piganiol*, Paris, 1966, pp. 1373–86.

[59] There are no grounds for identifying this Beryllus with the commander of the Praetorian Guard, Burrus. Against such an identification, see Dessau, *op. cit.*, (n. 51), II, 2, p. 802, n. 4.

[60] On the *decaprotoi* of Tiberias, see Josephus, *Life*, 69, 296. On the *decaprotoi* of Gerasa, see C. H. Kraeling (ed.), *Gerasa*, New Haven, 1938, (Inscriptions by C.B. Welles), nos. 45–6. On its general occurrence in the Roman world, see E. G. Turner, *Journal of Egyptian Archaeology*, 22 (1936), pp. 7–19.

[61] For a rather sympathetic evaluation of Albinus, see A. Momigliano, *CAH*, X, 1934, p. 855.

[62] P. Horovitz, *Revue de Philologie*, 13 (1939), pp. 47–65; 218–37 has suggested that procurators were only sent to frontier territories, but this has no basis. Cf. also H. G. Pflaum, *Les procurateurs équestres sous le Haut-Empire romain*, Paris, 1950, pp. 26–7.

[63] For the suggestion that Felix was raised to the equestrian order, see P. R. C. Weaver, *Historia*, 14 (1965), p. 466; for the argument on the opposite side, see F. Millar, *Historia*, 13 (1964), p. 182, n. 13. Examples of freedmen in high administrative positions during the Julio-Claudian period include Licinus, the financial procurator of Gaul (Dio Cassius, LIV, 21), and Hiberus, Prefect of Egypt (Dio Cassius, LVIII, 19, 6).

[64] Cf. E. Birley, *Roman Britain and the Roman Army*, Kendal, 1953, pp. 133–53; H. G. Pflaum, *RE*, vol. 23, 1265–6; 1272–8.

[65] On the career of Tiberius Alexander, see: E. G. Turner, *JRS*, 44 (1954), pp. 54–64; H. G. Pflaum, *Les carrières procuratoriennes équestres sous le Haut-Empire romain*, I, Paris, 1960, pp. 46–9.

[66] Pflaum (*op. cit.*, I, p. 76) maintains that Albinus served in an administrative post in Alexandria.

[67] See E. Täubler, *Klio*, 17 (1921), p. 101 (according to *Ant.* XVII, 133.)

[68] See also W. Orth, *Die Provinzialpolitik des Tiberius*, Munich, 1970.

[69] See B. Dobson, *apud* A.v. Domaszewski,

Die Rangordnung des römischen Heeres, Cologne-Graz, 1967, p. XLIV.

70 See Cicero, *Pro Balbo*, 53; Dessau, *Inscriptiones Latinae selectae*, no. 3700, (Cauponius = Coponius).

71 G. A. Müller, *Pontius Pilatus der fünfte Prokurator von Judäa und Richter Jesu von Nazareth*, Stuttgart, 1888, p. 4.

72 The inscription was first published and edited by P. Fraccaro, *Athenaeum*, 18 (1940), pp. 136–44.

73 See S. I. Oost, *American Journal of Philology*, 79 (1958), p. 115. A new inscription published by M. Avi-Yonah, *IEJ*, 16 (1966), pp. 258–64, has been restored by the editor to imply a connection with Felix. Against this restoration cf. *L'année épigraphique*, 1967, no. 525.

74 See also: O. Hirschfeld, *Die kaiserlichen Verwaltungsbeamten bis auf Diocletian*, Berlin, 1905, pp. 384–5; A. H. M. Jones, *Studies in Roman Government and Law*, Oxford, 1960, pp. 115–25.

75 See e.g. Strabo, *Geography*, IV, 6, 4, p. 203; Pliny, *Nat. Hist.*, X, 134, and various inscriptions (see Jones, *op. cit.*, pp. 118, 195).

76 Dessau, *Inscriptiones Latinae Selectae*, nos. 1358–9.

77 See the inscription and the discussion on it in: A. Degrassi, *Atti della Accademia Nazionale dei Lincei*, Rendiconti, 19 (1964), pp. 59–65; H. Volkmann, *Gymnasium*, 75 (1968) pp. 124–35.

78 This is attested by the linguistic use in *Ant.* XVIII, 252; XIX, 274.

79 It is quite impossible to accept the explanation given by E. Schwartz, *Gesammelte Schriften*, V, Berlin, 1963, pp. 152–4, who claims that Judea in the limited sense, and as opposed to Samaria and Galilee, was directly included under Syria.

80 An exaggerated view of the independence of the procurators is found in P. Horovitz, *Revue belge de philologie et d'histoire*, 17 (1938), pp. 53–62; 775–92.

81 Dio Cassius, LX, 25, 4–6, on the relations of Claudius to the provincial governors. To allow for legal processes against a governor, the emperor did not usually send him directly from one province to another. For a general treatment of these problems, see P. A. Brunt, *Historia*, 10 (1961), pp. 189–227.

82 On the power of the influential provincials, see Tacitus, *Annals*, XV, 20–2.

83 Tacitus, *Annals*, XIII, 31, 3 (in 57 A.D. Nero forbade the use of gladiatorial displays as a means of winning popularity among the provincials).

84 On the census in Egypt, see M. Hombert et C. Préaux, *Recherches sur le récensement dans l'Égypte romaine*, Brussels, 1952.

85 Concerning the census in the Roman world, see H. Braunert, *Historia*, 6 (1957), pp. 192–214.

86 M. Rostovtzeff, *Social and Economic History of the Roman Empire*, Oxford, 1957, p. 572, n. 6.

87 H. I. Bell, *JRS*, 28 (1938), pp. 1–8; G. Chalon, *L'édit de Tiberius Julius Alexander*, Olten et Lausanne, 1964, pp. 53–68.

88 For the edict of Germanicus, see A. S. Hunt and C. C. Edgar, *Select Papyri*, II, no. 211; for the edict of Capito, see Dittenberger, *OGIS*, no. 665; on the corvée, see M. Rostovtzeff, *Klio*, 6 (1906), pp. 249–58.

89 C. F. Hill, *British Museum Catalogue of the Greek Coins of Palestine*, London, 1914, pp. 248–68.

90 M. Grant, *From Imperium to Auctoritas*, Cambridge, 1946, p. 131.

91 *Supplementum Epigraphicum Graecum*, IX, no. 8, Edict, 4. 11. 65–6.

92 Valerius Messalla was brought to justice before the Senate. Augustus himself intervened in the case by sending a directive to the senators to show no mercy to the accused. See D. Magie, *Roman Rule in Asia Minor*, I, Princeton, 1950, pp. 489 and 1347, n. 60.

93 Pflaum, *Les procurateurs équestres*, etc., pp. 147–8.

94 P. Garnsey, *JRS*, 58 (1968), pp. 51–9.

95 A. N. Sherwin White, *Roman Society and Roman Law in the New Testament*, Oxford, 1963, pp. 61–2.

96 The first suggestion comes from T. Mommsen, *Römisches Strafrecht*, Leipzig, 1899, p. 244, n. 3. The other opinion is Dessau's (*op. cit.* [n. 51], II, 2, p. 778 n. 1.)

97 Pflaum, *op. cit.*, p. 117; A. H. M. Jones, *op. cit.*, pp. 51–65.

98 On the location of the legions and their

movements in the Julio-Claudian period, see Ritterling, *RE*, vol. 12, pp. 1211–65.

[99]   Cf. War II, 186, where the number is three legions. Philo (*Legatio ad Gaium*, 207) refers to "half the army of the Euphrates."

[100]   There is no clear evidence from this period of cohorts numbering one thousand men (*cohortes milliariae*). Josephus does mention such cohorts in connection with the Roman force which conquered Galilee in 67 A.D. (*War*, III, 67). The first documentary evidence dates from 85 (A.D.) and comes from Pannonia (*C.I.L.*, XVI, no. 31).

[101]   On the garrison in Judea at this time, see: Schürer, *Geschichte*, I, pp. 458–66; T. R. S. Broughton, *The Roman Army, apud.* F. J. Foakes Jackson and Kirsopp Lake, *the Beginnings of Christianity*, London, 1, ,5 1933, pp. 439–41.

[102]   It seems that this cohort was the *Cohors II Italica civium Romanorum*: Gabba, *Iscrizioni*, nos. XXV-XXVI.

[103]   On the fleet of the province of Syria, see D. Kienast, *Untersuchungen zu den Kriegsflotten der römischen Kaiserzeit*, Bonn, 1966, pp. 88–97.

[104]   The material on Gerasa is gathered in C. H. Kraeling (ed.), *Gerasa, City of the Decapolis*, New Haven, 1938. The inscriptions were edited by C. B. Welles, *op. cit.*, pp. 353–494.

[105]   The importance of the trade routes for the development of the town has been especially pointed out by M. Rostovtzeff, *Caravan Cities*, Oxford, 1932, pp. 55–90.

[106]   A survey of the history of the town in the first century is given by R. O. Fink, *JRS*, 23 (1933), pp. 109–24.

[107]   See H. Seyrig, *Revue numismatique*, 6, (1964), p. 59.

[108]   The annexation of these territories occurred *ca.* 56 A.D., as may be seen from the new era used on the coins of Agrippa II. See T. Frankfort, *Hommages à Albert Grenier*, 1962, pp. 662–3. On the problems of the chronology of Agrippa's reign and his coins, see mainly H. Seyrig, *Revue numismatique*, 6 (1964), pp. 55–67.

[109]   See J. A. Crook, *American Journal of Philology*, 72 (1951), pp. 162–75.

[110]   See Seyrig, *op. cit.*, pp. 62–3, on the epigraphic material. This contradicts the remarks of Photius (*Bibl. cod.* 33, p. 6b), according to whom Agrippa II died in the third year of Trajan's reign. It follows that we must either discard Photius' date or presume that Agrippa ceased to rule some years before he died. See T. Frankfort, *Revue belge de philologie et d'histoire*, 39 (1961), pp. 52–8. A new inscription has been published by H. Seyrig, *Syria*, 42 (1965), pp. 31–4. It is dated 108 A.D., and refers to a former officer in Agrippa's army who later served Trajan.

CHAPTER V

THE ECONOMY OF JUDEA
IN THE PERIOD OF THE SECOND TEMPLE

1 "She makes linen garments and sells them; she delivers girdles to the merchant" — Prov. 31:24.

2 Josephus, *Against Apion*, I, 12.

3 "A Seah from Judea is equal to five from Galilea" (B. Batra 12a; Kᵉt. 112a).

4 The *Letter of Aristeas* (ed. by K. Wendland, 1900, paras. 107, 112–117) testifies to the high standard of farming in Judea in the period of the Second Temple. This source also exaggerates, but its panegyric of contemporary Jewry is not wholly without foundation.

5 See S. Krauss, *Talmudische Archäologie*, II, Leipzig, 1910 p. 164. The Hebrew word *ba'al* signifies land or crops which do not need irrigation but are watered by the rains. Similarly *'ishtari* (*Attari*; Himyarite: *'Attar*) is land that does not require watering; cf. Robertson Smith, *The Religion of the Semites*, Edinburgh, 1879, pp. 84 ff., 116.

6 "The fertile land of Jericho" (Sifrei Num. chap. 1, ed. Ish-Shalom, 21, p. 100; ed. Horovitz. p. 77).

7 M. Mᵉn. 8, 1.

8 *ibid.*

9 Cf. H. Graetz, *Geschichte, der Juden von den ältesten Zeiten bis auf die Gegenwart* (5th ed.), III, 1, Leipzig, p. 290, note.

10 Gen. 26; 12: "And Isaac sowed in that land, and reaped in the same year a hundredfold." Of special significance are the words "in the same year": they signify that it was an exceptionally fruitful year.

11 On the storehouses of the individual and of the king, cf. Tosef. Dᵉm. 1, 12–14; A. Büchler, *The Economic Conditions of Judea after the Destruction of the Second Temple*, London, 1912, pp. 57–9.

12 Acts 12:20.

13 *Ant.* XV, 305–314.

14 Cant. 4:13.

15 M. Ma'as. 2, 5.

16 Sifra Lev. Tazri'a, 3, ed. Weiss, p. 68b.

17 *War* IV, 468; cf. also J. Taglicht, "Die Dattelpalme in Palästina," *A. Schwarz-Festschrift*, Berlin–Vienna, 1917, pp. 403–16.

18 Pliny, *Nat. Hist.*, XIII, 44.

19 Tacitus, *Histories*, V, 6.

20 Yer. Ma'as. Sh. 4, 1.

21 Yoma 6a; Naz. 4a, Sanh. 70b.

22 Kᵉt. 111b (end).

23 M. Nid. 2, 7.

24 Nid. 1 (beginning).

25 M. Mᵉn. 8, 6.

26 *Ibid.* This could be Shiḥin (Asochis) in Galilee or Siknin in the Golan (Σωγάνη) mentioned in Sifrei Deut. ed. Ish-Shalom, 135, p. 2.

27 Cant. 8:2.

28 Yer. Yom ha-Kippurim 1, 4.

29 Mark 15:23.

30 Pliny, *Nat. Hist.* XVI, 15.

31 M. Tᵉr. 1, 9 *et al.*

32 Tᵉr. 11b; Bᵉr. 38a; M. Nᵉd. 6, 9.

33 Cf. S. Klein, "Weinstock, Feigenbaum und Sykomore in Palästina," *A. Schwartz-Festschrift*, 1917, pp. 389–402.

34 M. Mᵉn. 8, 3; Tosef. Shᵉvi'it 7, 15; Pᵉs. 53a. On Tekoa in Galilee see *Tᵉshuvot ha-Gᵉonim*, ed. Lik, X, 104, p. 33, and the note of Solomon Buber at the end of these *responsa*, p. 25.

35 "Like the olive of Netofah in its season" (Pe'a 7, 1).

36 "Shifḳoni and Beshani oils" (M. *loc. cit*). Traditional derivation links Neṭofah's name with the root נטף = to drip or flow, referring to its flow of oil; similarly Shifḳon was named after the oil spilt there (נשפך) These are obviously etiological explanations.

37 M. Mᵉn. 8. 3.

38 Mᵉn. 5b; Sifrei Deut. ed. Ish-Shalom, 148, 1. Gischala's abundant oil production is discussed in S. Klein, *Neue Beiträge zur Geschichte und Geographie Galiläas*, Leipzig, 1923, p. 9.

39 *War* II, 591–592; Josephus, *Life*, 7, 4.

40 Pliny, *Nat. Hist.*, XII, 54.

41 Strabo, *Geography*, XVI, 2, 41; Dioscorides, *De materia medica*, I, 18 (beginning).

42 Concerning En-gedi before the destruction, see Büchler, *op. cit.* (cf. above n. 11), p. 26, n. 4.

43   Pliny, *loc. cit.*

44   Cant. 1:14.

45   M. Shab. 14, 4.

46   On the practice of animal husbandry in Palestine up to the destruction of the Temple, see Büchler, *op. cit.*, p. 45. He is opposed by Krauss, *Qadmoniot ha-Talmud*, 1924, I, Vienna, pp. 192–3.

47   M. 'Eruv. 10, 9. Some are of the opinion that פטמים refer to spices (מפטמי קטורת). However, the remark of R. Jose (*loc. cit.*) that there was wool-dealer's market there favors the first interpretation. The Rabbis also support this: Rashi explains it as meaning "butchers" and R. Obadiah di Bertinoro as "cooks who fatten cattle for slaughter." *Aruch Completum*, ed. by A. Kohut (2nd ed.), Vienna, 1926 gives "fatteners — poulterers." Elsewhere, too, (Beza 29b) Rashi interprets פטם to mean "one who fattens poultry."

48   Cf. M. 'Eruv. *loc. cit.* and *War* V, 331.

49   M. B. Qamma 10, 9; cf. also R. P. Schwalm, *La vie privée du peuple Juif à l'époque de Jésus-Christ*, Paris, 1910, pp. 203–4.

50   Cf. S. Krauss *op. cit.* (cf. above n. 46), I. pp. 104–5.

51   On Herod's pigeons, see J. Klausner, *History of the Second Temple* (Hebrew) (2nd ed.), IV, Jerusalem, 1951, p. 21; also notes 35a–37a for a bibliography.

52   Neh. 3:3; 13:16.

53   *War* III, 509.

54   Its real name is Beth-yeraḥ (cf. the form Beit Ariaḥ in Yer. Kil. 1, 4; Mᵉg. 1, 1). See J. Klausner, *Jesus of Nazareth* (Hebrew) (6th ed.), I, Ramat-Gan, 1954, pp. 244–5; II pp. 52–3.

55   Strabo, *Geography*, XVI, 1.

56   *War* IV, 481.

57   *Nat. Hist.*, XVI, 25.

58   Nid. 62a; Shab. 90a (where it is erroneously spelled אנפונטרין. E. Leiff supports the latter reading, as in the Syriac *afanitron* (from Greek *aphronitron*); however, see Krauss, *Talmud-Archäol.*, I, 577, n. 348.

59   *War* IV, 454.

60   M. Suk. 3, 1.

61   Targum Jonathan, Num. 34; 3–4, 11.

62   Jerusalem Targum, *ibid.*

63   Tosef. Bᵉr. 7, 2; *Avot dᵉ-Rabbi Nathan:*

64   M. Avot 1, 10.

65   A. Büchler, *op. cit.*, p. 50.

66   Justin Martyr, *Dialogus cum Tryphone Judaeo*, LXXXVIII.

67   Acts: 8:3. Some maintain that Paul was a saddler; cf. G. A. Barton, *The Apostolic Age and the New Testament*, Philadelphia, 1936, p. 30.

68   M. Qid. 4, 14.

69   See note 47 above.

70   Suk. 10a.

71   J. Klausner, *In the Days of the Second Temple* (Hebrew) Jerusalem, 1954, III pp. 219–20.

72   Ben Sira 38:31, It is this very section which is missing in the original Hebrew from the Cairo Geniza. I therefore use the Greek text translated by M. Z. Segal, *Sefer Ben-Sira ha-Shalem* (Hebrew), Jerusalem, 1958, pp. 251.

73   Zech. 3:9; II Chron. 2:6.

74   'Av. Zara 50b (beginning).

75   Neh. 3:8; 3:31.

76   F. Bühl, *Die sozialen Verhältnisse der Israeliten*, Berlin, 1899, p. 43.

77   M. Yoma, 3, 11.

78   I Chron. 4:21; fine Judean linen is also mentioned in Pausanias, *Periegesis*, V, 7, 4–5.

79   Mo'ed Qaṭan 13b; Pᵉs. 55b.

80   A. L. Sukenik, *Sefer ha-Zikaron lᵉ — A. Z. Rabinowitz*, Tel-Aviv, 1924, p. 112–21.

81   Ruth R. 1, 5.

82   Gen. R. 86.

83   Joseph ha-Levi, *Shᵉmot 'Arei Erez Yisra'el* (Jerusalem, A. M. Luncz) IV, pp. 11–20.

84   M. Dᵉm 3, 1.

85   M. B. Mᵉzi'a 5, 8.

86   On Rabban Gamaliel and his great wealth, see Büchler, *op. cit.* (cf. above n. 11), pp. 37–8.

87   Matt. 20:8; Luke 16:1–8, etc.

88   Yoma 35b.

89   Cf. Krauss, *Talmud. Archäol.*, II, 102.

90   On wage standards of the Jews in ancient times, see L. Herzfeld, *Handelsgeschichte der Juden des Altertums*, (2nd ed.) Braunschweig, 1894, pp. 195–6.

91   Tobit 5:4.

92   Matt. 20:2, 9–10, 13.

93   S. Raphaeli, *Maṭbᵉ'ot ha-Yehudim*, Jeru-

text, A, ch. 11; text B, ch. 21, ed. Schechter pp. 44–6.

salem, 1913, pp. 39–40; J. Z. Lauterbach, "Weights and Measures," *Jewish Encyclopedia*, XII, p. 485.

94 "Apprentice (שוליא) of a carpenter" — P^{es}. 108a; "apprentice of a smith" — B. Qamma 32b; "apprentices (שוליהן) of curtain-weavers," according to the *Aruch Completum* (Shab. 96b).

95 *Ant.* XX, 219–22.

96 Matt. 20: 1–7.

97 These are collected in D. Farbstein, *Das Recht der umfrein und der freien Arbeiter nach jüdisch-talmudischen Recht*, Frankfurt, 1896.

98 "These are the lessees of the estates of the elders [lit. fathers]" — B. Batra 46b. The expression "estates of the elders" (Tosef. T^er. 2, 11) has the implications of *latifundia*.

99 Matt. 21: 33–42.

100 Krauss, *Talmud. Archäol.*, II, 101–2.

101 R. Zadok Cohen, *Ha-'Avodot 'al-pi ha-Tora w^e-ha-Talmud*, transl. from the French, with notes by J. S. Fuchs, Cracow, 1892; Simeon Rubin, "Ein Kapitel aus der Sklaverei im talmudischen und Römischen Rechte," *A. Schwarz-Festschrift*, pp. 211–19.

102 M. 'Arak. 8, 5; this is contradicted in Qid. 16a, Qid. 28a and B. Qamma 113b.

103 Qid. 20a; 22a.

104 Ben Sira (Hebrew) 42:6; 33:28–32; 7: 21–22.

105 E. Meyer has shown, however, that classical scholars often exaggerate the number of slaves in ancient Greece and Rome, as well as the extent of their influence on agriculture and urban industry; see *Die Sklaverei in Altertum*, Jena, 1895; idem, *Wirtschaftliche Entwicklung des Altertums*, Jena, 1895.

106 *War* IV, 508.

107 Gen. 9: 25–7.

108 II Macc. 8:11.

109 M. B. Qamma 4, 5.

110 Simeon Rubin, *op. cit.* (above n. 101), p. n. 1.: p. 224 n. 3; the branding of slaves was unusual and was reserved for the slave who had attempted to escape (*fugitives*). Cf. S. Krauss, *A. Schwartz-Festschrift*, pp. 573–4.

111 Nid. 17a; M. Giṭ. 7, 4.

112 Lev. R. 9 — obviously a late section.

Pheroras (Herod's brother) had a serving-maid with whom he was in love and who was undoubtedly his mistress (War I, 484), Cf. also M. Y^ev. 2, 5. Hillel the Elder said, "The more bondwomen, the more lewdness" (M. Avot 2, 7).

113 Giṭ. 7b.

114 B. Qamma 27a.

115 M. B^{er}. 2, 7.

116 Yer Nid. 1, 9b (end).

117 S. Krauss, "Ha-K^erak̲, ha-'Ir w^e-ha-K^efar ba-Talmud," *He-'Atid*, 3 (1923), pp. 50–1.

118 Yer. M^eg. 1, 1.

119 *Life*, 45 (ed. Niese, 235).

120 *War* III, 540.

121 Dio Cassius, LXIX, 14.

122 The word חנוני should be punctuated with a *qamaẓ* as in the Syriac, and as in the noun חנות from which it is derived.

123 This word first appears in Ben Sira (37:12; 42:4). Both תגר and מתגר are derived from it. It is of Sumerian origin and was early absorbed into the Semitic languages, appearing in Akkadian as *tamkaru; tamgaru; tagaru;*, in Syriac as *thagara*, and in Arabic as *tajar*.

124 This word is modeled entirely on the Greek form τραπεζίτης, from τράπεζα = שולחן (table), though of course the Phoenicians preceded the Greeks as money changers.

125 Cf. "her merchandise (סחרה) and her hire" (Isa. 23:18).

126 Ezek. 27:15.

127 Neh. 10:32 uses מקחה for סחורה, , as a pure Hebrew word.

128 This is the correct reading, and not with a *samek̲* as the word comes from *sagum*, a Celtic loan word in Latin.

129 In the singular it is spelled with a *samek̲* and in the plural with a final *mem* — hence the verbal form מלסטם in the phrase מלסטם את הבריות ("robs mankind") in Sanh. 72a.

130 Krauss, *Talmud. Archäol.*, II, pp. 355–6; Schürer, *Geschichte*, II, 67–82 (a summary). Both these authorities regard certain words as Greek which possibly belong to the Semitic group, having reached both Hebrew and Greek through the Phoenician, e.g., אויר (air); קופה (box), מפה (coverlet), which is found in Punic and is hence

Semitic. See Quintilian, *Institutiones Oratoriae*, I, 457.

131 Tosef. B. Mᵉẓiʿa 3, 20 and M. Mᵉg. 1, 1–2; 3, 6.

132 The word יריד is from the root ירד — "to descend", since the majority of the fairs were at first held in low-lying coastal cities. The term later came to include fairs held inland, e.g., the fair of Batanaea, east of the Jordan.

133 The spelling of איד with א is late. Its biblical meaning is "calamity" and was probably substituted deliberately for the earlier עיד, which even the Jerusalem Talmud preserves.

134 L. Herzfeld, *op. cit.* (cf. above n. 90), p. 73.

135 Tosef. Pᵉs. 4, 3; Babylonian Talmud *ibid.*, 64b.

136 *War* VI, 421.

137 *Ibid.*, II, 280.

138 D. Chwolsohn, *Das Letzte Passmahl Christi, und der Tag seines Todes* (2nd. ed.), Leipzig, 1908, pp. 49–54.

139 Herzfeld, *op. cit.*, pp. 194–270 and n. 34; pp. 244–336.

140 *Ant.* XIV, 112–113 (Strabo *apud* Jos.).

141 Cicero, *Pro Flacco*, XXVIII *passim*.

142 Cf. *above* on agriculture.

143 Herzfeld, *op. cit.*, pp. 129–30.

144 This and the preceding items are mentioned in M. Pᵉs. 3, 1; Maʿas 5, 8; Kel. 17, 12; Nᵉg. 6, 1.

145 M. ʿAv. Zara 2, 4; the reading should be גבינה ביתוניקית or גבינת ביתוניקי rather than גבינת בית אונייקי.

146 M. Shab. 22, 2; M. Makshirim 7, 3.

147 Sanh. 106a.

148 M. Soṭa 2, 1.

149 Shab. 30b; Kᵉt. 111b.

150 M. Sanh. 10, 5.

151 S. Klein, "Derek Ḥof ha-Yam" *Qedem vi-Yhuda*, 1 (1923), Jerusalem.

152 Herzfeld, *op. cit.*, pp. 22–3, 141–2; Krauss, *op. cit.*, II, p. 327; Bühl, *op. cit.* (n. 76), pp. 7–8.

153 Herzfeld, *op. cit.*, pp. 46–7; Krauss *op. cit.*, p. 142.

154 *War* IV, 659–663.

155 The word is of Syriac origin.

156 Amos 4:2.

157 Yer. Shab. 4, 7.

158 Cf. Tosef. Shᵉv. 6, 26; Tosef. Qid. 4, 18; Nid. 14a (top) in contrast to M. Qid. 4, 14.

159 For a list of Hebrew nautical terms, see Krauss, *Talmud. Archäol.*, II, pp. 833–49.

160 *War* II, 635.

161 A. Fuks, "Marcus Julius Alexander" *Zion*, 13–14 (1948–1950), pp. 10–17.

162 Yer. Yom ha-Kippurim 5, 3.

163 Beẓa 5a; R. ha-Sh. 38b; Moʿed Qaṭan 13b.

164 Krauss, *op. cit.*, II, p. 366.

165 M. Kᵉr. 3, 7; Ḥul. 91b.

166 Suk. 51b; Yer. *ibid.* 5 (beginning); M. Maʿas. 2, 3 *passim*.

167 M. Kil. 9, 5; Shab. 9b; Pᵉs. 26b.

168 "Markets and their dining-rooms" — Sifrei Num. 159 ed. Ish-Shalom 72; ed. Horovitz, p. 215.

169 Tosef. Dᵉm. 1, 11.

170 *Pᵉsiqta Rabbati* 41, ed. Ish-Shalom, 173a.

171 ʿAv. Zara 16b.

172 Tosef. Oholot 18, 18.

173 Yer. Dᵉm. 2, 1.

174 II Macc. 3:4.

175 *Ant.* XVIII 149; see Chap. 4.

176 Cf. J. Klausner, *Hist. of the Second Temple*, II, pp. 174–5.

177 Gen. R. 99.

178 Klausner, *op. cit.*, pp. 67–8. According to Bühl (*op. cit.*, p. 119, n. 2), הלך was an import-export tax, while מנדה and בלו were income taxes, etc. My suggestion in the above book (*loc. cit.*) seems to me more plausible. For it I drew on: B. Meissner, *Babylonien und Assyrien*, I, Heidelberg, 1920, pp. 123–7, 129–30; L. Waterman, *Royal Correspondence of the Assyrian Empire*, IV, Ann Arbor, 1936, p. 25; L. Ginzberg, *A. Schwartz-Festschrift*, 1917, p. 337.

179 I. Macc. 10: 28–33; 11: 34–6. See also Klausner, *op. cit.*, p. 167–9.

180 *Ant.* XVII, 205.

181 *Nat. Hist.*, XII, 65.

182 M. Kel. 15, 4.

183 M. B. Qamma 10, 1.

184 M. Shab. 8, 2; Tosef. *ibid.*, 8, 11.

185 M. ʿAv. Zara 5, 7; Shab. 145b; Beẓa 21a. See M. Rostovtzeff, *Geschichte der Staatspacht in der römischen Kaiserzeit*, Leipzig, 1902.

186 Sifra Lev. Qᵉdoshim, 10, ed. Weiss, 91b; Shᵉv. 39a.

187 Tosef. Sanh. 5, 5.

188 M. Ḥag. 3, 10; Tosef. Ṭᵉhorot 8, 5.

189 Sanh. 25b.

190 M. B. Qamma 10, 1. A list of nearly all the references to tax collectors and publicans in the Mishnah, Barayta, Tosefta and Midrash is to be found in A. Büchler, *Der galiläische Am-Haarez des zweiten Jahrhunderts*, Vienna, 1906, p. 8, n. 2; p. 177, n. 3; pp. 185–90. Büchler believes that the hatred for the publicans reached its peak in the second century, a view I do not endorse.

191 Matt. 9:10–11; Mark 2:15–16; Luke 5:30.

192 On the rich citizens of Jerusalem before and after the destruction of the Temple, see A. Büchler, *The Economic Conditions of Judea after the Destruction of the Second Temple*, London, 1912, pp. 34–41.

193 On the money changers (חלפנים, שולחניים) — the bankers of the Second Temple era — see R. P. Schwalm, *La vie privée du peuple Juif à l'epoque de Jesus Christ*, Paris, 1910, pp. 376–408.

194 On the murderers and brigands in Judea immediately after the Destruction, see Büchler, *op. cit.*, pp. 55–6 and n. 5 (end).

CHAPTER VI

JERUSALEM IN THE HELLENISTIC AND ROMAN PERIODS

1   See in particular the account of Herod's constructions, *Ant.* XV, 380–425; *War* I, 401–2.

2   These texts have been partly collected by T. Reinach, *Texts d'auteurs grecs et romains relatifs au judaisme*, Paris, 1895.

3   For a bibliography of excavations at Jerusalem see L. A. Mayer–M. Avi-Yonah, *QDAP*, 1 (1932), pp. 163–88 and its continuation in subsequent volumes of *QDAP*; also the current bibliographies by Milka Cassuto-Salzman in *'Atiqot*.

4   See the reports of C. Schick, *PEFQS* and *ZDPV*; the Chronique of L. H. Vincent in *RB* and its continuation by P. Benoit; also the reports of W. Masterman in *PEFQS*, and since 1948 the *Alon* and the *Ḥadashot Arkeologiyot*, both published by the Department of Antiquities.

5   B. Bagatti–J. T. Milik, *Gli Scavi di "Dominus Flevit"*, 1, Jerusalem, 1958, (Bethany); V. Tzaferis *et al.*, *IEJ*, 20 (1970), pp. 18–59 (Giv'at Mivtar).

6   Cf. the New Testament form "Bethesda" (John 5:2) and the *Biz'ata* of the Talmudic sources.

7   Ezra 6:15.

8   Ezra 3:12.

9   Neh. 10: 38, 39.

10   *Ibid.*, and Zech. 3:7.

11   Neh. 13:4.

12   *Ibid.*, 13:13.

13   Ben Sira 50:1–2.

14   M. Mid. 2, 3.

15   I Macc. 4:60; 6:62; 9: 54–7; 10:11; 12:53.

16   *War* V, 245.

17   *Ibid.*, I, 143.

18   *Ant.* XIII, 307; *War* I, 75.

19   Although by now the valleys have filled up with debris, the height of the Western Wall is still 19m. and that of the southeastern corner 25m. above ground level. These data will probably soon be changed as the result of excavations now in progress.

20   *War,* V, 245.

21   *Ibid.*, 186.

22   *Ibid.*, 188.

23   If we try to fit the measurements quoted by the Mishnah to the Herodian esplanade, taking the altar (or the Holy of Holies) as center of the 250m. square, we notice that the east and west boundaries of the sacred area correspond more or less to the existing limits of the Herodian enclosure, whereas on the south and north — exactly where the Herodian additions were most evident, — the enclosure extended beyond the limits specified in the Mishnah.

24   Charles W. Wilson, *Ordnance Survey of Jerusalem*, London, 1865.

25   R. W. Hamilton, *QDAP*, 10 (1940), pp. 6, 19, 26 and Pls. III, 2, 3; VI, 2.

26   M. Avi-Yonah (ed.), *Sefer Yerushalayim*, Jerusalem, 1956, p. 417.

27   M. Mid. 2, 2.

28   This gate was perhaps named after the first Roman procurator who resided in Jerusalem after the deposition of Archelaus, in 6–9 B.C.E. (*War* II, 117).

29   The present-day Golden Gate was built in the Byzantine period (C. Watzinger, *Denkmäler Palästinas*, II, pp. 144–5); possibly even in the time of the Umayyads. We cannot agree with the attempt to identify the position of this gate with that of the Susa Gate by diagonally reorienting the whole plan of the Sanctuary; see F. J. Hollis, *The Archaeology of Herod's Temple*, London, 1934. For references to the two ramps see M. Sheq. 4, 2; M. Para 36.

30   *War* V, 190.

31   *Ant.* XV, 411–6.

32   *Ps. Aristeas* 89–91 mentions a "spring" in the Temple area; on the possibility of a Hasmonean aqueduct, see below.

33   M. Hecker in *Sefer Yerushalayim*, pp. 210–1, 418; for a map of these cisterns, see Wilson, *Ordanance Survey*, note 24 above.

34   *Sefer Yerushalayim*, p. 210, fig. 10, cistern no. 28.

35   Yadin, *Sefer Yerushalayim*, p. 187.

36   *War* V, 192.

37 M. Mid. 2, 3.

38 One complete text has been found of this inscription, and one fragment, both in Greek (Iliffe, *QDAP* [1938] 6), pp. 1–3.

39 This court was so called not because only women could enter it, but because it was accessible *also* to women, whereas the other court was closed to them save in exceptional circumstances.

40 M. Mid. 2, 5; M. Suk. 5, 4.

41 M. Mid. 2, 3; Yoma 38a; Yer. Yoma 3, 8–41a.

42 Avi-Yonah, *Sefer Yerushalayim*, p. 408 ff.

43 *Ibid.*, p. 406.

44 M. Mid. 4, 7.

45 Avi-Yonah, *Essays in Memory of E. R. Goodenough*, Leiden, 1968, pp. 327–335.

46 Yadin, *Sefer Yerushalayim*, p. 188.

47 *War* V, 244; M. Mid. 4, 6.

48 Suk. 51b.

49 *War* V, 212; Yoma 54a.

50 *Ant.* XIV, 34–6; *War* V, 211; M. Mid. 3, 8.

51 B. Batra 3b.

52 E.g. K. Zimmermann–K. Schick, *Karten und Pläne zur Topographie des alten Jerusalem*, I–II, 1876.

53 Avi-Yonah, *IEJ*, 18 (1968), pp. 122–5.

54 L. A. Mayer–E. L. Sukenik, *The Third Wall of Jerusalem*, Jerusalem, 1930.

55 *War* V, 136.

56 *Ibid.*, 142–5.

57 C. Warren–C. R. Conder, *Survey of W. Palestine: Jerusalem*, London, 1884, p. 271.

58 J. T. Milik, *Discoveries in the Judean Desert*, III, Oxford, 1962, pp. 244.

59 Parts of this wall were already found by Sir Henry Maudslay; see C. R. Conder, *PEFQS*, (1875), pp. 87–9; see also F. J. Bliss, *Excavations at Jerusalem*, 1894–7, London, 1898.

60 C. N. Johns, *QDAP*, 14 (1950), p. 126 ff.

61 K. Kenyon, *Jerusalem*, London, 1970, p. 161.

62 C. Wilson–C. Warren, *The Recovery of Jerusalem*, London, 1871, pp. 292–308.

63 *War* V, 146.

64 *Ibid.*, 158.

65 See n. 63.

66 Avi-Yonah, *Sefer Yerushalayim*, p. 312 and fig. 3.

67 *War* V, 331, 337.

68 *War* V, 468; on the pool called Amygdalon, see below, p. 246.

69. *Ibid.*, V, 259, 468.

70 A. Kümmel, *Karte der Materialien zur Topographie des alten Jerusalem*, 1904, p. 23, nos. 7–8.

71 *War* V, 149.

72 *War* V, 260.

73 *Ibid.*, 153.

74 *Ibid.*, 147.

75 *Ibid.*, 260.

76 Avi-Yonah, *IEJ*, 18 (1968), p. 98ff.

77 J. J. Simons, *Jerusalem of the Old Testament*, Leiden, 1952, pp. 459–503.

78 L. H. Vincent–M.A. Steve, *Jerusalem de l'Ancien Testament*, I, Paris, 1954, p. 146 ff.

79 *Ibid.*, p. 170.

80 *Ibid.*, p. 171 ff.

81 Mayer-Sukenik, *op. cit.* (n. 54 above) and C. S. Fisher, *BASOR*, 83 (1941), pp. 4–7; R. B. Y. Scott, *ibid.*, 169 (1963); E. W. Hamrick, *ibid.*, 183 (1966), pp. 19–26.

82 *War* V, 260.

83 Neh. 7:2.

84 I Macc. 4:60.

85 *Ibid.*, 7:62.

86 *War* I, 75.

87 II Macc. 13:52.

88 *Letter of Aristeas*, 104.

89 *Ant.* XIV, 61.

90 *War* I, 147.

91 *Ibid.*, I, 351.

92 *Ant.* XIV, 477.

93 *War* I, 401.

94 *Ibid.*, V, 238.

95 *Ibid.*, II, 332, 422, 430.

96 *Ibid.*, V, 238–44.

97 Vincent-Steve, *op. cit.* (note 78 above) p. 193 ff.; a different view has been advanced by P. Benoit in *HTR*, 64 (1971), pp. 135–67.

98 *War* V, 467.

99 I Macc. 1:35–8.

100 *Ant.* XIII, 216–7.

101 *War* I, 50.

102 *Ibid.*, V, 137.

103 E.g. V, 253.

104 *Ant.* VII, 63, 65, 66.

105 See note 99 above; *War* V, 143.

106   See above, page 228.

107   Kümmel, *Materialien*, map (note 70 above).

108   Avigad, *IEJ*, 20 (1970), p. 5.

109   *War* I, 402.

110   R. Amiran–A. Eitan, *IEJ*, 20 (1970), p. 9ff.

111   *War* V, 161–71.

112   *War* V, 161 ff.

113   *Ibid.*, II, 440.

114   *Ibid.*, V, 159–60.

115   This became evident as a result of the excavations at the northwestern corner of the Old City carried out in the spring of 1972; cf. D. Bahat–M. Ben-Ari; *Qadmoniot*, 5 (1972), pp. 118–119.

116   *War* V, 158.

117   *Praeparatio evangelica*, IX, 56.

118   *Ibid.*, III, 13.

119   *Against Apion*, I, 198.

120   *Geography*, XVI, 2, 36.

121   Avigad, *IEJ*, 20 (1970), p. 130ff.

122   II Macc. 4:9.

123   *War* II, 305, 315, 339; V, 137.

124   *Ibid.*, II, 429.

125   I. Macc. 1:15; cf. II Macc. 4:9–12.

126   Avigad, *op. cit.* (note 121 above), p. 136 f.

127   *War* V, 304; cf. *ibid.*, 284.

128   *Ibid.*, V, 145.

129   J. Germer-Durand, *RB*, 22 (1914), pp. 71–94, 222–46.

130   *War* II, 426.

131   Avigad, *op. cit.*, pp. 6–7.

132   *Ant.* XX, 189–92.

133   *War* II, 344.

134   See note 129 above.

135   *War* V, 137.

136   *Ibid.*, VI, 354.

137   *Ibid.*, II, 448.

138   *Ibid.*, VI, 354.

139   *Ibid.*, IV, 567.

140   *War* V, 252; M. Men. 32b.

141   C. N. Johns *PEFQS*, 80 (1948), p. 92.

142   *War* VI, 354.

143   *Ibid.*, V, 144.

144   *Ibid.*, II, 428.

145   V. Tcherikover, *IEJ*, 14 (1964), p. 61 ff.

146   *War* V, 140.

147   *Ibid.*, 136.

148   II Sam. 17:29.

149   Among the suggestions were *Gei hatoref* and *Gei ṭura ẓiyyon*, neither of which makes much sense.

150   *War* V, 337.

151   *Ibid.*, II, 530.

152   John 5:2.

153   See below, pp. 303 f.

154   M. Mid. 2, 5.

155   Personal observation of the writer.

156   War V, 148–52. Whatever Bezetha might mean, it certainly makes no sense as "New City."

157   *Ant.* XX, 326; *War* II, 218.

158   *War* V, 246.

159   *Ibid.*, II, 328.

160   *Ibid.*, V, 260.

161   *Ibid.*, 504.

162   *Ibid.*, 303, 504.

163   Matt. 21:17.

164   M. Men. 11, 2; Matt. 21:1.

165   Book of Baruch, poem; cf. Abel, *RB*, 44 (1935), p. 61.

166   *War* V, 507.

167   *Ibid.*, 57.

168   *Ibid.*, 107–8.

169   *Ibid.*, 147.

170   *Ibid.*, 506.

171   *Ibid.*, 304.

172   *Ibid.*, 259, 304, 356; VI, 169.

173   *Ibid.*, V, 108, 507 (the text of the latter passage is corrupt).

174   R. A. S. Macalister, *PEFQS*, 33 (1901), pp. 397–402.

175   *War* V, 55, 119.

176   *Ibid.*, II, 95; V, 147.

177   Pausanias VIII, 16, 4.

178   Hieronymus, *Epitaphium Paulae*, 22.

179   L. I. Rahmani, *IEJ*, 17 (1967), p. 95 ff.

180   M. Hecker, *Sefer Yerushalayim*, pp. 191–218 and bibliography; for a recent study of the aqueduct and its date see A. Mazar, *Qadmoniot*, 5 (1972), pp. 120–124, map.

181   Hecker, *ibid.*, p. 211.

182   Frey, *C. I. Jud.*, II, Roma, 1952, No. 5.

183   *War* V, 468.

184   *Ibid.*, 467.

185   John 5:2.

186   Benoit, *HTR*, 64 (1971), p. 140 ff.

187   *War* V, 108.

188   Hecker, *op. cit.* (n. 181), p. 203.

189 *War* V, 145.
190 II Kings 18:17.
191 Hecker, *loc. cit.*
192 *War* II, 187.
193 *Ibid.*, 175–7.
194 M. Sh^eq. 4, 2.
195 By A. Mazar; see n. 180 above.
196 M. Ma'as. 1, 5; Sh^evi'it. 7, 6.

CHAPTER VII

JEWISH ART AND ARCHITECTURE IN THE HASMONEAN AND HERODIAN PERIODS

1 P. Lapp *et al.*, *BASOR*, 165 (1962), pp. 16–34; *ibid.*, 177 (1963), pp. 8–55; see Vol. VI of this *History*, Figs. 57–59.

2 *Ant.* XII, 233.

3 M. Mᵉn. 13, 10.

4 M. J. B. Brett, *BASOR*, 171 (1963), pp. 45–55.

5 I Macc. 13: 27–30; *Ant.* XIII, 211.

6 Y. Meshorer, *Jewish Coins of the Second Temple Period*, Tel Aviv, 1967, Nos. 18–29 (cf. Vol. VI of this *History*, Figs. 75–76).

7 Meshorer, *op. cit.*, Pls. III–IV.

8 N. Avigad, *IEJ*, 20 (1970), p. 5, Pl. 2A.

9 F. J. Bliss–R. A. S. Macalister, *Excavations in Palestine*, London, 1902, Pl. 12.

10 L. Y. Rahmani, *IEJ*, 17 (1967), pp. 61–113; see Vol. VI of this *History*, Figs. 60–62.

11 G. Gromort, *L'architecture en Grèce et à Rome*, Paris 1947, p. 114, Fig. 76.

12 Rahmani, *op. cit.*, pp. 70–1.

13 N. Avigad, *Ancient Monuments in the Kidron Valley* (Hebrew), Jerusalem, 1954, pp. 37–90; cf. Vol. VI of this *History*, Fig. 56.

14 H. E. Stuchbury, *PEFQS*, 93 (1961), pp. 101–13.

15 N. Avigad, *IEJ*, 22 (1972), p. 198.

16 N. Butler, *Princeton Archaeological Expedition to Syria*, II, Leiden, 1922, A fasc. 6; E. Littmann, *ibid.*, IV, A, No. 882.

17 Y. Meshorer, *op. cit.* (n. 6 above), Nos. 89-93; cf. Fig. 29-31 of this volume.

18 C. N. Johns, *QDAP*, 10 (1940) Pls. XLVII-XLVIII.

19 B. Mazar, *Excavations in the Old City of Jerusalem, First to Third Season*, Jerusalem, 1969–1971.

20 L. H. Vincent–F. M. Abel–L. Mackay, *Le Haram de Hebron*, Paris, 1922.

21 H. Frankfort, *The Art and Architecture of the Ancient Orient*, Harmondsworth, 1954, Pls. 12, 52, 55, 78.

22 Mazar, *op. cit.* (n. 19 above), 1971, pl. XXIV.

23 N. Avigad, *IEJ*, 20 (1970), Pl. 31.

24 *Ant.* XV, 381–90.

25 B. Batra 3b; Suk. 51b.

26 *War* V, 222–3.

27 B. Batra 3b.

28 M. Mid. 2, 3; Yoma 38a; Yer. *ibid.*, 3, 8–41a.

29. *Ant.* XVII, 151 ff.; *War* I, 648–55.

30 *Ant.* XV, 277–9.

31 Josephus, *Life*, 65.

32 V. Corbo, *Liber Annuus*, 13 (1962/3), pp. 219–77.

33 A. Segal, *IEJ*, 23 (1973), 27–29.

34 Y. Yadin, *Masada*, London, 1966.

35 M. E. Blake, *Memoirs of the Amer. Academy, Rome*, 8 (1930), pp. 97–109.

36 N. Avigad, *IEJ*, 20 (1970), pp. 1 ff., 129 ff.

37 *Ibid.*, Pl. 4 A.

38 M. Broshi, *IEJ*, 22 (1972), p. 171 f.; Ruth Amiran–A. Eitan, *ibid.*, 20 (1970), p. 9ff.

39 M. Kon, *The Tombs of the Kings* (Hebrew), Tel Aviv, 1946.

40 N. Avigad, *IEJ*, 1 (1950–1), pp. 96 ff; L. H. Vincent — M. A. Steve, *Jerusalem de l'Ancien Testament*, I, Paris, 1954, pp. 313–71.

41 N. Avigad in M. Avi-Yonah (ed.), *Sefer Yerushalayim*, I, Jerusalem, 1956, pp. 336–7.

42 N. Avigad, *Ancient Monuments*, pp. 91 ff.

43 Most of the known ossuaries are illustrated in E. R. Goodenough, *Jewish Symbols in the Greco-Roman Period*, III, New York, 1953, nos. 105–224; see also L. Y. Rahmani, *IEJ*, 18 (1968), p. 220 ff. and *ibid.*, 22 (1972), p. 113 ff.; also V. Tsaferis, *ibid.*, 20 (1970), p. 18 ff.

44 Goodenough, *op. cit.*, Nos. 232–250.

45 B. Bagatti–J. T. Milik, *Gli Scavi di "Dominus Flevit"*, I, Jerusalem, 1958, Pls. 14–18.

46 N. Avigad, *IEJ*, 21 (1971), p. 186 ff.

47 *Idem, ibid.*, 12 (1962), Pl. 22.

48 On this problem in general see M. Avi-Yonah, *Oriental Art in Roman Palestine*, Rome, 1961.

49 *Ibid.*, Chapter I.

CHAPTER VIII

THE HIGH PRIESTHOOD AND THE SANHEDRIN
IN THE TIME OF THE SECOND TEMPLE

1 R. de Vaux, *Ancient Israel* (transl.), London, 1961, p. 376 ff.

2 H. Graetz, *Geschichte der Jüden von den ältesten Zeiten bis auf die Gegenwart* (5th ed.), I, Leipzig, 1908, p. 262; R. Kittel, *Geschichte d. Volkes Israel*, III, Stuttgart, 1929, pp. 425 ff.; R. H. Pfeiffer, *Introduction to the Old Testament*, New York–London, 1941, p. 792; O. Eisfeldt, *The Old Testament* (transl.) New York–Evanston, 1965, p. 433; W. O. E. Oesterley, *A History of Israel*, II, Oxford, 1932, p. 102; M. Noth, *The History of Israel*, London (2nd ed.), 1960, p. 316; J. Bright, *A History of Israel*, London, (1960) 1967, p. 360; J. Klausner, *History of the Second Temple* (Hebrew), I, Jerusalem, 1951, pp. 220–3; E. Bevan, *Jerusalem under the High-Priests*, London, 1912, p. 5; W. Foerster, *Palestinian Judaism* (transl. G. E. Harris), Edinburgh–London, 1964, p. 17.

3 The implication of this argument — that Zerubbabel was also in charge of internal matters while succeeding governors were not (Kittel, *op. cit.*, p. 468) — is not proven. However, Zer-Kavod interprets Zechariah 3:7 "and will also judge my house" (וגם אתה תדין את ביתי) as referring to the "house of Israel" (as in Gen. 49:16) (M. Zer-Kavod, *Haggai, Zechariah, Malachi* [Hebr.], Jerusalem, 1957, p. 78). This would indicate that the High Priest was the supreme judge or ruler.

4 Neh. 5:15.

5 Originally read as "Hezekiah Yhd"; see E. L. Sukenik, "Paralipomena Palestinensia," *Journal of Palestine Oriental Society*, 14 (1934), pp. 178–82. The correct reading has now been established by Y. L. Rahmani, *IEJ*, 21 (1971), pp. 158–60. For the later literature, see W. F. Albright, *BASOR*, 148 (1957), pp. 28–30; F. M. Cross, Jr., "Judean Stamps," *Eretz-Israel*, 9 (1969), 20–7 (Engl. Sect.); Y. Aharoni, *Excavations at Ramat Rahel : Seasons 1959 and 1960*, Rome, 1962, pp. 58–9. According to Professor Cross "jars of standard weight were fabric-ated "by potters' guilds under the regulation of the crown," both in Phoenicia and Judea (art. cit., p. 22).

6 B. Porten, *Archives from Elephantine*, Univ. of California Press, 1968, p. 290.

7 N. Avigad, "A New Class of Yehud Stamps," *IEJ*, 7 (1957) pp. 146–53.

8 P. C. Hammond, "A Note on Two Seal Impressions from Tell es-Sultan," *PEQ*, 89 (1957), pp. 68–9, Pl. XVI.

9 Ezra 1:2.

10 Strabo, *Geography*, C 535, Loeb ed., V, pp. 352–3.

11 Herodotus, III, 89 ff., Loeb ed. II, p. 116 ff.

12 H. Frankfort, *Kingship and the Gods*, Chicago, (1948), 1966, p. 222.

13 Strabo, *ibid.*

14 *Ibid.*, C 537, pp. 358–9.

15 *Ibid.*, C 558, pp. 434–5.

16 See note 10 above.

17 *Ibid.*, C 537, pp. 358–9; C 556, pp. 430–1.

18 See note 10 above.

19 *Ibid.*, C 537, pp. 357–9.

20 *Ibid.*, C 558, pp. 436–7.

21 M. Rostovtzeff, *Studien zur Gesch. des römischen Kolonates*, Leipzig-Berlin, 1910, pp. 270–3.

22 Pfeiffer, *op. cit.*, pp. 602–15; Eisfeldt, *op. cit.*, pp. 426–43.

23 Ezra 9:9: כי עבדים אנחנו.

24 *Ibid.*: לרומם את בית אלהינו ולהעמיד את חורבותיו ולתת לנו גדר ביהודה ובירושלים. Even the uncomplimentary references to the High Priests testify to their supreme religious (Ezra 10:18; Neh. 13:4–8, 28) and political (Neh. 3:1) position.

25 *Ant.* XI, 297.

26 Judith 4:6–7.

27 Concerning its date, see Y. Grintz, *The Book of Judith* (Hebrew), Jerusalem, 1957, pp. 11–17; M. Avi-Yonah, *The Holy Land from the Persian to the Arab Conquests* (536 B.C. to A.D. 640), Grand Rapids, Michigan, 1966, p. 64.

28 Yoma 69a; *Meg. Ta'an.* pp. 339–40.

29 *Ant.* XI, 317–8 (does not name the High Priest); 326–39 (calls the High Priest Jaddus).

29 Neh. 3:1.

30 Frankfort, *op. cit.* (above, note 12) p. 221.

31 *Against Apion* I, 183.

32 *Letter of Aristeas*, 35 ff.

33 *Ant.* XII, 158.

34 Ben Sira, chapter 50, first alludes to the political greatness of the High Priest Simeon, and only then refers to his religious activities.

35 Oesterley, *op. cit.* (above, n. 2), pp. 42–5; Klausner, *op. cit.* (above n. 2), pp. 78–81.

36 Oesterley, *op. cit.*, pp. 51 ff., 71 ff.; Klausner, *op. cit.*, 178 ff., 233 ff.

37 The first to note similarities between the temple servants of other deities and the Nethinim was, to my knowledge, R. P. Dougherty, *The Shirkûtu of Babylonian Deities*, New Haven, 1923, pp. 90–1; see also Kittel, *Geschichte*, III, p. 418.

38 Ezra 8:20 merely gives the historical origin of the "Nethinim, whom David and the princes had given for the service of the Levites," rather than a description of their function in the Second Temple, as R. de Vaux believes (*Ancient Israel*, p. 89). B. Mazar's suggestion that two of the names of the Nethinim's families may signify their specific functions in the Temple (*Pirsumei ha-Ḥevra lᵉ-Ḥeqer ha-Miqra bᵉ-Yisra'el*, vol. IX, p. 111) is relevant only to the First Temple, as the names of the Nethinim were inherited from their ancestors. (For other possibilities of the name's significance, see W. Rudolph, *Ezra u. Nehemia*, Tübingen, 1949, p. 12.) Regarding the term "Nethinim," B. Mazar (*op. cit.*, pp. 108–110) has shown that it was a professional, not an ethnic designation, and B. Levine ("The Nethinim," *JBL*, 82 [1963], pp. 207–12) concludes that they were a cultic guild, whose "exact function must remain a mystery" (p. 212).

39 Ezra 2:43–58; (Neh. 7:46–60).

40 Ezra 3:12.

41 Ezra 2:36–9.

42 Ezra 2:40–2; Neh. 7:43–5.

43 Ezra 7:24; ׳פלחי בית אלהא דנה

44 Neh. 10:35: והגורלות הפלנו על קרבן העצים הכהנים הלויים והעם להביא לבית אלהינו לבית אבותינו לעתים מזמנים שנה בשנה. לבער על מזבח ד' אלהינו. See also *Mᵉg. Ta'an.* pp. 331–2.

45 *Ant.* XI, 128; I Esdras 5:29 in its rendition of Ezra 2:43. However, the LXX merely transliterates Nethinim (ναθινατῖοι and ναθεινιμ).

46 Ezra 2:58; Neh. 7:60.

47 L. W. Batten supposes that פלחי בית אלהא דנה — "servants of this house of God" (Ezra 7:24) — refers to Solomon's servants (*Ezra-Nehemiah*, I.C.C., p. 313).

48 B. Levine, "The Nethinim", p. 210, also cites Rudolph and Mendelson. See also S. Zucrov, *Women, Slaves and the Ignorant in Rabbinic Literature*, Boston, 1932, pp. 162–3.

49 Ezra 7:24; Neh. 10:27.

50 I Chron. 9:2.

51 The term ראשונים in I Chron. 9:2 is not equivalent to ראשים in Neh. 11:3, as suggested by E. L. Curtis — A. A. Madsen, *The Books of Chronicles*, I.C.C., Edinburgh, (1910) 1952, p. 169. היושבים הראשונים literally means "the earliest settlers", not "the foremost residents," as is thought by B. Levine (art. cit. p. 208).

52 Dougherty, *The Sirkûtu*, pp. 89–90. Though there may be points of similarity between the *sirkûtu* and the Nethinim, they are far from being identical. Thus the *sirkûtu* had been dedicated by their fathers or masters, while the Nethinim were a hereditary group. See Dougherty, *op. cit.*, pp. 88–9.

53 Neh. 13:10.

54 E. Bevan, *Jerusalem Under the High-Priests*, London, 1912, pp. 5–8; J. Wellhausen, *Israelitische und jüdische Geschichte*, Berlin, 1958, p. 182; V. Tcherikover, *Hellenistic Civilization and the Jesus* (transl. S. Appelbaum), Philadelphia, 1961, pp. 119–20; idem, *Ha-Yehudim wᵉ-ha-Yewanim* (Hebrew), Tel Aviv, 1963, p. 97–8; J. Jeremias, *Jerusalem in the Time of Jesus Christ* (transl. F. H. & C. H. Cave), London, 1969, pp. 96–8.

55 Jeremias, *op. cit.*, p. 98. Wellhausen's assumption that all the priestly gifts brought to the Temple were simply appropriated by the High Priests (*Prolegomena*, Berlin, 1905, p. 160), is not supported by

our evidence. According to Neh. 13:13 the distribution of the gifts was made by a committee consisting of two ordinary priests a Levite and a singer (on the inclusion of a Levite, see M. Zer-Kavod, *ad loc.*).

56 Diodorus, XL, 8 (T. Reinach, *Textes*, Hildesheim, 1963, p. 19).

57 Deut. 18:1.

58 L. Finkelstein, *The Pharisees*, I, Philadelphia, 1962, p. 21.

59 S. W. Baron, *A Social and Religious History of the Jews*, I, Philadelphia, 1952, p. 149.

60 *Ant.* XVIII, 16. See R. Leszynsky, *Die Sadduzäer*, Berlin, 1912, pp. 48, 85 ff.; see also H. [D.] Mantel, in *Studies in the History of the Jewish People*, in Memory of Zvi Avneri (Hebrew), Haifa, 1970, pp. 66–7.

61 Finkelstein, *op. cit.*, p. 20.

62 See Schürer, *Geschichte*, II, p. 311.

63 See Oesterley, *op. cit.* (n. 2 above), p. 170.

64 Num. 18:14.

65 Ezek. 44:29.

66 *Ant.* IV, 69–75, 205.

67 Finkelstein, *op. cit.* (n. 58 above), p. 21.

68 See, for instance, Ezra 4:1–24, 5:6–6:15, etc.

69 Frankfort, *op. cit.*, (n. 12 above), p. 222.

70 Deut. 18:1.

71 I Macc. 7:6.

72 Herod was wont to confiscate the property of his enemies (*War* I, 358–9, *Ant.* XV 5–7), presumably for distribution among his supporters.

73 *Ant.* XII, 138–41; 143–4.

74 I Macc. 10:31.

75 *Ibid.*, 10:32.

76 See R. Marcus, *Josephus*, Loeb ed. VII, p. 84, note d; also A. Schalit, *König Herodes*, Berlin, 1969, p. 308, note 580 (Hebr. p. 453, n. 562).

77 *Ant.* XII, 175 ff. See also M. Rostovtzeff, *Social and Economic History of the Hellenistic World*, I, Oxford, 1957, pp. 346–51.

78 *Ant.* XII, 161.

79 Marcus, *ibid.*

80 See Wellhausen, *op. cit.* (n. 54 above), p. 231.

81 See Tcherikover, *Hellenistic Civilization*, p. 127. (Hebr. *Ha-Yehudim we-ha-Yewanim*, p. 103 ff.); S. Zeitlin, "The Tobiad Family and the Hasmoneans," *Proceedings of the American Academy for Jewish Research*, 4 (1933), p. 170.

82 M. Stern, "He'arot le-Sippur Yosef ben Ṭuviya," *Tarbiz*, 32 (1963), pp. 37–47, shows that the Tobiad story was composed in Ptolemaic Egypt. In Egypt it was unknown for a High Priest to be a political ruler as well.

83 See Oesterley, *op. cit.* (n. 2 above), p. 273 ff; Klausner *op. cit.* (n. 2 above), III, pp. 83 ff., 155 ff.

84 *Ant.* XV, 254; see also *Ant.* XIII, 254–8. Zucker thinks that Simeon was given the title *Sar 'am El* — "Prince of God's People" (I Macc. 14:41) and Judah Aristobulus took the title of king (*Ant.* XIII, 301; War I, 70) because these titles represented independence, whereas High Priesthood implied subordination to a king. (H. Zucker, *Studien zur jüdischen Selbstverwaltung*, Berlin, 1936, p. 43). But *Sar* was the title of nobles, not of kings. If the two terms were synonymous, why did the people object to Jannaeus' assuming the title of king, since the title *Sar* was voluntarily conferred by the people upon the Hasmoneans?

85 *Ant.* XIII, 318–9.

86 *Ant.* XIII, 256.

87 *Ant.* XIV, 41.

88 *Ant.* XIII, 288 ff.

89 Qid. 66a. See I. A. Halevy, *Dorot ha-Rishonim*, pt. III, Frankfurt, 1906, p. 397, n. 13; also J. Derenbourg, *Essai sur l'histoire et la géographie de la Palestine*, Paris, 1867, pp. 79–81; p. 80, n. 1; p. 95, n. 1 (Hebr. pp. 38–9; p. 38, n. 1).

90 Qid. 66a.

91 According to *War* I, 70, it was Aristobulus, the son of John Hyrcanus, who "transformed [μεταθείς] the government into a monarchy, and was the first [πρῶτος] to assume the diadem." So, too, *Ant.* XIII, 301. Strabo, *Geography* XVI, 2, 40 attributes the innovation to Jannaeus Alexander. See Marcus, *Josephus*, Loeb ed. VII, p. 379, note c.

92 The Talmud contains several stories indicating that its authors were well aware that the Hasmoneans were priests. Of

John Hyrcanus it is related that he heard a divine voice when he entered the Holy of Holies on the Day of Atonement to perform the services of the High Priest (Soṭa 33a).

93 *Ant.* XIII, 291.

94 See Psalms of Solomon, as interpreted by J. Wellhausen, *Die Pharisäer u.d. Sadducäer*, Hannover, 1924, p. 112 ff. Derenbourg thinks that the Pharisees were afraid that Hyrcanus might give priority to his temporal over his priestly duties (*Essai*, p. 90; Hebr. p. 39). But had he acted in political matters in accordance with Pharisaic principles, the Pharisees would have applauded him.

95 The Pharisees' demand may also contain the principle of opposition to combining the two offices in one person, since the High Priest chosen by the Pharisees in the days of the First Revolt, Phanni (= Phineas) the son of Samuel, seemed to have had no authority in secular matters (*War* IV, 155; *Ant.* XX, 227).

96 *Ant.* XIII, 372.

97 *Ant.* XIII, 320.

98 *Ant.* XIV, 41.

99 *War* I, 92.

100 *Ant.* XIV, 41.

101 See especially Tcherikover, *Ha-Yehudim wᵉ-ha-Yewanim*, p. 200 ff. (Eng. transl. p. 250 ff.); E. Bickerman, *Die Makkabäer*, Berlin, 1935, p. 49 ff. (Engl. *The Maccabees*, N.Y., 1947, 75 ff.).

102 *Ant.* XIV, 74.

103 *Ant.* XIII, 288. See also Jeremias, *Jerusalem*, p. 262 ff; H. Mantel, *Studies in the History of the Sanhedrin*, Cambridge, Mass., (1961) 1965, p. 100 (Hebr. pp. 113–4).

104 *Ant.* XX, 181; Pᵉs. 57a.

105 *Ant.* XII, 142 ("the senate, the priests, the scribes of the Temple and the temple-singers").

106 *Against Apion* II, 165 (Θεοκρατίαν).

107 The title of king was usurped by the Hasmonean princes, as the people appointed Simeon merely to be their "leader and High Priest" (ἡγούμενον καί ἀρχιερέα), and "general" (στρατηγόν) "until a true prophet shall arise" (I Macc. 14:41–2).

108 *Ant.* XX, 244.

109 This was also the case with Aristobulus II (*Ant.* XX, 243). He was made "High Priest of the nation" (ἀρχιεράτευεν τοῦ ἔθνους).

110 The omission of the latter title in *Ant.* XIV, 73 must therefore be an oversight. Dio Cassius (XXXVII, 16) may be inaccurate in saying that "the kingdom" (τε βασιλεία) was given to Hyrcanus, but his "error" certainly indicates that Hyrcanus was more than a High Priest. See also Strabo, XVI, p. 765.

111 *War* I, 170.

112 *Ant.* XIV, 91.

113 *Ant.* XIV, 91; also *War* I, 170.

114 T. R. S. Broughton, "Roman Asia Minor," in T. Frank (ed.), *An Economic Survey of Ancient Rome*, Baltimore, 1938, pp. 641–3; see also W. M. Ramsay, *The Cities and Bishoprics of Phrygia*, Oxford, 1895, p. 103.

115 R. Marcus, *Josephus*, Loeb ed. VIII, p. 495, note g.

116 *Against Apion* II, 184.

117 Neh. 5:7. See also A. Cowley, *Aramaic Papyri* 30:18: יהוחנן כהנא רבא וכנותה ... וחורי יהודה — "Johanan the High Priest and his associates... and the nobles of Judah."

118 Judith 4:8; 15:8.

119 *Ant.* XIV, 164.

120 I Macc. 14:28. See also 7:33; 11:23.

121 M. Rostrovtzeff, *The Social and Economic History of the Roman Empire*, I, p. 270.

122 *Ant.* XIV, 205–207.

123 *Ant.* XIV, 191.

124 *Ant.* XIV, 199.

125 See Mantel, *Studies*, pp. 237–9, (Hebr. pp. 271–3). While the High Priest may or may not have been in charge of the routine administration of the Jewish communities, he was their official "protector."

126 See A. Schalit, *King Herod* (Hebrew), Jerusalem, 1960, pp. 61–5 (German transl. *König Herodes*, Berlin, 1965, pp. 101–5).

127 Jeremias, *Jerusalem*, p. 148.

128 *Ant.* XX, 251.

129 *War* II, 240.

130 *War* II, 243.

131 *Ant.* XX, 162; *War* II, 240 ff.

132 *War* II, 563 *passim*; *Life* 193 *passim*;

133 *War* IV, 160, 238 ff.; *Life* 193, 204.

134 For references, see Jeremias, *Jerusalem*, p. 224.

135 *War* II, 411.

136 Luke 19:47. The same view is held by Schürer, *Geschichte* (1898), Hildesheim 1964, II, pp. 251–4; A. Kuenen, *Gesammelte Abhandlungen* (transl. K. Budde), Frieburg i.B. — Leipzig, 1894, pp. 60–2.

137 For references, see Jeremias, *Jerusalem*, p. 225.

138 John 11:50.

139 Acts 5:37 ff.

140 *Ant.* XIV, 74. For references, see Jeremias, *Jerusalem*, p. 262 ff. and H. Mantel, *Studies*, p. 100 (Hebr. p. 114).

141 For the various views on the composition of the Sanhedrin, see Mantel, *Studies*, pp. 55–63 (Hebr. pp. 64–75).

142 See F. M. Cross, Jr., *The Ancient Library of Qumran*, Garden City, N.Y., 1961, p. 72, note 33; for halaḵic differences, see: S. B. Hoenig, "Dorshe Halakot in the Pesher Nahum Scrolls," *JBL*, 83 (1964), pp. 119–38; H. Mantel, "The Nature of the Great Synagogue," *HTR*, 60 (1967), pp. 69–91. "טיבה של הכנסת הגדולה", דברי הקונגרס העולמי הרביעי למדעי היהדות, תשכ"ז, עמ' 81–88).

143 *War* IV, 155. See C. Roth, "The Zealots in the War of 66–73," *Journal of Jewish Studies*, 4 (1959), 332–55. Roth assumes that "it was necessary for him [i.e. the High Priest] to work in close collaboration with the Zealot leaders" (p. 344), though no "work" of any kind is ascribed to him by the sources. B. Kanael ("The Transition from Priestly Predominance," *Congresso Internazionale di Numismatica*, 2 [1961], 87–92) shows that the coins indicate the rise of non-priestly power even in the Temple, during the Great Revolt.

144 *Ant.* XIII, 291. See also Qid. 66a.

145 *Ant.* XIV, 41. See above, notes 94–95.

146 Peʿs. 132:11–12.

147 Hor. 13a.

148 I Macc. 14:41.

149 *Against Apion* II, 21, 185.

150 R. de Vaux, *Ancient Israel* (*Les institutions de l'Ancien Testament*, Paris, transl. J. McHugh), 1961, pp. 376–7.

151 S. W. Baron, *A Social and Religious History of the Jews*, I, Philadelphia, 1952, p.

152 ff.; T. C. Vriezen, *The Religion of Ancient Israel*, (transl. 1963), Philadelphia, 1967, p. 201 ff.; G. von Rad, *Old Testament Theology* (transl. 1960), N. Y.-Evanston, 1965, p. 50 ff.; D. Neumark, *The Philosophy of the Bible*, Cincinnati, 1918, p. 11 *passim*.

152 Neh. 8.

153 Meg. 17b and parallels ("120 elders, of them several prophets"); Yer. Sheʿq. I, 74d ("85 elders, of them 3, or 30 prophets").

154 See Mantel, "The Nature of the Great Synagogue," *HTR*, 60 (1967), 69–91. "טיבה של הכנסת הגדולה", דברי הקונגרס העולמי הרביעי (למדעי היהדות, ירושלים תשכ"ז, עמ' 81–88).

155 *The Scrolls of the Rule*, IX, 11, p. 94, "Until the coming of the Prophet and the Anointed of Aaron and Israel," in A. Dupont-Sommer, *The Essene Writings from Qumran*, Cleveland–N.Y., 1960, p. 94. "עד בוא נביא ומשיחי אהרן וישראל" מגילת הסרכים, פרשה חמשית, פרק ג'. בעריכת יעקב ליכט, ירושלים, תשכ"ה, עמ' 190 = מגילת מדבר יהודה, א. מ. הברמן, תש"ט (ט), 11, עמ' 68.

156 See I Macc. 5:62.

157 M. Peʿs. 1, 6 and parallels. Also, Acts 4:1 (στρατηγὸς τοῦ ἱεροῦ).

158 Yoma 39a.

159 M. Yoma 3, 9; 4, 1; 7, 1; M. Tam. 7, 3.

160 A. Büchler, *Die Priester und der Cultus*, Vienna, 1895, p. 106 (Hebrew, הכוהנים ועבודתם, תרגם נ. גינתון, ירושלים, תשכ"ו, עמ' 79); Jeremias, *Jerusalem*, Göttingen, 1962, pp. 184–5 (English, F. H. & C. H. Cave, London, 1969, p. 163).

161 Büchler, *op. cit.*, p. 117 (Hebrew, p. 88).

162 Acts 5:24, 26.

163 *War* II, 409 f.

164 Büchler, *op. cit.*, pp. 107–11 (Hebrew, pp. 79–83).

165 Peʿs. 57a.

166 Tosef. Sheʿq. 2, 15 (p. 177; ed. Lieberman, p. 211).

167 *Ibid.*, 2, 14.

168 M. Sheʿq. 5, 1.

169 Jeremias, *op. cit.*, pp. 187–95 (Eng. pp. 165–75). A somewhat similar suggestion had been made by Büchler, *op. cit.*, pp. 93–8 (Hebrew, 71–4).

170 Tosef. Sheʿq. *ibid.*

171 *Ibid.*

172 Büchler, *op. cit.*, pp. 93–4 (Hebrew, 71–2).

173 M. Tam. 1, 1; M. Mid. 1, 8.

174 Isa. 22:23 (*The Bible in Aramaic*, Leiden, 62, ed. A. Sperber, III, p. 43.) "amarkal" may here not refer to an office in the Temple, but to one with "the House of David."

175 Büchler, *op. cit.*, pp. 102–3 (Hebrew, 77–8). See also L. Finkelstein, *Ha-Perushim we-Anshei Keneset ha-Gedola*, N.Y., 1950, pp. 14, 16–17.

176 Tosef. Sheq. 2, 15.

177 Tosef. Hor. 2, 10 (p. 476); Yer. *ibid.* 3, 7.

178 M. Yoma 3, 9; 4, 1.

179 Yer. Sheq. 5, 3.

180 See discussions in Büchler, *op. cit.*, pp. 93, 104 (Hebrew, pp. 70–1, 79).

181 On the question of how the Greek term *synedrion* penetrated into Judaism, as well as on the Jewish usage of the term, see the Hebrew edition of H. Mantel, *Studies in the History of the Sanhedrin*, Cambridge, Mass. (1961) 1965; מחקרים בתולדות הסנהדרין, תל-אביב, תשכ"ט – 1969, עמ' 117–121.

182 See Mantel, *ibid.*, chapter 2.

183 See A. Schalit, *Roman Administration in Palestine* (Hebrew), Jerusalem, 1937, pp. 17–19. See also B. Kanael, "The Partition of Judea by Gabinius," *IEJ*, 7 (1957) p. 102 ff.

184 *Ant.* XIV, 90–1. Hyrcanus now had charge only of the Temple.

185 *War* I, 170.

186 See Mantel, *Studies*, p. 144, n. 18 (Hebrew, p. 166, n. 18).

187 *Ant.* XIV, 194, 196.

188 *Ibid.*, 197.

189 *Ibid.*, 195.

190 See F. Rosenthal, "Die Erlasse Caesars," *MGWJ*, 3 (1879), 176–183; J. Juster, *Les Juifs dans l'empire romain*, I, Paris, 1914, p. 391; also p. 216, n. 3; A. Büchler, *Studies in Jewish History*, Oxford University Press, 1956, pp. 7–11; H. Zucker, *Studien z. jüdischen Selbstverwaltung*, Berlin, 1936, p. 58; S. W. Baron, *A Social and Religious History of the Jews*, I p. 218.

191 E. Täubler, *Imperium Romanum*, Leipzig, 1913, p. 161, n. 3, believes that the High Priests' religious authority extended only

over Judea. See, however, *Ant.* XIV, 241–3, where Hyrcanus protected the religious rights of the Jews in **Laodicaea**.

192 Acts 9:1–2.

193 Juster, *op. cit.*, p. 394.

194 See Mantel, *Studies*, pp. 198–206 (Hebrew, 226–36).

195 The expression ובא מעשה לפני החכמים ("the matter came before the Sages") means before the authoritative body of the scholars, namely, the Sanhedrin. See M. Kil. 4, 9; M. 'Eduy. 2, 3; 7, 3; M. Bek. 4, 4; 5, 3 (twice).

196 ובא מעשה לפני חכמים. Tosef. Ket. 4, 9 (pp. 264–5); Yer. Yev. 15, 1; B. Mezi'a 104a.

197 משם הלכה יוצאה ורווחת בישראל. Tosef. Hag. 2, 9 (p. 235); Tosef. Sanh. 7, 1 (p. 425); Yer. Sanh. 1, 7; Sanh. 88b. See also *Meg. Ta'an*, p. 323 (אמרו להם חכמים). Men. 65a has R. Johanan b. Zakkai instead of Sages. But R. Johanan was *Av beth din* even during the time of the Temple. See Mantel, *Studies*, pp. 28–32 (Hebrew, 34–8); *ibid.*, ch. 11, p. 329 (נתנו להם חכמים רשות) (also Sanh. 91a); *ibid*, ch. 13, p. 331 אמרו להם (חכמים). In all these places the "Sages" represent the final authorities in Judaism.

198 This is the view of E. Rivkin, "Defining the Pharisees," *HUCA*, 40–1 (1969–70), pp. 205–49.

199 *Ant.* XIV, 163–84.

200 *War* I, 208–15.

201 Sanh. 19a.

202 See Mantel, "Mishpat Horedos," *Bar Ilan*, 1963, pp. 165–71, for an attempt to reconstruct the events.

203 *War* I, 211.

204 *Ant.* XV, 173.

205 *Ant.* XV, 176.

206 *Ant.* XV, 220.

207 *Ant.* XVI, 357.

208 *War* I, 357.

209 *Ant.* XVII, 160–1.

210 *Ant.* XVII, 163.

211 M. Jastrow, *Dictionary*, pp. 815–6, *s.v.* מעילה; *Aruch Completum*, (ed.), by A. Kohut (2nd ed.), Vienna, 1926, *s.v* מעל

212 *Ant.* XVII, 158–63.

213 The fine for *me'ila*, according to Lev. 5:14–16, is a guilt offering and restitution plus a fifth.

214 See Mantel, *Studies*, pp. 308–9 (Hebr., 347–8).

215 *Ant.* XX, 199–200.

216 The Mishnah (Sanh. 7, 2) refers to a Sadducean court (Sanh. 52b) as one that is "not expert."

217 *Ant.* XX, 201.

218 *Ant.* XX, 216–8.

219 See 'Arak. 11a–b. For discussion and bibliography, see A. Büchler, *Die Priester u.d. Kultus*, pp. 136–40 (Hebr. pp. 105–102).

220 L. H. Feldman (*Josephus*, Loeb ed., IX, p. 504, note a) cites H. A. Wolfson to the effect that Agrippa II exercised his scriptural prerogative as king to appoint judges (Wolfson, *Philo*, II, 346). Though Agrippa II was by Roman appointment only king of Chalcis, by Jewish law he had inherited the title of "King in Jerusalem" from his father (Deut. 17:20; Sifrei, Deut. 162, p. 106a, ed. Finkelstein, pp. 212–3; Hor. 11b). Thus "King Agrippa" in M. Bik. 3, 4 may refer to Agrippa II (H. Albeck, *Untersuchungen über d. Redaktion d. Mischna*, Berlin, 1923, pp. 89–121). From the Roman point of view Agrippa's authority stemmed from the fact that he was "curator" (ἐπιμέλειαν) of the Temple (*Ant.* XX, 222).

221 *War* II, 562–5.

222 *Ant.* XX, 251.

223 A. Kuenen, *Gesammelte Abhandlungen* (transl. from the Dutch by K. Budde), Freiburg i.B. — Leipzig, 1894, p. 62.

224 Schürer, *Geschichte*, II, p. 252, n. 42 (Eng. transl. by T. P. Christie, Second Division, vol. I, p. 178, n. 484).

225 J. Jeremias, *Jerusalem zur Zeit Jesu*, Göttingen, 1962, p. 254 (Eng. transl. by F. H. and C. H. Cave, p. 224).

226 *War* II, 562.

227 Schürer, *op. cit.*, pp. 251–2; Kuenen, *op. cit.*, pp. 61–2; Jeremias, *op. cit.*, p. 167 ff. (Eng., 148 ff.)

228 *Life*, 62.

229 *War* IV, 334–6.

230 See discussion in Mantel, *Studies*, pp. 254–300 (Hebr., pp. 254–339).

231 Mark 14:53.

232 Acts 23:6–9.

233 Mark 14:53 and parallels. See Mantel, *Studies*, p. 290 ff. (Hebr., 328 ff.)

234 Mark 14:53–4; Matt. 26–57 ff.

235 Luke 22:66; see Mantel, *Studies*, p. 254 (Hebr., p. 289).

236 Acts 23:6–9.

237 M. Sanh. 11, 2; Tosef. Sanh. 7, 1 (p. 425) and parallels.

238 M. Pe'a 2, 6; M. 'Eduy. 7, 4.

239 M. Mid. 5, 4; Tosef. Hag. 2, 9 (p. 235); Tosef. Sanh. 7, 1 (p. 425).

240 Tosef. Hag. *ibid.*; Tosef. Sanh. *ibid.*

241 M. Sanh. 1, 5.

242 M. Sanh. 11, 2.

243 Tosef. Sanh. 3, 4 (p. 418).

244 M. Soṭa 1, 4.

245 M. Soṭa 9, 1. Akabya b. Mahalaleel was not appointed *Av beth din* because the holder of this office was in charge of four things in the Temple. See Mantel, *Studies*, pp. 114–8 (Hebr., pp. 135–9).

246 I Macc. 14:41.

247 Tosef. Hag. 2, 9 (p. 235); Tosef. Sanh. 7, 1 (p. 425). See A. Weiss, "Li-She'elat Tiv ha-Beit Din," *Sefer ha-Yovel li-Kevod Levi Ginsberg* (Hebrew section), N.Y., 1946, 189–216.

248 M. Sanh. 2, 1.

249 M. Sanh. 2, 2.

250 Schürer, *Geschichte*, II, pp. 248, 249, 254 ff. (Eng. 180 ff.); A. Geiger, *Urschrift und Übersetzung der Bibel* (2nd ed.), Frankfurt, 1928, ירושלים, המקרא ותרגומיו, גייגר .א
.עמ' 77 תש"ט,

251 M. Hag. 2, 2.

252 Shab. 15a.

253 M. Ned. 5, 5.

254 S. Safrai, in his review of H. Mantel, *Studies in the History of the Sanhedrin*, Kiryat Sefer, 39 (1964) pp. 69–75.

255 For the various types of *synedrion* see Liddell-Scott, *A Greek-English Lexicon*, Oxford, 1966, p. 1704, *s.v.* τό συνέδριον. For its usage in Ptolemaic Egypt, see G. Semeka, *Ptolemäisches Prozessrecht*, Munich, 1913, pp. 192–9.

256 M. Yoma 1, 5; see also M. Para 3, 7–8.

257 R. ha-Sh. 22b. See also M. R. ha-Sh. 1, 7, which states that the witnesses testified before a court of Pharisees. The Pharisaic *Nasi* also sent epistles notifying the Jews in the Diaspora of intercalations in the year, etc. See Mantel, *Studies*, p. 3 (Hebr., p. 5).

258 M. Pe'a. 2, 6.

259   M. K^er. 1, 7; Sifra, Tazri'a, (7). f 59 b-c (ודרש)

260   M. Yoma 1, 6 (אם היה רגיל לקרות קורא, ואם לאו קורין לפניו); *Life*, 9, where Josephus relates that when he was merely fourteen years old, the chief priests used to come to him for information about the law.

261   For a bibliography and an analysis of the various views, see Mantel, *Studies*, p. 55 ff. (Hebr., 65 ff.)

262   J. Wellhausen, *Die Pharisäer u.d. Sadducäer* (2nd ed.), Hannover, 1924, pp. 26–43.

263   Schürer, *Geschichte*, II, pp. 248–58.

264   J. Jost, *Geschichte des Judentums und seiner Sekten*, Leipzig, 1857, pp. 280–1.

265   D. Hoffmann, *Der oberste Gerichtshof*, Berlin, 1878, pp. 40–5.

266   A. Geiger, *Nachgelassene Schriften* (Hebrew section), V, Breslau, 1885, p. 128.

267   J. Derenbourg, *Essai*, Paris, 1867, pp. 90–3 (Hebr., pp. 44–5).

268   S. Schreier, "L^e-Tol^edot ha-Sanhedriya ha-G^edola," *ha-Shiloah*, 31 (1914/15), pp. 404–15.

269   Yer. Sanh. 2, 6; *ibid.* 1, 7. Also Tosef. Hag. 2, 9 (p. 235) Tosef. Sanh. 7, 1 (p. 425).

270   Tosef. Sanh. 4, 7 (p. 421); Sanh. 88b. For a discussion of these corrections, see Mantel, *Studies*, pp. 58–60, notes 26–9 (Hebr., pp. 68–71). See also the rejoinder to S. Safrai in the Hebrew edition, p. 71, n. 32.

271   A. Büchler, *Das Synedrion*, Vienna, 1909, pp. 1–114.

272   See Mantel, *Studies*, pp. 60–3.

273   Liddell-Scott, *Lexicon*, p. 1744.

274   F. Poland, *Geschichte des griechischen Vereinswesens*, Leipzig, 1909, p. 8 ff. and p. 152.

275   H. Frankfort, *Kingship and the Gods*, Chicago, (1948) 1962, pp. 3, 47, 51–2. Wellhausen (*Die Pharisäer und die Sadducäer*, pp. 36–9), assuming that there was only one Sanhedrin, argues that the High Priest in Jerusalem was always the political head of the state.

276   S. Safrai, *Kiryat Sefer*, 39 (1964), p. 70.

277   *Ant.* XIII, 408 relates that Alexandra "permitted the Pharisees to do as they liked in all matters, and also commanded the people to obey them" etc.

278   Herod and the Pharisees did not have a common language on the meaning of law, as shown by A. Schalit *König Herodes*, Berlin, 1969, pp. 659–60 (Hebr., pp. 331–2).

279   M. Yoma 1, 5: אמרו לו [זקני בית דין]: אישי כהן גדול, אנו שלוחי בית דין, ואתה שלוחנו ושליח בית דין.

280   *Ant.* XIII, 297; "The Pharisees had passed on to the people certain regulations handed down by former generations and not recorded in the Laws of Moses, for which reason they are rejected by the Sadducaean group" etc.

281   *Ant.* XIII, 296.

282   *Ant.* XIII, 408 (see above, note 91).

283   See H. [D.] Mantel, "M^egillat Ta'anit w^e-ha-Kittot," *Studies in the History of the Jewish People*, in Memory of Zvi Avneri, 1970, pp. 51–70.

284   M. Sanh. 1, 6.

285   *Ibid.*, 5. During the period of the Second Temple, the term "tribes" probably meant "region"; see G. Alon, *Tol^edot ha-Yehudim*, I, Tel Aviv, 1952, p. 129. See also H. Mantel, *Studies in the History of the Sanhedrin*, Cambridge, (1961) 1965, p. 311, n. 44. (Cf. Tosef. Hag. 2, 9 (p. 235; ed. Lieberman, p. 383), and *ibid.*, Sanh. 7, 1 (p. 425).

286   Sanh. 86b. 87a; Sifrei, Deut. 152 (ed. Friedmann, p. 104; ed. Finkelstein, p. 205); Yer. *ibid.*, 11, 3.

287   See H. Mantel, "Ordination and Appointment in the Period of the Second Temple," *HTR*, 57 (1964), pp. 334–5: also *idem*, מחקרים בתולדות הסנהדרין, תל־אביב, תשכ"ט, עמ' 377–378.

288   M. Sanh. 1, 4.

289   Schürer, *Geschichte*, Hildesheim, 1964, II, p. 227 (Eng., Division II, vol. I, p. 154).

290   *Ant.* IV, 214; *War* II, 571. See Schürer, *op. cit.*, p. 226 (p. 153).

CHAPTER IX

THE TEMPLE AND THE DIVINE SERVICE

1 The three names mentioned in it — R. Eliezer b. Jacob (5, 2), R. Judah (7, 2) and R. Eleazar b. Diglai (3, 8) do not belong to the Mishnah itself; see Ginzberg, *Tamid* etc. p. 38f.

2 This is the conclusion of 7, 3. The following *mishna* enumerates the Psalms that were sung in the Temple, and it is not part of the *mishna* itself; see J. N. Epstein, *Mavo le-Nusah ha-Mishna*, Jerusalem, 1948, p. 979.

3 Tosef. Zev. 6, 13; Yer. Yoma 2, 39d; Yoma 14b.

4 M. Pe'a 2, 6 has: "The story is told of R. Simeon of Mizpeh that he once sowed his field [with two different kinds] and came before Rabban Gamaliel [probably R. Gamaliel the Elder]. They both went up to the Chamber of Hewn Stone. . ."

5 Yer. Yoma 2, 39d; Yoma 16a.

6 See D. Hoffmann, *Mishna Rishona*, Berlin, 1913, p. 14f. The view is widely held by scholars that these *mishnayot* refer to Agrippa I, the assumption being that a king who acted with the piety described in the Mishnah and was more strict with himself than required by the *Halaka* could have been none other than Agrippa I, who was known to have kept to tradition during his reign. However, even Agrippa II was capable of acting piously — carrying the basket of firstfruits on his shoulder or reading the Torah while standing, even though permitted by *Halaka* to sit — if only for the sake of appearance and the pretense of pious conduct before the congregation. Furthermore, both for chronological reasons and because of the Tannaitic tradition concerning the many who were slain on the day he was praised (Yer. Sota 7, 22a), it is preferable to attribute that incident to the time of Agrippa II. This is also implied by the Tosefta (Sota 7, 16) for R. Tarfon, who continued to live until close to the Bar Kokhba revolt, was present on that occasion and testifies about it. It is certain that R. Tarfon could only have testified about the time of Agrippa I. See A. Büchler, *Die*

Priester und der Cultus, Vienna, 1895, p. 9f.

7 One of the Oxyrhynchus papyri (V, No. 840) contains a fragment from a non-canonical Gospel in which Jesus debates with a Pharisee priest who rebukes him and his disciples for their effrontery in coming into the Temple to see the holy vessels without first purifying themselves. From the debate it is possible to gather many details of Temple life during a festival. These details illuminate and supplement information derived from Tannaitic literature (Yer. end of Hag.; Yoma 54a), and all are of great historical importance (see Büchler, *JQR*, 20 (1908) p. 330 f., in contrast to the views of the editors, who had misgivings about the authenticity of the historical traditions embedded therein).

8 John 10:23 and elsewhere.

9 M. Sheq. 11, 2; end of Tosef. Sheq.; Sanh. 88b. The version of the Talmud seems preferable to that of the Tosefta which reads (7, 1) "courts of three each." See J. Derenbourg, *Essai sur l'histoire et la géographie de la Palestine*, Paris, 1867, p. 91. G. Alon, *Mehqarim be-Toledot Yisra'el*, Tel-Aviv, 1956, p. 96 f.

10 Tosef. Sanh. 7, 1; Yer. Sanh. 1, 19 c.

11 M. Sheq. 1, 3; 5, 3; 7, 2.

12 Keritot; Matthew 21:12, and parallels.

13 M. Mid. 2, 2. All actions in the Temple were begun on the right side of the person as he faced the sun. See Zev. 6, 3, and cf. Büchler, *op. cit.*, pp. 46–63.

14 End of Tosef. Sheq.; Sanh. 88b.

15 II Chron. 20:5, "And Jehoshaphat stood in the congregation of Judah and Jerusalem, in the house of the Lord, before the new court." The words "the new court" almost certainly mean a court annexed to the Temple court, and are most appropriate to the Court of Women. This is also the view of the Talmudical tradition (Yev. 7b and parallels). Ezekiel, too, speaks several times of two courts, an inner and an outer one (ch. 44). He cannot be referring to the Court of Priests and the Court of Israelites, since he places

a gate in the inner court at the east (46:1) through which the populace entered, and this is certainly not appropriate to the Court of Priests proper which never had a wall or gate on its eastern side; the four chambers which he places in the outer court (48:22) we know were all in the Court of Women (M. Mid. 2, 5). Büchler (*JQR*, 10 [1897–8], pp. 678–718) and several earlier scholars are inclined to regard the Court of Women as having been added in the time of Herod or even later. However, from the sources indicated, and many more which may be added, it seems to have already existed in early times.

16 *War* V, 199. In the description of Solomon's Temple in *Ant.* VIII, 95–97 there is no mention of the Court of Women, despite its detailed description of the Temple court.

17 *Ant.* XV, 418–419; *War* V 98–99.

18 In *Ant.*, *ibid.*, and *War* V, 198–199, 227; Josephus says that women were forbidden to cross the border of the Court of Women. However, there is no mention of such a prohibition in Talmudic literature, whereas the Tosefta ('Arak. 2, 1) states explicitly: "No woman was seen in the court save at the time of her sacrifice." Thus in order to offer her sacrifice she approached even the altar in the Court of Priests.

19 Tosef. Suk, 4, 1; M. Mid. 2, 5.

20 *Ibid.*; Josephus, however, in *Ant.* VIII, 95 says that this partition, which he calls γεισίον, was three cubits high; in *War* V, 226 he says it was only one cubit.

21 This is not mentioned in the Talmuds, but several early authorities transmit this in the name of the Jerusalem Talmud, e.g., *Sefer Rokeaḥ*, No. 221 (at the beginning); *Or Zaru'a*, No. 315, *et aliter*. Cf. *Midrash Psalms* 17, Buber's ed., p. 128.

22 M. Mid. 1, 7–8: "There were two gates to the Chamber of the Hearth, one opened toward the Rampart and one toward the Temple court ... The Chamber of the Hearth was vaulted; it was a large chamber and around it ran a raised stone pavement; and there the elders of the father's house used to sleep" etc.

23 M. Mid. 3. In Yoma 16 a-b the Tannaitic tradition is divided on whether it stood exactly at the center or extended slightly to the south.

24 Soṭa 1, 5; "They take her up to the eastern gate which is over against the entrance of the Nicanor gate, where they give suspected adulteresses to drink [the water of bitterness], purify women after childbirth, and purify lepers."

25 Yer. Ma'as Sh. 5, 56a; Acts 2:5–11; *et aliter.*

26 See J. B. Frey, *C. I. Jud.*, II, nos. 1222, 1226, 1233, 1236, 1284, 1372–5.

27 See the latest publication by M. Schwabe in the *Sefer Yerushalayim*, Jerusalem, 1956, p. 362. A Jerusalem synagogue connected with the Diaspora is mentioned in Acts 6:9. To these may be added the synagogue of the men of Tarsus (Meg. 26a) or, according to another reading, of the Alexandrians (Tosef. Meg. 3, 6).

28 M. Zev. 5, 8; *Ant.* IV, 205.

29 Matthew 26:18 and parallels.

30 Jubilees 49:20, in connection with eating the Passover in the Temple; 32:11, in connection with fruit of the tree's fourth year of planting which in the *Halaka* is subject to the same law as second tithe. See Büchler, *ZAW*, 25 (1905), p. 40.

31 Tosef. Sanh. 3, 4; Shevu. 16a, and parallels.

32 The things mentioned in M. Shevu. 2, 2: "the [Holy] City and the Temple courts may not be added to save by the decision of a king, a prophet, Urim and Tummim and a Sanhedrin of seventy-one."

33 As amended by the Babylonian Talmud.

34 Verse 106; cf. M. Sheq. 8, and Yer. Sheq. 8, 51a.

35 Tosef. Nega'im 6, 2 and parallels.

36 *Ant.* XIV, 285; *War* I, 229.

37 M. Zev. 3, 1; the slaughtering is valid if performed by a non-priest. However Josephus (*Ant.* III, 228) does not imply this. The Talmudic sources too, when describing the life of the Temple, speak of the priests as the slaughterers (M. Pes. 5, 8; M. Mid. 4, 7; Ket. 106a).

38 See J. Liver, *Chapters in the History of the Priests and Levites* (Hebrew), Jerusalem, 1969.

39 Tosef. Ta'an. 2, 2; cf. the reading of Yer. Ta'an. 4, 68a.

40 Tosef. Hor. 2, 10 and parallels: Mid. 1, 8; but cf. 2, 8.

41 II Macc. 2:1; Tosef. Yoma 1, 4; Yer. Ta'an 4, 67d and 69a.

42 M. Tamid 1, 1 and Mid. 1, 8.

43 M. Yoma 2 and Tamid 3.

44 M. Mᵉn. 11, 7, and Mᵉn. 100a.

45 M. Zᵉv. 12, 1; *Ant.* III, 278.

46 M. Mid. 2, 5; Yer. Suk. 4, 54c; Tosef. Soṭa 7, 8.

47 *Ant.* XIV, 65–66; IV, 318–322.

48 Ezra 6:16–17; Neh. 12:46.

49 I Macc. 4:35–57, particularly v. 52.

50 See particularly 50:17.

51 M. Mid. 1, 2. The keys of the court were in the possession of the elders of the priestly father's house, who were wakened only in the early morning (M. Mid. 1, 9 and Tamid 1).

52 M. Suk. 5, 4; Pᵉs. 5, 5; Tamid 7, 3.

53 Philo, *De Spec. Legibus* II, 188; Sifrei, Bᵉha'alotḵa, 75.

54 M. Tamid 7, 3; Mid. 2, 6; 'Eruv. 2, 6.

55 M. 'Araḵ. 2, 3–4; Tosef. 'Araḵ. 1, 15 and 2, 1–2.

56 Cf. the incident of R. Joshua b. Hananiah, who was a singer, and R. Johanan b. Gudgada, a gatekeeper, in 'Araḵ. 11b; See *Ant.* XX, 218.

57 Philo, *De Spec. Legibus*, I, 156.

58 Sifrei, Deut. 15; M. Makkot 1:3; see Büchler, *ibid.*, pp. 150, 180.

59 *Ant. loc. cit.;* concerning the differing traditions see *Ant.* VIII, 94 and I Chron. 9–27.

60 M. Ḥul. 1, 5; Sifrei, Bᵉha'alotḵa, 62, *et aliter.*

61 Yᵉv. 86b; but the problem was never finally decided; Yer. Ma'as. Sh. 5, 56b.

62 See especially Sifrei Zuṭa, 26, and Liver, *op. cit.*, p. 53 f.

63 M. Para 3, 3 and Tosef. Para 3, 14.

64 Tosef. Para 10, 2; 5, 6; 7, 4.

65 *War* I, 229; Acts 21:24; John 11:55.

66 M. Tamid 5, 6, which states that they were made to stand at the Nicanor Gate. This is not easily explicable, since those needing to be sprinkled were not permitted to approach as far as that; but see the commentators.

67 M. Tamid 7; Ben Sira 50; Luke 1:10.

68 This is how it is explained by R. Akiba in Sifrei at the beginning of Shᵉlaḥ; cf. the words of R. Huna in Yoma 19a.

69 See Ezek. 45:17; 46:13–15; II Chron. 31–3.

70 See M. Bik. 3, 2 and Tosef. 2, 8.

71 Ta'an 27b; Yer. Ta'an. 2, 68b.

72 So it states explicitly in a *barayta* in Yer. Yoma 3, 40b; it is also implied in Tosef. Nᵉg. 8, 9 and *War* V, 227. See the *Oxyrhynchus Papyri* (V, No. 840).

73 See the *Oxyrhynchus Papyri, ibid.;* Josephus, too, relates that Archelaus donned white garments before entering the Temple (*War* II, 1). The Essenes, too, wore white as a sign of piety (*War* II, 123).

74 This is how the *mishna* is explained by Alon in *Tarbiz*, 9, (1938) p. 278; those scholars who have directed their attention to this matter agree with him. Cf. also Acts 21:30.

75 Tosef. Yoma 2, 5–8, Tosef. Shᵉq. 2, and parallels in the Talmuds.

76 I Chron. 23:28–9, 9:26–32; thus, too, in a *barayta*, embedded in the Midrash ha-Gadol to Num. 3:6 (ed. Rabinowitz, p. 20).

77 Tam. 3, 1; Tosef. Shᵉq. 2, 14, Mid. 2, 4.

78 M. Yoma 1, 2; Bab. Yoma 17b.

79 Yer. Ḥag. 2, 78b; *War* V, 230.

80 I Macc. 10:15–21; *Ant.* XIII, 372 and XV, 51.

81 M. Para; Sifrei Ḥuqot, 123, *et aliter.*

82 M. Tam. 7, 3; M. Yoma 7, 1 and 4, 1; Yer. Yoma 3, 41a.

83 *War* II, 409; *Mᵉgillat Ta'anit*, beginning; *Sᵉmaḥot* 6; see Graetz, IV, 3, p. 885.

84 See Pᵉs. 89a and Ḥag. 2b. Yer. Ma'as. Sh. 5, 56a relates a series of legends about women pilgrims to Jerusalem and their miraculous experiences.

85 M. Nazir 3, 6; *War* II; 313–4; Tosef. Nazir 3, 10.

86 Frey *C.I. Jud.* Nos. 1390, 1372–4, 1383, 1384, 1226.

87 M. Sheq. 8, 5; this is the correct reading — see Alon, *op. cit.* (note 9), p. 297, n. 3. The Mishnah is supported by *baraytot*, the Syriac Baruch (1:19) and the Protoevangelium of James (10:1).

88 Pᵉs. 3b; Acts 21:29, John 12:20; *Ant.* XII end of ch. 3.

89 M. Sh^eq. 1, 5 and 7, 6.
90 Tosef. Suk. 3, 15; Tosef. R. ha-Sh. 1, 12 and parallels.
91 The watch is described at the beginning of M. Middot and M. Tamid; cf. the discussion in the Babylonian Talmud at the beginning of Tamid.
92 *Against Apion*, II, 9; there is no need to amend the number to make it conform with the twenty men mentioned in *War* VI, 294, for there he is referring to the shutting of the gates and here to the actual guarding.
93 Philo, *De Spec. Legibus*, 1, 159; *Ant.* XVIII, 30.
94 Yer. 2, 48d; cf. M. Sh^eq. 5, 1 and M. Tam. 3, 8.
95 M. Tam. 1, 2; M. Yoma 2, 1.
96 M. Suk. 5, 5; M. 'Arak. 2, 3.
97 *Ant.* III, 128; Z^ev. 55b.
98 See M. Tam. ch. 4 and beginning of ch. 5; the *barayta* in Yoma 37b: "Whosoever reads the Sh^ema' with the men of the priestly course has not fulfilled his duty," since these read it earlier.
99 M. Tam. ch. 5; Yoma 26b.
100 M. Tam. 6, 3; M. Kel. 1, 9.
101 See Luke 1:10: "and the whole assembly of the people prayed without while the incense was being offered." Judith, too, prayed while the incense was offered (9:1).
102 M. Tam. ch. 7; Tosef. Soṭa 7, 8.
103 Ben Sira 50; Qid. 71a; Eccl. R. 3, 11.
104 M. Tam. 7, 3; for details of the order of singing, see below.
105 M. Tam. ch. 7; this custom is already mentioned by Ben Sira, 50:15–16.
106 M. P^es. 5, 1; M. Tam. 6, 1; M. Yoma 3, 5; Tosef. Ta'an. beginning of ch. 3. Nowhere in the sources is it stated explicitly that the priestly blessing was given only during the regular morning offering, but this seems the case from Tosefta Ta'anit, beginning of ch. 3, and Yer. Ta'an. 4; this is also the view of Maimonides in *Hilkot Tefilla*, 14.
107 Sifrei Zuṭa, p. 325; cf. Yoma 26a.
108 See L. Ginzberg, *Perushim w^e-Ḥiddushim ba-Y^erushalmi* III, pp. 70–5.
109 M. Z^ev. 9, 6; M. B^er. 1, 1.
110 Cf. the *barayta* at end of Soṭa; *Ant.*, end of Book III. and XIV, 67.

111 The Sabbath customs in the Temple and the arrangement of the shewbread are mainly taught in M. M^en. ch. 11 and Tosef. M^en. 11.
112 M. Tam. 5, 1; Bab. B^er. 12a.
113 See M. M^en. ch. 11 and cf. Tosef. Suk. 4, 25.
114 Tosef. M^en. 11, 12–13.
115 Yoma 39a and parallels.
116 Tosef. M^en. 11, 18–19 and parallels.
117 M. Beza 2, 4, where the Schools of Shammai and Hillel differ on which sacrifices of the people were offered on the festival; see the discussions in both Talmuds. In the course of time it was decided that all the festival sacrifices, including the pilgrimage burnt offering which was not eaten, could be offered on the day of the festival.
118 M. Yoma 1, 8; *Ant.* XVIII, 29; *War* VI, 290.
119 M. Ḥag. 3, 7; *Ant.*, *loc. cit.*
120 *Ant.* III, 128; Yoma 54b. The practice of carrying out the vessels to show the people is mentioned in Mishnah Ḥagiga and the Talmudic discussions there. Evidence of this practice is also found in the *Oxyrhynchus Papyri*, V. No. 840.
121 M. Suk. 5, 7; M. M^en. 11, 7.
122 M. P^es. 7, 8 and 9, 8; Targum Jonathan to Ex. 12:4.
123 M. P^es. 5, 6 and Yer. P^es. beginning of ch. 6; *et aliter*. Philo, *De Spec. Legibus*, II, 145.
124 See the *baraytot* in both Talmuds, beginning of P^es. 6.
125 M. M^en. 10, 2.
126 Cf. II Macc. 10:6–9 and Plutarch in T. Reinach, *Textes des auteurs grecs et latins relatifs aux Judaisme*, Paris, 1895, paragraph 2.
127 M. 'Arak. 2, 3; Yer. Suk. 5, 51a.
128 II Macc. 9:10, at the dedication of the Temple; a crowd of celebrants also went to meet Jesus with palm branches in their hands (John 12:13).
129 M. Suk. 4, 9; Tosef. Suk. 3, 1 and 16.
130 Cf. Philo, *De Spec. Legibus*, II, 204–7; *Ant.* III, 245 T. Reinach, *op. cit.*, p. 143–4.
131 Several early authorities cite this in the name of the Jerusalem Talmud. See S. Safrai, *Pilgrimage at the Time of the Second*

Temple (Hebrew), Tel-Aviv, 1965, p. 212 n. 165.

¹³² M. Suk. 5, 4; Tosef. Suk. 4 and the Talmudic discussions.

¹³³ See Geiger, *Zeitschrift fur jüd. Theol.*, 3, p. 417; Rappaport, *Hashahar*, 4 (1873) p. 134; S. Lieberman, *Kiryat Sefer*, 12 (1936), p. 56.

¹³⁴ Tosef. Yoma 4, 17; M. Yoma ch. 1 and 6, 3.

¹³⁵ M. Yoma 3, 8; Yer. Yoma 3, 10d; cf. the versions of the order of the service.

¹³⁶ M. Yoma 1, 6; Tosef. Yoma 1, 9; Yoma 19b.

¹³⁷ Yoma 53b; Yer. Yoma 5, 4, 2c. Concerning the unstable houses of the people of Sharon, see also M. Soṭa 8, 3.

¹³⁸ Tosef. Yoma 4, 18; Yoma 70 a.

¹³⁹ Yoma 36b. The papyrus fragments were published by Cowley in *JEA*, 2 (1919), pp. 207–13; see Safari, *Yerushalayim, Review for Eretz-Israel Research* (Hebrew), II, Jerusalem, 1955, p. 40, n. 44.

¹⁴⁰ R. ha-Sh. 31b. Yer. Mᵉg. 4, 74b; Suk. 55a; M. Pᵉs. 5, 7; M. 'Araḳ. 2, 4; Yer. Suk. 5, 55a; cf. further M. 'Araḳ. 2, 3–6 and Tosef. 'Araḳ. 2, 2.

¹⁴¹ M. Shᵉq. chs 5 and 6

¹⁴² M Shᵉq. ch. 4; cf. Philo, *De Spec. Legibus*, I, 70–6.

¹⁴³ M. Mid. end ch. 3; Josephus refers to this vine several times (*War* V, 211), and Tacitus (*Histories*, v, 5) also mentions it.

¹⁴⁴ Tosef. Shᵉq. 3, 2; cf. the whole of Mishnah and Tosefta 'Araḳ.

¹⁴⁵ M. Shᵉq. 4, 2; for others who were paid rom the chamber offering, see M. Shᵉq. 4, 1 and Yer. Shᵉq. 4, 48a; Kᵉt. 105 a and 106a.

¹⁴⁶ *War* II, 175; *Ant.* XVIII, 60.

¹⁴⁷ See Epstein, *op. cit.* (note 2), 1, p. 72f.

¹⁴⁸ M. Shᵉq. 5, 2; 2, 1; Tosef. Shᵉq. 2, 15, M. Mᵉn. 8, 7; *et aliter*.

¹⁴⁹ Tosef. Mᵉn. 13, 21; Pᵉs. 57a.

¹⁵⁰ II Kings 12:5; II Chron. 24:5 and 34:8f.

¹⁵¹ Sifrei, Num. sec. 142: "Shall ye observe" (with reference to the daily offering), "that it be brought from she offering of the chamber alone;" cf. beginning of *Mᵉgillat Ta'anit*, where the *barayta*

describes the festival held from the 1st to the 8th of Nisan in commemoration of the victory of the Pharisees over the Sadducees. (Mᵉn. 65 and parallel).

¹⁵² M. Shᵉq. ch. 1. Regarding the conflict with the priests, see M. 'Eduy. 8, 3; Büchler, *Die Priester*, p. 9; Alon, *op. cit.*, I, p. 255 f.

¹⁵³ M. Shᵉq. 1, 3; "the province" in the Mishnah sometimes refers merely to Jerusalem, but in this case it is certain that other cities throughout the land are intended. This is also implied in Maseḳet Sofᵉrim 21, 5 and in Yer. Shᵉq. end of ch. 1, where reference is made to the expenses of the journey which the money changers defrayed from the offering of the chamber. This can certainly only mean the expenses for the journey to the cities of the provinces; cf. further Shᵉq. beginning of ch. 2 and Tos f. Shᵉq. 1, 8.

¹⁵⁴ Yer. Ta'an. 4, 69; Lam. R. 2 2; the records of three cities — Kabul, Shihin, and Migdal Zebo'aiya — were carried up to Jerusalem in a wagon.

¹⁵⁵ Matt. 17:27; *Ant.* XVIII, 19.

¹⁵⁶ *Ant.* XVIII, 312; cf. Philo, *Legatio ad Gaium*, chs. 40 and 42.

¹⁵⁷ M. Shᵉq. chs. 2, 3, 4; Tosef. Shᵉq. 2, 3–4.

¹⁵⁸ *Ant.* XIV, 214, 245; see also *Ant.* XVI, 28 as well as the whole of that chapter; cf. Cicero's speech in defense of Flaccus, the governor of Asia (*Pro Flacco*, 28f.).

¹⁵⁹ M. Ḥag. ch. 3; see Yer. Ta'an. 4, 69a.

¹⁶⁰ M. Mᵉn. ch. 8; Tosef. ch. 9; for the lambs from Hebron, see Mᵉn. 87a and Soṭa 33b.

¹⁶¹ Yer. Ta'an. 4, 69a; Lam. R. 2, 2.

¹⁶² Mᵉn. 21a and Tosef. Mᵉn. 9, 15.

¹⁶³ Kᵉr. 6a and parallels.

¹⁶⁴ Midrash Cant. ed. Grünhut 4:13. The name "Mt. Moriah" interpreted as a reference to the myrrh growing in Jerusalem; see the Targum to Cant. 1:13. For gardens in the valley of Kidron, see M. Yoma 5, 6.

¹⁶⁵ M. Beẓa 1, 6; Tosef. Pe'a 4, 7; Sifrei Qoraḥ 117; *et aliter*. The whole subject is clearly set forth by Alon, *op. cit.*, I, p. 83f.

166   *Life*, ch. 12; *Ant*. XX, 181 and XX, 206.

167   Malachi 3:10, Neh. 10:36–38 12:44, 13:5–12, II Chron. 3:5f.

168   This is how the words αἱ δεκάται καὶ τὰ τέλη are to be understood. They were so interpreted by Kautsch, Charles, and Zeitlin in their eds.

169   *Ant*. XIV, 245: καθώς ἔθος αὐτοῖς; the words are explained well by Büchler in the *Steinschneider Jubilee Volume*, (1896), p. 95.

170   M. Ma'as. Sh. 5, 15: "Johanan the High Priest did away with the avowal concerning the tithe." In explaining that this refers to the time of John Hyrcanus II (end of the sixties B.C.E.), I am following the view of Alon, *op. cit*. In the Talmud some interpret this regulation "unfavorably" and some "favorably". In our explanation this act is treated as unfavorable. See Yer. Ma'as Sh. end of ch. 5 and parallels. Cf. A. Oppenheimmer in the *De Fries Memorial Volume*, Jerusalem, 1969, p. 7of.

171   M. Yadayim 4, 3; Epiphanius Panarion 129; 30–34, 30.

172   Büchler, *Die Priester*, p. 6of.; G. Dalman, *Die Worte Jesu*, Leipzig, 1898, p. 7f.

173   Yer. Suk. 5, 55a: "Said R. Jonah: Jonah b. Amitai was one of the pilgrims on the festival. He entered during the rejoicing of *Beth ha-Sho'eva* and the holy spirit possessed him." Cf. Acts 2.

174   See especially Midrash Tannaim, p. 77–8.

175   *War* I, 88; II, 10; V, 244.

176   Ex. 23:17 and 30:23; Deut. 16:16. Deuteronomy typically adds the phrase: "in the place He shall choose".

177   See Ḥag. 6a; *et aliter*. This difference in the discussions of the Babylonian and Jerusalem Talmuds is striking.

178   Ḥag. 6b and parallels.

179   Pᵉs. 70b; this Sage lived after Shemaiah and Abtalyon and belonged to Hillel's generation. See the Talmudic discussion.

180   Tobit 1: 6–10; Midrash Tanhuma, Buber ed., Tᵉzawe (51b); Luke 2:41.

181   *Ant*. IV, 203–204; Philo, *De Spec Legibus*, I, 67–8. In *Allegoria*, III, 11, Philo again deals with this topic, but only repeats the Torah verses. For all details of the pilgrimage, see S. Safari, *Pilgrimage at the Time of the Second Temple* (Hebrew), Tel-Aviv, 1965.

182   *Ant*., *ibid*. The Talmudic sources also support this; see, e.g., Yer. Hor. 1, 46a and Gen. R. 5, 8.

183   *War* II, 43 and 515.

184   The most explicit source is in *War*, *ibid*. For other proofs see Klein, '*Ever ha-Yarden ha-Yᵉhudi*, Vienna, 1925, especially pp. 25–31.

185   Yer. Ma'as. Sh. 5, 56a, and parallels; Eccl. R. 1, 1 and parallels.

186   Tosef. B. Batra 10, 12 and parallels; M. Yoma 6, 3: "It once happened that Arsela of Sepphoris led it [the scapegoat] away." This is the reading in all the principal versions.

187   See the numerous verses in John, and also Luke 2:41.

188   *Life*, 52; *War* II, 232–33; *Ant*. XX, 118.

189   See Dalman, *Worte*, p. 222–56.

190   Philo, *De Spec. Legibus*, I, 69. For Philo's own pilgrimage see *De providentia*, 64.

191   Philo, *De Spec. Legibus*, I, 78; *Ant*. XVIII, 313.

192   *Ant*. XXII, 26; Acts 2:9–11, 6:9, 8:26; Mᵉg. 26a; *et aliter*.

193   Tosef. Mᵉg. 3, 2, Mᵉg. 26a; Acts 6:9. The inscription of Theodotos has been explained and translated into Hebrew by M. Schwabe in *Sefer Yerushalayim*, I, p. 362.

194   D. Chwolsohn, *Das letzte Passahmahl Christi und der Tag seines Todes* (2nd. ed.), Leipzig, 1908; J. Jeremias, *Jerusalem, Zur Zeit Jesu*, Göttingen, 1962, p. 89 ff.

195   Pᵉs. 64b; *War* VI, 421.

196   *Ibid*., *ibid*.

197   *Aggadat Shir ha-Shirim* (ed. Schechter), p. 28. With regard to the text, see *idem*, p. 108.

198   Ps. 42–3, 84, 122, 134–5 etc.

199   *Ant*. XVII, 26.

200   Ḥag. 6b and parallels.

201   *Ant*. XI, 109; Pᵉs. 89a and parallels; Luke 2:41–3.

202   Tosef. Suk. 2, 1.

203   *War* VI, 290; I, 229; John 11:56; Acts 21:26.

204 M. Ḥag. 1, 6; Ḥag. 17b; Bab. Mo'ed Qaṭan 24b.

205 *Ant.* XVII, 213; *War* II, 10; P⁰s. 80a.

206 *Ant.* IV, 2034; M. Ḥag. 3:6–7 and both Talmuds *ad loc.*; M⁰g. 26a.

207 Sifrei Num. 151 and Deut. 134. For the custom of Jesus, see Matt. 16:1 and parallels.

208 *War* II, 425–6; Tosef. Ta'an. 4, 6.

208a So is the correct text, see Safrai, *op. cit.* p. 221.

209 Z⁰v. 97a, and Tosaf. Bab. to Ḥag. 17b beginning "For it is written."

210 M. Yoma 7, 1; M. Soṭa 7, 7. On the number of synagogues in Jerusalem, see Yer. M⁰g. 3, 73d.

211 See Neh. chs. 8 and 9. This view of the origin of the synagogue inclines to the views of M. Rosenmann, *Der Ursprung der Synagoge*, Berlin, 1907, p. 17, and L. Herzfeld, *Geschichte des Volkes Israel*, III, Braunsweig, 1857, p. 131.

212 See B⁰r. ch. 4, Mishna, Babylonian and Jerusalem Talmuds.

213 R. ha-Sh. 31b; Soṭa 40a.

214 On the blowing of the shofar, see M. R. ha-Sh. 1, 4; on the holding of the palm branch, Tosef. Suk. 2, 10. This question is clarified by Alon, *op. cit.*, I pp. 106–14.

215 *Ant.* XVII, 140–163; Luke 21:37 and elsewhere; Acts chs. 2–4; P⁰s. 26a.

216 Yoma 71b.

217 Yer. Sanh. 2 20c; M. Mo'ed Qaṭan 3, 4; *et aliter.*

218 *Letter of Aristeas*, 46; *Ant.* XII, 56.

219 Yer. Sh⁰q. 4, 48a; Num. R. 11, 3; Ket. 106a.

220 Sifrei Deut. 356. See also Yer. Ta'an. 4, 68a and parallels.

221 *Ant.* V, 61 and III, 88; *Against Apion*, I, 30–38.

222 *Halaḵot G⁰dolot*, Venice ed., 141c; Berlin ed., p. 615, *Sefer Beit-Ḥashmonai.*

223 Shab. 13b; the *barayta* at the beginning of M⁰gillat Ta'anit, see Graetz, *Geschichte*, III, p. 802 ff.

224 Shab., *op. cit.*

225 Sanh. 52b; Midrash Tannaim, p. 102.

226 Philo, *Vita Mosis*, II, 177 ff.; *Ant.* III, 146 and *War* V, 217–218; Suk. 55b.

BIBLIOGRAPHY

INTRODUCTION
THE RISE OF ROME

A. Alfoeldi, *Early Rome and the Latins*, Ann Arbor, 1965

H. Bengston, *Grundriss der römischen Geschichte und Quellen*, München, 1967

M. Cary, *A History of Rome*, N.Y., London, 1954

G. De Sanctis, *Storia dei Romani*, Torino, 1907

T. Frank (ed.), *An Economic Survey of Ancient Rome*, I-V, Baltimore, 1933–1940

E. Gjerstad, *Early Rome*, Lund, 1953–1960

A. Heuss, *Römische Geschichte* (2nd ed.), Braunschweig, 1964

M. Holleaux, *Rome, la Grece et les monarchies hellénistiques*, Paris, 1921

J. Kromayer, *Rom's Kampf um die Weltherrschaft*, Leipzig, 1912

D. Magie, *Roman Rule in Asia Minor*, I-II, Princeton, 1950

F. B. Marsch, *A History of the Roman World From 146 to 30 B.C.* (2nd ed.), London, 1953

Th. Mommsen, *Römische Geschichte*, Breslau, 1854–5

E. Pais, *Storia critica di Roma durante i primi cinque secoli*, I-III, Roma, 1913–1920

L. Partei, *Storia di Roma e del mondo romano*, Torino, 1952–1960

A. Piganiol, *Histoire de Rome* (5th ed.), Paris, 1962

T. Rice Holmes, *The Roman Republic*, Oxford, 1923

M. Rostovtzeff, *The Social and Economic History of the Hellenistic World*, I-III, Oxford, 1941

H. H. Scullard, *A History of the Roman World from 753 to 146 B.C.*, London, 1966

CHAPTER I-II
THE FALL OF THE HASMONEAN DYNASTY AND THE ROMAN CONQUEST; THE END OF THE HASMONEAN DYNASTY AND THE RISE OF HEROD

F.M. Abel, *Géographie de la Palestine*, I-II, Paris, 1938

M. Avi-Yonah, *The Holy Land from the Persian to the Arab Conquests* (536 B.C. to A.D. 640), (translated from the Hebrew), Grand Rapids, Michigan, 1966

H.I. Bell, *Jews and Christians in Egypt*, Oxford, 1924

J. Derenbourg, *Essai sur l'histoire et la géographie de la Palestine*, I-II, Paris, 1867

R. Dussaud, *Topographie historique de la Syrie antique et médiévale*, Paris, 1927

T. Frank (ed.), *An Economic Survey of Ancient Rome IV*, Baltimore, 1933

H. Fuchs, *Der geistige Widerstand gegen Rom*, Berlin, 1964

M. Gelzer, *Pompeius*, München, 1949

J. Juster, *Les Juifs dans l'empire romain*, I-II, Paris, 1914

E. Kuhn, *Die städtische und bürgerliche Verfassung des römischen Reichs*, I-II, Leipzig, 1864

J. Klausner, *History of the Second Temple* (Hebrew) (2nd ed.), I-V, Jerusalem, 1951

R. Laqueur, *Der jüdischen Historiker Flavius Josephus*, Giessen, 1920

D. Magie, *Roman Rule in Asia Minor*, I-II, Princeton, 1950

J. Marquardt, *Römischen Staatsverwaltung* (3rd ed.), I-II, Darmstadt, 1957

Ed. Meyer, *Cäsars Monarchie und das Prinzipat des Pompeius*, Gotha, 1920

B. Niese, *Geschichte der griechischen und makedonischen Staaten seit der Schlacht bei Chaeronea*, I-II, Gotha, 1903

W. Otto, *Herodes : Beiträge zur Geschichte des letzten jüdischen Könighauses*, Stuttgart, 1913

A. Paretti, *La Sibilla babilonese nella propaganda ellenistica*, Firenze, 1943

T. Rice Holmes, *The Roman Republic*, I-III, Oxford, 1923
The Architect of the Roman Empire, Oxford, 1928

M.I. Rostovtzeff, *The Social and Economic History of the Hellenistic World*, I-III, Oxford, 1941

A. Rowe, *Topography and History of Beth-Shan*, Philadelphia, 1930

A. Schalit, *Roman Administration in Palestine* (Hebrew), Jerusalem, 1937
King Herod (Hebrew), Jerusalem, 1960
König Herodes, Berlin, 1969

A. Schlatter, *Geschichte Israels von Alexander der Grossen bis Hadrian* (3rd ed.), Stuttgart, 1925

E. Schürer, *Geschichte des jüdischen Volkes im Zeitalter Jesu Christi* (3rd 4th ed.), I-III, Leipzig, 1901–1909

H. Willrich, *Das Haus des Herodes zwischen Jerusalem und Rom*, Heidelberg, 1929

CHAPTER III-IV

THE REIGN OF HEROD; THE HERODIAN DYNASTY AND THE PROVINCE OF JUDEA AT THE END OF THE PERIOD OF THE SECOND TEMPLE

F.M. Abel, *Histoire de la Palestine*, I, Paris, 1952

E. Ciaceri, "Agrippa I e la politica di Roma verso la Giudea," *Processi politici e relationi internazionali*, Roma, 1918

H. Dessau, *Geschichte der römischen Kaiserzeit*, II, 2, Berlin, 1930

J. Dobiás, *Dějiny rimské provincie syrské*, Prag, 1924

J. Felten, *Neuetestamentliche Zeitgeschichte* (3rd–4th ed.), I, Regensburg, 1925

H. Graetz, *Geschichte der Juden von den ältesten Zeiten bis auf die Gegenwart* (5th ed.), III, 1, Leipzig, 1905

A.H.M. Jones, *The Herods of Judaea*, Oxford, 1938

J. Klausner, *History of the Second Temple* (Hebrew) (2nd ed.), Jerusalem, IV, 1951

Ed. Meyer, *Ursprung und Anfänge des Christentums*, II-III, Stuttgart, Berlin, 1921

A. Momigliano, "Herod of Judea," *CAH*, X (chap. XI)
"Ricerche sull'organizzazione della Guidea sotto il dominio romano," *Annali della R. Scuola Normale Superiore di Pisa*, 3 (n.s.) (1934), 183–221; 347–396

W.O.T. Oesterley, *A History of Israel*, II, Oxford, 1932

W. Otto, *Herodes : Beiträge zur Geschichte des letzten jüdischen Königshauses*, Stuttgart, 1913

S. Perowne, *The Life and Times of Herod the Great*, London, 1956

A. Schalit, *Roman Administration in Palestine* (Hebrew), Jerusalem, 1937
König Herodes, Berlin, 1969

A. Schlatter, *Geschichte Israels von Alexander dem Grossen bis Hadrian* (3rd ed.), Stuttgart, 1925

E. Schürer, *Geschichte des jüdischen Volkes im Zeitalter Jesu Christi* (3rd–4th ed.), I, Leipzig, 1901

A.N. Sherwin-White, *Roman Society and Roman Law in the New Testament*, Oxford, 1963

J. Wellhausen, *Israelitische und jüdische Geschichte* (8th ed.), Berlin, Leipzig, 1921

H. Willrich, *Das Haus des Herodes zwischen Jerusalem und Rom*, Heidelberg, 1929

S. Zeitlin, *The Rise and Fall of the Judaean State*, II, Philadelphia, 1967

CHAPTER V

THE ECONOMY OF JUDEA IN THE PERIOD OF THE SECOND TEMPLE

A. Aptowitzer-S. Krauss (eds.), *A. Schwartz-Festschrift zum siebzigsten geburstgabe*, Berlin-Vienna, 1917

A.G. Barton, *The Apostolic Age and the New Testament*, Philadelphia, 1936

A. Büchler, *Der galiläische Am-Haarez der zweiten Jahrhunderts*, Vienna, 1906
The Economic Conditions of Judea after the Destruction of the Second Temple, London, 1912

F. Bühl, *Die Sozialen Verhältnisse der Israeliten*, Berlin, 1899

D. Chwolsohn, *Das letzte Passamahl Christi und der Tag seines Todes* (2nd ed.), Leipzig, 1908

D. Farbstein, *Das Recht der unfreien und freien Arbeiter nach jüdisch-talmudischen Recht*, Frankfurt, 1896

H. Graetz, *Geschichte der Juden von den ältesten Zeiten bis auf die Gegenwart* (5th ed.), III, 1, Leipzig, 1905

L. Hertzfeld, *Handelsgeschichte der Juden des Altertums* (2nd ed.), Brunschweig, 1894

J. Klausner, *History of the Second Temple* (Hebrew) (2nd ed.), I-V, Jerusalem, 1951
Jesus of Nazareth (Hebrew) (6th ed.), I-II, Ramat-Gan, 1954

S. Klein, *Neue Beiträge zur Geschichte und Geographie Galiläas*, Leipzig, 1923

S. Krauss, *Talmudische Archäologie*, I-III, Leipzig, 1910–1912
Qadmoniot ha-Talmud, I, Vienna, 1924; II, Tel-Aviv, 1929

B. Meissner, *Babylonien und Assyrien*, I-II, Heidelberg, 1920–1925

Ed. Meyer, *Wirtschaftliche Entwicklung des Altertums*, Jena, 1895
Die Sklaverei in Altertum, Jena, 1895
(Both reprinted in *Kleine Schriften*, I, Halle, 1924, 79–212)

S. Raphaeli, *Matbᵉot ha-Yehudim*, Jerusalem, 1913

M.I. Rostovtzeff, *Geschichte der Staatspacht in der römischen Kaiserzeit*, Leipzig, 1902

R.P. Schwalm, *La vie privée du peuple Juif à l'époque de Jesus Christ*, Paris, 1910

E. Schürer, *Geschichte des jüdischen Volkes im Zeitalter Jesu Christi* (3rd–4th ed.), I, Leipzig, 1901

R. Smith, *The Religion of the Semites*, Edinburgh, 1879

L. Waterman, *Royal Correspondence of the Assyrian Empire*, I–IV, Ann Arbor, 1930–36

CHAPTER VI

JERUSALEM IN THE HELLENISTIC AND ROMAN PERIODS

M. Avi-Yonah (ed.), *Sefer Yerushalayim*, Jerusalem, 1956
Essays in Memory of E.R. Goodenough, Leiden, 1968
"The Third and Second Walls of Jerusalem," *IEJ*, 18 (1968), 98–125

B. Bagatti-J.T. Milik, *Gli Scavi di "Dominus Flevit*," I, Jerusalem, 1958

P. Benoit, "L'Antonia D'Hérode le Grand et le Forum Oriental D'Aelia Capitolina," *HTR*, 64 (1971), 135–167

F.J. Bliss, *Excavations at Jerusalem* (1894–97), London, 1898

F.J. Hollis, *The Archaeology of Herod's Temple*, London, 1934

K. Kenyon, *Jerusalem*, London, 1970

A. Kümmel, *Karte der Materialien zur Topographie des alten Jerusalem*, Halle, 1904

L.A. Meyer–E.L. Sukenik, *The Third Wall of Jerusalem*, Jerusalem, 1930

J.T. Milik, *Discoveries in the Judaean Desert*, III, Oxford, 1962

T. Reinach, *Textes d'auteurs grecs et romains relatifs au Judaisme*, Paris, 1895

J.J. Simons, *Jerusalem of the Old Testament*, Leiden, 1952

V. Tcherikover, "Was Jerusalem a 'Polis'?"
IEJ, 14 (1964), 61–78

V. Tzaferis, "Jewish Tombs at and near
Giv'at ha-Mivtar, Jerusalem," *IEJ*, 20
(1970), 18–32

L.H. Vincent–M.A. Steve, *Jerusalem de
l'Ancien Testament*, I, Paris, 1954

C. Warren–C.R. Conder, *Survey of W. Palestine : Jerusalem*, Leiden, 1884

K. Watzinger, *Denkmäler Palästinas*, I–II,
Leipzig, 1933–35

C.W. Wilson, *Ordinance Survey of Jerusalem*,
London, 1865

C. Wilson–C. Warren, *The Recovery of Jerusalem*, London, 1871

K. Zimmermann–K. Schick, *Karten und
Pläne zur Topographie des alten Jerusalem*,
I–II, 1876

CHAPTER VII

JEWISH ART AND ARCHITECTURE
IN THE HASMONEAN AND HERODIAN PERIODS

N. Avigad, *Ancient Monuments in the Kidron
Valley* (Hebrew), Jerusalem, 1954
"Excavations in the Jewish Quarter of
the Old City of Jerusalem, 1971," *IEJ*,
22 (1972), 193–200

M. Avi-Yonah, *Oriental Art in Roman Pales-
tine*, Rome, 1961
"Jewish Art," *Encyclopaedia of World Art*,
VIII, 898–920

F.J. Bliss–R.A.S. Macalister, *Excavations in
Palestine*, London, 1902

N. Butler, *Princeton Archaeological Expedition
to Syria*, II, Leiden, 1922

E. Cohn-Wiener, *Die jüdische Kunst*, Berlin,
1929

H. Frankfort, *The Art and Architecture of the
Ancient Orient*, Harmondsworth, 1954

E. R. Goodenough, *Jewish Symbols in the
Greco-Roman Period*, I–XII, New York,
1953–65

M. Kon, *The Tombs of the Kings*, (Hebrew),
Tel-Aviv, 1946

E. Littmann, *Princeton Archaeological Expedition to Syria*, IV, Leiden, 1922

F. Landsberger, *History of Jewish Art*,
London, 1946

B. Mazar, *Excavations in the Old City of
Jerusalem First to Third Seasons*, Jerusalem,
1969–71

Y. Meshorer, *Jewish Coins of the Second
Temple Period*, Tel-Aviv, 1967

V. Nedomački, *Stara jevrejska umetnost u
Palestini*, Belgrade, 1964

A. Reifenberg, *Ancient Hebrew Arts*, New
York, 1950

C. Roth (ed.), *Jewish Art*, Jerusalem, 1961

A. Segal, "Herodium," *IEJ*, 23 (1973),
27–29

V. Tzaferis, "Jewish Tombs at and near
Giv'at ha-Mivtar, Jerusalem," *IEJ*, 20
(1970), 18–32

L.H. Vincent–F.M. Abel–L. Mackay, *Le
Haram de Hebron*, Paris, 1922

L.H. Vincent–M.A. Steve, *Jerusalem de
l'ancien Testament*, I, Paris, 1954

Y. Yadin, *Masada*, London, 1966

CHAPTER VIII

THE HIGH PRIESTHOOD AND THE SANHEDRIN
IN THE TIME OF THE SECOND TEMPLE

M. Avi-Yonah, *The Holy Land from the Persian
to the Arab Conquests* (536 B.C. to A.D. 640)
(transl. from the Hebrew), Grand Rapids
Michigan, 1966

S.W. Baron, *A Social and Religious History
of the Jews* (2nd ed.), I, New York,
Philadelphia, 1952

E. Bevan, *Jerusalem Under the High-Priests*, London, 1912

J. Bright, *A History of Israel*, London, 1960

A. Büchler, *Die Priester und der Cultus im letzten Jahrzehnt des Jerusalemischen Tempels*, Vienna, 1895
Das Synedrion, Vienna, 1909
Studies in Jewish History, Oxford, 1956

J. Derenbourg, *Essai sur l'histoire et la géographie de la Palestine*, I–II, Paris, 1867

L. Finkelstein, *The Pharisees*, I, Philadelphia, 1962

A. Geiger, *Nachgelassene Schriften* (Hebrew Section), V, Berlin, 1885
Urschrift und Übersetzungen der Bible (2nd ed.), Frankfurt a.M., 1928

H. Graetz, *Geschichte der Juden von den ältesten Zeiten bis auf die Gegenwart* (5th ed.), I, Leipzig, 1908

D. Hoffmann, *Der oberste Gerichtshof*, Berlin, 1885

J. Jeremias, *Jerusalem zur Zeit Jesu*, Göttingen, 1962 (English transl: *Jerusalem in the Time of Jesus Christ*, London, 1969)

J. Jost, *Geschichte des Judentums und seiner Sekten*, Leipzig, 1857

J. Juster, *Les Juifs dans l'empire romain*, I, Paris, 1914

J. Klausner, *History of the Second Temple* (Hebrew), I, Jerusalem, 1951

R. Leszynsky, *Die Sadduzäer*, Berlin, 1912

B. Levine, "*The* Nethinim," *JBL*, 82 (1963), 207–212

H.D. Mantel, *Studies in the History of the Sanhedrin*, Cambridge, 1961
"The Nature of the Great Synagogue," *HTR*, 60 (1967), 69–91

"Megillat Ta'anit we-ha-Kittot," *Studies in the History of the Jewish People*, in Memory of Zvi Avineri (Hebrew), Haifa, 1970, 51–70

M. Noth, *The History of Israel* (transl. from the German), London, 1960

W.O.E. Oesterley, *A History of Israel*, II, Oxford, 1932

M.I. Rostovtzeff, *Studien zur Geschichte des römischen Kolonates*, Leipzig, 1910
Social and Economic History of the Hellenistic World, I, Oxford, 1941

A. Schalit, *Roman Administration in Palestine* (Hebrew), Jerusalem, 1937
King Herod (Hebrew), Jerusalem, 1960
König Herodes, Berlin, 1969

M. Stern, "He'arot le-Sippur Yosef ben Tuviya," *Tarbiz*, 32 (1963), 37–47

E. Taübler, *Imperium Romanum*, I, Leipzig, 1913

V. Tcherikover, *Hellenistic Civilization and the Jews* (transl. from the Hebrew), Philadelphia, 1961

R. de Vaux, *Ancient Israel* (transl. from the French), London, 1961

J. Wellhausen, *Die Pharisäer und die Sadducäer*, Hannover, 1972
Israelitische und jüdische Geschichte, Berlin, 1954

S. Zeitlin, "The Tobiad Family and the Hasmoneans," *Proceedings of the American Academy for Jewish Research*, 4 (1933), 170 ff.

H. Zucker, *Studien zur jüdischen Selbstverwaltung*, Berlin, 1936

CHAPTER IX

THE TEMPLE AND THE DIVINE SERVICE

G. Alon, *Meḥqarim be-Toledot Yisrael*, I–II, Tel Aviv, 1956

M. Avi-Yonah (ed.), *Sefer Yerushalayim*, Jerusalem, 1956

A. Büchler, *Die Priester und der Cultus im letzten Jahrzehnt des Jerusalemischen Temples*, Vienna, 1895
"The New Fragment of An Uncanonical Gospel," *JQR*, 20 (1908), 330–346

D. Chwolsohn, *Das letzte Passamahl Christi under der Tag seines Todes* (2nd ed.), Leipzig, 1908

G. Dalman, *Die Worte Jesu*, Leipzig, 1898

J. Derenbourg, *Essai sur l'histoire et la géographie de la Palestine*, I–II, Paris, 1867

J.N. Epstein, *Mavo le-Nusah ha-Mishna*, Jerusalem, 1948

L. Ginzberg, *Perushim we-Hiddushim ba-Yerushalmi*, III, New York, 1941

H. Graetz, *Geschichte der Juden von den ältesten Zeiten bis auf die Gegenwart* (5th ed.), III, Leipzig, 1908

L. Herzfeld, *Geschichte des Volkes Israel*, III, Braunsweig, 1857

D. Hoffmann, *Mishna Rishona*, Berlin, 1913

J. Jeremias, *Jerusalem zur Zeit Jesu*, Göttingen, 1962

S. Klein, '*Ever ha-Yarden ha-Yehudi*, Vienna, 1925

J. Liver, *Chapters in the History of the Priests and the Levites* (Hebrew), Jerusalem, 1969

A. Oppenheimer, "The Separation of the First Tithes During the Second Temple Period," *De Fries Memorial Volume*, Jerusalem, 1969

T. Reinach, *Textes d'auteurs grecs et romains relatifs au Judaisme*, Paris, 1895

M. Rosenmann, *Der Ursprung der Synagoge*, Berlin, 1907

S. Safrai, "To the History of Worship in the Second Temple" (Hebrew), Tel-Aviv, 1955

Pilgrimage at the Time of the Second Temple (Hebrew), Tel-Aviv, 1965

INDEX OF NAMES AND PLACES